Between Courses
A Culinary Love Story

Karla Clark
Copyright ©2003

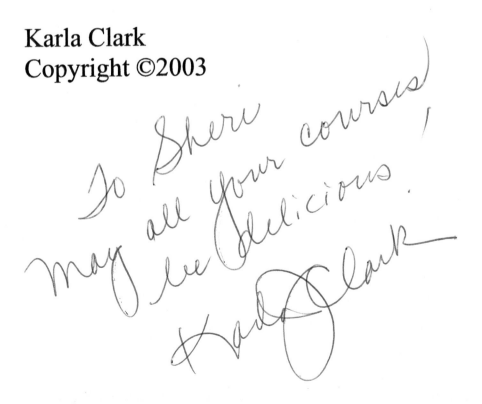

To Sheri
may all your courses
be delicious!

Karla Clark

ISBN: 1-4107-5970-9 (e-book)
ISBN: 1-4107-5969-5 (Paperback)
ISBN: 1-4107-5968-7 (Dust Jacket)

Library of Congress Control Number: 2003094030

This book is printed on acid free paper.

Printed in the United States of America
Bloomington, IN

1stBooks – rev. 09/11/03

For my mother and father,
Marge and Frank Manarchy

and

For my sister, Dana Manarchy,
Aunt Extraordinaire

Acknowledgments

I am deeply grateful to the following: My father who introduced to me the universe of books; my mother who taught me how to love in the present tense; my Nana who taught me how to make bread; my husband Scott who is love in the real world; my two sons Jordan and Jonathan who defined love; my siblings Linda, Dana, Paula, and Frank who share our family's collective consciousness; and my friends who make it fun. Special thanks to my editor, Linda Cleary, and my trusty readers: Frank Manarchy, Dana Manarchy, Paula Sentovich, Rose Ciaccio, Sue Ciaccio, Marcey Sink, Mary Halbin, Judy Prisby, Joy Parlapiano, Jane Sudderberg, Nonie Broski, Lisa Greco, Kris Rummel, Suzanne Untersee, Kay Sentovich, and Lori Michalsen. Your love and support propelled me to the finish line. God bless you all!

1

Ne Carne Ne Pesce
(Neither Fish Nor Fowl)

By day I am a waitress in my father's Italian market and café. By night I am something else again—"Aunty Fun" to my thirteen nieces and nephews. Right now it is day, in fact, my birthday, and I'm standing at the top of the back stairs that lead from our apartment down to our store. I'm stalling.

You'd stall too if you had a family like my family, a family that puts birthdays right up there with national holidays. You know the kind. My sisters hire singing birthday-grams, they "balloon" people at work, they stage surprise parties, and once, on the occasion of my brother-in-law Ed's fortieth birthday, my sister, Rosa, the rich one, rented a billboard a block down from my father's store and had Ed's face plastered on it for God and all of Chicagoland to see, and it read: "Hey, Ed, Thank God you're not dead! You're forty instead!"

1

My thirtieth was this pseudo-surprise soirée hosted by my four sisters right downstairs in the store. And I have to admit, it was a beautiful party, all cozy and candle-lit, with just my family and a few close friends. But that was then, ten years ago when my life was still an unopened envelope, and this is now. The way I see it, there should be a law prohibiting birthday parties after the age of thirty. They could stick it in there with the law against cruel and unusual punishment.

This year I had a little talk with my sisters, asking them to please save the fancy parties for their kids. My nieces and nephews are the recipients of the world's most lavish birthday parties. My oldest sister, Rosa, the rich one, actually rented a hot air balloon once for her daughter's eighth birthday. It was tethered, but still... Another year she had a dress-up theater affair where she and Ed escorted another daughter and five of her friends in a limo to see Donny Osmond in *Joseph and the Amazing Technicolor Dreamcoat.* And just last month my other sister, Marina, the hypochondriac nurse, rented out a movie theater for a private showing of the latest Disney film for her son and forty of his closest friends. I say to my sisters: "These are not parties, these are extravaganzas." But when it comes to celebratory events of any kind, my sisters don't listen to me.

They promised me, this year, just a family dinner at Rosa's. They promised. But they've promised before. I've found out the hard way that when it comes to surprise parties, anything goes: lying, forgery, voice disguise, and, I'm ashamed to say, once, in a desperate last-ditch effort to save the surprise, my sister Rosa, the rich one, even stooped as low as kidnapping. That's what I said, kidnapping. She abducted my baby sister Angie right out of her dorm room. Angie's roommate was this close to calling the police.

So you can see why I'm hoping that downstairs I'll find only a few helium balloons, a hand-lettered butcher-paper banner reading *"Bona Ano, Sabina!"* and my mother's famous birthday bread. But I'm worried because my sisters are sneaky. They can't pass up the opportunity for a good party, especially for an "eth" birthday party—twenti*eth*, thirti*eth*, forti*eth*. Add to that the guilt my sisters feel because they are married and I am not, and they are mothers and I am not.

Only Mama knows how I feel about turning forty. To be perfectly honest I've been nervous about coming face to face with it. There are so many things I thought I'd have by now: a husband, children, a home, a bridge group, a car pool, a stroller. Reasonable cravings, to be sure.

I'm leaning here against this cold plaster wall, deep in thought. For the most part, I live right here in the present, day to day, minute to minute, without mothball nostalgia or airy hopes, because what is hope if not expectations with confidence. And I have neither.

I promise you, I will not whine about my life. There are no complaints there. Nowadays people consider themselves lucky if they had two straight, non-alcoholic, non-abusive parents who raised them. I consider myself blessed because I have two loving, faithful, hard-working, unselfish parents and four wonderful sisters. Not to mention an extended family including aunts, uncles, cousins, nieces, and nephews. You won't find a loser in the bunch...well, I do remember some whispering way back when about a second cousin once removed on Papa's side who was an inventor, which in our family is good, but I guess he invented some kind of kinky sexual device, which in our family is bad, really bad. But other than him...

And I promise you I won't complain about the family business. My sisters and I had to pull our own weight, even when we were very young, but we certainly weren't held prisoners; we weren't chained to a stove. We missed a football game or two and we worked all summer while our friends sunbathed. We complained about cleaning the grills and the bathrooms; we detested taking inventory and waxing the hardwood floors. There were times when certain customers gave us histamine headaches, and we worried constantly about smelling like garlic. To this day I for one can't even look at *babalucci* (land snails) without my stomach turning, but I wouldn't call that scarred.

I may be in the minority, but I'm not the kind of person who looks back on her life and grades each year as either good or bad. First of all my mind doesn't function on such a linear basis. Secondly, my long-term memory for dates stinks.

Now my father, he's a different story altogether. A whiz with numbers, Papa is famous for pulling dates out of thin air. "Nineteen hundred and fifty-three," he'll say to his friend, Mr. Barbiere, whose barbershop is right next door. "Now you're talking about a good year, mister. In fifty-three I moved to America, married my beautiful wife, and got my first American paycheck. Well, it was actually cash back then, and just a few bucks, but what a year, what a year! Probably the best year of my life!" To hear Papa talk, they were all the best years of his life.

That's how Papa is, running around with his good memories stuffed like a clean white handkerchief in his shirt pocket. And he has this amazingly selective memory—he chooses only to remember the good stuff. He says his brain is like a wine cellar in which he only allows the best vintages. There's simply no room for sour grapes. I guess you could say he's an optimist, but he's the worst kind, subscribing to the doctrine only when it relates to his family, then his attitude automatically defaults to Optimism, like the way a computer defaults to the C drive. "Only the best for my girls," he'll say. He pretends that the rest of the world can go to hell in a hand-basket. But anyone who knows Papa knows that he's a lot like a loaf of his own bread: crusty on the outside, but a softy through and through.

But he keeps you guessing. His isn't so much a dry sense of humor as a confounding one. You find yourself asking, "Was he joking, or what?" And his temper is full-blooded Sicilian: many times his fist has met the top of a counter. He's also been known to throw a drunken or disorderly customer out of the place every now and again. And he loves a good argument with Mr. Barbiere, who he harasses mercilessly every morning by peeking his head into his barbershop and saying, "Hey, does the bus stop here?" This is major razzing because five years ago a city bus skidded on ice and crashed into Mr. Barbiere's shop.

As for me, you couldn't really peg me an optimist, but I'm in no way a pessimist either—both require looking to the future and that is something I avoid like a bad batch of garlic. I'm too impractical to call myself a realist and not imaginative enough to call myself an idealist. I wish I had it in me to say that the past is just the past: memories that are pleasing, regrets that are mournful, successes that make you grow taller, and failures that you simply chalk up to experience. But I can't. The past stays with you, sticks to your ribs like a heavy lasagna dinner, so that by the time you reach my age you feel heavy, bloated, weighty.

I guess I fall somewhere on middle ground, just like my placement within the family, where I'm number three, sandwiched between two older best-friend sisters and two younger best-friend sisters. I am what Papa says Sicilians from other villages used to call people from his little town of Agrigento: *"ne carne ne pesce,"* loosely translated as "neither fish nor fowl."

My father, the optimist, tells me: "Think good thoughts! Make a plan! Map out your future!" You can almost hear the exclamation points at the end of his sentences. What Papa doesn't understand is that some people can't read maps. To some people, a map looks like a gigantic bloodshot eye or a tangled cluster of varicose veins.

The truth is I'm like Papa in one way: I also have this incredibly selective memory. But all my memories are of Vito. I can play back Vito memories in my head like home movies, in full, living color. And unlike Papa, my wine cellar houses buckets of sour grapes.

I'm standing here, playing for time, leaning against the wall in this dark hallway, thinking that something has got to give, because suddenly I am forty and my life has not changed a whit since I was twenty. I'm still here, pouring coffee, sweeping floors, and slicing *provolone*.

I walk down the stairs the way I have since I was a kid, slowly but with a bit of a skip because I like to hear my heels click on the steel strips that hold down the worn linoleum. I turn the corner… and I am relieved and horrified at the same time. There is no surprise party, but Mama or Papa—

surely not Papa—has rented one of those stupid lighted signs and it's screaming in big red letters: *"Lordy, Lordy, Sabina is forty!"* The thing is a monstrosity and I'm wondering how they ever got it inside when I hear my mother calling, "Surprise, *bedda!*" (Sicilian for beautiful) She hurries around the counter, grabs me and wraps me up in a hug, enveloping me in her softness and scent. "My *bambina!*" she says as she pinches my cheeks.

"Yeah, Ma, your forty-year-old baby. Forty! I still can't believe it." I point to the sign and say, "Thanks for helping me to forget!"

"Forget nothing. You're forty and you're wonderful."

"Well, I don't feel wonderful. I feel forty."

"So you feel forty and look twenty. Isn't that better than feeling twenty but looking forty?"

"I think," I answer, but I'm not so sure.

"You think?" she says, patting my cheek. "Well, I know."

I walk over to the sign to get a better look. It's probably four feet high and eight feet long and it clashes with the decor to say the least. Mama comes up beside me and hooks her arm around my neck. I look at her face. It has always reminded me of the happy sunshine faces that children draw. My mother is sun-like: round, warm and radiant. Papa always teases her, saying her mother should have named her after the sun, rather than the moon—Luna. Out of the blue, my father will walk across a room just to take my mother's face in his hands and say, *"Faccia la sole* (face of the sun), and then kiss the sun. She has dark brown hair and these deep, dark brown eyes that sparkle even when she's sad. She's what people mean when they say "pleasingly plump" with her full, soft cheeks that are perennially rosy, never needing even a pinch of blush. Her lips are full and her skin is smooth and milky in color, so light for someone with Sicilian blood. There are no sharp edges to my mother; she's just soft and wonderful.

Mama and I stand here and stare at this sign as if it's going to do something or say something else, when all of a sudden it does, it says: Y*ou're old! You're old! You're old as mold!* I blink my eyes once, twice, and the real-life message returns to view. "A simple Hallmark would have sufficed," I say.

"I had nothing whatsoever to do with that thing," Mama says, pointing to the sign as if it were a dirty old dog. "Just enjoy yourself today. Forty or not, make it a happy day. There's still a lot of life ahead."

"Yeah, half of my life if I'm lucky."

"Maybe the best half. Good things are ahead, *bedda.*"

"I know, I know," I say, but all I really know is that Mama and Papa have convinced themselves that any minute God will be rolling out his special plan for me.

"Just be happy your sisters didn't get their way this time," she says, heading for the kitchen with me like a puppy at her feet. "You can't imagine what those girls had in mind."

"Oh, Mama, don't even tell me." I pause for effect. "Okay, tell me."

She stops at the kitchen door. "No, I can't, but you know them, either too much time on their hands or too much money to burn." Mama bites her index finger. It's hard for her to keep anything from me. She lets the secret teeter on the tip of her tongue for a few seconds, then she sighs and says, "Oh, all right, but don't tell them I told you."

"I promise."

"They wanted to rent a hall and do one of those *Sabina Giovanotti, This Is Your Life* kind of parties. You know, a roast. Invite all your friends, relatives, teachers, classmates, old boyfriends...everyone you know."

"Oh, geez! I was guessing another right-out-of-bed party or something really disgusting like a Chippendale dancer. Those idiots! I would have died. How did you stop them?"

"I just told them the truth."

"That I have no old boyfriends?"

"Oh," she says, waving her hand at me, "yes, you do." But then she pauses because she knows there is only one old boyfriend to speak of—Vito Salina—and if anyone actually did speak of him in my presence he or she would certainly use the more accurate term of "ex-fiancé."

Mama does this thing with her face whenever she thinks of Vito, pulling it into a pouty squint. She holds him in her thoughts for a few seconds and then relaxes her facial muscles and lets out a small "humpf." She pushes through the door to our warm kitchen—a study in shiny stainless steel—with me still at her heels. Mr. Maggio, our bread maker, has been here before dawn working his magic with high-gluten flour.

"Good morning, Mr. Maggio," I say in that patronizing, singsong voice pupils use with their teachers. Then I say, "Maaaaaaaaaaaa!"

Mama washes her hands at the sink, slowly, deliberately, lathering and massaging every finger like a surgeon scrubbing up. She actually looks like a surgeon as she presses her foot down on the trundle pedal. (Papa installed a foot pedal for the faucet years ago because we wash our hands and use the sink so much.) She's taunting me.

Mr. Maggio watches us but says nothing. A permanent fixture in our kitchen all these years, he's privy to all our comings and goings, but he never lets on, just goes about his business kneading and forming and braiding and slashing and pulling golden loaves of bread from Papa's brick oven with his ten-foot-long baker's peel. His face looks like one of his loaves: perennially brown, crusty, and irregular in structure. He's as old as an olive tree and just as stoic.

Mama is pulling me by a string. Finally she speaks. "I just told those girls it would break Papa's heart if *their* surprise upstaged *his* surprise," she explains while wiping her hands on a clean white dishtowel.

"Oh, no!" I pound my forehead with an open hand, which I know is a stereotypic Italian-American gesture, but I can't help it, this family drives me crazy around birthdays. "Please, Mama, what surprise? I can't take any more surprises. Mr. Maggio, you don't know about any surprises, do you?" He draws in his thin lips and shakes his head.

"Don't bother Mr. Maggio," Mama says, her mantra since we were little girls. She slaps her dishtowel at me, striking me right on target, at the top of my thigh.

"That hurt!" I lie. "What surprise?"

"Sabina, you're so melo-dramatic. It's just that silly blinking sign. Now don't hurt your father's feelings. That thing was expensive." She pats my cheeks with baby taps.

"That's the surprise?"

"That's it." She throws the dishtowel at me and goes to prepare herself the first of the many pitchers of ice water she drinks all day long, in all seasons, instead of coffee. Mama thinks caffeine is bad for you. Sugar and fat and little white lies, on the other hand, are perfectly fine.

***

A key turns in the front door and my father, Sunny Giovanotti, enters his store as he has every day for the last forty years: backwards, shouting happy greetings to the neighbors, and juggling his keys, a cup of coffee, and the Tribune.

"*Buon giorno*! *Buon giorno*! Where is she? Where's my birthday girl?"

"Oh, Papa, I'm over here. You're a bad man." He pockets his keys, sets down his coffee and paper and wraps me in a hug. I ask him where he got the sign.

"You like it? Only the best for *numero tre*!" He pats me on the back, *hard*, and we admire the sign together as if it were a famous sculpture.

"I think it's great, Papa. I mean it's short. It's pithy. You spelled my name right, you got my age right. It's perfect." I reach up and kiss his cheek. "You're not a bad man," I say. "You're a nice man." He's a handsome man, too, my father, looking more like fifty-four than sixty-four thanks to good olive-toned skin and a thick crop of wavy brown hair lightly salted with gray. He claims to be five-ten but I think gravity and time have

7

probably stolen an inch or two. He's solid, with powerful arms, and hands that are soft to touch but firm to grip. As for his face, his gray-blue Sicilian eyes steal the show. If Mama had a jealous bone in her body there could have been trouble along the way, but Mama knows Papa's heart.

"Good things, my Bina. There are good things floating around in the air. Maybe even a breadman for you, you think?"

"Oh, Pa, stop with the breadman. There aren't anymore left. You were the last one God made." Mama comes from the kitchen and says I'm right, that after Papa, they broke the mold.

Papa scowls. "Don't think like that. If I let myself think like that I wouldn't have all of this." He gestures to include the store, Mama, and me, as if we were castle, queen, and princess. "You think good thoughts, Bina, and good things will come. You deserve some nice surprises." I tell him that I don't like surprises. Papa shoots me a look that's somewhere between disbelief and where-did-I-go-wrong. "But, *bedda*," he says, talking with his hands, "surprises are the best part of life." He and Mama saunter off to the kitchen, leaving me with that little jewel.

Aunt Emmalina, Mama's oldest sister, is at the front door fiddling with the lock. She's been having trouble with her key for six months now. I unlock it from the inside and Aunt Lina with her fiery "from-a-box" red hair enters like a gush of wind. "Sunny, when are you going to fix this lock?" she shouts to the general vicinity of the kitchen. "Egads, it's cold. More like December than October. The trick-or-treaters will have to wear snowsuits under their costumes tomorrow. Happy birthday, you. I know I'm late but I had to go back for your gift." She pulls a small box out of her Gucci purse and waves it in front of my face, saying I can open it later after the rush. Then she yells for my mother. "Luna, *dove sono tu* (where are you)? *Si sbrighi* (hurry up)! It's going to be a busy day. Luna?!"

Aunt Lina is something else. She and Mama look like sisters but they're as different as butter and butterscotch. Sixty-five looks good on Aunt Lina and she knows it. Smooth skin, healthy hair (notwithstanding the "I Love Lucy" henna dye) and a shapely full-figure make her a *junior* senior citizen. But her clothes scream, her jewelry blinds, and her perfume lingers.

Mama calls to her from the kitchen. Where else would Mama be I would like to ask her. Where has she been every morning since Aunt Lina started working here six months ago? My aunt will tell anyone who'll listen that she left a glamorous life on Long Island to come back to Chicago to cook with her sister. Truth be told, she left husband number *three*. Now Aunt Lina calls out to Mama to hold on a minute, as if it were Mama who was rushing *her*. She's searching for a safe place to store my birthday present, which must be treated like a gift of the magi. She finally decides it will be safe yet appropriately displayed until its unveiling on a shelf reserved for *cornetti* (croissants).

To the background kitchen-bickering of Mama and Aunt Lina I prepare for another day at Mela's Market. I sweep the hardwood floors because even though my job title is *assistant manager,* I am everything here at Mela's Market except cook and delivery boy: janitor, stock girl, busgirl, hostess, waitress, and cashier. To be fair I must say that we all—Mama, Papa, Aunt Lina, and me—wear these hats. That's just how it is in a family business. And I should also mention my nineteen-year-old cousin, Jimmy, who also helps out. Jimmy's a good kid, working here during the day and taking journalism classes at night. Why night classes? He'll tell you with a serious mug that the "babes at night class are *babier* than the babes at day class."

Speaking of Jimmy, here he is now…late as usual. Nothing is a rush for this kid, he has one pace and he moves at it. There's no speed control button on his body. Believe me—I've checked. I unlock the door for him (Papa doesn't trust him with a key) and he enters with an entourage of swirling leaves. He greets me with this headline: "*Sabina Giovanotti Turns Forty,*" and hands me a small brown paper bag, scrunched and twisted at the top, the way only a boy would close a lunch bag. "Hey, hey, cuz. Happy birthday." I open the bag and find a jumbo pack of Kodak film. He knows I like to take pictures and he knows about my childhood dream of becoming a photographer so he fantasizes that someday we'll be partners, journalist and photojournalist. I humor him and say, "I'm too old now." He humors me and says, "You're not old, you're just not new anymore."

"Wow, thanks, Jimmy. Really," I say, hugging his neck. I whisper, "This is the best gift so far." I point to the blinking advertisement of my age.

"Lordy, Lordy, look at this thing!" Jimmy says.

I whisper, "Papa."

Jimmy shrugs. "Hey, forty is a big damn deal. Right?"

"Right." I smile and watch as my cousin heads for the kitchen, led by his nose.

"Damn, something smells good!" he says (today and everyday), barreling through the door.

I smile again, thankful for Jimmy, who makes me laugh and helps dilute some of the tension that spills over from the kitchen where the gourmet sister partnership grows more competitive each day. Things have really heated up in there. Mama started out with patience, but after six months of culinary harassment, she's starting to snap. Papa's had to come to her defense and now he and Aunt Lina have been really going at it. In desperation, Mama's been recruiting my help, and now I feel like an emulsifier: trying to coax two unfriendly ingredients together. Papa and Aunt Lina are oil and vinegar. I just wish I had a wire whisk for a weapon. Instead I've been trying flattery, which works only up to a point.

Like yesterday morning, after I heard her bawl out Papa about the lock and lambaste Mama about the temperature of the kitchen, I said in passing, "Aunt Lina, that shade of blue is so pretty on you. You should wear that color more often." And Mama, catching on, added, "It makes you look thinner, Lina." Then Papa chimed in, "Yeah, blue makes you look thinner. Yesterday you wore yellow. Yellow made you look fat. I wouldn't wear yellow no more." I don't know what rumples Aunt Lina's feathers more, Papa's insults or the fact that he purposely uses poor English when speaking to her. He tells her over and over how people out East "talk funny." Ever since Aunt Lina came, Papa has replaced the word *ask* with *ax*, just to get her goat. I used to think that when it came to Aunt Lina, Papa just didn't get it, but Papa gets it just fine.

Mama was quick with damage control. "Don't listen to him, Lina, you're thin as *asparagi* (asparagus). Are you on a diet?"

"Diet, Schmi-et! I'm like Mae West when it comes to diets. The only carrots that interest me are the number you get in a diamond."

At exactly two minutes before seven I open up. My day begins. I pour coffee, serve giant squares of Mama's Artichoke and Cheese Strata and say, "Of course I'm grateful to be alive." I endure the good-natured ribbing our morning regulars dish out about the sign. Later, during the lunch hour, the customers who don't know me ask, "Who is Sabina?" and Jimmy points to me like I'm the prom queen. It's so embarrassing. Believe me, I've been tempted to pull the plug on the twenty-four hour commercial of my age, but I don't want to hurt Papa's feelings. Seeing that he doesn't easily part with his money, I should be very grateful for the sign and the cash outlay it represents.

At one-thirty Penny from *Penny's Pastry* down the street comes over with this enormous iced sheet cake—the size we usually order for wedding showers. Penny is one of Mama's closest friends so I have to be nice. Mama and I *ooohh* and *aaahh* and I say, "Penny, how sweet of you! You shouldn't have." But I'm glad she did because I have this thing for bakery cake with lard frosting roses. The cake is definitely the best surprise so far. The cake, then the film from Jimmy.

The whole place erupts into a perfectly pathetic version of *Happy Birthday* and then Penny actually slaps me on the butt forty times. When Mama gives me a "pinch to grow an inch" I have to wonder—am I forty or am I four? Mama hands me a colossal slice of cake with copious amounts of frosting and then she cuts the rest of the cake while Aunt Lina tells her the pieces are too damn big. Mama cuts smaller pieces even though I wish she wouldn't just because you-know-who told her to. Aunt Lina says, "That's more like it," and I watch her as she carries plates off to the lunch customers. Honest to God, I think she shakes her butt like that on purpose.

At three o'clock Darth Vader walks into the store and I have to wonder if he has anything to do with the surprise my sisters are concocting. But as it turns out, he's just a college kid from the University of Illinois, which is down the block from us, on his way to a Halloween party. I've always hated that my birthday is the day before Halloween.

At last it's four o'clock. I turn the sign around to *closed* and lock up. This has been the longest day of my life, like a day on the planet Venus, where one day is two hundred and forty-three earth days long. Jimmy and I clear tables and head to the kitchen balancing trays of dirty dishes. We find Mama and Aunt Lina arguing over whose daily special was more popular: Mama's "Sabina's Birthday Special," *Penne con Pescespada* (tender cubes of swordfish sautéed in olive oil with tomato, pine nuts, fresh sprigs of parsley and basil, and raisins served on penne pasta), or Aunt Lina's "Halloween Special," *Spaghetti alla Siracusana* (homemade spaghetti with a sauce of tomatoes, anchovies, olive oil, sweet basil, and topped with fried breadcrumbs).

Aunt Lina practically knocks Mama down as she makes her way over to me with a fork twirled with her spaghetti. Then Mama follows with her own fork. For the last six months this has become a daily thing: the dreaded taste test. I'm tasting…

"Sabina?" It's the one who needs constant praise. Talk about a rock and a hard place. To be disloyal to one's own mother would be the greatest Italian sin, but to offend Aunt Lina would be like offending Mother Nature: you might as well prepare for a natural disaster.

I sample each forkful, smacking my lips for effect, closing my eyes as if each bite were a bit of heaven. But as usual, this is not enough fuss, so I have to moan and groan and *ooooh* and *aaaah*. Finally, I chicken out altogether and say, "It's a tie."

Now Aunt Lina calls Jimmy over for a second opinion. He tastes Aunt Lina's, then Mama's. Aunt Lina's. Mama's. "I don't know," he mutters. "I just don't know." He keeps chewing away until Aunt Lina gets tired of waiting and says, "You're right. You don't know. You don't know nothing." She pushes him in the direction of the pots and pans and tells him to get scrubbing.

I load the dishwasher while Mama makes the floor clean enough to eat off of, Aunt Lina scours the stove, and Papa fiddles with his big old brick oven. "I think your dish could've used a little more salt, Luna," Aunt Lina says.

"You think so?" my sweet Mama says, going about her business.

"And a little less *basilico*. *Basilico* can be so overpowering."

"Yeah, like a punch in the nose can be overpowering," Papa yells over. He flashes Mama a knowing look, winks at me and then starts singing this little tune:

> *"This is my little wife Luna,*
> *her pretty face shines like the moon-a,*
> *I met her the fourth day of June-a,*
> *in six months she made me a groom-a."*

They make me smile, these two. Papa is sixty-four, Mama, sixty-two. They have worked side by side for most of their married life and they still get along. Living under the same roof with my parents all these years, I have witnessed the secret of their forty-plus year marriage: my mother always gives my father whatever the hell he wants.

I load the dishwasher and think this thought: yesterday, I was the thirty-something daughter of Sunny and Luna Giovanotti; today I am a forty-year-old *zitella* (old maid) with no prospects. Aunt Lina used to send me a birthday card from Long Island every year, each one ending with the question, "When ya' gettin' married?" Now she is here, a constant reminder of my singular state. "I loved being married," she tells me. "All three times!"

Zitella…it sounds like a dirty word. Oh, but this is nothing if not dangerous, this kind of thinking, about what I am and what I am not, about what I have and what I have not. I have a lot—Mama, Papa, my sisters, and my nieces and nephews. And someday I will have this place. You see the plan is that daughter *numero tre*, the one with the business degree but no husband, no children, no home, no life of her own, will take over the store and carry on the family name and the family tradition and the family honor well into the twenty-first century. But all I can think about is what I don't have. And what I don't have is Vito.

Papa is still singing, but now he's serenading Aunt Lina:

> *"This is my sister-in-law Lina*
> *She looks good but she's kinda mean-a*
> *She wishes that she was a queen-a*
> *'Cause she hates to cook and to clean-a."*

"You are such a liar, Sunny. If I hated cooking and cleaning, do you think I'd be here wrecking perfectly good silk-wrapped nails five days a week? I think not, hot shot." Then she says to me, "Sabina, tell your father to stop singing." I hum softly and pretend I don't hear her. Why should I be dragged into every quibble? "He's piercing my ears with that voice," she says, covering her ears. Papa just smiles and switches over to whistling.

Aunt Lina grabs my arm. "Sabina, go and get your present. I want you to open it now, before we go to Rosa's tonight. I don't want your sisters to see what I'm giving you. It's going to have to be our secret."

"But how—?"

"Just go get it. I wrapped a fake for you to open at the party tonight. It's a white lace slip. Give it back. *Capice* (understand)?"

This, I know, is not going to be good. I go out front to retrieve the gift, and as I carry the tiny box, exquisitely wrapped in purple foil paper and satin ribbon, over to the counter, I wish I was on a game show where I could trade my box for whatever was behind door number one. I know what it is before opening it. I've been handed hints now for over a week. "Aunt Lina, it's too pretty to open," I say as Mama, Papa, and Jimmy gather round.

"Don't be stupid," Aunt Lina says. "And don't be so sure when people say big things comes in small packages. *Little* things come in small packages, little *expensive* things. And don't listen when they say it's the thought that counts. You can't wear a thought on your finger, can you, or wrap a thought around your shoulders now, can you?"

"Just let her open the present," Papa snaps. He looks annoyed. Mama looks anxious. My cousin Jimmy looks…well, this might sound silly but just standing there he looks like a young Frank Sinatra. I slide off the ribbon, gingerly tear the paper, open the box, and remove a turquoise blue velvet ring box. *Please God, don't let this be what I think it is. I don't want to be engaged to my Aunt Emmalina.* But it is. A diamond ring smiles up at me, actually winks at me. I know nothing of cut, color, clarity, or carats; all I know is that this is an exquisite ring.

"Aunt Lina!" is all I can get out.

"Emmalina, what do you—" is all Mama can get out.

"Now listen to me," Aunt Lina interrupts. "You know all about me and my jewelry," she says, pointing to the diamonds on her ears, wrists, fingers, and ankle. "One of the many advantages of being married to a Long Island jewelry wholesaler. You know that I have more bobbles than I could ever wear—at least in *this* city. No daughters or granddaughters to accessorize. Not even a decent daughter-in-law—they're not even getting the costume stuff. So I've decided I'm going to start giving some pieces away, but only to people I love, people who treat me properly. Sabina's a good girl, Luna."

"I know she's a good girl. But it's too much."

"Ha! It's a Can Hardly diamond."

"A Ken Hardley diamond?" (I can't believe Mama actually falls for this.)

"Yeah, you *can hardly* see it. Haven't you ever heard that joke, Luna? I swear, you Chicagoans are at least five years behind us New Yorkers." Mama rolls her eyes. "Now, Luna, here's my way of thinking. No woman should be without diamonds. I know you have no interest in jewelry but maybe Sabina does. My first husband, Joey number one, gave me this engagement ring. I told him it was too small and if it represented his love for me then he didn't love me enough. So he got a second job and bought me a respectable ring. This one sat in my jewelry box for forty-something years. I had some baguettes added and now it's a stunning cocktail ring. Try it on, Bina. No, not on your left hand, you do-do. Do you want all the men to think you're married?" I want to tell her that all the men already know I'm not married because she's told them. "On your right hand. There. It would look a hellava lot better if you took care of your nails. If only you would let me buy you a makeover, I'd have you married by Christmas! See, the trouble with you is—"

"There's no trouble with her," Papa says. "She's perfect."

"Like I was saying, Sabina, the trouble with you is easily fixed— it's a merchandising problem. You're a pretty girl, maybe the prettiest of the bunch, you just need a little polish...nail polish, lipstick, eye shadow, eye liner, blusher, foundation..."

"This face needs nothing," Papa says, seizing my face by the chin and holding it up for all to see.

Mama says, "Lina, she's fine the way she is."

"Is that so? Then why doesn't she have a ring on her finger? Well, other than mine."

"Aunt Lina, it's a beautiful ring," I say and hug her. "But how can I accept it? It's too generous." I've never had a diamond before. When I was engaged it was vogue for brides-to-be to get rings set with their birthstones, so mine was an opal, which I've since given to my oldest niece, Lauren, on her thirteenth birthday. (Hmmm, maybe we've started a tradition in this family of dumping ex-engagement rings off on our unsuspecting nieces.) I hold out my hand in front of my face and turn it this way and that until the ring catches the light. I admire the glitter. There is little about my life that glitters. It *is* a beautiful ring.

"You *have* to keep it. It's a gift," Aunt Lina says. "Enjoy it. Maybe it will bring you luck. Get you another breadman, if that's what you really want. I'd go for a CEO or a broker or a jeweler, but that's just me. Anyway, I'll see you tonight. I gotta go. I've got an appointment with Richard." Richard is either her broker or her masseuse. Who can keep track?

When Aunt Lina leaves the store, you can almost hear a sigh. It's like turning off a fan after running it for hours and being startled by the silence. I look at my ring and admire its sparkling energy and think about how Aunt Lina is sucking the energy out of all of us. I lock the door behind her and look at Mama. She sighs, shakes her head.

"She's *your* sister," Papa says to Mama, his standard line whenever Aunt Lina acts up. I know that Aunt Lina's spotlight can be blinding so I very dramatically remove the ring from my finger, return it to its box, and stuff it in the drawer where we keep pens and sticky note pads.

Mama says to me, "You had better wear it to the party tonight or we'll all be in misery here tomorrow."

"Tomorrow's Saturday," I remind her. (We're closed Saturdays.) "Besides, she has a fake gift for me to open at Rosa's."

"*Dio mia!* (My God)."

"It's a slip."

"A slip."

"And she wants it back."

"Sabina?"

"Hmmmm?"

"You know what Papa and I get you girls every year for your birthday."

"Mama, I look forward to my season tickets. I enjoy all the shows! Don't think for a minute...I mean it's a beautiful ring but we have to consider the source!"

Mama grabs me and we hug. How can a human being be so soft? When I was little I thought everyone's mother was soft but then I hugged some of my friends' mothers and they were about as soft as breadboards. "Oh!" Mama slaps her cheeks. "I almost forgot your birthday bread."

"My bread! I can't wait to see what it is this year." When we were small, Mama started a tradition on our birthdays of baking us bread formed into little shapes—suns, moons, stars, hearts, musical instruments, animals, even people. These are not big loaves to be shared at our big family parties, but special *pane* to be shared just by mother and daughter.

We sit at a table by the window and I open the small white bakery box that Mama has set down in front of me. I pull out a delicately shaped, golden brown hand. Almost to scale, it truly is a work of art. It's a left hand because I am left-handed.

"Mama, it's your best! It's just beautiful!"

"Sunny, get Sabina's camera, will you?" Mama calls.

I pose with my bread hand, cradling it like a bouquet of roses as Papa snaps my picture. He says, "*Mangia,*" and tells us that he's heading upstairs to get cleaned up for Rosa's.

We always eat the bread; Mama insists. As I pull off the thumb and hand it to her, I say, "It's too beautiful to eat. We should varnish it or something and save it."

"You say that every year. What would you do now with forty loaves of stale bread?"

"Open a bread museum?"

"Sometimes you're a foolish girl."

"I know, Mama. That's why I'm forty and single. Very foolish."

"Hmmmph," she says. "That foolishness wasn't any of your doing. That was Vito's." She shakes her head and squints her face into that million-miles-away pouty look. When she returns to the present she tells me what I already know: "Your foolishness lies in the fact that you have waited eighteen years for a foolish boy to come back to you. Sabina, look at me. He's not coming back, *bedda*. Ever."

"That's what you think, that I've been waiting for him?"

"Well?"

I bite off the pinkie. "Not him so much as someone like him." Chew. Swallow. "Someone like him, that's all."

"*Mangia* your bread," she says.

"Wait, Mama, I have an idea." I run to the drawer where I stashed Aunt Lina's ring. Mama gives me a she-must-be-crazy look, but I take the ring from the box and try to fit it on one of the three remaining fingers of my birthday bread hand. Of course it won't fit; the bread fingers are thick as cigars.

"Bina, what in the world are you doing?"

"I thought we'd put the ring on a finger of the bread and then tell Aunt Lina that one of us accidentally swallowed it."

We both laugh. When Papa shouts from the back hallway (hadn't he gone upstairs to clean up?), "She'd probably lock you in the bathroom until nature took its course and you returned the damn thing to her," we laugh so hard Mama has to cross her legs.

We head upstairs to shower and change for what better be just a family birthday dinner at Rosa's. When I emerge from my bedroom in clean jeans and black turtleneck sweater, Mama is waiting for me in the hallway, dressed in black dress slacks and a royal blue silk blouse.

"You're not wearing that, are you, *bedda*?" Mama asks.

"Yeah, why?" I ask, looking down at myself.

She shrugs. "No reason. I just thought you might get a little more dressed up for your fortieth birthday party, that's all."

"Mama! It's just us at Rosa's, right? You said the sign was the surprise."

She pats my cheek twice. "Don't worry, it's just us." She covers her mouth with her hand and mumbles something that I don't make out.

"What was that? What did you say?"

"Nothing," she says, smiling a perfectly naughty smile.

"Geez!" I say as I head to the hall closet for my jacket. Something tells me I'm in big trouble.

In Papa's car, on the way to Rosa the rich one's house, I torture myself considering all the demoralizing possibilities that await me: clown, mime, performance artist, caricature artist, barber-shop quartet, harpist, handwriting analyst, Chippendale dancer, line dancing instructor...who knows. And I know what Rosa will say after she screams "Surprise!" She'll say: "But, Bina, you just can't turn forty without a big bash."

We're a little more than halfway to Rosa's house in Hinsdale, when suddenly, Mama gasps and Papa hits the brakes. I jerk forward in the back seat and scream, "What's wrong?" as Papa pulls off to the shoulder.

Mama pats her chest to calm her heart. "I'm sorry. I didn't mean to scare you, but I just realized I forgot the cake."

"Luna!" Papa shouts. "I almost went off the road!"

"Well, I told you to remind me to grab it from the downstairs refrigerator," Mama says.

"That's all right, Ma, you know Rosa will have enough food for an army," I say, not wanting to turn back now and prolong this day another minute.

"But, Sunny, it's my *Cassata*," Mama whines.

I'm tempted to ask Mama why she bothers with a cake at all. We have this odd tradition in our family of wrecking every birthday cake we bring to a party. We've dropped cakes, sat on them, melted them, elbowed them, spilled wine on them. They've slipped entirely off of plates. And one winter, we even lost one (my sister Colina found it weeks later, frozen solid, right where she'd hidden it, on a shelf in her garage).

Papa exhales through his nose and takes the off ramp. No one says anything as we head for home. The heavy winds tug and pull at Papa's car. "We should probably give Rosa a call and tell her we'll be late," I say and pull out my cell phone.

"Here, let me," Mama says, holding out her hand for the phone. "I want to make sure she has room in her fridge for my *Cassata*. It's huge."

We pull up in front of the store. Wanting to hurry things along, I tell Mama that I'll run in and get the cake. She opens her door, but then shuts it. "Okay, but don't drop it, *bedda*."

As I turn the key in the front door, I could swear I hear a muffled "sssssshhhhhh!" I open the door to Italian lights and horns and balloons and confetti and jack-o'-lanterns and "SURPRISE!"

"Oh, geez!" I say out loud. I scan the room to see if Mama was telling the truth and it really is just family. But everyone is dressed in Halloween costumes so I don't recognize anyone right off. As "Cleopatra" approaches though, I can tell it's Rosa the rich one, and I prepare myself for her spiel about how you can't turn forty without having a big bash. She hugs me and then surprises me a second time when she says: "No, this is not a surprise birthday party, Bina, it's a Halloween party. Happy Halloween, Bina!"

"Happy Halloween, Sabina!" dozens of voices say.

Then Frank Sinatra, who looks an awful lot like my cousin Jimmy, swaggers over, grabs me by the shoulders, and throws out this headline: "Sabina Giovanotti Celebrates Her Fortieth Halloween!"

2

Don't Let Them Eat Cake

I pan the room again and even in the soft light I quickly deduce that the number of people here far exceeds the number of people in my family. This leads me to a terrible revelation: that my Aunt Lina's inborn talent for craftiness is rubbing off on my mother. Used to be, Mama was a terrible liar.

"You really had no idea?" she asks me now. "That whole ride in the car was a scam—just to give everyone time to get here, to decorate, and to hide. And that sign—that was just to throw you off, too. I was sure you suspected."

"No, honest, I've never been so surprised in my life." Even if this weren't the case, I've learned early on, that, in my family, it's the right answer.

"Happy Birthd— I mean Happy Halloween, Aunt B!" a three-foot tall black-widow spider says to me. Then he whispers, "Don't worry, forty's not so old. You're not even six in dog years."

"Is that you, Nino?" I ask, but he runs away.

Rosa the rich one brings me a mug of hot cider, takes me by the arm and says, "We did it simple, Bina, just *antipasti, pizza, calzone,* and Mama's tossed salad. Nothing fancy. No big deal. Come and see who's here."

As it turns out, everyone I know is here: every single member of my family, all our morning regulars from the market, aunts and uncles, cousins, and even my hairdresser, Joey Jr., Mr. Barbiere's son. I plaster on a party smile and make the rounds.

Some people are only half-disguised, like Mr. Barbiere, who is easily recognizable despite the cowboy hat covering up his bald head, and Mrs. Zinsia, another of our morning customers, who kind of looks like a gypsy anyway. But I can't identify the two guys who are dressed up like Hans and Franz, those body-builders from Saturday Night Live, until I get closer: Nick and Tony Radanza, more friends from the market. When I turn around and come face to face with Charlie Gradezzi, my all-time favorite customer, he looks so handsome I let out a little gasp. He grabs me and delivers a big hug. "Happy birthday, little girl," he says. He's dressed in a crisp naval uniform that I'll bet is his own. It fits him perfectly and he knows it—his sixty-eight-year-old brown eyes twinkle like a teenager's. He's unusually tall for a Sicilian and has a full head of silvery gray hair, but what I find most appealing about Charlie Gradezzi is his generous Roman nose. Once when someone commented on it, he said, "It's a Roman nose all right…it's roamin' all over my face!" Ever since then I've harbored a secret crush on Charlie Gradezzi.

He rocks me in his arms and whispers this is my ear: "Man oh man, if only I were a few years younger…" I have to smile. If only he knew how often I've thought that myself. Take twenty years off him, hell, take ten, and he'd be the man for me.

But there's no time for dawdling. Rosa the rich one pulls me away from Charlie so that I may greet my other guests—even though this is a Halloween party and not a surprise birthday party. She says she "did it simple," but honestly, once again, she's gone all out. The store is transformed into an autumn wonderland with the balloons, pumpkins, Indian corn, squash and gourds, the Italian lights, and all the votive candles. There are trays upon trays of *antipasti,* overflowing with *prosciutto,* olives, cheese, *bruschetta,* marinated mushrooms, *peperoncini, caponata,* and *salami.* There's beer and wine and hot chocolate and apple cider to drink.

Look at Rosa. She loves this. How she could pull this off is beyond me. She makes it look like nothing. Rosa's the oldest of us girls but she looks the youngest. She has short, wavy brown hair, dark brown eyes, and a beautiful, full Renaissance figure. Not only is she beautiful, she is indefatigable in spite of being the mother of five. I tease her now and ask if she's still able to bend at the knees because she never sits down.

"Of course I sit, silly...when I'm driving. Now come and kiss your sisters."

My sisters. After Rosa comes Marina. That's Marina, standing near the kitchen door. She's dressed as a nurse, which is some original costume because she *is* a nurse. I'm sure she's standing by the door to keep warm. She's always "chilled" and fighting off some kind of bug. Plus, whenever you see her she's either just getting, just ending, or right smack in the middle of her period, and this means her menstrual bitchiness spans the course of about three weeks. God love her, but Marina the hypochondriac nurse is a person with just enough medical knowledge to make her dangerous. Marina is just as pretty as Rosa but she needlessly loads on the makeup and tends to over-accessorize. I lean in to kiss her, finding her cheek as warm as a bun fresh out of the oven. She jumps at my touch. "God, Sabina, you're so cold. And your hands are like ice. Happy birthday, anyway," she says, hugging me. "I mean Happy Halloween."

Marina's husband, Ross, a pharmaceutical salesman in real life, but outfitted as a surgeon right now, comes over and brushes his face against mine. This is about as affectionate as Ross gets with anyone except his wife, whom he can't keep his hands off of. I've been waiting years for their newlywed behavior to wear off. It hasn't. Ross, like Marina, is also equipped with just enough medical knowledge to be dangerous. "Welcome to forty-something, Sabina!" he says.

"Hey! No way! You guys are forty-something," I say, pointing to Ross, Marina, Rosa and now Rosa's husband, Ed, who has just joined our little huddle. "I'm just forty."

"Technicalities," Rosa says.

"Hey, who are you supposed to be?" I ask Ed, who is in tan Dockers and a denim shirt.

"I'm just me," he says, "and I'm a little confused. I thought this was a surprise fortieth birthday party."

"It most certainly is not," says Rosa, kissing her husband and explaining to me that Ed had to come directly from work. I hate playing favorites, but Ed is my most favorite brother-in-law. And Mama and Papa would never admit it, not even under torture, but I'm sure Ed is their favorite son-in-law. Mama calls him a "piece of bread" which translates idiomatically to "a sweet guy." (My parents have employed three bread metaphors over the years to describe our boyfriends and potential husbands. Two are good and one is bad. "Breadman" is the best, an Italian or Italian-

American man representing all the sublime virtues of bread—food for the body and soul. "A piece of bread" is just below a breadman, a non-Italian man who is sweet, kind, and sensitive, but not wimpy. The third, "a breadball," is a foolish man, a meatball, only worse. Marina's husband, Ross, teeters precariously between the latter two.) Quiet-mannered, Ed was at first taken aback by our lively, animated dinners. I would watch him open his mouth to say something, only to be cut off by one or another of my vociferous family members. Eventually, he learned that if he was to be heard, he had to speak quickly, loudly, and with a sense of urgency. Let's just say he's assimilated well. Now Ed just yells when he wants to be heard. And he's done quite well for himself as you may have guessed by my repeated references to his wife, Rosa, as the rich one. He owns children's shoe stores with these neat little Italian, German, and Swedish shoes that come in funky colors and continental prices. Catchy name, too—he calls them "Shoestrings." I think he has eight stores now, one in the city and seven in the suburbs. But shoes aren't what's made Ed rich—it's all the real estate he owns.

Here come some of the little feet that Ed has outfitted in those vogue little shoes. I think this is Lauren, sixteen, dressed as...gulp!...Madonna. Ed's double take confirms that it is Lauren. Sophie, fourteen, wearing a nun's habit, brings about a nod of approval from her father. When Ed sees Claire, twelve, usually a serious and sensible girl, scantily clad as a cave woman, he gasps. "I'm Pebbles!" Claire tells him. Ed and Rosa's boys, Eddy, eight, and Franky, seven, are nowhere in sight.

Colina and Angie, my two little sisters, approach with wide smiles and plates of food. Colina pushes a plate heaping with cheese and olives and such at me and I accept it. Check out her costume: Tinkerbelle. The skinniest Tinkerbelle I've ever set eyes upon. Really, you could blow her away. Sometimes I think Colina prefers to eat vicariously. Watching other people eat must satisfy something inside her...and she doesn't gain an ounce.

Then there's Angie, the baby. All muscle and tone, not one thing on her body jiggles. She's either come directly from the gym or this is her costume—personal trainer or aerobics instructor or something along the lines of fitness fanatic.

Everyone thinks Angie and Colina are twins because they look alike, dress alike, and laugh alike, but actually, they're a year apart and as different as mustard and ketchup. They do look like twins, except Colina's got Papa's gray-blue eyes, and Angie's got Mama's deep brown ones. Colina is the good girl. In high school, she sang in the choir, worked in soup kitchens, and raised money for homeless shelters. Now, Angie, she's way over there—a comedian, a daredevil, a wise guy. She's got spunk or what Papa calls "oven spring" which is a baker's term for the last bit of rising that bread dough does in the oven before the yeast dies completely. In high school, Angie ran wild, chased boys, and smoked pot. Thank God she found Art, who reformed her. But she's okay. She makes us all laugh.

Angie takes hold of my hand, swings our arms back and forth and says, "I promise, no jokes about the big *four-o.*"

Ross feigns shock. "Four-O! Four-O! No one told me she was Four-O!"

Angie, who can get away with it since her muscles are bigger than his, tells Ross to shut up. "And no jokes about saggy boobs or gray hair, either," she assures me.

Marina adds, "And definitely no jokes about the big *M* for menopause."

"Menopause!" Ross roars.

"Well, peri-menopause anyway," my sister the nurse says.

"Give her a break, will you, Marina?" Ross says. "The poor thing hasn't even had the big 'O' for orgasm yet."

"Ross!" I scream, reaching over to slap the air in front of his cheek. I'd like to slap his cheek, but, well, you know. I scan the room to see if any of the kids heard him. I stare at my sisters, and at Ross and Ed. I'm sure they'd all bet millions that I'm still a virgin. Well, they'd lose. "I had a life before you came around, you know," I say to Ross, hoping he can't see through me and know that I'm talking about *one* time in my whole life. I kid you not, there was just this one time and that was it.

I'm wishing for a distraction when my wish is granted: I spot my best friend, Virgie, gift bearing and costume-less, coming through the front door. I make my escape before anyone sees the tears that are beginning to blur my vision. Ross teeters no more; he's definitely a breadball.

The first thing that hits you when you see Virgie is her size: she's got to be close to six feet tall and she's big-boned. Papa says she's built like a linebacker; Mr. Barbiere says she's built like "a brick-a shit house-a." I try to stick to kinder similes. As a matter of fact, from the waist up, Virgie kind of looks like a winged corkscrew with her long neck, squared shoulders, and long arms. In spite of her big bones, Virgie is gorgeous, with skin that seems to glow and mounds of vibrant, natural vermilion-colored hair. A true redhead, though another redhead I know begs to differ.

"Lordy, Lordy, what have we here?" Virgie says, pointing to the lighted sign.

"Papa," I say. "Did you know about this party?"

She laughs. "Rosa knows better. She didn't even invite me until yesterday."

"Where's Pauly?" I ask, just to be polite, since Virgie's husband hasn't accompanied her to a social function in years. She doesn't even bother with an answer, just lets a small burst of air escape through her lips as she hands me a gift. "But this is a Halloween party," I whine, trying to push the gift back at her.

Rosa comes up looking all bothered. After hugging Virgie she explains that she's been holding off dinner until Aunt Lina gets here, and now Aunt Lina just called and said not to wait. "She got a better offer. Somebody's taking her to Charlie Trotter's for dinner. Papa's worried that it's one of his customers."

"Well, we know it's not Mr. Barbiere, or Charlie, or the Radanza brothers, anyway," I say. "They're all here."

Rosa claps her hands and calls out, "Time to eat, everybody!" Dinner is served buffet-style, so while everyone lines up, I chat with my Uncle Silvio and Aunt Anna, and my cousins, Ambra and Carlian. Then I round up the rest of my nieces and nephews. I find Rosa's two boys, Eddy and Franky, both dressed as space aliens, and give them "no-lipstick" kisses. Not far behind are Marina's two older boys, Mark, twelve, and Carl, nine. Mark, who claims to be too old for a costume, won't let my lips near his cheeks even though I assure him I am lipstick-free, but he does say, "Happy Birthday, Aunt B." He says "Aunt B" just like Opie from Andy Griffith so now I feel fifty instead of forty. Carl is a hilarious Albert Einstein with wild white hair and thick mustache.

The spider, Nino (his real name is Nathan, but he wanted an Italian name like mine, so I started calling him "Nino" last year and it stuck), runs over and fills me in on second grade: "Well, Monday I puked on the playground because Michael D. picked a big black and green booger and wiped it on the swing set."

Okay.

Nino does something to me. His older brothers are both brilliant like my sister (I will not give any genetic credit to Ross) but Nino's different. We don't really know what's going on with him. They've done every test possible, researched everything imaginable. The tests have come out okay, showing above average intelligence and no genetic syndromes, but there's just a little something special about him. He's like a sensory sponge, taking in sight, sound, taste, smell, and touch more intensely than most people. As a baby he was hypersensitive to sounds and he couldn't tolerate sunlight at all. He has an acute sense of smell, can sniff out a gas leak better than that weird contraption the guys from the gas company use. He see shapes in clouds, has spotted more rainbows in his seven years than I've seen in my lifetime, and sometimes makes inappropriate, but dead-on comparisons, like when he told his father's great Uncle Larry that his nose looked exactly like a hot dog.

That's Nino. And the thing is Marina doesn't appreciate his...his uniqueness. The way he seeks out geometry in life. The way he blinks his eyes really, really fast when he's contemplating a deep thought. The way he impersonates someone right down to the arching of an eyebrow. Marina gets so frustrated she sometimes doesn't know which way to turn. I wish Marina would just let me have him. After all, she has two other sons.

I grab my sister Colina's baby from her just as Papa delivers his famous, shrill whistle. "A prayer before we eat," he bellows, then waits for silence and for us all to join hands. We listen as he prays and then laugh at the end when he says, "Oh, and one more thing, Lord, please let Lina *not* be out with one of my customers tonight. Amen."

I stand here in the food line, holding Chelsea and extracting kisses from Colina's other two girls, Nicole, five, and Morgan, three. I'm taking it all in—all these beautiful children. As Papa says, "There's not a dog in the bunch." I'm nothing if not nuts about these kids and I ache for one of my own. I am visited by the thought that at this point in my life I'd be almost willing to by-pass the husband altogether if I could just have a child of my own. But then I watch as Angie's husband, Art, pulls her to him and kisses her smack dab on the lips, and I change my mind. I want what my sisters have, I want it all. But the truth is it's hard to meet people at this stage in the game.

I've always been fascinated with how people meet. Maybe because Vito and I never really met, we simply were born knowing each other. He was always there, intertwined in the everydayness of my life. I often wonder what it would be like to meet a total stranger and get to know him little by little, inch by inch, weaving in and out of childhood, adolescence, and adulthood until you get to the present time and he is the person who is sitting right across from you. I've had dates, mind you, post-Vito, but not one ever amounted to anything.

My sisters all met their husbands in such interesting ways. Romantic ways. Ed sat behind Rosa in a college philosophy class. He stared at the back of her head for weeks before he worked up the nerve to ask her out. He finally did one day after her long brown hair got caught in his book on Socrates.

Marina and Ross met (how disgustingly appropriate) in the ER. Marina had driven a friend in who was having an asthma attack and Ross had brought his younger brother in for a deep laceration on his leg. While Marina's friend was hooked up to the nebulizer and Ross' brother was being stitched up they started up a conversation in the waiting room. Romance blossomed among the blood and the breathing treatments, and Marina says that they barely even noticed when the older man sitting across from them had a myocardial infarction (can't she just say heart attack?).

Colina and John were an unlikely couple if ever there was one, but they've made it work. Even after she graduated from college, Colina remained a pretty straight-laced kid. She went into social work, devoting her life to her clients, rarely dating or whooping it up like Angie. One night a couple of friends persuaded Colina into going to Rush Street. She went. She danced. She met John, a handsome and charismatic investment banker. She drank. She danced some more. She made love for the first time in her entire life. She got pregnant with Nicole. She married John. They both swore they wouldn't be a statistic and have worked hard on their relationship. Rosa didn't like John at first. She said he thought he was a "perfect plate of pasta," but she has grown to care for him, even if she can't like him outright. I'll admit, he has an ego the size of Lake Michigan but I know he's just crazy about my sister and their three little girls.

My favorite "how'd-ya-meet?" story is Angie's. She met Art while white-water rafting in Colorado the summer between her junior and senior year of college. Geez, she was a wild one—uninhibited, unrestrainable, *unbelievable.* She got all the thrill-seeking genes in our family. Anyway, while going down the final drop Angie fell out of the raft and hit her head on a rock. In a moment of heroics, Art, a total stranger, abandoned his raft (with his girlfriend in it), swam over to the rocks and rescued Angie from the water. Ever since, Art has had this kind of calming effect on my sister. Mama and Papa adore Art, the man they believe saved their daughter from a life of pot smoking, bungy-jumping, and hang-gliding. Now Angie's a mommy, which she says is more life-threatening than anything else she's ever tried.

Now Papa's shouting, "Toast, toast," and I brace myself for his *I remember the day you were born* speech. "Sabina Alana, *numero tre,* I remember the day you were born—the date, the time, the hour, the minute, the second. You were number three and it was no secret that we wanted a boy. Your Nano Melarosso had five daughters and five granddaughters. He wanted a boy. The doctor thought you were a boy. All the old ladies insisted you were a boy by the way your mother carried you. Your mother herself, she was sick as a dog. She just knew you were a boy. And then you were born, a terrible delivery, you were breech. It was touch and go for a while. I was out in the waiting room praying to God, please just let them live. And you did and I was not disappointed for one second that you were not a boy. I mean that *bedda.*" He clinks his glass with Mama's, which sets off a chain reaction of chimes. But Papa's not finished; I know because he's been telling this same story since the day the hour the minute the second I was born. He gulps down some wine, wipes his mouth with the back of his hand, and says, "Now your Nano Melarosso was a different story. When I told him he had a sixth grand-daughter, he said, 'Shit, I wanted a G.D. boy!'"

I wish you could try some of Rosa's pizzas. Tonight she's made three different kinds: *Pizza Margherita* (a classic Neapolitan pie), *Calzone* (another kind of pizza in which the crust is folded over to enclose the ingredients) and a Sicilian style pizza with crust as thick as bread. My personal favorite is the *Pizza Margherita*, which has only a few ingredients—fresh *Mozzarella*, sliced tomatoes, fresh basil leaves, and a few drops of olive oil. Pizza perfection. All the men love Rosa's *Calzone*, which she stuffs with mushrooms, onions, artichoke hearts, cheese, and olives. (I've read in some cookbooks that *calzone* means "shoes," but the word *calzone* actually translates to "trouser legs.")

We let our guests sit at the tables while my sisters and brothers-in-law and I stand on either side of the counter. Art tells Rosa that her pizza crust is the best he's ever eaten and asks her secret. As Rosa explains her dough secrets—you can't rush it, make it the day before, let it rise six hours, don't use too much yeast—I can't help but think that she's giving him a little too much information, but Art seems genuinely interested, following every word while biting into another slice. And Papa, he's over there quizzing the grandkids like he used to do with us every night at the dinner table. Tonight, he says he'll give a buck to anyone who knows when and where pizza was first introduced.

This thought comes to me: is my family obsessed with food? Where other people talk wistfully of places they have never traveled, my family talks of foods or spices we have never tasted, like silver beet or rutabaga or blancmange or headcheese or sea cucumber or mace or crazy water or okra or divinity or summer savory or crab Louis or celeriac or turmeric. Do other families talk about food as much as we do?

This worrying all started the other day when I was sitting in my doctor's office waiting to have my annual gynecological check-up (what my sister Angie calls her "annual open house") and reading a magazine article about new brain science. I about fell out of my chair when I read about a newly reported syndrome called, "Gourmand syndrome." Apparently a couple of psychiatrists found a link between a sudden fixation on food and a brain lesion. This is not good news for my family. I know for a fact that Ed and Rosa have more than once decided upon a vacation spot specifically for the food. Who cares about the sights, can you get good seafood?

I look over at my brother-in-law Art who is built like a linebacker. He probably weighs what two of us do and probably can eat what four of us can. "Why, oh, why," he moans between bites of pizza, "didn't your mother teach Angie how to cook?" Angie punches his arm and we all laugh. But

27

it's true, Angie can't cook. Whoever said, "It always tastes better when someone else cooks it" has never had Angie as the "someone else." Colina can't cook either, and what's worse, she thinks she can. As young girls they weren't interested in learning. Rosa was interested, and Marina and I were, too, although to a lesser degree. But it's Rosa who shines in the kitchen.

After dinner I dance with Charlie Gradezzi, my cousin Jimmy, and even Ross, who actually apologizes for embarrassing me earlier. All right, so that moves him back up in between "piece of bread" and "breadball." I dance with Papa last and it's a good thing because the song is Dean Martin's *You're Nobody 'Till Somebody Loves You*, and for glaringly obvious reasons that song always makes me tear up. Papa kisses my hair and whispers, "You are loved, *bedda*. You are loved." I lay my head on his shoulder. I feel like I'm sixteen.

When the song ends, I say goodbye to Virgie, who has to make an appearance at a *real* Halloween party, and I head to the kitchen to help my sisters clean up. As the birthday girl I'm not supposed to help but this isn't a birthday party, right? Besides, I want to help because there's something about the sound of running water that makes my sisters loose at the lips. I can't afford to miss any good kitchen gossip. Like now, Angie has us in stitches telling us about her morning: Alexandria, two, sucked up one of Angie's good earrings with the vacuum cleaner; Victor, eighteen months, pooped through three outfits; the dishwasher broke and leaked water all over the kitchen carpet; and when the meter-reader rang the doorbell, it wouldn't stop ringing and Angie finally had to rip the unit out of the wall. All this before nine o'clock in the morning.

"Be glad you don't have kids, Sabina," Angie says to me. My sisters are always saying stuff like that to me when they've had a hard time with their kids. Or, it's: "Be glad you're not married," when they're mad at their husbands. They just don't get it.

Marina hands me the rinsed dishes and I load the dishwasher. Her long nails are painted blood red and it's not just for Halloween, they're always that color. I've often wondered how many of her patients suffer stab wounds. I'm trying to avoid being stabbed right now.

"Oh, guess who I ran into yesterday at Nordstrom's?" Marina asks no one in particular. "Remember Tammy Cipolla?"

"Sure, she was in my class," Rosa says.

"Yeah, pug nose, skinny, dyed her hair blond. Kinda looked like Joan Rivers," Angie says.

"That's her," Marina says, "only now she's even skinnier. I think she's anorexic. She was looking at a size two dress and it would have just hung on her. But get this: she told me that she stays thin by eating only on Tuesdays and Thursdays."

"You've got to be kidding," Rosa says. "That's crazy."

Colina reaches around me to get another dishtowel from the drawer. "Well, I only eat on Mondays, Wednesdays, and Fridays and I'm not anorexic," she announces.

We all stop and watch each other's jaws drop.

"What do you mean?" Rosa asks.

Colina snaps her dish towel at Rosa and says, "What do you mean, what do I mean?"

Marina the nurse takes it from here. "Are you telling us that you really only eat three days a week and you starve yourself the other four?"

"I don't starve myself the other four. I eat well on Mondays, Wednesdays and Fridays. Like tonight, I had a piece of pizza and some salad. Then I drink liquids on the other days—orange juice, tea, and chicken broth." All eyes are on her. "Well, sometimes I cheat and eat sugar-free gelatin. But look at me, I'm fine."

We look at her all right. We look at her tiny body, the body of a not-yet-developed thirteen-year-old. "You worry me, girl," Rosa says hugging her. "I mean you've always been skinny but I didn't know you had to starve yourself to be that way."

"Well, I never had a problem until after the kids. Then my whole body changed. But you don't need to worry. I'll tell you when you need to worry. You need to worry if and when I ever get fat because John has made it perfectly clear to me that he doesn't approve of fat women."

"Doesn't *approve?!*" Rosa screams. "Where the hell does he get off?"

"Now, Rosa…"

"Now, Rosa, nothing! That makes me really mad. He must not approve of Mama then because she's heavy. And what about me? I'm probably a moose by his standards."

"Oh, Rosa, you are not. That's not what I meant. I meant he doesn't approve of fat wives," Colina says, as if this will clear up the whole misunderstanding.

It's hard stopping Rosa once she gets started. "But I'm a wife; Mama's a wife."

Now Colina is crying. "I mean *me*, Rosa. He wouldn't approve of me if I were fat. That's what I mean." She throws the dishtowel down on the floor and runs out of the kitchen.

Angie turns to run after her, but then stops in mid-step, looks back at us and says quietly, "She thinks John is having an affair," then she follows after her. Rosa, Marina, and I are left standing speechless in the kitchen. Just when I'm about to call John every name in the book, he walks in with baby Chelsea.

"Look who just woke up and wants her Aunt B," he says as he deposits her into my arms. We all give him daggers. He takes a step back and says," What? What'd I do?" We just ignore him and one by one head out front to do damage control.

I find Colina dry-eyed and smiling, sitting by Mama and my Aunt Connie, with her three-year-old, Morgan, in her lap. She's rubbing Morgan's swollen tummy. She says to me when I come over: "Too much pizza for this little girl." I kneel down and lightly touch Morgan's stomach. I knock on it gently. "What's in there, Morgy, rocks? Want me to kiss it?" She nods, so I do, and then she jumps up from Colina's lap, proclaiming that it's all better now. I think to myself, really, people around here can't decide if they are hurting or not.

I spy Angie and Rosa whispering near the front door. Angie will give Rosa the scoop and Rosa will pass it on to Marina and me. I carry Chelsea around the room while she tugs at the helium balloons and I let myself believe for a second that John is actually having an affair. I hate to say it, but of all my brothers-in-law, John would be the most likely: he's great looking, a charmer, and he travels a lot. Plus, he's always had that attitude. Maybe Rosa and her "perfect plate of pasta" theory was right. Doesn't he know Papa will kill him?

Mama announces that it's time for dessert. She heads to the kitchen with Rosa trailing. We all hold our collective breath as she emerges with her beautiful *Cassata*. "Nothing is going to happen to this cake!" she promises our guests as she sets it down on the counter. We exhale and give a round of applause as she and Rosa insert not one less than forty candles into it.

My mother's *Cassata Alla Siciliana* is to die for. *Cassata* means treasure chest and this smooth decadent dessert is truly a treasure. These days it's made commercially with various flavors of ice cream but Mama makes the traditional recipe with *ricotta* cheese. And since Mama's motto is "the richer the better" she adds a layer of green almond paste.

If you've never had C*assata,* you don't know what you're missing. It's so easy to prepare. You simply dissolve water and sugar in a sauce pan, add *ricotta*, chocolate chips, candied fruit, and pistachio nuts. You then layer sponge cake that is moistened with sweet dessert wine in a large mold. Fill the center of the mold with the *ricotta* mixture and top with layers of sponge cake. Refrigerate for several hours, unfold onto a platter and serve with whipped cream. Mama triples her recipe and uses a stainless steel mixing bowl in place of a dinky mold to make the cake party-size.

Morgy says, "I want a gigantic piece please, Aunt Rosa."

"What about your tummy ache?" Rosa asks.

"It's gone now," she insists.

I sit on a stool at the counter, with Morgy on my lap, and for the second time today I suffer through another round of *Happy Birthday*. I feel my face turning red—partly due to embarrassment and partly due to the heat that forty candles put forth. Morgy, poised to help me blow out the candles, is literally hanging over the cake. She's high enough that she's away from the flames but I'm afraid she'll drool in it. I'm just about to pull her back when suddenly she turns green and throws up all over herself and me and the *Cassata*. If this isn't bad enough, there's a chain reaction of puking— first Nino, then Carl. Some of the little ones are crying. I look at Mama who is holding her face in her hand. She's shaking her head and I think she's crying, too, but when I hand off Morgan to Colina and approach Mama I see that she's laughing, laughing so hard that she has to cross her legs. She starts to lose her balance and falls into me, causing me to fall into Rosa. We grab each other and laugh and laugh as we watch Colina and Marina wiping up the pukers. The other kids are gagging and choking and repeating over and over: "Sick, sick!"

"Happy Birthday, Sabina!" my Mama says, teetering as if she were drunk.

"Mama, your cake!"

"No, *your* cake! She laughs some more. "Aw, *merda* (shit)," says my mother, who never swears. "Next birthday I'm buying the stupid cake."

Nino, the black-widow spider, looks up from the floor where he is sitting in his own mess. "Nana owes me a quarter for swearing," he says. Marina bops him on the head, while she positions a potato chip bowl under his chin like a hospital emesis tub and says, "Nino, be quiet and finish puking, will you please?"

Rosa comes out of the kitchen with a huge tray of cupcakes. "Don't worry everybody, Sophie and Claire made these just in case!" Mama laughs again, crossing her legs at the knee to keep from wetting her pants. I laugh, too, not even caring that I'm splashed with Morgy's yuck.

The only good thing about what will be known forevermore as the "*Cassata* Catastrophe" is that it forces the night to end early. After cupcakes, we see our guests off, and Marina and Colina gather up their little pukers and go home, leaving me to open my gifts later, which is fine with me.

***

Later that night, I sit in the living room in my favorite flannel nightgown, the one that's so soft and worn it's almost threadbare, and I open my gifts. Even though it's late, Papa built a fire in the fireplace, and now I'm warm and content, thinking about what a nice day it turned out to be.

Mama and Papa are sitting across from me in their recliners, and I tell them that, once more, everyone has spoiled me—Mama and Papa with season tickets to the Drury Lane Theatre; Ed and the rich one with a taupe colored cashmere sweater; and Marina, Colina, Angie, and their families with a wide angle lens that I've been wanting for my Pentax. (I'm not the world's greatest photographer but I like having a hobby that is as far removed from food as possible. I have found holing myself up in a dark, pungent-smelling, closet-sized darkroom to be very appealing.)

"Well," I say, clapping my hands together, "that's it. It's four minutes after twelve and my fortieth birthday is officially over. I've lived through a lighted sign, a diamond ring, and a surprise Halloween party. Tomorrow will be just another day."

"Not so fast," Mama says as she pulls another gift from out of nowhere. "There's one more." She sets the flat rectangular-shaped box on the coffee table and pushes it my way.

I try to protest because I'm thinking maybe the ring Aunt Lina gave me intimidated Mama into buying me an additional gift. "But, you already gave—"

"Just open it," Mama says.

I do. It's a framed eight-by-ten black and white photograph of the exterior of Mela's Market. "Nice picture," I say. "Hey! Wait a minute! I took this picture."

Papa laughs. "Of course you did. We're not giving you a picture of the store, Bina, we're giving you the *store*. Mama and I are ready to retire."

"Retire? Now?" These are the only two words I can get out. But why should I be surprised? They've been talking about it for a long time. Running the market is hard. You end up with dishpan hands, arthritic knees, heel spurs, and backaches. You go to bed, get a little sleep, but you still wake up the next morning feeling spent and looking like a dehydrated diffenbachia. Then you start all over again. No, I shouldn't be surprised. They're getting older; they can't go on forever.

"Yes, now. We know it's a little earlier than we'd planned, but your mother and I are ready," Papa says, leaning over the coffee table to pat my hand.

"But I'm not ready," I say quickly, pulling my hand back.

"What do you mean you're not ready? You know the store inside and out." Papa says. "The timing is right, *bedda*. Mama and I really need a rest. We want to travel a little, see some of my cousins in Sicily."

"It's what you always wanted, isn't it?" Mama says.

"Of course it is," Papa answers for me. "She's wanted this store for her very own since she was a kid. She can't wait to spiff it up. So, now you can redecorate. You can put up foo-foo curtains if you want. You can

32

change the menu. Hell, you can serve sushi if you want. It will be all yours. But not right away. We'll work out some kind of transition period and I'll help you hire new people. Mr. Maggio's going to retire too, Bina, so you'll need a new breadman. We haven't told Emmalina yet, but you know she's only working to annoy your mother. But don't worry. We're talking four to five months before everything is finalized. Mama and I aren't going anywhere—we'll just be moving to the other side of the counter!"

"Surprise!" Mama says, lifting her arms in the air.

"Very funny. I don't know. I don't know if I can do it without you."

"Nonsense!" Papa says.

"This is supposed to make you happy, *bedda*. I thought you'd be happier," Mama says.

"I am happy, Mama, but I guess I'm scared, too. You know me, I hate change. It's just so much. Nothing will be the same and—"

"Good things, Bina," Papa says. "Good things are ahead. Maybe right around the corner."

"Yeah, right," I say.

"Damn right!" Papa says as he delivers one of his famous slaps on the back, the kind intended to slap a little hope back into a hopeless person.

3

A Wine Worth Getting To Know

Taking over the store was not supposed to be a solo enterprise. Vito and I were supposed to do it together. Back then Mela's Market was just a small grocery and bakery. It was Vito and I who wanted to expand it into a café. Now, I'm to take it all—grocery, bakery and café—on myself. What if I screw up? What if I run it to the ground? I got myself so worked up I couldn't sleep, so now I'm in the tub. I've been macerating for almost an hour and my fingers are all wrinkled, but the water is so soothing I hate to get out.

It's windy now and the wind always reminds me of Vito. The wind and little boys with forever-rosy cheeks and brown curly hair, and those kind of long, dark, thick eyelashes that girls say they would die for. Outside the bathroom window the wind whips through the trees and scrapes the bare branches against the house. Even though I'm soaking in a hot bath I get the shivers.

By filling the tub with the shower sprayer instead of the faucet, I have created my own personal poor man's hot tub. Ours is the old fashioned kind of tub where the water level can reach up to your chest, unlike the newer tubs where you're lucky to be immersed up to your navel. In here, I feel like I'm hermetically sealed inside three walls and a plastic curtain, away from the world of dishes and food and people who chew with their mouths open. I just close my eyes and let the water envelop me. I think people have forgotten about baths.

The wind is howling now and it's beginning to blow some memories around in my head, memories that I am usually able to keep safely tucked away. Memories of Vito. You see, he's got a monopoly on my memory bank. I try not to dwell on the past. I attempt to keep it in this little pocket in my brain. And I try to keep my hands out of the pocket, but sometimes I can't help myself. Like now. It's the damned wind, "mad air" as my nephew Nino calls it. I hate the wind. But not nearly as much as Vito hated it. For years after his mother died in a windstorm, he'd break out into hives whenever the wind started to blow, even on a relatively benign kite-flying kind of day.

We were both thirteen, Vito and I, in the eighth grade at Our Lady of Pompei Catholic School. Eighth grade proved to be a metamorphic year for Vito. He'd started out at five foot four, a hundred and twenty pounds, and by year-end, he'd grown five inches, gained twenty-five pounds, and sprouted some fuzz on his smooth-skinned face. Suddenly he spoke with a voice that changed octaves in mid-sentence and he walked in a way that made you think he wasn't comfortable in his own shoes. He was almost there—on the brink of manhood—but then his mother died and he was just a kid again.

He was at our store the day she died. It must have been a few days before Easter because we always closed a couple days before to do spring-cleaning and to prepare *Taano* (a Sicilian Easter pie made by layering rigatoni pasta, eggs, sausage, and four kinds of cheeses) and special holiday desserts. Mama, Rosa, and Marina were upstairs cleaning every inch of our apartment, while the rest of us helped Papa in the store. Colina and Angie cleaned cabinets and closets, I touched up the window trim and door frames with fresh paint, and Vito and Papa moved the furniture so we could wax the hardwood floors.

Vito always jumped at the chance to help out my father at the store. Certainly he was eager to earn extra money but it was more because he preferred the company of my father to that of his own. Mr. Salina was a stern, undemonstrative man, with a face so deeply grooved it looked like brown corduroy. Vito was the youngest of three children. Mr. Salina was forty-five by the time Vito came along and seemed disinterested in his only son. Vito's mother, Sara, was a kind lady, gentle and melancholy. I always wondered how such a sweet woman could have made such a bad choice in a husband, until one day I asked Mama about it, and she explained arranged marriages to me. Sara's parents had emigrated from a small island off of Sicily called Salina. When Sara was eighteen, she was informed that a husband had been chosen for her: a young man, educated in Milan, from the oldest family in Salina, a Salina himself. Before Sara could explain to her parents that she was already in love with someone else, she was engaged to a man she never even knew existed.

Around Papa, Vito acted like a puppy. He'd nuzzle up to him, eager for pats on the head, slaps on the back, even affectionate kicks in the butt. A special bond formed between them and I'm ashamed to say I was often jealous of their relationship. Papa would share off-color jokes with Vito, jokes he told me were not meant for my *orecchi delicato* (delicate ears).

Sometimes at school, I would catch Vito staring at me from across the room. It made me nervous and it got me wondering if Papa had divulged some family secret about me: that I had been a bed-wetter, a nail-biter, a sleep-talker, that I sang in the shower, whistled like a boy when I worked, read books while sitting on top of the clothes dryer in the basement (for warmth and privacy only, nothing kinky), or acted out musicals with my sisters, including *Fiddler on the Roof, Oliver, White Christmas,* and *Showboat.* My worst fear was that Papa would tell Vito that whenever his name was mentioned around our house I blushed. I would rather have died than have Vito know that.

What did I know at age thirteen about boys? It wasn't like it is now, where thirteen-year-olds have sex. If you even held hands with a boy when I was in eighth grade, you were considered loose. Hell, we were still playing with Barbie dolls at that age. But we did like boys, and when I say *like* I mean just that and nothing more. We didn't even *go steady* until high school.

All the girls in my class at Our Lady of Pompei liked the same three boys: Johnny Joe (J.J.) Fratello, Joseph Francis (J.F.) Sandino, and a Polish boy named Leonard Trupanski. These were the well-built, good-looking, loud-mouthed boys who teased girls mercilessly. They pinched our butts, asked us if we knew what the "F" word meant and if so, would we like to try it out with them. Nowadays these same boys would be sued for sexual harassment. They brutally made fun of our various physical features, calling us by cruel nicknames: Knob-knees Nancy, No Boobs Bartoli, Garlic-breath Gail. They had a name for each one of the seventeen girls in our class; the list was posted in J. F.'s locker. Mine was "Sabina Betweena." To this day

I have absolutely no idea what it meant, only that surely it was something dirty and sophomoric.

Vito wasn't popular with the girls, but not because he wasn't attractive—he was, with his clear skin, rosy cheeks, curly brown hair and lush brown eyelashes that were so long they used to brush against the lenses of his small-framed wire glasses. He had a nervous habit of constantly taking off and putting on his glasses in order to see things more precisely. He gave the appearance that he wasn't interested in girls. He wasn't quick with comebacks or "come ons" as the other boys were, and he never teased us. He was kind to everyone, a champion of the underdog, treating each of us with friendly respect, from the "nerds" to the "dweebs" to the "queers." He was so good and straight that the nuns saw a future priest in their midst. In fact, Vito was open about his "calling" and we all assumed that he would indeed become a priest.

I could go on and on about him. He was the kind of boy you wanted for a friend, someone who would be a pleasure to sit near because he wouldn't pull your hair or try to copy from your paper, or tell you your butt looked fat during morning prayer, or lean over to ask you a question then burp in your face. He was polite (in spite of his definite opinions), friendly (in spite of his competitive nature), and astonishingly brilliant. When he felt like rebelling, he did so in a constructive way, with his intelligence, by challenging the little, limited minds of the Dominican sisters who were our teachers: "But S'ter, tell me, do you think Judas Iscariot was forgiven for betraying Jesus? Or do you think he's rotting in hell, because if he is, is there really any hope for the rest of us?"

He was so serious in school. He knew his catechism inside out and I am not kidding when I say that the nuns would begin to visibly perspire whenever he raised his hand during Religion class. Often they responded by saying: "Why don't we save that one for Father Pucci. He'll be coming by on Friday."

His inquisitive mind frightened me as well. He excelled at everything academic. I was good-grade smart but Vito was intelligent deep beneath a surface that I only walked upon. He lived in a world much bigger than the four walls of Mela's Market. His father did give him that much, the love of learning. Mr. Salina was a research scientist at the University of Chicago and taught his children that information led to knowledge and knowledge led to wisdom and wisdom led to heaven, but he forgot to include love and tenderness in the equation.

I could live contentedly in a world whose form and function I did not understand, but Vito could not. He had to have answers. He soaked up information like a sponge and then never released it. He wasn't an intellectual arrogant, but he did find my ignorance to be fantastically

37

entertaining at times. Mine was a short-term memory. This allowed me to test well, but my brain was like a sieve—facts were gradually sifted out.

"We learned that last year!" Vito would chide when I'd forget something that he'd easily retrieve. Some insignificant fact (insignificant to my world anyway) like the distance of the planet Pluto from the sun. Vito felt the world would be a better place if human beings took the time to understand science a little better. We'd have heated arguments about his dogged philosophy. "What do I care about engines and pistons," I'd say, "as long as a car gets me from point A to a gas station." Or, I'd say, "So Pluto is three billion six hundred and sixty-four thousand miles from the sun, so what? I could live my entire life knowing only that it's the farthest planet from the sun."

"That we know of," he'd correct me. He never corrected anyone else, but I was a free target. And I remember how smug he was when years later he informed me that Pluto was in fact not the farthest planet anymore, that Neptune had switched places with Pluto and would be the farthest planet from the sun until the year nineteen ninety-nine.

Geez, he could make me mad. I remember one night when Vito and I were probably eleven or twelve and we snuck outside with Rosa to sit on the roof of our building in the middle of a summer thunderstorm. I know what you're thinking, *real smart,* but such is the mentality of youth. Up high on the roof, we were living lightning rods, but we were immortal, invincible, incapable of being harmed.

The thunder was magnificent; the lightning was terrifying. We were huddled in a corner, getting drenched and loving every minute of it. The thought of how we would explain our dripping selves later never even crossed our minds. Vito played meteorologist, explaining the ins and outs of an electrical storm. How the cumulonimbus clouds often spread out in the shape of an anvil and extended to great heights. That lightning is a discharge of atmospheric electricity from one cloud to another or between a cloud and the earth, and that thunder was the sound caused by the sudden expansion of air in the path of the electrical discharge.

"The bolt of lightening heats up the air in a fraction of a second and the air actually explodes," he said, addressing Rosa more than me, to impress her, I'm sure.

Rosa was impressed. "Oh," she'd said, looking beautiful even when dripping with rain, "I thought thunder came from two clouds bumping together." She giggled. "Silly me."

I just sat there, absorbing the rain, keeping my mouth shut. I wasn't about to admit that I'd always thought thunder was angels bowling, but by the smug smile on Vito Salina's face, I knew he already knew what I thought.

Oh, yes, he intimidated me. Plus, our families' close association caused us both to be easy targets at school. Our schoolmates didn't understand that, if anything, Vito and I were like cousins. Our mothers had lived next door to each other until they got married. Vito and I were born in the same hospital two days apart. My parents were Vito's godparents; Vito's parents were Marina's godparents. Vito's oldest sister Jenny used to baby-sit for us. Vito's other sister, Becky, was best friends with one of my cousins. We were thrown together for countless occasions at each other's homes. Our lives were intertwined like grapevine. There was no avoiding him. Still I tried, in the simple effort to avoid the teasing that came along with our association. You know how grade-school children can be, how they try on surnames for size: If Rosa Valetti married Peter LaRosa, she'd be Rosa LaRosa; if Franca Carmina married Antonio Manca, she'd be Franca Manca; and if Sabina Giovanotti married Vito Salina, she'd be Sabina Salina.

At thirteen this was my nightmare: to wake up one day and find that I possessed an alliterated, rhyming name, something I'd always loathed. As it was, the eight-syllable name I had was challenge enough, especially learning to write it in kindergarten, but I began to appreciate the musicality of Italian names in high school when I finally sat in classrooms that were not comprised of ninety-eight percent Italian-American students. At attendance, I remember rolling my eight syllables off my lips and feeling sorry for the kids Papa would have called *Americani* but I called *dunt-duhs* because that's how many of their names sounded to me: Joan Hill, Jim Clark, Tom Hayes, Beth Cole, Dunt-Duh. How could two little syllables represent an entire person? How could these syllabically challenged students ever discover their authentic selves?

Papa says a name should introduce you well, should sing out to the world your essence. "A name is not simply a word that a person calls you," Papa used to say. "A name is a holy thing, it laughs, it cries. I gave all you girls beautiful Italian names. All our friends and relatives gave their children American names, but your mother and I wanted our daughters to have Italian names: Rosalina is a lovely rosebud, Marina is the seashore; Colina is a little hill; Angelina, an angel." When I asked him what Sabina meant, he said, "It doesn't mean a damn thing, *bedda*, your mother just liked the name. It's a good name." The funny thing is that our last name, Giovanotti, means *young men*, or *bachelors*, an ironic fact that Mr. Barbiere doesn't let Papa forget.

If I couldn't avoid Vito altogether at school, I would at least pretend that he was nothing more than a casual acquaintance. But he would always give it away. He would share something during lunch or recess, something about me. Whatever he said, he said in a good-natured way, no ill will

39

intended, but it would throw me for a loop. This incident sticks out in my mind: once when we were short a carton of chocolate milk at lunch and J.F. wanted to trade his white milk for my chocolate, Vito traded his instead. I thanked him and he said, "It's okay, I know chocolate's the only kind you like." He may as well have said, "I know you only like to kiss with your eyes closed," for all it revealed about how well he knew me. I wanted to shrink, but then I looked around the table and no one else seemed to think anything of the fact that Vito knew my likes and dislikes so well. The conversation smoothly continued on about milk with Vito confessing that when he was little he thought skim milk was "skin" milk, made from cowhides. And then someone else said that his little sister thought chocolate milk came from brown cows, and with all the fascinating conversation going on, I guess I was the only one who noticed that Vito had removed his glasses and was staring at me.

In the end, I would find out that what Vito knew about me did not come from Papa at all, but from a feckless baby sister named Angelina, who at the age of seven was more interested in boys than in Barbie dolls. My sisters all loved Vito, but Angie was infatuated. To the others, Vito was like a cousin, part of the family (we even called each other's parents *aunt* and *uncle* out of respect) but to Angie, Vito was an *older* boy and she would get dreamy eyes whenever she was around him.

My parents adored Vito. "That boy is good as bread," Mama would say. "He wouldn't hurt a fly, or a mosquito for that matter." And she was right. Vito never stepped on ants, never intentionally hurt any living thing on God's green planet. Once he told me how the Native Americans apologized to an animal before they killed it and thanked the animal for providing food or clothing or whatever. He could be depressed for a day if he accidentally ran over a squirrel. And of course it was worse when he accidentally hurt a person. Once he and his friend, Mikey Pinotta, collided on their bikes and Mikey had to get stitches in his lip. Vito felt so terrible he kept buying ice-cream for him. And another time, when we were playing baseball, Vito accidentally hit me in the forehead, right at the hairline, with the bat. The gash required ten stitches. The poor guy felt so bad. I told him that it didn't hurt much and that my hair would hide the scar, but he still insisted on being my "servant for the day." And so I bossed him around one Saturday from nine in the morning until seven at night. He fetched me food and drink, played round after round of double solitaire, read to me, and acted as my human remote control for the television. It was fun for me but Vito's face was furrowed in concern the entire day as he tried for reparation.

The day of the spring-cleaning I painted the window trim while Vito and Papa carried furniture out to stack in the kitchen. Vito and Papa laughed and joked. I listened while Vito told Papa stories about his one-year old nephew Benny. He really did love kids. Every chance he had he visited his sister Jenny in Oak Park to play with little Benny. So I knew how much he must really love Papa, because he'd chosen Papa and the store over visiting Benny that day.

I hate to admit it but I was jealous of the good time Papa and Vito were having. I hated painting and I wasn't much good at it. I always made such a mess, dripping all over everything. Later in the morning, when all the furniture had been moved, Papa came over to the windows to inspect my work. I remember his words exactly: "Painting must not be one of your strong points, *bedda*. Why don't you help me with the waxing and we'll let Vito finish painting."

Maybe it wasn't really such a big deal, but standing there with white paint on my hands and clothes and in my hair, I felt about *this* tall. I'll be honest, I wanted more than anything to slap that smug smile right off of Vito's face.

"You're certainly enjoying yourself," I said to him later when he came into the kitchen to wash out some brushes.

"Uncle Sunny's great," he shrugged. "My Dad has never told a joke in his life and he wouldn't know an anecdote if it bit him in the ass."

"Don't let Papa hear you swearing," I said. I liked admonishing him.

"What do you mean?" he asked me. "Your father is the only person who lets me swear!" He flashed those white teeth that I rarely saw and shook his brush out at me, splattering me with pale white droplets.

"There's still paint on that brush," I yelled after him. He turned back and flicked the brush at me again. I shrieked, ran for cover, and pretended to be annoyed. And if I had to pinpoint it, I'd say it was at that moment, when the watery paint hit my face like a spring mist, that I fell in love with Vito Salina. He was changing…he'd become more comfortable at our house and more playful with me. I stood there in the store kitchen wiping paint splatters from my face and smiling. My destiny was sealed.

Late in the morning the weather went crazy. We had awakened to April sunshine, but it quickly turned into the kind of Chicago day that couldn't make up its mind: first it was sunny, then rainy, then windy, then sunny again. All in a matter of minutes. By noon it had begun to snow, then hail, dropping pellets the size of shirt buttons on the street. Moments later bright sunshine broke through the clouds. Gale-force winds hit, knocking out power, upending trees, whirling garbage cans, and stirring up the lake.

Vito, the storm-lover, had his face plastered to the front window. He called me over and pointed out a garbage can rolling down the street.

"I've never seen a storm like this before!" he said. He smiled at me when he realized I was afraid.

Mama and Rosa came down to inform us of the weather alerts. "Sixty-mile-an-hour winds," Mama said, shooing Vito and me away from the windows.

"This is scary," Rosa said.

"At least we still have power," I said and then—BLINK—we were in the dark. Everyone looked at me as if it were my fault. The phone rang and I tried another attempt at optimism. "At least the phone still works. That's good news."

The phone worked all right, but the news was all bad. It was Vito's Dad calling. There had been an accident. Vito's mother was dead.

Papa was there to catch Vito when his knees went weak and his legs gave out. Papa lowered him to the floor and held him like a baby. Vito cried for a long time. Mama and Rosa and I cried, too. I was so distraught; I wanted to punch something. I felt violent, like the weather.

At first they weren't going to let me go to the hospital with them. Papa asked Rosa to get me upstairs and to take care of us girls while he and Mama drove Vito to the hospital. But when I handed Vito his jacket, he whispered, "Come with." So I did.

At the hospital we found out what happened: Vito's parents had been driving on the Eisenhower to Oak Park to visit Jenny when the wind and snow hit. Blinded by a whiteout Mr. Salina reflexively hit the brakes in the middle of the expressway, causing his car to be rear-ended. Sara hit the windshield and was killed instantly. Mr. Salina suffered some deep lacerations, bruised ribs, and a crushed knee.

The funeral was so sad. The only way Vito got through it was by holding his baby nephew all day. He remained dry-eyed through Mass and even at the cemetery. But later when we gathered at his grandmother's house he broke down and wouldn't go home with his father. It was agreed that he would stay with Nana Lilli while his father recuperated, but when Mr. Salina was well enough to return home and went to retrieve his son from his mother-in-law, Vito wouldn't budge. He told Papa that he preferred living with his grandmother who barely spoke English, but cooked well and laughed a lot, than with his own father, whom he could scarcely talk to. Vito told me that he never regretted the decision even though in many ways it was as if he had lost both his parents in the accident.

Soon they fell into a routine: Mr. Salina joined his mother-in-law and son for dinner each evening, made attempts to help Vito with his homework (he needed no help), and then walked the three and a half blocks home.

On Sundays Vito and his father would alternate going to his sisters' homes for dinner. Vito was always happy to go to Jenny's. He loved playing with his nephew and he loved eating Jenny's pasta. Sundays at Becky's, well, that was a different story. Becky, a newlywed, was trying hard to master the art of cooking…but I guess she never did. Vito described his sister's dinner as "pasta la pusa" (overcooked pasta) with sauce that "tasted like she opened a can of tomato soup and seasoned it with a little ketchup, and meatballs that were more like breadballs, hard on the outside and mushy in the middle." The food was bad enough, but according to Vito, the company was worse. Becky was married to a disk jockey who loved to hear the sound of his own voice and thought that everyone else did, too. But Vito was very close to Becky and so one Sunday a month he endured the food and the brother-in-law.

Sometimes—oftentimes—when Benny was sick, Jenny would call to cancel Sunday dinner. Needless to say Vito was disappointed, but it was the thought of spending the entire day alone with his father that sent him quickly to the phone to ask Papa if he had any work that needed to be done at the store. Of course, there was usually something and if there wasn't Papa would invent some job or another for Vito. Afterward, Mama would always invite him to stay and have pasta with us.

"Invite your father, too," Mama would say to be polite. But Mr. Salina had an appetite neither for food nor for happy people who enjoyed each other's company. Not once did he ever accept Mama's invitation. Who knows, maybe Vito never actually invited him. Back then I hated the man, thought him to be the meanest person alive, but now when I think about him I realize that I should have felt sorry for him. Losing Sara took everything from him. Before the accident, he was a man who held his emotions in check, but afterward, he seemed to have none at all.

And that is how Vito Salina infiltrated the Giovanotti household. He was always there, every time I turned around, helping Papa or picking up groceries for his Nana. He became a semi-permanent fixture, keeping extra sets of clothes, pajamas, even a toothbrush at our house. Mama had always loved Sara's mother so Nana Lilli was a common guest in our home as well.

Sometimes, I didn't know what to make of it all. Sometimes it was like having a brother or a cousin around, but at other times when I'd see him asleep on our couch, I'd think: that's Vito Salina, a boy in my class, asleep on my couch. What would my teacher think? Or the kids in my class? Sometimes, for me anyway, it was weird. But Mama and Papa had just sort of adopted Vito. They never imagined that we would fall for each other. Over the years I'd openly expressed my indifference toward him—he was too smart, too serious, too boring. Papa disagreed with me, saying Vito was a wine worth getting to know. He said there was more to Vito than what

43

you saw, that he was like a nice Merlot: soft, charming, and accessible. What Papa didn't know then was that Vito, like some vintage wines, lacked "long finish." Besides, back then we all thought Vito was going to be a priest. Everyone knew that after high school he was headed for the seminary where he thought he could get all the answers.

Mama's heart ached for Vito. She was his godmother after all, and once I'd overheard Mama asking Papa if he thought there was any way that they could adopt him. Papa said no, the boy still had a father. Mama said, "Just barely." And Papa said, "Nevertheless."

Once when Vito had eaten the last *cannola* in the refrigerator, one I'd been saving for myself, I groused to Mama, "Why does he have to be here so much anyway? He has a home. He has two homes."

"Bina, you be nice to that boy!" she told me. *"Bedda matre* (beautiful mother) the child lost his mother. Instead of complaining, see if you can get him to talk to you."

"About what?"

"His feelings. You know, how he's getting along. I don't think he has anyone he can really talk to." Mama was worried that without his mother's influence, Vito would draw inward, clam up like his father. His Nana was a spunky old gal but she didn't speak much English and she couldn't read or write. Sometimes when Vito was fishing for an invitation to stay the night or the weekend (or for summer vacation), he would complain to Mama that his Nana was getting a little weird. She would make him put his hand over his heart and sing the National Anthem whenever they watched a baseball game on TV. She rubbed Vicks Vapor Rub on his chest at the merest sniffle and made him drop to his knees to pray whenever Billy Graham's face appeared on the television screen. But I knew she was fun, too. He told us that on Saturday nights they played a loose version of *Charades* and a card game called *Scopa* (with rules that changed as his Nana saw fit). And she loved rock and roll music and would even dance to it! She was feisty, too. If a nun needed a good talking to, it was Nana Lilli, not Mr. Salina, who would button up her black coat over her black dress, pull her silver hair tight in a bun, walk to Our Lady of Pompei, and in a few English words and lots of hand language, get her message across quite clearly.

Vito certainly did not lack attention, but his Nana's hands were not his mother's and sometimes in the middle of class he would lie his head down on his desk and cover himself with his arms. You couldn't hear him cry and when he lifted his head to return to the school work at hand, his eyes, cheeks, his face, gave no indication of his breakdown. But I sat behind him and one row over. I could see the teardrops glistening on his desktop.

One time, he ran away...well, sort of. Nana Lilli had to go to away for a week and Vito was supposed to stay with his father. He only made it three days. Mr. Salina called our house one night looking for him. Mama got panicky, wanted Papa to get in the car and go look for him. Before she could talk Papa into it, Mr. Salina called back and said that Vito was at Becky's house, that he'd *walked* to Franklin Park after school. The next day when I asked Vito about it, he said he just couldn't handle the stress of his father and his house and his mother not being there.

I felt so sorry for him. His home wasn't like mine, a place of comfort and support. And so I did as Mama said and I began to be extra nice to him. At school, I sought him out. I picked him when it was my turn to pick a milk partner, or a square-dance partner, or an eraser cleaner. I tried to get him to talk about his feelings like Mama said but I either wasn't going about it the right way or else it was too late and his emotions had already dried up, because all Vito wanted to talk about was Papa. He'd become obsessed with my father. I loved Papa, too, but let's face it, what thirteen-year-old girl wants to talk about her father all day?

What was there to know that he didn't already know? After all, Vito had known Papa for as long as I'd known him. He knew he'd come to the States at age eighteen, knew that Papa had so fallen in love with the ship on which he'd come that he dreamed of owning a boat himself but then met Mama and baked bread for her father before taking over the store. I answered all the questions I could on the days we walked home from school together. When I had no answer, Vito would try to guess, which exasperated me to no end.

"If Sunny had stayed in Sicily, I wonder what he would have been?" he asked. I knew he didn't walk with me to be nice or because he liked me; he walked home with me because he hoped I'd complain about some chore I had to do at the store, and then he'd pounce on the opportunity to do it for me.

"I don't think there was anything *to be* in Sicily. That's why so many people left."

"Yeah, but if he'd never come here, he would've had to have been something, like a fisherman, or maybe a hotel manager, or maybe an artist."

"Geez, Vito, Papa's from Agrigento. His father was a shepherd. They were dirt poor. There weren't any hotels back then and even now Papa says there's not much tourism."

"But Agrigento has some of the finest Greek ruins anywhere!"

"Listen, my father is just an ordinary guy. He's not Superman. You've put him on this pedestal. But basically he makes bread and sells olives."

He looked at me like I was crazy. "If that's all you think you're father does then you don't know him at all!"

"I know my father very well, thank you, now let's talk about something else."

"Like what?"

"Like feelings."

"Whose feelings?"

"Yours."

"My feelings about what?"

"Well…well, like how are you feeling about, about, about that math test we just took?"

Vito let go a little smile, but quickly pulled it back in. "Well, now that you asked, I guess I'm *feeling* good about that math test. As a matter of fact, I *feel* great about that math test. I *feel* like I aced it. I *feel* like I know more about this section than Sister does. I *feel* like that test was so easy that I should *feel* insulted. Yes, that's how I *feel*, Sabina, good and insulted. Thanks for asking."

He could be a real pain in the ass. He'd gotten cocky, what the nuns called "fresh." *"Now listen here, Mr. Salina, don't you get fresh with me. Just because your sweet mother, God bless her soul* (sign of the cross)*, has left us, don't think for a moment you are excused from good manners. What's happened to you, child?"* But just at the very moment you decided to be mad at Vito Salina, his brown curls would bob on his head like a toddler's, or you would come upon him in the hall helping Oleg Rushkov (one of the only two non-Italian students in our class and the brunt of continuous practical jokes), or you would find him in our neighborhood sticking up for Joey Barbiere Jr., when somebody called Joey a "queer." Yes, Vito had a heart for the underdog, a brain for math and science, and cheeks that mothers and grandmothers loved to pinch. You just couldn't stay angry with him for long. You just couldn't.

It was sometime during that first year after his mother died that Vito finally confided in me about his feelings. After months of asking him how he felt about this or that I finally mustered the courage and asked him straight out, "How are you handling your mother's death?" I just blurted it out as we were walking home from school, with only one day left of the eighth grade. I'd waited until we were a safe distance ahead of Colina and Angie who'd been trailing us and calling us "Mr. and Mrs."

He couldn't look me in the eye but he said, "I'm handling it. It's a piece of shit, but I'm handling it. I don't think I could have without Sunny. And Luna, too, of course, and well, all of you. Thank you, Sabina." Then he took my hand and squeezed it, quickly letting go when he heard giggling behind us. He started walking faster and then he said, "Sabina, ask me how I feel."

I laughed, not knowing if he was being serious or silly, but he waited, so I asked, "Vito, how do you feel?" I was prepared for him to spout off about feeling very confident about starting high school in the fall or very pleased with the honor roll report card he would be receiving the next day, but instead he exhaled deeply and said, "Relieved."

"Relieved? How come?"

I don't know why but he reached over and took my books and carried them for me. He had never done that before. "Because I've come to a decision," he said, so seriously.

"What's that?"

"What's a decision?"

"Geez, Vito, what decision?"

"Well, I'm not going to pursue the priesthood after all. I don't think I really had the calling. I think maybe I was just trying to please my mother. She was kind of sour about marriages, you know. Even *un*arranged ones."

"A scientist then?"

"No, not that either. That was just to please my father."

Was this the same boy who at twelve had mapped out the rest of his life—to start a medical research monastery and follow in the footsteps of his hero, Gregor Mendel, the Austrian monk, biologist and botanist, who gave us among other things, the principles of factorial inheritance?

"So what's it going to be?" I asked. "A fisherman? A hotel manager? Certainly not an artist. That's the only thing you stink at, the only A *minus* you ever got."

We were home now. Colina and Angie shot us one more singsong "Mr. and Mrs." remark, and then went inside. Vito and I stood out in front and continued talking about his feelings.

"Sabina, I got it all worked out," he said. "It's so simple. Jesus himself knew it: you've got to feed people first. Food is the universal language. Sister Alta thinks music is the universal language but she's wrong. Jesus knew: you have to feed the body before the soul." (I didn't know where he was going with this revelation so I just let him go.) "I mean, look, two of Jesus' big time miracles were food-related: the wedding at Cana and the fishes and the loaves."

"So you *do* want to be a fisherman. You're going to Salina or Sicily or somewhere to become a fisherman. Congratulations. You'll be the smartest fisherman that ever lived," I teased.

"Sabina!"

"Okay, I'm sorry. It's just that for months you won't share a single personal feeling and now it's like a flood."

He removed his glasses to pierce my eyes with his.

"Okay," I said. "I'm sorry, go on, finish."

As he leaned against the glass window of Papa's store, the sun shone on his curls and his naked brown eyes. "It's just that now I know the truth, Sabina. You can talk until your lips fall off and never get anywhere with a person, but feed him...feed him!"

"Okay, but what does all this mean?"

"It means I know what I want to be, what I want to do. I just have to talk to your father."

"Papa? Why?"

"Because that's what I want to do—learn the business, be a breadman like him. I want to go to chef's school or culinary college or whatever they call it, and someday I want to buy the market from your father. Keep it going for him. After all, I am his godson and since he doesn't have a son of his own to take over the business, it makes perfect sense."

I guess I was overcome with shock. Why else would I say what I said next: "But *I'm* taking over the business, Vito, *I'm* the one who is taking over the business. Papa wants me to." It was a big fat lie, a lie embroidered out of shock...and yes, jealousy.

"Sabina, I'm surprised. You talk about the store and your chores like they were burdens. I never imagined you loved it so much."

"Well, I do, and I want to expand it someday, turn it into a café or something."

Vito looked at me funny, so I just kept on talking, even though I could feel my nose growing longer by the minute. "Yes, a café, and I would run it, too. I'd be the chef."

He smiled at me indulgently and said, "You can't be a chef, silly, only men can be chefs."

I wanted to strangle him right then and there out in front of our store, but instead I said calmly, "Who says?"

Vito smiled again, as if he couldn't believe how sweet and naive I was. He opened up his backpack and withdrew his Webster's New Collegiate Dictionary (which explained why he seemed to be listing to the right on our walk home). He fanned the pages of the dictionary until he came to the page headed "*cheesy* to *chess*" and pointed to the word *chef.* "Look," he said. And then he read aloud: 'chef—a skilled *male* cook who manages a kitchen.'" Just as he was about to snap the book shut, I wedged my hand between the pages and pointed to the second meaning, which was simply: *cook.*

He clucked his tongue at me and said, "Sabina, you know that the first definition is the preferred."

"That is not true," I said and stomped my foot on the ground, validating his very thoughts of my childishness. "Give me that thing," I said and snatched it from his grip. I flipped to the Explanatory Notes section, found in the front of the book, before the history of the English language section (we had to read this once in English class) where Mr. Webster explains the order of the definitions, but I was flustered and couldn't find the page.

"Come on, you know I'm right," he said, taunting me.

Just as I was about to bop him on the head with his own dictionary, I detected movement in the store window. I thought it was Mama coming out with an after school snack and I was afraid Vito would expose my whopper of a lie, so I steered him over to Mr. Barbiere's barber shop, one door down from the market. I wasn't through with Vito Salina. "What about Julia Child," I said, "is *she* not a chef?" I thought Julia would be an impressive person to have on my side. Back then, there weren't as many celebrity chefs as there are nowadays. I can only think of two: Julia Child, the "French Chef," and Graham Kerr, the "Galloping Gourmet." We'd been watching Julia Child on educational television (what public broadcasting was called at the time) for years.

"I don't think so; I think she's a cook."

"She's the *French Chef* for Pete's sake, not the French Cook. Geez."

"I love Julia, but she's neither French, nor a chef. She's from Pasadena, California, and she only went to cooking school for six months."

"Yes, but at the *Cordon Bleu!*" I screamed.

He smiled and seemed to relent. "I know, I know," he said, giving my shoulder a little pat.

"You think you know all there is to know about just about everything, Vito Salina, but you don't know all there is to know about a lot of things, including me," I said plopping down too hard on Mr. Barbiere's wrought iron bench and hurting my tailbone.

He sat down next to me and right before my eyes he turned into someone else. Someone worlds older. He took my hand again, squeezed it and said, "You're right, I don't. But maybe I know what your Papa knows, that man *can* live on bread alone. Figuratively speaking, of course. Listen, Sabina, maybe our dreams are the same. Maybe this is our destiny. Maybe God wants us to be the next Sunny and Luna. Why can't we *both* run the store—together! I don't know, all of a sudden this just feels so right. Like it was meant to be. Maybe this is our calling!"

And then he took my face in his hand and gave me the first kiss I ever had, possibly the best kiss I ever had. And I was so taken with his eyes and his curls and his rosy cheeks and his God-inspired plans, that who was I to tell him that I really had absolutely no desire to be a chef or a cook at all, that I had my heart set on being a photographer and a world traveler? Who was I to remind him that we were going into high school, not college, and that you didn't have to have your life's plan set in stone at age fourteen? Who the hell was I?

Besides, Vito was the smart one. He was right ninety-nine point-nine-nine-nine percent of the time. And he had vision. Wide-angle vision. Vito could map out a life plan quicker than you could say double chocolate brownie. And now he was including me in his life plan! He was a goal-setter, a dream-weaver, a calculated risk-taker. He saw his projects through. He knew what he was talking about. Period. So who was I to question his plan? He was always right and here's proof: years and years after our little argument about Julia Child, I read an article in a magazine about her where she called herself a *cook*. She admitted that she was not a chef. Vito was right about so much. Except about us.

I win the Guinness World record for the longest bath. My fingers are wrinkled as raisins. I pull the plug, step out of the tub, pass the towel against my skin, and wrap my robe around me. I wipe the steam from the mirror and then I apply some outrageously expensive anti-wrinkle cream to my face. I look at my forty-year-old face in the mirror and remember this old proverb: A man is as old as he feels, and a woman is as old as she looks. I look forty. I feel fifty. I look myself straight in the eye and stick my tongue out at my reflection.

4

Real Friends Never Say "Let's Split Dessert"

I'm picking up Virgie from the bookstore at seven and we're going to see the new Mel Gibson movie. Virgie loves Mel Gibson. Okay so do I, but Virgie *really* loves Mel Gibson. She talks more about Mel Gibson than she does about her husband Pauly. Which is fine by me. I can't wait to tell her about the store. She is going to flip. It's not often that either of us has exciting news. Any excitement in ours lives usually comes from seeing a Mel Gibson movie.

I'm trying to maneuver my father's Buick through traffic. I don't like to drive, in fact I hate to drive, but Virgie's car is getting a new starter and Pauly won't let her drive his car, a virgin white Chrysler LaBaron convertible, which he loves more than life itself.

I'm looking forward to spending an evening with someone over the age of three, since I've spent the last two nights at Angie's house, taking care of her two little ones so she could tag along on one of her husband's business trips. They went to Toledo, Ohio, of all places. But Angie didn't care. She'd begged Art to take her with him, and then she begged me to take the kids. I never say no. How could I even if I wanted to? Victor is almost nine months old and Angie hasn't been away from his side for a minute. I told her that it was kind of pathetic calling two days in Toledo a dream-get-away, but that I would be happy to stay with the kids. I like to play mom. It's a good wake-up call for me. My sisters always make it look so easy. What I want to know is how they can function on so little sleep.

I'm circling the area, trying to find a parking place and it makes me wonder just how much time in years is lost in this city looking for a parking place. I find one, three blocks up from the bookstore. I walk through the misty rain and feel like a soggy sandwich by the time I reach the door.

Virgie is still checking out customers, so I head over to the cookbook section to browse. It never ceases to amaze me how some of these books make it to print. Maybe that's my green-eyed monster showing its teeth—it is my secret wish to see a cookbook of my own perched happily on these very shelves someday: *Recipes and Friends from Mela's Market.*

Here's a new one: *Cooking With Beer,* by Lucy Saunders. I never would have imagined that an entire book could be written on this subject, but here it is. And this one is a must for my sister Rosa: *Healthy Yummies for Young Tummies,* by Ann L. Schrader. Ahh, *Food In History,* by Tannahill Reay. This one looks interesting and I'm trying to find the price when Virgie comes up behind me and says, "Look at you. You need another cookbook like you need another birthday."

"I know, I know, but this one looks good."

"I have it. It is good. I'll lend you my copy."

I shrug, slide the book back into its place and say, "Okay, but you're not going to sell many books that way."

We stand there looking lovingly at the hundreds of cookbooks perched so cheerfully on the shelves. "What is it about cookbooks, do you think?" I ask Virgie who owns as many as I do, possibly more.

"I don't really know. Most people never even try most of the recipes in them."

"I'm guilty of that," I say, knowing that I'd rather read the recipes than actually prepare them.

"Look at all of them," she says. "All of a sudden, everyone can cook—from monks to prostitutes." She pulls one off the shelf called *Dishes From the Red Light District,* by Bernard Hemp. "Maybe it's because they're happy books," she muses. "They're comforting. The pictures are pretty. A person can vicariously eat her way through a good cookbook and never gain an ounce. Plus, there's no tragedy in a cookbook, no dysfunctional families, no conflict."

"Man versus nature," I point out.

"It's going to be woman versus woman if I miss the beginning of the movie. Let's go."

***

Twenty years ago when we heard that Paul Rosinni was bringing home a bride, none of us could believe it. Pauly was a Mama's boy who still lived at home at the age of thirty. (I should talk, but back then, who knew what the future held for me in the line of housing?) We met Virgie at the wedding shower Pauly's aunt threw for her in our church basement. She was five years younger than Pauly but five inches taller and five times smarter. While everyone commented on her more-than-average girth, Mama, sensitive herself to size issues, reminded us girls that it was the size of a person's heart that counted. History has shown: Virginia Rosinni is in possession of a good-sized heart.

I took a liking to Virgie right away. She was shy but inquisitive, and when she found out about our store, she expressed a desire to learn everything she could about Italian food and Italian style cooking in order to please her husband and mother-in-law. She was a fast learner, too. Since Pauly wouldn't let her work and she couldn't seem to get pregnant (did she subconsciously consider the gene pool and opt out?) she had plenty of time for cooking classes and experimentation. Now she's a gifted cook. I've encouraged her for years to open up a little place or at least to get a cooking job, but she lacks the confidence because she wasn't formally trained. She's been working at the bookstore for five years now, and although she likes the job well enough she still dreams about cooking professionally someday.

There's a plate in front of me upon which sits the most perfect wedge of cheesecake I have ever seen. Red raspberry sauce dribbles down the sides and I simply stare at it for several moments before I take my first bite. Oh, oh, oooohhhhhh. I say a quiet thank you to God for the creation of sugar and to the Arabs for the cultivation of it. I'm going to eat this entire piece of cheesecake. By myself. That's what I love about going for dessert with Virgie: unlike my sisters, she never offers to split something.

Virgie's in a talking mood, going on and on about Mel Gibson. I know her well enough to know that when she jabbers about nothing, something is wrong. "Everything's fine," she insists when I ask. I decide to hold off telling her about the store.

We eat slowly, relishing every delicious moment, analyzing every flavor, commenting on content, presentation, and service. Tonight it's four stars for content and presentation, but a half star for service. I think the waitress thinks this is a backwards party (Once Rosa threw her son a backwards party: the children arrive with their clothes on backwards and in-side-out, you greet them with good-bye, then open presents, then eat cake, then sing happy birthday, then play games, then you bid your guests hello as they leave for home) because first she took our drink order, but then brought our desserts before our wine, then she brought our wine, and finally our water. When we leave, Virgie says, "Thank you and hello," and the waitress says, "Whatever."

We walk the three blocks to the car. It's cold, it's drizzling, and it smells like worms. I ask Virgie when she gets her car back.

"Tomorrow, I hope. I hate being car-less. I don't know how you do it. I mean I understand why you do it, but I need my car. I hate feeling dependent on Pauly." Suddenly, she grabs my hand. "Sabina, I was going to tell you over dessert but I didn't want to ruin your cheesecake...I'm leaving Pauly."

I stop walking. It's like I hit a board. I look at Virgie, way up at Virgie. At this moment, in spite of her height, she looks about ten years old.

"There, I said it." She exhales deeply. "You're the first person I've told."

"You haven't told Pauly?"

"He'll be the last person to know."

"Virgie! Geez! I'm so sorry." And I am sorry. But I'm not surprised, I'm not shocked, and I'm not wondering what-the-hell-happened either. I don't even have to ask her if she has another man or if Pauly is seeing another woman. I know what this is about, it's about one person growing and the other person never even growing up. I say I'm sorry again.

"I know, I know. I'm sorry, too. But you know what the really sad thing is? Pauly won't be sorry."

"Oh, Virgie, yes he will be."

"Well, maybe a little sorry, but he won't be devastated or anything. He certainly won't try to talk me out of it."

I'm choosing my words carefully. Mama always told me to use caution in situations like these because the minute you badmouth your friend's boyfriend, fiancé, husband, the two of them get back together and you are left with the words *bastard* and *good-for-nothing lout* hanging from your mouth like a long strand of spaghetti.

"What are you going to do? What are your plans?" Virgie always has a plan; she's more organized than a labor union, more calculating than a computer, but never in a mean-spirited way. She looks through pragmatic eyes, problem-solves, and then carries out a clean, well-thought-out plan. Usually.

"I don't know yet," she says, slamming the car door shut.

I was about to start the engine, but I stop. "What do you mean you don't know yet? You know what you're going to have for breakfast tomorrow, lunch even."

"I know, but God, Sabina, this isn't food, this is my life."

"You're right, I'm sorry." I start the car and pull out into traffic. Dead wet leaves cling to my windshield so I flick on the wipers. As we drive through the drizzle and the silence I can't help but think about Virgie's wedding all those years ago. She and Pauly had looked a little ridiculous up there on the altar, to tell you the truth. Virgie had Joey Jr. do her bright red hair up in a big pile on her head. The veil on top of the up-do added inches to her height so she just towered over Pauly. I can remember overhearing my Uncle Silvio say, "That's a lot of woman for little pee-wee." I guess Uncle Silvio was right, Virgie is too much woman for pee-wee.

"The weird thing," Virgie says as we pull up to her house, a brown bungalow the color of a Hershey's kiss "is that I feel bad for Pauly. I do. He's not a bad guy. I can't even come up with a single instance where he's said one unkind word to me. I don't hate him. But I don't love him. I mean, he's just, he's just…oh, I don't know, I can't describe him."

I can describe him. I have adjectives. I could help her fill in the blanks: dull, boring, dim, bland, wimpy, monotonous, wishy-washy. Take your pick. And I don't hate the guy either. You can't hate what you don't know and no one knows Pauly, not even Pauly. Maybe his mother knows him, but that's just speculation, I couldn't say for sure.

Virgie opens the car door, but she doesn't get out. She's deep in thought, not even noticing the rain she's letting in. After a few seconds she sighs and says, "He's just, well, he's kind of like a prune. You know? What's a prune but a dried-up old plum. I've always felt sorry for prunes. They're kind of pathetic, really. I mean I wouldn't care if I never ate a prune again for the rest of my life, would you?" I shake my head no, and it's the truth, I wouldn't.

"Remove prunes from the grocery shelves and would anybody care? Would anybody complain to the grocer?"

It's a bad habit of mine, but sometimes I answer rhetorical questions. "Old people might," I say. "You know, prune juice."

She breaks a smile, shakes her head, and I'm afraid any second she's going to turn into one of my sisters and say, "Sabina, it's times like these that you should be glad you're not married," but she doesn't, she just says thanks for listening, the movie was great, the cheesecake was great, and she'll call me tomorrow.

If I were Papa I would say: "Virgie, make a plan; map out your future; there are good things ahead." And if I were Mama I'd say: "Pray about it; ask for guidance; everything will turn out all right." But I'm just me, and so I say, "Oh, Virgie," and lean over and give her a hug.

She pats *my* back. "It'll be all right, don't worry." She slams the door and heads up the walk, not even bothering to open her umbrella. I guess rain can be cleansing. I always wait until she gets in, and it's a good thing, too, because this time she doesn't even make it to the stairs. She's heading back to the car. Maybe the poor thing can't face Pauly. Maybe she wants to stay with us tonight. I know Virgie, she puts up a good front, but she's probably just a wreck. I unlock the door but she shakes her head and motions for me to roll down the window. When I do, she says, "I just remembered. You said you had something important to tell me."

"Oh, Virgie, it can wait."

"You sure?"

"I'm sure."

***

Back home in bed, I toss and turn. I think about Virgie and Pauly, about how I could have predicted this all those years ago. I think about Colina and John. What if that jerk really is having an affair? I think about my cousin Ambra, who is getting married in a few weeks to a man she's been going with on-again-off-again for something like eight years. And inevitably, I think of Vito and me. Finally, I'm too tired for this line of thinking. I drift off and dream that I finally make it down the aisle. Papa is walking me down, my sisters are waiting at the altar in silver taffeta. Papa lifts my veil, kisses me and hands me over to my groom—Mel Gibson. I wake up happy, with a glow that lasts for about twenty-five seconds.

5

Brownies, Medium Rare

Outside my bedroom window, Saturday lies before me. It looks like one of those rare fall days in the city where the sky is a blanket of baby blue, with just chips of white cloud interruptions here and there. I am so thankful for sunshine since we've had a week of miserable drizzles. Chicago can be so gloomy this time of year. With days as gray as concrete, you can feel engulfed in the gloom if you're not careful. Sometimes it's hard to distinguish the streets from the buildings from the sky. I have nothing planned today other than a simple haircut at Joey Jr.'s place. The day lies open before me. It's a good feeling.

"So who's going to cut your hair?" Papa asks me when I stop in the kitchen for a quick cup of coffee, "that *finocchio* (fairy)?"

"Papa, be nice. Joey Barbiere's one of the sweetest guys I know. A lot sweeter than his father."

"Yeah, yeah, he's sweet all right.   He's *fairy* sweet, like Tinkerbelle." (Papa just *pretends* that he doesn't like Joey.)

As I head toward the back steps I almost escape the predicted slap on the back. Papa smiles big. I guess I'm not as fast as I was at thirty-nine.

The November air feels like an after-dinner mint in my throat. It's cold but I don't mind.   I'm inside all day long and it gets so hot in our kitchen that sometimes you feel like you're smothering. I walk to Joey's every six weeks regardless of the weather. I walk a lot. It's my main means of transportation and my exercise of choice. I walk to Joey's shop, to the bank, to the camera shop, to Virgie's, to Jimmy's, to the cleaners, the video store—almost anywhere in our neighborhood. I really don't miss having a car. Geez, I've been so long without one, eighteen years now. Besides, I can borrow Papa's car or the delivery van whenever I need to.

Joey's shop is only four blocks up on South Racine so it takes me just ten minutes to get there. It's an entertaining walk. There's street theater on South Racine. I pass a young father pitching a ball to his little redheaded son. Nice hit! I nod to a white-bearded black man leaning against the brick wall of the video store as he passes a bottle in a wrinkled brown paper bag to another old man. A tough looking teenager with a pierced nose whizzes passed me on his bike. I inch closer to the edge of the sidewalk just in time to dodge another boy, a younger, chubby boy, who whooshes by on a skateboard, only this is funny, he's on his stomach, with knees bent and feet straight in the air. Mama worries about me walking everywhere (like other neighborhoods, ours is evolving) but I would hate to think I couldn't walk my own neighborhood anymore.

Like most Chicagoans born and bred here, I nurse a love-hate relationship with this city. The good parts are the lake, the skyline, and the people. The bad parts are the lake, the skyline, and the people. I wonder sometimes if we city dwellers are a totally different animal. Do people in Des Moines, Iowa, or Rockford, Illinois, or Madison, Wisconsin, transfer their living room furniture to their front yards on hot summer nights and then gather the neighbors to play cards, drink beer, and listen to jazz? And do they—like the Italian lady in that tidy brick bungalow on the corner— become so protective of the parking spaces in front of their houses that they'll haul chairs (anything from cheap lawn chairs to good mahogany dining room chairs) out into the street to reserve parking spaces for their kids when they come for Sunday dinner? Bent-backed, babushka-headed Mrs. Tatino is an Academy Award. After she arranges the chairs in the street, she'll sit in her porch swing and hurl dirty looks at curious passersby.

Halfway to Joey's place I look at my watch and pretend to realize that I'm ten minutes early for my appointment. My feet automatically take a left, turning down Lexington Street. I deliberately walk in crispy leaves, crunching them as I pass Our Lady of Pompei Church, and then my Uncle Silvio and Aunt Anna's house, where my cousin Jimmy still lives. I hurry by. If I'm seen I'll be invited in for coffee and a bun and I really just want to walk. When I come to the run-down brown brick house, three up from Uncle Silvio and Aunt Anna's, my feet stop. This was Vito's house. Of course way back when, it was well tended, with overflowing flower boxes, neatly trimmed hedges, and a clean, swept walk. If I squeeze my eyes almost closed I can take myself back twenty-four, twenty-five years easily...

After Vito kissed me on Mr. Barbiere's bench and engineered our life plan, he suddenly didn't want to be apart from me. "Bina, let's go study at my Nana's house," he said.

"Study what? Tomorrow's the last day of school."

"Oh, yeah."

Before he could come up with another idea, Mama peeked her head out of the store and asked if we were hungry. We told her we weren't. She frowned at first. How could we not be hungry? But then her face turned all smiley, and it made me think it pleased her to see Vito and me sitting and talking together.

"Well, then, if you're not hungry, would you mind delivering some bread to Aunt Anna?"

She was talking to me, but it was Vito who answered. "Sure, Aunt Luna, we'll deliver it."

Mama shot me a look and a wink that said: "Now's your chance to get him to talk about his feelings." Little did my sweet mother know: we were way beyond that.

At my Aunt Anna's there was no turning down her offer of milk and biscotti, so Vito and I sat on her porch swing, nibbling and sipping, while my aunt reminisced about Vito's mother Sara, who'd been her favorite neighbor. "She'll dance in heaven the day you are ordained, *beddu*," she told Vito, while dabbing at her eyes. I almost choked on my cookie.

When the cookies were gone and Aunt Anna went inside, Vito left me waiting on the swing while he walked three doors down to tell his father that he wasn't going to be a priest, that he wasn't going to be a scientist, that he was going to be a breadman like his godfather.

He looked like a dejected puppy when he came back. Apparently Mr. Salina had little to say about his son's future. Vito plopped down on the swing beside me and said, "He said okay, whatever I wanted."

"That's good, right?"

"It doesn't matter to him. The guy checked out a long time ago."

Vito was right about that, Mr. Salina had grown increasingly depressed and withdrawn after Sara died. Neither Vito nor his sisters knew how to help him.

A few days later, Vito told my father about his plans, explaining it all carefully: his short-terms goal of attending a good cooking school and his long term goal of working with Papa and one day taking over the market for him. I was certain that Papa would try to talk him out of it. I thought he'd say something noble like, "The world of science awaits you, my boy," or "Your vocation, my son, is the bread of life, not the bread of Mela's Market." Or, "You're so young, don't decide yet. There's plenty of time." Instead, he was ecstatic.

Nana Lilli was enthusiastic as well, but I'm quite certain the little old thing had no idea as to the extent of Vito's intellect. It was Mama who was shocked, who made a fuss. She slapped her cheeks and said, "What about the priesthood?"

Vito and I started high school with grand plans for our future together (all of them secret) as business partners. He had it all planned out: he would go to culinary school and I would get a business degree. This way we'd have both ends covered. Even back then I wondered who was getting the better end of that deal since Vito would get to cook beans while I had to count them. I didn't want to be a bean counter; I wanted to be a photographer. But that kiss Vito had given me outside of Mr. Barbiere's shop was still wet on my lips.

At school the boys laughed at Vito for taking Foods 101 but do you think he cared? We were in the same class and he cooked his way into becoming teacher's pet. "Teacher" was young Miss Compton, fresh out of college and a little flighty. Vito ended up much like an assistant, often out-performing cute little Miss Compton. He quickly developed a competitive streak, something that lay dormant in grade school. At Our Lady of Pompei everyone knew that Vito was the smartest student by a long shot so he had nothing to prove. High school was a different matter. Guys like Vito—potential valedictorians—were around every corner.

Vito spent hours upon hours with Papa and Mr. Maggio learning his way around the kitchen. He grew especially good at bread making, which pleased my father immensely. He'd always liked Vito's hands, always knew he had good hands for bread.

Vito grew fiercely competitive of me, vying for Papa's attention, always trying to prove himself worthy of taking over the store someday. Once we had this first semester baking project: brownies from scratch to be prepared at home, taste-tested by Miss Compton at school, and then served as refreshments at parents' night that evening. On the bus home, Vito was gloating. He said he'd gotten his hands on a special brownie recipe.

Couldn't wait to get home to try it. Mama had a great brownie recipe, too, I told him.

"I know," he said. "That's whose recipe I'm using. With some secret additions and omissions of course."

"*My* mother's brownie recipe?"

"Yes, ma'am."

Well, I wanted to know how he happened to have *my* mother's brownie recipe. He said he'd found an index card in his grandma's recipe box labeled "Luna's Fudge Brownies."

"But like I said, I'm adapting it, so go ahead and use it if you want to. I won't mind."

That night after dinner, Rosa helped me make Luna's Fudge Brownies downstairs in the store kitchen. My first mistake was asking for Rosa's help. My second mistake was telling her about Vito's planned improvements to Mama's perfect recipe. It ignited *her* competitive spark.

"Let me at this recipe," Rosa said. Then she proceeded to break all Mama's rules about the integrity of ingredients and not overdoing it, as she threw into the batter marshmallows, walnuts, almonds, raisins, and two different kinds of semi-sweet chocolate chips. While we waited for the timer to go off, Rosa and I drank bottles of Coke and shared a bag of salted pumpkinseeds.

By the time I realized that I had never even *set* the timer, the smell of burnt brownies assaulted my nostrils. The results vaguely resembled a piece of asphalt. I released a very dramatic, "AWWWW!" but Rosa insisted all was not lost. A stickler for details, she pointed out that a nine by thirteen pan didn't divide evenly into twelve three by three squares (the required brownie size). "They're really three by three and a quarter inch squares," she explained, gesturing with the knife, "so we'll just cut off a quarter inch of the burned part and they'll be just fine."

We sat at the counter and shared another bag of pumpkinseeds while the burnt asphalt, which counted as one-third of my semester grade, cooled. "What's going on with you and Vito anyway?" Rosa asked me.

"What do you mean?"

"Well, it seems like he's crazy about you but then he's so competitive, too."

I twisted my lips into a sideways pucker then shrugged. "I don't really get it myself. I guess he wants to impress Papa."

"Mama's a little worried about you two."

"Why?"

"Well, now that Vito's not going to be a priest and all, she was asking Papa if he should be spending so much time here and sleeping over and everything. You know, it's different now. And you'll be dating when you're sixteen and…"

It *was* different now. Very different. I was confused by it all, and I didn't want to discuss it until I had thought it through. "Look Rosa, right now I have to worry about these brownies."

"Well, I'm sorry honey but these aren't brownies, these are rockies." She tried to cut them, first dipping the knife in a glass of water, but she couldn't even get the knife to penetrate. Well, we got to laughing and then to giggling and then we tried so hard to get that knife through those brownies that the whole pan slid off the table and even then the brownies didn't budge from the pan. We laughed and laughed until it occurred to me that I was going to get a zero on this project, then I got teary. "What are we going to do?" I asked Rosa.

"Don't worry, it's only seven o'clock. We'll make another batch, the regular way."

And so we mixed and measured to Mama's exact specifications but then one of us unknowingly bumped the oven dial, turning it up to four hundred-fifty degrees. This time we had a piece of concrete. Now it was close to eight o'clock and our lips were swollen from the salted pumpkinseeds. "I guess I better go up and get Mama," I told Rosa. But I hated to because I knew Mama was busy helping Marina with a school sewing project that counted as one half of her semester grade.

"No," Rosa said, blocking my way. "Better yet. I'll go get Betty Crocker." She sneaked out to the convenience store and came back with two boxes ("just in case") of Betty Crocker fudge brownie mix. We mixed and baked and this time they came out pretty good, but after cutting them into squares I said, "Miss Compton warned us not to try to use a mix; she said she'd be able to tell."

"Tell, Schmell. Just make sure she tastes yours last or almost last. After tasting thirty different brownies her *tongue* is going to taste like a brownie. Don't worry about it."

But I didn't sleep well that night. The next morning on the bus Vito wanted to see my brownies.

"No," I said, pulling them out of his reach. "They're wrapped just so. I don't want them to get squished."

"Just a peek," he said. "Just lift the foil, that's all."

"Geez, Vito, they're brownies. They're just like yours—Luna's Fudge Brownies. Exactly like yours."

"Let's see."

"No!"

"Come on."

I flipped the foil for a split second, like a woman flashing a peek at her breasts. He couldn't have seen anything but a blur of brown, but he looked up at me and clucked his tongue. "Sabina! I can't believe you used a mix!"

I looked over my shoulders to see if anyone was listening. "You jerk!" I whispered loudly. "You can tell just by looking?" I began to perspire in anticipation of my impending embarrassment and failure. After all, the Giovanottis were "food" people. Mama had never bought a boxed mix of anything in her life. What about her reputation?

Fortunately for me, Miss Compton ended up getting a sick stomach after taste-testing brownies from her first and second hour classes. By third hour, Mr. Monsanto, our principal and self-proclaimed "brownie connoisseur," volunteered himself as ringer. Mr. Monsanto thought *all* our brownies were wonderful, but he proclaimed Vito's brownies to be "brownie perfection." He went on tasting and praising until he was covered with crumbs. While he licked his fingers, I sighed in relief. I'd pulled it off. I smirked at Vito who was sitting across the room. He did a thumbs up.

Weeks later Vito and I and our gang of friends stopped by a diner after a school basketball game. We were supposed to stay with the group (group dating policy), but Vito and I sneaked off to a booth of our own to share a brownie a la mode. In a sweet moment, he reached across the booth to wipe some powdered sugar from my chin. He licked the sugar from his fingers and said, as if weeks hadn't gone by, "I saw Rosa at the store that night buying the Betty Crocker."

I was shocked. "You jerk!" I said. "Hey, wait a minute. What were *you* doing there? You weren't buying a brownie mix by any chance were you?"

"Sabina," he scoffed. "Pa-lease. Mr. Monsanto called my brownies 'brownie perfection.' I just wanted to get some fresher eggs, that's all."

I wasn't so sure. But that's when our food competition was born. That night I went home and informed Mama that I wanted to learn how to cook and bake, just like her. Rosa said, "Me too," and Mama said well it was about time.

I never told Vito what Rosa said the night we were making brownies, but as time went on, Vito became nervous around Mama, for no reason at all. But Mama took it for guilt of some kind or another and had a serious talk with Papa who in turn had a serious talk with Vito. We would both be turning sixteen soon, getting our licenses, and going out on "couple dates" rather than group dates.

Vito met Papa after the store closed and they scrubbed the grill while they talked so they'd have something to do with their hands. I stayed upstairs and watched *I Love Lucy* with Colina and Angie. After what seemed an eternity Papa came up the back stairs and called me into the kitchen. He smiled and said, "You can go down now. Vito's going to help you with your Geometry homework." He slapped me hard on the back. "You're a good girl, Bina. And you know I love that kid."

Vito and I sat on stools at the counter and worked on proof theorems, which I despised and he loved. Then he told me about the "little talk." Basically, it was: "you're turning into a fine young man" and "you're always welcome in our home" and "you're like a son to me." Papa told Vito that he knew he and I were attracted to each other which was fine with him, but to go slowly, not to get too serious at such a young age and to date other people. Then Vito said Papa got really serious and said, "Just so you know: every single one of my daughters is going to college." Vito told Papa he understood his wishes clearly and was glad they had the little chat. Then Papa lightened up and said, "One more thing kid, no more slumber parties," and gave Vito one of his famous slaps on the back.

That night I ended up getting what my sisters dubbed the "virgin talk." Mama came into our bedroom and kicked Rosa and Marina out for a few minutes. We sat at the edge of the bed staring at the floor. She slung her arm around my neck and drew me closer.

"Papa talked to Vito," she started.

"I know."

"It's just that once he decided not to be a priest, it—well, it changed his presence here."

"I know, Mama."

"I mean before it was like having a nephew or a cousin around. I never dreamed you'd fall for each other. And there he was asleep on our sofa."

"Mama, you don't have to feel bad. Nobody thinks bad about it or anything."

"Not bad. Just strange. I just feel like I stuffed him in your face. You're young, *bedda*, you have choices."

"I know that Mama, and for right now I'm choosing him. You still love him, don't you?"

"Like a son, *bedda*, that's what makes it so hard. He's the sweetest boy I've ever met. Sara would be so proud—even if he doesn't become a priest."

"Oh, he's not going to be a priest, Mama, that's for sure." I guess I said this in a way that made her wonder how I knew for sure. She looked at me with suspicious eyes. "At least that's what he's told me."

She stood up suddenly. "Sabina, we have to talk about sex."

"Mama, we had our sex talk years ago."

"Yes, I know, but your hormones weren't raging then, and now look at you." I felt my cheeks with my hands and wondered if you *could* actually see a person's hormones raging. "I'll tell you the same thing I told your sisters: It's best to wait. And Papa and I expect you to wait. I'm not one of these mothers that helps her daughter have premarital sex by either getting her on the pill or supplying her with rubbers (oh, how I hated that word), or by closing my eyes and pretending I don't see raging hormones."

Maybe you *can* see hormones, I thought again.

She came back and sat next to me on the bed and took my hands in hers. "Sabina, you're a good girl, but this is a different world, what with this sexual liberation and feminist stuff, and I agree with some of it—but within the confines of marriage. You're going to be tempted, and I just ask that you remember this: you are special, your body is special, and every time you have sex with someone you give away a very intimate piece of yourself. Some girls end up feeling very empty—like they've given away everything. Just remember that and always do as I've taught you, always ask 'What would Jesus say about this?'" She patted my cheeks and kissed my forehead. "Be a good girl and then you'll be a happy girl, too. Jesus, Mary, and Joseph, I've got five girls to keep my eyes on, five beautiful girls, and I think that little Angelina is starting early with the goo-goo eyes! Set a good example for her, Bina."

Rosa and Marina came back in laughing. "So you got the virgin talk!" Rosa said. "Congratulations! It's a right of passage." My sisters were "good" girls and I vowed to be a good girl, too. I hated to see Mama so worried. She didn't need to worry about me.

No, she didn't need to worry her little heart about anything in that area, at least not yet anyway. Vito certainly wasn't a hopeless romantic. After all, he'd only his father as a role model. In our high school days we held hands and kissed but mostly we "planned" for our future together. It was as if both the business and the romance lie somewhere out in the future. I wanted to tell Mama that I didn't think Vito ever really thought about sex—at least he never acted like it was foremost in his mind, like most boys his age. Rosa and Marina talked about fighting boys off, but that had never happened to me. Sometimes, I had to wonder, why not?

At times, Vito's demeanor annoyed me, but usually I was glad he respected me and that at least one of us had hormones that weren't raging. Sometimes though I'd lie in bed and torture myself with doubts. *Maybe he doesn't really love me. He's never said in words that he loves me. He talks about our plans and our future and our destiny. About running the store together, about cooking together...partners...a team. Maybe we've known each other too long and we're mistaking familiarity for love. Maybe it's all because of his mother's death—he wants a family, my family.*

Once I got started it was hard to stop. But just when my doubts would surface to the point where I could actually look at them as real possibilities, Vito would say or do something that would end up laying all my worries to rest.

Like this one night, we'd been out to a movie and I'd worn a new outfit and there'd been no compliment, and the goodnight kiss could have been from my uncle for all the passion it held. I was really in the dumps. Then he called…

"Bina, just wanted to say goodnight."

"Goodnight."

"You all right?"

"Yeah, just tired."

"I forgot to tell you what Mr. Maggio and I made this morning."

"Whoopie?"

"Sabina!"

"What did you make?" I asked in between an enormous yawn.

"Raisin bread."

"Yum."

"And as I was stirring in the raisins it occurred to me that your eyes are as dark as raisins."

"Is that a good thing?"

"Raisins are good."

"But are raisin eyes good?"

"Very good."

"Oh. So am I like a gingerbread woman or something?"

"Then I got to thinking about your whole face."

"While you were stirring in the raisins?"

"Actually while I was kneading the dough."

"I don't think I like the symbolism in that."

"No, no, listen. I was thinking what a beautiful face you have. You really have a beautiful face."

"I do?" I said. This wasn't like him.

"Yes, and you have a beautiful body attached to it. *You* are beautiful."

"And *you* are embarrassing me."

"It's just that I was thinking, I've known you, well, forever, and sometimes you just take for granted that something is beautiful and sometimes you even forget that something is beautiful, because it's so familiar. But then something or someone reminds you and then it hits you in the face."

"Who or what reminded you?" I demanded.

"Brad Burns." (Brad Burns was that year's Homecoming King, Mr. Muscle-builder, Star Quarterback—you know the kind.)

"What? What did he say to you?"

"Just that he thought you were...I think the word he used was luminous."

"Luminous?"

"Yeah, luminous. Or he might have said luminescent. No, it was luminous, because then he added voluptuous, and I started to get pissed off, but before I did I remember that I was impressed that a guy like him had those two words in his otherwise limited vocabulary."

"Vito!"

"What?"

"What did you say to him?"

"I said, 'Don't you think I know that?'"

"And what did he say?"

"He wanted to know what the story with us was. He'd heard we were cousins."

"Cousins!"

"Yeah. I felt like a jerk."

"Well, what does all this tell you?"

"That I'd better stop treating you like a cousin?"

"Yeah, and?"

"That other guys are interested?"

"Bingo."

"The thing is, I don't think we've been acting like cousins; I think we've been acting like an old married couple. I'm sorry, Bina."

"You don't have to say you're sorry, just tell me what I was wearing tonight."

"Uh, uhmmmm, jeans and a, jeans and a—"

Imagine, a forty-year-old woman, and these are the conversations that are carved on my brain word-for-word. I can't remember how to conjugate a single Spanish verb, but I can remember every sophomoric conversation I ever had with Vito Salina.

***

That same chubby kid doing the stomach thing on his skateboard snaps me out of my daydream. This time he falls off. I give him a hand and he gives me a million-dollar smile. I look at my watch. If I power walk to Frederick's, I'll be on time.

Joey's place is hopping. He runs a nice business, the works, with hair stylists, manicurists, cosmetologists, and a couple of tanning beds. My

67

only complaint about Joey would have to be his relentless cross selling of services: "Would you like a half-price pedicure with that manicure?" or, "How about ten dollars off your next makeover with any perm or color?"

Joey greets me with a kiss that never quite touches my cheek. "Sabina. I had fun at your fortieth Halloween party. Girl, you don't look a day over thirty-five. Swear to God."

"Thanks a million, but you're just saying that because I'm one of your oldest customers."

"Oh, honey, I've got lots of customers older than you."

"You know what I mean. I've probably been coming here for twenty-five years. I keep thinking one of these times, you'll get it right."

He practically strangles me with a purple plastic cape and then cranks me up in the chair. "Your nails don't have to look like that, Sabina," he singsongs.

"Cut it out, Joey."

"Just tell me this one thing," he says to the "me" in the mirror. "Why oh why won't you let me cut this hair, I mean really cut this hair?"

"Joey—"

"I could take five years off this face with a stylish cut."

"Say ten and you got yourself a deal, Barbiere."

He flips my hair this way and that way and over and under and around and says, "I'm an artist, honey, not a magician."

"Just trim off an inch please."

"Yes, Ma'am."

But before he can start snipping, he gets called away to handle some catastrophe or other and I am left here to stare at myself in the big-lighted mirror before me. If you must know, I haven't changed my hairstyle in twenty-five years. My dark brown hair is still parted down the middle and shoulder-length. When I'm working I pull it back with a barrette. Boring, but me. I shake my hair like the girls in the TV commercials do and then feel stupid. Maybe forty is too old for long hair.

Joey comes back with "the book," a slick, hardcover with black and white photographs of models with the latest hairstyles. He pushes this book in front of my face every time I come in. Today he throws it on my lap, flips to a page marked with a sticky note, and points his finger to a photo of a woman who looks remarkably like me. Her hair, the same color as mine and seemingly the same texture, is parted on the side, chin length, and layered stylishly. She has my dark brown eyes, olive skin, my wide mouth.

"I'll take it," I blurt out.

"You're kidding me."

"No, really, I like it. Cut it off. Just twirl me around so I don't have to watch.

He starts to snip. I bite my lip. "So what'da get for your birthday, doll?" he asks.

"Cashmere sweater from the rich one."

"You go girl." Snip. Snip. Snip. Snip.

"A new camera lens."

"And season tickets from Sunny and Luna?"

"Yes, but they threw in a little extra something this year."

"Oh, do tell."

"The store."

"The store?"

"The store. They're retiring earlier than planned."

"That's great news, Sabina! It's what you've always wanted. Even if that *traditore* didn't stick around to be your partner, the idiot fool. Can I help you redecorate?"

"Of course you can," I say. He starts rattling off ideas about a fifties theme complete with jukeboxes and sock hops on Saturday nights. I let him talk. Everybody knows Joey is all talk and no action. He hasn't redecorated his own place in years, but he talks about it all the time.

Finally, he spins me around to see my new do. I have to admit, I like it. It feels nice—lighter, but not bouncy.

"There, you look like a businesswoman. But really now you're going to have to let Gary do your nails. A proprietor should be well groomed. Let's find Gary and make an appointment. He's booked solid for months, but we'll just squeeze you in—my birthday present to you, girlfriend."

Well, I think, as Joey leads me by the hand to Gary's cubicle, won't Aunt Lina be pleased that I'm finally polishing up the merchandise.

6

Kitchen Crimes Punishable By Death

I'm up to my elbows in cookie dough. I'm here, believe it or not, in the kitchen of my high school Foods class. Yes, Miss Compton's class, only Miss Compton is long gone. My mother, three of my aunts, three of my cousins, and all of my sisters are here with me. We've gathered here on this gray November Sunday to bake hundreds of Italian cookies to serve at my cousin Ambra's wedding next week. We're wrapped in floral aprons, we're wearing our most comfortable shoes, and we're armed with wire whisks and wooden spoons.

If you've ever been to an Italian wedding, even a small one, then you know about the tradition of serving trays upon trays of Italian cookies. Cookies for the guests to consume by the plateful, to enjoy with their slices of wedding cake, and to dunk in their cups of coffee or *vino*. The cookies, all from my Nana Melarosso's recipes, are so good—moist or chewy or crunchy—that they usually out stage the wedding cake. In our neighborhood, the reputation of a woman's wedding and holiday cookies precedes her. Mama and her sisters, Lina, Josie, Gina, and Connie make cookies that are so delicious and well-known in our circle that strangers (not strangers so much as uninvited neighbors) have been known to crash our weddings just to sample a few of the legendary cookies.

We've been using this kitchen for ten years now, ever since my cousin Natalie started teaching here. When I first came back, it was kind of weird. I had this gnawing feeling that even after all these years, somehow, some way, someone was going to find out about my boxed brownie mix. Plus, everything in the room reminded me of Vito. But what other kitchen has six ovens and six kitchen stations and a definite requisite of Mama's—room to dance?

We've paired ourselves off by experience: one master to one assistant. I think this is the third time in a row that I've been stuck with Colina, who hates baking, could care less about cookies, and probably hasn't even bitten into one in years. At the very least, her steady hand and attention to detail usually make her an excellent measurer, but today she's definitely distracted. She has a way of pouring "high up," hence creating a fine dust that assails my sensitive nostrils and gives rise to a series of six or seven consecutive sneezes. What makes this even more annoying is that afterwards I have to stop and wash my hands, and as anyone who bakes knows, it is so easy to forget where you left off—did I just add the second cup sugar or was I just about to? Mama and I have always agreed that true baking success comes from solitary kitchen confinement.

I seek out Rosa's eyes, make contact, and ask in a telepathic fashion if she's found out anything else about John. She shrugs back in answer. Colina and I continue baking. I read off what I need, she measures it and pours it in, and I mix or combine or fold or cream or blend. At least we make an efficient team if not a cheerful one. But everyone else is cheery, even merry.

There's music because Mama always brings a tape player and it's booming out what she calls "cookie music," a medley of Sicilian folk songs about weddings or food. Mama's favorite is this silly Sicilian folk song (Lou Monte covered it in the fifties) about a daughter talking to her mother about marriage. They play this tarantella at all the Italian weddings (even in the first *Godfather* movie where the wedding guests take turns singing choruses).

In the song, a daughter tells her mother that the moon is over the sea and so she wants to marry. The mother asks the daughter who she wants. Verse after verse follows with the mother considering the baker, the butcher, the fireman, and the fisherman. The old song is replete with double entendres—the fish, sausage, bread, and fire hose all representing a phallus, the moral of the story being: "Honey, it doesn't matter who you marry, they're all going to want the same thing."

When Mama and her sisters hear this song they go crazy and start dancing arm-in-arm around the room. The rest of us are quick to join in. Mama starts pantomiming—pretending to hold a fish, a sausage, a loaf of bread, or a fire hose right below the belt. We laugh so hard and loud, sometimes we don't hear the oven buzzers going off.

I'm making Italian Chocolate Cookies. There are many different recipes for these particular cookies—some that taste like cocoa-flavored cardboard, others like undercooked fudge. Of course my Nana Melarosso's recipe is perfect. This recipe takes a bit of time since it makes two hundred cookies, plus you have to allow time for the cooled cookies to be dipped in icing and dried. But they're worth it. Bite into one and you will find a chocolate flavor so deep and so bold you just have to cut it with a glass of ice-cold milk. Men love these cookies, but beware, the union of chocolate and raisins creates a chemical reaction known in Italian as *flatulenza*. If my brother-in-law Ross consumes too many of these cookies Marina makes him sleep on the couch.

Mama and Natalie are making Fig Cookies. Aunt Lina and Angie are making Almond Biscotti. Aunt Josie and Annie are making Sesame Seed Sticks. Rosa and Franny are making Orange Cookies. Aunt Connie and Marina are making Pineapple Cookies.

You'd have to ask Rosa if you want to know how many pounds of flour, sugar, and shortening she bought or how many dozens of eggs we've gone through because she was in charge of those purchases. All I know is that we will walk out of here with more than a thousand cookies, about fourteen dozen of each variety. This is a labor of love, a dying tradition that the older ladies are trying to preserve, but to be honest, Franny, Natalie, Annie, Colina, and Angie are here only because they love and respect their mothers, not because they love cookies or respect the tradition. I'm afraid by the time all of their children get married, it will be only Rosa and me and maybe Marina here in this kitchen. But for now, I'm happy to be here with these ladies.

Somewhere in between the dancing and the baking, my sister Angie gets the devil in her and starts chasing Aunt Lina around the kitchen, threatening to give her an almond biscotti dough mustache. This because Aunt Lina told her she should seriously look into getting a boob job.

"Sabina," Aunt Lina says, mustache-free, out of breath, and using me as a human shield, "show me where the bathrooms are, will you?"

As we walk down the long dark hall Aunt Lina complains about Angie's cooking skills. I'm hearing only half of what she's saying because my old high school walls start talking to me, and suddenly I am taken back in time...

In this very hallway Vito opened up his letter from the California Culinary Academy and announced to his best friend, Mikey Pinotta, and me that he'd been accepted. We jumped and hugged, and when I dropped a folder, papers went flying like confetti.

Vito's dream was finally coming true. We'd spent hours in the library researching cooking schools, only to find that the really good ones were in New York. The best known and most influential cooking school in the country was and still is the Culinary Institute of America, in New Haven, New York. Even back then the CIA was known as the Harvard of cooking schools. I told Vito to go for it. But when we added up the total cost including housing, it was astronomical.

Then we came across a brand new school called the California Culinary Academy in San Francisco. The cost, while still high, was more reasonable. Vito got excited about this one. The more he found out about it, the more excited he became.

"Why San Francisco?" I whined. "It's soooo far!"

"San Francisco is a world-famous culinary Mecca."

"Yeah?"

"With award-winning wine regions nearby."

"Yeah?"

"With access to some of the world's greatest restaurants and markets."

"Yeah?"

"They have all these kitchens, Bina, including three baking and pastry kitchens, two Garde Manger kitchens, and two demonstration kitchens."

"You're starting to sound like a brochure."

"Plus they have student-run restaurants."

"Well, one thing I know they don't have."

"What? They've got everything, Sabina."

"They don't have Sabina."

He took my hand and squeezed it. "Yes, I know. This *is* a problem."

There were other problems as well, like the fact that the Academy's Culinary Arts Degree Program including Baking and Pastry Arts ran only two years, and I'd be attending the University of Illinois for four years.

"What will you do for two years while I'm finishing school?" I wanted to know.

"I thought I'd help your father at the store. I've got some improvements in mind." You could almost see the wheels turning in his head.

The night before he left, we threw him a going-away party at the store. Actually, my idea was to invite over a few close friends, make pizzas and have a quiet night together. But of course Rosa got wind of it and even though she wasn't the rich one yet, she still had a penchant for parties. She turned my little gathering into an all-out surprise *bon voyage* party, complete with gag gifts and everything—wooden spoons, a pornographic apron, a broken mix-master, and my gift: a box of Betty Crocker fudge brownie mix.

Vito was truly touched by the whole affair, getting choked up at the toast and at the end when he thanked everyone for coming. When the party was over, we kicked my sisters out saying we would finish cleaning up. We really just wanted to extend the last bit of time we had together. When everything was put away we sat at the counter sipping bottles of Coke. Vito leaned over and gave me a peck on the lips. "It was a great party. And I really was surprised."

"You can thank Rosa for the surprise part."

"Man, I can't believe I'm really going."

"Tomorrow."

"Tomorrow. Man, Bina, I'm sitting here kind of shaking." He splayed his fingers out in front of him. He was shaking. "I'm scared shitless," he said.

"It'll be okay. You're just nervous."

"I've never been anywhere, never been on a plane, never lived alone. I don't know, I've been thinking maybe this isn't the right decision, maybe I should work at the store for a year and then go to school. Maybe—"

"Vito." I took his hand and squeezed it. He hadn't been this vulnerable and confused since his mother died. "It's going to be just fine."

"It's going to be hard as hell."

"You're smart, you'll blow them away."

"I mean to be apart from you."

"I know."

"Bina, you know how much I respect you. And your Dad would murder me if we ever, well, you know. But it's been so hard."

I didn't know what to say, but I got shivers.

"I mean I've always assumed that we'd wait, that you'd want to wait, you know, until we got married. That's what you want, right?"

"Of course," I said. "But you know you've never formally proposed to me, don't you? I have no ring, no date, no—"

"I did so propose!"

"Oh yeah? I must've missed it."

"When we were fourteen years old. In front of Joey the Barber's place. That's when it all started."

"Geez, we were young," I said, remembering that day and that kiss as if it were yesterday.

"Babies."

"What did we know about anything?" I said.

"Nothing. But we're not babies now are we?"

"No, but I still think it's best to wait, don't you?" I asked.

"Course I do. We're mature. We love each other. What's a couple of years anyway?"

"Seven hundred…and…thirty days to be exact."

"Man, Bina!" He threw his head down on the counter with a thump. I lay mine down, too. An onlooker may have thought we were deep in prayer. I was. I was doing exactly what Mama had told me to do when faced with this situation, ask the Lord what to do. But I didn't really have to ask—every cell of my body was Roman Catholic. Every cell said to wait. But were hormones cells? Because all the hormones were saying: Go for it!

I let out a big sigh of resignation. Vito took it for what it was. He popped up and looked over at me and smiled. He didn't say anything, just laid his head back down, but facing me this time and then he started gently rubbing the back of my calf. We were suspended in time, just staring at each other, until finally he broke the trance and said, "We better make a promise right here and right now that we're going to wait so when I come home after the first part of the program, I'll know what to expect or I guess what not to expect."

"Okay," I said, extending my hand for a handshake, "let's promise." We shook hands, and then hugged, and then kissed, and then Vito took me around to the other side of the counter, and we broke our promise right then and there on Papa's hardwood floor. Afterwards, between kisses, he kept saying "I love you" and "I'm sorry." But I didn't feel bad, honest I didn't. I felt wonderful. Vito and I had shared a part of ourselves that up to this point had never been expressed. It was like a seal of our love. Vito and I were special: we weren't two immature sex-crazed kids fooling around with fate. Our future was secure! We had a plan! More than you could say about most eighteen-year-olds, right?

But as I lay there on that cold hard floor, I grew nervous. I tried to rationalize what we had done. It had all happened so quickly. There wasn't time to think. It was so spontaneous, so unplanned. Then this thought shot through my head: if this was so spontaneous, how come Vito just happened to have a condom on hand? I looked into Vito's eyes and found the answer…he loved me! He wanted this! He had planned this! I felt better.

Vito held me for the longest time. But then the doubts returned and I started to cry. Why did we do this? Wouldn't it change everything? Wouldn't it just complicate things? Make it harder to be apart? Vito read my thoughts and tried to soothe me. He said we could renew our promise to wait, which was ridiculous really, you either waited or you didn't. I guess we didn't.

The next day he left me for his "world-famous culinary Mecca" in California, and a week or so later I started at UIC. While Vito stirred sauces, flipped omelets, and drizzled olive oil, I absorbed all I could about supply and demand, debits and credits, and free trade laws. I hadn't expected the theory of business to be more boring than real life business, but believe me, it was. I couldn't sit still at a desk. I day-dreamed about working at the store with Vito. I could picture us behind the counter teasing our customers just like Mama and Papa. I thought about the children we would have. Vito wanted five or six. I missed him so much and wondered how we would survive being apart for so long. I lived for his letters. Luckily, one came every other day or so.

> *Dear Bina,*
> *I miss you! I miss you! I'm finally settled! For a guy who's never left Chicago proper, this trip has really been a trip! First of all, San Francisco is gorgeous—the hills are even hillier than I thought! (Isn't that an intelligent remark?) Anyway, everything went smoothly and I've got myself settled in. I'm rooming with this guy named Hoss (yeah, like the guy from Bonanza). He's about six-four, three hundred pounds, and my hand hurt for an hour after our first handshake. He told me he's from "Tex-ass" and he's been cookin' up Bar-B-Que and grits in his uncle's restaurant for years. He says now he wants to learn to cook "some of them fancy-schmancy foods." I think he's going to be all right. I'm going to be really nice to him so he doesn't ever get the urge to smoosh me! Actually he's full of "Tex-ass" good cheer, and I think that will suit me fine.*
> *Man, this place is so different from the Midwest. It looks different. It sounds different. It even smells different. I miss the smells of home...I miss you.*
> *Well, tomorrow I begin my rigorous journey—seven hours a day, five days a week for the next eighteen months, then on to pastry school. I guess I'm really on my way to becoming a culinarian.*
> *Write soon and tell me all about UIC! Love, V.*

Dear Bina,

Wow! This is a hectic schedule. I really love what I'm doing and I'm learning so much, but it's overwhelming. The chef instructors are geniuses but I say they can't hold a candle to your mother.

Hoss is working out well. We don't really see each other that much—just in and out. Call me on Saturday—about noon would be a good time because I'll be here studying thickening agents; I'm trying to perfect my roux.

I miss your face—but I have it memorized right down to your raisin eyes. All day long, I stir you into sauces, I toss you into salads, I whip you into soufflés and I drizzle you on vegetables...you are here with me. This is for us. Love, V.

Dear Bina,

I can't get enough of this stuff! When you finally get to study the subject you love exclusively it's a little like heaven. I am eating this stuff up—pun intended!

I never realized how many different kinds of chefs there are: executive chef, sous chef, chef saucier, chef routisseur, chef emetier, chef grade-manger, chef patissier, chef tourant. And I'd never ever heard of a sugar chef, have you? A sugar chef creates these amazing edible art objects out of sugar syrup. I will learn the art of sugar creation when I get to the baking end of the program. Talk to you Sunday! I'll call you around noon. Love, V.

Dear Bina,

Well, believe it or not, I have now completed Introduction to Gastronomy and Culinary Math. The Math was easy! Questions like—you are catering a luncheon for 200 people; you estimate that each person will eat three quarters of a cup of potato salad; how many pounds of potato salad should you order? I'm also finished with Product Identification, and Sanitation and Nutrition. I don't know what I was thinking, but I thought I would be cooking more and studying less, but anyway, next comes Meat Identification and Meat Fabrication.

How did your Statistics exam go? I'm sure you did fine. Your professor really sounds like a jerk, but hang in there! Well, I think my brain is caramelizing, so I better wrap it up. I can't really explain it, but there's such a sense of urgency here. Even when you're not in the classroom it spills over into the rest of your life. Love, V.

P.S. Hoss is starting to drive me a little crazy—he's skipped a.m. classes and is watching a lot of M.A.S.H. reruns. I'm not sure he's going to make it. They say ten percent of us will drop out and if he keeps it up, he might end up on the list of culinary casualties. This place is not for the weak-kneed, weak-backed, slow-moving person. It's all about method and speed.

Dear Bina,
You will be proud to know that I can now identify any and all retail cuts of beef, veal, pork, and lamb.
Now I'm really cooking! I've got this awesome Skills teacher. He demos everything—even how to peel a carrot. Everyday we cut two pounds of mirepoix—one part celery, one part carrot and two parts onion. We made tomato cancasse—a fancy name for chopped tomato. Now we're learning to make the perfect stock, the perfect consomme, the perfect roux, the perfect Béchamel.
Big test tomorrow! I'm going to take a nap before I hit the books. Kick some butt on your Econ test. Love, V.

Midpoint through the year Vito's letters started to include requests: Go and buy this cookbook—it's marvelous. Take your mother and father to such and such a restaurant in Chicago—my instructor's brother owns it. See if Papa can get his hands on a rennetless, basil pesto Monterey jack cheese—it's sublime.

That is how my cookbook collection got started. Every time Vito said buy a book, I not only bought it, but in between my own studies, I read it as well. Then I brought the books home for Mama to read, and only then did Mama realize what a great cook she was. She learned the names of some of the culinary techniques she used everyday, things that were second nature to her. And this is when Mama really started to experiment with cooking foods from other Italian regions and putting a new twist on old classics. It was as if Mama knew her cooking was good, but somehow seeing it in books, gave her validation. She soaked fruit in liqueur or wine to soften it and release its juices, but she never knew there was a name for it—to macerate. She didn't realize that by melting butter, letting it stand until the milk solids settled to the bottom and then skimming and straining, she was "clarifying" it. That stirring and scraping the residues from a roasting pan was called "deglazing." That a mixture of flour and fat used as a thickening agent was a "roux," or that cooking vegetables over a low heat until they were soft and translucent was called "sweating."

By the time Vito began the thirty-week baking and pastry program we had an impressive cookbook collection. Back then there weren't that many from which to choose. Virgie tells me that nowadays there are over fifty thousand cookbooks on the shelves, everything from the best midnight snacks to cooking with flowers.

It was after reading all of those cookbooks that I got the idea to write one of my own. I knew I wasn't a great writer, but I knew I could get my sisters to help me polish it up. Here's what I have after all these years: an orange colored pocket folder filled with a half dozen of lunch recipes and some photos I took of customers enjoying Mama's dishes in our store. So much for about twenty years of work. But now with Mama and Papa selling me the store, I have to write the cookbook. I have to get it all down, so that even if I run the business to the ground, the food and the spirit of the food will live on forever. I have to write the damn cookbook.

Aunt Lina's voice pops my daydream bubble. "I *said,* did I tell you I like your haircut?" she asks me, running her fingers through my hair.

"Yes, several times," I say, flipping it back to the proper direction.

"That's because I can't believe how nice it looks. I've been telling you to spiff up the merchandise. If only you'd let me treat you to a makeover at Le Franc's, I could have you married by Christmas."

"Oh, if it were only that easy, Aunt Lina."

There are eight stalls in the bathroom, but of course, my aunt has to go in the stall right next to me. I can see her feet; her shoes are the only thing that gives away her age.

"It *is* that easy," she says as she flushes. "Look at me. I kept myself looking good. I found myself three husbands, Sabina, one in my twenties, one in my thirties, and one in my forties." She comes out of the stall and adjusts her slacks under her apron. "Oh, did I tell you about the guy at my salon? David does him right after me, so I see him every month. Last week I ask David, I say what's up with this guy? I didn't see a ring, is he married or what? And David said to me, 'Isn't he a little young for you, Emmalina?' And I said, 'Not for me you idiot, for my niece. I got this beautiful niece.'"

"Uh-oh."

"Now listen," she says as she washes her hands, "he's forty-two, divorced, one daughter, twelve. He gets her on Tuesdays and every other weekend. He's a police detective—"

"Fancy word for cop."

"And I showed him your picture."

"You didn't."

"I did. But it was with your old hairdo. Wish I'd had a picture of you now. But no matter, baby, he liked your face. Said he'd like to meet you."

"Aunt Lina."

"His name is Ron Donald. He's nice-looking. Don't you like a man in a uniform? I've always liked the sight of a man in uniform. He's very tall and has a nice head of hair, too, for a cop."

"I thought he was a police detective."

She gives me a look and then pulls a pack of cigarettes out of her purse and lights one up. I say, "Aunt Lina, you can't smoke in—" She just blows a forceful cloud my way. I ponder over the possibility that this guy's real name is Ronald Donald, which is silly enough in itself, but way, way too close to Ronald *Mc*Donald. I'm not desperate enough to settle for a clown, even a famous one.

I opt not to comment on the name and instead say, "Look, I appreciate what you're trying to do here, and I don't want to hurt your feelings, but, well, I'm sure he's nice and I'm sure he's very tall, and he's probably a fantastic cop, and once you get passed the name he's probably Mr. Wonder—"

"What's wrong with the name?"

"Nothing, nothing, only when you hear it, don't you get hungry for a cheeseburger and fries?" I can't stifle myself.

"Sabina!"

"Well, I've picked up that bad habit from you. You're the one who's always butchering people's names to death."

"Well, I never even made the connection. You'd like him. And he likes to eat."

"You don't understand."

"But I do. I understand that you gotta get out there, baby. This is a big city. You gotta start somewhere. You go out with him. You don't have to marry the bastard, just get out. See a movie, get some Chinese."

"Or a quarter-pounder with cheese."

She chokes on her cigarette smoke and asks me when I became such a smart-ass.

"Since I've been hanging around with you. Listen, let me think about it, okay?"

"What's to think about? It's not like they're lined up."

"Well, he got to see a picture of me. How come I don't get to see what he looks like?"

"What?" She punches me in the arm. "You don't trust me? You think I'd fix you up with some ugly guy? Sabina, *bambina*! If there's one thing I got, it's an eye for a good-looking guy. All three of my husbands were lookers. Oh! Joe number one was good looking but stupid, Joe number two was good looking but lazy, and Joe number three was good looking and good for nothing, but at least he left me very, very comfortable." I smile because it always strikes me as funny when rich people compare their wealth to a good-fitting pair of underwear. "Anyway, if I could have combined the three of them into one man, taken number one's looks, number two's brains, and number three's mula, I'd probably still be married today. But then I wouldn't be here to help you, now would I?" She pats my cheek. I just hate it when she pats my cheek.

She's trapped me in here you know, in this smoky, dimly-lit, prison green rest room. She's leaning on the door, and I know her all too well: we will not be leaving this room until a promise is made to go out with Ron Donald, the cop, not the clown.

I can play her game. "Well, let me ask you this, what are his hands like? Does he have nice hands?"

"Hands! What the hell are you talking about, hands? Who the hell cares about hands?"

"Hands are very important to me, Aunt Lina. They tell a lot about a person. I could fall in love with a nice pair of hands."

"Okay, okay. That's it. God knows I've tried to help you." She opens the door and waves me through. "I got one request before I die, honest to God; I want to get my hands on that Vito Salina. I want to tell him what a rotten excuse for a human being he is. Tell him how he messed up your life forever. What a bastard. What a pathetic piss. What a goddamn fool!"

"Aunt Lina!"

"Sorry," she says, dragging out the "ree."

Just to shut her up I say, "Okay, okay, maybe I'll go out with him."

She drapes her arm around my neck in a "gottcha" kind of way. "I think you'll like him, I really do. Did I mention how tall he was? Anyway, just give him a chance, try him on for size."

Sure, Aunt Lina, I'll give him a try I think as we walk down the hall. She thinks she knows all about my life. She knows nothing. I've had dates. Geez, I've had dates. There was Carl, this male nurse Marina knew, who'd worked trauma at Cook County Hospital for a year. Try eating a bowl of chili while being fed graphic details of head injuries and stab wounds. There was Simon, this construction guy who helped build one of Ed's shoe stores. He was like adventure-boy—bungie-jumping, skydiving, and hang-gliding his way through life. Everything was a "rush." He kept saying, "You should try it." Little did he know he was talking to a girl who holds onto railings when descending stairs.

Believe it or not, it was Mr. Barbiere who fixed me up with an "almost." Thomas French was a med student just finishing up at the University of Chicago when we met for dinner and a play. I thought maybe there was something there, but then he moved to California to do his residency. I remember his hands—intelligent, capable hands.

If I had a penny for every time one of my relatives said, "Go out with him, Bina, as a favor to me," I could cash in big. As a favor, I've dated a plumber (they make good money, Sabina), a car salesman (you'll always drive in style), an electrician (he'd be handy to have around the house), and a guy who sold vitamins by day and was a comedian by night, ba dump bum.

I've had some doozies all right. But here's the clincher: only one of the guys I've dated ever asked me out for a second date. So then you think, maybe it's me. I guess it's only fair to look at the situation from the guy's side, right? "Please, please Pete, or Tony, or whoever, do me a favor and take out this girl, huh? She's a nice girl, a pretty girl. And she can cook too. As a matter of fact she works at her family's Italian cafe. She's a waitress. Yeah, a waitress."

I don't think I'm uninteresting, it's just that my topics are limited. I guess I do talk about food a lot. I found out very quickly on dates that most men don't like to talk about food the way women do. They just want a plate of something wonderful set in front of them so that they have something to munch on while they talk about themselves. Just so the food is nice and hot and primarily animal fat, who cares how it was prepared, which spices were used, or from where the recipe originated. All of this has led me to a very prejudicial conclusion: that people should stick to their own kind—royalty to royalty, politicians to politicians, actors to actors, and foodies to foodies.

I really need to find a breadman. Who else is going to appreciate someone like me? No one else but a fellow foodie is going to care about the culinary minutiae swimming around in my brain. Like, in China, for example, it's an insult to the host if you *don't* slurp your soup. Or, that the color of wine is not determined by the type of grapes. That the first doggy bag originates back to ancient Rome where diners brought with them small linen bags to use both as napkins and sacks to carry home leftovers. That weight for weight, truffles are the world's most expensive foodstuff. That there is a pasta dish called *Pasta alla Puttanesca* which means literally "in the style of a prostitute." (The sauce for this dish, found mostly in and around Rome, is made with tomatoes, garlic, black olives, anchovies, and capers. It's thought that the name originates from the idea that because this dish can be made quickly, the prostitute could have a delicious meal between clients. That, or else that the sauce for the dish is rather spicy.) But no one seems to care, at least no one since Vito, who was the one who told me all that stuff anyway.

Aunt Lina and I smell disaster as we walk back into the kitchen just as Colina is pulling out a pan of my chocolate cookies. They're burned beyond recognition.

"Colina!" I scream, but Rosa shoots me a look from across the room, like, go easy on her. "What happened?"

"I forgot to set the timer. Sorry."

Know this about me: ever since the infamous brownies I had to make for food class, I consider burning food a senseless and preventable crime. But in light of Colina's frayed nerves, I say in my big sister voice: "No problem, Cocalina, we'll just make another batch."

I stick another pan in the oven, set the timer, and turn around to see that the bride-to-be, my cousin, Ambra, and her mother, my Aunt Gina, have arrived. They've just come from a huge wedding shower thrown by Ambra's father's sister, and when I say huge, I mean the kind where they rent a hall and set up a microphone at the head table for the bride to use to announce her gifts. My sisters had these kinds of showers.

I hug Ambra and ask how her shower was.

"Fine until my little sister wrecked it," she tells me, popping a hot cookie in her mouth.

"What did Carlian do now?" I ask. Ambra and Carlian are always at each other's throats.

"Stole my thunder, that's all. After I opened all my gifts, I do the bride thing and thank the guests. I tell them that I'll see them at the wedding on November nineteenth, blah, blah, blah, and then Carlian pulls the microphone toward her and I think she's going to say something about what a great sister I am and how proud she is to be my maid-of-frigging-honor and instead she says, 'I have an announcement to make, I'm getting married too.' And then she flashes her engagement ring at everybody."

"Is it a 'can hardly' diamond?" Aunt Lina wants to know.

"Sure is. It's so frigging big you 'can hardly' keep your jaw from dropping."

Mama rolls her eyes to heaven.

Aunt Lina comes closer, wiping her hands on her apron. "You know what this means, Sabina? You know, don't you?"

"Emmalina," Mama warns, one step ahead of her.

"It means you are the last. Dead last. All seventeen of the grandchildren are married or will be married soon. All of your sisters. All of your cousins—some of them twice!"

"Emmalina, leave her alone!" Mama says. But no one can stop Aunt Lina once she gets up on her high horse and starts looking down on the rest of the world. "This is what I mean, Sabina. Your life is passing you by!"

All eyes are upon me. My mother. My sisters. My cousins. My aunts. I know they think I'm going to fall apart. I've heard their whispers: So-and-so is engaged, but don't tell Sabina just yet, it's so hard on her. I say slowly, calmly, as if speaking to a child, "I don't see it that way, Aunt Lina, that my life is passing me by. You think I'm very, very foolish, but did it ever occur to you that I just might be very, very patient?" As if on cue, three timers go off in succession and everyone runs to the cookies. We still have several hundred to go.

I hear Mama whispering loudly to Aunt Lina, but then Rosa turns on the music, turns it up loud, and their voices disappear behind the song about a daughter who wants to get married to a butcher, or a fisherman or a breadman, or damn it, to anyone. I guess she's not as patient as I am. That, or she needs to get away from a domineering mother, someone not unlike my Aunt Emmalina.

***

It's later that night. I lie in bed under a sheet, two blankets, and a down comforter. I have a robe on over my flannel nightgown and slippers over my socks. I can't seem to get warm. I keep reading the same sentence over and over in my book. I can't concentrate. I keep thinking about Aunt Lina and thanking God that she's only my aunt and not my mother. I sometimes try to imagine the kind of childhood my Aunt Lina's three boys must have endured. I don't know them that well since they live out East, but when they visited I got to see Aunt Lina in action.

"When I was on the phone," Aunt Lina told me once, "my boys were not allowed to interrupt me. And if one of them did, I threw a shoe at him."

I have witnessed Aunt Lina reprimanding her sons. "Don't speak to me when I'm speaking to you," was one of her favorite lines. I could imagine her pitching commands at her sons like baseballs: "Jump!' "Go." "Eat." "Shut up." "Go to sleep." I'm not saying she didn't love them, of course she did—she removed every seed from every slice of watermelon they ever ate—but I don't think she was the snuggling kind. The funny thing about Aunt Lina is that the kids all love her. They like her accent, and beg her to say car (*cah*) or brother (*bratha*). Or they point to things and ask, "What do they call this out East?" It's funny to them that jeans are "dungarees" and panties are "bloomers" and a drinking fountain is a "bubbler." A "smear" is something you put on a bagel, and out East, you don't wait *in* line, you wait *on* line. The fact that she likes to play games is not diminished by the fact that she plays to win. They like to hear her talk about New York, how different it is from the Midwest. How? She'll tell you that everything is bigger and better and brighter and more expensive. "And out there it's okay to swear. Everybody swears. Here, people only cuss in private. What a waste! Out there we swore at friends, relatives, even strangers—we weren't prejudiced."

What am I going to do with Aunt Lina? What will happen when I take over the store? Will she retire, too? What if she wants to stay on? I don't think I could handle her without Papa and Mama. I could take Marina's advice and "fire her sorry ass." But we all know I won't do that. Nothing to do but wait it out and see what happens. Be patient. After all, wasn't I the one who just told Aunt Lina that I was very, very patient?

I hear footsteps outside my bedroom door and I wait for a knock, but instead I hear a faint swish under the door and I see a piece of paper slide through. I get up, pick it up, get back under the covers and unfold it. It's Papa's writing and it says:

Bina,
Mama told me about your Aunt Pain-in-the-Ass.
She also told me you put her in her place. Reminded
me of a quote I like: "Never think that God's delays
are God's denials. Hold on; hold fast; hold out.
Patience is genius." (Buffon) Love, Papa

I smile and burrow deeper under the covers. Papa started writing me notes when Vito left. We'd always been able to talk face to face, but Vito's abrupt departure was so painful for all of us that our entire household became monastery-mute for days. The whole family avoided making eye contact with me, certain I would fall apart. They avoided mentioning Vito's name, which thank goodness was not a common one that popped into our daily conversations, like Mike or Jim or Joe. For awhile they avoided me completely. Rosa and Marina, who were already married, didn't telephone. What could they say to me? Colina and Angelina, themselves caught up in teenage love, even giggled in whispers. Mama made my favorite foods. Papa switched from dispensing advice through silly little songs to pithy little notes. After all this time, they're still coming.

I lie back and read the quote again. *Hold on, hold fast, hold out.* That's exactly what I've been doing all these years and where has it gotten me? I know Mr. Buffon, whoever he may be, was speaking of holding on to faith, to hope, to dreams. I guess I've been holding on to memories, which are the opposite of dreams. I want to tell Papa that maybe we got it wrong, that maybe what I need to do is to move on, think fast and get out, but that would necessitate asking an important follow-up question: HOW? I close my eyes and see the letters H, O, and W, written in block letters on the black and gold snowy screen that is the undersides of my eyelids. I sleep. I dream. I wake up a day older.

7

Stir Occasionally

I'm awake. But I feel like a piece of stale bread. I hit the snooze button for the third time and seriously consider spending the whole day in bed, alone, under the covers, and in the dark. Maybe I'm coming down with something. Definitely coming down with something. I hear the shower running. Mama's up. Her alarm clock has no snooze button because she is her own alarm clock. Wakes up at 5:30 a.m. regardless of what time she turned in. Her arms won't even be sore from all the baking we did yesterday.

The faucet shuts off abruptly and I hear Mama singing "Amazing Grace," her all-time favorite song. I roll over. When I hear Papa whistling that happy face song—*something, something, cheer up, put on a happy face, spread sunshine all over the place, just put on a happy face*—that's when I pull the covers over my head. It's not always easy living with such sunshine-happy people. How is it that these two sixty-somethings can greet the day with such vim and vigor, and I can barely place my feet on the floor? Something's wrong with this picture.

I lie here contemplating forty. I'm trying hard to honor my father and take an optimistic view: Okay, if I live until I'm ninety then right now I'm in the top of the second scene of Act II. I lay out a matrix on the ceiling from age zero to forty so I can look at my life as a linear equation. I can't do it, but one thing is for sure, the current output that is me is not directly proportional to all the input. I could be wrong, but optimism might just be another word for fooling yourself.

There's a knock. It's Mama, I can tell. My parents' knocks have personalities all their own. Mama's is a series of five soft, tentative taps. Papa's, three forceful blows: blam, blam, blam.

"I'm up," I call out, removing the covers from my head.

Mama comes in and sits down on my bed. "Oh, you're up all right. Tell me what's going on with your sister."

"Oh, I don't know, I think she's planning a surprise party for someone…anyone."

"You know who I mean."

"I know who you mean. What do you know so far?"

"Just that she's been crying at the drop of a hat and snapping at the girls. When I ask her what's wrong she says nothing."

"She and John are having some trouble, Ma, but I don't have details. If you want details, talk to Angie."

"I already did. Everybody's so hush-hush."

"Well, you're the one who warns them not to complain about their husbands because they make up and you stay mad."

"I know, and it's good advice, too," she says as she pats my foot. "Well, I'm not going to worry until there's something to worry about. Somebody said, 'It's no use putting up your umbrella before it rains' and I think it's good advice."

I tell Mama as I finally force myself out of bed, "Maybe it's nothing. You know Colina, she invents trouble."

"Not so much invents it," Mama says, rising from the side of my bed, "as invites it over for dinner."

***

I'm down here in the store sweeping the hardwood floors. And although sweeping is nothing more than one of the many routine tasks I perform each morning, today it's different. For soon this floor and everything that sits upon it will be mine. All morning I have been looking through different eyes. I notice things, like, how the floors need waxing again, and how the ceiling fans, when turned to high, shimmy.

And people look different, too. Like Mr. Maggio. Now that I know he's ready to retire, he looks ancient, a hundred, at least. And Jimmy, now that I know he'll soon be in my employ, he looks less like a young Frank Sinatra and more like one of Jerry Lewis's goofball characters. I watch him as he mops the area I've just swept. He's using the mop alternately as a cleaning tool and a microphone to the tune of Frank Sinatra's *I've Got You Under My Skin.* I stop, rest my chin on the top of the broom handle and watch him until he notices me. When he finally does, he smiles at me, dips the mop, and then gives her a very long, very passionate kiss. My sweet Lord, I think, we have the same genes coursing through our bodies.

My favorite part of the day is right before we open. Soon this place will be buzzing with people, but until they arrive, Jimmy and I have the place to ourselves. This is our time of peace before we get so busy we can only visit the bathroom on an emergency basis. The store is blanketed with the warm, yeasty aroma of fresh baking bread. Later in the morning, the aroma of fresh brewed coffee overpowers that of the bread, but there's a short time, just a minute or so, when your nose can detect both scents equally. There's a subtle interplay of the two aromas, and it's such a delicious smell I told Papa he just had to create some kind of coffee bread. Within days he came up with a cappuccino cheese bread that Mr. Barbiere says will "make-a you cry." It actually tastes like *Tiramisu* in a bread. Honest.

Papa's outside sweeping the walk, something he does every day. Even in the winter after he shovels, he'll take the broom to the remaining snow. "You got to look welcoming," he says. "The outside of your place should scream out to people, 'Come on in! It's warm, it smells good, there are good things to eat, and people who will treat you decent and make you laugh.'"

Again I see through different eyes as I observe Papa's silhouette on the window shade as he sweeps the leaves that have accumulated on the doorstep. He takes brisk, deep swipes and I am visited by the thought that this is the way Papa handles all of life's little problems—simply sweeps them out of the way. It makes me wonder how I will handle the problems that arise at Mela's: that one incorrigible customer who finds his way inside once or twice a week, the dependable vendor that suddenly isn't, the debilitating mechanical breakdown, not to mention the stroke-inducing surprise health inspection.

I find myself staring at the window shade even after Papa's silhouette has disappeared. The yellow glow of morning light filters around the shades, and when I raise them, the whole place is flooded with sunlight. I feel better, almost reassured by the soft rays of light.

I do love this place. Really, most of my life has been lived out down here in the store. It's been my living room, my dining room, my place of study and discovery, my playground. All the important news of my life—births, deaths, engagements, accidents—has been delivered to me right here in this room. And if I close my eyes and think "there's no place like home, there's no place like home," home ends up being this bright sunlit space and not the darker, quieter apartment that lies above it. Home is and always was the store.

They all call it the *store*—Mama, Papa, the whole family—but I never felt that *store* was the right word for the place. "We sell things, so it's a store," Papa would retort. My grandfather opened the doors to Mela's Market on Taylor Street in the heart of little Italy sixty years ago, after his door-to-door business grew too much for one person. When he came to Chicago from Sicily, he didn't know much about America (he truly expected the streets to be paved with gold), he didn't know much of the language (although he had memorized the phrase "God Bless America"), and he didn't know many people (his three brothers and their families). But he did know food—Sicilian food—so he bought a small wooden cart, knocked on neighbors' doors, and peddled his goods. Soon people in the neighborhood came to count on my grandfather for their olive oil and cheese and *babalucci* (snails). With every customer, he left a wine sap apple to help him or her remember his name: *Melarosso*, which means "red apple." Imagine, marketing gimmickry even back then!

I hear a key jiggle in the lock on the front door. I swear, Aunt Lina will never get the hang of that thing. The door opens, the little bell rings, and I hear Papa say, "See, it's nothing. Turn the key to the left *while* you pull on the knob."

"Well, for cripes sake, Sunny, a lock shouldn't be so damned complicated."

My time of peace is over.

"Wait until I tell you about my date last night!" Aunt Lina calls to me, singing the word "night" as if it had two syllables. "I had a very, very nice time and another scrumptious meal at Charlie Trotter's: yellow fin tuna served with lobster and garnished with sprouts and mushroom caps in a shellfish vinaigrette—"

"Who with this time?" Mama, who has just come from the kitchen, asks. Papa, finished with his sweeping, slams the front door closed just in time to hear Aunt Lina's answer.

"Benjamin Roan."

"Mr. Roan?" I yell.

"He was very, very nice," she retorts.

"Well of course he was," Mama says. "He's a very, very nice man."

I'm waiting for Papa to say something like, "Too nice for you," but he doesn't comment at all, just walks past us with his broom. But before he pushes open the kitchen door, I hear him mumble, "Ben Roan," in a way that makes you think Mr. Roan robbed a bank or something.

Mr. Roan, one of two professors from University of Illinois who take their breakfast daily at Mela's, is a persnickety bird-boned man with close-cropped dark hair and a pencil mustache. (I think he teaches Ancient Philosophy.) When I first introduced Aunt Lina to Mr. Roan, she extended her hand for a shake and said, "What's your first name, honey, Testoster?" Mama about died. Since then Papa has tried to keep Aunt Lina in the kitchen as much as possible but she still manages to escape just long enough to meet and nickname customers. She calls Mr. Barbiere "Joey the Baldy" to his face! The Radanza brothers—Nick and Tony—she calls "Mac" and "Roni." My favorite Mr. Charlie Gradezzi is *Capitano Naso* (Captain Nose), and mean old Aunt Lina calls poor Mrs. Zinsia "Helen Keller." Her answer when I asked her why: "She's almost blind, might as well be deaf, and she sure is dumb." With Aunt Lina, nothing is sacred and no one is safe.

But that hasn't stopped her from having more dates in the last six months than I have had in my entire life. To my father's horror she has dated just about every man between the age of fifty and death who has walked in this place—even Charlie Gradezzi, which just about broke my heart. But maybe *date* is too strong a word. She has *allowed* various men to escort her around the city of Chicago, a city that, she reminds us daily, cannot hold a "measly birthday candle" to "my" New York.

Mr. Barbiere is probably the only customer she hasn't gone out with and I think it's his new goal in life, to get a date with her. She makes these men take her to the most expensive restaurants in town, where she orders the highest priced entrée on the menu, the priciest bottle of wine, the costliest dessert.

Mama warns her for the millionth time that her suitors are going to want something in return. Aunt Lina tells her not to worry, they get something in return. Mama gasps. "Lina, you're not having relations with all of these men, are you?"

"Cripes, Luna, give me a break, will you? Most of these old geezers can't handle anything more than a little necking."

Papa told her months ago that if he loses one customer because of her, she's fired. Aunt Lina just laughed. She patted his cheek and said, "Don't worry, Sunny, I guarantee they'll keep coming back."

And she's right. But it's not her charms that keep them coming back—it's her cooking. Even though her cooking skills are identical to her people skills (she bosses food around too) the results are delicious. The food here is out of this world. Even though neither has been formally trained, Mama and Aunt Lina are truly connoisseurs of good Italian food. They both feign modesty and describe themselves as "just two old ladies who know how to cook," but they have come (naturally and by research and experience) to know and understand the details, techniques, and principles of fine cuisine.

Aunt Lina likes to think she's a gourmet, an epicure, a gastronome. But it's Mama who is truly all of these, a literal bon vivant. Some people think in words, some in images. Mama thinks in flavors. Don't get me wrong—Aunt Lina is a good cook, too, but she's more by the book. Mama's not afraid to experiment and by juggling flavors she's come up with some tasty surprises. Mama's dishes are more abstract; Aunt Lina's more concrete. Mama's a messy cook, chaotic and spontaneous, guided by her taste buds. Aunt Lina's neat and tidy and likes authentic renderings. In the end, they're like two plates at the pass: you won't be disappointed either way.

Before Aunt Lina came to help at the store our menu was pretty straightforward: *focaccia, calzoni,* soups and sandwiches on fresh baked bread. When Aunt Lina came, she and Mama agreed to each prepare one authentic regional entree of the day. And now their rustic dishes are packing them in. People leave here happy, lulled by the carbohydrates that we now know positively effect brain serotonin levels. Plainly speaking: carbohydrates make us happy!

It's not just the food—people love Mama and Papa, too. Papa, with his incessant teasing, his counterfeit grouchiness, and his affectionate slaps on the back keeps them coming back. And Mama, with her golden smile, empathetic ear, and tender heart keeps them coming back.

Aunt Lina drags Mama by the arm to the kitchen. I shake my head because I know that all morning my poor mother will have to endure an exhaustive critique of her sister's dining experience at Charlie Trotter's.

When the kitchen door closes and he's sure she can't hear him, Jimmy and mop come closer. He says, "You can't really blame her, Sabina. Shit, *I'd* go to Charlie Trotter's with Mr. Roan if he asked me."

***

At exactly two minutes to seven I turn the front door lock and flip the open/closed sign around to *open*. Mr. Barbiere is waiting for me, which is no surprise because Mr. Barbiere is always waiting for me. You could set your clock by this guy. A bald man of diminutive size, he attempts to compensate for his shortcomings by walking on his tiptoes and combing what few hairs are left on his head into complicated swirls around his scalp. He greets me with a grunt and enters with an "I'm-in-with-the-owner" attitude. In all the years I've known him, he's barely given me the time of day. Most the time he doesn't even remember my name, calling me by one of my sister's names or just "Ina"—the common ending of all our names. He's really only interested in two people here: Papa, to harass and Aunt Lina, to entice.

As for Aunt Lina, she has made it perfectly clear that in spite of his money Mr. Barbiere would never find himself in the running. "Everything but his pocketbook is very, very small," she told Mama and me one day. "I'd bet good money he has nothing but a Tootsie Roll in his pants." Honest to God, she said that. So there you go: logic alla Emmalina.

Even though they're friends, Papa pretends to have little time for a man who legally changed his surname of *Barbiere* to *Barber*. Barbiere means barber in Italian and coincidentally (give me a break) Mr. Barbiere is a barber. The sign on his shop right next door says *Joey the Barber*, and that's what everyone except for Papa, Aunt Lina, and me calls him, as if "the" were his middle name. I call him "Mr. Barbiere" because Papa has always demanded respect for the customers from his daughters. Papa calls him simply "Barbiere"...to rub it in that the man betrayed his heritage by changing his name. And you already know what Aunt Lina calls him.

Papa has mellowed over the years but he used to be so disgusted by all the Italians, who, when they came to this country, wanted so badly to assimilate that they Americanized their names and disassociated themselves from their heritage. Papa calls them *Italiani annacquato* (watered down Italians). Once Papa went so far as to criticize his own father-in-law for calling his store *Mela's* Market, instead of *Melarosso's* Market. Mama said that didn't count because, one, her father didn't legally change his name, and two, it wasn't Americanized so much as shortened—it wasn't like he called it *Apple's* Market.

Papa has confided in me more than once about wishing he hadn't promised my grandfather that he would never change the store's name. Sometimes I catch him staring up at the sign outside while sweeping the front walk and I know he's picturing how it would look if it said *Sunny's Market* or *Giovanotti's Market & Cafe*. But Papa was and is a man of his word. It is the Italian way that family honor supersedes personal ego. Even so, I hear him mutter every once in a while when he's sweeping the sidewalk: "Never is a long time."

Mr. Barbiere pushes his way past me to his stool at the counter, as if there were someone waiting to steal it from under his big Mediterranean nose. He doesn't bother to order; his daily order is "understood"—*cafe latte* and toasted Italian bread that is almost, but not quite burned, with Italian cream cheese.

Before long the bell on the front door rings and our other morning regulars stream in. The place is alive. I am pouring coffee and getting the scoop on everything from the new soup diet Mrs. Zinsia is trying (nothing but soup for breakfast, lunch, and dinner) to the latest love escapades of the Radanza brothers (a double date with two check-out girls from the video store). Mrs. Zinsia is trying to get her two preschool-aged granddaughters to quit spinning on the stools and eat their French toast. Charlie Gradezzi grabs a stool next to Mrs. Zinsia. He's been pursuing her for years (the only explanation being that loneliness must do something to a fellow's eyesight), but he has gotten nowhere with her simply because she is too vain to wear a hearing aide so she never understands what he's saying. This morning the talk turns to pro basketball (everyone is disgusted with the Bears), and Charlie asks Mrs. Zinsia what she thinks of "them Bulls."

"Thimbles? What do I think of *thimbles*? Well, I don't know, Charles, I don't even sew! Elizabeth quit spinning on that stool!"

Mr. Barbiere waits until he's had his first bite of toast and his first sip of coffee before he starts in with the daily badgering of my father. "Mr. Melarosso," he calls to the kitchen. "Mr. Mela. *Dove sono tu?* (Where are you?)"

Papa emerges from the kitchen and pretends to look around the store. "Oh, it's you," he says. "I thought maybe I had a *real* customer." Then he greets his other morning regulars with a welcoming *"Buon giorno!"* A few "lucky" ones get slapped on the back.

"Where is Mr. Mela?" Mr. Barbiere continues. "The sign-a out-a front-a says *Mela's* Market. I wanna talk-a to Mr. Mela. I have-a some-a complaint."

"He just stepped out," Papa says. "Give your complaint to me. I'll file it in with the others." He gestures toward the wastebasket.

"Who the hell-a are you? I wanna Mr. Melarosso. Where is-a he?"

"I told you, he's out."

"Out-a where?"

"Out-a cold. He's dead. So what's your complaint?"

"You missed-a you appointment yesterday."

"I did not."

"Oh, so you-a telling me you-a were sitting in-a my chair at tree-terdy and I *did* cut-a you raggedy hair?"

"I told you that I had to make a run for *babalucci*, that Mrs. Zinsia was asking for them. I have a business to run here."

"Oh, an-a you tink-a I don't. You said-a you 'might-a' have to make a run, you left it-a open. You should-a called-a an-a canceled. I could-a filled-a you slot with a number of-a people."

"I said I had to cancel."

"You left it-a open!"

"I had to get the *babalucci*. Here," Papa says as he throws a ten dollar bill on the counter, "that's for the scalp job I didn't get. No tip. I'll ask Luna to get the butcher knife and go at it. It'll probably look the same. No, it will look better."

"Now Papa," I say, but there's no calming him.

Mr. Barbiere's bald head begins to redden and then he shouts, "Sabina!" (I guess when he's angry he remembers my name.) "Please, get-a the toast-a for Joey. And wrap it-a two times-a in the foil. Then bring-a me my check-a for this breakfast I did not-a even-a eat." He leaves Papa's ten right where it is.

I bring the toasted and buttered Italian bread, wrapped twice in foil, which he buys everyday for his son Joey Jr. We're all waiting for him to leave (I didn't say "hoping for") when he plops back down on the stool, scoops up the ten dollar bill, and says to Papa, "Well-a, seeing that-a you prepaid-a, I guess I can-a squeeze-a you in today. Come-a at tree-terdy."

"Three-thirty?" Papa says.

"That's-a what I-a say, tree-terdy."

"Today?"

"Today."

Papa looks around the room. All eyes are on him. We're all thinking the same thing: it can't be that easy. Usually Papa and Mr. Barbiere spend half the morning arguing. Mostly about dumb stuff. They don't argue about sports or politics or religion or even ancestry. My father and Mr. Barbiere wrangle over nothing: whether Reynolds Wrap is tin foil or aluminum foil, the correct pronunciation of the word *Caribbean*, if it's better to be blessed with five daughters (Papa) or one son (Mr. Barbiere), or whether or not Humphrey Bogart actually said, "Play it again Sam."

Papa whips his dishtowel over his shoulder, and says, "I'll be there, Barbiere."

"Good," Mr. Barbiere says. I shrug my shoulders and head for the kitchen as he and Papa argue about whether Charlie is putting *ketchup* or *catsup* on his eggs. Normalcy reigns.

***

There's a lull late morning, so before the lunch crowd descends, Jimmy and I play this dumb game he invented—ABC Whatever—while we

95

ready the place for lunch. You pick a topic or category and start naming off items in the category alphabetically. Like yesterday, we played ABC pasta. We started the day with *acini* and kept it moving until we got to *ziti.* I don't know why I enjoy the silly game, but I do. I guess it's because Jimmy makes me laugh. Sometimes he makes me crazy the way he talks in headlines, but mostly he makes me laugh.

Today he wants to play ABC Geography but I want to play ABC Cheese: Alsation Munster, Brie, Camembert, Dietrich Blue, English Farmhouse Cheddar... I know what you're thinking; you think I need to get a life. But I can only tell you that this is my life. We fill in the slow spots where we can.

A little before noon, I'm filling the reach-in refrigerator with bottles of *Pellegrino* when all at once Aunt Lina appears from out of nowhere. "Pssssssttt!" she whispers. "Sabina!" Whispering comes hard to Aunt Lina so I just know I'm in trouble. "I've been dying to tell you this all morning. Did you know that Benjamin Roan has a son?"

"Oh, Aunt Lina, not again!"

"What do you mean, *not again*, you haven't gone out with a single person I've come up with. Besides, this one's a CEO."

"Of what?"

"Who cares?"

"You don't even know what *C-E-O* stands for, do you?" I say, because I'm finally learning that the best way to handle my aunt is to give her back whatever she dishes out.

She puts her hands on her hips and says, "I do, too... it means Cute-Eligible-Owner."

"Ha!"

"Charming-Enchanting-Old Timer?"

"Never mind."

"Chief-of-Excellent-Opportunities?"

"Aunt Lina!"

"All right, all right. But it means a guy with big bucks."

"Not interested."

"Egads!" she says as she marches back to the kitchen. "This family runs long on stupidity."

***

The lunch crowd has descended. I've been watching this young couple over in the corner table. They're like something out of the movies: perfect, young bodies, faces full of freshness and the future. The sunlight streaming through the window favors these two like a spotlight. The tabletop view is sweet: on one side of the table his hand covers her hand, and on the other side of the table her hand covers his. It's what's going on under the table that's got me peeping like a Tom. The girl keeps slipping her right foot out of her chunky-heeled pump and rubbing it up and down the guy's leg. Does she think no one can see? Is she just too young to even care? Or does she want an audience? Who knows?

All I know is that people rarely get romantic here. I've always wished we had booths. Things happen in booths: romance and affairs, engagements, break-ups. Like Booth One at the Pump Room, one of Chicago's best old restaurants in the Omni Ambassador East Hotel. The legendary Booth One...now there's a booth. It's quite possibly the most famous booth in Chicago, in the country, perhaps in the world. Booth One—just an ordinary looking booth—sports its own conventional telephone (a real luxury before cell phones) and is reserved for VIPs and celebrities. Many famous behinds have warmed the seats of Booth One. They say that Humphrey Bogart and Lauren Bacall shared wedding cake in that booth. And my cousin Ambra's uncle, a set designer, said that Robert Redford and Paul Newman had sandwiches and beer in Booth One in between the filming of the movie *The Sting.*

A while back I suggested to Papa that booths might be a good idea for us. We could fit six easily along the windows. He just looked at me funny and said, "People linger in booths." And, just in case I didn't understand English, he added, "Sabina, they stay too long!"

The lighting is so perfect that I'm tempted to ask the young couple if I may snap their picture for the cookbook I am going to write some time in this century. You know, for the section on romantic lunches and dinners. I would never intrude but I will admit that three-fourths of my body is seething with envy. From where I stand, this honey-haired, twenty-something girl seems to have it all. I'm sure in reality she's probably as normal as the dishwater blonde at the table next to her. It's even likely that she has a bitchy boss, an elephant-sized credit card balance, an expensive apartment, and a long commute. But right now she's got something no one else in this room has: a handsome someone to play footsie with.

"Sabina!" Aunt Lina yells. "Who gets the *Panzanella?*"

"That blonde over there in the corner, that's her salad," I tell Aunt Lina. I go to serve another customer, and just as I set his plate in front of him, I hear a squeal of tires outside followed by a loud crash. Then our front door opens and some big, bearded guy in a red flannel shirt screams, "Somebody call 911!"

I head for the phone but don't know exactly what to say to the dispatcher who answers the call. "There's an emergency in front of our store, a car accident I think." She fires a million questions at me but all I can say is that some guy came in and said to call 911. She stays on the line until I hear the sirens. Many of our customers are gawking with stretched necks at the windows. The footsie couple has remained seated but the blonde at least has the decency to put her shoes back on.

I go stand by Charlie Gradezzi. "Looks to me like the old lady in the blue car turned in front of the guy in the van," he says. "She looks pretty bad, the poor ol' gal." We watch as the paramedics transfer the lady to a stretcher and then to the ambulance. The guy with the van looks fine, gesticulating wildly to the police officer who has arrived on the scene. I look away. Somehow my stomach has climbed up my esophagus and is sitting at the back of my throat. I can feel the acid.

The guy in the red flannel shirt comes back in the store and proceeds to give all the gory details to those who have gathered near the windows. I'd rather be spared the gory details. I have a hard time with car accidents. Car accidents are the reason I am who I am today, and I am where I am today. And the reason that I didn't drive for years and don't own a car of my own even now.

You already know about the car crash that took Vito's mother's life, but I don't think I've told you about Vito's father's car accident. What are the chances of losing both of your parents in separate car accidents? Really, what do you think would be the chances?

***

Talk about timing. Vito had just gone back to California, back to the CCA, after being home for a break the whole month of July. He had only one class left to complete, the three month Baking and Pastry Art class. Three days after Vito left, Mr. Salina, who walked everywhere, was on his way to meet with his accountant, downtown, when he was struck by a car driven by a seventy-nine year old lady on benzodiazapines (anti-anxiety drugs that my brother-in-law Ross says cause sedation). The lady told police her gas pedal had stuck. She was speeding out of control down Wabash Avenue when she struck a car stopped at a light. Her car veered over the curb and onto a sidewalk where it struck seven people, killing two. A witness said she heard a thump and then saw several people fly three feet up in the air. Mr. Salina died that evening at Northwestern Memorial Hospital after suffering head injuries and multiple trauma. The driver was cited for operating an unsafe vehicle, disobeying a red light, and failure to exercise due care. Later, her license was revoked, but not without a fight on her part.

Vito abandoned Baking and Pastry and flew home. We had just ended a glorious month together, the happiest time we'd ever spent. I was on summer vacation from UIC and Vito had come home happier and more relaxed than I'd ever seen him. He'd let his hair grow long and curly and he was trying out a beard. He looked so California! We ate out every night, visited friends, saw some movies, and played cards with Nana Lilli. Papa gave me some time off so Vito and I could look for an apartment he could move into when he returned in November. We found a clean little brownstone that Vito declared perfect—close to the store and Nana Lilli but not too far from downtown, where all of a sudden he had his heart set on working. "What about the store?" I'd asked. "I thought you were going to help Papa when you came home." He said he and Papa had revised the plan a bit. Papa wanted him to work at some downtown establishments for a year or two, while I was finishing up school. Once I graduated we would both work at the store. I wanted to say something like thanks for consulting me, but everything was going so smoothly that I didn't want to mess it up. The important thing was that we would be together, wasn't it?

Secretly, I wanted to talk about the wedding details—the date, the size, the guest list—but the closest he got to talking about the wedding was saying how the built-in cabinets in the dining room of the apartment we wanted would be perfect for our wedding china. That or our cookbook collection, I'd teased.

One night Vito cooked a huge meal at Nana Lilli's for our two families. It was the first time we'd all been together since Sara died. Mr. Salina actually made attempts at warmth and friendliness. It was enough to make Vito believe that just maybe there was something there. At the end of the evening, he told me that before he went back to San Francisco he wanted to tell his father that he loved him.

It never happened. The timing wasn't right or the mood wasn't right or one of his sisters would walk into the room or his father would be aggravated about something or other. "Maybe I'll write him a letter," Vito said shortly before he went back to California. "Being away has made me appreciate him. I guess I grew at school, Bina."

"I know," I said, "and you grew hair, too!" I rubbed his scratchy beard.

He patted my hand while it still lay on his chin. "You say the word and it's gone."

"No, I like it, really. You look so different though, with your hair so long and the beard and all. Mama said you look like Jesus."

"Jesus is good."

"Angie says you look like Cat Stevens."

"Who do you think I look like?"

"Not who, but what."

"What then?"

"A Californian."

"Don't worry, Bina, I do love it out there, but I love Chicago more and you the most. I'll be back in three months."

He was back in three days. I went with Papa to O'Hare to pick him up. His sister Jenny waited at our house with her kids. She was up to four now, the most recent being a colicky little boy that even Mama, who usually had a magic touch with babies, couldn't settle down. Jenny was a wreck.

I almost didn't recognize Vito at the airport. He was almost face to face with me before I realized it was him. His hair was pulled back in a ponytail, his eyes were bloodshot, and his skin was patchy. He fell into my embrace, but it was in Papa's that he remained for minutes upon minutes, until I said we'd better get his luggage. He said he just had the duffel bag he'd carried on.

Papa insisted that we both sit in the back seat of his car even though Vito said he didn't want him to feel like a chauffeur. Papa said, "Awwww," and so we got in the back. Vito didn't say a word the whole way to his Nana's house, just held my hand and stared into my eyes. I could only see him when the headlights of an oncoming car flashed us for a second. Over and over. It was chilling.

The funeral was grim. Closed casket, not very many people. Jenny and Becky, who had made all of the arrangements, were zombies. I felt so bad for all of them: Jenny with her four little kids; Becky, who, in a week, would be moving to Atlanta with her DJ husband; and Vito, who looked like a little boy again. I never thought anything could be more painful for Vito than losing his mother when he was thirteen. But at least he and his mother had a wonderful relationship; his memories of her buoyed him up. His father was altogether a different story. And Vito had never written the letter to his father so he was beating himself up over that.

And as if losing both his parents wasn't bad enough for Vito, another terrible thing happened when he was home for his father's funeral. After the burial, our families gathered at Nana Lilli's for the luncheon. Even though we weren't hungry we ate the casseroles that friends, relatives, and neighbors provided. After lunch Angie and I went out on the back porch so that she could sneak a cigarette. Angie was fifteen, selfish, and bored. She may have been high, too. She was trying to cheer me up, to get me to crack a smile. And I finally did when she started imitating Becky's husband, Jerome, the D.J. Well, how were we supposed to know that Becky was lying down in the bedroom off the kitchen? The window was open. She not only heard the perfect imitation, she heard my howling.

It sounds so cruel now. I'm filled with shame even thinking about it. How could we have been so insensitive? But if you could have heard my baby sister lower her voice a couple of octaves, and seen her contort her face just so, twist her mouth to one side and say, "You're jamming with Jerome on W-J-A-M fm," you would have cracked up, too. Becky never forgave me. It was that day that she turned against me. Vito said she over-reacted but I think he was hurt, too. It was one thing for him to make fun of his brother-in-law; it was another thing for Angie and me to do it.

Afterward, when Papa and Jenny and I put Vito back on the plane, I just ached. I'd wanted him to stay home a while, to grieve and heal, but he said if he didn't get back right away he'd be forced to withdraw from the Baking and Pastry class and he'd have to wait three months for the next program to start. He said the best thing would be to get his hands in some dough. He was afraid he'd never finish if he waited. I knew he was right.

When Vito kissed me good-bye, I looked into his eyes and I knew he would never be the same. Death without peace, without forgiveness...well it does something to a person, robs them of something.

His face looked sad and serious, like the old Vito. He gave me one last peck on the cheek and I watched him walk away, carrying his old brown duffel bag. Suddenly I was seized with what Mama calls "what-if" fear. What if the plane crashes? Or what if he never comes back? Or at the very least, what if he comes back changed—depressed, inconsolable? If I'd known then what was ahead for us, I would have kissed Papa's cheek and hopped on that plane to California. It's dangerous to think when things are going bad that they couldn't possibly get any worse, and of course Papa forbids that kind of thinking, but I've learned the hard way: the possibility is always out there. And in spite of growing up in a household filled with optimism and hopefulness and confidence and faith and assurance, I started entertaining bad thoughts about the future. After all, every single day, somebody, somewhere, burns a second batch of brownies.

***

"Bina."

"Yeah, Jimmy."

"Cop Questions Waitress," he says and writes in the air.

"Come on, Jimmy, what?"

"Cop here wants to ask you about the 911 call."

"Oh. Okay, thanks." I see this very tall, very stiff cop with cropped red hair and dark sunglasses standing by the door. I walk over.

"Sabina Gio-"

"Vanotti," I finish for him.

"Giovanotti, that's a mouthful."

"For some people, I guess," I say. It comes out a little snottier than I intended, but all my life I've had to deal with comments about my name.

He says, "I'm Detective Donald..." and that's all I hear him say because my mind can't take this in. Very tall...police detective...Donald. And I realize, geez, this is Aunt Lina's cop. This is either an unlucky coincidence or a dirty set-up.

"Ma'am?"

"Oh, sorry. Can you repeat your question? It's been a long day." He asks me about the accident and I tell him that I didn't witness the accident, and no, I didn't know the victim. No, she didn't have lunch in here, at least I didn't think she did, we were pretty busy. No, busy or not, I would have remembered.

He asks me a few more questions and then tells me to call him if I come up with any other information. He hands me his card. I wait until he is out the door before I look at it. Right there in plain letters: Detective Ron Donald. So not my type! I'm just relieved that he didn't make the connection.

I look back at the door, it opens and I'm afraid he's coming back, but it's not him, it's Colina, and she's carrying Chelsea and dragging Morgan who's pulling Nicole. When she deposits Chelsea in my arms I can see that she's been crying. Her eyes are bloodshot and the skin around them is pink and puffy. She doesn't say a thing but she starts to spring a leak so I practically push her through the kitchen door before she calls attention to herself. She runs into Mama's arms, and Mama says, "What? What?"

Aunt Lina rushes over, ready to pounce.

Mama says, "Lina, take Morgan and Nicole out front and get them some *gelato*, will you?"

Aunt Lina looks kind of disappointed but she says, "Sure, come on you two."

As soon as she's gone Colina lets go like a river. She blubbers out all this stuff about John and his assistant Monica and how they travel together all the time and how she's confided in him that her marriage is going downhill and he actually invited her over last month for Nicole's birthday dinner.

"Colina, *bedda*, you think he's having an affair?"

"Well, wouldn't you think so, Mama?"

"I don't know. Maybe they're just friends. Maybe, oh, I don't know. I just hate to think it, that's all." Mama rubs her eyes, then her whole face. "*Jesu mia*, I hate to think it. Three little ones."

"Well you might as well think it, Mama, because I'm thinking it."

"Tell me why you think it. What's going on?"

"It's been a lot of things over the past couple of months." She pauses to blow her nose with a tissue I hand her. "You know how much

102

he's been traveling. Well, one morning I call him, early, at the hotel. Morgan is having a conniption because her school is having this doughnuts with your Dad thing and her Dad can't come, can't ever come to anything because he's always off somewhere. I call at 6:30 a.m. because I know they always start the meetings so early. Well, this woman answers the phone, and I say, 'Oh, I'm sorry, I asked them to ring John Andrew's room.' And she says, 'This is John's room. He's indisposed or undisclosed or indecent or whatever you're supposed to say when someone's in the little boy's room. He'll be out in a minute. Care to hold?' I say, 'No thank you, just tell him his daughter wanted to say good morning,' and I hang up."

Did I tell you that Colina talks a lot? And that she talks really, really fast? Well, she does. She pauses for air and then continues: "So he calls back like two seconds later with his cheerful morning voice—'Hi, hon, what's up?' Then he proceeds to tell me that he and Monica and two other women from his department are all meeting in his room to study for their test. Well, I didn't even know he had a test." She holds her hands out in front of her, palms up.

Mama says, "Well, I think he could have chosen a better place to study, but honestly, Colina, that sounds innocent enough."

"Sabina?" Colina wants my opinion.

I shift Chelsea to my other hip and scrunch my nose.

"See, Mama," Colina says.

"*Bedda*, you say that like you think I'm on *his* side. I'm on your side. I just hate to think it, that's all."

"There's more. Florist entries on our credit card."

"How does he explain that?" I want to know.

"That they were all for customers and that sometimes he pulls out his personal credit card instead of his business card. He has perfectly legitimate and logical excuses prepared for every accusation. And of course he throws it all back to me. I'm the one who's over-reacting."

"Well, it's not like you're melo-dramatic or anything," I say and then immediately regret having said it. Mama shoots me a look.

"I'll give you dramatic, Sabina. Get this: our anniversary is this Thursday. I want to surprise him. I'm thinking maybe we need a little romance. Angie says she'll take the girls for me, so I order theater tickets and call the Italian Village and make a dinner reservation for John Andrews, party of two, seven o'clock. And the maitre d' says, 'Oh, so you want to move your eight o'clock reservation to seven o'clock, Mrs. Andrews?' And I tell him that I never made an eight o'clock reservation. And he says, 'Very sorry, Mrs. Andrews, my mistake.' And I hang up the phone and say to myself, no, it's my mistake."

Aunt Lina peeks her head in. "Nicole has to go big potty and I'm sorry but I don't wipe."

"I'll wipe her, Aunt Lina, hold on one second. Hurry, CoCo what happened?"

"So that night in bed I ask what his plans are for the rest of the week, and he says that he talked to his boss about cutting down on the travel, but he's got an emergency in Atlanta Thursday and Friday, home Saturday late afternoon. And I say something like, 'Well then, why would you need an eight o'clock dinner reservation at the Italian Village for Thursday night?' And without missing a beat he says, 'You stinker, you wrecked my surprise!' He didn't have to go to Atlanta after all and was going to surprise me with a night out. I told him I just didn't buy it. He said I was a piece of work and I said he was a piece of crap and we haven't said one word since. Well?"

Mama, who never swears, says, "That bastard!" with an Aunt Lina-like inflection.

I say: "I'll go wipe your daughter's butt." When I exit the kitchen door Papa blocks my way.

"What's going on, Bina? Is she all right?"

"Oh, Papa, let Mama tell you. Please."

"All my life with you girls and I'm always the last to know. Last to know when that one in there gets pregnant and has to get married; last to know when Ross almost moves my daughter and my grandchildren to Portland, Oregon; last to know when Rosa lost the baby; last to know when Vito left town. What am I anyway, chopped liver?"

I hug him. "You're not chopped liver, Papa, you're just liver. Mama will tell you all about it. I have to go wipe Nicole. I guess Aunt Lina doesn't do windows and she doesn't do butts.

***

Finally, we close. Mama takes Colina and the girls upstairs. I run the dishwasher while Aunt Lina mops the floor and talks on her cell phone to her masseuse or her manicurist or her hairdresser. Jimmy helps Papa scrub pots and pans and tells us about school. "I'm trying to get an article published in our school newspaper," he informs us.

"What's it about?" Papa asks. Sometimes Papa feels like being nice to Jimmy and sometimes he doesn't.

"Road rage in the campus parking lots," he says proudly.

"Psssshhh," Papa says, waving a hand at Jimmy. "Road rage. Old news. Overdone."

Like I said, sometimes he doesn't feel like being nice. But Papa's remarks never faze Jimmy, who was born optimistic, like a black ant at a summer picnic. "Hey! Hey! Uncle Sun, you just gave me a great idea. Instead of writing about *road* rage I'll write about *sidewalk* rage."

"Sidewalk rage?" Papa says.

"Yeah, sidewalk rage. Like the other day I come out of Starbucks with a double cafe mocha and, okay, so I'm not looking where I'm going 'cause I'm looking at this blonde, and I kind of crash into this old dude. And he just goes ballistic on me, shaking his fist. Screams: 'Watch where you're going you caffeine-intoxicated son-of-a-bitch.'"

Papa can't help but laugh. "Oh, *sidewalk* rage!" he says.

I drift out of their conversation and into more daydreams about Vito. We had our secret plan: "Project Mela" we called it. The plan wasn't comprehensive, just little things, really—fresh paint, new furniture, updated music, and something new to hang on the walls since both of us were sick to death of looking at the faded maps of Italy, Sicily, and Sardinia that dated back to my Nano Melarosso. Vito came up with the idea of me shooting some black and white photos of our customers laughing and enjoying their meals, enlarging and framing them, and then displaying them above the tables in the cafe section.

But all these ideas died out when he left.

And Papa lost some of his enthusiasm. Still, I tried to get him to make some of the changes we'd planned. "Things have changed, Papa," I tried to tell him. I told him how it used to be if the food was outstanding, people would forgive the decor, but diners were becoming so much more sophisticated, their expectations so much higher. Many of the family-run restaurants in Chicago's Little Italy had updated their buildings, decor, and menus to accommodate this new breed of diners, but Papa was stubborn. And it's not that I wanted to compete with the other restaurants and cafes in our neighborhood—we all had our own little niche and personality. We're one of those little Italian classics on Taylor Street. The kind of place where you are served old-fashioned Italian food by people who look it. We, like *Il Vicinato* on South Western Avenue, *Tufano's Vernon Park Tap* on Vernon Park, *Bruna's* on South Oakely, and Taylor Street neighbors like *Mario's* (best Italian ice in town), *Gennaro's*, and the fashionable *Tuscany*, do business side by side in one of the great old neighborhoods of Chicago.

"If it ain't broke, don't fix it," Papa said. "As soon as you start adding more tables, you got a different place. Bigger's not always better, *bedda*. The whole feel of the place changes and then the people aren't happy. You keep changing things and you'll never have a tradition. Too much change confuses people." I sometimes wondered if Papa's obstinacy had more to do with his deep pockets than his hold on tradition.

Finally he softened up a little (Mama's doings, I'm sure) and he agreed to a little cosmetic surgery. We got new—actually second-hand—tables and chairs for a steal from a friend of Mr. Barbiere's and sectioned off a larger space for the dining area. We scrapped the greasy oilcloth tablecloths and in their place put linen cloths topped with plaits of glass. Papa agreed to the long-overdue paint job but he nixed my idea of a soft, buttery yellow and chose the color himself, *sand*, but boring as it was, it was a definite improvement. He bought some old oak cupboards to display some of our imported olive oils and vinegars, a brand new reach-in refrigerator, and an espresso/cappuccino maker, but was shocked when I'd mentioned changing the store's name. He looked me in the eye and said calmly, *"Uno parola*, Sabina, *onore!"* (One word, honor).

The few changes we implemented certainly have helped to put some life back into the old place, while still keeping it a great favorite with the neighborhood. But it's Mama's and Aunt Lina's food that's responsible for packing them in. In six short months we've seen the business grow. Suddenly, Chicago's young and hungry have discovered Mela's. Now young executives power lunch here. People eat food here that they like to call *ethnic* and they buy bread here that they like to call *artisan.* They get their fuel injections of caffeine here. And although the place is so much more interesting now, it's not quite as innocent as it used to be. The good thing, the saving grace, is that the new crowd only invades us for lunch. Breakfast is still the same at Mela's Market. The same morning crowd is here day in and day out, catching a quick bite on the way to work or passing the time until the invasion of the lunch crowd.

Now Papa's waiting to be put on the map by Chicago Magazine. The day he opens up an issue and finds a favorable review of Mela's Market is the day he can breathe his last breath. Each month when the new issue comes out and he doesn't find a mention of Mela's, he pouts for an hour, but then old Mr. Optimism kicks in and he says, "There's always next month."

I'm nothing if not optimistically challenged, so I want to say, "Papa, don't hold your breath," but if you could see the look on his face, you wouldn't say anything either. Let him think his good thoughts: it makes him feel good, keeps him young and healthy. And in light of the fact that he'll soon be retiring, I'm rooting for a stellar review.

A loud snap sounds in my right ear, and I turn to find Aunt Lina attempting to smack me out of my daydream. "Snap out of it, Sabina. You look ugly when you frown like that. Not to mention the wrinkles you're inviting over for dinner. Where the hell were you, Russia?"

Besides cooking, Aunt Lina serves another purpose here: she does snap me out of my daydreams several times a day. But her utility is double-edged, like a pair of scissors—useful but dangerous. I don't know what it is but I've been daydreaming a lot lately. My body is here in the store but my thoughts are always elsewhere. It worries me to think that I'm losing the ability to stay focused on the present. Daydreams can be dangerous—especially the ones that take you back instead of forward.

As I head out front, I'm tempted to tell Aunt Lina to leave me and my daydreams alone. To hear her tell it, her life has been perfect. But I ask you, how perfect can a life be that included three different husbands, three different sons—one by each husband—and three ugly divorces? Still, this is the same woman who claims to have lived the "good life." She told me once that a good life can be reduced like a good wine sauce to four things: beauty, love, fine cuisine, and wealth. She claims that all her dreams have been fulfilled. In her youth she was a beauty and in her old age, a gourmet. In between, there were the three husbands, each one named *Joe*, or as she endearingly refers to them: Bastard Number One, Bastard Number Two, and Bastard Number Three. As for the wealth, well, she'll tell you all about that. "I left my first two husbands, the bastards," she likes to explain to anyone who will listen, "but my third husband left me...filthy rich!"

As I count the money in the register and prepare the bank deposit, I think about how quiet things were around here before Aunt Lina came. Now she corners me numerous times a day to tell me what's wrong with me and how to fix it, or else to set me up with some man with money. "The trouble with you," she keeps telling me, "is you're too nicey-nice. Always getting your toes stepped on. You gotta make your wants known. Shout out your needs and desires. You gotta knock people over the head—sometimes that's the only way." There's only one person in my whole life I've ever been tempted to knock over her red head.

Or she'll say with disbelief oozing from her voice, "You've been waiting *how* long for that good-for-nothing to come back to you? Are you crazy?"

I'll deny to the death that I'm still waiting for Vito Salina to come back to me. Still, I know I'm fooling no one. Maybe I am crazy.

I head for the bank, thinking about how predictable my days at the market are. Early morning at Mela's is a *festa Italiana* with all the neighborhood Italian-American customers who are now like family to us. Late morning brings customers picking up bakery orders for lunches and brunches and picnics and parties. The lunch crowd frenzy is just a blur. Early afternoon brings a smattering of shoppers who depend on my father for their authentic Italian foodstuff. By four o'clock the front door is locked. We clean up, and by five o'clock, we all go our separate ways: Mama and Papa upstairs for a catnap; Aunt Lina to various appointments with doctors, chiropractors, masseuses, manicurists, and hairdressers; Jimmy off to study *The Associated Press Stylebook and Libel Manual;* and Mr. Maggio, well, he leaves right before noon, since his day starts at three a.m.

As for me, I head straight to the bank. After that, I can be found at Rosa's or Marina's or Colina's or Angie's, playing backgammon, or chess, or Twister, or, my personal favorite, Barbie dolls... because by day I am a waitress in my father's Italian market and café and by night I am "Aunty Fun" to my thirteen nieces and nephews, who are without a doubt the best thing I've got going. There's nothing like the feeling I get when I walk into one of my sister's homes. They treat my like their hero, come to save the day. And all I have to do is burp this one, diaper that one, bandage this one, read to that one. Help with a math problem, drive this one to piano lessons, pick up someone else from soccer. Walk a fussy baby so the family can eat a meal together. Bathe a kid or two so that my sister can have a real life conversation with her husband. Wash a load of whites, fold a basket of towels.

But there are deep, dark, gray days that I can't bring myself to go anywhere but home after the bank. I head up to our apartment where I am greeted by the muffled denseness of the closed rooms. In my bedroom, I sit facing my computer screen and try to put down on paper my family's recipes. But sometimes, more often that not, my eyes blur at the computer screen and I turn it off, sit on my bed and look out the window at my fellow Chicagoans. I create lives for them as they pass by below, all the while wishing I could create one for myself. Then I lie back in bed and wonder what I would be doing right this very minute if Vito hadn't walked out on me eighteen years ago.

8

Water, Nice and Hot

"Get a load of this," Mama says to me as she shakes her head and hands me the telephone. It's Rosa, and she's all upset about Colina. She says someone keeps calling Colina's house and hanging up—all day yesterday and all day today. It's driving poor Colina crazy.

"Where's John?" I want to know.

"Atlanta."

"I thought he wasn't going to go to Atlanta."

"Well, he went."

"What do you think is going on, Rosa?"

"I have my ideas. But right now we got to get her out of that house before she loses it. She keeps thinking it's John calling to wish her a happy anniversary. It's their anniversary today, you know."

"Some anniversary."

"Really. But listen, here's my plan. Mama said she and Papa would take Nicole, Morgan and Chelsea, so we can take Colina and get her out of that house."

"Where are we taking her?"

"To the Four Seasons. My treat."

"Rosa!"

"Sabina…"

"When are we going?"

"Tomorrow night. We'll have dinner and then we'll have a slumber party. She needs us. We'll have room service—champagne and strawberries and cheesecake—and maybe even a pillow fight. I'm excited. We haven't had a sleepover since Natalie's bachelorette party last year. I'm psyched. I got us a suite. You're not busy are you?"

"As a matter of fact, Rosa, I have a date."

"Oh, shoot."

"Rosa, I'm just kidding."

"Oh, okay. Well, good. Not good that you don't have a date, but good that you're not busy. Oh, you know what I mean."

"I know what you mean."

"Anyway, let's see if we can't talk some sense into that sister of ours. First of all, she has to start eating seven days a week instead of three. And secondly, she and John have to get some counseling before this thing blows up in their faces."

"I just hope we're not too late. Does anyone know if that Monica person went to Atlanta, too?"

"I asked CoCo that. She said John swore it was just he and his boss."

"So this Monica person could be harassing her with the phone calls."

"It's possible *and* probable. Okay, well listen, you wait for Colina to drop off the kids and then the two of you meet us in the lobby at six-thirty. Bring something nice to wear for dinner. And some comfortable shoes for shopping. And your swim suit. Don't forget your suit. But if you do, they provide disposable ones. Isn't that a kick? And it's all my treat."

"Okay, Ivanna."

"Quit that. If I can't spend a little on my sisters, who can I spend it on?"

"You always say that."

"We've just got to help her, Bina."

"Poor thing. Do you think he's really cheating on her?"

"Yes I do, the bastard. Don't tell anybody, but Ed saw him one night at a restaurant with some woman and it didn't look like they were conducting business."

"Poor Colina and those poor babies."

***

I've always been of the opinion that Chicago is best at night. The days can be gray as mop water but the nights sparkle. If by day Chicago is the city that works, then by night it's the city that glitters. The black sky is the perfect backdrop for all the twinkling lights. The stars look like sequins on a black evening dress.

Colina and I are risking our lives in the back seat of a yellow cab. Colina's talking to the driver, a young Pakistani, who has been in the U.S. for three years. He left his wife and two children back in Pakistan. His English is very good and he and Colina are talking about family and she's telling him about ours and about how five girls (doesn't she mean four?) have thirteen children and about the Thanksgiving feast we'll have at Rosa's in a couple of weeks. This makes Jamil homesick and he tells her so. Colina tells him in no uncertain terms to get his butt home, that it's not worth being away from his family.

This is vintage Colina—she's one of the most genuinely friendly persons I know. She could hold an animated conversation with a doorknob. Colina gives a new meaning to friendly—exchanging good cheer and personal information (what I would consider *private* information) with anybody and everybody. She told the lady at the cleaners all about her emergency appendectomy last year, she talks to bus boys about getting a college education, she tells the meter reader about her kids' ear infections and her mail-lady rings her doorbell every afternoon just to say "hi." Mama calls Colina a cup of coffee because she's smooth, warm, and very social.

She's working her magic on the cabby. Jamil is crying now and I'm worried that he can see to drive. When he pulls up in front of the hotel, I am relieved. He gets out of the car and comes around with our bags and Colina pats his shoulder and wishes him well. I pay and tip him while he tells us we are the most beautiful American women he has seen in the three years he has been in this country. "Your hearts are on your faces," he says, wiping his eyes with a tissue I hand him. Any second Colina is going to hug him and tell him about her appendectomy, three cesareans and her marital problems so I try to direct her attention to the hotel entrance where Rosa is waving to us like we're celebrities.

The Fours Seasons is lit up like fireworks. It's always been Rosa's favorite hotel, and she's stayed at some of the best. She looks for excuses to stay here: bachelorette parties, Mama's and Papa's twenty-fifth wedding anniversary, shopping weekends, and get-aways with her daughters, sisters, sisters-in-law, husband, and friends. They know her by name here, and without being presumptuous, she walks about the place like the reigning queen. You forgive Rosa her wealth because of her generosity.

The bellhop escorts us up to our suite. When he opens the door and waves us in, even Rosa sighs. The room is like a residential palace, so spacious, so elegant, filled with classic European furnishings, tastefully upholstered in yellow and moss green tapestry fabrics. The woods gleam as if varnished with a coat of glass. Our attendant opens the draperies to reveal a twinkling, sparkling view of the city and we all gasp as if we have never before seen it all lit up.

I plop down on the sofa and think about how nice it will be to be served rather than to serve, even if just for a day and a half. It will also be nice not to have to make any decisions, for Rosa will have an itinerary, and of course it will be perfect.

"Okay, girls, I thought we'd get unpacked and go for a swim. Then we can come back and change for dinner. How does that sound?" Like I said, you don't have to expend a single brain cell worrying about what to do when Rosa's in the driver's seat.

***

The water is perfect, like bath water. And even though I am not a swimmer I like to splash around in it. Right now I'm sitting in the pool with Rosa and Marina on the steps leading into the shallow end. I'm immersed up to my shoulders. I lean back, supporting myself on my elbows and kick my feet slowly. This is my speed. Colina and Angelina, both champion swimmers in high school, are doing laps. It makes me tired just watching them.

I keep adjusting my swimsuit, which is a hand-me-down from Colina. She rarely hands down anything to any of us girls since she is so much smaller than we are, but apparently this suit was a gift from John who like many husbands is notorious for committing what Marina calls "Size-Crimes." This was a biggy. You don't buy a girl who takes a size two a size eight swimsuit. You just don't. Somehow, the thing found its way to me and in spite of it being red, and in spite of it being low cut in some places and high cut in other places, I decided to forego the agony of swimsuit shopping—which for me is right up there with tooth extraction—and keep it. But it's not *me*, really it's not.

Rosa and Marina are telling me story after story about my nieces and nephews. I can't get enough of them. Rosa says, "So after we set up

112

Lauren's new bed, Franky says to me, 'Mom, how come you and Dad get a king size bed, Lauren gets a queen size bed, and I only get a jack size bed?'"

"That is so cute," Marina says to Rosa while I wonder what a thirteen-year-old needs with a queen size bed.

"Listen to what Nino asked Ross the other night," Marina says. "He goes, 'Dad, how come we have only one opening for food to go in,' and he points to his mouth, 'but we have two openings for food to come out,' and he points to the front and back of his pants."

"How do they think of these things?" I say in awe of their thirsty curiosity. I think that when you are not around children you grow old faster.

"Oh, Nino's my little inventor," Marina continues. "He's got this invention notebook. You should see it. He invented cloud glasses. You wear sunglasses on sunny days to deflect the sun's rays. You wear cloud glasses on cloudy days. They're tinted yellow so even if it's rainy you have the illusion of sunshine."

I stop kicking. "Oh, my God, Marina, he hasn't told me about that one yet. He's a little genius. What else has he invented?"

"Well, let's see. He rigged this contraption in his bedroom with Ross's help. When his alarm goes off it triggers this thingy connected to a brick that pulls up his window shade."

"That's great. I've got to see it," I say. Inside I'm aching. I long to have that kind of wonder and creativity following me around all day.

"And he was working on this thing-a-ma-bob that would heat up a cup of coffee at my bedside, but it involved candles so I nixed it. But it's still in his notebook for someday when he's a grownup and drinks coffee."

"Oh, Marina," I say, "just let me have him. You have two other boys. Just give me Nino. I'd take good care of him and I'd send him to the best inventor college in the country."

"Well, you could have had him today. Sometimes, I just don't know what to do with that kid. Now he's going through this stage where he sees scary faces everywhere—in windows, in closets, on the TV screen when the TV is turned off. He's driving me crazy."

"He's a very sensitive kid," I say. "Maybe—"

I'm cut short by Colina who has finished her laps and is calling us over to the hot tub which has just emptied out.

"Maybe—" I continue, but then Marina puts her hand up to stop me.

"You know what, Bina? I don't want to talk about Nino right now. I just want to relax and forget that I'm a mom for a few hours. Is that so terrible?"

I want to say, "Yes, it is," but I'm not a mother, I'm only an aunt, so who am I to say? I just pretend it was a rhetorical question and leave it hanging there.

I climb the steps out of the shallow end and look for my towel. Realizing that I left it on the *chaise lougne*, I start to walk over to retrieve it when I catch this really nice-looking guy sitting in the chair next to mine watching me. I look over my shoulder to see if he's watching someone else, but no, he's definitely looking at me. I absolutely loath being looked at in a swimsuit—especially in this fire engine red suit that I had no business pouring myself into—so I forgo the towel and "fast-walk" over to the hot tub. On my way, I do something really stupid: I turn around to see if he's still looking. He is. This unnerves me and prompts me to do something even more stupid: I *jump* into the hot tub. My sisters scream in unison as the one-hundred-plus degree water splashes their faces. A part of me wishes to drown.

I give in to the idea of living, but I don't give in to the idea of embarrassment. I'm nothing if not a good liar when the need arises so I "Pinocchio" my way through an explanation: "I fell! The floor was slippery and I just fell in." Then I feign pain—another defense mechanism I find useful at times like this. "Geez, I twisted my ankle a little."

I should have known better to use the twisted ankle ploy. Nurse Marina has to take a look at it. "It's a little puffy, Bina, but I don't think it's sprained," she says as she turns it gently. The others watch with concern. Colina, skin and bones in her tiny orange bikini, looks so worried and pathetic that my guilt gets the better of me. I start laughing and then I can't stop.

"What? Sabina? What?" they're all saying. And through my own laughter I hear Marina speculate that maybe I bumped my head. I take some deep breaths and come clean about the guy. I steal a quick look at him. He's reading a magazine now so I point him out to my sisters. Marina kind of gasps and Angie lets go a soft whistle. I slide down a little deeper into the hot water and wait for my sisters to stop gawking.

They finally do, but then the razzing starts. My sisters can tease you without even uttering a word. Rosa will arch an eyebrow, Marina will hum, and Angie will smile a conniving smile. Colina, of course, uses her words. "Guess my red swimsuit is attracting a little attention," she says, hitting my shoulder.

Rosa says, "It's not the suit, Co, it's what's in it." She splashes me in the face and then I splash her back. Then she kicks some water at me and in two seconds we're all kicking and splashing each other until this baby-faced lifeguard walks over and tells us to CUT IT OUT. He points to a sign that lists "no splashing" as one of the rules. I am completely embarrassed by this, but my sisters are not. They are laughing hysterically.

I want out of here. "Anyone getting hungry?" I ask.

"No, but I am a little thirsty," Colina says.

"How about some water?" Rosa asks and starts to splash again like a deranged dolphin. This time we get kicked out. *KICKED OUT!* I've never been kicked out of anywhere in my life. When my cousin Jimmy hears about this he'll take his right hand and draw this headline across the air: *"Five Sisters Kicked Out of the Four Seasons Hotel For Unruly Behavior."* Geez!

Now, like it or not, I have to walk over to the chair to get my towel and sandals. I fold my arms across my chest and trudge over with my head hung down like a bad dog. As I gather up my things I can't avoid the guy. He looks up from his magazine and smiles at me as I wrap my towel around as much of me as possible. He keeps smiling, this nice-looking guy with piercing blue-green eyes, a full head of thick wavy brown hair, and slightly hairy chest. Then he takes one forefinger and brushes it over the other, as if to scold me. And I know I turn as red as my one-piece swimsuit, the one Colina gave me, the hot, bold, red one that I would have never chosen for myself in a million years. Anyway, I just smile and shake my head and walk quickly away, knowing that his eyes are following me until I reach my sisters and we push our way through the double glass doors and out into the ice-cold hallway.

Back in the room, we're like co-eds running around in our bras and undies, drying our hair, putting on fresh make-up, and comparing stretch marks and cesarean section scars. I have no scars to boast of save for the one on my forehead that Vito gave me when we were kids. But how can that compare with the magnificent stretch marks on Rosa's and Marina's hips or the deep incision scars on the abdomens of Colina and Angie? And then there's the sad fact of varicose veins. Rosa is showing us what bearing five children will do to your legs. Hers look like the work of a bad cartographer. I stand back and watch their public display of war wounds. My sisters wear their injuries like purple hearts.

"Look at you," Marina says to me, staring at my half-naked body. "Your body is perfect. No pouchy stomach, no saggy boobs, no scars or veins. It's times like this Sabina you should be glad you don't have kids."

Geez, I hate when they say that. Don't they know that I'd gladly take the scars—bring on the mutilations—if it meant having a child of my own? I want to ask Marina—how can you say such a thing. But this night is for Colina and I don't want to make waves where there are already too many ripples.

It takes Rosa forever to order, it always has. Even when we were kids she'd ask the wait-person to take her order last. Tonight it's either the charred peppered tuna steak or the roast pheasant with sweet potato pancake and wild elderberry vinegar. She just can't decide. Our waiter is a young Asian-American man named Edison. He is an excellent server and right away senses that he can have a little fun with our party.

Rosa starts ordering nice bottles of wine and we embark upon our journey of overindulgence, Rosalina-style.

Tonight the wine feels like liquid velvet as it glides down my throat. All my senses are engaged: my eyes take in the lovely decor, my ears the familiar drone of voices and the clatter of dishes, and my nose detects a vast array of aromas as waiters pass our table with trays upon trays of food. My taste buds are tempted and I almost order something different—sage-onion gnocchi with Oregon chanterelles—but then I chicken out and order the grilled lobster, my absolute favorite food. I sit back. Being here, together with my sisters is as nice as it gets for me.

Like all sisters and girlfriends we pee in pairs. So, before our main course arrives, Rosa and Marina go, and then Angie and Colina go. Mama's not here so I go alone. Usually I don't mind, but now that I'm here in the bathroom, I can't find a hairbrush in my tiny purse and I wish I had a sister nearby so I could borrow one. My fingers make do as the teeth of a comb. I check out my face, add lipstick, mash my lips together, and decide I look all right. Relaxed. Okay, very relaxed. Okay, a little buzzed.

On my way back to the table I get lost. Did I turn the wrong way? No, but I can't find our table. This is silly, the restaurant isn't even that big. I must look lost because I hear a voice behind me say, "Looking for your cohorts in crime?" I turn around to see the guy from the pool. He looks different—his tan, slightly hairy chest now covered up with a nice dark blue shirt and tie, but I know it's him. He's seated alone at a table.

"Oh, hello," I say.

"Hello," he says as he stands. He flashes that smile again revealing teeth that are perfectly straight and white as breath mints. His eyes are green-blue, or else they're blue-green. He points ahead a few tables. I follow his finger and see Rosa throwing her head back in laughter.

"Oh, thanks," I say. "I guess I should have used my ears instead of my eyes. I didn't realize we were so loud."

"No, no, not at all. It looks like you're having fun. Sisters? Co-workers? Girlfriends?"

"Sisters," I say, backing up to let a waiter pass.

"Thought so. You look like sisters. So what's the occasion?"

"No occasion really. My oldest sister is just filthy rich and she likes to pamper her little sisters every once in a while."

"Well, have fun."

"Thanks, you too," I say.

"Well, I'm here on business. Alone. So it's not much fun," he tells me.

"Oh, I'm sorry."

"There's no need to be sorry," he says.

"Well, enjoy your meal," I say by means of a good-bye.

"Actually, I've just finished and it was wonderful."

Of course I have to ask. "What did you have?"

"The grilled lobster. Very simple, no fancy smothering sauce, just warm, drawn butter, and this perfect wine. All ten thousand of your taste buds savoring just three perfect flavors—lobster, butter and wine."

"What a coincidence...*I* ordered the grilled lobster. I can't wait to have it." A waiter bumps into me and the glasses on his tray teeter. If looks could kill I'd be at least maimed.

"You'd better get out of the way before they kick you out of the restaurant, too. Sit down for a minute, won't you? Let me pour you a glass of this wine. You can drink it with your lobster." He points to the bottle on the table and waves down the waiter for another glass. I look at his hands. He has these really nice hands, with strong, nicely shaped, ring-less fingers.

"Oh, no, thank you, really, I'd better get back to my sisters."

"Please, sit down. They won't miss you for a couple of minutes. What's a missing sister or two when you've got four of them?" He gestures politely for me to sit. I look over at our table and I hate to admit it but he's right, they are laughing and sipping wine like there's no tomorrow and no sister named Sabina.

I sit, and so does he. "I'm surprised that you would want to associate with a trouble-maker like me," I tell him as the waiter appears with another glass and pours wine for me.

"Trouble-maker?"

"Back at the pool—getting kicked out."

"That was one of the most entertaining things I've ever seen in my life. Grown women!"

"My sisters have made an art out of growing up without maturing. It's a gift actually," I say and take a sip of wine. "Oh, what is this, it's just wonderful."

"I'm glad you like it. It's a Chevalier-Montrachet from Leflaive, 1983. I love this wine. I could say that it's very complex—full-bodied and fruity—but then I'd sound like a wine snob, wouldn't I?"

I smile and sip more wine. "Do you eat here often?"

"When I come to town, yes. I love to eat in Chicago. This is an eating town. I'm a food-is-everything kind of guy."

I sip more wine and think this thought: Oh, my dear Lord, he's a foodie. "You seem to know a lot about food and wine."

"Yeah, well," he says and pats his stomach, "I put food right up there with…well, you know, some of those other important bodily needs. I love to eat. I was born hungry. I weighed eleven and a half pounds at birth. Never had a problem cleaning my plate. Speaking of plates, I think they're serving yours now. You don't want it to get cold. Please take your wine with you."

"Thank you. It was really nice talking with you."

As I walk back to our table I can feel him holding me in his gaze, just like at the pool. I walk carefully. I don't want to trip and fall.

When I sit down at our table, Rosa says, "We thought you got lost," and Marina says, "Hey, where'd you get the wine?"

I sit down. Should I tell them or not? I know they'll make a big deal about it and end up embarrassing me.

"Well, I ran into this guy."

"What guy?" they all say at once.

"The guy from the pool. Now don't all turn and look at once but he's behind me, over near that fig tree." Of course they all turn to look and, God help me, Rosa even waves. I don't dare turn around and look. I just want to dive into my wine glass and drown in Chevalier-Montrachet.

"Hey, he's even cuter with clothes on," Angie says.

Colina, who may have gotten loaded in the short time I was gone (she's so tiny it only takes a glass) finds Angie's comment hilarious.

"You're blushing," Rosa says to me.

Marina says, "Yeah, Sabina you're as red as your wine."

"Yeah," says Colina and downs the rest of her wine.

Edison places the grilled lobster in front of me. It smells like heaven and right here and now I decide that if I had to choose my last meal it would be this grilled lobster and this wine. I sip the wine. And if I could choose only the lobster or the wine, my choice would leave me hungry but not thirsty.

After serving each of us, Edison comes back to our table with a bottle of 1983 Chevalier-Montrachet Burgandy from Leflaive, compliments, he says, of the gentleman at the table near the fig tree. He uncorks it with a flourish and then we all look over at…oh, I don't even know his name. He nods and smiles.

Colina, who has had quite enough already, says, "Goody, more wine." And Edison pours.

"Go and ask him to join us, Sabina," Rosa says.

"No! Stop it. It was just a friendly gesture. Now stop embarrassing me. I wish I'd never mentioned it."

"Oh, Sabina, but it looks like expensive wine," Angie says.

"It is," Edison whispers as he pours.

"That's not a friendly gesture, that's a flirtatious gesture," Marina tells me.

"And look, he's all alone."

"Please you guys."

"Well, you at least have to walk over and thank him," Rosa says.

"Obviously he's interested," Colina adds.

"Sabina, this could lead to something," Marina says.

"He's here on business. Probably lives on one of the coasts. Where could that lead?" I do wish I'd left well enough alone.

They all look at me like I'm stupid, but Rosa says it. "Don't be stupid, Sabina. It's just good manners to say thank you. Mama would tell you to say thank you." Rosa smiles. She knows she's got me. I always do what Mama says.

"Okay, okay, get off my back. But I would like to eat a bit of my dinner first before it gets cold. *If* you don't mind."

But my sisters are too excited. They are eating fast on purpose to hurry me along. They are watching every forkful I bring to my mouth. I can't stand it anymore. "All right already. I'll be right back. But don't let anyone take my plate, I'm not finished." I slide out of my chair and place my napkin along side of my plate. I think as I'm walking in the direction of his table that maybe I'll just keep going and make another stop to the ladies' room. But he sees me so of course I stop.

"My sisters and I want to thank you for the lovely wine."

"My pleasure, but I do apologize for the waiter's blunder."

"What blunder, did he spill or something?"

"No, no, but I could tell that he didn't ask your permission. A good waiter should always secure a lady's permission before allowing a gentleman to send over a bottle of wine."

I laugh. "Oh, well, that's way too classy for my sisters. They'd accept wine from just about anyone. Wait a minute, that didn't come out right. They're just not picky. No that's not what I mean either. I mean they're..."

"Gracious?"

"Yes, that's it. We were taught never to refuse a gift."

"Well that etiquette certainly supersedes the buying-a-woman-a-drink etiquette."

I extend my hand. "I'm Sabina. Sabina Giovanotti."

"What a beautiful name, so melodic, kind of sounds like a delicious Italian wine. I'm Ted Kallista, kind of sounds like a beer, doesn't it?"

I laugh and he asks me what I thought of the lobster/wine pairing.

"Absolutely perfect."

"Please, join me again."

"My sisters…"

"Your sisters—well, one of them is giving me the A-okay sign, so that must mean they give you permission to stay." I turn around and shoot Rosa arrows with a face that is all pinched and puckered, but I smooth it all out when I turn back around to face Ted Kallista and slide into the chair opposite him.

***

Back in the room, my sisters give credence to my point about their maturity level. They interrogate me high-school-girl style the moment I walk through the door. What's his name? What's he do? Give us all the details. Don't leave anything out.

"He's really nice looking," Angie says. "He reminds me of someone…one of Aunt Lina's sons maybe. Luke?"

"He does not!" I say, a little too fervently. For some dumb reason I want him to be totally original.

They all look so comfy in their pajamas and I know it's mean but I make them wait for the juicy details until I change into my flannel nightgown and wash my face. When I come out of the bathroom, I find Rosa doing the thing in life she loves most next to mothering: ordering room service.

"Okay, okay," I say, trying to act as if this is no big deal, as if this happens to me quite often in fact. But I know that they know what I know. "His name is Ted Kallista. He's Greek. He's forty-three and divorced. No children. He's a free-lance writer in town on business. He lives in San Francisco, but he's from Chicago and may be moving back here soon. That's all I know really, other than he's a foodie. But since I know that in the morning you two," I point to Rosa and Marina, "will sleep in and you two," I point to Colina and Angie, "will be on that roof-top track, I told Ted that I'd meet him for breakfast at seven o'clock."

"Good for you Sabina," Rosa says and then there's a knock at the door. Here comes our cheesecake and strawberries and a bottle, no two, no three bottles of wine. We're pouring it back like college girls.

Colina is officially loaded and is crying and now we're all referring to her husband as "that son-of-a-bitch." She's decided that when she gets home she's going to give him an ultimatum: get rid of Monica and get

120

counseling or get out. Poor Colina is so spent, physically and emotionally, that Rosa has to help her to bed and tuck her in.

Rosa returns and says, "Well at least she's made some decisions about John and she promised to let me take her to a doctor about this eating problem. So at least I feel like we accomplished something tonight."

I'm sitting here feeling kind of guilty because all these decisions must have been made when I was sitting at another table. Now I feel so selfish. This night was supposed to be for Colina and here I am worried about some guy.

Apparently, that is not how my sisters view the situation, for Rosa is brushing her hands together, as if now that the Colina dilemma has been addressed and put to bed, we can move on to Sabina. "So Sabina," Rosa begins and plops down beside me on the sofa.

"Rosa, you're such a mother hen," I tell her and click her wine glass with mine.

"I am, aren't I? Sooooo," she repeats.

I smile. "All I can say is: dot, dot, dot." I'm nothing if not a prognosticator, but now and then I like to throw in an ellipsis rather than attempt to predict the future. It's nicer than saying what I really want to say: hell if I know.

***

It's seven-o-five the next morning and I'm about to turn back. I'm in the lobby outside the cafe. Last night Marina told me to be a tinch late, not to seem too excited. But now that I'm late and Ted is nowhere to be seen, I wish I'd had sense enough to sleep in. But then there he is, walking briskly toward me. And when he reaches me he grabs me by the arm and directs me toward the cafe. "Sabina, I'm so sorry. My meeting was pushed up to seven forty-five. I've got exactly ten minutes before I have to get a cab. I'm so sorry. I tried to call you but your room must be in your rich sister's name."

I'm thinking to myself: I can tell a brush off when I see one. I'm not that experienced with dating, but this I know.

We slide into a booth. He orders coffee, black, and I order hot tea with lemon, just because it's four words instead of two and I want to use up these nine remaining minutes and get this over with.

"I feel terrible," he says and I must admit that he kind of looks like he feels terrible, but for all I know he could be an actor as well as a writer. "This editor, well, you can't please him. He's the red-pencil devil. I bet he proofreads his own dreams."

"I understand," I hear myself say, but inside I'm thinking that he's probably just blowing smoke. I can almost feel this little being on my left shoulder, a little devil, or maybe Aunt Lina, saying, you putz, you're too damn nice, give it to him good.

"No, really. I want to make it up to you. I've got a two o'clock flight out today, but I'm coming back to finish the job next week. Let me take you to dinner. I know a place that has really good Thai food. Do you like Thai food?"

"I don't know, I—"

"Oh, please. Can I call you when I get back in town?"

"I don't know, I—"

"Look, I know this must look bad. All I can tell you is that this editor is as bad as they come. He pulls this kind of crap with everyone; today's just my day. Well, actually, by the way things are going here, this is not my day. Please, give me your number and I'll call you next week."

"All right already. I don't want to make your day any worse than it is." I write my number on a scrap of paper he hands me, thinking while I do that maybe I'll just accidentally transpose a couple of numbers and put an end to this whole thing. But I find myself forming the real numbers, area code included. I hear the little voice. It's saying: sucker!

Another sip of his coffee and he's gone. The waitress returns and asks what will I be having this morning and I realize that he didn't even bother to pay for his coffee, black, much less for my hot tea with lemon. "What the hell," I say, not realizing that I've said it out loud until I see the funny face she makes, her pad and pen poised in her hand. "I'd like French toast please and could they sprinkle a little powdered sugar on them, and a side of sausage, but only if you have patties."

"We have patties."

"Oh, good, and a small glass of orange juice please, and a warm up on my tea when you get a chance."

When my food arrives, I take my time, chewing and savoring every bite. Sometimes, I think, food is the only thing that doesn't disappoint, but then I bite into the sausage patty and it definitely disappoints. I've decided I'm going to stay down here for as long as possible and comfort myself with fats and carbohydrates. There would be a bomb of questions if I went back up too early. This way, I'll just say I had a nice breakfast, which wouldn't be a lie, and that he took my phone number, which he did, and dot, dot, dot.

9

How Heaven Smells

It's Thanksgiving Day and I wake up without any sense of smell or taste. I'm not kidding. I am having a definite problem with my chemical sensing system. A little while ago, Mama brought me a nice hot cup of coffee (okay, so she spoils me a little, but I don't ask her to do these things, she just does them) and I couldn't even taste it. I'm puzzled because I don't have a cold or a sinus infection and it's not the season for my seasonal allergies. It's just weird. I start feeling my nose, pressing in the nostrils, bending the cartilage, poking at the bridge, but I detect nothing from my physical examination. And so I have to think, is it some kind of nose tumor? Can you get a tumor in your nose? I don't know. I guess I could ask my sister the nurse.

I am not a hypochondriac, honest I'm not, but on the other hand, I have been the picture of health for the past forty years. Maybe my time is running out. Maybe Marina is right, that after forty, everything is downhill.

I inhale deeply. Nothing. I take a swig of coffee. Can't even tell you if it's regular, hazelnut cream, or cinnamon mocha. This is not good.

I try to think about something else. I look at the time on my clock radio, but my eye catches the phone in my peripheral vision. The phone makes me think about Ted and the fact that he has not called.

When you want the phone to ring it never does. I should know, I've been staring at the thing for two weeks now and I guess it actually does ring, but it's Rosa or Aunt Lina or Marina or Colina or Angie or one of the kids or someone selling water softeners, discounted long distance rates, or replacement windows. I've done this before, waited for the phone to ring. I won't do this. I won't.

He said he was going to be in town next week. He distinctly said *next* week, not in a couple of weeks, or in a few weeks, but *next* week. He blew it. I said I'd give him until today, Thanksgiving Day, and now I'm going to put him out of my mind. I can barely remember how to pronounce his last name. Can't remember if his eyes were green or blue. Was his hair light brown or dark brown?

Lately it's been taking me longer to get out of bed. I haven't been sleeping well. Last night I lie awake half the night feeling guilty—guilty about being attracted to a nice-looking man who seems to be a single, straight, income-earning foodie. Guilty because somehow I feel like I'm cheating on a man who I've been faithful to for eighteen years. A man who could be anywhere: here in this country, or abroad, or maybe not living at all. A man, who, for all I know, could be married with five children, although it was because of children, or a certain child, actually, that he left in the first place.

It's funny but I don't feel like a single person. I feel like I'm attached, like the wife of a soldier missing in action or the fiancée of a prisoner of war. I want to move on, but as long as there is even the remotest chance that he'll return, I'm stuck in neutral. The past is heavy. I should know, I carry it around every day.

***

Everybody's here at Rosa's for Thanksgiving dinner, even "that son-of-a-bitch." Angie told Rosa and Rosa told me that John and Colina are seeing a marriage counselor and that they are trying to work things out. According to Rosa, John confessed to Colina that yes, he was attracted to Monica, that things were moving in the direction of an affair but hadn't come to anything sexual yet, and that he'd come to his senses and ended the relationship. Monica quit her job and apparently is moving back to Ohio to live with her parents. Now I guess Colina has to decide if she can forgive John and trust him again.

He's awfully quiet today, spending most of his time with the kids and avoiding eye contact with the rest of us. I think to myself as I watch him giving Chelsea a horsy ride—if Colina can forgive I guess I can.

Suddenly, I have a strong urge to hold a baby. I walk over to John. "Can I take her?" I ask. He looks up at me and I can see the pain in his eyes. I'm probably the first person to say anything to him today besides Art, Angie's husband. I take Chelsea from him and hold her tightly, taking a deep whiff of her hair that always smells like Johnson's Baby Shampoo. Nothing. I smell nothing. I nuzzle her anyway, carry her over to the window and set her down on a chair. The light is just right so I grab my camera and start snapping. She's a natural—already knows how to pose for the camera. How could John even think about breaking this little heart?

Chelsea won't pose for long so I set my camera down and we cuddle in the chair and I guess we both doze off because the next thing I know Rosa's calling us to the table. My sisters prefer that I play with their children rather than help them in the kitchen, which is fine by me.

Colina comes to fetch Chelsea from me. "Did he call?" she asks. I shake my head no. "What a jerk." She's the last sister to ask about Ted so at least I have that out of the way.

As usual, Rosa has gone all out. The dining room table is right out of a magazine, beautifully set with her wedding china, crystal, and flatware. She's scattered the table with clove-studded oranges, Indian corn, gourds, grapevine and bittersweet. Instead of a floral centerpiece, she's filled four large glass bowls halfway with water, placed a pillar candle in the middle, and floated fresh cranberries and kumquats in the water. The table beckons us to sit, eat, and enjoy. Since Thanksgiving is an American holiday we serve all the traditional foods: turkey with dressing and gravy, potatoes mashed with garlic, sweet potatoes, green bean casserole with those French-fried onions on top, cranberry gelatin salad, cauliflower in cheese sauce, and tossed salad. Mama always says this year she's not going to, but then she always does, she makes one pan of baked *mostaccioli* or baked *ziti* with *ricotta*. We anticipate it all—but we wait for the bread. Tradition has it that Mama bakes the bread for Thanksgiving and so there are clover leaf rolls for the adults and fist-sized bread turkeys for the kids.

Aunt Lina's here…but she's not herself. She's actually subdued. Even her hair color seems toned down. Her oldest son Thomas, his wife Barbara, and their thirteen-year-old daughter Jean Marie, flew in yesterday from New York. Aunt Lina gets cranky around all three of her daughters-in-law, but Barbara seems to have an even more toxic effect on her. The last time I saw Barbara was probably at Aunt Lina's youngest son's wedding, some fifteen years ago. And I would never admit it to Aunt Lina but Barbara hasn't aged well at all.

As my sisters bustle around the table getting their children situated, I sit quietly and try to find something to do with my hands. At this moment they seem not to have a worthwhile purpose, so I fold them and drop them in my lap. I wait for food. But I don't really feel like eating because I know I won't be able to taste anything.

I look around the table at my sisters and their families and I wonder if I've just fooled myself into thinking I'm not envious of them. What has led me to this bad humor? I know very well what has brought me here. Please don't repeat this to anyone, because it's so embarrassing, but I guess for the last week or so I've had a different picture of today in my head. Put it this way, in my version, I'm not sitting next to my seven-year-old nephew, Nino. I know it was stupid to think that Ted would be here, even if he had called me. But at my age, you start running out of things to hope for. Geez, this is stupid thinking. I sit up straighter and smile at Marina, who is looking at me funny.

"Bring on the food," I whisper to Nino.

He turns to me, sighs, and smiles. "Aunt B, what do you think heaven smells like?"

"What, honey?"

"What do you think heaven smells like?"

I don't even have to think about that one. "Fresh baked bread and just-brewed coffee."

"I think it smells like Thanksgiving dinner," he says and takes in deep whiffs of roasted turkey-infused air. It makes me wish I could smell.

Papa clears his throat and stands to pray his usual "Hey-God-here-we-are-the-Giovanotti-clan-nice-eh?" prayer. Mr. Optimism ends his prayer today with, "Thank you for all of our blessings, Lord: for those of which we are aware, for those of which we are not aware, and for those of which are right around the corner." Then he winks at me, making me wonder which one of my big-mouthed sisters went and told Papa about Ted after swearing she wouldn't mention it. Angie, I bet; she never could keep those lips locked.

Rosa and Mama, who insist on serving us, enter the dining room with the turkey. It's beautiful! Golden and brown. They follow it with bowls and trays and dishes of colorful, beautiful food, but damn, if I can smell any of it.

I look down at my plate, piled high with food. I start with the turkey (which could be chicken or pork for all I can tell) and head clockwise around my plate, eating (but not tasting) my food in courses, the dressing next, then the mashed potatoes, then the cranberry sauce. I know I'm weird

126

about food. I get to about half past on my plate when I realize that this food is not sitting well in my stomach. I don't think it's the food so much as the fact that I've just come to the sudden realization that maybe there are no more surprises right around the corner for me, that I've had my share of surprises, that the rest of my life will run itself out in right turns and left turns, but no U-turns or one-eighties or three-sixties or short-cuts or long-cuts or back roads. Nothing like that, just turn left, turn right and you're home.

All of a sudden I can't swallow, nor can I catch my breath. My chair makes a rude sound on the hardwood floor as I slide it out from the table. I hear Papa say, "Is she choking? Bina, are you choking?"

I make it to the bathroom. I close the door and lock it. I slap the toilet seat down and I sit on it. I try to breathe and yes, there's a breath. I'm okay. I take another breath, and another. I begin to breathe normally and then I take in my surroundings. You cannot believe how big this bathroom is. It's all done up in ivory and black with gold fixtures and it is such a nice bathroom I have a mind to stay in here forever.

But of course there's the predictable knock. I can tell by the force of it that it's Aunt Lina, the very, very last person I care to speak to right now. "Sabina, it's me." (It's *her*.) "You okay?"

"My stomach's upset, that's all. Too much antipasto. I'll be fine. Go and eat. Please."

"Let me in."

"Please, Aunt Lina, I'll be out in a minute."

"Let me in now."

"If you must know, I'm sitting on the toilet."

"Sabina Alana, open this door or tomorrow I'll call Detective Ron Donald and tell him that you've been talking of nothing else ever since you laid eyes on him the other day in the store."

I open the door on the word *day* and she penetrates yet another of my hiding places. She does have the courtesy to lock the door behind her. She looks around as if this is the first time she's ever set foot in Rosa's bathroom. She steals my seat which leaves me to lean against the counter.

"So?" she says.

"So." I echo.

"So it's not your stomach, is it?"

"Sort of. Not really. Oh, I don't know, it's either digestive, or respiratory, or maybe it's pulmonary."

"Oh, for cripes sakes, Sabina, I didn't ask for a biology lesson, I just want to know what's wrong."

"What's right? That's the ten-thousand dollar question." I don't know what it is, but Aunt Lina brings out something different in me. With

Mama and Papa and my sisters, I put on my happy face. I'm always nice; I'm not sarcastic or cynical. Words don't come out sounding like satire. It's like my parents and my sisters know that sometimes I feel bad about my situation and I know that they feel bad for me, but I don't want them to know that I feel bad and they don't want me to know that they feel bad for me. For some reason, Aunt Lina won't let any of us feel bad privately. I don't think she knows the definition of private. Her presence in this room attests to that.

She allows herself to stray from the topic (me) for just a second to make rude comments about her daughter-in-law. "Did you get a load of Barbara? I didn't even recognize her. Last time I saw her she had brown hair. Honest to God, I thought maybe my Tommy divorced her, got himself a new wife and forgot to tell me. She looks older than me and she's your age. Jesus, baby, that alone should lift your spirits. You might not have a man, Bina, but at least you got your looks."

"Oh, thanks for the compliment. Besides, Barbara doesn't look that bad."

"No? Mrs. Potato Head would beat her in a beauty contest."

"Aunt Lina, you are so mean!"

"I am not, I'm just so honest."

"Okay then, but it's your honesty that makes you mean."

"So be it," she says, waving a hand at me. "You'd be wise to take some lessons from your old aunt."

"Why? I don't want to be mean."

"Forget the mean stuff, you're hopeless in that category, I'm talking about the honest stuff."

"I need lessons in honesty? Me? Take a look at my tax return sometime. My accountant says I'm too honest."

"I'm not talking numbers here. Have your father check for carbon monoxide poisoning in the store, will you? I think you're losing brain cells."

"Can we do this without the insults? Wait, can we not do this at all? Don't you think there's something strange about a woman who traps her niece in bathrooms to discuss her love life? We've got to stop meeting like this."

"This isn't about your love life, this is about the rest of your life. No one in your family has the guts to tell it like it is."

"Oh, and how is it, Aunt Lina, I'd like to know." I tell her this face-to-face but then I conveniently turn around and wash my hands in the sink so I don't have to look her in the eye when she unravels the fabric of my life. Someone knocks.

"Yes?" My voice cracks.

"It's Rosa. Are you sick? I hope it wasn't the food."

I talk through the door. "Rosa, no, it wasn't your wonderful food. Don't be silly. It's not my stomach. It's not a digestive thing. First I thought it was more respiratory-related, but since Aunt Lina has joined me, now I'm thinking it's more of a neurological issue."

Aunt Lina slaps her thigh. "More of the biology class."

"What?" the door says.

"Rosa, I just have a really bad headache, that's all. Go and eat. Don't let my little headache spoil everyone's dinner. Just tell me if you have any Excedrin."

"In the second mirrored cabinet, the one on the right."

"Thanks. I'll be out in a little bit, okay?"

"Hop in the Jacuzzi if you want to, that might help."

"Okay, thanks." Like I'm going to get naked in front of my aunt.

When I turn around, Aunt Lina has a cigarette in her mouth. "You know you can't smoke in here, the kids—"

"Have allergies. I know. I know. It's not lit."

"It's not just allergies, it's asthma, too," I say, feeling as if I have to justify Rosa's no smoking rules.

"I just want it on my lips, that's all. Don't give birth or anything."

I search and find the Excedrin. "Aunt Lina, why don't you just say what you want to say and then we better get out of here. The longer I'm in here the harder it's going to be on everyone."

"You see that's your problem, you worry about everyone. You've got to start thinking about *numero uno*."

I hold my head—it really is aching now—in my hands. "I'm not up for this, Aunt Lina."

"You said I could speak my piece."

"You're right, go ahead." I wave her on.

She looks at me, up and down, with an expression that's something like disgust or disbelief. "Rosa and her sleepover at the Four Seasons. All to talk some sense into Colina. Forget about Colina, she'll do what she has to do—although I do worry that she suffers from the same nicey-nice disease that you do. I know what I'd do to the bastard. But that's for another day."

I can't help but snicker. "Aunt Lina, did you come all the way from New York to solve all our problems?"

She takes a puff of her un-lit cigarette, and says, "Don't go getting disrespectful. Somebody has to kick you girls in the butt. Look at you all. Not one of you knows how to live."

"You mean live it up."

"Rosa could be spending some of her husband's money in style—cruises, an East Bank Club membership, jewelry, furs—but all she wants to do is bake bread and cart these kids around. Marina wishes she was a man or a doctor or something. Colina spends more time in soup kitchens than in her own kitchen."

"Now that's not true."

"And Angie, well, that girl used to have some spunk. Now every time I see her she's asleep."

"Geez Louise, she's got two babies, neither of whom sleeps through the night. What do you expect?"

"I expect nothing, from them, that is. You're right, you're right. It's like your Nana Melarosso used to say: 'When ya' got kids, ya' got nothin' but kids.' But with you, I expect more."

"Oh, you do."

"Let me tell you a story, Sabina. I've never told you this story, and even if your mother has already told you about this, it was her point-of-view."

I have to admit, she has my curiosity piqued. I unfold my arms and hop on top of Rosa's ivory marble counter. I lean back against the mirror and nod to Aunt Lina to go on. She never tells stories; she only lectures.

"You may not know this, but you and me, we have some things in common. You've got four sisters, I've got four sisters. Your father owns the store, my father owned that store. You worked in the store—"

"*Work*," I correct her. "Present tense."

"Yes, but I meant when you were young, just like I worked in the store when I was young."

"So we're twins, right."

"I'm just trying to say there are some…"

"Parallels?"

"Yes, but differences, too. I was the oldest, not crammed in the middle like you. They were like my baby dolls, my little sisters. And they worshipped me. I was a little Mama to them since your Nana Melarosso was so busy in the store. I was the leader, the organizer, the boss. And I loved the role. I was so good to them—let them borrow my clothes, introduced them to my friend's little brothers, smoothed the way for them in school. I tell you, I was a hot-shot."

"You're still a hot shot."

"Ha! No one listens to me anymore. But that's not part of the story." She gets up from the toilet seat. "*Maronna*," she says, rubbing her behind, "that's not the most comfortable seat in the house, is it." She moves to the marble ledge of the tub. "What I'm trying to tell you is that I was *too* good to my sisters. I started putting their needs ahead of my own: '*Sure

Connie, I'll take your shift at the store tonight,' when she wanted to go out with Franky Tandini. And *'That's okay Josie, I'll send it to the cleaners,'* when she spilled marinara sauce on my white silk blouse. And before long it was me who was giving my mother a permanent every other month and me that took over the book work for my father, and then I blinked my eyes and bang, your mother got married, and then two years later Connie got married, and then two years later Josie got married, and in another year, it was Gina. And there I was, the oldest, and, even if I say so myself the best damn looking one of the bunch, passed over because I was too busy playing nicey-nice for my sisters, too busy being loyal to my parents and the family business. I didn't put myself out there, and so there I was slicing *provolone* and passing *mortadella* over the counter, while your father baked bread in the kitchen and your mother nursed baby after baby in a little apartment up the street." She takes a pretend puff on her cigarette and even exhales.

"Everyone talked. They couldn't understand how it could be that I was not yet taken. My father used to tell the old timers that he was saving the best for last. And then I went and broke his heart when Joey *numero uno* walked through that door. I owe my first marriage to a sweet little old lady named Margerita Panepiano. I was all dressed up in black that day to attend Miss Margerita's funeral. As you know, I look good in black. I bought that dress especially for that funeral. I figured there would be a lot of people there, maybe some nice young men. How ironic that Joe number one would walk into the store ten minutes before I was to walk out. That was that. We got married and we moved to his hometown in Bridgehampton, on the island."

"So you got a happy ending and you want a happy ending for me, too."

"Happy ending! Sure, sure, three husbands and three rotten sons later, some happy ending. Joe number one used to hit me, Sabina. A lot. But I remember thinking I'd rather take the hits than be called an old *zitella*. So I stayed in New York and let everyone think that Joey and I hobnobbed with uppities. He was a bum. They were all bums, they just got progressively richer, that's all." She walks over to the toilet, lifts the lid, throws the unsmoked cigarette in and flushes. "So, now you know why I can identify with your situation. I hate to see it, Sabina. You remind me too much of myself. I was too damn nice and look where it got me. Right back to the store slicing cheese. I made a complete circle. For the love of God, Sabina, beat it out of here while you still can."

"Beat it out of where?"

"The store. Your Mama's house. This city. There is a whole world out there."

"If there's a whole world out there, how come you came back here?"

She waves me off, "Well, me, I'm too old for adventure, and well, I guess I'm just like an old dog whose come home. There're people here who love me."

"Exactly."

I hear five soft, tentative taps on the door, and I know it's Mama. I climb down from the vanity-top and open the door. Her face looks funny—mad, jealous, and confused all at once.

"What's going on, *bedda*? You've missed the whole dinner. And you," she points to Aunt Lina, "your son is looking for you."

"Okay, okay, I better go see if Barbara's changed her hair color while I was gone." She pats me on the cheek, hard, as she goes around Mama and me. We both watch her walk out the door, shaking her butt on purpose.

I just look at Mama and say, "She took me hostage, Mama, and I just couldn't get out of here."

"I'm not worried about her, *bedda*, I'm worried about you. It's that boy isn't it?" And when she says this, at first I think she means Vito. But then she adds, "Rosa told me about this fellow you met at the Four Seasons."

"Geez, what a big mouth. Next thing I know she'll rent a billboard on the loop that says, I don't know, "Ted Kallista Where Are You?""

We're still standing in the doorway, which is the narrowest part of the bathroom, and I'm this close to Mama. It breaks my heart when she says, "We never had secrets, Bina. You tell me everything."

"I know, Ma, I just didn't want to say anything in case nothing became of it, which is exactly what has happened. It's just too hard to deal with."

"But you told *her* about him?"

"Geez, Mama. *No!* She'd be the last person I'd tell, honest. I've just learned that I handle rejection better in privacy."

"I understand, *bedda.*" She puts her arm around my neck. "But don't give up yet, maybe he'll call. What with the holiday and everything. Let me heat up your plate. Maybe you'll get your appetite back."

"I'm not hungry, Ma."

"How can you not be hungry? It's Thanksgiving."

10

Bring To a Rolling Boil

It's another day. I'm in the store, doing what I do. I still can't smell. And for the life of me, I can't maneuver my facial muscles into a smile. Both my parents and the redhead have accused me of moping. Jimmy's trying to get my attention by telling me something I didn't know: that the *tortellina* was fashioned after a woman's navel, which is information I could have lived the rest of my life without knowing. Now every time I sit down to eat a plate of *tortellini*, I'm going to think of innies and outies. How absolutely disgusting.

We start to get busy so my body goes into automatic. Charlie Gradezzi tells me that he's going to spend Christmas with his oldest son in San Francisco, and now I have San Francisco on the brain. I'll never forget our trip out to see Vito graduate. Papa, Mama, Colina, Angie, and I flew out. They were so excited to see San Francisco, but I was just excited to see

Vito. It had been torture being apart for so long. I could hardly believe that he was finally coming home.

He'd changed again! Gone were the long curls and the beard. His cropped hair and clean-shaven face made him look robust and happy. He ran to us at the airport and kissed me for at least ten seconds before coming up for air. He got us settled in at the Westin St. Francis Hotel and then gave us a tour of the city. We took in the sights down on Fisherman's Wharf and enjoyed people watching.

The day before graduation the students hosted a pig roast for family and friends. Why they wanted to do more cooking was beyond me, but Vito said, "Bina, this is what we love to do." He was more animated than I'd ever seen him before, running here and there, grabbing buddies that he wanted to introduce to us. He kept saying, "Come over here and meet my family," and I at first wondered if he meant adoptive family or the family he would be marrying into. He smoothly presented Mama and Papa as his godparents and me as his "girl," but when he got to Colina and Angie, he stumbled. "And this is Colina and this is Angie, my—" and he rolled his hands in front of him to indicate that it was coming to him. "My girlfriend's sisters...or my godparent's daughters...or, well, anyway, they're like my cousins," he got out finally and hugged Colina who was nearest to him.

Meeting Hoss was a shocker. I guess I'd pictured a big teddy bear of guy, but in reality, he looked like a Hell's Angel, with his scraggly hair and beard, dirty jeans and tattoo. But a *sweet* Hell's Angel. Vito said he was graduating by the skin of his "Tex-ass" teeth. Upon meeting me, Hoss picked me up, twirled me around, and declared me a "cute one."

The party ran a little wild. The air smelled of relief and deliverance. Two years was a long time; now it was time to party. Someone turned the music up and that alone was the cue for parents and anyone else who was not ready to celebrate in a big way to leave. Papa and Mama took the cue and told Vito that they were heading back to the hotel. Vito asked Papa if I could stay, that he'd bring me back by midnight. When Angie asked if she could stay I said "no" a little too emphatically and I saw Mama's eyes register concern.

"I wasn't asking you," Angie said, "I was asking Vito."

I thought it was stinky of Angie to put Vito on the spot like that. She knew he had a soft place for her. I thought he would give in, but instead, he looked at me, squeezed my hand tighter, rocked on his heels a couple of times, and said, "Maybe not this time, Ang. There's going to be drinking and everything." Mama's pupils dilated at the word *everything*.

Colina said, "Besides, Angie, they'd probably like a little time alone." Neither of us said a thing but time alone would be better than gold.

We sat at a picnic table with Hoss, his girlfriend Mary, and some other students who'd been in Vito's group. We drank ice-cold beer from bottles and ate plain potato chips, which struck me as kind of funny, like, where's the gourmet dip? Vito slung his arm around my neck and I listened and laughed while he and his friends shared horror stories and success stories about their last two years together. Like the three-fifteen a.m. Breakfast Cookery Class, which after daylight savings time was really the two-fifteen Breakfast Cookery Class. Like the time George sliced off the tip of his index finger. And the time, when Chef Johannes was demonstrating how "a sharp knife is a safe knife" and it slipped out of his hands and punctured his shoe. About the time Hoss spilled the fat bucket (which I understood to be the bucket containing all the fat that had been skimmed from stock) then slipped and fell when he was mopping it up.

This guy named Julian told about the time he used his side towel to blot his forehead. Someone—obviously a non-student—said, "So?" He puffed up and imitated one of his chefs declaring that side towels were not for wiping your knife or your board or your hands for that matter, they were for grabbing hot things. They talked about how competition ran fierce and passions ran high. They talked about arguments over blond roux and brown roux.

"Damn, I hated making roux," Hoss said, shaking his head.

"You must rue roux," Mary said cleverly.

A guy named Barry or Perry told how his consume almost got the better of him. Vito explained that a perfect stock is so clear that you can read the date of a dime at the bottom of a gallon. "Hell," Barry or Perry cried, "I couldn't tell who the hell's *face* was on that damn dime, let alone the date." We all laughed and someone said, "Who the hell's face *is* on a dime, anyway?" People shouted out their guesses. Lincoln? Jefferson? Eisenhower? Someone produced a dime to prove it was in fact Franklin Delano Roosevelt, but then someone else wanted to know who was on the nickel then. Some guy with a long brown ponytail said, "I don't know, some dude with an f-ing ponytail," as he swung his own back and forth.

"That's Jefferson, isn't it?" said Vito, and before long they were all digging into their pockets to see who was who in American currency.

Looking around the table, there was a part of me that was envious. There was a bond here. Things were a lot different for me at UIC. Most of my fellow students in the business college didn't get all that excited about what we were doing. These people were passionate about food and about what they could do with their diploma, namely give pleasure to anyone who ate their food. What a gift.

At ten o'clock Vito pointed to his watch, and I said my "nice-to-meet-yous" to all his friends and we walked the short walk to his dorm room. "Hoss and Mary are going to the bars," he said, giving me a little wink.

In his room we sat on the bed with our legs crossed, facing each other. He'd opened a bottle of wine, some special bottle from the chef he had externed with at a restaurant in the Napa Valley. (All students had to complete a three-month off-site externship before they could graduate. Vito said the externship was the fun part—like when you finally get behind the wheel in driver's ed class.) We clicked our glasses together and I asked him how it felt to be a real honest-to-goodness chef. "I feel like Julia Child," he said, referencing our debate all those years ago, the debate that really started all of this in motion.

He couldn't stop talking. He wanted me to know every single thing he'd learned. He told me for the millionth time about his different chef instructors, his favorite being his Skills teacher, Chef Torma. He showed me his knife set with its leather carrying case embossed with the CCA logo. He showed me his textbooks and his notebooks. "You know, Bina, the goal here is to get a solid grounding in the fundamentals, to master the basics, to become an expert in navigating the kitchen. It's about skills and technique and speed." He paused to take a sip of his wine. "But if I had to boil it all down to one thing it would have to be something your mother taught me years ago: it's all about a respect for food, and about knowing what a particular food needs to taste its best. Kind of what Italians have been doing all their lives. Oh, I almost forgot, I have a present for you," he said with a little-boy smile.

"For me?" I don't know why I thought it would be an engagement ring but the timing seemed so perfect to me. Apparently not to him though because the gift was a sterling sliver charm bracelet dangling with little culinary charms: a spoon, a fork, a knife, a cup, a pot, a frying pan, a wire whisk, a coffee pot, an oven mitt, and I think a toaster, but it's been ions since I've fished it out of the bottom of my jewelry box so I can't be sure. It was adorable. He'd seen it at a museum gift shop and thought I would love it.

I did and told him so as I held out my hand so he could put it on me. I dangled it so we both could admire it, but I wondered if he could see the disappointment in my face. I don't know if he actually did or if it was all part of the plan, but then he told me that as soon as we got home and settled we'd pick out a ring.

"So, is this the formal proposal I've been waiting for?" I teased.

"I told you, Bina, I proposed when we were fourteen!"

I shook my head and smiled. "I guess I'll have to take that as a proposal."

"And I guess I'll have to take that as a yes."

We set down our wine glasses and snuggled close with our heads together. I leaned my head on his shoulder and he leaned in and kissed me slowly and tenderly. It felt so wonderful to finally be reunited. I wanted him so much. But then I saw the clock. It was eleven-forty. Vito told Papa he'd have me back by midnight. I broke our kiss to say, "Vito, look at the time! How long does it take to get to the hotel?"

"Shit," he screamed, straining his eyes to see the clock. "Twenty minutes if we walk, fifteen minutes if we run...if we're lucky!"

We ran a few blocks, but luckily a trolley came by and we hopped on. Vito got a little wild, hanging off the side, whooping and hollering. The trolley driver told him to knock it off or he'd kick him off, but Vito was too hyped. He started singing the "Rice-A-Roni" song and so we all joined in. Then he belted out that song from Mr. Roger's Neighborhood: *"It's a beautiful day in the neighborhood...please won't you be my neighbor?"* Everybody on the trolley cracked up. Everybody except the driver. He said something like: "I always wanted to go after that guy with a shotgun." Vito held on to the pole for dear life and let his legs go flying. Then the driver pulled the brake lever and said, "Get the hell off my trolley." So we did.

We ran the rest of the way down Powell Street and arrived with only minutes to spare. Vito was ticked, said he had a very romantic evening planned for us. Where had the time gone, he wanted to know. I told him had there been a little less talking there might have been time for a little more smooching. He said that he had a little bit more than smooching on his mind. I gave him a pretend hit on the shoulder. He squeezed my hand, brushed his lips briefly against mine, slapped me on the butt, and sent me on my way up to the room.

None of us was surprised to find out the next day that Vito had graduated at the top of his class. He absolutely beamed from the stage, looking so distinguished in his whites. I wondered if the glow that emanated from his body was that elusive something people called an aura. That day, if you measured our lives on a bar graph, our indicator would have bled off the page. That's how high our highs were.

The next day, Vito took us to lunch at Kuleto's Italian Restaurant, then we hung out in Union Square, fed pigeons and people-watched. A black man dressed in a gray tuxedo with top hat and cane serenaded shoppers in front of Saks Fifth Avenue. Another man who had spray-painted himself bronze posed as a statue of a soldier. It was amazing! How anyone could freeze himself into one position like that was beyond me. *Why* he would do it was also beyond me. "It's his art!" Vito proclaimed. Sometime in his stay in San Francisco, Vito had become a connoisseur of art in addition to cuisine.

Back at home things were far different than either of us imagined. Vito worked at the store two weeks before starting his new job at Mezza's, a highly rated Italian/French restaurant where reservations were required and jackets and ties for the gentlemen were as well. I would come home from school and find him in the kitchen with Mama, Papa, and Mr. Maggio instructing, demonstrating, and showing-off. He devoured their attention. My parents and Mr. Maggio seemed in awe of his knowledge and skills and listened with interest to everything he told them.

As for me I found it all a little annoying. He'd come back such a professional, picky and precise. Once when I was helping him make dinner at the apartment, he asked me to hand him a sauce whisk and I handed him a balloon whisk instead. When he realized that I didn't know the difference, he gave me a crash course on kitchenware, beginning with Knife Identification 101. He even tested me.

Night after night, after I finished my own studying, we would scour his CCA textbooks. I never knew there were so many different kinds of knives! He didn't stop at knives either. He wouldn't let up until I knew the difference between a granny fork, a pot fork, and a spaghetti fork. The difference between a cheese plane, a cheese cleaver, a cheese marker, and a cheese slicer. Soon, I could identify and describe utensils and gadgets that I never knew existed: taco tongs, zucchini corers, avocado skinners, tuna squeezers, chocolate frothers. By the time he was through with me, there wasn't a gadget—handy or ridiculous—that I couldn't identify.

The new job at Mezza's had Vito working day and night for little money, but in less than six months he progressed from prep cook to the lead line position. He was shooting to move up to sous chef, but then he heard about a more attractive opening at another excellent downtown restaurant. He took that position but only stayed there for about three months, claiming that the executive chef was certifiably mad—he kept threatening to kill the kitchen staff's first-born children if the food was not perfect. Then, Vito ran into an old high school friend whose cousin was preparing to open up a bakery café near the loop. "Bina, a chance to help create something from the ground up!" It was there that he ended up and it was there that he went wild developing original breads and simple dishes. He started to earn some decent money and started to make a name for himself.

The owner was a young Sicilian-American man, about Vito's age, named Carl DiMontaggio. Carl called the place *The Bread and Salami* because he said that's what Sicilians in Palermo used to call his father, meaning he was an easy person to be around, friendly, and informal. And that's just the kind of place it was, friendly and informal, like Mela's. But it was also hip and trendy, unlike Mela's. They served comfort food—breads, soups, muffins, and cookies. Vito was ecstatic, saying he'd had enough of cooking food that was almost too fancy to eat. He wanted to get his hands back into dough, his first love.

I hardly ever saw him. He went in at three a.m. and on the three afternoons that my schedule allowed me to stop by his apartment for an hour or two, I would find him wiped out on the couch, barely able to move much less hold a conversation. I tried not to take it personally. I knew how physical his job was, not to mention how hazardous it could be with high flames, wet floors, and sharp knives. He was working twelve-hour days. But he was in heaven. Bread heaven.

Papa wasn't the least bit worried. "Let him get his feet wet, *bedda*. Let him be."

So I let him be.

Before long, Carl got Vito involved in all aspects of the café—food ordering, equipment ordering, menu planning. Our time together shrunk like a ground beef patty cooked too long. But while I was pouting, Vito was baking. Carl gave him free reign in the kitchen and Vito started creating artisan breads, one new one each week. He was never happy with his sourdough rounds though. I guess there is a particular kind of yeast that is only found in San Francisco and makes a sourdough that is superior to all others. Still, he created an inspired sourdough, with a good crumb and a crispy golden crust, and I think it was the bread that finally untied Papa's heart.

You should have seen Papa's eyes when he bit into a slice of that bread. It was just for a milo-second, but I saw something. After that day, it seemed that every time I came home from *The Bread and Salami*, Papa would ask me, "So what's going on with Vito? Any new breads? He likes it there, doesn't he, Bina?" And then I knew that Papa was just as worried as I was about Vito ever coming back to work at the Mela's.

Just when I'd worked up the nerve to ask Vito about his career plans, our marriage plans (he referred to me as his fiancée, but there never was a ring or a date), and our business plans, Carl decided to send him on a trip. One afternoon when I'd arrived at his door, miracles of miracles, he wasn't dead on the couch as I usually found him. Instead, he was bouncing off the walls he was so excited. He told me Carl was sending him on a food tour of Sicily. "I leave Monday, Bina. Isn't that great?" He grabbed me and hugged me and said, "Man, I wish you were finished with school so you could come with me."

I pouted a little, but he took my chin and turned it up to him and said, "When I get back, we'll go get a ring. I've saved some money now. And then let's set a date. As soon after your graduation as possible." That alone made the trip easier to swallow. Although in the back of my mind I felt that if Carl was investing so much time and money into Vito, how would he ever be able to leave? I told myself that I just had to have faith.

He left on a Monday. He came back the following Tuesday. In those nine days he became another person. It wasn't just his appearance, although he did look different; he'd gained some weight and sprouted a beard. It was as if he'd been "Italianized" or something.

For weeks upon weeks he talked about nothing but Sicily until I got tired of even hearing the word. He told Papa how Sicily had surprised him, how he'd expected peasants, poverty, gangsters and black-veiled widows, and while it was some of that, it was also mountains, volcanoes, beaches, temples, open fields, and endless sunshine. He told Mama about the food, how he knew it would be good, but he never imagined it could be *that* good. He said the flavors were almost three-dimensional.

He expounded upon the bread to Mr. Maggio, he told my sisters about the *gelato,* proclaiming it the best ice-cream in the world. Even his own grandmother tried to change the subject after enduring all she could about the superior fruits and vegetables. I'd stop into *The Bread and Salami* and find him telling a customer how the best food in Sicily could be found in tiny *cafés* that were really just someone's living room, complete with the owner's teenage son slouching in a chair, reading a comic book.

Once I overheard Vito lecturing my father about the history of restaurants in Sicily, about restaurants being a pretty recent thing on the island. Papa told him: "When I lived there, there *were* no restaurants. People who had some money had their own chefs; the rest of us cooked at home. There was no such thing as eating out; we had barely enough food to eat in." Either Vito didn't detect the terseness in Papa's voice, or else he ignored it, for he continued with his lecture, explaining how restaurants came about after World War II. Out-of-work chefs from rich families started teaching cooking and in turn their students ran the first real restaurants on the island.

After his trip, Vito started speaking more Italian, pronouncing all the words with an exaggerated accent. And even when he spoke in English, he sounded like a European the way he dropped words completely ("You like?" rather than "Do you like it?") or ended sentences with yes or no ("Tastes good. Yes?"). And he looked more Italian, too—he'd let the beard grow in full and left his hair long and curly. Who was this person? Did I even know him?

My senior year at UIC was a blur. I raced to classes, I studied, and I visited Vito at *The Bread and Salami* in between. We small-talked in the kitchen while he cooked or baked, but he couldn't give me his undivided attention. And that's all I wanted, a little attention...that, an engagement ring, and a wedding date.

Again I started doubting Vito's love for me. He was so wrapped up in his passion for Sicily and his passion for cooking and his passion for *The Bread and Salami* there seemed to be no passion left for me. One would think, after being apart for so long, that I would have had to fight him off. I wished for the chance, but the few opportunities we had to share some quiet time together at his apartment Vito ended up falling asleep on the couch. Often I felt like an old married woman before I was even married.

He'd promised that we'd pick out a ring when he got back from his trip but months had gone by and he never mentioned it. I racked my brain trying to come up with a clever way to bring up the subject without actually bringing it up. But it ended up I didn't have to. One night we actually got out to see a movie and we bumped into Brad Burns from high school. Brad Burns who all those years ago told Vito he thought I was luminous or luminescent or maybe loony. Anyway, the big hug he gave me must have triggered something in Vito because the next day he bought me a ring—the opal that I later gave to my niece. I guess the jeweler convinced Vito that it was vogue for brides-to-be to get engagement rings set with their birthstones. I'll admit, I was disappointed at first, but I knew Vito didn't have much money, and he still had a hefty school loan to pay off.

Honestly, I wasn't *that* disappointed that I didn't get a diamond. I was different than my sisters who wanted rocks. I just wanted romance. The night he gave me the ring was about as close as I got...

We were sitting on his sofa watching TV. He asked me to grab him a can of pop. I was kind of ticked at him about something or other and I almost told him to get it himself, but he never asked me to serve him like that, so I thought maybe something was up. When I opened the fridge door I found a small white ring box sitting next to the six-pack of pop. I got the shivers.

"Bina?"

"Yeah?"

"Did you find it?"

"I found it."

"And?"

"And...do you want ice?"

"Bina!"

I was still standing at the refrigerator, door open, staring in at the box, when he came in and hugged me from behind. "Aren't you going to open it?"

"Is there a proposal that goes with it?

"Bina! How many times do you want me to propose? I've loved you since I was thirteen, actually it was more like ten or eleven."

I turned around to face him. "But that's just it. We were kids. I want to hear it from the adult you, not the thirteen-year-old you."

He hugged me harder. "What do you want, you want me down on my knees?"

"I do."

"I do—you'll marry me? Or, I do—you want me down on my knees?"

"The second one."

"Then I'm down."

"Okay then. Now, ask me like you've never asked me before. I need to hear it."

He knelt on one knee and took my hand in his. "Bina—Sabina—Oh, you know I'm not good at this!"

"Go on."

"Any memory I hold inside my head includes you. Every major event in my life I experienced with you. You are part of my past and I want you to be part of my future. I love you so much. So marry me, will you?"

"Yes, I will." I kissed him and he kissed me back. He picked me up, carried me to his bedroom and lay me gently on the bed. He kissed me all over my body and whispered wonderful things to me in Italian. "*Che bellezza!*" (How lovely) "*Innamorate.*" (Sweetheart) "*Ti amo.*" (I love you.) He asked me what I wanted, and I said I wanted to wait, but deep down inside I wished he wouldn't have listened to me. Even now there's a part of me that thinks maybe he wouldn't have left if we'd been…more connected.

***

The year dragged on and I trudged through Principles of Management and Business Law while Vito baked beautiful breads and created sumptuous desserts for *The Bread and Salami*. A new generation of espresso-fueled executives flocked to feast on his baked goods. Carl's place flourished, and in just a year it was such a success that Chicago magazine reviewed it, which in the restaurant biz is the equivalent to being nominated for an Academy Award.

The review was the sword in my father's side.

There was a second trip to Italy without me, this time to the mainland where Vito uncovered glorious regional desserts, returning with more recipes and history and trivia than Papa had daughters or letters in his name. If Papa was the breadman than Vito was becoming the dessert man because his desserts started to draw a lot of attention. At that time, a typical American dessert was a slice of pie or cake, a couple of scoops of ice cream, or a dish of tapioca pudding. But Vito started offering other-world desserts like *Zucatto*, a chocolate and almond cake that is similar in shape to a halved pumpkin (*zuco*), hence its name. It's made with sponge cake, rum, toasted almonds, candied fruit, double cream, and maraschino liqueur. He made *Crostada di ricotta*, a *ricotta* cheese tart. Then there was *Ravioli Dolci* from Liguria, a sweet ravioli filled with *ricotta*, sugar, chocolate, candied fruit, nuts, cinnamon, and orange liqueur. My favorite was something called, "*Dolce delle Monache*," or Nun's dessert. It was made with eggs, *ricotta*, chocolate, and marmalade. Vito's favorite was "*Gatto Dolce di Riso*," a sweet rice cake consisting of Arborio rice, almonds, eggs and orange flower water. There was a Roman cheesecake that even Mama proclaimed to be the best cheesecake ever. American-style cheesecake is made with cream cheese, but the Roman version is a crustless cake made with *ricotta*, white rum, and double cream.

One night when I was typing up a paper that was due the following day, Vito called and said we needed to talk and could I go for a ride. He knew about the paper so I figured it must be important. I bribed Colina into finishing it for me.

Vito had inherited his father's nineteen-seventy-something Impala Chevy, a boat of a car with a lot of give to it. One thing I hated was when girls practically sat on top of their boyfriends in the front seat so that from behind it looked like a double-headed driver. I sat on my side. Out of nowhere there was an ocean between us. He parked in front of his Nana's house and I started to open my door, but he said, no, we weren't going in, he just wanted to park here to talk. "In that case," I said, "keep the radio on so I can hear the end of this song." Seals and Crofts' *Play For You* was on... "*Here the band, hear the band, won't you let the music take you, hear the band.*" He let the song run out and then killed the engine. It was quiet; the street innocent of people and cars.

He was acting weird, like he didn't know how to break it to me—whatever *it* was. So in the quiet I fantasized... either he wanted to break up (it's been one big, long mistake); or he wanted to move to Sicily (just quit school and let's go); or else he was sick of celibacy and wanted me right then and there in his father's car (hop in the back, Baby).

"Bina," he said as he draped his arm across the back of the seat in what seemed like an effort to bridge the gap between us, "I don't know how you're going to take this, so I'm just going to say it. Carl wants me to go in with him. Partners. Fifty/fifty. I'd own half the store. *We'd* own half the store. You and I."

I was stunned. I didn't say anything.

"We're doing great, Bina. People are going crazy for our food. Carl and I are talking about opening up a second place, but more of a coffee and dessert bar kind of place. An after-the-theater kind of place. People are going loopy for our desserts, honey. They tell me that they're better than sex and I say well I'm sorry for you but I'm glad to hear it just the same." He was trying to get me to laugh. He laughed nervously and ran his hands through his curls. "We want to call the new place *Sweet Thing.* What do you think, Bina?"

What did I think, Bina? Here's what I wanted to tell him: that I was pissed, major pissed, big time pissed. I wanted to ask him how come he always got to make all the decisions: "I'll go to culinary school, you go to business school, then we'll run your father's store together and live happily ever after." I wanted to ask him what ever happened to "Project Mela?" I wanted to say, "What about me, Vito?" but it sounded so selfish, so instead I said, "What about Papa?"

"Your father's the one who wanted me to get my feet wet. They can't get any wetter than this!"

"Yeah, but he thought you'd come back."

"I know, but you don't think he really expects me to now, do you?" He slid closer to me. I couldn't look at him so I fiddled with my thumbnail instead. "You know how I feel about your parents, honey, I practically worship them. They're like parents to me and they gave me a great start. I don't mean this as an insult but I've just gone beyond what Mela's Market can offer me. I know that sounds arrogant as hell and I don't mean it to be, but Bina, you know how I am about food." He gave my arm a squeeze. Finally I looked at him. It scared me to see that look in his eye—the same look he had all those years ago in front of Mr. Barbiere's shop when he'd planned out our future. Now, just as then, I knew there was nothing I could say or do to change his course.Right then and there I decided that the polish on my nails just had to go, so I commenced with some major chipping. He let me get to my ring finger, the one with the opal on it, before saying, "Talk to me, Bina." He moved closer. "You're probably wondering about our plan, right?"

"Yes, what about Project Mela?"

"It's still the same. You graduate, we get married, we run a place together—it's just a different place, that's all. The thing is, honey, I caught the bug. You go to school and it's all about getting your own place, that's the end-all. And it usually takes years. This kind of opportunity comes along once in a lifetime, maybe twice if you are extraordinarily talented and fantastically lucky. Bina, there're guys I graduated with that are still doing prep or line. This is unheard of."

"It's going to break Papa's heart."

"You underestimate your father. He loves us. He wants what's best for us. Besides, he's a foodie. He caught the bug. He knows what I'm going through. Come on Bina, it's going to be a great ride. What do you say?"

What could I say? I loved him. "If it's what you really want."

He practically jumped on me. "Thank you, thank you, thank you! You won't regret it, Bina. It's going to be great. Of course I told Carl I had to talk to you first. And we won't rush into this, I promise. Carl is an excellent businessman, he's got a good head on his shoulders. I told him that we wouldn't do anything until after your graduation and our wedding. There's so much to be done before we open the doors. There's the location and financing. Do we build or renovate?" He went on and on until the windows steamed up and he had to start up the car and run the defrost before he could drive me home to my term paper.

"One thing," I said before I got out of the car.

"What? Anything."

"You tell Papa."

"We'll *both* break it to him," he said. "Tell you what. Invite your parents over for dinner tomorrow. Wait, Thursday would be better. I'll cook for him. Then we'll tell him. We'll tell them both."

***

I was so nervous Thursday I almost flubbed up an exam. On the drive over to Vito's I felt like a traitor. There they were, Mama and Papa, in the front seat of Papa's car, innocently anticipating an evening of good food and animated conversation with their daughter and godson slash future-son-in-law.

"What's he fixing?" Mama asked as we pulled up in front of the brownstone.

"I don't know. He wanted to surprise us."

"Well, I hope he didn't go to too much trouble. I know he's been working so many hours."

When Vito opened the door to let us in, we were greeted by the wonderful smell of garlic and onions and some kind of roasted meat. The apartment looked clean and tidy. Vito looked a little nervous. He wouldn't let Mama or Papa lift a finger, so there they sat in the tiny front room sipping their wine and watching Wheel of Fortune. I went to help Vito in the kitchen and I couldn't believe my eyes. Food was everywhere—in pots, in pans, in bowls, on trays. "Vito! What the heck—?"

He smiled sheepishly. "I guess I went a little overboard."

"We'll have leftovers for a month. Geez, it smells like heaven. What is it?"

"You'll see," he said and slapped my hand just as I attempted to lift the lid on one of the pots simmering on the stove.

We heard Papa scream from the other room, "An 'O' *stupido*, buy an 'O'."

Then Mama said, "Can you solve it, Sunny? I have no idea."

"Not yet, I thought the second word was *why*, but it's not. Must be *way*."

I looked at Vito and we both shook our heads. What was the deal with my parents and that TV show? We just didn't get it. It was weird, too, the silly game show was the only thing at which Mama and Papa ever competed. They worked side by side every day without a harsh word. Mama otherwise cared nothing for word games, but there was something about the spin of that wheel that set one against the other.

"I hope you timed it so that you can serve dinner *after* Wheel of Fortune," I said to Vito, only half-teasing.

We walked into the living room with our wine glasses and just as we turned the corner, there was Vanna turning a square, revealing an 'A'. Before he knew what he was doing, Vito blurted out, "The way to a man's heart is through his stomach," and solved the puzzle. Papa shot Vito a look that was like bullets. "Sorry, Sunny, I guess I just saw it fresh and you'd just been looking at it for some time. Okay, is everybody hungry or what? We've got food. To eat. So…let's eat…the food."

Solving Papa's puzzle proved to be a bad omen. Papa set his face in a scowl as we sat down to eat. Vito did his best to play gracious host. "Sunny, I didn't realize until I was in Sicily that there was no tradition of antipasti," Vito said, as he placed a tray of cooked shellfish in front of Papa.

"We were too poor for food before the food," Papa responded with a grunt. He could have just as well ended the sentence with "and we liked it that way." I watched Papa's eyes as he chewed and swallowed some of the calamari and shrimp, and here's what his eyes said: damn, this kid can cook!

For the first course, which in Italian is the pasta course, called *il primo*, Vito served *maccheroni alla chitara. Alla chitara* means guitar style, the name deriving its meaning from the devise on which the pasta is cut. The freshly made pasta is cut into strips by pressing it through steel wires anchored in a wooden box. The one Vito used tonight was a homemade contraption he and Papa designed and put together one snowy Saturday afternoon many years ago.

For the second course, or *il secondo*, Vito served *agnello a cutturo*—lamb that is boiled for two hours, defatted and then cooked in wine, cognac, parsley, carrots, onion, sage, salt, peperoncino, tomatoes and garlic. The garlic, Vito informs us, is a particular red garlic that he had shipped back from Italy from a town in the Abruzzo region called Sulmona.

By the time Vito served the cheese course Mama and Papa were completely blown away. Everything was so delicious, and the seasonings he used were so different from what we were used to in Sicilian style cooking. The cheese was a pear-shaped shepherd's cheese that had been grilled. It was so smooth and flavorful.

"Vito, it's all so wonderful, *beddu*," Mama praised him. "You must be dead on your feet."

"I'm fine, Luna. Look at all the extraordinary meals you've cooked for me. I really wanted to cook for you and Sunny tonight. Carl said I could come in late tomorrow, so I'll sleep in a little."

I was a nervous wreck all the way through to dessert, a buttery almond cake covered with bitter chocolate. I couldn't take my eyes off of Papa, but he seemed to be more relaxed now. You could always tell if Papa liked what he was eating by his posture. If he liked something, Papa sat like a bowl full of jelly, all loose and relaxed. If something was distasteful, he became more rigid. Tonight, he sipped his espresso and sat back in his chair, looking contented.

I turned to Vito and tried to tell him with my eyes—now, tell him now. But Vito just smiled at me as he listed the ingredients of the cake for Mama.

"Vito has discovered so many wonderful desserts in Italy, many that I'd never heard of. Tell them, Vito," I began, hoping he'd take my cue and lead into the real reason they were here.

"Oh, I never imagined the *dolci*, it's like dessert heaven. I mean the best dessert in Italy is truly the fresh fruit. But the cakes and cookies and all the special desserts they make for the holy days and the holidays and the festivals are outstanding."

"Desserts are really getting more popular these days," I offered as another lead in. "I think people are getting tired of cake and pie. They want something new to tempt their sweet tooth…"

Instead of picking up from there, Vito just turned to Papa and said bluntly, "Sunny, I have something important to tell you."

Papa, who was still in his jelly state, set down his coffee cup and sat up straighter. "I'm all ears. What is it?"

"Carl wants to make me a partner," Vito said and instead of allowing his proclamation to sink in, he continued talking. "We're throwing around the idea of opening up a dessert coffee bar in addition to the cafe. Sabina's right, the desserts are really becoming popular and we're looking at some locations near the theaters and movie houses, that sort of thing." Silence. I looked over at Mama, but she was watching her right hand twirl the wedding band on her left hand around and around and around. "So, of course I've talked this over with Sabina, and after she graduates and we get married, we'd open up the new place and run it together." I caught a few exchanged glances across the table, but still silence. Then Mama looked at me with the most pathetic face.

"Sunny, I want you to know how much I appreciate all you have done for me," Vito continued. "I can't ever repay you. And it's not that I think I'm a hot shot now and I'm too good to work with you. It's not that at all. I can't explain it, it's just the excitement of starting something new and seeing it grow—that's what's so appealing. Can you understand?"

Papa grabbed Vito's shoulder. "Vito, Vito. Listen, I'm surprised, but I'm not. I've known for a long time that my little Ma and Pa joint was not going to satisfy your hunger. I'm not insulted, I'm just a little disappointed."

"We want what you want," Mama said.

Vito and I both breathed a sigh of relief. "You're not mad?" I asked Mama.

"How can we be mad?"

"I've thought about this for a long time, Sunny, honest, and I'm not just saying this, but Mela's Market is a little jewel of a place, and if I started working there it would change, inevitably, it would change, and I don't want it to change. I hope that it never changes because it's such a unique little place."

Papa nodded and with each nod Vito relaxed.

"Sunny, thank you, thank you for everything," Vito said, leaning across the table toward Papa.

Papa gave him a nice, hard slap on the arm and said, "You don't have to thank me." He slapped him a couple more times. Then his eyes got glassy and he said, "Coffee went right through me," and he headed for the bathroom.

***

What I took as resignation on my parents' part Vito took as an out-and-out blessing. He became obsessed with the new cafe, thought of nothing else night and day. Everyone thinks I lost Vito the day he left town, but I really started losing him the day after we told Mama and Papa. I lost him little by little. I lost him in bite-size increments.

Driven by his ambition he worked day and night at *The Bread and Salami* and then spent half the night at Carl's house planning the new place. Carl's young wife, Tina, with whom I'd become friends, was seven months pregnant with their second baby, and she was starting to complain about Carl and Vito's hours, too, so I knew it wasn't just me.

I began to slowly resent Carl, which really wasn't at all fair because he was really a sweet guy and a good businessman. But I thought it odd and unfair that no one was asking for my input, even though I was the other half of the team. I lay in bed at night thinking, "I might as well have majored in Spanish for all the good this business major is doing for me." What did two foodies know about accounting and cash flow and liability insurance and computers and debits and credits and marketing and demographics anyway? Then I thought about my own father and grandfather and how the owners of Mela's Market had succeeded all these years without the benefit of a college degree.

I know this sounds so whiney but there was just no time for me. Vito was hardly ever even at the apartment anymore. I would go there to study sometimes or work on papers. I'd haul my Smith Corona typewriter up the stairs and listen to my own clickety-click in the quiet coolness of the stucco walls. Is this how it would be? Both of us at the cafe all day, then me here alone half the night? I had the notion to call him at the B.S. (what we'd been affectionately calling *The Bread and Salami*) and tell him to look for a place with an apartment above it. All of a sudden I had a vision of my life: it was a duplicate of my mother's. I started to question whether that is what I really wanted. It wasn't that my mother's life was so bad—she really had a wonderful, blessed life. But there was something about living above the store; you felt so anchored to it. It was in high school that I came to the realization that we were different from other families. We lacked their get-up-and-go. We were so stuck to that store.

***

One night Vito tracked me down in the school library. "Guess who?" he asked, sneaking up from behind and covering my eyes with his hands.

"What are you doing here?" I said, happy to see him. "I thought you and Carl were deciding on a location for the new place tonight."

"We were. We did." He pulled out the chair next to me. "But first things first. You got a calendar with you?"

I nodded and fished my calendar out of my backpack. Vito took it from me and flipped to June. "Pick a Saturday, any Saturday."

"For what?"

"For what, she asks. For a wedding day! What else? We've got to set a date. We've decided on a location and Carl wants us to get married as soon as possible so he can coordinate the opening date."

149

"Geez, Vito," I whispered loudly. "You're just about the most romantic man I've ever met. 'Hurry up and set a date so we can open the stupid store.'" I snatched the calendar out of his hand. "Geez!"

He grabbed my hand. "Hey, hey, hey. Where did this come from? Bina. Honey. I didn't mean for it to come out sounding like that." He rubbed my hand harder. "Man, Bina, I am just kind of stressed out. I'm so hyped about this whole thing—I'm not sleeping well, I'm not eating well. Everything's so intense right now."

"I know, I know. I don't mean to act like a baby, but we haven't had a lot of time together and it's hard. And if we really are going to set a date, there's a lot involved in planning a wedding. I'm going to need your help."

"You got it. I'm here for you, Bina. Nothing else is more important."

"Not even Sweet Things?"

"Not even Sweet Things."

"Vito?"

"Yeah?"

"You're really not going to name it Sweet Things, are you?"

"You don't like it?

"It sounds like one of those dirty lingerie shops."

"It does?"

"It does."

"Hmmmmm," he said and began to chew on the side of his thumb. "You may have a point. But it's just a working name, nothing's been set in stone. You're the one with the marketing expertise. Come up with something and we'll present it to Carl. Okay? But now let's come up with a date."

"How about June seventh? Before it gets too hot," I suggested. (Our Lady of Pompei wasn't air-conditioned then).

"How about it," he said. Then he grabbed one of my textbooks and said, "Want me to quiz you on anything?"

***

Virgie stops into the store and snaps me back to the present. She still hasn't told Pauly she's leaving him. "I just haven't had the heart," she tells me as she drops cans of anchovies and bottles of capers into her basket. "I thought it would be easier. The weird thing is now that I know I'm leaving him he's not bugging me nearly so much. Now I have to wait till after Christmas to tell him. This news is not what you would call good tidings. He still hasn't called, has he? I can tell by your face. The asshole."

I shake my head. I really don't want to get into it. Not even with Virgie.

"Well, Pauly will be available after the holidays."

"Virgie, how can you joke about such a thing? Besides, you know I don't go for bald men with beards. They seem inverted or something."

"You should get a look at his...oh, never mind." She waves the thought away. "Let's see, I need a fourth pound of *prosciutto* and a pound of *ricotta*." She makes her way around the store, filling her basket until it can hold no more.

Before she leaves, she turns to me and as if it's an afterthought says, "Did I tell you there's a new guy at the bookstore?"

"Oh, Virgie, not you too! I'm not interested."

"I meant for me, Sabina, not for you."

"Oh," I say, because it's the only thing I can come up with.

11

Heart Attack on a Plate

After Virgie leaves I close up and head to the ladies' room. I catch my reflection in the mirror and am startled by my own sour expression. Getting hit over the head with the news that my best friend may have a new man in her life even before she's gotten rid of the old man in her life has puckered me up. I haven't even finished peeing before there's a knock on the door. I know that knock.

"I'm almost done, Aunt Lina."

"Open up."

"I'm washing my hands."

"Open it up."

I open the door. "Geez, what's the rush?"

"Your mother went out for a minute and I need to talk to you before she comes back. She is so mad at me."

"And why is that? Did you criticize her cooking again?"

"No. She says I trapped you in the bathroom at Rosa's. I got the silent treatment all day."

"I'll tell her you didn't trap me." I try to get past her but she doesn't budge.

"Good, because I didn't." She pushes her way into the bathroom and shuts the door quickly. "But I am now."

"What? Not again."

"Listen, Bina, your mother has forbidden me from talking to you about your personal love life. She told me to back off or else. My sister has never threatened me in her life so I know she means it."

"Wow."

"Yeah, wow. So I think to myself, I don't get it. I must be missing something here. Maybe I don't know everything that went on with that Vito Salina."

"Oh, geez."

"I wasn't here then and I want to know what the hell happened. In your own words. All I know is that a week before the wedding your mother calls me and says cancel your flight to Chicago, the wedding is off. Vito was in a car accident. She told me it was your decision and she left it at that. What the hell happened, baby, did you get cold feet?"

"That's what they told you, that *I'd* called it off?"

"That was the gist of it."

I sit down on the toilet seat. "You know, I never really knew what they told people. I guess I always thought they said we were postponing the wedding rather than canceling it. I mean, that's how I saw it—as a postponement. I didn't even return the shower gifts until a whole year later."

"Tell me, baby, tell me what happened."

"Aunt Lina, you know Papa needs help."

"I'll stay late, I promise."

"Let Mama tell you what happened."

"No, I want to hear it from you."

And so I find myself starting to tell her. I don't really know why—maybe to get her off my back once and for all. Maybe I just need to hear the words myself, since I haven't talked out loud about the incident in eighteen years.

***

At first Mama was against the date that Vito and I chose for the wedding because she said it was too close to my graduation. It was a tradition in our family to celebrate big when someone earned a college degree. Rosa and Marina before me had had huge family parties. I told Mama that I didn't need a party, that graduating wasn't all that big of a deal to me.

"Don't let your father hear you say that," she snapped. Mama, who never snapped. It was then that I knew that she was hurt about Vito not coming back to work at the store. I wanted to explain to her that it wasn't that I was ungrateful; I was soured because I felt somehow I'd cheated myself and Papa by earning a degree in a field for which I had absolutely no passion. Sometimes I thought about my childhood dream of working for the National Geographic and it seemed so...so childish. And sooooooo wonderful. I wanted to tell Mama that I appreciated all the sacrifices she and Papa had made in order to send us girls to college and how I knew Papa put a college degree up there with American citizenship, but Mama's movements became sharp and jerky and I decided to leave well enough alone.

In the library, Vito'd said, "I'm here for you, Bina." But I had to drag him to Marshall Fields in March to do the bridal registry thing. Rosa, who still wasn't the rich one yet, but was still Rosa, was in a big hurry to throw me a bridal shower. Vito and I roamed the aisles in Field's, but he was cranky and uncooperative. He acted like a five-year-old dragged there against his will. I told him if he was a good boy I'd take him to the candy counter but he didn't even crack a smile.

"Who invented this idea of registering, anyway?" he said. "It's stupid. Rude, too. It's kind of like begging."

"It is not. It's supposed to be helpful to the guests. Plus, it will protect us from receiving fourteen spice racks and twenty-nine crock pots."

"I like white," was his only input for choosing linens. When it came to outfitting the kitchen though, he took a turn for the better. Actually he went a little overboard, registering for every little kitchen gadget ever invented. He allowed me to select the china and everyday dishes so long as he could choose the cutlery, flatware, stemware, and cookware.

He did choose the menu for the wedding dinner, fussing with it for over a week. And he was wonderful about the cake, selecting this extravagant and outlandishly expensive whipped cream and strawberry number. After that his involvement was minimal. "Whatever you want," or "Anything is fine with me," were his pat answers to questions about the ceremony, the music, the invitations, the band, the hall, the flowers. And so because she was so much more experienced in these things, Rosa effectively took over the organization of the entire affair.

"You just leave everything to me," she told me. "You worry about your final exams. I'll take care of everything else."

And she did. Before long, the wedding I had pictured since I was fourteen—a modest affair with a simple, reverent ceremony, a nice dinner, and a fun dance—began to take on the qualities of a royal ball. In all actuality it was simply turning into a repeat of Rosa and Ed's wedding, only new and improved. The funny thing is that I really didn't mind that she took over. The fact that I'd stopped caring so much about the plans made the fact that Vito didn't care that much hurt a little less. It was Mama who was getting a little upset with Rosa. "What are you going to do, let her plan your honeymoon, too?" Mama asked me one day. I told her no, Vito was doing that. She looked at me like she couldn't believe I'd missed her sarcasm. "Let me at least take you to pick out your peignoir. Just you and me. No sisters."

Picking out a honeymoon peignoir with my mother proved to be a mistake. I kept looking at the satin and slinky, and Mama kept gravitating to the sleeveless but respectable. Finally, she talked me into a pretty white eyelet cotton gown and robe set that she proclaimed to be "simple, but sexy." I said fine. My heart just wasn't in it. At that point I would have bought a zippered muumuu if she'd wanted me to. But at least now I had my gown and veil, some new shorts and sandals for the honeymoon, and my peignoir and new slippers for my honeymoon night. I was ready.

Vito wasn't. He completely forgot about his appointment to get fitted for his tuxedo. All the groomsmen were there, even his boss, Carl, but Vito was nowhere to be found. Later, he told me he had been buying weathered barn wood from some guy in Woodstock, Illinois, to use in the new café and he just plain forgot.

Carl ended up helping me pick out the tuxes. "You can't go wrong with charcoal gray, Sabina." I scheduled another appointment for a fitting for Vito and went home with a tension headache.

Mama started to worry about me. "You look pale and your clothes are hanging on you. This should be a happy time and yet you're miserable."

Two months before the wedding, on a rainy, windy Sunday in April, Rosa threw a kitchen shower for me. She rented a hall and a microphone, and invited fifty-five of our aunts, great-aunts, and cousins. Three toasters, two crockpots, and a spice rack later, Vito and I drove back to the apartment to store the gifts until after the wedding. Mama and Rosa wanted to display all the gifts on card tables in our dining room (as they had for Rosa), but Vito refused, saying it was the dumbest thing he'd ever heard of. "So first you beg for gifts, then you display the gifts you begged for to show off what you received? Where do you guys come up with this stuff?"

Lately, I'd had to pick my battles with him and this one was simply not worth the fight. "Fine. It's not that big of a deal to me," I said in the car as we headed to the apartment. The trunk and back seat were piled with

155

gifts and I was just too happy and excited, thinking about all the wonderful things we'd received. My brother-in-law Ed was right behind us in his van, which was also loaded down with packages. Even the heavy rain couldn't dampen my spirits.

It was really coming down. Vito took a corner a little too fast. "Isn't it a little slippery?" I asked. "It looks like it might be slippery."

"I'm more worried about the wind," he said. "It's really tugging me."

I was just about to say, "Slow down then," when I felt the car swerve abruptly and I heard Vito scream, "Heeeeyyyy!!" There was a crunch of steel and that rainy sound of shattering glass. I was thrown hard into the passenger door, wrenching my neck and banging my elbow. My heart was pounding and I felt tingles all over, but I was okay. I looked at Vito. He was doubled over in pain.

"Are you okay?" we both asked at once.

I held my elbow and turned my neck from side to side. "I think so. What about you?"

"Oh, man," he winced, "I banged up my hand. Shit! That car came out of nowhere. Did you see him?" He shook off some glass that had shattered on him.

Ed was there before I knew it and then some neighbors gathered and finally the police. The guy who hit us was so blatantly intoxicated that he didn't even resist arrest. He didn't seem to be hurt in the least, or else maybe he was just too drunk to feel anything. We found out that he'd been driving without a license, without insurance, and without his headlights on.

Ed drove us to the ER where they x-rayed Vito's hand and knee and my elbow and neck. I was lucky—I was bruised, but not broken. Two of Vito's fingers were broken. They were only broken bones, but you would have thought his hand had been severed at the wrist.

"What am I going to do?" Vito whined over the phone to me the next morning. "How can I work? I won't be able to mix or knead my dough or anything. I called Carl. Told him I needed at least a day."

I tried to look on the bright side of things, an attempt at optimism. "At least you're right-handed and you broke fingers on your left hand, and I'm left handed and I banged up my right elbow."

"How is your elbow? And your neck, too. Are you okay?"

"I'm fine, really."

"Bina, I feel so terrible that you got hurt. I'm so sorry, I just didn't see that guy. I just didn't see him. I should have slowed down. The roads were pretty slippery."

"It wasn't your fault. The guy was drunk and he didn't have his headlights on. How can that be your fault? Listen to me, I'm okay. And you're going to be okay?"

"My car's not okay. Ed said it was probably totaled."

"You'll just have to get another one."

"No, I don't think I'll replace it, Bina. I've been thinking, listen, I mean with my Mom and my Dad and now me—I don't think members of my family should drive. What do you think, do we really need one? Or maybe we could get one, but you drive it. I'm not kidding, I don't want to drive in this crazy city anymore. Man, next time, I might kill someone. Or another crazy drunk gets behind the wheel like that guy and we don't get by with just minor injuries. The roads are not safe. I couldn't handle hurting someone, Bina. I couldn't deal with that. I—" His voice cracked. I could tell he was near tears.

"Vito. Vito. I'm coming over. I'll skip my morning classes. I'll catch a bus. Please settle down. I'll be there as soon as I can."

He was a mess. He hadn't bathed or shaved or even run a comb through his hair. He skin was almost the same color as the gray sweats he wore. Even with the painkillers he'd slept fitfully. He started pacing around the room, rubbing his forehead and his eyes. I'd never seen him like this. It scared me. He breathed in and then exhaled deeply as if he were practicing Lamaze. Finally he sat down beside me. He took my hand and said, "I'm sorry that I'm so out of it. I am really out of it." He came closer and brushed my hair back off of my forehead so that he could look at the scar he gave me when we were thirteen. He did this every so often and it always broke my heart that he couldn't let it go, that he had hurt me, had scarred me. But honestly, *that* scar was nothing.

"How can I help?" I said. "I want to help you."

"But Bina, that's just it—this is all about what *I* have to do. I feel like I'm being pulled in three different directions: Carl still wants me baking all morning, I've got to be at the new place all afternoon and half the night, and you need me for the wedding stuff. And now, just when I need three hands to get everything done, I'm down to one. I don't know if I can do everything that everyone expects me to do. No, I *know* I can't do it all."

He rubbed his eyes with his fingers and pinched the bridge of his nose, but I could still see the tears. I just hugged him and held him and told him not to worry, we'd work it out. I said I'd finish the rest of the wedding plans. The only thing I couldn't do for him was to get fitted for his tuxedo; he'd have to do that.

He blew his nose and said, "You don't know what day it is, do you?"

"Monday? April fourth? Oh, April fourth. Oh, Vito, I'm sorry, I just forgot." It was the ninth anniversary of his mother's death. "I just completely forgot."

"Kind of freaky, huh?"

"What?"

"Just that my mother's car accident was April fourth and then we're in this car accident the day before. It's just too close for comfort."

"Vito, that's just a coincidence. The weather gets crazy in the spring. I bet there are actually more car accidents in the spring than in the winter—at least around here. Total coincidence. You're spooking yourself out. Now stop."

"Bina, I have to tell you something that I've never told you— anyone—before. After my Mom died, I started having these weird nightmares. They're all different, but the same, in that I drive around the streets of Chicago in a red convertible, like a madman, slamming into every car I see. You know the kind of dream I'm talking about, first it's so real, you're really going ballistic in this car and the next thing you know you're in bumpers cars at an amusement park. Then you're back in a real car, crashing and bashing. The worst part of it all is that I'm enjoying myself immensely. I'm laughing my head off, like revenge is so sweet or something. But I'm killing people, Bina, lots of people."

"In your dreams."

"Yeah, but laughing all the while."

"Vito, I'm no Freud, but it's probably your subconscious working out the anger over your parents' deaths. It's perfectly normal. Everyone works out their emotions in their dreams. It's not like you're going around crashing into people when you're awake."

"No, but, honest to God, my nerves are so frayed, I just about punched out a cabby the other day."

"You did?"

"This close, Bina. I didn't know I had that kind of anger in me. It scared me. Man, I wanted to hit that guy."

"Yeah, but everyone wants to punch out cabbies. That's just life in the big city."

"I know, I know, and that's why I really think that I don't want to get another car. I'll get you one if you want one, but I'm not going to drive anymore. Honest, I'm afraid I'm going to hurt somebody, and then I'll never be able to forgive myself."

I just had to have a car, I thought. How else would I sneak over to visit Mama and Papa after we were married? "We have to have a car, Vito, we just have to," I told him.

"Okay, okay, we'll get you one. It's got to be a used one, okay, or else a honeymoon is out of the question." He cracked a smile.

"Hey." I punched him lightly in the arm. "How are the honeymoon plans coming along, anyway?

"You had to ask."

"What?"

"Well, unless you have a dowry I don't know about we can't afford anything fancy."

"Vito, we're only two months away."

"I know that. I'm working on it. Would you be really disappointed if we had to stay in the states?" he asked.

"I don't care where we go, honest. Just somewhere sunny and quiet," I said.

"Well, don't worry, I'm on it. My sister's got a friend who's a travel agent and she's working on some ideas. How about if I just surprise you?"

"I don't like surprises."

"Yes, you do."

"No, I don't."

"Yes, you do."

"No, I really don't—not for something this important."

"You're serious."

"Yes."

"Oh."

***

I doubt if he ever did finalize any honeymoon plans. After he left, I called every travel agent in the city of Chicago to see if there were tickets waiting to be picked up for a Vito or Sabina Salina. No one even recognized the name. I still wonder, what was he going to do, tell me after the reception that he just never had a chance to firm anything up? Or maybe he picked up our tickets and went on our honeymoon himself. I guess I'll never know but I've never stopped wondering.

He'd gone back to work after sulking for a couple of days. The banged-up knee caused him to limp, but he got around. He tried one-handed kneading stints in the kitchen, but got frustrated and gave up. In the end, he recruited one of the waitresses to help him knead the dough.

He was not only preoccupied, cranky, and stressed out, but his fuse was so short, he started snapping at people, including and particularly, me. One day I called him in between classes from a pay phone at school. He was at the new place, where he'd been spending afternoons and evenings overseeing the work crew. When he answered the phone, I honestly thought it was one of the workmen, this gruffly old guy named Lou. But it was Vito. The stress was taking a toll—even his voice sounded old.

"What is it, honey, I'm really busy."

"Father Mike wants us to meet him tonight to pick out the readings for the ceremony."

Even over the hammering and drilling I could hear him sigh. "Didn't we do that already?"

"No, Vito, we chose the read*ers*, but not the read*ings*."

"Man, Sabina (he only called me *Sabina* when he was mad at me), the sign guys are here. Carl and I are trying to pick out the color and typeface and all that. Can't you just tell Father we'll do the standard stuff? *Love is patient, love is kind.* The thing about a man leaving his mother and the thing about the rib."

I couldn't believe my ears. This from a guy who up until the testosterone kicked in was going to be a priest! I was too angry for words.

"Sabina, did you hear me?"

"Fine," I said, "I'll meet with Father myself."

"Thanks. Whatever you choose will be great." And he hung up with absolutely no clue I was angry. I stood there at the pay phone, holding the receiver in my hand, steaming at his cavalier references to some of his favorite scripture passages. Then it hit me, what else he'd said—that he and Carl were picking out the sign, which meant they'd chosen a name for the place without any input from me. I fished in the bottom of my purse for more change. This time that Lou guy really did answer and it took him forever to find Vito.

When he picked up, I got right to the point. "Look," I said, "I know you're busy, and I'm going to be late for my class, but I have a right to know what you decided to call *our* place, since you never even bothered to consult me."

"Hey, you were supposed to come up with something, and you hadn't mentioned anything, and look, honey, time is running out. We have to have a name. There's the sign and the telephone listing and the business cards and the menus and the advertisements and the—"

"Well, I have some ideas, but I had two tests this week, not to mention my senior project, plus I met with the florist, the caterer, and the church organist. I'm doing the best I can."

"Well, so am I."

"So you just decided without me?"

"Actually, Carl decided."

I just stood there, my skin prickling with anger. I was going to be late for class, but I didn't care. All I could think about was the fact that I'd only gotten three or four hours of sleep the last few nights because I'd been racking my brains out after studying all night to come up with some pithy name for the new place. Maybe I didn't have a winner, but I had some contenders: *Sweet Endings, Sweet Cuisine, The Sweet Life, The Sweet Tooth, Sweet E. Pies, Sweet Dreams, Sweet Expressions, The Dessert Spoon, Sweet Dough, How Sweet It Is, and Sweet Street.*

"So, what's it going to be, Vito?" I asked after a drawn-out pause.

"C. V. Sweets."

"*C. V. Sweets?*"

"Yes, C. V. Sweets."

"And the C is for…?"

"Carl."

"I see. Well then, I know what the V is for, don't I? *VERY SELFISH!*" I hung up on him. Later he told me that the 'V' was for Victoria, Carl's daughter, but that didn't make me feel any better.

I skipped my class to sit outside on a bench and stew. I didn't like being shut out. What a waste, I thought, soon I would be graduating with honors, and for what? To plop a couple of *cannoli* down in front of someone who will think they are better than sex?

If I were someone else, someone like Marina or Angie, someone with a little ooomph, I'd have marched over to C. V. Sweets and…and…and what? I didn't even know how to plot my revenge, much less to see it through.

What was it about Vito that made it hard to stay mad at him for long? Sitting there in the spring sunshine, I started thinking about all Vito had on his plate. After all, he was just trying to get things done. I guess he was doing his best. My anger started to evaporate, but by then my head was pounding, so I skipped my last class and went home to nap, forgetting all about the appointment I had at the bridal shop for our fittings. Mama, and my bridesmaids—Rosa, Marina, Colina, Angie, and Vito's sister, Jenny, (Becky had turned me down when I'd asked her to be in the wedding, using the excuse that it was too hard to get back to Chicago for the fittings)—all waited there for me for over an hour. I felt stupid when I picked up the phone and had to tell Mama, "Geez. I forgot all about it." I borrowed Papa's car and flew to the bridal shop. I had to laugh a little as I put the car in park. Here I was all over Vito's case for forgetting everything and then I go and forget my own fitting.

***

I graduated. I had my nice party. The next day, I used my graduation money as down payment for a car. We bought a used brown

Datsun. Vito wouldn't even test-drive it, but he did ride along with the salesman and me. When it was time to sign the papers, he told me he didn't want the car in his name at all, but since he was the one with the steady income, I needed him to co-sign. So he did. Reluctantly.

Three weeks before the wedding. Everything was set. Everything except one thing: Vito had never gone to be fitted for his tuxedo. He'd lied and told me he had. But then the store owner of Tuxedo World called one night when I was at the apartment writing out thank-you notes. I lit into Vito. It was the same old story—he had to meet with a plumber or a carpenter or a banker or a somebody or other.

I lost it. I'd never screamed at him that way before in my life. "Go!" I pointed to the door. "Get in the car and go and I don't want to see you or talk to you until you have been fitted for your stupid tuxedo. They're only open until five!" I threw my keys at him and then I threw myself oh so dramatically on the sofa and didn't look up until I heard the door slam. Then I ran to the window and watched the little Datsun pull out and head down the street. Tearfully, I went back to the job from which I had been interrupted—writing out thank you notes for the gifts I'd received at my last shower. But after writing out a few cards, I got restless. I was all worked up. I left the thank you notes on the table and went into the spare bedroom to drool over my shower gifts. I opened up a big white box that held a place setting of my china. It was so beautiful! Plain ecru with a thick gold band around the edge. Rosa didn't say so in words, but I knew she thought my choice was boring, but I loved it. Vito and I had always felt that a plate shouldn't be more beautiful than the food that's in it. This china would allow whatever food Vito and I placed on it to shine.

Since Vito had been so uncomfortable about all the gifts we'd received, I hadn't really had the chance to enjoy them yet. I'd felt funny about even taking an item out of the box to admire it. Now was my chance to peek again at all the lovely things we'd been given. I spent a good while that night in the small bedroom organizing the gifts by the rooms in which they would go. The boxes of china, crystal, flatware, and table linens I stacked near the window. Kitchen items I stacked near the closet. I couldn't wait to put everything away, to set up house.

My back ached by the time I was finished. I looked at my watch. It was seven o'clock. Where the heck was Vito, I thought. We'd never even had dinner. We were going to order a pizza and then put the final touches on our wedding program before I dropped it off to the printer. I turned the TV on and went back to thanking friends and relatives for fondue sets and casserole dishes. He probably stopped at C.V. Sweets for something or other I told myself. But when I called over there, the phone just rang and rang. I went back to my thank you notes. Maybe he stopped by his Nana's house or by Mikey Pinotta's to complain about what a hassle all this wedding stuff was. I sometimes wonder, does the brain assign specific anatomic destinations for certain emotions? I always feel happiness from the head up. Anger and fear get me in the heart. I feel romance in this ticklish little spot on my back. But dread, dread I feel in the pit of my stomach. Why is that? I started to feel dread at about seven forty-five. He'd left at four-thirty; the store was only open until five. So then your mind takes over, the fantasizing begins. Oh dear Lord, he's lying dead in the street and the last words I said to him were mean ones. That, or else he'd had enough of my whining and was leaving me forever. I called the tuxedo store, but the phone just rang and rang there, too.

Just before eight o'clock, Mama called from Marina's to tell me to remove Marina's mother- and father-in-law from the guest list. Ross's mother had just called to say that her husband had to have a hemorrhoidectomy next week and that he wouldn't be up to traveling for a while. Mama, under the influence of my sister the nurse, started to get into the nitty-gritty...telling me about the lubricants, the hot and cold compresses, the sitz baths. I wanted to say, "Ma, that's more information than I need," but I'm nothing if not polite, so I just listened and then said how sorry I was. Then I sighed.

My mother is not a mind reader but she is something of a voice reader. She immediately detected something in my voice and asked me what was wrong. I told her what had happened with Vito and that I was worried that he wasn't back yet. She and Papa were planning to stop by on their way home to drop off Ross's parents' wedding gift, so she said they'd be right over.

When they arrived Mama made some coffee and addressed some envelopes for me. Papa watched a cop show. I bit my nails. It wasn't like Vito not to call when he was running late; it wasn't like the *old* Vito anyway. Lately, he'd been unpredictable—sometimes early, sometimes late, sometimes forgetting and not showing up at all.

At eight-thirty I said maybe I should call Nana Lilli, but Mama said, "Why worry her, Bina?"

"Well then I'll call Jenny," I said.

"Don't bother that poor girl," Mama said. Jenny had had yet another colicky baby. Her fifth. Vito thought this one might just do her in. Mama was right, I couldn't bother her.

So we waited. I called home several times, but lately Colina was always on the phone and I couldn't get through. I banged the receiver down. My hand wasn't even off of it when it rang again. I picked it back up. "Yes, Hello."

"Yeah, is Vito Salina there?" a man said.

"He's not here right now, can I take a message?" I said.

"Yes, is this Samantha by any chance?"

"This is Sabina," I said not sure what to make of the call.

"Oh, I'm sorry, yes, Sabina. This is Ray Tultz, from Tuxedo World."

"Oh, yes, Mr. Tultz." I covered the mouthpiece and told Mama and Papa who it was.

"I was calling to let you know that your fiancé left his wallet here when he was in earlier."

"He did?"

"Yes, he did. I just discovered it now while I was cleaning up. Must have taken it out of his pocket when I was taking his measurements. Actually I find quite a few wallets. I could have a hey-day if I wasn't such a scrupulous fellow."

"I'll bet," I said just to be nice. "What time did that fiancé of mine leave anyway—I'm still waiting for him to come home."

Mr. Tultz told me that Vito arrived a little before five but that he'd had to wait while he finished up with another groomsman. Mr. Tultz had closed the store before he even got to Vito. "By the time I was done with him, it must have been around five-thirty, five-forty-five. He told me he was in hot water with you for forgetting his appointment for the second time. He said something about picking up dinner. I was teasing him, told him maybe he'd better throw in some candy and flowers. I bet that's where he is. Now you act surprised, Samantha."

"I will."

"If you can get here within the hour to fetch the wallet, I'll stay put. I'm kind of in hot water with the Mrs. myself. Planned on sticking around here tonight as long as I can."

I covered the phone, explained the situation to Mama and Papa, and Papa said he'd drive over and get the wallet.

"Maybe he went to the B. S.," Mama said after Papa left, and I had to smile because even Mama had started calling The Bread and Salami the B. S. I told Mama I'd tried earlier, but there was no answer. I tried again. Still no answer. Then I called Carl's home—no answer there either. Finally, I called Mikey Pinotta's house, but Mikey said he hadn't seen Vito since yesterday when they'd chatted at the B. S.

When Papa came back, Mama asked him if he would drive by the new place just to make sure Vito wasn't there. "Sure," Papa said, tossing the wallet on the kitchen counter. He left again.

Mama and I continued to work on the thank you cards until they were finished, stamped, and rubber-banded together. Papa returned in an hour, saying the place was completely dark. By now it was almost ten-thirty. We didn't know what to do. "Where is he?" I screamed. Mama hugged me and tried to calm me down. "If something's happened to him, Mama, I'll never forgive myself. I was so mean to him before he left."

"All right, all right. Calm down."

"But where could he be?"

"He could be anywhere really. Let's not start imagining the worst. He could be just driving around town for all we know."

"Yeah, *bedda*," Papa said. "That boy has been under so much pressure lately—he's like Mount Etna waiting to erupt. Maybe he needed some down time." But they knew as well as I did that Vito had become terrified of driving. I could tell that they were worried, too.

We sat and waited some more. Other than one phone call from Colina, the phone hung silent on the kitchen wall.

At eleven, Papa said that we should probably call the police.

"The police?" Mama gasped.

"Yes, maybe we can report a missing person and—"

"Missing person?" I gasped. "I don't think a person is considered missing unless it's been over twenty-four hours."

"Just let me call them and see what they say. They'll have a better handle on things," Papa assured us.

I bit my thumbnail to a jagged edge as I listened to Papa answer matter-of-factly the questions the dispatcher was asking of him. Then he said, "I'll let you talk to my daughter for a description." He handed me the phone and walked over to the window.

The officer wanted to know Vito's full name, address, telephone number, age, race, sex, height, weight, hair and eye color, any distinguishing features, clothing worn when last seen, last known location and time seen there, the make and year of the car, and the circumstances leading to his disappearance. I told him everything plus the fact that Vito had left his wallet at Tuxdeo World. He told me that the information I'd given him would be entered into the National Crime Information Center's computer files and would then become available to all other law enforcement agencies in the country.

"Do you contact the area hospitals?" I asked.

"Yes, Ma'am."

"So I should just wait until I hear from you?"

"Yes, Ma'am. And if he comes home, please notify us immediately so the case can be closed."

"Yes, thank you," I said and hung up the phone.

Less than a half an hour later, the officer called back and said that they'd located Vito. He'd been involved in a three-car collision and had been transported to the ER at Rush Presbyterian St. Luke's Medical Center. They had not listed his condition yet.

In the back seat of Papa's car, all I could think of was Vito telling me that he never wanted to drive again. I made him get behind that wheel. Why hadn't I driven him to the stupid tuxedo store myself? I had to act like such a baby. I prayed that he would be all right, that he would forgive me, and that he would recuperate before our wedding in three weeks.

By the time we got to the hospital, my chest actually hurt from my heart beating so violently. The triage nurse in the ER told us that Vito'd already been admitted. We made our way through corridors and down long hallways. Hospitals can seem so eerie with the quiet whispers of visitors, the plaintiff wails of patients, the everyday working voices of the nursing staff. I didn't have the stomach for it. We took an elevator up to the fourth floor and walked and turned and walked and turned until we came to room 413. I opened the door ever so gently and I heard soft moaning from behind one of the curtains in the double room and loud snoring from behind the other. I didn't think Vito snored, but at that moment I desperately hoped that he did. But when I peeped behind the curtain I saw a pale old man— had he not been snoring I would have thought him dead. I turned to Mama and motioned to the other curtain.

At first I didn't even think it was Vito. His face was bruised, cut, and swollen. His lower lip looked like a hot dog that had split open on the grill. He was either moaning in his sleep or else he was semi-conscious. I turned to Mama and buried my face in her neck. "Come on now," she whispered.

He was hooked up to an IV. A yellowish liquid dripped into the tube. I just stood there looking at him, wondering what other parts of him were hurt. When the doctor came, he took Papa and Mama and me out into the hall. The first thing Dr. Rose wanted to know was our relationship to Vito. Papa explained that he and Mama were his godparents and that I was his fiancée. He told us that Vito was in fair condition. He'd suffered a concussion and a whiplash injury, and he'd broken his left arm at the elbow and possibly fractured a rib. They'd had to stitch up several lacerations on his face, but actually he was very, very lucky: all his injuries would heal. I exhaled in relief and Mama and Papa hugged me. "Thank you, Jesus," Mama said and made the sign of the cross. "Yes, thank you," I repeated.

A police officer walked down the hall toward us and asked if we were Vito Salina's family. We said we were and he asked us to meet him in the waiting room when the doctor was finished with us. The doctor nodded. "We've got him on some antibiotics and we've given him something for pain. He'll be dozing in and out tonight, but tomorrow morning he'll wake up with a first prize headache, not to mention the stiffness in his neck muscles. Plus, he may have fractured a rib; we're waiting for the radiologist to look at the x-rays. Oh, and I wouldn't be in a hurry to let him look in a mirror, if you know what I mean," he smiled.

I hated to ask, but I had to. "Doctor, we're getting married in three weeks. Will he be okay by then?"

"Well...you might have some interesting wedding pictures," he said and broke a smile. "He's got the neck brace and the arm cast, and depending on the x-ray, we might have to splint his chest with an elastic belt. He's definitely going to need time to heal. I'm concerned about the possible rib fracture. His breathing is rapid and shallow and he seems to be in pain when he breathes in. Let's see what the x-rays show. Rib fractures can be pretty serious if the bone is splintered or the fracture is displaced. Then you have to worry about sharp fragments piercing the lung. But I didn't hear any crackling of bone fragments when I listened to his chest, so hopefully we won't have to worry about that. But it all depends." He patted my shoulder and said, "I wouldn't call the wedding off just yet." He smiled a smile that I'm sure was supposed to be reassuring, but it wasn't. All I could think of was that my fiancé was injured and possibly would not recover before our wedding. To postpone the wedding would be a nightmare—the invitations were out, non-refundable deposits had been placed for everything from flowers to food—but on the other hand, how fun would it be for Vito to walk down the aisle looking like a war hero? Dr. Rose patted my shoulder again. "Listen, the good news is that he's going to all right, right?"

"Of course," Mama said, answering for me. Then the doctor led us to the waiting room where the officer sat writing on a clipboard.

He stood up when we approached and he said, "I'm Sergeant Collins," and invited us to take a seat.

Papa introduced us.

"I was the officer called to the scene tonight. I understand your godson is going to be all right. I can tell you he's one lucky young man. His car looks like a crushed pop can."

I covered my mouth in horror. "What happened, officer?" I asked.

"First of all, you should know, Ma'am," he said to me, "your fiancé will not be charged in the accident. It wasn't his fault. But it is a tragedy."

He told us that they were still investigating the accident, but that there were three cars involved. The preliminary report was that the driver of the first car, a teenager who had just robbed a gas station, was fleeing the scene of the crime. Driving at high speed, he lost control of his car and smashed into the rear end of Vito's car, which was stopped at the red light. A witness said that Vito's car shot like a pinball into the cross traffic and collided into another car that had just pulled out into the intersection at the green light. The teenager suffered a broken collarbone. The driver of the car that Vito hit escaped with minor injuries, but his two-year-old daughter, who had been properly restrained in her car-seat in the back seat, was killed instantly. I looked at Mama and then just buried my head in my lap and sobbed.

Papa told the officer that he didn't understand, so the officer tried to explain it again, this time making scribbles on his clipboard to help illustrate. I looked up to see what he was drawing and I'll never forget his crude renderings—his long lines that depicted the streets, the rectangles that were the cars, the circle marking the spot where the baby sat in her car seat, the two X's that marked the areas of impact.

I heard Papa ask the officer, "Does Vito know about the baby?"

"I doubt it, sir, he was unconscious when they put him in the ambulance."

I cried even harder knowing that I would have to tell him. He would never forgive himself. Poor Vito. That poor little baby. The poor parents. Life as we knew it was over.

It was hospital policy that visitors could not sleep in the patient's room, but a sweet nurse pulled over a reclining chair for me and said no one said you couldn't sit up all night. Mama and Papa left me, promising to call Vito's sisters tonight, even at this late hour, and to bring Nana Lilli over in the morning.

I couldn't even hold his hand—his right hand was hooked up to the IV; his left arm was in a cast. The two fingers on his left hand that he'd broken in the other accident weren't even all the way healed. I was afraid to touch him. He slept fitfully. I saw the clock hit three-o-clock, as I sat there, trying to keep my eyes open, listening to Vito's soft moaning and his roommate's loud snoring. I heard two nurses talking about the dates they'd gone on the night before and I remember thinking how can they be so cheerful? Didn't they know? How could they act like it was just another day? For some people, it was the worst day of their entire lives. Finally I slept, but I dreamed about the accident, and although I hadn't witnessed it first-hand, my own recent accident with Vito was still fresh in my mind, and so my brain, in its dream-state, combined the police officer's pencil drawings and my own real-life visual and audio memories into a terrifying nightmare. I woke in a sweat, with a stiff neck, and a confused sense of not knowing where I was for a second. Vito was awake, staring up at the ceiling. I got up from the chair and a blanket fell to the floor. That nice nurse must have covered me. "Vito," I said. He turned his head slightly.

He managed a weak, hoarse groan.

"Are you in much pain?" He gave me a moan for an answer. "Do you need anything?" I asked.

He couldn't answer, he just closed his eyes as if he hadn't the strength to deal with my presence. I waited for a few moments to see if he'd open them again, but then I went back to my chair. The phone rang and scared me to death. It was a hysterical Nana Lilli, speaking half in English and half in Italian, and I could understand none of it. I told her Mama and Papa would be coming over soon, but then Mama got on the phone and I realized they were already there. She asked how Vito was and said they'd be up in a half hour.

When I hung up Vito opened his eyes again. He tried to call my name but his lip was so swollen and distended that it came out "Ina" and the thought zipped through my head that he sounded like Mr. Barbiere. Imagine, thinking about Mr. Barbiere at a time like that.

"I'm here, Vito, I'm right here. And Papa and Mama are bringing over your Nana soon and I'm sure Jenny will be coming as well."

"Ina," he said again and looked me straight in the eye. "Who died?"

I pretended to mishear him. "Your eye? Does your eye hurt? You cut it pretty bad. But we talked to the doctor and you're going to be okay. You're pretty banged up, but you're going to be just fine."

"No," he said, then winced in pain. "No, who died?"

"Oh. Well, listen now. The police said you were not responsible for the accident. You were a victim, too. There was this kid and he robbed a gas station and he was speeding and he crashed into you and sent your car flying into another car."

"Who died?"

"Just rest right now. You need your rest."

"Who?"

"Oh, Vito, a little girl, but it wasn't your fault. You were sitting there innocently at the stoplight. It's a tragedy, but it was not your fault. Do you understand?"

He said nothing. Just closed his eyes. Tight. Closing me out completely.

Later that morning, Dr. Rose came to talk to Vito, but Vito just stared at the ceiling, avoiding eye contact. The doctor told us that the x-rays showed a break in the fourth rib on the left, but that it wasn't splintered so there was no danger to the lung. This was good news, but Vito didn't even blink an eye. He was completely unresponsive.

Our neighborhood paper covered the accident, complete with a photograph of the wreck. Looking at it you wondered how anyone survived. Near the bottom of the column was a picture of the kid who'd robbed the gas station and hit Vito's car. Bobby Pendall was his name. I wondered if he knew how many lives he'd ruined. He had these dark, haunting eyes. He looked old for nineteen, and sad.

There were no pictures (thank God) of the little girl, Grace Kallistaphulos, but there were angry quotes from neighbors: "What is this crazy world coming to?" and "Where are the police when you need them?" (Apparently it had taken the police forever to arrive to the scene.)

The writing was on the wall. Vito would never forgive himself. He wouldn't talk to his Nana, or his sister, or Carl, or Mikey Pinotta, or Mama, or Papa, or the nurses, or the doctor. Even Mr. Maggio came up later in the afternoon, but Vito didn't even acknowledge his presence with a nod. I asked Papa to talk to him and then I sat in the waiting room to give them some space. Later, when Papa joined me, I could tell by his face that he hadn't been able to get Vito to open up either. Papa sat down next to me and banged his fist repeatedly against his open hand. Then he said, "I think Vito should have a lawyer."

"What for?" I asked.

"I just think he should," he said. "There's probably going to be a trial of some kind and Vito will probably have to testify. Plus, the boy's innocent and we don't want anyone to question that. You know how things get when insurance companies and lawyers get involved. People want justice and sometimes they think justice is money. I'm going to call Charlie Gradezzi's son, Frank. He'll help us out."

Later that day when Frank Gradezzi showed up, Vito wouldn't talk to him either. Frank gave me his business card and I put it in Vito's wallet.

The next day, I talked to the doctor about Vito's detachment. He said Vito had taken quite a blow to the head and had experienced great trauma. He told me about a newly diagnosed mental disorder called Post Traumatic Stress Disorder. People who suffered a great emotional wound would often withdraw, feeling detached and estranged from others. He wanted to bring in a psychiatrist to evaluate Vito. He patted me on the shoulder and said, "These things take time."

The psychiatrist was somewhat noncommittal at first. "Post Traumatic Stress Disorder was introduced into the American Psychiatric Association's official manual only a few years ago. It's a very new and very complex condition," he said, in a hushed voice, as we were speaking right outside of Vito's door. "In a case like your fiancé's, where he was both the victim in the first car accident and then seconds later, an indirect cause of the death of the child in the second collision, it's a very strong possibility that it is PTSD."

"So what can we expect?" I asked him and hoped he would use layman's terms.

"In some cases, like in your fiancé's, possibly, the post traumatic reaction begins immediately. Other times, we see a delayed onset with symptoms emerging only after days, weeks, months or even years, as I've seen with some adults who were sexually molested as children."

"What kinds of symptoms?"

"The things you have been describing are common—detachment and withdrawal. Many times a person will have recurrent and distressing recollections of the event—we call these intrusions—either consciously or in nightmares, hallucinations, or in disassociative flashback episodes. A person suffering from PTSD will attempt to avoid stimuli associated with the trauma, for example, a woman who was raped in an elevator never rides elevators. Or in your fiancé's case, he may find it extremely difficult driving a car or even riding in a car. A person may suffer from a markedly diminished interest in things that they loved prior to the traumatic event. Some show a restricted range of affect. And in severe cases, a person is unable to have loving feelings."

"How long does this last?" I asked.

"We specify PTSD as acute if duration of symptoms is less than three months and as chronic if the duration of symptoms is three months or more."

I asked when he would be able to make a specific diagnosis. He said to give him another day to observe him. "We'll look at how he sleeps, if he's irritable, if he shows outbursts of anger, if he's having difficulty in concentrating, if he's hyper vigilant or displays an exaggerated startle response."

"How do you treat this?"

"As I said, PTSD is new, but it is getting so much attention right now in the mental health industry that the journals are filled with articles and studies. There are some medications and some therapies that have proven helpful—hypnosis, cognitive behavioral therapy, and exposure to systematic desensitization. Often, a combination of drugs and therapy is indicated. There's so much we can do."

"But what can I do?"

"Be there for him when he's ready to talk to you. Don't push him. Don't take his anger and his withdrawal personally. It won't be easy. But people do get better."

"Do you have any statistics?"

"I'd say symptoms usually last less than six months in about half of the cases I've seen."

"And the other half."

"It can go either way, I'm afraid, depending on the emotional health of the person and the severity of the event. A woman who is raped once in her life may recover more quickly than a child who was sexually molested for ten years. But let's not get ahead of ourselves. The human spirit is an amazing thing. And just as the body is programmed to heal itself, I believe the mind is as well. Keep that thought."

"I will. When will you start to observe him?"

"First thing tomorrow, after you give me his personal and medical history. Can you be here by eight?"

"I'll be here," I said. Afterward, I went back in the room to check on Vito. He was sleeping, though fitfully. I could see his eyeballs rolling spastically under his almost transparent eyelids. I thought about him re-living the terrible accident. I ached for him. I sat back in the chair and let the tears silently roll down my cheeks. He stirred, and when I opened my eyes, his eyes were open. "Vito," I said softly, "I'm here. Can I get you anything? Do you need anything?"

"Hi," he got out.

"I know it hurts to talk, your lip is still so swollen."

"It doesn't matter."

"You look a little better today, you really do. Each day will get a little better. Little by little."

"I need you to do something for me."

"Anything, you know it."

"I want you to go to her funeral. The little girl."

"Oh, Vito, please. I think I'd better stay here with you. You need me."

"I don't need you," he said, without emotion. "The nurses are here. And I don't want to talk about it, I really don't."

"I won't ask you to."

"But you want to. You want to know about it. What the hell happened."

"You'll tell me when you're ready. Don't worry about it right now."

He grunted. "Don't worry about it? It won't leave me, Sabina. I keep seeing it, over and over. And it's real, but each time I get closer and closer. To her." His face began to convulse with terror.

"Honey, you don't have to talk about it right now."

"I keep re-living it."

"Oh, Vito."

"And each time I turn the steering wheel a little more to the left, because I keep telling myself, if I can swerve to the left I can miss her, hit the rear of the car. But no matter how far left I turn that wheel, Sabina, I keep hitting dead on."

"I'm so sorry," I cried, touching his hand softly.

All of a sudden he grabbed my wrist with a strength I wouldn't have thought he possessed lying there in that bed. "You have to go to the funeral,

172

Sabina. You have to tell them I'm sorry. Her parents. You have to make them forgive me." He squeezed harder and said, "You owe me that." Those four words hurt more than the squeezing of my wrist. He *was* blaming me for making him drive.

I wanted to say, "No. I won't go. I can't go. Don't ask me." But I was too afraid for him and he was squeezing my wrist so tight with his good hand.

"Don't worry," I heard myself say, "I'll go."

***

Mama and Rosa came with me. We sat in the last pew at St. Basil's, a beautiful Greek Orthodox church. The casket was closed. We prayed and we cried and we listened to haunting music. I only saw the parents from a distance—the mother hid behind a black veil and the father, with his long dark hair and thick beard, hung his head so low I worried he would fall over. They looked young—probably in their mid twenties. I wondered if they'd survive. I'd read statistics on the marriages of couples that had lost a child. The odds were not in their favor.

I knew that I would never have the courage to approach the parents, to explain who I was and that my fiancé was begging for their forgiveness. I'm sure forgiveness was the last thing on their minds that day. I knew that I had absolutely no right to approach these grieving people. After the Mass, Mama, Rosa, and I slipped out of the pews and ran quickly to the car. That little girl's funeral was the saddest thing I had ever experienced in my then twenty-two years of life.

Rosa drove us home. It was raining hard and I could tell she was driving slower and more cautiously than ever—we had all been spooked by the accident. We left each other alone to our own thoughts, but I could hear Mama softly humming *Amazing Grace*, which someone at the funeral had strummed gently on a guitar as people were coming in. I overheard someone say the little girl's daddy sang *Amazing Grace* to her at night when he rocked her to sleep. I wanted Mama to stop humming, but I knew it would be rude to ask her to stop.

Vito was so angry with me when I returned to the hospital and told him that I had not spoken with the little girl's parents. He couldn't believe that I didn't approach them, introduce myself, offer my condolences and ask for forgiveness for him. "You broke your promise!" he screamed at me. "Why'd you go at all then?"

"To pay our respects."

His eyes darted back and forth between me and the window, me and the window, me and the window. "What do you suggest I do now?" he asked, his eyes still on the window.

Of course I had my answer all planned out ahead of time. "I was thinking you could write them a letter expressing your thoughts and asking for forgiveness. Include your phone number and your address—it might be easier for them to respond by phone or mail." I set a card and some notepaper that I'd purchased downstairs in the gift shop on the table next to him. I'd found the couple's address in the telephone book and had pre-addressed and stamped the envelope. Oh, yes, I'd thought it all out—right down to the perfectly timed arrival of Father Mike, our associate pastor, who was going to marry us in two weeks. I thought he could help Vito write the letter by helping him to find the appropriate words.

Father Mike did help Vito write the letter. He mailed it for him, too. But of course, there was never any kind of response. Had it been me, I wouldn't have written back to the person who was responsible—even if inadvertently—for the death of my baby daughter. Vito wasn't thinking straight. He started complaining the very next day about not receiving an answer. I told him Father had just mailed the letter the day before. He needed to give it a little time. He demanded that I check his mail each morning before I came up to his room. And I did just to humor him, because I knew of course that there would be no letter.

The psychiatrist confirmed the Post Traumatic Stress Disorder, started Vito on some medication, but wouldn't release him just yet. He wanted to keep him in for another day or so. He told me to be patient, that these things couldn't be rushed.

I thought about writing a fake letter. It would be simple, saying only this: *we forgive you.* I would forge the parents' signatures. What would be the harm? They would not be hurt by my deception and Vito might be helped immensely. It might mean the difference between being ill and being well. But I didn't write a letter. Instead, after practically living at that hospital for days on end, I just went home. I stayed home the entire next day. It was the end of May, but it still felt like winter. It was cold and damp. Mama fed me tortellini soup. It warmed me to my bones, and I slept deeply throughout the day. Then I lay awake all night tormenting myself, wondering what the future held.

The following day, they discharged him. They said they couldn't keep him any longer. I wheeled him out to Papa's car. Mama helped me get him settled in the back seat with various pillows propping him up here and there. On the way home, Vito said: "Please take me to my Nana's. I want to stay with her for a while." I looked at him in disbelief. I simply assumed he'd go back to the apartment where I, his fiancée, would nurse him back to health. I was so hurt, but I could think of nothing to say that wouldn't sound selfish, so I said nothing. I let Mama help Nana Lilli get him settled in his old room. Then I went in and sat on the side of the bed and rubbed his good arm. "Vito," I said.

He just turned over and said, "Sabina, I really need to sleep." And then he slept. And slept. And slept.

I went home with the same intentions: to sleep off the stress and the worry. But before I could climb into my bed, Mama stopped me in the hallway and asked me what Vito and I had decided to do about the wedding. I told her that I hadn't even had the chance to discuss it with him, that he would barely make eye contact. "Two weeks, *bedda*," she said, as if I didn't know the date of my own wedding.

"I'll talk to him," I told her. And I tried, honest I did. Each day I walked over to Nana Lilli's in the morning. All day long I sat on a chair next to his bed and watched him sleep. Nana tried to feed me lunch and dinner. But who could even think about food? Each night at seven o'clock, I walked back home.

Finally, after he'd been at Nana Lilli's for five days, I lost my patience. I sat on the edge of the bed, took him by the shoulders and shook him, gently but firmly. "Vito," I pleaded, "we have to talk. Please talk to me. The wedding is in a week and a half. Are you going to able to do this, or do we need to postpone it? I'll understand if you think we need to postpone it. I know you're hurting physically and emotionally. If you think it's best, we can wait a month or two, or whatever it takes."

I waited a long while for him to respond. I'm nothing if not patient, but he just sighed and stared at the ceiling. I had to make a decision. "Okay," I said, "so I guess we'll postpone it."

When I got home I told Mama, "We'd better call it off. He's in no shape to get married right now." She suggested we give him a couple more days, but I insisted that we do it now. So while I took a long nap, Mama divided up my guest list and she, Rosa, Marina, Colina, and Angie each called fifty people and told them that the wedding was postponed indefinitely—"until the groom-to-be recovered." Then Rosa undid all her doings: she called Father Mike, the florist, the hotel caterers, the bakery, the printer, the bridal shop, and the tuxedo store, and canceled everything, forfeiting all the deposits.

I stayed in bed wondering how long we'd have to wait. Would he be better in July? August? September? Would I have to wait for a fall wedding? My bridesmaids would have to have new dresses; I would have to reimburse them for their old ones. What about our honeymoon? I was sure Vito wasn't thinking about contacting the travel agency. The only thing he was thinking about was that little girl. There were so many things I needed to talk to him about, but Vito wasn't talking, he was only sleeping.

And then, just like that, he was gone.

After I'd pleaded with him to talk to me, I stayed away for two days. I couldn't bear to see him. I stayed in bed myself, sick about my canceled wedding. Finally, Mama made me get up, told me that although things seemed terrible, it really wasn't the end of the world. "But it is the end of *my* world," I told her. She encouraged me to keep trying to talk to him about his feelings and it made me remember all those years ago when Vito had lost his mother and Mama had told me the same thing—to talk to that boy about his feelings.

The next day I walked to Nana Lilli's in the new pair of sandals I'd bought for our honeymoon. After walking just two blocks a blister had formed on the back of my heel. The only thought on my mind when I knocked on Nana Lilli's door was getting those killer sandals off of my feet and getting a bandage.

When she opened the door, Nana Lilli was crying. In Italian, English, and sign language, she told me that while she was fixing lunch, Vito'd packed his duffel bag and left. And no, she didn't know where he went because he didn't bother telling her.

I ran home, blister and all, and got the keys to Papa's car. He must be at the apartment, I thought. Maybe he wanted his own bed. I don't even remember driving there. All of a sudden I was just there. I sat in the car in front of the apartment for a few minutes. These little kids were playing with a basketball in the street and it accidentally hit the windshield and scared me to death. It felt like a gunshot to my compromised nerves. Finally, I climbed the front steps. My legs were like rubber. I knew even before I put the key in the lock that he wouldn't be there. When I opened the heavy wooden front door, I didn't call out his name. Nothing looked out of place as I walked through the living room, the bedroom, the bathroom, the kitchen. I searched every surface in the place for a note, a letter, some words of explanation. Finally, I found an envelope with my name on it in the basket where Vito kept bills and mail.

I sat on the sofa for the longest time just holding that damn envelope in my hand. I let the phone ring three different times, the third time it rang twenty-two times before the caller hung up. I bit my stupid fingernails—the ones that I'd promised Rosa I wouldn't bite before the wedding. I hit the envelope nervously against my right hand, over and over. Stupid thoughts ran threw my head about how long it was going to take me to pay back Mama and Papa for all the money they'd spent, about how we would probably have to wait a year before we could book the hotel again, about how someone in my Uncle Dino's band might kick the bucket by the time we set a new date. I knew Vito was gone, but I really deep in my heart thought it would be a temporary thing. Until he got well. Down time. Time away to find himself, that kind of thing. I could wait, I told myself as I put my finger under the seam of the envelope. I *would* wait.

Damn it, if it wasn't just some legal papers from Carl that we were both supposed to sign for C. V. Sweets. That's when I started laughing. Peels of laughter, uncontrollable laughter. Tears streaming from my eyes kind of laughter. Leg slapping, can't breathe kind of laughter. Holding your stomach in pain kind of laughter. When it stopped, I locked the front door and drove Papa's car home.

12

Serve From the Right, Clear From the Left

Mr. Barbiere has dragged Joey Jr. in today for toast. He starts in on Papa before his rear end even hits the stool.

"Mr. Melarossa, Mr. Mela. *Dove sono tu?* I have-a someone I want-a you to see," he calls out to the kitchen even though Papa is standing three feet away from him.

"Joey," Papa says, extending his hand. Joey grips Papa's hand and gives him a nice, firm handshake, just like Papa taught him years ago. (Way back when, both Papa and Mr. Barbiere thought they could *teach* Joey how to be straight.)

"Hey, Mr. G. Good to see you," Joey says.

Mr. Barbiere is almost glowing. Joey rarely eats breakfast with his father. He's never had the time. He heads for the salon at the crack of dawn (walks down the back stairs, same as I do) and doesn't go back upstairs until well into the evening. I pour them coffee and bring them their almost-but-not-quite-burned toast. Joey grabs me by the arm and brings my hand closer to inspect the manicure that Gary gave me last week. "Look how nice!" he says. I smile and leave them to harass and be harassed.

Papa tells me that Mama could use my help in the kitchen so he'll take the counter. I think he just doesn't want to miss anything good out here, but I head for the kitchen as I'm told.

It must be twenty degrees hotter in here and let me tell you it's not all due to the ovens. This time after Aunt Lina and I spent bathroom time together I found Mama in tears. "I don't like to feel like this," she said between sniffles. "Jealous of my own sister, but what is going on between you two?" I explained to her that I shared the Vito story with Aunt Lina in hopes of getting her off my back once and for all.

I think it worked, too. But maybe too well. Now Aunt Lina looks at me and sighs. With Aunt Lina, it's either sweet or sour, there's no in between.

The way this all manifests itself here in the kitchen is through blatant competition. I really would rather not be in here, wedged between them like the cream in an Oreo, but here I am.

"What are you making today, Mama?" I ask, tying a white apron over my green apron.

"Charlie said he's been dying for some *Bruscioluni*."

"*Bruscioluni*?" I am surprised because *Bruscioluni* is a rolled meat, a fancy dish usually reserved for holidays or special company.

"He said it's the one thing he can't make like his wife did. I figured it's probably not that much more work than making sixty meatballs," she says.

Not that much work! Who's she kidding? It's a ton of work, but well worth it. Here's how you make it: ask your butcher to cut you two nice pieces of sirloin about a fourth inch thick. First sauté some onion, garlic, celery, and shredded carrots in olive oil. When this mixture is cooled, sprinkle generously with a mixture of seasoned breadcrumbs, Parmesan cheese, salt, and pepper. Take a couple of slices of *provolone* cheese and lay them on top of the steak. Add a couple of slices of *prosciutto* and a few slices of *salami*. Spread some of the vegetable and breadcrumb mixture on top of the salami slices. Now, here's where Mama and Aunt Lina differ in their recipes. Aunt Lina likes the traditional version where you wrap your meat around one or two hard-cooked eggs (sans the shells). I'll admit it looks beautiful when sliced, but Mama never liked the taste the hard-cooked egg lent to the *sugo* that the *Bruscioluni* is cooked in. Aunt Lina thinks the egg omission is something like a mortal sin. I agree with Mama, I love eggs, but not in my tomato sauce. Roll up the meat and tie it with string to hold it together. Brown it on all sides in olive oil and then add it to your pot of *sugo* to cook for a couple of hours. It's very tender and very delicious, with or without the egg.

We're making ten of them, Mama and me. Aunt Lina is close by, watching our every move. She wants me so badly to pay her some attention. I watch her as she chops vegetables by hand. There's a perfectly beautiful Cuisinart on the counter next to her, but today I think she'd just rather be a martyr and cut it all by hand. She must be making soup. St. Joan of Arc soup. She calls it that because it's so time-consuming to make. It is a delicious soup, but it's not a practical soup to make at a restaurant. She spends hours preparing the stock for it—using chicken bones and her secret ingredient: chicken feet. Maybe I shouldn't have told you that. I hope it doesn't keep you from trying it.

Aunt Lina does make a mean soup. St. Joan of Arc Soup is a curious concoction of chicken stock, cabbage and meatballs. Simply start with a good chicken stock and add chopped onions, carrots, celery, and fresh asparagus. Chop and add to the stock one fourth head of a medium cabbage. To make the meatballs, mix one pound of ground round or sirloin with breadcrumbs, grated cheese, minced onion, salt, pepper, garlic powder, one egg, and dried garden mint leaves. Form into one inch balls and drop into the stock. Before serving, add a pasta—*farfalle*, *tortellini*, or *penne*. This soup has a deep flavor, and I must admit, it is my most favorite soup ever.

The kitchen is way too quiet and way too hot for me. I tie up my last meat roll and hand it over to Mama to brown. "Okay, I better get ready for the lunch crowd. So, the specials are angel hair pasta and *Bruscioluni*...and what's yours, Aunt Lina?"

"You can't tell by the fragrance?"

"Joan of Arc soup?" I ask.

"*Saint* Joan of Arc Soup. Cripes Sabina, the woman was burned at the stake for God, don't forget the *saint* part."

"All right already." And I am out of here.

***

Today's the first day of December so this morning Papa and I came down early and strung little white Italian lights all over the store. I hung up a few ancient Christmas decorations and Papa put up a small fresh tree on a little wooden table near the pasta shelves. The place looks cheerful.

Someone says, "Hey look! It's snowing!" and we all look out the window to see for ourselves. Sure enough, it is. What is it about the first snow? It makes everyone act like characters in Frank Capra's *It's A Wonderful Life.*

Our lunch customers bring good cheer as they come in from the cold, kicking the snow off their shoes and brushing the frosting of snow from their shoulders. They rub their hands together and take in deep whiffs of the glorious, but unidentifiable blend of aromas wafting out of the kitchen.

The race is on. I have to explain to many people what *Bruscioluni* even is. I almost wish Mama would have provided me with a prototype, although it's really the kind of dish that tastes better than it looks. There are some adventurous diners though who want to try it. But the first snow day is also a good soup day, so I take a lot of soup orders, too. I'll tell you one thing, I am staying out of the kitchen.

I go into overdrive as I take orders, serve, and clear. Jimmy, with a little help from caffeine, is actually working at a quick pace. No time for ABC Whatever today. In the middle of the rush, cranky old Mr. Lazio comes in to pick up his bakery order of five dozen buns. He wasn't supposed to pick them up until three o'clock and now he's got his nose in the box, counting the buns. "There's only sixty in here," he tells me. I want to inform him that sixty is in fact the product of five times twelve, but I'm nothing if not an ambassador of goodwill, so I say as sweetly as possible, "Didn't you order five dozen, Mr. Lazio?"

"Yes, I did. But your father always gives me a baker's dozen, so I was expecting sixty-*five* buns."

I tell him it's no problem and go back to the kitchen to fetch five more buns. When I come back out, the front door opens and two tall dark-haired men, one in a gray tweed overcoat and one with no coat on at all, enter the store. It's not until I hand Jimmy the bakery box and watch him lead Mr. Lazio out to his car that I realize that the dark haired man without a coat is Ted Kallista. My hand automatically slaps my heart. I think it missed a beat. What in the world is he doing here? I can't help but stare at him. He sees me. Does a double take of sorts, or at least attempts to get me into focus. There. It registers. I can tell by his face. He and the man he's with are approaching the counter.

"Hello," I say, giving my nicest "welcome customer!" smile, the one Papa drilled into us when we were little girls.

"Hello," says the other man. Ted simply nods and gives me half of a smile.

"Have you had time to decide what you'd like?" I ask politely, directing my attention to the other man, who is older, taller, and more distinguished-looking than Ted.

The man says, "Well, something warm, that's for sure. Believe it or not, I just moved here from San Francisco. Yesterday. When I left, it was seventy-one degrees. I just bought this coat today."

"It's a beautiful coat. You'll be glad to have it. We have two specials today. One is a delicious meatball and cabbage soup."

"I'll take that," the man in the beautiful coat says without bothering to hear the other special.

"The other is an Italian delicacy specially made by my mother. It's a meat roll made with sirloin, stuffed with vegetables, cheese, breadcrumbs and *prosciutto*. It's cooked in a thick tomato sauce. It's wonderful."

"I'll take that," Ted says. He looks at me with those blue-green eyes of his. I know he remembers me, that much is obvious, but he doesn't acknowledge it.

"Anything to drink?" I ask routinely.

"Cup a coffee, Ted?" the man in the beautiful coat asks.

"Yeah, that's fine."

I ring up their total and tell them to help themselves at the coffee bar. They pay and go sit near the windows, Ted taking the back seat that faces me. I can't believe this! It doesn't make any kind of sense! He says he'll call but he doesn't call, he shows up. His eyes say he knows me, but he doesn't say a word. My heart is beating so fast I have to take a couple of deep breaths to calm myself down. My hands are clammy too. I think I may be having an anxiety attack.

I will myself to play it cool. I place their orders and then serve soup to two young corporate type women—girls, really, they can't be more than twenty-five. One girl, who has flung a monstrous fur cavalierly over the back of her chair as if she had two or three more at home says, "If I don't like this soup, can I please get something else? I'm not sure I like cabbage." She says this in a way that makes you think she considers cabbage peasant food. I want to tell her that I'm pretty sure she wouldn't like cabbage, but you already know I never say what I really want to say. I tell her of course and stand over her and wait. She dips her spoon delicately and properly—away from herself—then brings the soup to her lips and slurps loudly. So much for good manners. "It's delicious!" she exclaims in utter surprise. Her dining companion says, "Told ya so," and they go at it.

When I carry out Ted and his companion's order, I'm careful not to "thumb" the plates. "There you are," I say, setting the plate and the bowl in front of the two men. "Can I get you anything else?" They both shakes their heads, so I say, "Enjoy your lunch." I'm afraid to make eye contact with Ted, so I don't. I go about my business. Thank God we are busy. Even so, my eyes find their way back to his table. He catches me looking at him a couple of times, but I really don't care. It's a free world; I can look.

I steal another glance and decide he looks different. Stiffer. Uptight. He looks like any one of the corporate types that lunch here. He's dressed in a pinstriped suit, crisp white shirt, conservative striped tie. His loafered feet seem fidgety under the table. I'm successful in ignoring him for a while. I must pass his table six or seven times at least without so much as a glance. I'm proud of myself, proud that I'm keeping it together so well.

It seems like they will never go. But finally, they get up. The man with the beautiful coat makes eye contact on his way out. He lifts his hand in sort of a wave and says, "Thank you, the soup hit the spot."

And Ted says, "Everything was delicious."

I say, "Thank you," but don't follow it up with "come back soon" for reasons that are obvious. The door slams behind them and the bell jingles. I breathe a sigh of relief. The torture is over. I hope I never see him again in my life. Isn't it great how I can lie to myself with a straight face?

***

Our last lunch customers leave and I head to the kitchen with dirty dishes. Papa's scrubbing the stove and singing an insulting little song to Aunt Lina:

> *"This is my sister-in-law Lina,*
> *She makes me so mad I could scream-a,*
> *But things aren't as bad as they seem-a,*
> *Just pinch me and I'll say it's a dream-a."*

"I'll pinch you all right," says Aunt Lina, shaking her broom at Papa. "*Marone*, Sunny, you're no Sinatra."

"Oh and Engelbert Pumpernickel is," Papa retorts. (Engelbert Humperdinck is Aunt Lina's favorite singer. I swear.)

"Well, everybody's gone," I say, ignoring their bantering. "And the soup and the *Bruscioluni* were both big hits. Everybody raved."

Mama turns from the sink and looks at me in a way that makes me think I should have said "*Bruscioluni* and soup"—in that order.

Aunt Lina swishes by and whispers, "Did you ever try to contact him?"

At first I think she means Ted, but she doesn't even know about Ted—she better not know about Ted—so I realize she means Vito, did I ever contact Vito.

"Aunt Lina, please," I whisper, not wanting Mama to hear, "I don't want to talk about it anymore. Okay?" She frowns but doesn't say anything else.

I head out front to help Jimmy stock shelves. "Hey, Bina, he says. "For one of my journalism classes, I gotta do a restaurant review."

"Yeah?"

"Yeah. Where do you think I should go?"

"You can go anywhere?"

"Yeah."

"Charlie Trotters."

"Get real. I don't have a hundred and fifty bucks a plate."

"How much do you have?"

"Ten bucks."

"Ten bucks?"

"And some change."

"There's a burger joint up the street," I tell him.

"Sabina."

"Well? What do you do with all your money anyway? I know you don't make that much here, but geez kid, your tuition is paid and your parents give you free room and board."

"Hey, so do yours," the little snot says.

"I pay rent I'll have you know," I tell him as I bop him on the head. "Plus, I've saved a lot of money. Where does all yours go?"

"Beats me. I cash my check on Friday and by Monday it's gone."

"Yeah, well, maybe you're just buying too many CDs."

"Hey, why don't you come with me? You know a lot more about food than I do. You're good with all those food words, too…fricassee, canape, piccalilli."

I stop unpacking. "And I'm also good at *paying*, right?"

"No, no, no, It'll be my treat. I'll pay you back Friday."

"No, you won't."

"Yes, I will."

"No, you won't."

"Yes, I will. And I'll take you somewhere really nice."

"Not too nice," I say. "Since I'm paying."

"Oh, right."

Papa calls him to the kitchen and I am left to think my own thoughts. I refuse to think about Ted right now so instead I think about what Aunt Lina asked me…

Of course I tried to contact Vito. But not right away. I waited a good month, thinking he'd show up any minute, rested and well again. When he didn't, I went over to Nana Lilli's and cried and begged for her to tell me where he was. She swore she didn't know. I called his sister Jenny but she also swore she didn't know. All she would say was that he'd called her about a week after he'd left and said that he was okay, that he was looking for a cooking job so he could afford some therapy and get himself straightened out. I think Jenny would have told me if she knew where he was, I really do. Nana Lilli never would have. Those old Italian ladies are loyal until death.

When I called Becky in Atlanta I expected her to hang up on me—she never did forgive me for laughing at Angie's imitation of her husband. She didn't hang up on me but she didn't help me either. She denied any knowledge of Vito's whereabouts. The anger in her voice transmitted clearly through the telephone wires, from Atlanta to Chicago. Finally she just came out and said: "What did you expect, Sabina, after all, *you* called off the wedding."

That got my blood boiling. I should have just told her that the reason I called off the wedding was because her brother was too sick to get out of bed. Instead (and regrettably) I blurted out this: "Well, if you had bothered to get on a plane and come and see your only brother in the hospital, you would have known just how sick he was and why I had to *postpone* the wedding." Becky's response was a nice loud *Click,* and I knew I had just cut off any hope of help from her. But I also knew Vito was there. I even entertained the idea of flying to Atlanta to see for myself—peek in Becky's windows or something—but I'm nothing if not a chicken, afraid of confrontations and of flying.

The only person left to call was Mikey Pinotta. By then Mikey was back at school out in Pennsylvania, working on his masters in psychology. I called five or six times a day for two weeks before I finally reached him. He stuttered his way through some small talk and then tried to lie to me: "Sabina, why would you think he's here? I'm busting my butt with this master's program. I don't have time to nurse anyone's wounds, not even my own." But I could detect the empathy in his voice. After all, he was home when this all happened. He saw Vito in the hospital. He knew how messed up he was.

I told Mikey right out that I didn't believe him. "I've known you all of my life—I know when you're lying, even if I can't see your face, I can tell by your voice."

"All right, all right, he was with me, but he's gone now. Cripes, Sabina, right after you called off the wedding, he called me."

"I didn't call off the wedding, I postponed it!" I yelled into the phone.

"Okay, okay, postponed. Anyway, he was wigged out, didn't know what to do. He wanted to go somewhere, get away for a few days. Think about things. I wasn't planning to leave for school until the following week, but I was anxious anyway so I told him he could come with me and hang out for a few days. He vegged out here for a few weeks, sacked out on my couch. But I could tell he wasn't getting any better. He just couldn't sort things out in his mind, couldn't get over the accident and couldn't understand why you called off the wedding."

"I called off the wedding because I thought my fiancé couldn't get out of bed. Apparently he could."

"He was in no condition to walk down that aisle, Sabina. It would have been a mistake. Maybe it has something to do with never grieving his parents' deaths adequately, and now it's like he's reliving both of those losses plus the little girl, too."

"Why didn't you call me, Mikey? I would have come and got him."

"God, Sabina, he begged me not to call you or anyone. I've never seen him like that before and it scared me. I thought he'd stay a few days, get some sun, and then go home to you, get some therapy and medication and heal. Set a new date for the wedding. But I don't know, here I am studying to be a psychologist and I couldn't even help my best friend. I'm seriously thinking of dropping out of the program."

"Mikey, don't do it. It's not your fault. Sometimes we're too close to the people we love to help them. You'll be a wonderful psychologist. So where is he now?"

"He's in bad shape, Sabina. He really needs help. It's pretty crappy, the whole thing. I'm most sorry for you."

"But where is he now?" I asked again.

"I don't know. And that's the truth. My roommate kicked him out a couple of weeks ago. My roommate's an asshole." I knew by his voice that he was telling the truth.

"He blames himself, Sabina. He doesn't blame you."

"But he must, otherwise he'd be back."

"Listen, this must be hell for you. Pray that he gets some help. If he gets good therapy and some medication, he can get better. I've read a few case studies—people do get better. The thing to remember is that he loves you. He's only ever loved you. He'll be back, you watch."

My conversation with Mikey made me feel better…and worse. Better because I knew Mikey was right—Vito did love me, had always loved me. Worse because I still didn't know where he was.

After that, I decided time was what Vito needed most. I didn't bug Nana Lilli, Jenny, Becky, or Mikey anymore. I would just give him time. But then Rosa had a brainstorm: hadn't Papa said something about a trial? Certainly there would be some kind of court proceeding for Bobby Pendall, the guy who'd robbed the gas station and caused the accident. Vito would likely be summoned or subpoenaed, or whatever. I kissed my sister, told her she was brilliant, and called Frank Gradezzi, Charlie's lawyer son.

Frank said yes, that Vito would definitely have to appear in court. Lucky for me, Frank Gradezzi had harbored a life-long crush on Colina, and that might have had something to do with him promising to look into the case for me. I told him I would pay him to represent Vito…but first, he had to find him. The fact that Frank did find Vito proves the power behind the law. He *was* with Becky in Atlanta. Apparently Vito flew down there after Mikey's roommate kicked him out. Becky wanted to protect her brother's wish for privacy, but she didn't want him to be in contempt of court either, so she and Vito flew to Chicago in October, three days before my birthday.

It ended up that there wasn't a jury trial but plea-bargaining and all that kind of judicial stuff. I wasn't allowed in the courtroom, but you can bet I waited for Vito on a bench outside the door.

Well, you wouldn't have believed it was the same person. His arm cast and neck brace were gone, his lacerations were all healed, but he'd lost so much weight. His hair was a long tangle of matted curls. His wire glasses were taped together at the nose with what looked like electrical tape. I just stared at him, then looked at Becky. She sent daggers my way. I wanted to tell her that yes, maybe I was the one who called off the wedding, but I wasn't the one who'd run away.

"Vito," I said. Becky didn't move. "Can I have a minute, please?" I asked her, although it wasn't a question. She made a face and then went and stood by the water fountain, her eyes never leaving us.

Vito couldn't look at me. His eyes darted here and there, anywhere but on mine. He fidgeted like a hyperactive kindergartner.

"Vito," I said again.

"Did you see them?" he said to me, as he banged a clenched fist nervously against his lips.

"Who?"

"The parents. The little girl's parents. They're really young and—"

"No," I said. I wanted to say something stupid like, "Can't you stop thinking about them for one minute and think about us?" But of course I didn't.

"Jesus Christ, they look like hell," he said, then he reached in his pocket and grabbed a pack of cigarettes. He shook one out and lit it, while I stood there in shock. Vito smoking? Vito using the Lord's name in vain? Who was this guy?

I could see he was shaking. He inhaled and exhaled and then said, "They looked at me the same way they looked at him. They won't forgive me…ever."

I chose my words carefully. "Maybe it's too soon. Maybe in time, they will forgive you."

He drew on his cigarette. "What a mess, huh? The whole thing. And I'm the biggest mess, Sabina, I'm a mess. Christ Almighty, just look at me. I'm scared all the time. I know you want answers from me, but I don't have any. How do I know I'll get better?" Then his face turned pale and he started to cry. He said, "I feel sick," and he turned to go. I watched him walk passed Becky at the water fountain and push open the men's room door. I walked over to Becky who stood leaning against the wall. She sneered at me. "I didn't mean to upset him," I said sheepishly.

"Yes, you did. That's exactly what you meant to do," she said. "And just for your information, Jerome was just promoted to morning drive time. Thought you and Angie would like to know."

I held up the wall for what seemed like forever, waiting for Vito to come out of the men's room. When he did, he walked right over to me and placed both his hands firmly around my arms. His touch was like electricity running through me. "Vito," I said, and leaned in to hug him. But he pulled back, holding me at arms length.

"Sabina, listen. I love you, but I'm a mess." And then they called him into the courtroom. And that was the end of it.

I decided to erase the entire conversation we'd had in the courthouse from my memory, except for three words: "I love you." That's all that mattered, wasn't it? He'd said he loved me. And I held on to those three words for eighteen years, ignoring the important word that had followed them, the big, bad "*but.*"

When Nana Lilli died a year later, I thought for sure he would come home for her funeral, but he didn't. Becky and Jerome came from Atlanta but they didn't bring Vito with them. Jenny told me that he just wasn't up for another funeral. She said he was getting psychotherapy but felt he had a long way to go.

A few weeks after Nana Lilli's funeral I somehow found the nerve to call Becky again. I'll never know where I got the guts, but I just called, said it was Sabina, and asked to speak to Vito. Becky was brisk. Vito was not staying with her anymore. Jerome had kicked him out. If Vito wanted me to know where he was, he would call me. Please stop calling her.

At one point, Papa came to me and offered to hire a private detective. "If we find him, we can bring him home, *bedda,* and we can help him. We can get him the doctor he needs, the medicine he needs. He just needs time. So, first we'll find him and then we'll get him fixed up."

But all I could think of was this: what if he didn't want to be found? And I knew that we couldn't fix him—as if he were Humpty Dumpty or something—he had to fix himself. Besides, I had my pride. He had to come back on his own. So I never hired a detective, but that was back when I still thought he'd come back.

Papa and Mama, my sisters, everyone, they were all sick for me. They hated to see me moping around. I filled the days doing what I always did, working at the store. Finally Papa said that maybe I needed a change of pace. Why didn't I go out and get a job in an office or a bank or wherever you go when you have a business degree. But you know how it is when you're job hunting—you have to be at your best, self-confident, your own greatest advocate. I just wanted to lie in bed all day.

At first I waited by the year. After the first year, I returned all the wedding gifts. It took four Saturdays to return everything. I thought as soon as I returned the gifts, he'd come back, because isn't that how it goes? The minute you get your car washed, it rains. You finally get a doctor's appointment and the pain goes away.

Then it was, okay, I'll give him one more year. Okay, I'll give him another year. Now then, this is it, this is the last year. Or when I'm thirty, then I'll stop waiting. And when I was thirty I talked myself into believing that I had stopped waiting, because that's when I did start dating, but I was still waiting. I was the queen of waiting.

I became obsessed with Post Traumatic Stress Disorder, sitting in the public library and medical libraries trying to glean whatever information I could from the journals. Then I bought a computer, got on the Internet and had a hey day. There were horror stories, but the most severe cases seemed to be people who had suffered for years. People who had witnessed or been a victim to a single, isolated event—such as a car accident—seemed to fare better.

So then I got angry. He should be better by now—why hasn't he come back? But then I'd give him another year until I stopped counting and then the theme and the thread of my life become waiting for Vito—whatever else I may be doing at any given moment in time, first and foremost, I was waiting for Vito.

I couldn't for the life of me figure out what was keeping Vito from coming home. If he'd told me that he just couldn't live in the city anymore, I'd have moved anywhere in the world with him. If he needed therapy for the rest of his life, I'd have worked two jobs to pay the doctor bills. And if he really needed that little girl's parents to forgive him, I would have knocked down their door and begged for their forgiveness on his behalf.

I had so many questions, the primary one being: who left whom? Vito left me physically and emotionally the moment he was discharged from that hospital and chose to go to his grandma's house instead of to the apartment where I could have cared for him. He knew exactly what he was doing because later I discovered that he had withdrawn exactly half the money in our savings account. I knew he blamed me, but not for calling off the wedding, but for forcing him to get behind the wheel of a car that killed an innocent child. Maybe it wasn't little Grace's parents who couldn't forgive, maybe it was Vito.

I needed answers. I needed closure. I was certain he'd come back sooner or later but I guess his misery kept him away. What was Chicago but a place where he'd lost everyone—his mother, his father, a little girl, his fiancée.

At least that's how I had it in my head. Sometimes, though in my dreams, things were different. Sometimes he was married with five children, sometimes he was married with no children, sometimes he was a cook out in San Francisco, sometimes he was a missionary in South America. Once I dreamed he was working and living on a cruise ship— away from cars and traffic and accidents—where he baked bread all day long. Even now I wonder about self-retribution. How was he punishing himself? Maybe he ran a homeless shelter, offering his culinary services as recompense for the injuries he thought he caused. He was always big on reparation—both in his personal life and in his business life. If he accidentally broke something that belonged to a friend or a classmate, he replaced it. If a priggish customer was unhappy with an order, Vito would give him something else at no charge.

Most of the time though, I saw him living a very modest life in the mountains of his beloved Sicily, where there were no real roads, no cars, and most important, no traffic fatalities. He cooked simple, consummate dishes for the humble locals that had adopted him as one of their own. He was alone. Happy. Life was good. He had been right about leaving. Right as rain.

I don't believe in a lot of things: I don't believe Elvis is still alive, I don't believe no two snowflakes are alike; I don't believe in writing your account number on your check when bill-paying; I don't believe Jerry Springer is a journalist, I don't believe politicians are capable of telling the truth; I don't believe in bread machines or in Italian Fast Food; but I always believed that Vito would come back to me—sooner or later.

13

A Pizza is Not a Dumping Ground for Leftovers

Jimmy won't tell me where we're going. We're zipping through the city in his old emerald green V.W. Beetle, the pride and joy of his life. The best way I can describe Jimmy's driving skills is to say that my eyes have been closed for most of the way. I open my eyes as he sneaks into a parking place that no other car could fit into. "Oh, *Volare*," I say, looking up at the marquee. "I've been hearing a lot about this place," I say as cheerfully as possible. Inside I'm cringing. Jimmy doesn't know—he couldn't possibly know—that this chic pizzeria occupies the space that was once *C.V. Sweets*. After Vito left, Carl still opened the place. He had to; he had so much invested in it. He hired a couple of pastry chefs, and although I'm sure they were talented, neither one was Italian and neither one had been to Italy to sample the desserts, and so it ended up being what Papa called "nothing much." They served pie and cake and tortes and cookies and custard and cheesecake—the very things Vito would have omitted from the menu. But it was a cozy spot in an excellent location and it was frequented by the theater-going yuppies that Vito and Carl were looking to serve. After a few years though it began to falter and Carl got an offer that was too good to pass up, so for many years it was *Papa P's* (the *P* was for Peterson and the pizza was no better than frozen pizza from the grocer) and now it was *Volare.*

Once we're seated I ask Jimmy when his review is due.

"Shhh!" he says, looking around. "My instructor said not to let anyone in the restaurant know that we are reviewing them—it will taint the service."

"Sorry!"

"I couldn't even bring a pencil or notebook in. He said restaurant people are always on the lookout for dining critics."

I want to tell him that we aren't on the lookout at Mela's but I know we'll get into a philosophical argument about the store and what it really is—a cafe first, or a bakery first, or a market first, so I decide not to go there. Even so, it makes me think about how badly Papa would like to have Mela's reviewed by a dining critic.

"All I can say is that this assignment is a lot less painful than last week's was," Jimmy says as we peruse our menus.

"Why is that?"

"We had to write our own obituary."

"Well, that's a really morbid thing to have college students do," I say, thinking for a fleeting second how short and uninteresting mine would be.

"That's what I thought at first, because I was looking at it from the wrong perspective. It's really morbid to think of dying right now at this point in time, but my instructor never said we had to write the obituary as if we died now, so I projected myself well into the future. I had myself kick-off at the ripe ol' age of ninety-five." He laughs and says, "I hope this turns out to be a self-fulfilling prophecy."

"Leave it to you, Jimmy."

"Right, and can you believe I was the only one in the whole class who thought of this? All the other losers wrote these banal obits. Stuff like, 'Joe Blow, sophomore at so-and-so, died today after a short illness. Blah, blah, blah.'"

"Okay, so let's hear yours."

"Well, I don't have it memorized or anything but the gist of it was that I'd carved out a stellar career for myself in print journalism, landing a senior editor position at the New York Times at the young age of twenty-nine. After thirty years at the Times, covering such significant pieces as the fall of the leaning tower of Pisa, the crash of two thousand and thirty, World

War III, and the first life station on the moon, I retired in Africa to devote my senior years to the preservation of the rain forest and to the stock market. I was survived by my third wife, seven children and twenty-two grandchildren. A school, hospital, playground, and several park benches were named in my honor. My estate, upwards of eighty-three million dollars, was divided among my heirs. Services will be held, blah, blah blah."

I clap my hands. "Congratulations on such a sparkling existence. I guess I could say I knew you when."

"You'd be dead, Sabina. If I was ninety-five, you'd be a hundred and five."

"I'd be a hundred and fifteen. Good thing you don't want to be an accountant."

"I hate numbers. Hey, how's your pizza?"

"Save it for the review," I say.

"Shhhhh!" he says, looking around.

The pizza is really good—up there with some of the best I've ever had. The entire meal is pretty straightforward and I'm thinking a review wouldn't be too difficult to write, but then it occurs to me that it's probably easier (and more fun) to write a bad review than a good one. Plus, I remember the obituary—that could have been pretty straightforward, too, but not when you're dealing with a guy like Jimmy, a guy who can turn a fender-bender into a three-car crash, a light drizzle into torrential rains, and a couple of picketers into a full-fledged strike. I take a sip of beer and think: now this could be interesting.

On the way home, I try to give Jimmy some tips about writing the review but he's concentrating on trying to see through a clear spot on the windshield that is maybe all of six inches in diameter. He doesn't believe in scraping the ice from the windshield. "How can you *not* believe in scraping ice from your windshield?" I ask him now. "It's not something that's up for believing in—like ghosts or psychics or purgatory. It's just something you do." But he just lets the defrost and the wipers do their job as we zigzag through town. Only when we reach my house is the windshield totally see-through. "I thought you wanted me to help you write the review," I say as I get out of the car. He says thanks just the same but he thinks he's got it. I thank him for the meal, climb the stairs up to our house and wonder if I'll ever see my money again. Even if I don't, I'll still be thankful to Jimmy tonight. He saved me from an evening of sulking about what's-his-name, Ted Kallista.

***

Jimmy's early to work the next morning and hands me his review, neatly typed, appropriately spaced and margined. I tell him to get mopping and I walk over to the window where the light is better. He leaves me to read and heads for the kitchen, calling out his usual greeting of *Damn-something-smells-good!*

Here's the review:

Restaurant Review by James Giovanotti

    Bella Luna's has pizza that "will knock your socks off" says Chicago Sun Times restaurant critic, Pat Bruno. Edwardo's has won Chicago Magazine's "best pizza" award. Spago's invented designer pizza. But Volare has pizza like nothing I've ever tasted before—other than in my own mother's kitchen. Volare's pizza tastes like the genuine article.

    No, you're not going to find foo-foo toppings like shrimp or pineapple or salmon or goat cheese or asparagus or Canadian bacon. I have nothing against spinach and zucchini and artichokes and hearts of palm—I just don't want these things on my pizza. The folks at Volare don't think pizza is a dumping ground. Volare's just offers the basics: cheese, sausage, pepperoni, black olives, peppers (okay, red) mushrooms, onions, anchovies. Nothing fancy. Just plain ol' perfect.

    In Naples, where pizza was born, they judge a pizza by its crust. Volare's owner, Vince Natali, was born in Naples. Yes, his family moved him here when he was only six years old, but obviously Vince was in Italy long enough to develop Italian taste buds. Vince's crust—whether you'd swear by a razor thin crust or kill for a think pan crust—is just right, crispy but not weighty.

    And the sauce! It's his mother's recipe. Tangy. A bit sweet. But not overpowered by oregano, like so many pizza sauces I've tried. You can taste the fresh basil and the garlic and the crushed red peppers. And I'd bet my next paycheck that Mrs. Natali poured a generous amount of vino rosso into that sauce.

    My dining companion and I shared a deep-dish pie with cheese, sausage, onions, olives and extra sauce. And I have to confess, we didn't have even one corner piece left to bring home for the next day's breakfast. So if you're like me and love cold pizza, I'd recommend ordering a large.

    The decor at Volare is pretty basic, but in my dining travels I've found this often to be a good thing. More times than not, it means the management is spending more money on quality food and ingredients than on designer paint and wallpaper. We sat at an antique (maybe just old) wooden table (a little wobbly), on wooden chairs (a little too straight-backed for my poor posture), and listened to Dean Martin sing Volare over and over and over again (once is quite enough, thank you). The tables are covered in red and white-checkered tablecloths and upon every table sits a candle in a cliché Chianti-bottle. Had I not been dining with my cousin, it could have been a very romantic setting.

To complete the meal, we both had a generous slice of ricotta pie that was so smooth it simply slid down my throat—no masticating necessary. Here again, Mr. Natali doesn't waste time with fancy plate art. His desserts look good (not gorgeous) and they taste superb. My philosophy has always been: foods don't have to look marvelous to taste marvelous. You don't agree? Otherwise who in their right mind would ever eat an artichoke? squid? frog legs? cottage cheese? See what I mean? Volare's desserts won't be displayed in the Museum of Modern Food Art, but they will satisfy all your sweet-craving senses.

To make this meal an absolutely perfect one, get your dining companion to spring for the very, very reasonable bill. I did. I owe you, cuz.

This isn't half bad, I think, in fact, it's pretty good. Maybe he'll make it as a journalist after all. But then I look over at him and see that he's making love to that mop again so now I have to wonder.

"Hey, Jimmy," I call over, "this is good. It's really good."

He and the mop come closer. "You think?"

"I do. And you didn't go crazy with the Thesaurus—well except for *masticating.*

"I love that word. It stays."

"It's your piece."

"It was a damn good pie, wasn't it?" he says.

"Yes, it was. But you still have to pay me back." I hand him back his review, which he folds into twenty-fourths and stuffs into his shirt pocket. I hope that's not the copy he's handing in. He starts mopping again and says, "So what'll it be today? ABC Berries? Bilberry, blueberry, blackberry, boysenberry..."

"You forgot black currant," I say.

"Or maybe ABC exotic fruits. Guava, Kiwi Fruit, Litchi, Mango, Papaya, Passion Fruit, Persimmon, Prickly Pear..."

I look at him funny. "What the hell's a litchi?"

"Sabina, unlock the door," Aunt Lina shouts from the kitchen, "it's time to open."

It's snowing again this morning and when I open the door I'm expecting to find a shivering Mr. Barbiere, dusted with snow, grumbling as if it were thirty below. Instead, I come face to face with Ted Kallista.

I gasp. Hurt my throat even.

He doesn't smile and he doesn't enter right away so Mr. Barbiere does show up and cuts right in front of Ted. Mr. Barbiere doesn't say a word to me and for the first time in my life I don't bother to say good morning to him. He'll probably mention this to Papa, what do you want to bet.

"Hello, Sabina," Ted says, standing in the doorway without a coat, his hands jammed in his pants pockets. I want to say, oh, so you do remember me, but what I do say is, "Good morning, Ted. Why don't you come in out of the cold?" And when he does, I say, "You really need to get yourself a coat, like your friend."

"That's my *boss*," he says, brushing away the snow that has accumulated on his shoulders.

Outwardly, I do not react to this statement as I walk to the counter, but inwardly, I'm thinking *boss*, well, that could explain some of his behavior yesterday, but certainly not all of it. I know that I'd better throw Mr. Barbiere's toast in first, or else I'll hear about it all day, so I ask Ted to excuse me for a moment. Once my back is to him, I catch my breath. I actually have to think about what are usually rote actions: slicing the bread, inserting the slices into the toaster, pushing down the lever... He came back! I can't believe it! I wonder if I am smiling on the outside.

When I return to the counter I ask Ted what I can get him. "Latte? Cappuccino? Flavored coffee?"

"Just plain would be fine."

"Breakfast? My mother makes these stuffed pancakes. Crepes filled with *ricotta* and raspberries."

"Maybe next time. My stomach's a little nervous. Do you have raisin toast?"

"Cinnamon toast."

"That's fine."

He pays. I tell him to help himself at the coffee bar and that I'll bring the toast over shortly.

The morning regulars start filing in and some of them eye the newcomer up and down—very few new people venture in for breakfast.

There goes my heart again—someone's doing a drum solo in my chest cavity. I can't think of what I'm supposed to do next. Oh, yeah, cinnamon toast. I really am jumpy. What's he going to say to me anyway? That he lost my phone-number? That he couldn't remember my name? That he has been so busy trying to get moved here that there was just no time to call? That he happened to stop in here yesterday with his boss, purely by coincidence?

I look over at him. He's got his coffee and the Tribune that Papa always leaves on the counter by the coffee thermoses for anyone to pick up.

But he's not reading, I can tell. He's really checking out the place, watching Jimmy, Mr. Barbiere, Charlie, and Mr. Roan. I realize how loud everyone is, intimate and earthy. A stranger might think he walked in on a private party, a family reunion. I'm ashamed to admit it, but all of a sudden I'm embarrassed of my parent's little Mom 'n' Pop place, which seems about as folksy as you can get. Down home. Quaint. Totally unsophisticated. I'm just thankful that I finally talked Mama and Papa out of the tradition they had for years where, every time a certain song by Dean Martin would play, they would waltz out of the kitchen and dance around the store. When the song was over, the customers would applaud and Mama and Papa would bow and then disappear back into the kitchen. Could there be anything more embarrassing! Oh, our regulars loved it, and many of them were angry with me when I convinced Mama and Papa that the little dance wouldn't be appropriate with our new lunch crowd.

Aunt Lina comes out of the kitchen and spots Ted right away. "Who's that?" she asks me, punching me in the arm. I spill some coffee on the counter.

"Geez, Aunt Lina, if you must punch me could you please not punch my coffee arm?"

"Who's the guy?"

"Nobody. Okay, somebody. But I don't want to tell you right now, okay?"

"Excuse me for breathing. I'm getting the silent treatment in the kitchen and verbal abuse out here. *Marone*, why do I put up with it?"

"I'm sorry. I'll tell you later—after I tell Mama."

After serving another customer, I pass Ted's table, and he leans over and whispers to me, "I lost your phone number."

I don't know what possesses me to say it, but I reply, "It was a fake anyway."

My remark elicits a wide smile. "It was not!"

"Was so."

"Really?"

"No, it was real, but when you didn't call, I wished I'd given you a fake."

"And I couldn't remember your last name...Giovanni, Gionetta, Gio-something."

"Giovanotti," I say, hitting each articulatory target.

"Okay. Sure. I had parts of it I guess. You wouldn't believe all the people in this city I called whose name began with Gio or Gia."

"Really?" Now it's my turn to smile.

"Yeah, really."

Just then Aunt Lina passes in front of me, clears her throat and serves the Radanza brothers their frittatas. I get her oh-so-subtle hint.

"Listen, I've got to get to work."

"What time do you finish up?"

"Five o'clock or so."

"How about dinner?"

"I don't know."

"Come on, I promise by the end of the night I'll have your last name and your phone number memorized."

"Maybe you could just write it on a bigger piece of paper this time."

"Don't worry, I think I've got it. G-I-O-V-A-N..."

"O-T-T-I," Aunt Lina finishes as she walks by. I give her my best mean look. What is it with this woman? First, it's her life's mission to find me a man, and then when I find one on my own, she tries to sabotage it. The woman is predictably unpredictable.

"O-T-T-I," he repeats. "Should I pick you up at seven?"

I pause, pretending to consider the invitation and all that I have going on in my life.

"Do you need to check your planner?"

I laugh. "Planner? I don't even own a calendar. I keep it all in here." I point to my head, hoping he can't tell that I'm throwing out a big, fat lie. I don't have a calendar or a fancy day-planner because those things are made for people with busy lives, important jobs, hectic social lives. I accepted a long time ago the fact that I am closer to Social Security than a social life. I look at Ted. Maybe my luck is changing.

"Lucky you. I couldn't function one day without mine. How about it, Sabina. Seven o'clock?"

"How about six? I know it's vogue to eat late, but my stomach can't take it."

"Actually, six is perfect. Lately, my stomach can't take it either. Six it is. See you later then," he says. "And Sabina?"

"Yes?" Here it comes, I think, the romantic part, the moment when he tells me how he finally tracked me down.

"That was the best cinnamon toast I've ever had in my life."

I look at him to see if he's kidding. I honestly can't tell so I just say, "Well, I'm really glad."

I leave him to finish his coffee. I head to the kitchen to tell Mama that he's here, the *boy* that Rosa told her about. But Aunt Lina's beat me to it. I almost knock them both in the head when I push through the kitchen door because Aunt Lina was just pointing him out to Mama. I try to contain my excitement, but I can't.

"Mama," I say and hug her tight. "It's him! It's the guy Rosa told you about. From the hotel. He lost my phone number, but he found me."

Mama hugs me back. She's all smiles. "He looks nice, *bedda.*"

"He looks tall," says Aunt Lina. "Very, very tall and a nice head of hair at that. You won't have to worry about male pattern baldness."

"I'm having dinner with him tonight."

Mama claps her hands. "Oh, good! An answered prayer!"

"Don't get too excited, it's dinner, one dinner."

"Oh, but I have a good feeling about this. He has a good face," she says as she squeezes mine. "I'm so happy for you."

"It's about time you got out," you-know-who says.

I go back out just as he's getting up from the table. He opens the door to leave, but before he goes, he looks back at me and waves, he actually waves. A lot of guys wouldn't wave, but he waved.

14

A Sip of the Good Stuff

I'm sitting down here in the store, in semi-darkness. While I was getting dressed it occurred to me that I never told Ted where to pick me up. I'm assuming I told him that I live upstairs but I can't really remember. I know I told him about the market, I just can't remember if I'd revealed my current housing arrangements. Let's face it, it gets a little embarrassing.

I'm early; it's only five thirty-five, but I'm so nervous I told Mama and Papa that I'd just as soon go down and grab a can of pop before he came. I know Papa wanted me to bring Ted up so they could meet him, but I think I'll wait and see how tonight goes. I hate feeling like this, like a teenager. Geez, I'm forty years old. I could have teenagers of my own. But here I am, doing what I do best...waiting.

When Ted arrives at the door, he tries the handle first, then knocks. I turn the lock, open the door, but then I don't know if I should go out or have him come in and so we both kind of stutter at the threshold for a few seconds. It's awkward. But it's cold, too, and so I say, "Do you want to come in or just get going?"

"I made a reservation for six-thirty so maybe we should just get going."

"Okay then," I say and lock the door.

He's not wearing a coat, just his sports jacket, and the mother in me says, "You still don't have a coat? It's freezing." He leads me to his car, some kind of spiffy SUV.

"You know, I have a coat, I do. Somewhere. I just can't find it."

"Well, you can't live here without a good coat and some gloves, too. You have to have gloves."

"How about a hat, can I live here without a hat?" He smiles the nicest smile and opens the car door for me. I climb in. I'm pleased to see that he has scraped every flake of snow and every crystal of ice off of the windshield. It's pristine. I'm relieved that I won't have to fear for my life like with Jimmy.

He turns the heat on high and says to tell him if it gets too hot. He asks me how the rest of my day went and tells me that my family has a nice little place. "Who's the lady with the Lucille Ball hair?"

I laugh. "That's my aunt, my mother's sister. She came from Long Island to cook with my mother about eight months ago."

"How's that working out?"

"I don't know yet," I lie.

"The only reason I ask is that my mother and her sister used to cook in my uncle's restaurant—a little gyros joint not far from here as a matter of fact. They lasted exactly nine months. My uncle fired both of them. Actually fired his own wife."

"It might be headed in that direction," I say.

We chit chat a little about Mela's Market. He wants to know how we got started, how long we've been in business. He tells me how Chicago has and hasn't changed in the ten years he's been gone. He asks how my sisters are and then we drive without talking for a little while. He sticks in an Eric Clapton CD and sings softly along to "Tears in Heaven."

"I love that song," I say, "but it's so sad. Isn't that the one he wrote after his little boy died?"

"Yeah, I think so," he says, and then without explanation skips to the next song. This strikes me as rude. I just say I like a song and then he skips over it. I don't get it.

Before I can think anything more about it, we pull up in front of the Four Seasons Hotel and he says, "I thought it might be kind of nice to go back to the hotel tonight." The way he says it makes it sound like he means for the night. He must read the look on my face because he quickly adds, "For dinner, I mean."

"That'll be nice," I say.

***

"I'm actually staying here for a few days," Ted tells me as we wait for the matre d'. "Until my apartment is ready. They were supposed to paint it last week but you know how that goes."

"Actually, I don't. Did I tell you that I live upstairs from our store?"

"Yeah, with your parents, right?"

"Right."

"Don't tell me Lucy lives up there, too."

"Lucy?"

"Your aunt with the Lucy hair."

"Oh," I shudder at the thought. "God forbid."

He smiles at me. "She's a firecracker, huh?"

"More like a heat-seeking missile," I say, as the matre d' seats us in the dining room. Ted orders wine and when our glasses are filled, he lifts his and says, "Here's to finding you!"

I click his glass. "How did you anyway?" I ask as I sip the wonderful wine—the same wine that Ted bought for my sisters and me that night.

"Pure luck or destiny or fate or God's will or something, because to be honest, I'd given up."

"I about dropped dead when you came in the store."

"You? What about me? Here I am with my boss, trying to be cool, trying to make him believe he made the right decision in moving to Chicago in the middle of December. The guy gets frostbite if it's below fifty."

"How did you know about Mela's? It's such a neighborhood place."

"That was Clay's idea, my boss. He says he loves to eat at family-run ethnic restaurants and a guy we work with told us about your place. Said it was great, and it was."

"Thank you."

"Clay's a good guy. We go way back. We both worked for San Francisco Magazine. I'd been there eight years. Clay, ten."

"How did you end up back here?"

"My mom is here and we had to put her in a nursing home last year, so I wanted to be close. Plus, I felt like I was being called back home. Maybe I'm getting old or something. I still have a lot of friends here. Clay has no friends out here—but his wife's family is here. I'm the one who talked Clay into moving here and his wife is still a little mad at me. She left Chicago fifteen years ago, saying she'd never move back. She's a sun-worshipper, one of those eternally tan people. But we brought her back and wined and dined her and she finally acquiesced. The fur Clay bought her may have helped, too."

"So," I say, "is Clay a writer, too?"

"He's an editor. See I got this offer, and it was attractive, exactly what I wanted, but the editor was a crazy bastard and I knew I couldn't work with the guy. Come to find out, they wanted to can the guy anyway. I tell them about Clay. So they fire the other guy and hire Clay. It was one of those fluky things—never would have worked out this way if you'd planned it. Hey, let's look at the menus, you're probably starving."

"I'm fine, really. So are you and Clay with a magazine now?"

"Oh shit, Sabina," he says and I get a *de ja vu*, like any second he's going to jump from his seat and say he's got to catch a cab or a plane. He does jump up. He grabs his cell phone from the pocket of his sport jacket and says, "All this talk about Clay and I almost forgot, I told him I'd call him at six-thirty. I'll just be a minute."

I didn't realize how nervous I was until he leaves the table. I wipe my clammy hands on my napkin. I feel so rusty, so out of practice. I look around the room. Everybody seems so young, so sophisticated, so comfortable. I feel like a daisy in an expensive vase (pronounced *voz*).

Ted returns apologizing for the interruption. "Sorry about that, but I had to know where we're eating tomorrow."

"Where you're *eating* tomorrow?" I ask, wondering if I'm sitting across from someone with that Gourmand Syndrome, that neurological thing where these people plan their day, their vacation, their life around food.

"I mean where we're *meeting* tomorrow." He opens his menu with a flourish. "Now then, Sabina, what looks good?"

But nothing does. My nerves have sabotaged my appetite.

Ted says, "Shall we get that wonderful lobster again?"

I smile and say, "Sure."

"So, Sabina Giovanotti, 3-1-2-5-5-5-2-1-1-3, tell me, what's your story?"

Here it is, I think, so soon into the meal, too. The question they all ask: "What's your story? Your claim to fame? Tell me about yourself." This is where it all starts and ends for me.

"All I really know is that you have four beautiful sisters, and that you work at your father's store, which you will take over for him sometime next year, right?"

"Right." I take a sip of wine to stall. I swallow. "That's it. I don't really have a story."

"Everybody's got a story."

"Yes, but not everybody's got a *good* story."

"Oh, come on. Start with where you were born."

I laugh, this is so embarrassing. "Okay, okay, let me get this over with so that I can drill you about when you got your first tooth. I was born here, in Chicago. I've lived above the store my entire life. I went to a Catholic grade school, Catholic high school, and UIC. After college, I continued to work in the store. Eighteen years later, we're at the end of the story. That's it. See? You're getting sleepy, I can tell."

"I am not. But I'm sure you left out all of the good parts. Aren't you going to tell me about the good parts?"

Luckily, before I can tell him that the good parts are my nieces and nephews, the server comes with our salads and asks if we want fresh ground pepper and we do, so that puts a little time between his question and my answer.

"Mmmmm," he says, "this dressing is delicious. I detect a hint of cilantro."

"You really know food. Do you cook?"

"Oh, but now we're getting to my story and we aren't done with yours."

"Yes, we are. Believe me."

"Well, I used to cook a lot. You happen to be dining with a graduate of the Culinary Institute of America, but before you get too impressed, let me tell you that I only cooked professionally for nine months. Then I quit. But I like to cook for friends, although I haven't had the opportunity much lately. And I do like to experiment, but I only experiment on myself."

"I am impressed. That's the best cooking school there is. You're the one with the story. Tell me what happened."

"Should I start with my first tooth?"

"But of course.

"The first tooth I got or the first tooth I lost?" He smiles the nicest smile. "I grew up here, too, in Greektown, over on Adams. Went to Northwestern. Got a journalism degree. Even got a job at the Sun Times. Started out writing the obits."

"Somebody's got to do it."

"That's what my mother said. I did it, but I hated it. I covered crime, city council, then I moved up to the mayor—I'm talking about Ms. Jane Margaret Bryne. Now there was a tough old broad." He looks at me funny and says, "Do you mind me saying *broad?*" And when I shake my head no, he says, "It's just that I've found out the hard way that some women do mind me saying *broad*." He laughs and accidentally spits a piece of lettuce across the table. "Anyway, she was a tough old broad, and I got sick of following her around. So I quit. Just like that. No two weeks, no nothing. I was pretty immature. Hell, I was a jerk. My father died when I was a senior in high school and I tried to blame everybody and everything. My mother remarried when I was a sophomore in college. This rich guy, this filthy rich guy, who was always trying to win my brother and me over with his bucks. Which never worked. But I spent a lot of time and he spent a lot of money before we came to that conclusion. Anyway, he wasn't the bastard I thought he was—he did have the decency to die an early death and leave my mother a very comfortable woman." He puts his fork down and makes a look like he's surprised at himself. "I don't know where all that came from. See Sabina, just start from your first tooth and it'll just start flowing."

I smile at him. I could listen to him talk all night. He makes it easy to be with him.

"So then you went to the CIA?" I ask.

"Yeah, with Papa Howard's money, and it wasn't cheap."

"How'd you get interested in food?"

"You'll probably hate me if I tell you. You being a genuine foodie and all."

"I won't, honest."

"It was all because of a bet."

"A bet?"

"A bet. After I'd quit the paper, Howard and my mother were on my case. They wanted me to decide what I was going to do with the rest of my life. Wanted me to choose a new career, as if it was as easy as choosing a new suit. But I didn't know what I wanted to do. One night we were having dinner, the three of us, and I said something about the lamb chops being tough and I didn't mean it as a criticism of my mother's cooking as much as I meant it as a criticism of the sheep itself. Howard was incensed, said I was rude, and asked if I could do better. I said if I knew how to cook I could do better. I know it sounds like I was the king of spoiled brats, but I was really a nice kid until my father died. It was all just to get back at her. Anyway, Howard, a gourmand in every sense of the word, thought it would be grand to have a chef in the family and offered me a free ride for two years at the CIA. I accepted."

"The Culinary Institute of America," I say dreamily. "I've read so much about it. Was it all that they say it is?"

"It was living hell. I grew up, anyway. You cannot be a spoiled brat at the CIA. The curriculum was grueling, the hours ungodly, the pace exhausting, and the instructors were like army sergeants." He shakes his head and smiles, and for a moment I see that same glint in his eye that Vito used to get whenever he spoke about the California Culinary Academy. "It was the best damn thing that ever happened to me, that's for sure." He takes a big sip of wine and leans back as the waiter serves our lobster.

"So what made you quit cooking?"

"Well, first of all, I wasn't that good. I mean I learned all the fundamentals—roux, stock, pastry, forced meats—and I had the technique, but I was never fast enough. The guys, back then it was mostly guys, that made it, that were great at it, were so fantastically fast. They had this efficiency of movement about them. I can't describe it—like a dancer almost. No wasted steps. It's a talent, honest it is."

I wanted to tell him I knew exactly what he meant. Vito had moved with that kind of efficiency.

"Howard said I lacked the passion and I guess he was right. You've got to have a passion for cooking if you want to cook and something even more than passion if you want to be a chef—something like an obsession. I was a good baker though. I get along well with dough."

"So you went back to writing?"

"Yes, I did. But that doesn't mean I can't whip up a mean Creme Brulee. Speaking of, theirs is quite good here. So save some room. Then after dessert I have something else in mind."

"What," I ask, hoping it's not an invitation up to his room.

"We could go for a nice swim."

"A swim?"

"Yes, don't tell me that you don't remember the nice pool they have here, not to mention that beautiful hot tub that you and your sisters were summarily kicked out of?"

"Oh, I remember all right. That was so embarrassing."

"What do you say?"

"I didn't bring my suit."

"They have disposable ones."

"You're supposed to wait an hour after eating."

"That's just a myth mothers dreamed up to get a little rest at the beach."

"But I'm so stuffed."

"Work off a few calories."

Other thoughts start running through my head: where will I change and dry my hair? What about make-up? But I look across the table and he's sitting back in his chair looking at me with those incredible blue-green or green-blue eyes and these straight white teeth and this head of almost curly hair, and I hear myself say: "Okay, that sounds nice."

Now we're sitting here in the hot tub with two young women. Very attractive women, I must say, filling out their bikinis quite nicely. Here I am in this disposable suit, which isn't as bad as I'd anticipated (I thought disposable meant paper), but I'd be much more comfortable if these two little bathing beauties would call it a night. Ted acts as if he doesn't even notice them, as if he only has eyes for me, which makes me feel both wonderful and self-conscious.

Finally they leave and Ted and I have the tub to ourselves. It feels nice, worlds away from my real life, from Aunt Lina and the store and Mr. Barbiere's almost-but-not-quite-burnt toast. It's been so long since I've even entertained the idea that my life could be different. I've allowed my entire life to be planned by others—Papa decided I would go to college, Vito decided I would major in business, that we would get married, that we would run *C. V. Sweets* together. Wouldn't it be weird if all of a sudden I had some control over my own destiny? And even more weird if my destiny started right here, right now?

I get gooseflesh just thinking about it. Ted says, "Sabina, you're shivering, but you can't be cold can you?" Before I can answer he moves closer and puts his arm around me. Then, not even one drop of blood in my body is cold. "I like your suit," he says, smiling.

"Oh, right."

"I do, but I like your red one better."

I bite my bottom lip. He remembered my suit, Colina's hand-me-down. This is not my life. I haven't had even a smidgen of romance since bread costs fifty cents. This can't be happening. But, please God, let it be happening.

"I might get in trouble for saying this, but you know all that time that I couldn't find you?"

I take a deep breath; my eyes are watering. Why are my eyes watering?

"Whenever I thought about you, you were always wearing that little red suit."

I hit him lightly on the shoulder.

"It's just the image that stuck in my head," he says, with a little shrug. "I can't help it." He leans in closer and kisses me. I kiss him back, not even caring if anyone sees.

The nice thing is that he doesn't even try to get me to stay. We go upstairs to his room and I dry my hair and dress, and then we come down and sit in the lounge for a glass of wine. He tells me a little about his marriage and divorce. "What I want to know is why the hell do opposites attract? What was God thinking? I'm pretty laid back. Lizette is this driven person, brutally competitive, fiercely ambitious. I think maybe I was attracted to the qualities I lacked. Maybe nature seeks to balance itself out. I don't know. She never liked that I was a chef. Maybe that was another reason I quit. To her food was food, something better off avoided if you want to stay fantastically thin. Anyway, she's still a prosecutor, still out in California, hoping the next trial will make her famous."

I look like I'm just listening politely, but actually, I'm playing what my social-worker sister Colina calls "face detective." I'm scrutinizing Ted's facial expressions for underlying emotions. What I want to know of course is whether or not he's still in love with his ex-wife. He uses a flat, unemotional voice when he speaks about her, but still I wonder.

Now we're almost home and I just don't want the night to end. He's holding my hand while he drives. It's snowing and a tiny part of me is thinking that maybe he should have both hands on the wheel but the rest of me is thinking about the electricity that is being transferred through our hands. I want to think that this might be something, but I'm too afraid.

We pull up in front of the store. Ted puts the car in park. I fiddle around in my purse for my house keys and wonder if all women find these few moments the most awkward part of a date.

"This may sound crazy," Ted says, "but I think I actually missed the snow."

"I only like it when it's coming down," I say.

"Do you ski?"

"No," I say, feeling as if it might be a character flaw. Skiers like girlfriends who ski.

"I don't either. Never liked it. Ice-skate?"

"Nope."

"Me neither. Weak ankles. What about sledding?"

"Now that I can handle," I say. "As a matter-of-fact, I'm taking my nephew sledding Saturday."

"Tomorrow Saturday or next week Saturday?"

"Tomorrow is...oh yeah, Saturday. Want to come?"

"Wow. I haven't been sledding in years. Decades even."

"Come on, it'll be fun."

"You sure your nephew won't mind?"

"Nino won't mind. As a matter of fact, he was kind of upset that his brothers weren't joining us but they both have basketball tournaments. You'll be appreciated as ballast if for nothing else. Nino's a real character."

"How old is he?"

"Seven."

"What's that, like fourth grade?"

"First, actually, but if you ask him if he's in the fourth grade, he'll be your friend for life. He's kind of little."

We agree to meet at the park at two. I tell him he'd better round up some appropriate clothing—a jacket and gloves.

He squeezed my hand. "And a hat too, right?"

"It wouldn't hurt."

He squeezes my hand again, then leans in to kiss me. He has these full, juicy lips and when he kisses me all the energy seems to drain out of my body. I almost go limp. I'd forgotten how nice kissing in a warm car on a cold night could be. Hell, who am I kidding? I'd forgotten how nice kissing could be, period.

15

Burnt To Crispy Perfection

Even though it's after midnight, I take the steps up to our apartment two at a time. If I wanted, I could probably fly up them. I unlock the front door and immediately sense that something's wrong. There's someone lying on the couch.

"Sabina?"

"Yeah?"

"It's me."

"Who's me?"

"Colina."

"Colina!" I say as I kick off my boots and throw my coat on a chair. I go over and sit at the edge of the couch.

"Careful," she whispers, "I've got the baby."

"Where are Morgy and Nicole?"

"In my old room."

"You should have taken my bed."

"I left him, Bina. I really did it."

"You did?"

"I did."

"Oh, Co, I'm so sorry."

"Me too."

"What happened? Tell me."

She gingerly hands me a sleeping Chelsea so that she can sit up and blow her nose. She pulls two tissues from a jumbo size box on the end table. She blows and then flicks the tissues on the floor. I look down at the floor. Now that my eyes have adjusted to the dark I can see that it has snowed used-tissues.

"Monica came back."

"Oh, Colina."

"She never went to Ohio. I've been an idiot." She cries, blows, and flicks. I hug her, smooshing Chelsea a little in the process. She moans and repositions herself in my lap. Colina cries harder. Blows. Flicks.

"How does this happen?" she asks. "You give someone five years, three children. You give up friends. You give up your career. Hell, you give up food."

"He's a rotten rat fink."

"Don't. Please. I don't want to blast him."

"Why not?"

"Because. It's not entirely his fault."

"Oh, right." I can't believe what I'm hearing.

"I've always known in my heart that he only married me because I was pregnant. He must really be in love with her." Cry. Blow. Toss. "You know how old she is?"

I shake my head.

"Twenty-three! Twenty-three. Fifteen years younger than him. But you want to know what the worst part is?"

"What?"

"She's fat."

"That's the worst part?"

"Sabina, she's fat, well she's not fat really, she's like Rosa— voluptuous. But the point is this—I've been starving myself to hang on to him and he leaves me for someone so, so, so meaty. It's so, so, so—" Cry. Blow.

"Unfair?" I say as she flicks.

"I've been a fool."

"You're nobody's fool. He's the fool. Oh, sorry, I forgot, I'm not supposed bad-mouth him," I say, not bothering to hide the sarcasm. "So what are you going to do?"

"I don't really know. Right now I just want my mommy and—"

"Some mint chocolate chip ice-cream?"

She looks at me and pauses. The only woman in the world that would have to *think* about getting intimate with a half-gallon of mint chocolate chip ice cream. Finally she smiles. "That actually sounds really good."

I hand her the baby and head to the kitchen to get the carton and two big spoons.

***

The next morning, I wake up to voices in the kitchen. Papa's and Colina's. They're laughing and the sound of it is good. No matter what, Papa can make Colina laugh. You never met a more serious and sensitive person than Colina. She cries for strangers. Just walk around this city with Colina. Go with her to a museum or to Navy Pier and watch her watch people. If a guy limps past you, look over at Colina and her eyes will be moist. Or if you spot a so-called mother spanking her kid in public, Colina's eyes will leak. And if you ever see a child in a wheelchair or in leg braces, try to block Colina's view or it may send her spiraling downward into a dark funk.

I turn to look at Chelsea, who is here in bed with me. I took her from Colina last night and brought her in with me. Colina thinks that I did it so that she could get a good night's sleep, but I also did it for me—there's nothing else in this world that compares with cuddling with a baby. She's awake, sucking on the toes of her yellow sleeper.

"Where's my little girl? Who's in Aunt Bina's bed?" She smiles and the whole room lights up. I take her and rock her and smother her with kisses. And then I think about her idiot father and what's ahead for her: stepmother, stepfather, stepsisters, stepbrothers, half-sisters, half-brothers, step-cousins, step-grandparents, and worst of all, step aunts. I bury my face in her brown ringlets. She coughs this sort of chesty-sounding cough and I get nervous. Maybe it's a good thing that I'm not a mother. I'd worry too much. I'd probably smother my kids. I'd probably go over over-protective. I wait for another cough, but it doesn't come and so I calm down a little.

"Let's go find Morgy and Nicole," I say and we hop out of bed. The floor is so cold it makes me wish I was wearing yellow footy pajamas. I feel for my slippers and we tiptoe down the hall. I gently open the door to the spare bedroom and find the two girls awake and sitting on the bed talking. They don't see us so I listen in for a moment. Nicole, the five-year old, has her arm draped around her three-year-old sister's neck.

"It'll be okay, Morgy," Nicole says, in a very big girl voice. "My friend at school, Brianna, you know, the one I hate? Her Mom and Dad got de-vorced and she gets to visit her Dad every summer and go to Disney World. It won't be so bad."

"But why does Mommy want a de-vorce?"

"I don't know. Maybe she just got tired of being friends with Daddy. You know, like I did with Brianna."

Listening to them, I get this choking feeling in my throat, but I'm thinking about choking someone else. How could John do this to them?

Morgy doesn't say anything else so maybe Nicole's explanation has satisfied her. I decide to let them have their time together. The more they rely on each other to get through this, the better. I start to shut the door, but then Chelsea blurts out "Mugga," which is her version of Morgy.

The two girls jump down from the bed. "Aunt Bina, Aunt Bina," they scream as they run to me. Nicole says, "We've come to live with you. Is that okay?"

I kneel down to reach them and then gather them in for a group hug. "Of course it is," I say pecking their cheeks, "I've been wanting to have a slumber party for the longest time. I'm so glad you all could make it." They giggle. Then Morgan gets all serious-faced and asks if I can keep a secret.

"Of course I can."

"It's a big secret."

"Is it top secret?"

"No, it's just bottom secret, but it's still secret."

"I see. Okay, shoot."

"Last night Mommy told Daddy she wants a de-vorce."

I look into her huge brown eyes, and honestly, the thought that goes through my head is this: hey, don't get me involved. But I can see she's expecting an answer so I bring her closer to me and I say, "I know honey, you're Mommy told me. Sometimes married people have fights. Sometimes they make up and sometimes they don't. Sometimes they say things they think they mean, but don't really mean, and yet sometimes they really do mean them." I rub my forehead. None of this is coming out right but I know I have to finish now that I started. "Sometimes married people can work things out and sometimes they just can't. It doesn't mean they love you any less though, sweetie. Even when parents do get divorced, it's never the children's fault. It's just that grown-ups don't always act like grown-ups, do they now."

Morgan looks at me funny, as if she's trying to decide if I'm one of those kind of grown-ups or if I'm the real kind. Nicole says, "I don't think I want to be a grown-up when I grow up. I think I'll be like Peter Pan and never grow up."

All of a sudden, Morgy breaks into a fit of tears. I'm thinking the poor thing's overwhelmed by the family crisis, but when I pull her up on my lap and ask her what's wrong, she says, "I want to go to Never Neverland, too!"

Mama calls us to breakfast. Just as we sit down to eat the thick slabs of French toast she's prepared us, the phone rings. "It's your sister," Mama says, as if I had just one. It only takes one word and I know it's Marina. She's calling to say that Nino has a sore throat and can't go sledding. "He is so mad at me, Sabina. Maybe you can drop by later and just say hi."

"How bad is it? How about if we just do lunch?" I say as I watch Morgy drown her French toast with maple syrup.

"Better not. I think he's feverish, too, but he won't let me get near enough to take his temperature." Her voice gets progressively louder. I want to tell her I think she's obsessing—I'm nothing if I'm not an amateur psychologist—but I'm afraid if I open my big mouth I'll find myself on the receiving end of a medical dissertation on streptococcal pharyngitis, and, I ask you, who needs that?

"I'll stop by later with a little treat for him. Maybe we can play a game of chess if he's up to it," I say. "Tell him I hope he feels better."

"Okay. The mom's always the bad guy. But this kid has been sick the last two Christmases. This year I'm going to keep him well if I have to shove antibiotics up his you know what."

How wonderful to have a nurse for a mother I think as I hang up the phone. I sit back down to my French toast. "Nino's sick. Or should I say, Marina *thinks* Nino is sick. Tell you what," I say, addressing the two sticky little girls on either side of me, "if you two are good girls today and help your Mommy, I'll take you sledding after lunch. How does that sound?"

"Great!" says one.

"Great!" says the other.

"Oh, Bina, you don't have to, really."

"Actually I need to. Ted's supposed to meet Nino and me at the park at two. So, you're really helping me."

"Another date," Papa teases. "Well, well, well."

***

214

Standing at the top of a clean white hill, I eat snowflakes with Nicole and Morgy and watch for Ted. It's windier than I'd anticipated and I can tell you right now these two little things aren't going to last long. In spite of being over-bundled, they're shivering. Nichole keeps repeating "burrrrrrrrrrrr" and "va-va-va-va-va" over and over again, but when I ask her if she's too cold, she says, "No, I'm hot. I say 'burrrrrrrrrrr' when I'm hot."

We watch as people load themselves onto sleds and scream their way down the hill. "Why are they screaming?" asks Morgy, who is about to embark on her first sledding experience.

"Because it's scary," her sister tells her.

"No, silly, because it's fun," I reassure her.

"And kinda scary," says Nicole.

"Okay, okay, it's a little scary, Morgy, but that's what makes it fun. You'll see. We'll put you in between us and you'll be just fine." I can tell by looking at her that she's not so sure but she'll do anything her big sister does. She watches intensely, soaking it all in, building up her courage while we watch for Ted.

"What does he look like, Aunt B?" Nicole wants to know.

"He looks really nice," I say. "He has dark brown, kind of curly hair, with blue or green eyes, I haven't decided which, and hopefully he's wearing a coat and a hat and gloves and boots."

Nicole looks at me as if I'm a little loony, like I'm half-expecting Ted to arrive in a bathing suit. "There he is!" I say a little too excitedly and wave to him.

"He's tall," Nicole informs me.

"Yes, he is," I say and we both check him out as he trudges over to us in these enormous leather work boots. He's wearing a navy blue ski jacket, jeans, and black leather gloves.

"Where's your hat?" I tease him.

"Right here." He pulls a black knit hat out of a pocket and pulls it down on his head. "I never wear hats you know, only for you would I wear a hat."

"Well, thank you. I think. Ted, I'd like you to meet my nieces. This is Nicole and this is Morgy."

"Morgan," she corrects me.

"Excuse me, Morgan."

"Well, nice to meet you girls." He shakes each of their little mittened hands. "Now let's see, Nicole, you must be in about the fourth grade, huh?"

"I'm in kindergarten, silly. I'm five and three-quarters."

Not to be outdone, Morgy says, "Well, I'm three and three dimes."

You are?" Ted says. "Then you're old enough to drive, right? You drove your Aunt Sabina over here, didn't you?"

"I can't drive yet, you Mister Silly," she says, giggling. She covers her mouth with her mittened hand.

"Well, I'll bet you can drive a sled though, right?"

"You have to drive?" she asks, her eyes big as saucers.

"You have to steer, honey, but don't worry about steering, we'll do the steering," I tell her. I explain to Ted that it's her first time sledding.

"Oh, well, it's my first time in probably twenty years, so I'm in the same boat as you. You think maybe I could sit in the middle with you?"

"If there's room," she says quite seriously.

He smiles and looks around. "Hey, where's your nephew?"

"Oh, his mother, the hypochondriac nurse, decided he has a sore throat today. These two are my baby sister's girls. There's one more who stayed behind. She's just a little over a year old."

"They're beautiful," he says. "Dark hair and dark eyes. They could be yours."

"Well, I'm crazy about them, that's for sure. But I don't think they're going to last long. It's colder than I thought."

"Especially for a California boy."

"I like your jacket, California boy."

"Thanks, just some old thing I picked up this morning," he says in a falsetto.

We walk over to a spot that looks like a good take-off strip. Nicole pulls at my jacket. "Aunt B?"

"What honey?"

"They're blue. Like blue jeans."

"What?"

She flutters her eyes oh so dramatically until I realize she means Ted's eyes. I look up and smile at him as he's gently placing Morgy on the toboggan and explaining what we're going to do. He looks over at me and smiles. Nicole's right, in this light, Ted's eyes are the color of denim.

We take our places: Nicole in the lead with me behind her, then Morgy, with Ted pulling up the rear. Ted pushes us off and down we go at great speed with the wet wind whistling in our ears and slapping our faces. Behind me, Morgy is squealing with delight, but in front of me, Nicole, the older one, is screaming for her life. We gently crash into the hay bales that are strategically positioned at the bottom of the hill for just this purpose. Morgy is still giggling as she and Ted scramble out of the toboggan. Ted yells, "Wow! That was fun! Wasn't that fun?" Morgy jumps up and down, shrieking, "Yeah! Yeah! Yeah!"

Nicole turns to look at me, tears streaming down her cheeks like satin ribbons. I hug her and give her "there-there" pats on the back. "Oh, Nicole," I say. "You didn't like it, did you?" But she can't settle herself down to answer.

When Morgy realizes that Nicole is crying she runs over to the aid of her big sister, the love of her life. She pats her on the head and waits for her to compose herself. Nicole finally does and opens her mouth to speak. I know what she is going to say—it was too fast, too scary, too cold, too windy, too dangerous, too crazy. But here's what she says: "Let's go again!" And so we do. Many times. Changing positions each time so that everybody gets a turn in the front seat, which is the most thrilling seat of all.

Each and every time we slide down the hill Nicole bawls. But after we crash-land she dries her eyes with her mittens and gears herself up again.

I tell Ted that I stopped trying to figure out Nicole a long time ago and he laughs good-naturedly. I wonder if he knew what he was in for when he accepted my invitation. This event would have definitely been different with Nino, I guarantee that. Nino's not raw emotion like Nicole is. If he were here now he would be taking a scientific look at sledding. What angle would give the best advantage? How could we go faster, straighter? I wonder how he's feeling anyway.

After our ninth or tenth descent, Nicole's eyes are swollen from crying and her voice is hoarse. When Morgy informs me that she needs to use the "ladies and gentlemen's room," I almost say hurray. Nicole thinks it's necessary to translate and says, "She's gotta go pee."

I think about how much fun it's going to be getting her snowsuit and all of these layers removed for her to go potty. We head for the rest rooms and call it a day.

Ted walks us to the car and suggests that we warm up with some hot chocolate somewhere, but we can't figure out where, and now Morgy wants her Mommy.

"Why don't you meet us at my house? There are some people there who are dying to meet you."

"Aunt Lucy?" Ted says, flashing white teeth at me.

"No, not her. Do you have a thing for redheads or something?"

He slams the door of Colina's mini van shut and snickers. "No, she just reminds me of my mother a little."

"Oh, please, say it's not true."

"No, really, she does. She reminds me of my mother twenty-years ago. She was feisty like that. Hell, she's eighty-two now, wait, eighty-three, no eighty-two. Anyway, she's mellowed."

"Well, I was talking about my parents and my sister." I motion toward the girls, who are secured in their car seats. "She and the kids are staying with us for a while."

He raises his eyebrows in question. I whisper, "She left their dad last night."

"Oh, no," he says shaking his head. "That's terrible."

"It's sickening is what it is."

***

At home I wait for him to pull up behind me. I want to ask him if he'll give me five minutes to run up and just make sure that Colina is okay. Who knows what state of mind I could find her in? But before I can say a thing, he's out of the car helping me get Morgy out of her car seat. "Here," he says, "let me. These car seats can be tricky." He has Morgy out in a second—which impresses me to no end because I always fumble with the belt and the button. The way he holds her in his arms makes you think he's had some practice. He looks at Morgy, who seems to be following his eyes with her own.

"You're a good sled driver, Mr. Man," she announces happily from her perch in his arms.

"His name is Mr. Ted, Miss Girl," I tell her. She giggles. I unlock the door to the store and we are greeted with warmth and good smells—even when the store is closed it smells good. "Tell you what," I say to the girls. "Let's get some hot chocolate started and then we'll go tell your Mommy we're back. Okay?"

Now that we're here, Morgy's in no hurry to see her Mom. Both girls want to stay down here with "Mr. Man." So I put a pot of milk to boil and then take the back stairs two at a time. Upstairs, it's quiet as a church. Too quiet. Someone-is-sleeping-kind-of-quiet. I walk down the hall, peeking into the bedrooms. When I get to mine, I find Colina and the baby asleep on my bed. Colina wakes and sees me. "Did you have fun?" she whispers. "Hey, where are the girls?"

"They're downstairs with Ted. I was going to bring him up. Where's Mama?"

"Papa had to bring her to the walk-in clinic, she was coughing so bad. Mama talked to Marina and Marina thinks it's bronchitis."

"Well, of course she does. She diagnoses all our ailments over the phone."

She hears the sarcasm in my voice and adds, "She did sound kind of wheezy, Bina."

218

"Oh, poor Mama. It's just that sometimes I wish Marina'd keep her hypochondria to herself." I have no patience for this thing my sister does, this morbid concern about everyone's health, accompanied by these delusions of disease.

"Try telling her that," Colina says. "We should engrave her own motto on her tombstone: *Just Because You're A Hypochondriac Doesn't Mean There's Nothing Wrong With You.*" She says this too loudly causing Chelsea to stir and cough.

"She doesn't sound good either, Co."

"I know, but I keep checking her temperature. She doesn't have a fever."

"Okay, well listen. You two rest. We're making hot chocolate downstairs. I'll keep the girls busy for a while." I pull the comforter up around her and shut the door.

Downstairs I find Morgy and Ted sitting at a table. Nicole is standing beside them with an imaginary pen and pad in hand, poised to take their order.

"Sorry, we are all out of French fries today. Would you care for a baked potato instead?" she asks.

Ted says that would be fine, but Morgy says, "I don't want a baked tay-ta, I want a Mr. Tay-ta."

Nicole puckers up her face and stares at her little sister. "Do you mean a Mr. Potato Head potato?"

Morgy says, "Yeah."

Nicole says, "That'll be extra." Then she turns to Ted and says, "My Mommy and Daddy are getting a de-vorce."

"Oh, Nicole," I say, heading for the table.

She looks up at me with china doll eyes. "Well," she says, "they are."

I hug her and say, "Maybe, Nicole, but maybe not. Nothing is for certain yet. Why don't we have our hot chocolate and—oh, no! The milk!"

I run to the kitchen anticipating a mess. Sure enough, the milk has scalded and boiled over and the bottom of the pan is covered with a burnt brown scum. I start over. The girls and Ted join me in the kitchen. The girls busy themselves by playing at the sink—they love the foot peddle. Ted asks if everything is all right upstairs.

"Actually, no," I say. "My father had to take my mother to the clinic—she may have bronchitis—and my sister and the baby are napping."

"Would it be better if I left?"

"No, not at all. It's better if I keep the girls busy down here so she can get some rest. If you don't mind playing restaurant, please stay."

"Those two are something else," he says, waving his thumb in their direction.

"They give my sister a run for her money."

"The little one kills me."

I smile. "Yeah, she's got spunk."

"Oven spring," he says.

"Yeah, oven spring," I say, remembering that I am talking to a foodie who knows about such things. "Oven spring," I say again.

Sitting at a table near the window, Ted and I drink hot chocolate, eat some almond biscotti, and watch Nicole spin on a stool at the counter. Morgy is lying below me on the floor, wrapped up in my cardigan sweater, humming softly to herself. It's weird to be in the store on a Saturday, without all the lights, without all the music, and especially without all the people. Morgy is falling asleep right before my eyes. "But I'm not sleepy, Mrs. Lady," she insists, kicking the air. I've been "Mrs. Lady" for the past half-hour now.

"*Aunt* lady to you. And yes, you are. I can tell." Before she can protest again, she's asleep.

Suddenly, I'm exhausted. I can't help yawn. It must be catchy because Ted yawns, too. "I could use a nap myself," he says. "Do you want to see a movie later tonight?"

I look at Morgy sleeping and Nicole spinning and I think about Colina sleeping and Chelsea coughing and Nino waiting and Mama sick. I can't believe it. For the first time in years upon years upon years, I'm actually getting asked out on a second date. I should say yes, yes, yes, yes, yes! I should march these two little girls up to their mommy, deposit them on the bed and just go. But I just say weakly, "Can you call me later tonight? Maybe I can make a late show. Things aren't usually this crazy around here. Honest."

He says not to worry, he'll call around eight. He gets up to go, walks carefully around the sleeping girl, leans over, and without even looking to see if Nicole is watching, plants a nice sturdy kiss on my lips. I hear giggling, but it's not coming from Nicole, it's coming from the one on the floor who I thought was asleep. She sheds her sweater like a cocoon, springs up and sings, "Mr. Man kissed Mrs. Lady!"

Ted actually blushes as I walk him to the door, which only makes me like him all the more.

16

Artichoke Hearts

Talk about timing. Just as I watch Ted's car pull away, Papa's pulls up. I open the door and Mama coughs her way in. "Bronchitis *and* sinusitis," Papa says and leads her straight up to bed.

In the kitchen upstairs, Colina tries to feed Chelsea a bowl of *pastina* (tiny pasta) but without a high chair, she finds the task almost impossible. You can hardly believe the mess on the table and on Colina represents the doings of a one-year-old. I look at Chelsea and underneath the layer of pasta I see the same kind of flush on her cheeks that I saw on Mama's. "How's she doing?" I ask Colina as I spoon some *pastina* into bowls for Nicole and Morgy.

"Still no fever, but she won't eat much."

"Do you want to take her in tonight?"

"I think I'll wait until morning. Last time it was viral."

"You sure? You could be in for a long night."

"It's going to be long anyway."

"I want cow juice," Morgy says loudly, banging her cup on the table.

Colina shoots her a look. "Is that how we ask for milk, young lady?"

"I want cow juice, please."

"No, say: May I please have some cow juice—I mean milk—Aunt Bina."

"May I please have some cow-juice-I-mean-milk, Aunt Bina?"

"Sure honey," I say, grinning at Colina. I pour milk and then answer the ringing telephone.

"Are you coming? He keeps asking if you're still coming," Marina says, without even saying hi or asking how Mama is.

"Mama's got bronchitis-sinusitis," I inform her.

"Bronchitis *and* sinusitis," she corrects me. "They're two separate respiratory infections, Sabina. Which antibiotic did they give her?"

"I don't know, it was a big white pill."

"Well, I hope it's the one Ross sells."

I look at the rooster clock above the sink. Six-o-five. I tell Marina I'll be over in about an hour.

"You're going to Marina's?" Colina says to me. The tone in her voice leads me to believe she feels as if I am deserting her.

"Do you need help getting the girls down?" I ask, only because I know she'll say no, she can handle it.

"Yes, thank you. This one is not going to let me put her down for a second," she says, wiping pasta from Chelsea's cheeks. "And B? Could you stick them in the tub first? Please?"

***

By the time I pull Papa's car into Marina's driveway, it's ten to eight. I told Colina to please tell Ted when he called that I'd have to take a rain check on the movie and to please call me tomorrow. Colina got all bothered and guilty about it. "Why didn't you tell me you had a date? For Pete's sake, Sabina, I wouldn't have asked you to help with the girls if I'd known you had another date." Something about the way she said the word *another* made it seem as if a second date was something along the lines of extravagance.

Here is how Nino greets me: "Where have you been? I've been waiting all day long!" He looks pitiable lying there in his bed under layers of blankets. This whole house is so warm I find myself breaking out into a sweat. I sit on the edge of his bed and put my hand to his forehead. He's cool as a cucumber. "You mean to tell me that from the moment you woke up until the moment I walked in your door you have done absolutely nothing but wait for me?"

"Quit teasing me."

"Well?" I lean over and kiss his cheek, which he allows. He's about to wipe it off though, so I quickly say, "That's an unwipe-able."

"Awwww," he moans and leaves the kiss where it is.

"So what have you really been doing all day?"

He sits up a little straighter and pretends to think. "Well, Nickelodeon's had a Brady Bunch marathon—twelve straight hours of nothing but Marcia, Marcia, Marcia!"

"How educational!"

"Aunt B, you know what really stinks?" This is his favorite line, a question he interjects into every conversation.

"No, what really stinks?"

"That I couldn't go sledding. I mean the snow is perfect. It'll never be this perfect again. Ever. How was it anyway?"

"Oh, not so great. Nicole was a big chicken. You should have seen her. Cry. Cry. Cry." He smiles widely at this news.

"Morgy, too?"

"Actually Morgy did great. But I missed you." I poke my finger on his nose. "Shall we go next Saturday?"

"Can't. Gotta go to Jeremy Given's birthday party."

"How about the Saturday after that?"

"Duh! That's Christmas Eve."

"It is? It can't be. And don't "duh" me, please."

"Sorry."

"Well, I better get going then because I haven't finished my Christmas shopping. I'm done with everyone but you. What did you want again—the Barbie Pop-up Camper?"

"Aunt B!"

"No, no, it was the Barbie supermarket." He looks at me like I'm a girl, and so I decide to let up. "I know you want more LEGOS, but tell me, where are you going to put them?" LEGOS masterpieces occupy every inch of his shelf space.

He ignores my question. "You know what else stinks?"

I want to say, yes, Nino, I know what else stinks. What stinks is that just when Sabina Giovanotti (now forty years and two months old) finally gets a man in her life, all hell breaks loose and it seems as if no one can live without her. That's what stinks. That's what I think. What I say is this: "No, honey, what else?"

Home. On the couch, due to the fact that there is a sister and a baby in my bed. I can't sleep because of all the coughing. First Mama has a coughing jag and then the baby hacks in reply.

Colina left me a note saying that Ted called and asked that I call him in the morning. I can hardly read the number though because she must have spilled cough syrup or grape juice or something on the note—it's all purpley-smudged. I hear Chelsea coughing again and I can hear Colina sending a telepathic message to me from my bedroom: "It's times like this Sabina you should be thankful that you don't have kids."

I should be lying here thinking about Ted, about the nice time we had today. Instead, I'm feeling like I let some people down today. Like Nino. And Colina. And Mama. And every time I hear that baby cough I think that I should have insisted that Colina take her to the clinic.

I can see the kitchen rooster clock from here. It's either one-fifteen or three-o-five, I can't tell which. Either way, I've been awake for hours. I'm restless. And I'm worried about Nino.

He's seeing "scaries" again. He swears people are looking in his windows or breaking into the house. Ross recently spent a fortune on new locks and dead bolts to appease him, but the kid has himself spooked. His older brothers haven't helped the situation, playing into Nino's fears whenever possible. And Nino's feeling threatened by Ted.

I'm lying here on this couch thinking about what I have done—I have spoiled them all. I've been available to everyone in my family all these years at beckon call. I've been chauffeur, nursemaid, cook, babysitter, tutor and cheerleader all these years. I'm not saying that anyone has taken advantage of me, because I've always wanted to be involved in their lives. It's just that I've been so accessible. I've been so dependable. Damn it, I've been so easy.

I hear footsteps and see Papa's silhouette. It's Sunday. He joins Mr. Maggio on Sunday mornings to make bread. That means it must be after three o'clock. He's trying to be quiet, to tiptoe even, but I whisper, "I'm awake Papa."

"How come?"

"Beats me."

"You want to bake some bread?"

"Sure." I'm in gray sweats, a tee shirt, and socks so all I need are my shoes. I grab them and follow him down to bread.

We are greeted by the voice of Perry Como singing Don MacLean's *And I Love Her So.* Mr. Maggio raises his eyebrows by way of a greeting. We've joined him just as he is shaping the dough—molding the risen dough into loaves. Some dough he has placed in proofing baskets, some in proofing cloths. I look at the marker board on the wall where he keeps meticulous track of his routine, logging his shaping and proofing times in the left column and his baking times in the right. It's a fiendish schedule, but he rises to the occasion (pun intended).

In wintertime, the six-hundred degree Fahrenheit heat from Papa's *dragone* oven is almost welcoming; in summer months it's oppressive. I watch Mr. Maggio move about the kitchen. His steps seem almost choreographed as he glides from work table to oven, manipulating dough one second, then stoking the oven, deftly moving around huge chunks of wood to prevent hot spots, and spritzing the oven with water.

Papa asks me to make Kalamata Olive Bread, so I pit and chop the olives, then rinse them and set them to drain. I pile two handfuls into the center of an oval of dough and then wrap the ends over to encase the olives. This bread is one of my favorites. I'm glad I came down. I feel better. I'm not even tired now. Making bread is one of my favorite things to do. I think it's so ethereal since it's the closest thing to creating a baby. The dough feels like flesh, soft and supple; when you touch it, it gives. The attention and lack of sleep that's required to make bread is like that of devoted parents. So is the joy you receive when you pull your creation from the wombs of the oven. And so I spend the rest of the early morning hours making little olive babies. When I use the peel to pull them out of the oven, I couldn't be more proud.

Once my loaves are cooling on the rack I look around for more work. But all of a sudden I feel as if I'm in the way, so I nod to Papa and head back upstairs leaving my olive bread offspring behind. Now I need sleep. I have to drag my legs up the steps.

When I open the kitchen door I find Nicole sitting all by herself at the table, her little sleeper-covered feet dangling from the chair. Her eyes are sparkling with tears. She's not startled when I walk in on her. "What's wrong sweetie?" I ask and squat down to talk face to face.

"Morgy peed on me."

"She what?"

"She peed the bed and it got on me."

"Oh, well that happens." I smooth her hair back, out of her eyes. "I used to wet the bed when I was little."

"You did? Why?"

"Because. Some kids can't help it. She'll outgrow it when she gets bigger, just like I did. Now let's get you and Morgy and the bed changed."

Afterward, I go back to the couch and get situated. I lie there until seven-thirty when I hear Colina go to the bathroom. Next thing I know she's standing over me. My eyes aren't even open yet but I can feel her presence.

"Sabina?" she whispers loudly.

"Yeah."

"What time does the walk-in clinic open on Sundays?"

I open my eyes. "One, I think."

With Chelsea in her arms she plops down in the chair next to the couch. "One?!" She sighs and rubs her eyes with her free hand. "Damn, it's going to be a long day."

I want to say, "You're telling me," but I just sit up and stare at the very pathetic sight of my emaciated sister and her feverish, wheezing child.

The rest of the day I spend cooking, playing nursemaid, and fielding phone calls. Colina and I took turns going to Mass. Thankfully, Colina was able to get a prescription called in for Chelsea and I went and picked it up. Finally I get a minute to myself to call Ted. He answers with a nice, pleasant *hello.* I am relieved. Once somebody fixed me up with a guy that answered the phone with a flat, nasal *yello,* and I know it sounds shallow, but I just had to hang up.

After asking me how Mama is, he says, "I move into my apartment tomorrow and I was wondering if after work you could come over and help me—get unpacked, hang up some things, show me which cupboard is for the plates and which is for the cereal. You know, that kind of stuff."

I'm nothing if not a quick thinker, so before I start feeling guilty about the time away from home, I say, "I'd love to."

***

Monday morning brings Rosa to the store to fill in while Mama is sick. "Am I glad to see you!" I say, hugging her tightly and taking her coat and scarf to hang up in the back. I whisper, "Are you sure you're up to working with you-know-who?"

"Piece of cake. Can of corn. Don't worry about me."

But I do, because even Rosa, who can hold her own with anyone, can get tangled in Aunt Lina's web. Aunt Lina comes out of the kitchen when she hears Rosa's voice and this is how she greets her: "Great! You're here! I've been asking your father for some kitchen help for months now and he's finally come through. Come on, now, get an apron and I'll show you what I want you to do. This is going to be great."

I hate to admit it but the morning runs pretty smoothly. Right before lunch, I'm refilling the toothpick dispenser when my cousin Jimmy shoves a piece of paper in my face. It's his restaurant review. He got an "A." And the best part is that his instructor has made only one change to the entire paper: he's crossed out the word *masticating* and he's written the word *chewing* above it. I want to say I-told-you-so but I don't. Instead I say, "This is great! I am so proud of you! Maybe instead of a reporter you should be a food writer."

"You know I never thought of it before, Bina, but it just might be the perfect thing for me." He smiles a big confident smile. I hand the review back and he folds it into twenty-fourths and slides it into his shirt pocket. "So, when do I get to meet this guy?" He raises and lowers his bushy eyebrows five or six times and I have to smile.

I'm about to say how about tonight when he picks me up at five, but then there's Ted walking through the door, five hours early, and so I say, "How about right now?" But I change my mind when I see that he's with his boss, Clay. He smiles at me when I wave, but when I walk over, I can tell by the way he's standing that something's wrong.

"Hello again," Clay says, friendly enough. "I enjoyed your mother's soup so much the other day, I decided to bring my colleague back again." (I know it was Aunt Lina's soup that Clay ate, but I'd just as soon let Mama get the credit.) "What's your soup today?"

"Sausage Tortellini," I say.

"Oh, wonderful," Clay says.

"And your other special?" Ted asks, addressing me as waitress.

"Fettuccine in garlic sauce with a stuffed artichoke."

"That's for me," Ted says and gives me a nice customer-sort of smile.

I ring them up. Clay pays, and I say, "Help yourself to the soft drinks." Then I storm into the kitchen to place their order.

In the thirty or so minutes that they're here, Ted doesn't so much as glance my way. I just don't get it. Unless he's ashamed that I'm a waitress, but I'm not really a waitress. It just looks like I am. And what if I was?

When I go to the kitchen to get Charlie Gradezzi his pasta and stuffed artichoke I find Aunt Lina lecturing Rosa on the correct way to trim the leaves of an artichoke. "I just don't like how yours look, Rosa, kind of jaggedy."

I'm nothing if not an escape artist, so I hightail it out of there with Charlie's order. After I serve him, I glance over at Ted's table. He's gone. They're both gone. He never even said good-bye. I say out loud, "How do you like that?"

Jimmy hears me and says, "How do you like what?"

"It was a rhetorical question."

"Oh," he says, then looks over at the table where Ted and Clay were sitting. "Hey, where's Ted? Weren't you going to introduce us?" I give him one of my looks and he says, "It was a rhetorical question."

My day has turned to dog poop, just like that. I trudge through the rest of the day. At four o'clock, after I lock the front door, I find that I have this incredible urge to hide. The best place available is the ladies' room, so that's where I go. I lock the door behind me, turn the water on hot and let the steam coat my angry skin. A headache commences in my right temple as I try to sort out the thoughts that are running chaotically through my head. Why did Ted act like he barely knew me? Why did he leave without saying good-bye? And most importantly, will he be showing up at five?

I say a prayer, asking for strength to get through the next few hours without losing my temper or putting my fist in contact with someone with red hair.

There's a loud knock on the door and then Aunt Lina's gravely voice says, "Sabina, are you in there?"

"No, I'm not," I say, surprised to find the words coming out of my mouth. Prolonged exposure to my Aunt Lina has proven hazardous to my health: I've become a cynic.

"Ha!" she says, "I knew it."

"Go away."

"Hey! Show some respect."

"Go away please."

"I have to go."

"Use the men's."

"For the love of God, Sabina, I'm going to wet myself."

I don't speak. I don't move. Finally I hear her footsteps and the door to the men's room close. I pat my face with a paper towel. "Ha!" I say to myself. "I finally won one."

But when I open the door, there she is, decked out in her bright purple tunic sweater and matching leggings—the fastest pee-er in the west.

"So tell me what's wrong."

"Geez, Aunt Lina, nothing is wrong. Where's Rosa?"

"Scrubbing pots. And with her bare naked hands. No rubber gloves. I told her, with her husband's money, she could get a manicure every week." She follows me to the kitchen. "What do you girls got against nice nails, anyway?"

The kitchen is hot and loud and steamy, with the dishwasher and the faucets running. Papa says: "There she is." I think he means me, but he's looking at Aunt Lina. "Lina, why don't you go? Rosa whipped this kitchen into shape in half the time it takes us. She's so quick."

"Well," Rosa says, "I'm used to whipping five kids into shape."

"Really, Lina, go," Papa says.

But Aunt Lina doesn't budge. She's afraid if she leaves, she'll miss something. She's right. She'll miss us complaining about her.

"I suppose you'll dock my pay."

"You're overpaid anyway, but I'm not docking your pay. I'm just trying to be nice. You worked hard. Go home. Put your feet up."

"My feet are fine. I'll go, but first I'm going upstairs to see how my sister is doing."

"Leave her alone," Papa yells after her, "she's just starting to feel better."

"Oh, shut up, Sunny," Aunt Lina yells back.

Papa smiles widely. "Maybe I will dock her pay."

After Jimmy and Rosa leave, Papa and I head upstairs. We are both surprised to hear Aunt Lina's voice coming from Mama's room.

"She's still here!" Papa says in a hoarse whisper.

"Poor Mama!" I whisper back.

On my way to the bathroom, I peek in Mama's room. What I see throws me a little off balance: Mama's sitting up in bed and Aunt Lina's sitting on the edge of the bed, *holding Mama's hand.* "I missed you today Luna," my aunt says, patting Mama's hand. "I didn't realize what a good thing we got going in that kitchen. We got a pace. We got rhythm."

I can't tell you how touched I am by this tender moment between my mother and my aunt. I'm so used to hearing harsh words from those bright red lips. I think I actually *like* Aunt Lina at this moment. I smile and turn to go run the water for my bath when I hear that aunt of mine say: "Yeah, I love that Rosa to pieces but the girl is slower than *babalucci*!"

***

This time, Ted is supposed to come upstairs to pick me up so Mama and Papa can meet him. Mama took a shower after Aunt Lina left and she looks better, some of the color has returned to her face. I'm still in my room trying to decide what to wear. I wish Colina was still here to advise me. She and the big girls are at Angie's for dinner. Chelsea's asleep in the spare room. Papa's in charge of her. He insisted on giving Colina a break. I'm sure jeans would be just fine—we're only going to Ted's apartment. He said he'd cook something for us there. I slip into some brown jeans and a tan colored, ribbed, mock-turtle neck sweater. I look in the mirror and frown. I'm blah. I guess this is why my sisters call me Miss Beige. I am partial to neutrals.

Papa and Mama are sitting in their chairs in the living room when the doorbell rings. I'm sitting on the coffee table, tying up my brown leather boots. I swallow the lump in my throat. Mama starts coughing.

"Hello, hello," Papa says as he opens the front door. He shakes Ted's hand. "Sunny Giovanotti. Good to meet you."

"Ted Kallista. Nice to meet you, too." He looks like an uncomfortable schoolboy. Probably a little rusty in the meet-the-parents department. Papa takes his coat and hangs it in the front closet. I wish he would have just laid it across a chair. Hanging up a coat implies an extended stay and I love my mother and father but I'd just like to get on our way. I'm much too old for this kind of stress.

I manage a smile and a "hi." Then I introduce Mama, or try to because she can't stop coughing. I'm afraid she'll wet her pants so I run to the kitchen and get her a glass of water. It does the trick and she apologizes and tells Ted to sit down and offers him a drink.

"I'll have what you're having," he says.

Papa says, "Water?!" like it's poison or something. "We have wine, beer, pop, coffee, tea."

"All right, you talked me into a cup of coffee, but only if it's already made." He turns his attention to Mama. "Sabina told me you've been under the weather. So many people are sick right now. Three in our office. And right before Christmas, too."

Mama says, "Well, I don't think I'm contagious anymore. I'm fever-free and have been on the antibiotic for more than twenty-four hours." Obviously, Mama's been talking to Marina.

I get up to go make coffee but Papa waves me back down. "I'll do it," he lips. It takes him forever, because of course the coffee is not made, but that gives Mama more time for friendly interrogation. Actually, I learn a lot about Ted myself. He tells Mama more than he's told me so far. I find out that both of his parents were from Greece, but he was born here. That his mother is in the same nursing home as one of Mama's friends. That his brother builds condominiums in Florida. Mama seems to like him, but when it comes up in the conversation that he is a trained chef, she goes crazy.

Papa brings out a thick, manly mug and hands it to Ted. "Careful, it's hot."

Mama says, "Sunny, Ted's a chef. A CIA graduate."

Papa's eyes open wide. He gives me a look. "I thought you said he was a free-lance writer."

Ted laughs and takes a sip of coffee. "I am a writer, Sunny. I guess my culinary career was never meant to be. It's a long story. A long boring story, but I'll tell you about it sometime. Besides, Luna, you're the one who can cook. Your café is great."

Papa is obviously impressed. "The CIA, huh?" And then I guess just to make conversation he says, "Our godson went to the CCA."

I almost stop breathing. My parents have hardly mentioned Vito's name in my presence in the past eighteen years and now Papa has to talk about him in front of Ted.

"Out in my old neck of the woods," Ted asks. "How'd he like it?"

"He liked it just fine," I say and add, "You know, Ted, we really better get going, uhmmm, because I can't stay too late tonight because I have to get up extra early tomorrow, so we'd better get going. If you don't mind."

Ted darts up a little too quickly. His coffee mug wobbles but doesn't spill and he is visibly relieved. "Of course," he says, "I've got an early day myself. It was good to meet you both. I hope I'll see you again soon."

I get his coat out of the closet and then mine. I'm thinking: this is not the same guy that was in the store today. Does he have a split personality or something? It must have something to do with his boss.

Papa shakes his hand. Mama says she better not shake his hand, just in case she's still contagious. We head down the front steps, then out into the bitter cold. In the car, Ted turns the heat—what will be heat—on high. "Your parents are great. Really warm people," he says, blowing into his un-gloved hands.

"My parents are great," I say.

"You're lucky."

"I know, I'm really blessed."

He pulls the car carefully out into the gray slush and says, with his eyes straight ahead, fixed on the road, "Okay, well, about this afternoon..."

I look over at his profile. I can see his breath as he speaks. And I say a silent prayer of thanks. I didn't want to have to ask.

"You probably think I'm a big jerk. And I almost called you before I came over, but then I thought this is better said in person."

"Well, to tell the truth, I am confused."

"I can imagine. I feel bad about it, too. Well, you know that I'm a writer but I've been intentionally evasive about exactly what I write and for which magazine."

"Yes, I've noticed that."

"Well, it's not been without good reason, believe me. See, I'm a food writer, a dining critic, for Chicago Magazine."

"Okay..."

"This is a crazy occupation, being a restaurant critic. The whole critique process is shrouded in secrecy. There's protocol, rules, codes, directives. You know what I mean, don't you?"

"No, I really don't," I say.

He keeps his eyes fixed on the road as he explains. "Well it has everything to do with being anonymous, working incognito. Here's how it works: there are four of us critics and we use pen names after our listings. You know what I mean, don't you? That little box at the bottom page of the reviews that gives the key to the symbols we use—like a little car means free parking and four stars means superlative, etcetera. Everything depends on our anonymity."

"I understand all of that, but I still don't get why you acted as if you didn't know me."

"It's a big no-no to fraternize with the restaurant owners, especially when you're reviewing them."

"Reviewing them? You mean us? You're reviewing us?"

"Yes, for this special section on Mom and Pop type ethnic places. That's why Clay wanted to come back today for lunch. It was between you and Mario's. Do you know Mario's on South Racine?"

"Yes, they're really good. But wait a minute, Mela's is going to be reviewed by Chicago Magazine? Papa's going to die! He's been obsessed with getting a review ever since Aunt Lina came. He is just going to die."

"Well, let's hope not, but I'm glad that he's going to be happy. But you can't tell him yet about what I do. As a matter of fact, please don't tell anyone in your family anything more than that I am a free-lance writer. You see this is such a funny business. You try so hard not to be recognized. Most critics think that being recognized affects the service and then the whole dining experience is changed. You want to be invisible. You shouldn't fraternize with the owners."

"Well, technically, I'm not an owner yet."

"Doesn't matter if you were the janitor. Someone would find out we were dating and would say I gave Mela's a positive review on that basis alone. It would be a bad thing for me—my credibility would be questioned—but it would also be a bad thing for Mela's. Plus, I'm telling you, Clay wouldn't like it."

We pull up to what I assume is his apartment complex. He inserts a card and the basement garage door goes up.

"Wow," I say. "I thought maybe you were ashamed that I was a waitress."

"You're not a waitress," he says, looking me right in the eye. "Not that there's anything wrong with being a waitress. As a matter of fact, I've dated a lot of waitresses."

"A lot?" I tease.

"A few. Okay two, but they were before I was a restaurant critic. This is really taboo."

"Hmmmm," I say. "I've never been involved in anything taboo before. Could you get fired?"

"I don't know. Maybe. Probably. Hell, I don't know. And I don't really care." He flashes me a smile and pulls into a stall. "But that's why Clay can't know about us."

"Not ever?"

"Not until after the March issue comes out."

"March?"

"That's when we'll review the Mom and Pop joints."

"March?"

He kills the engine and opens his door. "It's only a few months. And it doesn't mean we can't see each other, it just means Clay can't see us. That's all. Don't worry about it. But if he wants to eat at Mela's, you'll just have to treat me like a customer."

"And you'll just have to treat me like a waitress."

He takes my gloved hand and squeezes it. "Yes, but my most favorite waitress."

I look around the parking garage for—I don't know—Clay maybe? All of a sudden I feel like I'm doing something wrong. Like I've committed a crime or like I'm having an illicit affair. Couldn't this get complicated, I wonder, as I board the elevator, wishing for a wide-brimmed hat and a pair of dark glasses?

17

Grace After Meals

We've made it to his apartment without being noticed. At least I
think. Ted opens the door to his twenty-ninth floor apartment and I smell
fresh paint. He clicks on the light, kicks off his shoes, and then proceeds to
close every window blind in the place, as if Clay had Superman eyes. I
remove my boots and walk on tan carpet that is so cushiony slippers would
be redundant.

He tells me to please excuse the mess. "When I moved to San
Francisco it took me three months to get unpacked and another three before
I had anything up on the walls." He puts a CD into his player—Eric
Clapton again—and tells me to have a look around while he gets our dinner,
so that's what I do. The living room is sparsely filled with masculine
furniture: chocolate brown leather sofa and love seat, iron and glass coffee
and end tables, iron lamps. A study in neutrality. Nothing overpowers;

everything counterbalances. Definitely a "Mr. Beige" room. Come to think of it, I match this room perfectly.

There are boxes stacked everywhere waiting to be unpacked. His priorities are obvious, even typical for a guy. I'd bet money that he unpacked his stereo first and his computer second. He's got a few antique pieces—a large mission oak desk monopolized by his computer and scattered with papers (restaurant reviews?); a lawyer's bookcase not yet filled with books; a lovely Tiffany-look-alike lamp; a massive, crusty cast iron urn. Positioned near one of the floor to ceiling windows is a large black telescope, and I catch myself thinking, hmmm, either astronomer or voyeur.

"What smells so good?" I call to the kitchen, then think to myself, *oh my gosh, I can smell again!* I breathe deeply—my sense of smell has returned just as suddenly as it disappeared. Very strange. Is this some kind of sign?

"I just made a salad and some focaccia, that's all," he says as he joins me and hands me a glass of white wine. "Hope you don't mind if we eat here. I don't have a table yet."

I say it's fine and he insists that I sit while he fiddles in the kitchen. I listen to Eric Clapton while sipping my wine and think about how sad it was when his little son fell out of the window of his mother's high-rise apartment building.

Ted comes in balancing the salads and a plate with the focaccia. He sets them on the table and then goes back for the silverware, then goes back again for napkins. "I said I was a good cook, presentation is not my department." We sit on the floor, with our legs folded under the glass table.

"Mmmmm," I say. "This looks and smells delicious. When did you have time to make the bread?"

"I had the morning off, so I got the bread made, but then Clay called and said he wanted to eat at Mela's again. I'm sorry I had to act like I didn't know you. If there was time I would have called you first to warn you. You were ticked, weren't you?"

"Yes."

"It's a weird line of work, let me tell you."

"I'm beginning to see that. But glamorous too, right?"

"Ha! You'd think so. But the glamour wears off fast. It's hard work actually. You've got to have a strong stomach. The thing most people don't realize is that you eat a lot of really bad food. More bad food than good food. And you work all the time. Sometimes I eat out four nights a week and lunch everyday. Sometimes you spend twenty or thirty hours a week at a table. And most of the time, you bring people with you to help divert the attention from you, so you feel like you're always entertaining.

And in November when we're finishing the year-end issue, I eat out every night for a month."

"Wow. I guess I never looked at it that way. Just thought about eating at all the really great Chicago restaurants like Charlie Trotter's and Frontera/Topolobampo and Zinfandel and Arun's and The Pump Room."

"Yes, but more often you're eating in the "wanna-be" joints and believe me you don't wanna be. I've been doing this for so long—eight years for San Francisco Magazine—that I was actually considering giving it up, going back to freelancing, but then I got the offer from Chicago. So I'm still a hired belly."

"You know, I always wondered how it worked with dining critics. How do you make a reservation and pay the check?"

"We use fake names and corporate credit cards. See most people in this business—and I'm one of them—think that being recognized can affect all aspects of the dining experience. Some critics think that we're all kidding ourselves if we think we can remain anonymous, but all the years I reviewed for San Francisco Magazine I think I was recognized only twice."

"Fake names, as in an alias?"

"Yes, and disguises, too. I've grown my hair and beard out. Sometimes I'll wear a suit. Sometimes I'll deliberately dress sloppily. Sometimes I'll dress in black leather. I have two wigs, a few hats, a couple of moles. One time I wore a pillow under my shirt to simulate a beer belly but it kept shifting so I'm staying away from prosthetics. Grew a goatee once. And once on a dare, I even got my ear pierced, see?" He pulls at his earlobe. "And so every once in a while I'll wear an earring."

"Wow. You have to be part-actor, don't you."

"Oh, yes. There's a lot of theater in it. It can be a little dangerous, too. Give a bad review and watch out. I got punched in the face once—this guy said my review closed his restaurant down."

"Did it?"

"Well, yes, but honestly, it was on its way out. The guy was serving literally rotten food. I'm talking about inferior ingredients—questionable cuts of meat and vegetables one minute away from being spoiled."

"Weren't you scared?"

"It shook me up. But really, it was an isolated incident. Mostly you get hate letters. Once I got a sympathy card from some smart-ass who said he was sorry to hear that my taste buds had died."

I can't help but laugh.

"Oh, go ahead and laugh. They passed that card around the entire office. This friend of mine got recognized and then got harassing telephone calls at all hours of the night. That was scary because it went on for a couple of months. And this other critic, well, he got a rock thrown through his window," he says, pausing to laugh, "but he said that could have been his ex-girlfriend."

"Geez. I never imagined. So what are some of your names?"

"Can't tell."

"Oh, come on."

"Can't."

"Come on!"

"I really can't."

"Please?"

"Okay, but I'll have to kill you afterward."

"Fine."

"All right, but I mean it, you can't tell anyone. I've used Teddy Adonis a lot. Adonis was my ex-wife's maiden name."

I'm thinking, *Teddy?* Did he say Teddy? I'm not sure if I should tease him so instead I say, "Adonis, as in the Greek god of vegetables?"

"As in the Greek god of *vegetation*," he corrects me.

"Sorry. I guess I need a brush-up on the gods. I thought Venus was the god of vegetation."

Ted laughs. "Venus is the Roman counterpart to Adonis."

He doesn't seem to be bothered by all my questions. I just feel like I'm involved with an FBI agent or something. I turn my attention back to my salad, which is delicious. I can actually *taste* the olive oil and the balsamic vinegar—maybe I'm growing new taste buds and new olfactory bulbs. The focaccia is so good. I can't believe that Ted can bake bread. But I also can't help but think more about his job. "Tell me some of the other names."

He gets up and goes over to the hall table and grabs his wallet. He sits down next to me and passes me credit cards one by one. I read them out loud. "Teddy Adonis. David Santerlin. Matt Leonard. Trent Terril. Ted Kallista. George Nikkos. Reed Howard. Cal Adotti."

"Wow. How do you keep it all straight? How do you remember which name you made the reservation under?"

"It takes a lot of time and planning and phone work and good note-taking. The logistics of it all can be daunting. But in the end, it beats writing obits and chasing politicians around."

"So how many other critics work with you?"

Before he answers he darts up and goes over to the CD player. It's that song again, *Tears In Heaven,* the one Clapton wrote for his son. He flicks to the next song. He's got a real problem with that song.

"I'm the chief dining critic and we have seven contributing critics. There's an editor and a deputy editor and that makes up the Dining

Department at the magazine. Great people, all of them. I think I made the right move."

"Teddy, huh?"

"Yeah, Teddy. From infancy to third grade I was Theodore. In fourth grade I refused to answer to anything but Teddy. I was Teddy until I got my first job at the paper. My boss told me from then on I was Ted."

"You certainly are a guy with a lot of names. How do I know who's who?"

"They're just names, Sabina. I'm just me. You don't have to worry about a multiple personality disorder or anything. I know it's kind of weird. But actually, I'm really lucky. There are only a handful of serious restaurant reviewing positions in the entire country. You know what I think? I think we've been talking too much." He leans in to kiss me and I taste balsamic vinegar on his lips. I enjoy the kiss very much, but I can't help but wonder just who it is I am kissing: Ted Kallista, Teddy Adonis, Cal Adotti, or any of the others.

Truth be told, I'd rather kiss than eat, but I'm also scared out of my mind. The last time I was in a man's apartment, I was twenty-something. "Shall we finish dinner and get unpacking?" I say when we come up for air.

"I guess that is the excuse I used to lure you to my apartment, isn't it?" he says.

I wipe some lipstick from his chin. "Lipstick. Sorry."

"Hey, don't be sorry. It's been forever since I've had lipstick on my chin."

"And why is that? Haven't you been divorced for a long time?"

"Twelve years."

"So why no lipstick?"

We head to the kitchen with the dirty dishes as he explains. "I guess I should say there hasn't been any lipstick for about a year. But it seems like forever. I dated on and off since my divorce. Pretty serious with one woman for about three years, but she got tired of eating out all the time—she gained ten pounds the first year we dated. And she got tired of all the people we ate out with because when you're reviewing it's best to eat with three or four or five other people. Anyway, I've been going it alone for about a year. And for months now I've been traveling to Chicago every month or so to see my mother and get her set up in the nursing home, so there's been no time for lipstick."

"Oh, I'm sorry about your mother," I say as Ted takes the plates from me.

"Me too, but we had no choice. She broke her hip while she was still recovering from knee surgery. She pretends to hate it there. Drives me crazy. I visited her the other day and I see her in the community room laughing with some other ladies. The minute she sees me though, she puts on this pathetic, poor-little-me face. So I ask her, Ma, how you doing today and she says terrible. This hurts and that hurts and her phone didn't ring once all day. So I ask her, did you play Bingo today, isn't today Bingo day? And she says no, she couldn't bring herself to play. And so I ask the lady next to her, Martha, didn't you play Bingo today? And Martha looks at me with these obscure eyes and shakes her head no. Then my mom punches Martha in the arm and says: "Yes you did Martha; you sat right next to me."

"That is so cute!" I say.

"Right, real cute. See why see reminds me of your Aunt Lucy?" He rinses the dishes and I load them into his bachelor-empty dishwasher.

"Really though, I've been a pathetic workaholic for the last two or three years. I was never like that before, when I was married. It was Lizette who worked like there was no tomorrow. Anyway, one of the big reasons I wanted to move back here was for the connections, the friendships. I've still got a lot of friends in town. Anyway, it seemed like something was calling me back home. It wasn't you, was it?"

"How could it have been? I didn't even know you yet, Ted-Teddy-Cal."

"Mr. Man to you," he says, poking my nose with his index finger.

"Hey, we'd better get unpacking. Where do you want to start?"

"The bedroom?" he says with a loopy grin.

"How about in here? That would be the most practical."

"Oh, don't tell me you're a practical girl."

We start unpacking the dishes. Ted starts whistling, just like Papa, a pleasant, pure whistle. The tune is *My Kind of Town* and I'm wondering if the melody came to him because he was talking about Chicago calling him back home. Maybe it *was* me calling him and I just didn't know his name. Or names.

You would never know this guy was a trained chef. He was right when he said presentation was not his department. The guy owns zippo gadgets. He's got only the basics: a cutting board, a good knife set, some stainless steel mixing bowls, some utensils, casserole dishes, some bake ware, and good cookware. One of these. Two of that. Mismatched wine glasses. Three different place settings of dishes.

He must notice me eyeing his kitchen stuff because he says, "I didn't leave with much from the divorce. I shouldn't say that, I left with my sanity intact. But I let her keep all the wedding-poop—china, crystal, flatware. I didn't want it. What would I do with it?"

Unpacking all this kitchen stuff makes me think of Vito's little brownstone apartment. Our kitchen was going to be better equipped than a luxury Cadillac. This kitchen that I'm standing in looks like it belongs to someone who eats cold pork and beans out of a can, standing up.

"My mother keeps buying me gift certificates to William Sonoma. She's the type that puts a candle and a place card on the table even when she's the only one eating."

I give him a look.

"I'm not kidding."

I give him another look.

He smiles. "Okay, I am, but just barely. Anyway, I just use the gift certificates to buy stuff for my friends. I don't cook much for myself since I eat out so much. That and it's depressing to cook for one person. The portions look so pitiful. Your plate screams, "You're alone!" When I do cook, it's to experiment with cuisines that I'm not familiar with so I know how things should taste."

We finish the kitchen in no time. Ted rubs his hands together. "Well, shall we move on to the bedroom?" Again, a twinkly smile.

"How about the living room? I can't stand to see an empty bookcase."

"That's funny, I can't stand to see an empty bed. But that's okay, we can save the bedroom for last."

"Ted!"

"You know I'm just kidding don't you?"

"How would I? After all, I just recently found out about your multiple personalities."

"Well, that shouldn't worry you, all of us are good in bed."

"Ted!"

"Oh, I'm just kidding. I like to see you blush."

"I don't blush."

"Yes, you do."

I touch my cheeks as we head for the living room. They do feel warm. "It's the wine. Wine always warms up my cheeks."

I dig into a box of books. Mystery novels. Biographies. Steinbeck. Hemingway. Creighton. Grisham. Ted has more books then shelf space. He keeps dragging more and more boxes over to me. This one is full of cookbooks, tons of cookbooks. "Do you want these arranged in any special way?" I ask, sitting among hills and mountains of books.

"Oh, yeah, good thinking. I keep all the cookbooks in this bookcase, and I have another one in my bedroom for the novels and other books."

"Look at all these cookbooks! Did you rob a bookstore? And I thought I had quite a collection."

"Tools of the trade," he says. "Over there by the window are two boxes full of nothing but restaurant menus that I've collected over the years."

"Wow! That's amazing! I collect restaurant menus, too!"

"Really? I've never known anyone—other than food critics—that collects menus. Got any good ones?"

"Jean Georges, Chez Panisse, Le Francais... Customers get them for me from all over the place."

"Hmmmm, maybe we can trade them like baseball cards."

I come to a box of magazines. "Where would you like these?"

He comes over and peeks in the box. "Oh, those. I should probably just pitch the whole box but it happens to represent my life's work."

"Wow! You have articles in all of these?" I pick them up one by one: *Cuisine, Cooking Light, House Beautiful, Food & Wine, Cook's Illustrated, Fine Cooking.* I rifle through the table of contents: "Trendy Italian Wines" by Ted Kallista; "And For Dessert..." by Ted Kallista; "Midnight Snacks" by Ted Kallista; "Pasta—Queen of the Table," by Ted Kallista, "A Zeal For Veal" by Ted Kallista.

"'Tempting Openers and Satisfying Closers?'" I quote from one magazine.

"Oh please, just because you write the article doesn't mean you get to entitle it. I fought with the editor on that one. It was a piece on appetizers and desserts but that title made it sound like an essay on foreplay and climax."

He squats down next to me. "Awww, you really don't want to see these, do you? It's like showing someone your baby pictures."

"I'd like to see those, too."

"Sure, they're in a box in my bedroom."

"You are bad."

"I know, I know. But you can't blame a guy for trying, can you?"

And I can't. I always secretly wished Vito would have tried a little harder. I know he was only trying to respect my wishes but sometimes I wondered if the only drive he had was for food. All his passion was wasted on fodder. Looking back, I can see that ours was a culinary romance: I was in love with him and he was in love with food.

I finish with the bookcase and Ted finishes moving boxes to the right rooms. "You thirsty? Want more wine? Or a pop? Water? Coffee? Oh, I almost forgot. I made dessert."

"You made dessert?" I follow him into the kitchen. He opens the refrigerator and there, behind a quart of milk and a million condiments is a beautiful *panna cotta*, a rich, delicious dessert, which is Italian custard, literally "cooked cream."

"You made me *panna cotta*! Wow! You must really like me."

"*You like me, you really like me,*" he says, providing a bad imitation of Sally Fields at the Oscars. "I do really like you. That and it's so easy to make."

It is easy. You just dissolve a packet of unflavored gelatin in water, add sugar, cream, and milk and cook slowly over low heat. Mama serves it with a fruit compote. It's so wonderful.

We eat our *panna cotta* bachelor-style: sitting on top of the kitchen counter. Ted has served it with a raspberry sauce, apologizing that he couldn't get fresh berries this time of year.

"Oh my God," I say when the custard slides down my throat. "Don't tell my mother, but this is even better than hers. Okay, what's your secret?"

"Buttermilk, instead of whole milk. It's lower in fat and adds a certain zip."

"It's delicious. Thank you for cooking for me."

"No, thank you for helping me."

"I haven't done that much."

"Wow," he says, glancing at his watch, "It's nine o'clock. Did you really need to get home early, or were you just saying that?"

"I was just saying that. My parents like to talk. A lot. It's just embarrassing, you know, that I still live with them."

"Why do you? If I can ask."

He takes my plate and spoon from me and puts it in the sink with his. "Let's go get comfortable," he says and I am relieved to see that he means on the sofa. "Don't get me wrong—I don't think that there's anything wrong with living with your parents, but I mean, look at you. I can't believe someone hasn't snatched you up. When I first laid eyes on you at the Four Seasons, I just knew you were married."

"You're embarrassing me."

We sit at either end of the sofa, half lying, half sitting, foot to foot, so we can see each other as we talk.

"Come on, Sabina, it's story time. Tell me what's been going on with you and then I'll show you my baby pictures."

"Oh, all right. There's not much to tell, really. I was engaged. We were proverbial childhood sweethearts. Our families had been friends forever. My parents were his godparents. But it didn't work out. Well, he left me, my fiancé, ex-fiancé, a week before our wedding."

"No!"

"Yes. Well, in all honestly, I called off the wedding a week before, okay, a week and a half before. Anyway, he ran away. He ran away fast."

"Why'd you call it off?"

"It's complicated," I say, hoping he'll leave it at that.

"I'm okay with complicated."

I don't know how to respond to this statement, so I say, "Well, you can't get any more complicated than this. See three weeks before our wedding I find out he never went to get fitted for his tuxedo, so I tell him to go and get fitted. He does but he gets in a terrible car accident on the way back. It was tragic, someone was killed but it wasn't his fault. Have you ever heard of Post Traumatic Stress Disorder?"

Ted sits up a little straighter. "As a matter of fact, I have."

"Well, he gets it, or develops it, or whatever. And he just cannot handle it all, so instead of getting help, he just lies in bed and contemplates the ceiling. He wouldn't talk to anyone, barely ate. He was just engulfed in guilt and self-pity. So when he got home from the hospital, one week before the wedding, I ask him, what should we do? Can he make it down the aisle? Or should we postpone the wedding until he is physically and emotionally better. No answer. So I just told him that I was going to call it off until he got better. He let me walk out of there, knowing what I was going to do. Then the next day, he gets out of bed easily enough, and takes off with his best friend. Takes half of the little money we'd put away in a savings account, heads to Pennsylvania, and hangs out with his friend until his friend's roommate kicks him out. Then he lived with his sister in Atlanta for a while. I lost track of him after that."

"Man."

"I know. Just left me, our wedding, our apartment, our business. We were just about to open this dessert cafe. You know where *Volare* is?"

"Yeah?"

"That was going to be our place. He'd put so much money into it. He'd put everything into it. He just left his whole life."

"Man."

"I know. So I wait for him. He comes back months later to appear in court, so I see him, talk to him for exactly three minutes. He was so messed up. But our short conversation gives me some hope that he'll get better and that there's still a chance for us. So I wait and I wait and finally I get some counseling and I think I'm no longer waiting. I date but it doesn't feel right, like I'm cheating on him or something. What if he comes back? What if he gets better and comes back?" I lower my voice a little, because now I'm getting a little worked up here. Getting angry at Vito all over again. "So eighteen years go by and I still live at home and work at the store because, because, I don't know really, it's either because I want to be there, right where he can find me if he ever gets back, or else it's just that I'm frozen in this unforgiving state where I can't move, can't make decisions about my own future. It's also because I love my parents and they're old-fashioned enough to think a daughter should live at home until she's married. That and I'm needed—someone has to take over the business, carry on the tradition. But I can't carry on anything because I can't move on. I mean people need closure, don't they? He's never contacted me. In all these years. Not a note, not a measly post-card."

I'm crying now, the tears are hot on my face. Ted sits up and scoots over to me. His arms are around me; his head is in my hair. "Go ahead, cry it out. Get it out. It's all right. It's all right."

My eyes are glued shut. I haven't the courage to open them. What have I done? I don't allow myself to cry in front of people, especially about Vito. I open my eyes. We are forehead-to-forehead, nose-to-nose. I think my nose may have just dripped on his shirt. "I am so sorry. I don't know what's come over me. I never talk about this. I never cry about this. It's been buried for years."

"Don't be sorry. It's okay. We're all black and blue. Sometimes you just can't see the bruises."

"I feel stupid. I should have said I live at home because I get to eat for free."

He laughs, but his eyes are serious. "He never contacted you, all these years? That's insane." He's quiet for a minute, then he says, "Sabina, I have to ask: are you still in love with him?"

I throw my head back and look up at the ceiling as if the answer could be found in the freshly painted eggshell white swirls. I don't answer right away. "That's the question that I've been asking myself all these years. If I say no, it's not quite true, because do you stop loving someone just because he's not with you? And if I say yes, that's not true either, because if I was still in love with him, I would be in love with the twenty-two year old boy he was when he left. He's forty now, if he's even still alive, and so the person that I loved doesn't even exist anymore, right?"

"Right." He kisses my tears. "So is that a *no*?"

"I think so. Yes, it's a no. I couldn't possibly be in love with him anymore."

"Good."

I sit up, blot my eyes. I'm sure my mascara is striping my cheeks. He kisses me and I kiss back with a passion that I didn't know I had in me. We are entwined, enfolded. I can't tell which parts are me and which are him. We start to slip on the leather and Ted whispers, "Do you want to go in my room, Sabina?"

And I do, I really do, every cell in my body wants to go. I break away from him and say, "Ted, I have to tell you one more thing." A look of worry scurries across his face. The poor guy's probably thinking how I seemed so nice and normal at first.

"What?"

"I've only made love once in my entire life. With him. When we were eighteen. Once and only once."

He laughs. Out loud even. I'm horrified. I want to crawl inside one of the boxes I just unpacked. I hide my face with my hands.

"Oh, Sabina, are you real?" He asks, gently peeling my hands from my face and then holding my face in his hands. "You are wonderful! Loyal and honest." He shakes his head. "The poor bastard."

"Who?"

"Your ex-fiancé. I feel bad for him, I really do. He has no idea who he left behind."

It's comfortable here, on his sofa, with my head in his lap. He's a solid man, but soft, too. His hands are large but his fingers are slender, with nicely shaped nail beds. Hands that I think I'd like touching my skin. I must doze off for a bit, because next thing I know, Ted is gently shaking me. "Hey, you. Hey. Come on, wake up. I'll take you home."

We're both quiet in the car. I'm looking out the side window, thinking that maybe I blew it tonight, dropping the Vito bomb on him the way I did. I mean let's face it, I come with a trail of baggage. Roberta Flack's song *Killing Me Softly* is playing on the radio. I love that song. I listen now and am visited by the thought that maybe that's what Vito did to me: killed me softly, quietly, one year at a time. I've been only half-living my life. Not really seeing, smelling, or tasting. It's exhausting to think about. A yawn escapes before I can suppress it.

"Tired?" he asks.

"A little."

He parks at my house, turns off the lights and the radio, but keeps the engine running.

"Thanks for everything," I say. "You made such a nice dinner. And the dessert, well, that will be hard to top."

"It was fun to cook for someone who can appreciate it but isn't intimidated by it. I dated a woman once who demanded that I stop cooking for her, said I was putting her cooking to shame."

"Crazy Californians," is all I can think of to say. But then I gain composure and say, "Listen, I'm sorry I lost it tonight. I don't know what came over me. I don't usually cry so easily."

He grabs my hand. "Hey, look, we all have baggage. *I* have baggage."

"You probably have carry-on."

"I wish. I've got suitcases. I've been through therapy."

"Really?"

"Years of it."

"Your divorce?"

"That was a big part of it. But then stuff about my father and my stepfather came out, you know, that family dynamics crap, the dysfunctional shit. But the big thing was, well, we, my ex-wife and I, we, we lost a baby, Sabina, a little girl, and it just about did the both of us in."

"Oh, Ted, I'm so sorry." He swallows hard and I can see that he can't say anything more. I squeeze his hand, rub his arm. I feel awful for trying to minimize his pain into carry-on luggage.

"It was a long time ago. Awww shit. You know what I think? I think everyone is screwed up. It's just a matter of degrees. By the time you get to be our age, and dating, you just look for someone who's screwed up in about equal proportions to yourself, like a compatible craziness or something. Then maybe there's a chance. Damn, that sounds cynical, doesn't it?"

"The scary thing is that it doesn't. It sounds just about right."

He fakes a brightening up. "Hey, what are you doing for Christmas anyway?"

"We all go to my sister Rosa the rich one's for dinner. Her house turns into a restaurant and department store all in one. Commercialism with a capital "Come." It's not a pretty sight. What about you?"

"Well, there'll be a big splash at the nursing home."

"Oh, Christmas in a nursing home is so sad."

"Actually the splash is on Christmas Eve. She'll be hell on wheels if I don't show."

"You have to show. It's Christmas. She's your mother."

"I know, but think of the food."

"I know."

"She's driving me crazy, now that I'm back. She's got my number at the magazine and she calls me five, six times a day, just to say something like, "A Pepsi would taste good right about now, Teddy." My mother, the only octogenarian who drinks Pepsi."

"Hey, can I call you Teddy?"

"Hell no, you can't. It's Mr. Man, remember? Anyway you totally missed my hint about Christmas."

"You want to come to Rosa's for Christmas?"

"Yes."

"Well, come then, by all means."

"Okay, I will."

"You totally missed my hint about Christmas Eve."

"You want to come to the splash?"

"Sure."

"You can't."

"Why not?"

"I'm not ready for you to meet my mother. She might scare you away. You don't like me enough yet to meet my mother."

I smile. "Who says?"

***

In my new bed again—the couch. I got home around eleven-thirty to a house engulfed in sleep. My thoughts are warding off sleep, the way thoughts will do until you give them their due consideration. I'm thinking about tonight. Of course about Ted, but what he'd said about—what did he call it—compatible craziness? I'm falling fast for him, but obviously we need to know more about each other. I don't even know his favorite color. I hear my little Aunt Lina devil on my left shoulder say, "Who the hell cares about his favorite color, you *stupido*. It's probably blue. All men love blue." Geez, I think, even an imaginary Aunt Lina is blunt and bossy.

How sad that he and his wife lost a baby. I wonder what happened. Miscarriage, stillbirth, SIDS, a terminal illness? Maybe his wife had had a difficult time getting pregnant and then maybe after they lost their baby they either couldn't have more children, or maybe they just couldn't bring themselves to have more children. Or maybe one of them blamed the other one for the child's death. Oh God, I pray, that *is* some heavy baggage.

The only comfortable position I can find on this couch is on my back, with my hands folded corpse-like on my stomach. Up until Vito's mother died, this was my favorite sleeping position. But after attending Sara's visitation, and seeing her in that coffin, it spooked me. I started forcing myself to turn over on my side. I was afraid that if I slept in the corpse position I might die in the night. Not so much superstitious as super-stupid. Sorry, it's just me. But here on the couch, the corpse position is the most comfortable position. So I resign myself.

I know what you are thinking: that I should discuss these hang-ups with a professional. Well, I have. It was Marina who made me see a psychiatrist. She's of the attitude that her nursing expertise runs the gamut of medical specialties: internal medicine, pediatrics, cardiology, allergy, and behavioral medicine.

It was my own fault really, how I got roped into it. After Vito left, there was nothing to do but throw myself into the store. And so I did, learning everything about the business, partly to busy myself and partly in an attempt to make it up to Papa for Vito. After all, Papa had put a lot of time and money into his godson, with absolutely no return on his investment. I wanted to show Papa that it was me all along who wanted to take over the business some day.

I started spending time with Papa and Mr. Maggio in the mornings. Sometimes, I'd even beat Papa downstairs. The kitchen was quiet like a confessional and working along side of Mr. Mute himself was like a good penance. I fell into a perfect routine: got up at three, baked until seven when the store opened, worked until five, then dropped dead into bed at seven-thirty, right after watching Wheel-Of-Fortune with Mama and Papa. No worries about a social life.

My other sisters accepted that this is what I wanted to do, what I had always wanted to do. But Marina got it in her head that I was hiding out, got it in her head that I should be dating. And so that's when the string of blind dates began. And I've already told you about how some of those turned out. But I don't think I mentioned this one guy, Ross's friend. I can't even remember his name now, it may have been Craig or Greg, but he met me at *Thank God It's Friday's* one night for dinner and we actually had a fun time. He was friendly and quick-witted and not altogether bad looking. I think he may have even been actually leading up to asking me out again. But then I said something stupid like I was still involved with someone. How was I to know that he would tell Ross and Ross would tell the nurse and the nurse would tell Papa that daughter *numero tre* was in need of some quick and cheap psychotherapy because she thinks she is still involved with Vito. I told Marina that he misunderstood me, that I'd said I was still *emotionally involved* with someone. I think Marina was worried that Vito had become the equivalent of an imaginary friend so she set me up with an appointment to see Dr. Richard.

He started our first session with this question: "What brings you here to see me, Miss Giovanotti?"

The answer was easy enough: "My sister, Marina."

The second question was: "What do you do, Miss Giovanotti?" I should have never answered, because once I told him that I worked in my father's store, the food metaphors started coming out of the woodwork.

We spent weeks on the subject of my self-esteem. Did I have any? What people or things gave it to me? How could I get more? Did I see myself as a wedding cake or a cupcake?

Then we went weeks on birth order, all the middle child psychobabble. Did I feel left out, sandwiched like an Oreo cookie, or more like ham between two slices of rye? All I got from this guy was hungry.

Diagnosis may be difficult, he told me. I had no clinical symptoms to speak of. It would be a diagnosis of exclusion. Rule out everything else: clinical depression, generalized anxiety disorder, agoraphobia, panic disorder, schizophrenia, delusions of grandeur, obsessive compulsive disorder.

"What do you think is wrong with you, Sabina?" he asked.

"Is there such a thing as a waiting disorder?" I asked him. Believe it or not he actually flipped through his DSM-IV manual, but that may have been purely for my benefit alone. The thing is, even back then I knew that waiting was not a benign action—it was a charged state of being. The only state of being I knew.

He did one thing for me, that Dr. Richard, I'll give him that much. At one point I told him I needed closure. So he had me write a letter to myself from Vito, the letter that Vito should have written to me when he left. The letter I'd thought I'd found at his apartment. My version was saccharine sweet, full of mush, and pretty, sentimental words that would never have come from Vito's lips, but it's what I thought I needed to hear:

Dear Bina,

How did this happen? One minute you're driving along to Pizza Fantastica to bring home a nice pie for your fiancée who is peeved at you for forgetting to get fitted for your tuxedo, and the next minute you're a cannonball ricocheting through the air, smashing to smithereens the lives of some innocent people. People who cannot forgive you.

I've always known that I couldn't live without love, but there is NO living without forgiveness. Isn't that the whole reason Jesus came, Bina?

Here's the thing: my life as I know it is over. There was a time when a beautiful loaf of bread could move me to tears, or a sublime dessert could lift my soul straight to heaven. All of a sudden, that passion is gone. How could food have been so important to me? I see now that I put my passion for food even before you at times. I'm sorry for that. How could I have been so stupid, so misguided?

You are right in calling off the wedding. This is for the best. I am no longer the person you knew, but a haunted man. I am not well. Mikey told me all about this posttraumatic stress stuff and I see a long hard recovery ahead.

Bina, I had to write this fast—before I lost the nerve. I can't saddle you with all this emotional baggage. The crossed out parts are where I started to say stupid stuff like wait for me until I get better, or I'll come home some day when I am whole again, but that's not fair to you. I can't do that to you. So instead, I say this with as much pain as if there were a sword in my belly: go on with your life and forget me. Find someone who will love you and who will give you the children you long for—for I know that I will never be emotionally able to father a child. That little girl's face is branded upon my heart and soul. When I look out of my eyes, I see hers. Pray for me, Bina, that somehow I can get over this pain, that even if the little girl's parents won't forgive me, that I can somehow forgive myself.

Please forgive me. I will love you forever.

I couldn't bring myself to sign his name to my self-serving words, but Dr. Richard said there would be no closure without a signature. So I printed the letters V, I, T and O, but it wasn't his signature. I couldn't do that.

Two thousand three hundred thirty-four dollars later, this is what the good doctor came up with: Life is like a six-course dinner. Some people get it all—antipasto, soup, salad, main entrée, cheese, and dessert. Some people just get a few courses. Some people only get one or two. In this scenario, supposedly I got one—dessert, which I ate first, like a child, out-of-order. I guess Vito was like the first bite of the best brownie in the world. After him, the law of diminishing returns came into play and everyone else was a disappointment. And so Dr. Richard's message was that I should grow up, forget about dessert and move on to the main course. I am not kidding you. This is what I shelled out good money to hear, that I was stealing the sweets.

And I never got my closure. That's why my room is still filled with Vito paraphernalia. The fact is, the letter made me feel better, but over the years, something bad happened: I began to think that Vito really did write that letter. On a conscious level, I knew I wrote it. But somewhere, under the layers, I would forget the author and just remember the words.

I think Vito got his closure though. I told Ted that Vito has never contacted me in all these years, but I guess I should have told him about the letter Mama got from Vito's sister Becky about five years after he'd been gone. One day I was in the store, sweeping, when Mama came out of the kitchen, holding worry on her face. She didn't say anything, just reached into the pocket of her apron and pulled out an envelope that'd been folded in half. She said, "This came yesterday," and handed it to me. It was addressed to "Mrs. L. Giovanotti." The return address was Atlanta, Georgia. Inside was a letter on plain college lined paper, and when I unfolded it, a check fell out and onto the floor. I bent to pick it up, the blood rushing to my head, mingling with the curiosity that had settled there. The check was for two thousand dollars and was signed by Becky. I opened her letter expecting it to be terse and direct, but surprisingly, it was warmer than I thought it would be. She did get her dig in at the end though.

Dear Aunt Luna,

Enclosed please find a check from Vito for two thousand dollars. He hopes this will cover some of the money that you and Uncle Sunny lost. I'm sorry things turned out the way they did, but after losing both of my parents, nothing surprises me anymore

I'm pregnant, due in June. I want a girl so badly—I don't know what I would do with a boy.

My brother desperately needs your prayers. You wouldn't know him if you saw him. Please don't be mad at him.

It seems like yesterday, we were sitting at your dining room table eating pasta. I guess life takes its turns.

Give my best to Uncle Sunny and the girls. Angie and Sabina will be pleased to know that Jerome has been promoted to station manager. Love, Becky

I looked up from the letter and met Mama's eyes. She nodded and so I tore up the check into minuscule pieces, and threw them into the air like confetti. They fluttered down around me, and when the last piece fell at my feet, I returned to my sweeping, blending the check confetti in with the dirt and the dust. I guess Vito and I both thought closure was a thing that could be bought.

Virgie's the one who helped me sort things out. She told me that Dr. Richard was the crazy one. "Everybody knows that people go into the field of psychiatry because they want to psychoanalyze themselves. All that stuff about eating dessert first is a bunch of bull crap. And so is all the stuff about some people getting six courses and some only one. Trust me, Bina, you'll get all the courses," she told me one night while we sat in the movie theater watching the credits to Mel Gibson's latest movie. "You're just between courses right now, that's all." And I've been hoping she is right.

I'm finally sleepy. Ted is a good man, I tell myself as I fade out. He's sweet, funny, good-looking, talented, and a gentleman to boot. Plus, he's wounded. But does that make him a breadman? I'm not sure yet. And in that layer of space between sleep and wakefulness, I allow myself to drown in the age-old fantasy that has faced many a daytime TV leading lady: the choice. What if Vito arrived at my doorstep today? What would I do? Who would I choose? These are the bizarre thoughts that visit me in my dreams. I wake up craving a double cheeseburger with extra pickles and mustard and I'd love to ask Dr. Richard—does that mean anything?

18

Hoarding Sweets

I'm in my room, lying on the floor, on my stomach with my head under my bed. I'm sort of stuck here. Well, I'm not physically stuck but in my search for the LEGOS set I bought Nino for Christmas, I have discovered a floral covered hat box, and I can't decide if I should open it or not. Actually, I'm lying when I say *discover*—the only thing I've discovered under here is dust. I know damn well that this box is under my bed, the same place it has been for years.

The box contains photographs of Vito. His whole life is in here. Baby pictures, childhood pictures, and all thirteen of his school pictures. If you stacked his school pictures from youngest to oldest and then riffled them by sliding your thumb along the edges of the photographs, you'd get a motion picture of Vito, morphing before your very eyes from age five to eighteen.

If I bring the box up into the light, I'll lose hours. You can get lost in this box, in that face, in those eyes. No, I tell myself, I have presents to wrap. My bed is piled with gifts. There is even a gift for Ted. Think about Ted, I tell myself. But it scares me to think about Ted. I get all worked up when I think about Ted. I mean who couldn't fall in love with a guy that's looking for a girl who's screwed up to the same degree that he is? I mean, really, how can you get any more romantic than that? Any more honest. Any more real.

I know I need to put things *to* bed and not *under* my bed. To move on, to make room in my life for this man. He's a good man. But I am scared. I just can't seem to gage how strong my heart is. Vito gave me a heart attack. I survived it, but I'm not sure if I could live through another.

Plus, at my age you get settled into your aloneness. You worry about who would want you, who would have you. I've got my bad habits and they cling to me like a good cream sauce. I won't empty a wastebasket until it's heaping—I'll walk right by without a thought. From time to time I allow myself to entertain irrational fears: What if something happens to my nieces or nephews while they are in my care? What if I have hurt someone deeply and I don't even know it? There's more. I'm constantly picking away at the clear acrylic nail hardening topcoat that I brush on my fingernails at night. I tend to put too much weight into first impressions. I'm a late-night Internet junkie. I criticize people's photographs: "You should have used 400 instead of 200 film." I vote for unfamiliar local political candidates solely on the basis of whether or not I like their names. I'm wishy-washy on certain issues: I vacillate between a perfectly natural female longing for a full length black mink coat and an equally perfectly natural disgust for the sacrifice of little furry animals for a garment that makes nothing but a snobbish social statement. (Still, I look at and try on Rosa's beautiful fur coat any time I get the chance.) I dress like a bag lady for bedtime. I spend an inordinate amount of my life in the bathtub. I'm not assertive enough. I'm too damn loyal. I let people walk all over me. I'm honest and patient to an absolute fault. Not to mention, I'm a terrible food snob. If I were twenty and not forty, someone might overlook this list. As it is, I'm hoping Ted will be open to taking me "as is."

I need air. I crawl out from under the bed, pulling the box along with me. I throw it on the bed, as if it were just another gift to wrap. I make a deal with myself: if I finish my wrapping before midnight, I'll just take a quick peek. But when I go to move the box off to the side of the bed, it tips and out pours Vito in good ol' black and white. Oh, here's one of my favorites: Vito with his nephew Benny on his shoulders. Vito's whole face is lit up in laughter. He was always happiest when he was cooking or playing with his nieces and nephews. I love this one, too. I took this picture one Easter at our house. Vito is hugging Mama. You can't see Mama's face because her back is to the camera, but you can see Vito's face. He's holding her tight and his eyes are squeezed shut. God, how he loved my mother. Looking at this picture, I can almost feel him hugging me.

This one's from Rosa and Ed's wedding. I was a bridesmaid and Vito was an usher. These I took at his graduation from the CCA. His hair was so short, it had no curl at all. This one's from a family picnic. Here's one when we went sailing on Mikey Pinotta's father's catamaran.

The camera always blessed him, even in profile. Captured on film, his skin looked smooth and clear; his nose, strong and regal; his eyes, intelligent and sparkly. I look closely at the eyes, always at the eyes. Looking for clues that I may have missed. Were there signs that I should have seen? Maybe what I always took for sparks of passion in his eyes were really sparks of pain.

I realize that I don't have the stomach for the whole box tonight. I return all but two pictures: the one of Vito hugging Mama and a photograph of the two of us at his graduation. I prop these two up against the box and direct my attention to the gifts that need wrapping. Once again I have gone overboard with Christmas gifts for the nieces and nephews. I wrap and tape and tie ribbon until my fingers ache. Why do I always wait until the last minute to wrap?

I've got to go to the bathroom, but I promised myself that I would not leave this room. I'm afraid that if I do, even to go pee, I'll lose my bed. Colina keeps apologizing about taking my bed; even so, she seems to end up in it almost every night. My back is aching, and I know this sounds selfish, but I just have to sleep in my own bed tonight. I told Colina that I would be glad to take Chelsea in with me. Then Colina could sleep in the spare room with Morgy and Nicole, who fight to sleep on the cot that Papa set up in there.

I love my sister, honest I do, and my nieces too, but right now, I would love them more if they would go home. Mama said that John has already moved out. He called Colina days ago to tell her the coast was clear, that she and the girls could come home now, that he would be staying at Monica's until they could work out the details of the divorce. That's how he put it, the jerk, that "the coast was clear." Then he had the nerve to tell Colina he wanted the girls Christmas day, that his mother wanted to see them. She told him over her dead body.

But Colina doesn't want to go home. She wants her mommy and daddy and her big sister. I am worried about her, but I really think she'd do better at home. The kids are getting restless here. They want their own beds, their toys, their neighbor friends, their comforting surroundings. Angie's trying to set up a schedule where we would all take turns spending the night at Colina's—to help her with dinner, baths, and getting the girls down. I think this would work out better for everyone than our current arrangements, but I don't think Colina is ready to face the walls of her big house.

I find the LEGOS set hidden in the back of my closet. I wrap it— the last gift—and stack it on top of the pillar of gifts that sits by my window. I look at my clock: it's ten to eleven. I decide my bladder can't wait any longer and I stuff the wrapping paper and supplies into my closet. I'm about to put the two pictures of Vito back in the box when there is a knock on my door. I jump. I look at the pictures in my hand and the box in front of me as if they were contraband. "Just a sec," I call, stuffing the pictures back in the box and then camouflaging the box with a pillow. "Come in," I say as I pull my right arm out of my flannel nightgown. When Colina comes through the door, I slide my arm back through the sleeve, trying pathetically for a just-putting-pajamas-on look. I think she buys it.

"Hey," she says and plops down on my bed. The pillow shifts and I have to adjust it.

"Hey."

"Everyone's asleep," she announces, leaning back, supporting herself with her elbows. She doesn't look like herself. Her thick brown hair lacks its usual luster and hangs limply around her face. Her skin is almost transparent in places; everything about her looks exhausted. "Mama's got the magic touch with Chelsea. Got her down like that." She snaps her fingers. "She fights sleep so bad, and I could sleep standing up." She looks around my room and then out of nowhere she lets go a laugh. It's good to hear.

"What's so funny?"

"This room."

"What's wrong with my room?"

"Nothing's wrong with it, Bina, it just hasn't changed much since we were teenagers."

I look around defensively. "Hey. I just redecorated last year. I spent a fortune on this room."

"I know and it's beautiful. The bed, the bedding, the rugs, and the window treatments are great, but everything else is Early American High School."

I don't want to admit she's right, but she is. I've redecorated this room four times since I've had it as my own. I've gone from Marimeko to Laura Ashley to Crate and Barrel to my current ensemble from Pottery Barn. The room itself is pretty. And why wouldn't it be? I had Rosa's help. She just took me by the hand and we walked into Pottery Barn for some ideas and came out with a receipt for a complete suite of bedroom furniture. Let me tell you, it's easy to splurge when you are with Rosa, but it does feel good to have something of my own, something that someday, I'll be able to take with me.

I bought this cool sleigh bed. It's stained a deep brown and one of the reasons I love it so much is that it looks a bit masculine with its traditional lines. I thought someday there might be a man in this bed. Okay, Rosa picked out the bed and matching bedside table and armoire. But I picked out my own bedding—a simple hydrangea design in white and light blue. I went back later and bought a periwinkle blue chenille rug, a swing-arm table lamp, roman shades with silver grommets, and a small desk for my computer. The room is subtle, with the soft shades of blue playing against the stark crispness of the white walls and the richness of the deep woods. I love it all. But I guess the kitschy memorabilia that fills my shelves and hangs on my walls negates the stylish look I've tried to achieve. It's the kind of stuff people say they save for sentimental value that fills my room. Stuff Vito bought me, stuff Vito won for me, stuff that I took from his apartment after he left. Stuff that every year I turn over in my hand, knowing full well that I should box it up for Goodwill. Stuffed animals in all shapes, color and size that Vito won for me in games of skill at different festivals and carnivals sit on wooden shelves that Vito made me in woods class.

Everything that hangs on my walls is connected to Vito. That ink drawing of a tree that's hanging by the closet door was something Vito did in art class senior year and that kind of odd-looking wooden framed picture box with a photo of Cat Stevens inside is something else he made in woods class. And those masks hanging from the closet doorknob are molds of our faces that we made with paper maché when we were both vacation bible school leaders one summer for our church.

My top dresser drawer holds a gold mine of nostalgia: concert ticket stubs, theater ticket stubs, mini-put score sheets, bowling score sheets, oil-spotted menus containing Vito's doodles. Every single letter that he'd ever written to me. Even some jewelry. The bracelet he bought me in California of course. A gold chain, assorted earrings, the watch he gave me as a graduation gift and the watch I gave him as a birthday gift.

Anything and everything that was associated with Vito I saved. Now I sit on my bed with my little sister and I feel embarrassed, ashamed. How much worse would Colina think of me right now if she knew about the box that I'm hiding under my pillow?

She sighs. "I'm just giving you a hard time. I like your room. It makes me feel like we're young again. We had a lot of fun in this room."

"That we did."

She lies back all the way on my bed, yawns, and closes her eyes, and I'm afraid that she's going to fall asleep right here and now and I'm going to lose my bed again.

"Co, you doing okay?"

She doesn't open her eyes but she says, "Yeah, just gearing up for a shitty Christmas."

Since the break-up, Colina has been doing two things that she rarely did before: swearing and eating. And I am visited by the thought that somehow the two phenomena are related, as if stuffing herself with so much bad food is forcing bad words to come out. All I mean is that it's so weird to see her eating all the time. And the swearing, well yesterday, Nicole asked me to "pass the damn ham please," and I couldn't decide if she was imitating Scout from *To Kill a Mockingbird* or her mother from…real life.

"By the way," she informs me, "I now give you permission to call the jerk anything you want. The time has come for anger and bitterness. I don't want revenge but I do want some justice. I can't believe the bastard has done this to me, to us."

"He must be out of his mind."

"Well, I'm not going to make this easy for him, Bina. Alimony, child support, the house, the works. He can have his stupid car and his stupid college loans and all the stupid Nautilus equipment in our basement."

"He's the one who screwed up."

"I've got an appointment the day after Christmas with Frank Gradezzi. Papa says he's a good lawyer, but I just remember him from high school as this nice, shy boy."

"He always did have a crush on you, Co."

"I'm through with men forever," she says. "I can do just fine with the girls. John was never around much anyway. Had to remind him to hug them every once in a while. Imagine that, Bina, I actually had to remind him!"

Colina talks on and on, a glimpse of her old loquacious self coming through. I really need to go to the bathroom, but I can't bring myself to interrupt her. This is the first time she's wanted to talk in days.

"You know what the worst thing is? Hey, you got anything to eat in here? The worst thing is that my girls will have to be around her, that Monica monster. And what if he marries her? That's the thought that's been preventing sleep of any kind for the last three nights. She'll be their stepmother! Oh, God!"

"It's so unfair," I say.

She sits up. "Well, I'm done with the tears, Sabina. Now I'm pissed. I'm not going to try to hold on to him." I expect her next sentence to be: "like you did." But here's what she says: "I'm hungry, are you hungry? Let's eat something."

Food comforts. Food also fuels a fire.

While Colina goes to raid the refrigerator, I go to the bathroom to relieve my poor, nearly bursting bladder. To have left Colina in the middle of her out-pouring would have been callous, but believe me, I almost didn't make it.

She comes back with a tin of Mama's Almond Anise Biscotti and two Christmas mugs full of milk. "You know what else stinks? That in the midst of all my crappola, there's Ted. And everyone is so involved, no, *consumed*, with keeping my head above water that everybody's forgetting about Ted. How is Ted?" She smiles and I bet it feels good to use those particular facial muscles again. It's been a while.

"Ted's good. I like him."

"You *like* him?"

"Okay, I really like him."

"Like is the only 'L' word you can use right now?"

"Yes, for now."

"Like? Or like-like?" she asks, reverting to our old adolescent boy-liking meter.

"Like-like," I concede.

"Well, my girls love him."

"He's great with kids."

"So, don't mess it up, okay?"

I stop just as I'm going to bite down on my cookie. "What's that supposed to mean?"

She pulls away the pillow and exposes the Vito box. "You know exactly what I mean."

"Hey," I say, covering the box back up. "Have you been snooping around in my room?"

"Yeah, but not now. Try twenty years ago. That box has been under your bed forever. Angie and I have seen every picture in that box."

So much for hiding places. Am I so transparent? Has my whole life been an open book?

"Listen Bina, you know that I dish out the advice regardless of whether or not anyone wants it, but life is only too short when things are going good. When things have turned to shit, life is long, long, long."

I brace myself for her "professional voice" as my sisters and I refer to the steady, confident, I-know-what-I'm-talking-about voice she uses with her clients. "When I did social work, Bina, these poor people would sit on the other side of my desk with no options and I was supposed to help them make choices. I can't for the life of me figure out my own life right now, but yours is easy. Yours is simple spring-cleaning. Clean out this room, Bina. Get him out of here."

"I know."

"I know you know, but you need a little push. Give me that box."

I pick up the box, hold it for a second, then hand it over to Colina. "Wait. Let me keep just two or three pictures."

"No!" she says sharply and pulls the box out of my reach. "Bina, you need to get rid of all of him. You can't keep even little pieces of him. You just can't."

I know she's right, but those pictures have gotten me through thus far. People talk about the magic of photography, and it's true, it keeps people alive.

"There's only one person in this world who would want these pictures," Colina tells me. "Well, two people, but Becky's not getting anything after the way she treated you. I'm going to mail this box to Jenny tomorrow, Bina. I'll send a note that says *Merry Christmas, Love Sabina.* Someday you'll thank me." She smiles and her own smile buoys her up. Helping people fix up their screwed-up lives has always been what's tripped her trigger.

"Wow," she says, "it's almost midnight but I'm not tired anymore, are you?"

"Yes, I'm tired."

"Well, you can go to sleep if you want to, but I'm going to stay up and clean your room. I'm talking about major spring-cleaning here. I'll go get some garbage bags and you go get us some more milk."

The thing about Colina—and all of my sisters will agree—is that when she starts using her professional voice, you do whatever she says. Only later do you hope she knew what the hell she was talking about.

***

I wake up the next morning, to sunshine, bare walls, bare shelves, and nothing but dust under my bed. It feels good. I feel cleansed, lighter, like I just got a new haircut. But I do have a confession to make. Last night, when Colina, at the end of her cleaning spree, asked if we got everything, I said yes, but secretly, I'd saved one item, one little, harmless item: the culinary charm bracelet Vito'd given me in California. Just a little token of such a big part of my life, I told myself as I slipped it under the liner of my dresser drawer next to the diamond ring that Aunt Lina gave me. Just one small bite of my past. It couldn't hurt anything, could it?

It's eight-thirty. I slept in. I didn't even bother setting my alarm since the store is closed now until after New Year's Day. It feels so good to sleep late.

Without warning my door swings open and Nicole and Morgy climb up on my bed to cuddle. They are the kissing-est little girls I know, planting big, wet kisses on my cheeks, and then sighing once they get settled in the comfort of my arms. I love holding them like this.

"Do you know what day it is?" Nicole asks me.

"No, what day is it?"

"Today is the *eve* of Christmas Eve."

"Oh, and what is so special about that?"

"You don't remember?" She asks, turning my face by the cheek so as to make eye contact.

"No, I don't remember."

"You people!" she blurts out, exasperated.

"Who people?"

"You and my Mom. She can't remember anything anymore either."

I tickle her under the arms. "That's because our brains are older and fuller than yours. Maybe we just need to do some spring cleaning in there to make room for new stuff to remember."

"Hey! My mommy told Nana that she did some spring-cleaning last night. That's good, now maybe she'll remember that we have to send Santa an e-mail tonight so that he knows we're sleeping at your house for Christmas."

I'm thinking about what a big mouth Colina has when Morgy, who's been quiet up to this point, wails, "What if he can't find us?!"

I pat her little tummy. "Don't worry, Santa always finds the good children. And you are good from your head to your toes, aren't you?"

"Aunt B, you really don't remember about tonight?" Nicole asks.

"I really don't," I tease, "please tell me."

"Tonight we go see the Nutcracker at the Arie Crown Theatre. Then we come home and have hot chocolate and cannoli and then we get to open one present each."

"Even me?"

"Even you."

The Nutcracker on the eve of Christmas Eve is a family tradition. And it just so happens that this year Rosa had an extra ticket so I invited Ted to join us. I'm not even out of bed and already I'm excited and a little nervous. The last few years I have been sitting with Nino, who would rather be seen at a Barbie Doll convention than at the ballet. He was four the first year we brought him and once the dancing began, he leaned over and whispered in my ear, "You gotta be kidding." Marina makes him go. All the cousins go whether they like it or not. It's just a family tradition.

When Nino heard that Ted was coming, he was really put out. Sharing has never come easy to him, but he's going to have to learn how to share me sooner or later. My hope is that once he meets Ted he'll love him, just like Nicole and Morgy.

Morgy tugs on my nightgown and pulls me away from thinking nice thoughts about Ted.

"Aunt B?"

"Yes, honey?"

"Is Mr. Man coming tonight?"

"Yes, he is."

"You have to share." She says *share* like it's a two-syllable word: shay-ya.

"Share what?"

"Him."

"Him? Oh, him. Oh, all right." I guess Nino isn't the only one who has to learn how to share.

***

Downstairs in the store kitchen, Mama, Aunt Lina, Aunt Connie, Aunt Gina, and Aunt Josie are preparing the desserts for tomorrow's Christmas Eve feast that we host for our combined families. Sixty-something people, right here in the store. Christmas Eve is our biggest event, part food festival, part religious ceremony, and part variety show.

It's Rosa's show, of course, but Mama and her sisters do the cooking. We close all the shades in the store and post a sign on the door that reads: *Closed For Family Gathering.* Rosa lights up the place with dozens of votive candles scattered on every tabletop, shelf, and window ledge. The festivities begin at six p.m. when our pastor, Monsignor Miles, opens with a prayer and a special family blessing. Then, one of the grandchildren will read the story of Jesus' birth from the Bible. A few other grandchildren will sing an Italian Christmas song that Papa taught them.

Then we eat. And we eat. And we eat. There is a tradition in the Italian region of Abruzzo for something called the *Panarda*, which is a mammoth-sized banquet the village people hold on special occasions where between thirty-five and forty courses are served. The feast lasts for hours and guests are expected to take a small taste of everything. Our Christmas Eve feast is not quite as magnificent as the *Panarda*, but still, it's impressive.

Mama and her sisters and sisters-in-law whip up their families' classic favorites for all to enjoy. So you take a taste of the antipasti, the baked lasagna, the Italian sausage, the stuffed artichokes, the *scampi*, the *calamari*, the breaded veal cutlets, the Eggplant Parmesan, the stuffed green olives, the garlic-stuffed pork roast, the *Bruscioluni*, the lemon and rosemary chicken breasts, the tossed green salad, the pizza bread, the garlic bread, the olive *crustini*, the *bruschetta*, then you unbutton the top button of your pants or you run to the bathroom to remove your pantyhose so that you can start on the desserts: *biscotti*, chocolate and pear cake, *cassatta, cannoli, tiramisu, panna cotta*, carnival fritters, something known simply as *refrigerator cake* (made with yellow cake, red and green gelatin, and whipped cream) and the special Christmas cake that my Aunt Connie makes every year, decorated with the likeness of the holy family, complete with marzipan fruit (the cake is more a work of art than a dessert).

Then we dance the food off to the music of my Uncle Dino's little trio, which is called *Musica Mangiarsi*, which loosely translated means: music to eat up. But over the years—and they have been around forever—they've been better known by their friends and *cugini* as "musicians that eat," because they are known for their half-hour food-grazing breaks. To give you an idea of how long these three old men have been together, they were booked to play at my wedding, and by then they'd already been playing together for twenty years.

When eleven o'clock rolls around, the music stops, the food is cleaned up and stored away and the big people put the little people to bed. Some of us—those who are not too full to sit in a pew—follow Monsignor Miles over to church for midnight Mass (something Papa dubbed *Midnight Mass with Gas* when we were kids). Those of us who are too tired or too stuffed wait until morning. I love midnight Mass but this year I promised Colina I would take her and the girls to the children's Mass Christmas morning.

All morning I help my mother and aunts in the kitchen until the extra tables, chairs, and tablecloths are delivered from the rental place, and then Papa, Jimmy, and I get them set up. At noon Rosa arrives with I don't know how many poinsettia plants which will be set around the store tonight and then carried by the midnight Mass-goers to church. After that I help my Aunt Anna wrap little grab gifts for the children: rosaries, holy cards, bookmarks, tiny statuettes, and other small items of a religious nature that she buys to help them remember that Christmas is a holy day first and a holiday second.

Angie and Marina show up mid-afternoon and help Papa convert the counter into a bar. Papa has agreed to let my cousin Jimmy play bartender tomorrow night even though he is underage. Papa said since it's just family and just beer and wine it would be okay. This is a huge deal to Jimmy, who is used to being treated like a baby. Jimmy saunters over to inspect Angie and Marina's work and when they go into the kitchen for something I spy him moving over a tower of glasses an inch or two.

By four o'clock, the place is all set up, the desserts are made, and many ingredients have been chopped or otherwise prepared for tomorrow's cooking. I head upstairs to get ready. Ted's picking me up for a pre-show dinner date. I haven't seen him in three days.

***

I have worn the dress I have on to the Nutcracker ballet so many times over the past few years that my sisters have dubbed it my "Nutcracker dress." It's a nice dress—simple, black, and comfortable—that started out expensive but was marked down three times. One of the nice things about being with Ted is that everything about me, even my oldest dress, is new to him.

"Oh, that's pretty," he says to me now, inside The Berghoff Restaurant, as he takes my coat and drapes it over my chair. He has this nice way of complimenting me that for some reason doesn't embarrass me the way some compliments do. He compliments me in a way that makes me feel like he likes the dress, he likes me in the dress, but that he's not just admiring a body in a dress. Do you know what I'm talking about?

He looks nice himself in a conservative charcoal gray pinstripe suit, with Christmas tie and tasseled loafers.

In my opinion, The Berghoff is the perfect restaurant for theatergoers. There's a certain bustle about the place so people don't linger here. You can get in and out. The consistently good German specialties make up for the consistently brisk waiters—from the old school in their black trousers, white shirts and aprons. You can't beat the Old World ambiance; the place is over a hundred years old.

Ted and I have a simple but nice dinner. He orders the schnitzel, I get the sauerbraten, and we both get the famed cream spinach. We catch up on the last three days, which for him included last minute Christmas shopping and wrapping.

"My mother wanted a scarf. A winter scarf," he tells me.

"What's wrong with that?"

"She doesn't leave the nursing home, Sabina. She won't leave. The scarf is just a way of making me feel guilty for putting her there."

"You make her sound absolutely impossible. She can't be all that bad. I want to meet her."

"I told you, not yet. And you won't be meeting my brother for a while either."

"And why is that? Is he single, better looking, smarter, and richer than you?"

"No, he's just not coming to visit till March. And for the record, Danny is single, but he is missing both front teeth and he limps."

"You liar."

We don't have time for dessert so Ted pays the check and we drive over to the Arie Crown. Chicago at Christmas is breathtaking, sparkling and festive. And if you have never visited the city, this is the time of year to do so, in spite of the cold and the wind.

Nino is already seated. As we descend the stairs to our row I can see his large brown eyes scrutinizing Ted. For my own good, I address Nino first, before my other relatives. "Nino, come here honey, I want you to meet Ted. Ted this is my nephew, Nino, the guy who was going to teach us how to sled last week." Nino, who looks stiff and uncomfortable in his hand-me-down suit, extends his hand and says, "Hi."

"Nice to meet you," Ted says, shaking Nino's hand. "I've heard a lot about you. We'll have to plan another day for sledding, won't we?"

"Sure," Nino says, then plops down hard in his seat and turns his head in the other direction. I pinch his arm to let him know I'm not pleased and then lead Ted up and down the aisle, introducing him to the rest of the family. I know that I have overloaded him with names and faces and relationships when he leans over and whispers, "Is there a review session later?"

When Colina and the girls arrive with Mama and Papa, there is a bit of a fuss on Nicole's part because she wants to sit by Mr. Man. The thought runs through my head that it's quite possible Nicole has formed an attachment to Ted in the absence of her father. Morgy wants to sit by Ted, too, but that's more because Nicole wants to. Colina gets them all settled and I take my seat in between Ted and Nino. Nino possessively grabs my hand and holds it—tightly—throughout the performance. Ted notices and smiles. Leaning over, he whispers, "Looks like I'm up against some stiff competition."

***

Now Ted and I are sitting on cushy seats around the piano at one of my favorites places in all of Chicago: The Red Head Piano Bar, on West Ontario. After the ballet Ted asked me where I wanted to go, and when I suggested the Red Head, he about died. It's one of his favorite places, too. It's an upscale, classy bar, not as smoky as you might expect. The russet colored walls, low lighting, black and white celebrity photographs, and the cushioned chairs, make it a lounge classic.

Between Courses

I tell Ted about how Rosa makes Ed bring her here for her "adult" family birthday party. We all look forward to it. All night long, Papa requests nothing but Sinatra songs and when we tease him about it, telling him that there are a few other great lounge singers, he says, "What? You gonna sue me just because I don't like Billy Joe?" My sisters and I laugh our butts off and tell him it's Billy *Joel*—with an 'l' on the end. We could tell him a thousand times and he would still say "Billy Joe."

I'm sipping a glass of Johannesburg Riesling. This guy on the piano is amazing. He's playing and singing Moon River and it sounds in my ears the way the wine feels in my throat.

"Okay, one more time," Ted says. "Rosa has Lauren, Sophie, Claire, and Carl?"

"Almost. Lauren, Sophie, Claire, Peter and Franky. Carl is Marina's middle boy. Marina has Marc, Carl, and Nino."

"Okay, I think I got it now. I'm just in awe of your big family, having come from such a small one. My parents intended to have more kids, but there was something odd about my mother's reproductive anatomy that prevented it."

I have no idea why but this statement strikes me as funny, hysterical even, and I choke on my wine and start laughing.

"What?" Ted says.

"The way you said that made me picture your mother with a Picasso-esque type body. A breast here, an ovary there, a fallopian tube…oh, I don't know, I'm sorry. I haven't even met your mother and here I am making jokes about her."

"The only Picasso-esque thing about my mother nowadays is the way she applies lipstick, on her lips and a quarter inch above and below." He demonstrates with an imaginary lipstick.

"So, you'll be at the nursing home tomorrow night for Christmas Eve?" I ask.

"Well, actually, my mother had the agenda wrong. It's not dinner at six at the nursing home, it's lunch at noon at the nursing home."

"Oh, then why don't you join us for dinner?"

"I would love to but Clay and his wife assumed I'd be alone so they invited me for dinner. I had to accept. You understand, don't you?"

"Of course," I say, but I don't really understand the whole thing with Clay at all.

"I know Rosa is having Christmas day," Ted says, "but who's having Christmas Eve again?"

"We have it in the store and my whole family comes, more than sixty people. It's probably better that you don't come—my family can be overwhelming."

"No, not *your* family," he says, smiling, and then he pulls a small, flat, wrapped gift out of nowhere and pushes it slowly across the table until it is sitting right in front of me. I wonder how he got it in here without me noticing.

"Ted! I have something for you, too, but I didn't bring it."

"Go ahead. Open it."

He looks on as I push my finger under the tape and gently pull back the paper. I don't know what to expect. We've known each other for such a short time. In a way I'm glad I'm getting my gift first, that way I can gage the climate and see if my gift represents equal value and/or commitment.

It couldn't be jewelry, I'm thinking as I tear off the last of the paper, the box is too long and flat. I open it and find an embossed black leather day-planner, one of those expensive ones my brothers-in-law use. "Oh my," I say, brushing my hand over the soft cover. "It's beautiful. So professional-looking." Down in the lower right-hand corner is my name in gold: *Sabina A. Giovanotti.* I am visited by the thought that this may not be the most romantic gift in the world, but very nice and very practical. Especially useful for when I take over the store. Besides, the book on astronomy and the cosmos that I bought for Ted isn't the most romantic gift in the world either. "Thank you so much," I say, "I wish I'd thought to bring your gift."

"Don't worry about it," he says, sounding like a person who enjoys giving gifts more than receiving gifts, someone like Rosa. "Open it up to January."

"What?"

"The calendar. To the month of January. Open it to that."

I do and here's what I see. Written in every single Monday, Tuesday, Wednesday, Thursday and Friday box of the month of January, in Ted's lefty-slant hand, is this note: "Dinner with Ted." In the Saturday boxes he's written: "Activity with Ted." And in the Sunday boxes he's written in: "Mass and Brunch with Ted."

Before I can say anything, he says, "Now turn to February. Look at the twenty-fourth."

I do. It says: "Ted's forty-fourth birthday—slumber party."

I look up and laugh. "Aren't you a little old for slumber parties?"

"It's not that kind of slumber party. It's just a small party, just two people."

"Oh, I see," I say, taking a sip of my wine.

"The way I see it, by then you'll know if you want me around or not. Now check out February twenty-fifth."

I find this entry on the twenty-fifth day of February: "March issue out—Ted to tell Clay about us."

I lean in across the table to grab his hand. I want to tell him that I think this is the most romantic gift anyone has ever given to me, but all I can say is, "Ted."

"What?"

"I don't know, I've just never had a man pencil his way into my life like this."

"Is that good or bad?"

"It's wonderful."

He squeezes my hand. "Oh, good, because look at March third."

I'm almost afraid to look. What if it says "Cruise with Ted" or "Move in with Ted" or "Do Ted's Laundry on Fridays." But here's what it says on March 3rd: "Meet Ted's Mom and Ted's brother."

I meet his eyes and he smiles sheepishly and says, "I figure if you still want me around by then, you should probably get a look at the gene pool."

***

Back at home the house is quiet as a cave. Quietly I walk down the hall, praying a silent prayer that my bed is empty. I open my bedroom door and find my prayer answered. I go and wash up and then slip into a flannel nightgown that has seen better days. You might as well know this about me: I love to wear old, soft, even tattered nightclothes. As I pass my dresser and see my reflection in the mirror, I have to ask myself what would Ted think if he saw me now? Ask for some white out? I think about Ted and my new day-planner and I start to get cold feet and it's not because my feet are cold. I guess it's because I'm out of my comfort zone. Things are starting to happen to me. My life has been playing in slow motion and it's just been turned up to high speed.

I climb into my beautiful Sonoma sleigh bed, pull the covers up to my chin and soak in the stillness. When you are forty and alone, you develop little compulsive habits to get to sleep, to get you through the night: I punch my pillow, I set my alarm and then check it twice to make sure I got that a.m./p.m. setting right, then I lie on my back with my arms folded behind my head. This is how I pray. Not on my knees, with hands folded, like I used to when I was little, but facing heaven. I've always been a person of faith, not even Vito's leaving could shake that. But I do wonder— have been wondering for a long time now—what God has in store for me. I thank God for all of my blessings because I am so richly blessed. Then I pray for everyone in my family in order: God bless Papa, Mama, Rosa, Ed, Lauren, Sophie, Claire, Peter, Franky...and I usually end with Vito. But tonight I don't bless Vito. I hope that he has someone else in his life who will bless him tonight. Tonight I bless Ted. I thank the Lord for sending me Ted.

I turn on my side to find sleep. Recently, I've noticed that my body feels lighter, unencumbered. I feel light as angel food cake. I feel as though a strong wind could carry me away and that I could fly. I hope I dream I can fly. I haven't had that dream in ages.

I sleep but then I wake up for no reason at all. The clock says two fifty-three a.m. No bad dream, no heartburn, no nagging worry, no caffeine before bed. I get up, pull up the shade and look out at the street below. Everything glows from the snow. The Christmas lights on the building across the street blink in a schizophrenic rhythm. The wind is really whistling and I realize that is what woke me up, the wind. There is one more thing I have to do. I know it. I'm only kidding myself.

I make my way across the cold wood floor to my dresser. I retrieve the charm bracelet that Vito gave me from the drawer. The winter light from my window catches the charms and they twinkle as they jangle. The thought that runs through my head is this: would this thing plug the toilet if I flushed it down? I'm thinking…probably. Instead I head for the kitchen, knowing that if I'm going to go through with this, I'd better do it now. One could mull over things in the morning. See things in a different light. Have a change of heart resulting in three steps backward.

Tiptoeing down the hall, I pass Mama's rhythmic breathing and Papa's sporadic snoring. I close the door to the bedroom and, once in the kitchen, I close that door, too. I don't dare turn on any lights. The moonlight reflecting on the snow provides sufficient light. I walk over to the sink—geez, the floor is cold!—and on the way I bang my toe on a chair leg. I want to scream far-reaching obscenities it smarts so, but I stifle the urge by stuffing a dishtowel in my mouth and I wait for the pain to emanate and then dissipate. For some reason, unbeknownst to me and abundantly irrational, I don't remove the dishtowel, but keep it stuffed inside my mouth as I proceed to the sink. I must look either entertaining or ridiculous, but since I can't see myself, I couldn't say which.

"Just do it, you damn fool!" the little red Aunt Lina devil on my left shoulder says. I do. I run the cold water, fling the bracelet into the sink aerator and flick on the switch. A terrible tinny, grinding sound growls up from the sink. I open the cabinet under the sink and feel for the flashlight that we keep there next to the SOS pads. I turn off the water and shine light into the drain. One by one I pick out little mangled charms and the links from the chain and throw them into the garbage. You are probably yawning, thinking so what's the big deal? But believe me, when you have held on for as long as I have and you finally let go, it is a big deal. As Jimmy would say, "a big damn deal."

When sleep falls upon me it covers me like a warm blanket. I dream that angels surround me. They stroke my hair, caress my cheeks, and sing me pretty melodies. And then I fly, high and strong. Me, Sabina Giovanotti, a woman with dates marked in her calendar. In ink pen, no less.

19

On With the Dough

h

I'm dancing with Frank Sinatra, a.k.a. my cousin Jimmy. My uncle's little trio, with their mandolin, accordion, and drums, is playing a tarantella, and Jimmy and I are cavorting around the perimeter of my father's store. I know we are a spectacle, but everyone is clapping and cheering for us. Their smiles say: poor, unmarried Sabina, thank goodness she has cousins to dance with.

When the song is over I give Jimmy a big hug and tell him to go and dance with his date, a pretty girl with creamy skin and long hair the color of pennies. She's waiting for him over by the makeshift bar. One of the "babier" babes from his night class. Geez, even Jimmy has a date. I catch myself thinking mad thoughts about Ted as I head over to the table where I left my glass of wine. He should be here dancing with me, that is, if he dances. I don't even know if he dances.

My baby sister Angie, who looks ravishing in a little black dress that shows off her toned and muscled body, hands me my wine glass and slaps me on the butt. "You look happy," she says. I remind her that I'm always happy at Christmas, but I have to wonder how I can look so happy on the outside, when on the inside I'm pouting. Tonight would have been a perfect opportunity for me to show off Ted. His very presence here would have shouted to my family, once and for all: "Stop worrying about poor Sabina! She'll be all right!" But of course, Ted had to go to Clay's for dinner. The very man, who, God forbid, cannot, must not, will not, find out about me until the March issue of Chicago Magazine is safely in the stands.

I wander about the room, catching up with cousins, kissing aunts and hugging uncles, all the while enduring their same old condolences: "I can't believe someone hasn't snatched you up yet honey," and "The boys in this town must be blind and nuts," and "Don't worry *bedda*, God must have someone real special for you." I smile. They mean well.

Nino has been on my tail all night, begging for hints about this year's Christmas present. He knows darn well I get him LEGOS every year. "Does it have a lot of pieces?" he asks, popping out from behind the fig tree near the front door. "Like two thousand three hundred and forty-two, to be exact?"

"I'm not telling," I say, pretending not to see him.

There's some ear-piercing static and then my Uncle Dino, leader of the band, speaks nasally into the microphone. "Okay now. Okay now, everybody." He gestures with his hand, as if pushing down the air, to get everybody to tone it down. "Listen up. It's time now for the beautiful Melarosso sisters to honor us with their annual and long-awaited rendition of 'Silent Night.' And we all know these five sisters sing as good as they cook. So let's hear it for the Melodious Melarosso Mamas!"

Mama and her sisters make their way to the "stage," all glittery and sparkly in their coordinating red and green beaded Christmas sweaters. They get situated, pushing each other a little to get closest to the microphone. After they trade places a couple of times, they settle down and sing. For me, this is the highlight of the evening. Their voices blend like ingredients in a good cake batter, smooth and harmonious, merging until all of their voices are incorporated. They sing three verses of "Silent Night" and then, a little irreverently, they go right into a bawdy execution of "Jingle Bells," complete with shimmying and line-kicking. I snap pictures left and right, using my zoom lens. If I could find someone in the room who didn't know any better, I would bet him or her a million bucks that Mama and Aunt Connie will both pee their pants. As sure as dough rises, Mama and Aunt Connie make a run for the ladies' room directly after they exit stage right.

Since nothing could top the stage show, Uncle Dino and his band take a break. I watch them, these three sweet old guys, as they shuffle over to the dessert table to inhale some *cannoli*. When Uncle Dino comes back to the microphone he has a little smudge of *ricotta* cheese on the corner of his mouth and another smudge on his tie, which makes me hope that he has completely swallowed his cannoli. Last year, his wife almost had to do the Heimlich on him. The music starts up but not before I hear a shrill scream that makes my hair stand up straight. I'm nothing if not a devoted aunt so I know it's Nino. Several of us—Mama, Marina, Ross, Colina, and I—run in the direction of the scream. Nino bolts across the room and into his mother's arms. "What happened?" she screams.

I give him a good once over with my eyes. He's not bleeding or limping. He's not even crying. But his eyes are the size and intensity of the moon, and his face is as gray as an oyster. "I saw someone!" is all he can get out.

Ross picks him up and carries him to the kitchen so we don't have to talk over the music. He sets him up on the counter and Mama gets him a glass of water. "Now, tell us what happened, big guy." Ross says.

"Me and Franky," Nino says, between breaths, "were crawling under the tables over by the windows. I was trying to get away from him so I ducked behind the window shade." He pauses and swallows hard. "And that's when I saw this man looking through the window."

"A man looking through the window!" Mama exclaims, covering her mouth with her hands. Marina and Ross exchange knowing glances. Ross exhales through his nostrils.

"Maybe he was just someone walking by, honey," Marina says, smoothing back his hair.

"No, Mom, his face was right up against the glass, like he was spying or something."

"Well, maybe he just saw all the lights and wondered what was going on inside," Mama says. "Some of our customers do feel bad that they aren't invited to our Christmas party, but we can't invite everybody."

"Then why did he run when he saw me, Nana?"

Ross looks at Marina. Marina looks at Ross. Marina says, "Now Nino, are you sure you saw somebody, or is this just like the other night when it was just the tree branches?"

"Mom!" he screams, "I saw someone. I did!"

"We believe you honey," I say. "What did he look like?"

"I don't know, he ran away so fast, but I think he had a black beard and oh, oh yeah, he had on a black hat. Or else his hair was all smooshed down. But he ran away fast, like he was doing something wrong or something."

Ross says, "I'll go get Sunny and have a look around." Then I hear him whisper to Marina, "They always have black beards and black hats."

I inch my way closer to Nino, hop up on the counter beside him and hug him closer to me. "You know what I think? I think Mama was right. I think one of our customers was spying on us because he felt left out and when you saw him, he was embarrassed at being caught and ran away. I'd run away, wouldn't you?" He stares at his dangling feet and gives me a half-hearted nod. "How about some cake? Have you had any cake yet?" I ask him, resorting to the great healer, food.

"He's already had two pieces," his mother says.

"Well then, how about a kiddie cocktail? You want me to mix you up a nice kiddie cocktail?"

"They're for babies."

"Well, how about a *supreme* kiddie cocktail? They're just for kids seven and older."

He squints at me to see if I'm serious. I keep a straight face. "What's the difference?" he wants to know.

"Two cherries instead of one."

"Did you say two?"

"Yes, two."

"Three and you got yourself a deal."

I hold out my hand for a shake and then pretend that I don't see Marina giving me the "you spoil him" look. He slides down from the counter and I lead him back out to the party. I open the door to cooler air, to louder music, and to Ted.

"Look who we just found knocking on the front door," says Ross, as if he's just cracked an unsolved mystery.

"Ted!" I say, "What are you doing here?"

"Yeah, what are you doing here?" Nino echoes me.

"Clay's wife got a migraine so they ended the evening early. I thought I would crash your party."

"Well, I'm glad you did." I give him a hug, but I feel self-conscious in front of everyone. "You weren't peeking in the windows by any chance, were you?" I ask, just because I have to.

He looks confused by my question, but says, "What? No, I just barely got to the door before your father opened it. He asked me the same thing. Said one of the kids thought he saw someone peeping in."

"I *did* see someone peeping in," Nino shouts, "and maybe it *was* you."

Ted looks to me for help. I take Nino by the shoulders, "But Nino, you said you thought the man had a beard. Ted doesn't have a beard."

273

He takes a good look at Ted's face and twists his mouth into a pucker. "Oh yeah. He did have a beard. And a black hat too, and yours is blue. I guess it wasn't you. Sorry."

"Hey, don't worry about it buddy. You know, now that you mention it, when I was parking my car up the street, I saw a guy walking along kind of briskly. He might have had a beard and a black hat, I didn't notice."

Papa comes through the front door. He slaps Nino on the back and says, "It's all clear kiddo, nobody's out there anymore. Don't worry now. Go play with your cousins." Off he goes, with a little corner of my heart.

Mama comes up and hugs Ted and then steals him right from under my nose. I'm standing here, by the kitchen door, and I watch as she leads him around introducing him to everyone as Ted Kallista, the trained chef. She's not usually so bold, but I know Mama sees the looks I get.

Now is as good a time as any to run to the bathroom to check my face, so I do. My face looks the same as it always looks. Sometimes, when you're at the peak of excitement, wouldn't it be nice to look in the mirror and look different? Ravishing or captivating or enthralling or some damn thing. Just not the same damn thing. I look at my watch. It's nine-thirty.

By the time I get back out there, Mama has filled a plate a mile high for Ted and seated him at a table with Uncle Silvio and my brothers-in-law. Papa brings over a glass of wine. Ted accepts it, smiling, taking it all with good grace. Mama's standing over him, waiting for him to take his first bite. He does, proclaiming it scrumptious. Satisfied, Mama leaves him to talk to the men.

I head for the bar to pour myself a glass of wine, when I catch Nino out of the corner of my eye. He's holding up the wall. I remember the drink I promised him. "Ready for your supreme kiddie cocktail?" I say casually, pretending I haven't forgotten.

His eyes light up, but he's stubborn as a strawberry stain. "It's about time," he says.

"Hey," I say, "speak respectfully to me, or you'll get the regular kiddie cocktail. What do you say?"

"Sorry."

"Okay," I say, as I pour cherry juice into 7-Up. "How many cherries did we say?"

"Five," he says straight-faced.

"Five it is."

***

Finally, Ted finds a way to excuse himself from his politically-correct-almost-empty plate of food, Papa, Uncle Silvio, and my brothers-in-law, and asks me to dance. How nice, I think, he does dance. "I'm in bad shape," he whispers in my ear as we dance to Uncle Dino's rendition of "Walking In A Winter Wonderland" which he plays in a sweet molasses tempo. I flatter myself by thinking Ted means he can't stand it that he can't kiss me or be alone with me or well, you know. "I ate so much at Clay and Sharon's and now I stuffed myself so as not to hurt your mother's feelings." He kisses my neck. "Got any Alka-Seltzer?" (You gotta love this guy.) I know I'll probably make more than a few people angry by disappearing without a word, but I lead Ted to the back stairs because the upstairs kitchen is the only place you will find an antacid around here. It would be a mortal sin to keep an antacid in the store kitchen. God forbid if a customer should see it!

Halfway up the stairs he grabs my arm and when I turn around to see what he wants, he sneaks a kiss, and it makes me feel like I'm sixteen. His lips taste like Mama's *sugo*. "I'm glad you came," I say.

"Me too."

In the kitchen, I have to gently shush him because he's talking loudly about Clay's boring Christmas dinner and I just remembered that Colina brought the girls up for bed a little while ago.

"Oh, sorry." He drinks down his fizzy water, releases a couple of good burps and a few pathetic moans. "Anyway, I thought to myself, what the hell am I doing here when I could be with Sabina? I just wish I felt good enough to *be* with you."

"You should have told Mama that you'd already eaten."

"Ha! I know better. You forget, Greek mothers, Italian mothers...same thing. Besides, your mother said she was just fixing me a snack."

"In our family, a snack can be a three-course meal. Come on in the living room and get comfortable."

The living room is all aglow with iridescent color, the source of which is the eight-foot fresh Christmas tree that sits in the corner. The lights are those large, bright-colored, old-fashioned bulbs, and whenever I pass by, I think of Bing Crosby. The room is so cozy and welcoming that I don't bother to turn on any other lights. I tell Ted to have a seat in Papa's recliner because it's the most comfortable. He does, moaning as he slides in. He loosens his belt a notch and sighs. We sit in the semi-darkness and speak in hushed voices so as not to wake up the little ones. Ted says, "Did you ever see that episode of the Andy Griffith Show or Mayberry R.F.D., whichever, where Andy eats a spaghetti dinner at his girlfriend's house and then another dinner at Aunt Bea's and then a third dinner somewhere else, and he just feels miserable?"

I can't help but smile, even though he's obviously in pain. "I did see that one. I loved that show."

"Well, just call me Ang."

"I haven't thought about that show in years. I always wanted to live in Mayberry where no one locked their doors and everyone knew everyone and the worst person in the whole town was that sweet little drunk guy."

"Hey, what the hell did the *R.F.D.* stand for anyway?" Ted asks me.

"R.F.D.? I don't know. Did I ever know? I don't know."

"I used to know. Now it's going to drive me crazy. Well, it'll come to me."

I look at him sitting there in Papa's chair. In this dim light it's as if I can see Ted as an old man. There are crow's feet around his blue eyes, but they don't diminish the sparkle. His hair, although salted with gray, is still thick and full. He looks like he belongs in Papa's chair. He looks like someone I'd like to be with when I'm old.

We talk a little about how things went at the nursing home and at Clay's and then I remember that I haven't given him his Christmas gift so I excuse myself and go to my bedroom to get it. I tiptoe into my room. Colina is on the bed with Chelsea, and seeing her there makes me remember that earlier tonight I promised that I'd help bring the girls' presents down from the attic. The moonlight shines on their faces, making them look celestial.

When I return to the living room, at first I think Ted has fallen asleep during my brief absence. But his eyes pop open as I approach him. "Merry Christmas!" I say and place the gift in his lap.

"Well," he says. I can tell he's embarrassed. I don't know why I say it but the next words out of my mouth are: "It's a book."

He laughs, ripping off a corner piece of wrapping paper. "Thanks for telling me, I've never seen one before."

I sit on the arm of Papa's chair and watch as he finishes with the wrapping. "It's just that I didn't know what to get you."

"Hey, all right. This is great." He holds up the book. It's called *Hubble Vision: Astronomy with the Hubble Space Telescope*, by Carolyn Collins Petersen and John C. Brandt.

"Well, I least I know you don't have it since I unpacked every book you own. And I saw your telescope and so…"

"I love it," he declares as he flips through the pages. It is a fascinating book, lavishly illustrated with fantastic photographs. Virgie helped me pick it out.

I slide off the arm of the chair onto his lap. He groans. "It's not you," he says, "it's my stomach. I do this every Christmas. And Thanksgiving and Easter. My birthday. I guess that's my way of celebrating: I eat till it hurts."

Men are such babies I think as I rub his stomach gently. When I hear footsteps in the hallway I jump out of Ted's lap and head for Mama's chair. I would just die if someone caught me sitting on Ted's lap, rubbing his stomach. It must be Colina. I fake a conversation with Ted. "Wasn't that weird about that guy looking in our window and spooking Nino?"

"Poor kid."

"You know, I'm sorry to say, if you hadn't come along and said that you did see some guy, we might not have believed him. He's been going through this stage. He sees lots of what he calls *scaries*."

"Hello," Colina says, holding a wide-awake Chelsea in her arms. She lingers in the hallway, but says, "Look, sweetie, it's Mr. Man." Chelsea is the only member of the family that Ted hasn't had the chance to meet. She was sick the day we went sledding and Colina left her home with a sitter when we went to the Nutcracker.

Ted rises politely from Papa's chair and stares at Chelsea. Chelsea, with her brown ringlets, heart-shaped lips, rosy cheeks, and deep brown eyes stares back, taking Ted in. The Gerber baby had nothing on my niece—Chelsea is nothing if not knockdown gorgeous at a little over a year old. And it kills me to say it but she looks just like her daddy. "This is Chelsea," I say to Ted, as I walk over and take her from her mother. I tell Colina to come and sit down.

"Thanks, but I'm just going to get her a bottle. She woke up from a sound sleep. I think she was looking for her daddy."

"Oh, Colina, come and sit down."

"No, but just hold her a minute, will you, while I get her some milk."

"Of course." Is there anything more irresistible than a chubby, cherub-faced baby? I ask you. I sit her in my lap and kiss her cheeks that are as pink as her sleeper. I turn her around to face Ted.

"Look at this face, will you?"

Without any kind of warning and completely spontaneously, Chelsea stretches out her arms to Ted.

"Look, she wants you," I say. Colina comes back with the bottle just as I'm passing Chelsea to Ted. You should see the look on Ted's face. For that matter, you should see the look on Colina's face. Neither can believe it. Chelsea checks Ted out, feeling his eyes and poking at his mouth. He doesn't resemble John even remotely, but even a baby can tell the difference between a man and a woman.

"Would you like to feed her, Ted?" Colina asks.

Ted looks like he's melting, the way he sort of reposes in this beautiful baby's presence. "Yes, I would," he says.

Aren't babies powerful? The way they know as they sit in your lap that you consider them wonderful and marvelous and awesome. Seeing Ted with Chelsea in his arms makes that little childless pain in my rib evolve to an aching throb. When Colina sees that Chelsea is quite comfortable in Ted's care, she asks if we would mind if she snuck in a quick shower. By all means, I tell her.

I can't keep my eyes off of Ted's face. In this soft light, Ted and Chelsea look almost holy and because it's Christmas Eve, I am reminded of Joseph holding baby Jesus. Ted doesn't say a word to Chelsea but they have locked gazes, equally mesmerized with each other. This man knows how to feed a baby, I think, noting that he holds the bottle at the perfect angle. I smile and say, "What is it with you and little girls, anyway?" I say this, blurt this out, before I think about his own little girl. My words hang in the air, I can actually see them floating above Ted's head. I feel horrible. Ted says nothing. He just keeps his eyes on Chelsea, who is sucking greedily from the bottle. With just a few sips left, the sucking stops, and Chelsea heaves a big sigh. She smiles in her sleep, burps, and then nestles her face into Ted's chest. Ted is bewildered. He has that sheepish look that we adults get when a baby steals our hearts and turns our souls to mush. Only when he looks up at me do I see that he's crying.

I don't know what to do, so I take the baby from him and return her to her freshly showered and powdered mother. When I come back Ted asks if I would like to take a walk. "Ted, I'm sorry about—"

"Don't be sorry. I enjoyed feeding her. She's beautiful. It, well, it just brought back so many memories."

We sneak down the front stairs so that we can avoid the party. But once outside we come face-to-face with the midnight-Mass contingency, processing with poinsettias in hand, over to church for the Christmas vigil. I kiss many cheeks before Ted and I start our walk. It's cold, but not freezing. Still, I wish Ted would hold my hand. He's walking rather briskly and I have to push myself to keep up. "This air feels good, doesn't it?" Ted says. "It's just what I needed. To walk off this indigestion."

We slosh through the snow that's left on the sidewalks. Funny how some people fastidiously remove every flake of snow that lands on their walk while others carve out a path only as wide as the blade of their shovel. We can't both fit in places, so he leads and I follow. Finally, I grab his arm.

"Hey, Mr. Man, my legs are a lot shorter than yours. What's the rush?"

"I'm sorry, Sabina, I'm lost in my own thoughts."

I thread my arm under his. "Do you want to talk about it? I unloaded on you the other night. Tell me what happened to your baby," I say, leaning in closer.

He stops short in his track. "Please, Sabina, I never talk about it anymore. They make you talk in therapy until they break you, and it's supposed to make you feel better, but it doesn't. I only feel better when I bury it. Don't be hurt, it's just the past and I try to keep the past behind me."

"Yeah, I know what you mean. I've been doing that for years. And I thought it was helping me, too, but it wasn't. You helped me to see that—that my memories were immobilizing me. Don't you feel that sometimes?"

He doesn't answer, but he pulls me to him. He is so much taller than me. The top of my head barely reaches his shoulder blade. He leans down and buries his face in my hair. We stay in this position for the longest time, rocking in our embrace. When Ted straightens up, he takes my hand and begins walking back in the direction of home. We're both quiet; his words hang between us. At least I get a chuckle out of him when we pass a house where the owners have placed their good dining room chairs out in the street to reserve their parking spots. Tomorrow, Little Italy will smell like *sugo* and overflow with visitors. This bit of levity breaks the spell.

"What kind of wine do you think I should bring to Rosa's tomorrow?" he asks. He doesn't wait for my answer, but adds, "I used to be a wine snob, you know."

"No, I didn't know," I say, deciding to give him his dignity. I'll play along.

"Oh, yes, the worst kind." He squeezes my hand.

"And how did this come to be?"

"Oh, just like cooking school, it was my step-father's idea. After I graduated from the CIA, cooked for a few months, and then decided that professional cooking was not for me, Howard issued another challenge to get me going on yet another career path. And so the dare was to become a wine connoisseur, with the possibility of landing a job as a sommelier in a four-star restaurant, which was in his opinion, the next best position after executive chef. So I studied, and I got quite good actually, but I knew deep down that I didn't want to be a wine steward any more than I wanted to be a chef. So instead I wrote an article, "Taking the Snob Out Of Wine." And to my surprise, *Food and Wine* bought it. As a matter of fact, that was the first article I published after shortening my name to Kallista."

I stop in my tracks. "You shortened your name?" I am incredulous. "You mean there's another name? Besides Ted Kallista, Teddy Adonis, Cal Whatever and all the others?"

Karla Clark

"Not another name, just shortened, like you told me your grandfather did—Melarosso to Mela. It was Howard's idea. If I was going to be a food and wine writer, I needed a name that was easy to remember. It didn't matter in newspaper writing, no one ever remembers the reporter's name, unless you were Mike Royko."

I must be looking at him funny. I hope not disdainfully, the way Papa looks at "watered-down *Americani.*"

"Sabina, it's no big deal. I just removed the 'phulos.' Although then after getting many more articles published, and in the heat of my snob appeal, I told Howard that I may have made a mistake. Why would a guy who writes about wine, change his name from *'Kallistaphulos'* which means 'with fine grapes' to *'Kallista'* which means 'most beautiful' or 'most excellent'?"

Just as I hear the word *Kallistaphulos,* I slip on a patch of ice. I hit the ground. Hard. *Kallistaphulos? Kallistaphulos?* Do you remember? Do you remember the little girl in the accident? She was Grace Kallistaphulos. Her father was Theodore Kallistaphulos. Also known as Teddy Adonis. Also known as Cal Whatever. Also known as Ted Kallista. Oh my God!

Ted squats down next to me and helps me sit up. "Sabina, honey, are you okay?"

"I'm fine." I'm actually sore, stunned, and sick to my stomach.

"Are you sure? Can you walk? I can carry you if you can't walk."

I shake my head. "Just give me a second. I'm okay. Really."

Then he looks down at my feet. "Sabina, you didn't wear your boots. And here you've been getting after me about wearing proper winter attire."

I want to tell him to shut up. I want to tell him right then and there, "Do you have any idea who I am? Who my fiancé was? What this all means? My ex-fiancé killed your baby daughter. Accidentally, inadvertently, indirectly, but bottom line, your daughter died because his car crashed into your car." But I'm nothing if not a coward. My past immobilizes me once again. What I say as I try to get up, is, "I think I'd better get back."

It's a long walk home. Ted insists on walking me upstairs, and if I would allow it, I think he would draw a bath for me and tuck me in as well. I wonder if he would be so attentive if he knew the truth. It's too much to even think about. In the living room he hugs me and asks me several times if I'm sure I'm okay. He makes me swallow two aspirins—knew right where to get them since he saw them when we got his antacid. "You're sure you didn't bump your head?"

"Yes, I'm sure," I say, failing to keep the impatience out of my voice.

"'Cuz you're acting a little funny, that's all."

Colina pokes her head in. "Hey, sorry to interrupt, but Bina, you said you'd help me bring the girls' presents down from the attic."

"I better help you, Colina," Ted says. "Your sister slipped on the ice and fell. She should get to bed."

"Are you okay?"

"I'm fine, really. Embarrassed more than anything," I say rubbing my butt.

Ted puts his arm around me and says, "Okay, well listen, I'm going to take Deidra to church tomorrow at ten. What time should I be at Rosa's?"

"Who's Deidra?"

"My mother, who'd you think?"

"I didn't think it was anybody, Ted, that's why I was asking."

"Uh-oh," says Colina. "She'd better get to bed, that edge in her voice means she's tired."

Ted gives me a look of surprise. I know it's not fair to take whatever I am feeling—I'm not even sure yet—out on him, but after all, it was he who changed his name. Had he introduced himself to me that night at the Four Seasons as Theodore Kallistaphulos or even Ted Kallistaphulos or Teddy Kallistaphulos, or for that matter, even Cal Kallistaphulos, I would have said, "Nice talking to you, gotta go."

He gives me a peck on the forehead and says, "Good night. Get some rest, okay?" He follows Colina to the door leading to the attic. I turn to head for bed, but not before I hear Colina say, "Why don't you come to Rosa's about two o'clock tomorrow. We'll eat at four. Are you picking up Sabina, or do you need directions?" Geez, do I feel like a jerk or what? All of a sudden there's a part of me that doesn't want to go to bed. All of a sudden I get this irrational fear that my sister Colina is going to hit on my boyfriend behind my back. Where does this kind of craziness come from?

It's not until I hear Ted's voice do I realize that I've been holding up the wall here in the hallway. Quickly I step into the bathroom, but I leave the door open just a bit, just enough to listen in. No, it's not eavesdropping, it's just determined listening. "This is kind of embarrassing," Colina says, in a voice perkier than it has been in weeks. "I guess I went a little overboard."

"Well, it is Christmas," Ted says.

Hmmm. Innocent enough. I close the door quietly and lock it. I will not stoop this low. It's humiliating to think that I am even capable of mistrusting my own sister. Ted, I'm not quite sure about. How do you trust someone with so many names—shortened, lengthened, and dreamed-up? I decide a bath would be a good idea, so I run the water good and hot.

Kallistaphulos! I think as I ease myself into the tub. Maybe it's just not possible to ever put the past behind you. Somehow it seems to creep up on you when you least expect it. I used to dream that I would find little Grace Kallistaphulos in odd places. She would just show up: in my closet, in the hamper, in the bathtub, under the dining room table, at the library, in my grocery cart. And I would call to Vito to come out of *his* hiding place. I would say, "Look! I found her! Little Grace. She's all right. Everything is going to be all right!" Because you see, I have never blamed Vito for the accident; I have always blamed myself. He never would have been behind that wheel if it weren't for a particular stressed-out fiancée.

There's a knock on the bathroom door and then Colina says, "Sabina, Nicole woke up. She's got to go."

"Hold on," I say. As I stand up in the tub I realize that I forgot to grab a bath towel from the linen closet. I pull the two hand towels from the towel bar and do my best to camouflage my important parts. I hit the light so as not to blind Nicole into a complete no-turning-back wakefulness. Colina says, "Sorry," and I make a mad freezing dash for my room. Someone is sleeping in my bed, and there she is! Chelsea. I hurry into my nightgown so as I can beat Colina into my own bed. She can have the couch tonight and I'll cuddle with Chelsea. I'm not even totally dry as I slip in beside her. Her warmth radiates toward me and I think maybe I will be able to sleep tonight after all. The door softly opens and I squeeze my eyes shut, pretending to be asleep or almost asleep or else just pretty darn not-getting-out-of-this-bed-unless-there's-a-fire comfortable. Colina closes the door just as softly as she opened it, and I am left with a warm baby and troubling thoughts. I think, how could I have not known that Ted was Ted? I guess I did only see him once—at the funeral. But back then he'd had a beard and glasses and a head full of curly hair. I think back to the funeral. I remember his head hung so low that I never really got a good look at him.

Somewhere between our walk tonight and Ted's revelation of his true identity, I figured out who the bearded man in the black hat was tonight. Of course it was Vito! I'm sure it was Vito—come back from wherever he has been just in time to rescue me from all of this. Wouldn't that be just like him to disappear from my life for all of these years and then return just as I have both found and lost love with another man? Yes, it would be just like him.

20

A Dish to Pass

Our Lady of Pompei is filled to capacity and then some. Nine o'clock Mass is the children's Mass where Monsignor tailors the entire liturgy for the little ones. Needless to say, this Mass attracts all the families with small children. Our church is all decked out for Christmas with lush greens draped on the altar, thousands of little white sparkling lights, and dozens of poinsettia plants. Don't you think the poinsettia is the perfect Christmas flower? I love how it shouts, "Merry Christmas!" in its showy assurance. Aren't you impressed with my good cheer?

I bless myself with holy water, genuflect, and then scoot down the pew to make room for Colina and the girls. Once situated between Nicole and Morgy, I kneel and say a prayer of thanks. I have so much for which to be thankful, but oh, we humans, we are never satisfied. And so after giving thanks, I begin my petitions. *Lord, please help Colina get through this difficult time. And Lord, please help John to make it right with his three girls. And Lord, please help Nino to get over this stage of seeing scaries. And Lord, please help me to get over Ted quickly after he dumps me.*

On the way home from Mass, Colina reminds me that Ted is picking me up at one o'clock. I was hoping he would meet me at Rosa's. I'm worried about the long drive and the awkward pauses. Obviously he knows something's bothering me, though the poor man can have positively no clue as to what it is. Besides, I will not tell him about my discovery today—this is not the kind of news to be delivered on Christmas day.

The disappointment I'm feeling must come across on my face because Colina hits my arm. "Hey, what's wrong with you? You should see your face. Everything is going great for you, Sabina. Your dreams are coming true—you're getting the store, you've got Ted. Ted is so great."

"Who's Ted?" asks Morgy from the back seat.

"Mr. Man," answers her big sister.

"I know Ted's great," I say. "I know that."

"Well, then, don't go getting overly picky. Nobody's perfect. And he does have nice hands."

I want to ask her what she is doing checking out Ted's hands, but after all, they're just hands.

"Honestly, Sabina, if you blow this one, I'll kill you."

Little does she know that I've already blown it.

***

"So, are you sore from the fall?" Ted asks me on our way to Rosa's house.

"No, I'm fine," I say and pretend that I see something fascinating out the side window. It's a cold, blah day, lacking any color. The sky is the exact shade of concrete; the air is so frigid it stings your nostril likes needles. There's freezing rain in the afternoon forecast. It just doesn't feel like Christmas.

Ted's free hand reaches across the gear shaft to find mine. He alternately rubs my hand, then squeezes it, and I know he's trying to say through touch that whatever it is that's bothering me will be all right. How can his hand make such promises? It doesn't have all the information.

I make an attempt at small talk. "How's Deidra?"

"Pouty."

"Is she upset that you're spending the day with us?"

"She's madder than a hornet. Like I said, I will not be introducing you to her until I'm sure you can't live without me."

I know this is my cue, and that I can turn this into a romantic moment just by saying, "I can't live without you," but instead I just let his words pop like a bubble in mid air.

Poor Ted is so confused by my behavior. He drives in silence for a while, then switches on the radio. I keep going over in my head different ways of breaking the bad news to him. *"Ted, I have something important to tell you. Ted, I have some terrible news. Ted, you're not going to believe this, but..."* It's no use practicing—I'll never find the courage to tell him. I can't help it. I start to cry. Ted sees the tear before I can wipe it away.

"Sabina, what's wrong?"

And then I say something that every woman, every feminist in the Western Hemisphere would hate me for saying...I say, "Don't mind me, I just have my period." Which is nothing more than a chauvinistic lie. I apologize to all the suffragettes, past and present, of the world. On the other hand, it does the trick. It shuts him up for a minute. It's a known fact that men hate to hear anything related to a woman's menstrual cycle. I think it was Marina, the perennially-menstruating feminist who taught me, when in doubt, site raging hormones. It works every time.

We drive in silence through the thick bleak grayness of the day. You can't tell where the highway ends and the clouds begin. Ted leaves me alone with my cramps and my bloating and my hormonally induced irritability. By the time we pull up to Rosa's I feel so miserable I might just as well have my period. It would serve me right.

Once inside Rosa's, Ted, still clutching the three bottles of wine he brought, is whisked away by Ed for a grand tour. I've always found it entertaining the way you can get two completely different tours of the same house depending on who gives the tour. Ted will get the "man's tour." He'll be shown the garage first, which would include the cars, the riding mower, the golf-cart and the snow blower. Next, a trip to the basement, featuring the big-screen TV, pool table, and bar. In the family room, Ed will explain the intricate details of his entertainment center where he has access to everything but sex with his wife through a myriad of remote controls. Ed saves the best for last: the master bathroom, complete with two toilets, two sinks, a hot-tub, a bidet, and a wall-hanging magazine rack like you see in doctors' offices. Ed wanted to put in one of those college dorm-type mini refrigerators, but Rosa was afraid the guy would never come out of there, so she put her foot down.

I busy myself in the kitchen, comforted by the feel and smell of food. There's enough to feed a subdivision: hot and cold antipasti trays, two stuffed capons, a bone-in glazed ham, baked *rigatoni*, cauliflower flowerets in cheese sauce, Caesar salad with homemade croutons, clover-leaf rolls, cranberry-cream-cheese gelatin mold, plus Italian cookies and other desserts. I don't know what has come over me, but all of a sudden, I'm famished. I start devouring food from the antipasti trays. A taste of this, a taste of that. Food never tasted so good! There's no mistake about it, my olfactory senses have been restored in full.

At the dinner table, Ted gets the guest of honor's chair, which up until now has been reserved for my Aunt Lina's derriere. She's not even put out by this. She likes Ted, I can tell. And why wouldn't she? Look at him, he's in his glory—right at home with the noise and the commotion and the chaos. One would think he grew up in a house full of children. Morgy has found her way over to Ted and is now sitting on his lap, picking at his food. Ted, for his part, is acting as if this is nothing, no big deal. He's carrying on a conversation—I heard something about the CIA—with Papa, all the while running his fingers through Morgy's hair. The whole family has taken to him and I catch myself thinking as I sip my second glass of wine how sad it will be after tomorrow when they find out they'll probably never see him again.

In the middle of dinner Rosa's doorbell rings or chimes—whatever it does—playing a complete verse of "America the Beautiful." We exchange puzzled looks, wondering who would be ringing the doorbell at four thirty-five p.m. on Christmas day. Rosa leaves to answer the door and then I hear John's voice. Colina hears it too and jumps up from the table. Then I hear raised voices and Colina shout, "Over my dead body!"

Papa slides his chair back and heads for the foyer. Good, I think, Papa will tell John to get lost. But when Papa comes back into the room, he whispers in Mama's ear and Mama gets up from the table and disappears down the hall. The rest of us continue to eat and make light conversation, but we can't help wonder what's going on. Morgy, who is under the impression that food on other people's plates tastes better than food on her own plate, is happily eating Ted's ham.

Mama returns with the girls' coats and hats and things and coaxes Morgy off of Ted's lap. Papa picks up Nicole and carries her to her Daddy. I hear shrieks of delight that pierce my heart. "Daddy! Daddy's here! Happy Christmas, Mr. Daddy!"

Well you can just imagine how things are after Rosa shuts the big, heavy oak door behind John. Poor Colina. She thought she could at least keep the baby, thinking that John wouldn't have had the foresight to bring a car seat. But he did. And so now Colina is in the bathroom, the very bathroom that I locked myself in on Thanksgiving Day. Aunt Lina gives me the eye and I give it right back, just daring her to try to force her way in on poor Colina. She gets up anyway and I'm about to follow her when I see Mama cut her off at the hallway. "I'll take care of this," Mama says, and I want to scream, "That a way, Mama!"

We all sit quietly—even the children, who usually fidget once they've finished eating. Nino gets out of his seat and walks across the table and whispers this in my ear: "Will we still get to open our presents and break the piñata, Aunt B?"

"Yes," I whisper. I'm annoyed at his selfishness but I remind myself that seven-year-olds believe the world revolves around them.

Papa says, "Why don't we have dessert so that the kids can open their presents." There is a chorus of hoorays and hurrahs and even a hallelujah from Carl. It hurts me to think that all they care about is more gifts after they have been showered with them this morning.

Angie and Marina start to clear away the dishes while I join Rosa in the kitchen to help get the coffee and the dessert. Or, more accurately, desserts. Rosa has arranged a beautiful tray of homemade Italian cookies—the same ones we make for weddings. She has a lovely tray of cannoli and a tub of spumoni ice cream. And there's also a cream-filled cake roll in the shape of a log, complete with edible pinecones which she formed out of almonds and almonds bark. Where does the woman find the time? When I ask her, she says, "Don't be silly, I have a convection oven." As if that were a real answer.

The cake is actually for Rosa's middle daughter, Claire, who has a December twenty-fifth birthday. When she was younger she loved to tell people that she shared her birthday with Jesus. After she grew a little older though, she realized that she was getting cheated by having Christmas and her birthday combined. Now, we are careful to make the day part-Christmas and part-birthday, making sure that she has her very own special birthday cake, apart from the traditional Christmas desserts.

Marina grabs the tray of cookies, Angie takes the tray of cannoli, Rosa carries the tub of ice-cream, I grab the log cake and we head for the dining room, hoping that a heavy dose of sugar will lighten everyone's spirits. As I turn the corner, I hear Marina say, "Hey! No rough-housing!" but not before Nino crashes into me, causing the cake plate to smash into my chest. In my bewilderment, I lose hold of the plate and it crashes to the floor. The log cake itself is glued to my chest, balancing precariously on the narrow shelf of my breasts. I don't know what to do, but my instinct says, "Save the cake! Save the cake!" I lean back to keep it from rolling to the floor, then I carefully walk the four feet or so to the dining room table, looking, I am certain, like I am attempting to do the *limbo*. Just as I reach the table, Rosa, quick as lightning, is there with a clean plate. I slowly lean over the plate, aim, and then with my bosom, project the cake onto the platter. I look up to see Claire with tears in her eyes. Right behind her, Mama and Colina, who have returned from the bathroom, are laughing like hyenas (Mama is crossing her legs to keep from peeing her pants) so I try for humor. "Who wants cake?" I ask. Everyone laughs except Claire and Ted. He can't for the life of him figure out what my family finds so funny about ruining a perfectly beautiful birthday cake.

Art fills Ted in about our family tradition of ruining birthday cakes, while Rosa helps me clean up and lends me a sweater to replace the chocolate-frosted one I was wearing. Rosa is more upset about my sweater (it's the cashmere she gave me for my birthday) than she is about the cake that she and Claire spent hours baking and decorating. She decides to keep it so that she can take it to her dry cleaner, who she says is a genius with stains.

Now everyone has gathered in the living room to open gifts. Ted smiles at me and pats the spot on the sofa next to him. My heart flip-flops. All these years, I have walked into this room feeling the same old feeling: someone is missing. Someone for me. And now here is someone for me, sitting here, beckoning. I sit down next to him and he moves in closer. I smile at him. There's a part of me that wants to believe that somehow we can work this out. I know two wrongs can't make a right, but I would like to think that two hurts can make a healing. Could there be healing in this whole freak coincidence? Or, maybe there are no coincidences.

***

It's only a little after nine o'clock when Ted and I walk outside into freezing rain. Neither of us has to work in the morning, but it's been a long, long day, and so after helping Rosa clean up, I suggest to Ted that we call it a night. Outside the driveway is like a skating rink. Ted and I slide to the car and load the shopping bag of gifts into the trunk. "Maybe I'd better run back in and warn everyone about this ice," I say, thinking especially about Art and Angie who live the farthest away. Ted agrees, saying it would be wise to get on the road now, before it gets any worse. On my way back out to the car, I slip on a patch of ice and take my second fall in two days. Luckily, Ted didn't see me slip because when I slide back into the passenger's seat I find him fiddling with his CD player, and he doesn't say anything about anyone falling. This time I really did hurt myself—not seriously, of course, but I'll be sore for days. As I slam the car door shut, Ted smiles and says, "Where to?"

I'm not sure what he has in mind—it's Christmas evening, nothing will be open—so I say, "I'm wiped. If you don't mind, I think I'll just go home."

"Oh, come on. Clay gave me this unbelievable bottle of wine for Christmas. I want to share it with you."

"Oh Ted, really, I would love to, but I can barely keep my eyes open." I am nothing if not a chicken. I am terrified of being alone with him. I know I have to tell him, but how can I tell him?

He looks at me, but I keep looking straight ahead. "Okay," he says as he accelerates in reverse, "I guess it will keep." We slip and swerve and then Ted gains control of the car. "Sorry, this ice is really bad."

I know, I want to say, keenly aware of the ache in my left buttock. I look out my window—it's beautiful! Everything is glazed with a layer of clear ice: tree branches, street lights, power lines, sign posts, guard rails. Ted slows down and turns the defrost on higher. "Sabina, this is treacherous. You have to remember, I haven't driven in this kind of weather in years."

The road ahead is layered with ice. I look at the speedometer: Ted is doing twenty, and even that seems too fast for conditions. He drives for ten or fifteen minutes, crawling at a careful pace. "It *is* bad," I say. "And I'm sure nothing has been salted because it's Christmas." As we inch along I can't help but marvel in spite of the danger at the beauty of it all. In the soft light of the street lamps, the whole city appears to be encased in icy glass.

"I'll be honest with you, Sabina, I don't like ice storms. I've got four wheel drive which helps in the snow, but nothing helps on ice. Once, when I was in high school, two of my buddies and I got caught in a terrible ice storm. The trees were so ice-laden they toppled onto houses and knocked out power. We got stranded at school and had to sleep there, believe it or not, for the night. I say we head for my place."

"You just want to get me to your apartment."

"No, I'm not kidding, we need to get off the road. It's that bad."

The second we get to Ted's apartment I call over to Rosa's, praying as I dial, that Mama and Papa haven't left yet. They haven't, and Rosa assures me that Mama, Papa, and Colina will be spending the night at her house. She reports that everyone else made it home safely. "Good," I say relieved. I tell Rosa that I'll be spending the night at Ted's. I say this nonchalantly, as if it were a frequent occurrence and give her the number.

"Have fun," Rosa says before hanging up.

I hang up the receiver and turn to hear a single, loud POP, the sound of a wine bottle being uncorked. I wonder how I will ever get through this night. In the short time it takes me to call Rosa, Ted has pulled together a plate of cheese and crackers, some wine glasses and a bottle, excuse me, *the* bottle of wine. Somehow, he's even found the time to light two ivory pillar candles that sit on his coffee table. There's some soft saxophone music playing. He pats the seat next to him on the sofa. "Come have some wine."

I go sit next to him and he hands me a glass. I'm careful to hold it by the stem since, God forbid, I am in the presence of a wine snob. He must read my mind because he says, "Not to be a wine snob or anything but this is an absolutely exquisite bottle of wine. Nineteen ninety-five Chateau Margaux Margaux. Yes, you say the *Margaux* part twice. Kind of nice having a generous boss; last year I got a fruit cake."

"You should have saved it for a special occasion."

"The fruitcake?!"

"No, the wine."

A smile spreads across his face. "This is a special occasion!"

"It is?" I ask.

"Sabina!" he says, gliding the back of his hand along my flushed cheek. "Don't look so scared. I just meant—it's Christmas!"

He clinks his glass against mine and then we sip simultaneously. It is the most beautiful wine I have ever tasted, slipping elegantly down my throat. I actually sigh, and a little part of me thinks that maybe everything will be all right. But then Ted exclaims, "Kallistaphulos!" in a loud booming voice.

"What?" I ask. "Why did you say that?"

"Don't you remember, it means *with fine grapes.*"

"Oh, right," I say, "I guess I forgot." And then he goes on in his professional sommelier voice about how this is the wine of the vintage, the greatest Chateau Margaux ever produced. A truly stupendous red. Full bodied and thick, yet kind of racy. Harmonious in structure with a long, long, long finish.

All of a sudden, while Ted rambles on about masses of tannins, I'm hit with a great idea. A great, great idea. An idea that will get me through the night. I'll just talk and talk and talk. I'll just keep my lips flapping, telling story after story after story of my life beginning with the day I was born, turned blue, and almost died. He's been begging me to tell him my story. Tonight's the night he's going to get it.

I take another sip of wine and look up at Ted. He rubs my neck and says, "Wish I had a fireplace."

Maybe this isn't going to be as easy as I thought. Well, here goes: "Ted, did I ever tell you about the time my sister Marina threw me into our fireplace?"

"Threw you into the fireplace? No!"

"Yes!"

"Why would she do a thing like that?"

"Well she didn't exactly *throw* me in, but..."

***

The bottle of wine is gone. I have been talking for three hours. I think Ted's clock says two-o-nine, but I can't be sure. One thing's for sure—he now knows my life story. Everything from the dog-bite in third grade to the tonsillectomy in high school. He knows about the time my family accidentally left me at the movie theater, the time I was interviewed on WGN for discovering counterfeit money that was being passed in our neighborhood, and about the time I performed the Heimlich maneuver on a little boy in our store and was said to have saved his life. I haven't even stopped talking to go to the bathroom. He now knows my favorite color, my favorite opera, my favorite rock band, my favorite author, movie, food, and singer. He knows my favorite dog, my favorite actor, my favorite actress, my favorite comedian. *Periwinkle, La Bohem, the Beatles, John Steinbeck, It's A Wonderful Life, stuffed artichokes, James Taylor, golden retriever, Johnny Depp, Kathy Bates, Steve Martin.*

He's been yawning for the last half hour but I pretend not to notice. "Hey, listen," he says, "why don't we get some sleep?"

"But I'm not tired."

"I thought you were wiped."

"But I got a second wind."

"Well, my wind has died. Come on," he says and pulls me by the arm, "I just bought a new mattress and box spring. It's so comfortable."

"Oh, well, I'm not ready for that. I'm sorry, I'm just not."

"Sabina, I'm only proposing sleep. Honest. I'm too tired for anything else. But I would like to sleep with you—in the literal sense of the word."

I say nothing, so he adds, "Or you can take the bed and I'll take the couch."

I'm just about to say I'll take the couch and you take your bed when the phone rings. He heads to the kitchen to pick it up and I can tell right away that it's his mother. "It was my mother," he says as he walks back into the room. "She woke up from a sound sleep certain that I'd been in a car acci—" He stops because he sees that I'm on the couch and that I'm fast asleep. I know it's a dirty trick, but since I am not experienced in these matters, it's the best thing I could come up with. I try not to flutter my eyelids. I feel a nice heavy blanket being pulled over me and I hear the lamp switch off and see the darkness against the inside of my eyelids. I really am asleep, I tell myself. I'm nothing if not a quick-thinker.

But now I'm lying here with my eyes scrunched shut, feeling very disappointed that Ted didn't kiss me goodnight. What is my problem? I never took myself for a woman who played games with a man's emotions, but I guess I haven't had that many opportunities. I have to wonder why God put women together this way. I fade off into a wine-soaked sleep.

My full bladder wakes me up. I can't see the time on my watch, but my inner clock tells me it's somewhere around four. Oh my, all that wine! I'm about to burst. I gain my footing and head for the bathroom, but then I hear water running, and I see that the bathroom door is shut. I'm afraid I can't hold it and I pace around the living room like a child, desperately trying to come up with alternatives. The kitchen sink? Disgusting! But I'm sure Ted doesn't have a second bathroom. Wait a minute—maybe there was a small master bath. I take a chance and tiptoe into his room. There is a door, but when I open it, I find only a closet. The scent of his clothes comes rushing out at me. It's the only door in the room—I'm out of luck. I turn to exit his room when I come face to face with him, still dripping, with only a towel wrapped around his waist.

"Sabina!"

"I'm sorry. I just needed to use the bathroom really bad and I thought maybe you had a second one in here." I don't wait for him to respond, I just rush past him and make it to the bathroom in the nick of time. When I come out, I see that he's thrown on a bathrobe and he's leaning against the wall in the hallway.

"Feel better?" he asks.

"Much. All that wine." He looks nice in his robe. "What time is it anyway?"

"A little after four. How'd you sleep?"

"Fine. Great. How about you?"

"Terrible. I just got up to take a cold shower, Sabina. You're driving me crazy."

"I'm driving you crazy?"

"Yes!"

"What? Was I snoring? I don't snore. My sister Marina snores, but I don't snore. Do I snore?"

He laughs and grabs me and presses me to him. "No, but you're here in my house, on my couch, and, well, I'd rather have you in there," he turns me toward his bedroom, "with me."

"I know." I pull away a little. "I told you, I'm just not ready."

He leans back against the wall again and lets out a sigh. "I know, I know. And I'll wait until you're ready, I promise."

I hug him. "Thank you, that means a lot to me."

"Uhhmmmm, have any idea how long it might take until you *are* ready?"

"Ted!"

"Just so I can, you know, pace myself. And you know, save up some money for the huge water bill I'm going to be getting from taking cold shower after cold shower after cold shower."

"I wish I could say. I guess I'll be ready when I'm ready."

"Months? Weeks? Days?"

"Ted!" I rub my temples. "Do you have anything for a headache?"

"Your head hurts?"

"Probably just from the wine."

"That was probably a two-hundred-and-eighty-dollar bottle of wine. It shouldn't have given you a headache."

I feel my jaw drop. "Two hundred and eighty dollars?"

"Something like that."

"Geez, I drank almost the whole bottle. How embarrassing."

"Come on," he says and slings his arm around my neck, "I've got something in the medicine cabinet." I take the two pills he hands me and wash them down. He looks exhausted, like he could fall asleep standing up. He says, "I'm going to try to get some sleep, okay?"

"Okay. I'm just going to use the bathroom again and then I'll do the same."

"Fine." He turns to go.

"Can I make us breakfast in the morning?" I ask.

"Sure, that would be nice."

"Would you like breakfast in bed?" I ask.

"I'd like you in bed."

I'm back on the couch, wrapped in the blanket. I've been finding myself on couches a lot lately. Maybe that means something, I don't know. I can't get comfortable. My butt cheek is really sore from falling at Rosa's.

I can't blame it on the wine because, other than the headache, I am thinking perfectly clearly, but out of nowhere, I am visited by that little Aunt Lina devil. She sits on my left shoulder and points an accusing finger at me. "There is a man in the other room who is crazy about you," she says. "You haven't been with a man in twenty years. As a matter of fact, you haven't ever been with a man, the other one was just a boy. This one is a man, a good man. Maybe too good for you."

I sit up straight and swallow hard. Ted deserves the truth. I pad across the carpet and down the hallway. When I come to his door, which he has left half-open, I knock lightly. "Ted? Are you awake."

"Yes."

"I have to talk to you." I open the door and slide through. "Can we just cuddle and talk?"

There is a window right above his headboard. I hear the wind pressing insistently on the panes. In the dim light, I see him sit up. He might be smiling. He throws back the covers and says, "Come on in."

I do. We snuggle but only from the shoulders up. The rest of his body he seems to keep at a safe distance, as if he's afraid to touch me. Can you blame him? I don't mean to torture him; but I have to tell him about the accident before we go any further. I bury my head in his neck—he smells clean and good.

"It's still raining," he says, his lips tickling my skin at the curve of my jawbone. "Everything must be encased in ice. Hey, your nose is like ice. Do you want me to turn the heat up?"

"The heat is up."

"I know. I'm glad you're here." He gives me a long kiss. "What's on your mind? You know what's on mine."

"Ted, listen. This is serious." He kisses my neck, the back of my ear, my ear lobe, the bridge of my nose, each of my eyebrows.

"This is serious, too."

"I know, but you're not going to like what I have to ask you. But I wouldn't ask you if it wasn't important. It's really important."

He stops kissing the individual features of my face. "What is it?"

"You have to tell me about your daughter, about what happened to your daughter. I don't think our relationship can move forward unless I know what happened to her."

He props himself up on his elbows, then scoots all the way up to a sitting position. "What? Why?"

I sit up, too. "Please, trust me. You have to tell me. Not all the details Ted, but please just tell me what happened to her."

"But I told you, Sabina, I don't talk about it. I can't talk about it. I never have—to anyone."

"But how can you release it if you can't talk about it?"

"Who says I want to release it? I embrace it, each and every day. It's pain I put on everyday like a pair of pants. I carry it with me everywhere, like a war wound." He slinks back down, burrows under the covers.

I remain sitting. It's cold by the window, and I let myself start thinking about why he would put his bed here underneath the window. I start rearranging the furniture in my mind just as a distraction. Safe and sound in this apartment, you can't hear the freezing rain the way you can hear ordinary precipitation. But you know it's raining ice because you feel the hair on your skin standing straight up, anticipating the danger of it all—the trees that fall on houses and power lines, the pipes that freeze, roads that become treacherous, sidewalks that turn unreliable, cars that run into ditches, or buildings, or—God-forbid—people. I shiver, and then I slither under Ted's covers, fully clothed in my sister Rosa's cotton cable knit sweater and my tan wool trousers, and feel the freezing rain as it drizzles down on me.

I'm quiet. He's quiet. It's a muffled quiet—the way the inside of your head sounds when you have a head cold. I'm the one who breaks the silence. "Was it a car accident, Ted?" I ask tentatively.

"Yes," he says, reluctantly.

"Was it more than one car?"

"Yes."

"Was her name Grace?"

"Yes." He turns to face me, his eyes questioning. "I don't understand. How do you know all of this?"

"I wish I didn't know. Please tell me, so I'll know if I know or not."

He turns away from me, to face the door. I snuggle up to him, putting my arm around his waist, fitting my knees into the bend of his knees. It's a good fit.

He says, "We hadn't seen my mother in a couple of days. Deidra adored her. Had to see her every couple of days or she'd have withdrawals. My wife—my ex-wife—was working late. She was a prosecutor, she always worked late. Back then I was freelancing—writing food and wine pieces for various magazines, and, believe it or not, I was working on a novel. So I had her a lot during the day. I wrote while she napped, I wrote while she played. I wrote a lot at night. We had this college student that watched her during the day, but I would often call her and cancel, saying I could handle it myself. We were buds. And of course she was amazingly smart and amazingly beautiful. My mother said she had me wrapped around her little finger, but really she had me wrapped around all her fingers. So we'd been to visit Deidra and she'd made soup and we had soup and she wrapped up some chocolate-chip cookies in waxed paper for Grace to take home. I loaded her in the car seat in the back of my car. On the right-hand side. We always put her on the right-hand side so you could see her and hand her a toy or a bottle or a cracker, you know?"

"My sisters always put their kids' car-seats on the right-hand side."

"Tell them not to; tell them to put them on the left."

"Okay, I will."

"So, we're driving along and we stop at a red-light and I peek back at her and see that she has unwrapped the chocolate-chip cookies. She's stuffed half of one in her mouth. She's starting to choke, which scares the hell out of me, so just as the light turns green, I pull out of that intersection fast. I gun it. I want to pull out and pull off the road as soon as I can." He swallows.

"Go on."

"Just as I pull out, this fucking—excuse me—asshole comes out of nowhere and slams into us. I don't even know what hit us—my eyes are fixed on the road ahead, on the place where I'm going to pull over. My head hits the side window. I'm not hurt, but I can't move. My head is frozen to the window, plastered to the window, because in my peripheral vision, I see the car that hit us. The front end of this little piece-a-shit of a car is inside of my car. And my little Grace... Oh, God..."

"Oh God," I say. My whole body feels like a raw wound. It dawns on me that I have also kept the accident—the accident itself—buried. It's too painful. And now I have felt the pain from both ends—Vito's and Ted's.

"Later, they told me that it was a three car accident. Some doped-up kid robbed a gas station and he was making his mad escape. He turned a corner at something like seventy and crashed into this other car that was stopped at a red light. When the kid hit that car, it propelled it into the intersection just as I was coming out. Sons-of-a-bitches, both of them. The one kid, the one who robbed the gas station, they put him away. Last year, though, he was up for parole. I'm not kidding, I almost lost it. Had dreams of doing him in with an automatic. They denied it. So then I could at least breathe until the next review came up. But then my attorney called and told me that the kid was stabbed to death in prison. And so, in a morbid way, I guess I should have felt some justice—that he was killed senselessly, too, but I didn't. I just felt worse, like I needed someone or something else to blame now that my original source of blame was gone. So then I started hating the other guy."

"The other guy?"

"The guy whose car actually hit us. That idiot had the gall to write Lizette and I a letter, asking for our forgiveness. Hell, I couldn't forgive myself much less anyone else. And Lizette, first she was numb, then her prosecutorial nature took hold and she blamed everyone and their brother for Grace's death. 'No matter what, it's always someone's fault' was her life's motto. It's a strange thing though, looking back, it wasn't even that guy's fault, but the thing was it was *his* face I saw, it was *his* car that was almost inside of my car. Lizette and I paired the two thugs together as one evil. I don't know what ever happened to the other guy. I do think about him though. Wonder about how it affected his life. Could you live with yourself?"

"No."

"Actually, I think about him more than I do about Ben Pendall, the robber. That kid was just bad inside and out. The other guy, though, he really was an innocent bystander, a victim too. But then why did I hate him so much? I guess because he has to live with it too. He wakes up everyday of his life and puts on the same pair of pants I do. And it bothers me to share it with him. It's my pain, not his. Does that make any sense?"

"Yes."

"It's *my* life that was ruined from that moment on. It's *my* wife that left me because I didn't grieve in the same way she did and because I didn't blame every single person on earth for our child's death. She went to support groups. I went inside myself, used my faith as a crutch. She wanted to talk about it every five minutes, wanted to include Grace in every conversation. We'd be out to eat and she'd say something like Grace would have loved this pizza or Grace would have gone crazy over that little puppy. I'm not put together that way, I tried to tell her. I feel my feelings deep inside. I don't want the world to watch me feel my feelings. She said I was in denial and of course I denied it. But later, much later, I realized, or I guess my shrink realized that yes, I am a denier. It's my defense mechanism of choice. Started after my father died."

He takes a long breath. "Lizette couldn't deal with me. And then the truth came out, that in fact she blamed me for the accident—I should have put the car seat on the left-hand side, I should have gone right home, not stopped at my mother's, and I never should have let Grave hold those cookies. What was I thinking? And Deidra never should have wrapped the cookies in waxed paper. Why hadn't she used a plastic bag? And then she went on this mission to sue the car-seat company and then the car manufacturer and the city of Chicago and the paramedics, and if she could have sued God, she would have. And so I do think about that other guy. Vito Salina was his name. And I think, is he as miserable as I am? Is his life as fucked-up as mine is? Has he ever found a way to forgive himself? And sometimes I dream about finding him. He shows up in the line at the bank, sitting in front of me at the movie theater, driving the cab I have just hailed. And I want to ask him these questions you see."

"Oh, Ted."

And now, with this all off of his chest, relayed without shedding a single tear, he turns to face me. "It's a piece of shit, Sabina. She was mine for such a short time. But to me, it was forever. So that's it. So what? You read about this in the newspaper?"

"Ted, I was at your daughter's funeral."

"What? You were? How?"

"Ted, Vito Salina was my fiancé."

Morning isn't even close to breaking through, but even in the soft, diluted light diffusing through the window, I can see his face go gray.

21

Service with a Smile

My Aunt Lina's second son, Luke, married a big time prima donna, Estelle Marie Sappington. Pampered and coddled by her wealthy parents—her mother served her breakfast in bed every single day of her life—she entered into marriage with my cousin with similar expectations. My Aunt Lina had warned Luke about the girl. She'd said: "She's a girl who'll need a lot of up-keep." Luke had said something like, "Ma, she's not a boat." But after two years of serving her breakfast in bed, he traded in Estelle Marie—for a boat.

The story left me with the thought that breakfast in bed—in the wrong bed—can be a dangerous thing, and should be reserved for special occasions only: birthdays, Mother's Day, Father's Day and an occasional sick day.

So why am I in Ted's kitchen whipping up a frittata and arranging a place-setting on a Chicago Bulls tray? Well, for one thing, I promised. And

299

for another thing, he has not said one word to me since I said, "Ted, Vito Salina was my fiancé." So now those six words are dangling in the air like a piñata waiting to be smashed to smithereens. Thirdly, this could constitute a sick day, since I think it's fair to say we are both sick about this whole thing.

I don't have much to work with—a couple of eggs, milk, a little cheese, a chunk of leftover ham from Rosa's, but I am able to whip up a nice frittata just the same. I toast and butter some bread, pour some orange juice and head for his room with the tray teetering in my hands.

Just as I push open the door with my foot the phone rings and Ted reaches for it from bed. His eyes are still closed. "Yeah, but that's okay. I was getting up anyway," he says into the receiver, and then opens his eyes and sees me. He squints and rubs his eyes, as if I am an apparition. He motions for me to come in and then motions again to set the tray on the bed. He scoots up, still listening intently, adding "Uh-huhs" and "I sees" and "that's greats" when appropriate. "Hey, I'm thrilled. I am. It's just that I just woke up. But I'm pumped. It'll be great. Okay then, I'll call you this afternoon, all right? Okay. Thanks for letting me know."

"Sounds like good news," I say, handing him a napkin and fork.

"It is. That was Clay. He got our first big project approved—the guy never stops, works in his sleep. I mean cripes, it's Christmas, but anyway, we're going to do this piece on how Chicago-style foods—thick-crust pizza, jumbo hot-dogs, T-bone steaks—have influenced other American cities. We leave for L.A. tomorrow. Probably be gone four or five days because from there we go to Dallas and then we finish up in New York City."

"Wow. That's great."

"We'll probably get back on the thirty-first."

"New Year's Eve."

"Oh yeah, New Year's Eve. Hey, this looks great. Thanks for cooking."

"Sure. No problem."

"Mmmmm. This is delicious," he says, but his voice sounds flat.

"Good."

"So," he says with a mouthful of eggs, "What are your plans for today? You know what I'll be doing—researching and packing."

"Oh, I've got promises to keep. I told Nino I'd build LEGOS with him. Rosa wants to shop for the after-Christmas sales. Papa likes to wax the floors in the store this week while we're closed."

"Well, looks like you've got a lot to keep you busy. Do you want to shower before I drive you home?"

All of a sudden, I get the feeling he wants me out of here. That he needs to get on with his day, his plan, his life.

"No, no, it's okay. I'll shower later."

"Okay then, I'll just be a minute. All right?"

"Fine."

He pecks me on the forehead and says, "Thanks again for breakfast," but to me it sounds just like "goodbye."

Before we leave, I make a few phone calls. Nino is ready and waiting: he's already sorted all two thousand three hundred forty-two LEGOS pieces into large margarine containers. Mama, Papa, and Colina are still at Rosa's so my plan is to play with Nino this morning, then spend the afternoon between Rosa's and the mall.

Ted says nothing on the ride over to Marina's, drives with the radio turned up high. Some oldies station blares out *Your Mama Don't Dance And Your Daddy Don't Rock 'N Roll* like that has anything to do with anything. I pretend to be preoccupied with the ice-glazed city. The sun is shining strong in the sky so now the city glitters and glistens as it thaws. Before my eyes the ice becomes prismatic, dispersing the refracted light. The tree branches seem to have been dipped in diamonds. Everything that was once a dull gray is now a sparkling silver. It is so devastatingly beautiful I want to cry.

When we pull into Marina's driveway, we both spot Nino with his face smashed up against the big picture window. "There's your biggest fan," Ted says. Then he turns to me and says, "Be sure to thank your family again for yesterday, it was great. And listen, I don't know if I'll have a chance to call you from the road...tight schedule...time changes...and Clay...you know how it is. So I'll call you when I get back, okay?"

I say "okay" even though I know he won't. And it's not like I know because of what I see on his face; I know because of what I don't see on his face anymore. He's pulled out. He's never even alluded to the conversation we'd had in his bedroom only a few hours ago. It's as if I'd never even brought up the subject. And now, I'm standing here, watching him pull out of my sister's driveway, realizing that I've left the shopping bag full of my Christmas presents in his trunk, and wishing I had never brought up the subject at all.

I play LEGOS with Nino all morning and shop-till-I-drop with Rosa, Lauren, Claire, Colina, and Mama in the afternoon. Then Rosa insists that we all stay for dinner to help polish off the leftovers. Throughout the day, my sisters have been teasing me about how convenient the storm was—what a great excuse to stay at Ted's. And just how romantic was it? And how happy they all are for me. "Ted's great." "Ted's great." I am sick to death of hearing how great Ted is. And now at the dinner table, Rosa informs me that Ed has agreed to let her throw one of her famous New

Year's Eve bashes (he swore last year's party was her last), and of course I just have to bring Ted. I remind her that Ted is away all week on business.

Rosa pouts and says, "But he'll be back by New Year's Eve, won't he? You just can't spend another New Year's Eve alone, Sabina." The people at the table freeze, but I say nothing. Even so, Rosa infers correctly from the look on my face that I am offended. "That didn't come out right," she says, and then, "Who would like some more dressing?"

***

I have decided not to sulk. The best thing, I tell myself, is to do what I always do during the week between Christmas and New Years—play with my nieces and nephews. So when I get home I get out my new day planner and arrange my week. I pencil in ice-skating with Rosa's kids on Monday and sledding with Marina's boys on Tuesday. Colina wants me to help her move back home on Wednesday and then stay the first night with her and the girls. Thursday I'll take Angie and the two little ones out to lunch and then to an indoor play center. I'll be way too busy to even think about what's-his-name.

But then I look at the box for Friday, December thirty-first. New Year's Eve. It's empty. Naked. I will leave it blank, I tell myself, just in case Ted gets home in time for Rosa's party and still wants to be with me. I pick up the phone to call all my sisters to make the week's arrangements and I can't help but think, who am I kidding? I will not be hearing from Ted Kallista again. Now I'm actually glad that I didn't sleep with him. Just imagine how different I'd be feeling now. The regrets. The humiliation.

I hang up the phone. Everything is set. Now I don't have to even think about Ted.

Monday I hardly thought about him. I had to devote all my mental energy to staying upright on ice-skates. The day slipped by and I thought I had it whipped—how nice that it only took one day to forget about Ted. But now it's Tuesday and I'm here sledding with my nephews and everything reminds me of Ted. This is mean to say, but Nino is getting on my nerves, asking me questions just to keep my undivided attention. "Aunt Bina, why does that kid have holes in his cheeks?" he asks as he helps me drag the toboggan up the hill.

"They're called dimples."

"Looks like someone took a screwdriver and went at it," Marc says.

"Be nice," I say.

"What's wrong, Aunt B?" Carl asks, his eyebrows all scrunched together.

Even they know I'm not myself.

On Wednesday, I help Colina and the girls move back home. Their house is quiet and dusty; there's a sadness in the air, in the walls. All day we clean while the girls play with their Christmas toys and get reacquainted with their rooms.

Colina's eyes are moist throughout the day. "Allergies," she tells Nicole. "At least he keeps paying the bills," she says to me.

"What's going to happen?" I ask her.

"I don't know. I'll get whatever I can from him, but I might have to get a job."

"It's not fair, especially for Chelsea."

"Well, I will *not* put her in a daycare. He can pay for a nanny if I need to work. I hate to be like this but I'm not going to make it easy for him. I just want things easy for the girls."

For supper we fix blueberry pancakes and eat them with tall cold glasses of milk. We bathe and bed down the girls and then we watch TV in Colina and John's bedroom. They have a massive bed and a television set suspended from the wall like in a hospital room. We watch David Letterman. Colina even laughs once or twice. When the show ends, we read for a while.

We're just about to turn out the light when Colina springs from bed and says, "Hold on a minute. I've got to show you something." I see her open up her jewelry box and slide a ring on her right hand. She walks over to me and extends her hand out to me. There's a beautiful diamond cocktail ring on her finger and for a moment I think she has taken her engagement ring and had it reset. "I'm not supposed to tell, but it's from Aunt Lina! What do you think I should do with it?"

I start laughing. "She gave me one, too! For my birthday."

"She did? That stinker! She acted like I was so special or something. So you kept yours?"

"I have it. I never wear it though."

"Why do you think she's giving away her jewels? And do you think she's given anything to the other girls?"

"I don't know."

"It's weird."

"It is weird."

She returns the ring to her jewelry box, standing there at her dresser for a while. She's tries on another ring, stares at her finger for a second and then removes it and throws it back into the box. "Bastard," she spits.

She tells me to go ahead and turn off the light, that she is just going to check on the girls. But I hop out of bed because I want to see them, too. I know I've been complaining about the sleeping arrangements at our house, but I am really going to miss my nieces. Each one looks so peaceful in her own bed.

Colina and I climb back into bed. I switch off the light, ready for a long, deep sleep. These kids take everything out of you. In the dark, I feel the bed shake as Colina tries to get situated. It crosses my mind that when your husband abandons you and your children, no position is comfortable.

"Sabina?" she whispers.

"Yes?"

"Thanks for everything. It's good to be home anyway."

"I bet it is."

"And Sabina?"

"Yeah."

"Ted's really great."

Hearing her say this makes me sad. And that long, deep sleep that I was preparing for only moments ago doesn't come until hours and hours into the night.

***

Angie and I are back at her house after our McDonald's run. We got both of the kids down for naps and now we are vegging out, each on a love seat covered with a soft cotton throw. I don't know why—maybe just to juxtapose myself against my nutrition-minded sister—but I ordered and devoured a quarter-pounder with cheese extra value meal. It tasted great going down. It gave me such satisfaction eating it as I watched my sister eat her salad with low-fat dressing. I even finished off Alexandria's fries.

This feels good. Just lying here. I haven't had this much alone time with Angie in a long time. "Should I make us some hot tea?" she asks.

"Don't even move."

"This is heaven, you know. You don't know how heaven this is for me," she says and sighs. "I don't know if I'm just unorganized or what, but I can't find one minute for myself. If you weren't here right now, I'd be scrambling—throwing in a load of laundry, filling the dishwasher. My ironing basket is like the loaves and fishes—you throw in three shirts that need ironing and the next thing you know the basket is overflowing."

"It's a miracle," I say.

She closes her eyes, repositions herself, and sighs again. I've heard that sigh before—all of my sister's sigh like that. I don't know exactly how to describe it, but it's a sigh that says, all in one breath, about how this parenting thing is so hard, so tiring, yet so unbelievably wonderful.

"Poor Colina," she says and yawns.

"Yeah."

304

"But lucky Sabina." She opens her eyes to smile at me. "Ted's really great."

"Yeah," I say, "I know."

***

It's five forty-five post meridiem, New Year's Eve, and I'm waiting in Papa's car outside of Virgie and Pauly's house. The temperature has plummeted again and the wind chill is minus five. I'm crazy to even venture outside on a night like tonight. I can't bring myself to go in— nothing could make this day more pitiful than laying eyes on Pauly—but I think it's rude to honk, so I'm just sitting here, idling, wasting gas, and hoping Virgie will peek out her window some time in this century and see that I am here.

No, Ted has not called. No, I have no idea if he's back or still on his trip, or if he's moved to Kalamazoo, but—and wait until you hear this— out of desperation (Rosa kept asking if Ted and I would were coming to her party tonight and Mama and Papa wanted to know how many lobster tails to buy since they like to have a quiet New Year's Eve at home) I called Virgie about an hour ago and inquired as to her New Year's Eve plans. Since Pauly hates New Year's Eve and she didn't have plans I begged her to do something with me. I told her I'd even see that Mel Gibson movie again if she wanted.

You see, I'm beside myself. I've done something so totally pathetic: I've lied to Mama and Papa and all of my sisters. Told them that Ted and I would be spending a quiet New Year's Eve at his place. Okay, okay, I know it was a stupid thing to do, that the lie will catch up with me sooner or later, but I just couldn't face the music. Not today, not on New Year's Eve.

I did tell Virgie the truth. But not all of it. Not over the phone. I just told her that something terrible had happened between Ted and me, that I'd tell her all about it tonight.

Virgie finally peeks out her window and waves. She navigates the icy sidewalks in her spiked, black leather, totally-impractical-for-this-kind-of-weather boots. The car comes to life when she slides in. Her cologne, a mixed bag of lemon and lime, permeates the interior of the car and makes me hungry for key-lime pie. Her big, pumpkin-colored hair, loose and frizzy today, seems to have a life of its own. I've missed her and am glad for the opportunity to catch up on what's going on with Pauly.

"Nothing," she tells me now, munching on a slice of Bruschetta as we share an early dinner at the Buona Fortuna Cafe, an unpretentious neighborhood place on North Milwaukee. We are here extra early because we want to be sure to miss the crowds of romantic couples that will emerge upon the city somewhere around eight tonight.

There is some major male-bashing going on at our table. "He's so pathetic," Virgie says about Pauly, "that I haven't been able to bring myself to leave the poor bastard."

"But he must know you're unhappy," I say.

"Hell no. He thinks everything is copasetic. Thing is, I have to get a better job before I leave him. Plus, I want to pay off my car—only three more payments. I've found an apartment I can afford but only without the car payment. I've got my savings, but I will not dip into that for everyday expenses. I wish I'd gone to college like my father told me to."

"You know, I've been thinking about something," I tell her. "And with everything that's been going on I haven't even had a chance to bring it up. Here it is: how would you like to have Mama's job when she retires? I'd even give you the title of head chef."

"Sabina!" she says way too loudly. She looks around the room. "God, just throw this at me, why don't you! Wow!"

"Well, I need a really great cook if I'm going to pull this off. I'm so scared, Virgie. I read something frightening about family businesses the other day—that a family can move from rags to riches, to rags, in three generations."

"Who said that?"

"I don't know, I think it was anonymous."

"Sabina, didn't you know? Anonymous is an asshole! If the quote was any good, somebody would take credit for it!"

"Oh, Virgie."

"Honest, you'll do great. It will never be exactly the same as it is now, but you'll do great."

The waitress sets our pasta in front of us. We have both always wanted to try the pasta with anchovy sauce, so this time —since neither of us will be kissing anyone at midnight—we go for it. "Mmmmm. It's divine," Virgie says. I taste and agree. The waitress told us that they cut the anchovies into little pieces and then cook them down in olive oil until they almost disintegrate. Then they add fresh breadcrumbs to the sauce. It's smooth and delicious and not as salty as you might imagine.

"God. Work at Mela's Market. I don't know, Sabina. I always said I'd never work for a friend. It's not a good idea. What if it doesn't work out?"

"Then I'd fire you, same as anyone else."

"Or I'd quit."

"Right. Come on, you love books, but cooking is your life. And maybe this will force us to write our cookbooks."

"Let me think about it." We eat our pasta, not caring a whit about our breath smelling of fish. "Okay I've thought about it," Virgie says. "I'm close to a yes, but I'd need to know who else will be cooking?"

"Don't worry, it won't be Aunt Lina. I'm sure she'll retire, too. She's just there to boss around Mama and annoy Papa. You can hire whomever you want."

"I'd like someone who knows his or her way around a kitchen but who is untrained so that I can teach the person the way I want."

"Fine, no problem. I'll be replacing everybody but Jimmy. Papa says Mr. Maggio will probably retire when they do, so I'll be starting almost from scratch. I'll need a good baker, a real breadman. Oh, Virgie, I'd love to have you cook!"

"You know it would be my dream come true, but Bina, let's be realistic, I'd need to make more money than I'm making now. Do you know about salary yet?"

We talk about salary and benefits over dessert and wine. Then I tell Virgie about Ted. For some reason, I can tell her everything—all the things that I cannot tell Mama and Papa and my sisters right now. They are too close. Virgie has the ability, like only a friend has, to stand two feet back from my problems so she can look at them objectively. Things always look different from her vantage point—not nearly as impossible, or devastating, or as bad as all that. Take the Vito situation for example. She only knew Vito for a couple of years. After he left, we talked about him once and only once. She admitted to me then that she'd had her concerns about his stability, which I can certainly appreciate since by the time Virgie met Vito he was wired for sound. She never knew the sweet, serious, boy with the long eyelashes and rosy cheeks. But she'd said her piece in so many words and never brought the subject up again.

This is why I can bleed my heart to Virgie. When I do get around to telling my family about Ted and the accident and that Grace was his daughter, they will react in predictable ways. Mama will be devastated. She'll cry and she'll light a million candles and she'll call her prayer chain, and they'll all pray to Saint Monica, the patron saint of unanswered prayers. Rosa will try to plan a sleep-over at the Four Seasons; Marina will recommend a good therapist; Colina will sink into an even deeper depression, wondering if she did me wrong by assisting me in excavating Vito from my room and my life at such a fragile time; and Angie will want Ted's address so she can send Art over to beat him up. Do I need this?

Here's what Virgie says: "For the love of God, Sabina, what are the chances? I am so sorry. It's a weird stroke of, of, of bad connections, I guess. You're crazy about him, aren't you."

"I really wanted you to meet him…"

"But why are you so sure it's over? Maybe he's not back yet from his trip. Maybe he'll call tomorrow."

"No, no, if he was going to call he would have called by now. I know it's over. I knew it on Sunday. I don't know how I know, I just know."

"Oh, Sabina," she says.

We leave a huge Happy New Year tip and walk across the street to the hardware store lot where we parked. Our next stop is Virgie's bookstore. Usually when people are off work, they don't want to step foot in their place of employment, but with Virgie, it's different. The bookstore is more of a home to her than her brown bungalow. And a bookstore is a happy place; not happy-happy, but happy-contented. Isn't it a harbor of sorts? A place offering some answers, or at the very least, some pretty good guesses.

I've been meaning to ask Virgie about the cute guy at the bookstore she told me about, but truth be told, I'm a little jealous. I mean she's got a husband, right? It's not anyone's fault but her own that she settled for beer when she could have waited for champagne. When I do ask her she says simply, "Dead end. Married with kids." He showed her pictures. Of his wife, even.

She and I have done this before—the dinner-bookstore date. Once inside we go our separate ways, Virgie to classic literature and me to photography books and travel books. Sometimes we hide out in Personal Growth and make fun of some of the titles: *"Be Your Absolute Best in Five Minutes!" "How to Succeed Without Even Trying!" "Don't Ever Say Never Again!"* And my personal favorite: *"How To Be an Upper When Your Life Is a Downer."* I like to linger in the Spirituality section, but I'm nothing if not a traditional Roman Catholic so some of the New Age stuff is really unsettling to me. But browse where we may, we always seem to find our way back to the cookbooks.

I'm looking through a new one right now—a celebrity cookbook whose proceeds are to be donated to AIDS research—but I'm not too impressed with the recipes since they run along the lines of unoriginal: Three Cheese Macaroni and Spinach Lasagna. Here's another new book—I haven't seen it before anyway—called *"Cooking in the Nude"* by Debbie and Steven Cornell.

"What will they think of next?" I hear a man say. I look up to find Clay, Ted's boss, standing next to me in the Cooking section. "Are there pictures?" he asks with a devilish grin. He *is* a good-looking man.

"Just of the food," I say.

"Have we met?" he asks, suddenly finding me familiar.

"I don't think so," I say as casually as I can, then I stand on my tiptoes and peer over the bookshelves pretending to look for someone.

"My mistake," he says politely, then, "May I?"

I hand him the book. "I've just returned from a business trip and I always bring my wife a gift. Well, this trip there wasn't a free moment, so I'm going to cheat a little and pick up something here."

"It's the thought that counts," I say, realizing that this comment is about as original as macaroni and cheese.

"You're right. What does it matter if I bought this book in L.A. or Dallas or New York? It will make a nice edition to our cookbook collection regardless. Is this the only copy?"

"Yes, but be my guest. I don't even sleep in the nude. There's not much chance of me cooking in the nude." I don't believe I just said that.

"I don't know," he says, that smirk returning to his face, "if my wife is up for it, it could be quite interesting." He laughs just thinking about it and turns to leave. "Happy New Year!" he shouts back at me.

I plop into the leather chair placed strategically between the Cooking Section and the bookstore cafe. How clever to put the cafe near the cookbooks. Drooling customers need only walk a few feet to satisfy their photograph-induced hunger. But I am suffering from pains other than hunger. I am having a pseudo-anxiety attack. Clay's appearance at the bookstore means that Ted is indeed back in town. It's like re-knowing what you already know: it's really over.

I can't wallow in my sorrows for long because Virgie emerges suddenly from either Personal Growth or Spirituality and is heading determinedly my way with a small book pressed to her generous bosom.

"I'm glad you are sitting for this. You are not going to believe this, Sabina. You are *so* not going to believe this."

"You are not going to believe who I just saw. Who I just talked to!"

She cuts me off. "No, no, honest, this is bigger. Unless it was Elvis...then yours is bigger."

"Virgie, what is it?"

She takes the book that is pressed to her breast and turns it so that the cover faces me. At first I don't get it. It's some prayer book. No, it's a cookbook. No it's a prayer book. I read the title out loud: *"Father Bonaventure's Food and Prayer Book.* Yeah, so?"

"So, open it up to the back flap of the jacket, Sabina." I give her a puzzled look. She says, "Go on, open it."

Nothing could prepare me for what I see on the back flap of the jacket. I repeat, nothing could prepare me. Father Bonaventure is a handsome, salt-and-pepper gray-haired man, with dark brown bespectacled eyes, and a full but trim beard. Father Bonaventure is Vito.

***

I let Virgie drive Papa's car to her house. I say it's because of the one and a half glasses of wine I had at dinner, but we both know that's not the reason. On my lap is a white paper bag from the bookstore. Inside of the bag is Vito's book. I could not bring myself to look through it at the bookstore. I was too worried about how I might react in public.

I keep my eyes peeled to the road. Virgie, admittedly, is not the best driver. She doesn't give it her total attention is the problem. And she doesn't give herself enough time to brake. I'm nothing if not a backseat driver, but not today, not now. I'm not so much numb as I am limp. I need to get home and in my room before I can sort this all out.

Virgie is doing her best to distract me, trying to make me laugh. She's knows I'm down but she can't conceal her "up." She tells me, yes, she definitely wants to come and work with me. She's decided she's going to tell Pauly tonight—everything—so that in the morning she can wake up a new woman and make a fresh start on the first day of the new year.

"But don't forget, Virgie, it will be some time before your start date."

"I know, I know. I'm not going to quit my job or anything. But I want to get the wheel rolling. We'll have to sell the house and everything." She looks at me and smiles. "It's time to tell him. That or I'm going to have to kill him."

"Virgie!"

"Sabina, you don't know what I've been living with. I've put up with the fifteen-minute rotations for all these years." (Pauly can only perform a function or a task for fifteen minutes at a time, then he has to stop and do something else for fifteen minutes.) "I've accommodated all of his idiosyncrasies: the way he stacks his loose change on his dresser at night into neat little towers of nickels, dimes, pennies, and quarters." She brakes inches from the green mini-van in front of us. My head jerks back, but she doesn't even pause to take a breath. "The way he puts on his right sock then his right shoe, then his left sock and his left shoe, instead of just putting on his socks first and then his shoes second like normal people. The man logs every phone call he makes. You know what he was doing before I left?"

"No, what?"

"You know how at Christmas they make red and green M 'n' Ms? Well, he was sorting them separately into two glass jars. Why? Then we can eat the red ones for Valentine's Day and the green ones for St. Patrick's Day. I'm not kidding."

"Wow."

"Wow nothing. He has two books of stamps at all times. One is marked with the letter 'O' on the cover and the other one is marked with the letter 'E'. If he needs an odd number of stamps, he removes them from the book marked with the 'O' and if he needs an even number of stamps, well, you see where I'm going with this. I'm going crazy."

"I never knew he was like that."

"Oh, Sabina. And the man eats like an alien. Here's how he eats his breakfast cereal: he pours cereal, then milk, eats a little, then keeps adding a little cereal, a little milk, so that the milk and cereal ratio stay at fifty percent until it's gone. He doesn't like different foods to touch each other on his plate, plus, he eats clockwise, finishing one food before moving to the next."

"Well I do that, eat the food on my plate in courses."

"You do not."

"Yes, I do."

"You do not."

"Yes, I do."

"I've never noticed and I've been eating with you for years."

"Well, I try not to do it in public, because I know it's a little weird."

"Well, see, you can control it. Pauly can't."

She pulls up in front of her house. I feel for Virgie. I wonder if I'd have the courage to walk through that front door. A blue glow from the TV emanates through the sheer curtains in the living room window. Virgie must see this too, because before she slams the door shut, she says, "And the man never cracks open a book either."

I am at a loss for words, so I say nothing as I come around to the driver's side. I hug her and thank her for saving me tonight.

"Hey, you know, maybe it's a good thing," she says. "Vito's book. If nothing else it's closure."

"I don't know what it is yet."

"I don't think he does either—what is it, a cookbook or a prayer book?"

"I don't know. I'll let you know tomorrow."

She starts to walk up her icy sidewalk, then turns around and says to me, "Hey, don't make a big deal about that book. It really has nothing to do with Ted and you."

But it does, it has everything to do with Ted and me.

I make sure she gets in and then I pull out onto the road. The clock on the dashboard says eleven twenty-seven. It's way too early to arrive home on New Year's Eve (Mama and Papa were already a little suspicious of New Year's plans that included me driving to Ted's house in this kind of weather), so I stop at Starbucks and get a decaf double latte. I drive around, take a pleasure cruise. The neighborhood Christmas lights sparkle cheerfully. There are people everywhere in spite of the frigid temperatures. They huddle in doorways, spill out of bars, walk hand-in-hand, hail cabs. I drive and I drive until I get sick of driving and I pull over onto a quiet street a few blocks from our store. With the engine running, I just sit here and listen as they count down the year's top one hundred hits.

Now it's eleven fifty-seven. My coffee is gone, they're playing the number one hit of the year (something I've never heard of and this makes me feel really, really old) and I decide to head for home. Just as I'm pulling out, my headlights dim out and Papa's car dies. I try to start it up again but it won't turn over. I wait a bit, then try again. Nothing but that uh-uh-uh, uh-uh-uh whine. Now what? Call Mama and Papa and say, "Just wanted to wish you a Happy New Year. And by the way, the car is dead. Can you come and pick me up?"

This is the very reason I have lived most of my life without telling lies—because I'm terrible at it. I'm not talking about the little white lies told in response to questions like "Do I look fat in this?" and "What do you think of my new boyfriend?" I'm talking about big whomping lies like the one I told tonight. I hope this is a good lesson to myself.

I pull the cell phone out of my purse and dial our number. When Mama answers, I say, "Happy New Year, Ma."

"Ted called," she says flatly.

"Ted called?"

"Yes! About, oh let's see, four hours ago."

A wave of emotions washes over me: joy, relief, then guilt and trepidation. "What did you tell him, Mama?"

"Sabina, where are you and why did you turn your phone off?"

"Ma, what did you tell him?"

"I said you were out."

"But you didn't say with whom, right?"

"If I did, I would have to have said, 'she's out with you.'"

"Oh, right. Ma, listen, I was with Virgie. We got a bite to eat and then we went to the bookstore. I'll explain when I get home."

"Where are you?"

"On Lexington, right off of Racine, not far from Uncle Silvio's. I don't know why but the car just all of a sudden died on me. Could you send Papa out to get me? It's too cold to have someone jump the battery tonight."

"Sabina, are you all right?"

"I've been better, Ma."

"Stay in the car. Papa's putting his coat on. I'll make some decaf and we'll talk about this. Won't we?"

I hit the end button and slip the phone back in my purse. My stomach has tied itself into knots. I hope Papa gets here soon. I can already see my breath.

***

My fingers are wrapped around a mug of hot hazelnut cream coffee and Mama has wrapped a heating pad around my frigid feet. She's sitting across from me in her recliner—Papa has left us alone to talk—patiently waiting for me to come clean. I hate to get into it. Where do I start? With Ted? Or with Vito, or should I say Father Bonaventure? And am I the only person left on earth who is using her real name?

I start with what happened with Ted. I tell her everything—everything except Ted's real occupation. About how I'm really falling for Ted and he for me. About my Christmas Eve discovery that he is Grace Kallistaphulos's father. And about how he froze up like an icicle when I told him about Vito. "After he left on his business trip I honestly didn't think I would ever hear from him again," I tell her.

"Now why would you think such a thing? The man is crazy about you—everyone can see it."

"Because, Mama, he said the way he deals with his daughter's death is just to bury it. I come along and because of who I am I've dug everything up. I don't think he could wake up to my face everyday. It would be too painful. I would be a constant reminder of what happened to his little girl. Geez, Mama, that's what broke up his marriage, he and his ex-wife dealt with their grief so differently."

She gets out of her chair and comes over to join me on the couch. "I think you're being melodramatic, as usual. Besides, the accident was not Vito's fault."

"Yes, but Ted still blames him."

"Oh, Sabina," she says, smoothing and patting the top of my hand. "He'll call tomorrow. He said he would."

She hugs me and I tell her that there's more. I tell her that Virgie found this book tonight at the bookstore. "Guess who wrote it?" I say.

"Sabina, just tell me."

"Vito."

"What? You mean you found him? He's alive?" (I think the only way Mama was able to deal with Vito's running away and never coming back was to convince herself that he was dead.) She covers her mouth with her hand and starts to cry. "Where is he?"

"He lives in Ohio. He's a priest, Mama, a Franciscan priest."

"*Marona!*" she says and then covers her mouth again. "Go wake up your father."

"No, Ma, let him sleep. I'll show you the book."

The first thing I do is show Mama his picture. She agrees that he looks exactly the same except for his salt-and-pepper hair and full beard. His eyes still look young and vibrant, and although I can't tell by the picture, I'm sure his lashes are lush and long. He's dressed in a dark brown friar's robe, the kind St. Francis of Assisi wore. His smile is so wide and genuine it makes me mad. How can he be so happy? What right does he have?

Mama flips through a few pages, shaking her head. "What do you make of this?" she asks me.

"I don't know. I've just thumbed through it myself."

"Well, you should read it first, *bedda.*" She closes the book and hands it to me. "Papa and I can read it tomorrow." She kisses my forehead and turns the lamp up a notch.

I start at the beginning:

FATHER BONAVENTURE'S FOOD & PRAYER BOOK

FEEDING YOUR FAITH

In God alone is there primordial and true delight, and in all our delights it is this delight that we are seeking. –St. Bonaventure

Introduction

Dear Kind Lady or Kind Sir,

I learned at a very early age growing up in an Italian-American family in Chicago's Little Italy that food has a spiritual component. It was on the end of a fork that I first found love. To show her love, an Italian mother dishes out hugs, kisses, pasta, and meatballs in equal proportions. My mother (like almost everyone's mother) was the best cook in the world.

To an Italian, food isn't just something you put into your mouth. Food has layers of meanings. In my father's family, if anyone took a bite of food before my grandfather did, it was as if that person had just slapped my grandfather across the face. And on my mother's side, competition ran fierce. My mother and her sisters didn't try to "one-up" each other when it came to clothes, decorating their homes, their husband's occupations, or their children's report cards, but look out if my mother's *cannoli* were better than my Aunt Mary's.

When Italians immigrated to this country, they brought with them two things: a tradition for family and a tradition for food. Taylor Street, in Chicago's Little Italy, where I was born and raised, is famous for that food. Taylor Street is packed with great places to eat authentic Italian-American food—from Mom 'n' Pop joints to trendy storefronts.

It was the food I ate on Taylor Street that made me, at the age of thirteen, revise my life's vocation. I had decided at a young age that I had a calling to the priesthood, but instead of entering the seminary upon graduation, I entered culinary school. I still wanted to spread God's word, but first I wanted to spread it on a piece of bread. You see I felt and still feel, that the Word of God is more palatable on a full stomach. Don't you think Jesus thought so, too?

After culinary school, I worked in some fine Chicago restaurants where I prepared food so beautiful it was almost a shame to eat and food so simple and honest it sang in your mouth. While employed at a marvelous Italian bakery and cafe I was afforded the opportunity to visit Italy, Sicily, and one of her small islands called Salina on a hunt for authentic Italian breads, dishes and desserts. The experience of this trip served only to intensify my passion for food.

My life has taken many turns, but the constant has always been my cooking. No matter what else I was or wasn't doing, I always cooked. And it is through cooking that I was led to the calling again. Years ago I found myself cooking in this dumpy diner in Atlanta, Georgia. The owner of the place was the worst kind of crank and he didn't really care about the food. I was just about to quit, when one morning, this priest came in and sat down at the counter. I remember he ordered "a nice stack of flapjacks." There was something I liked about him, Father Luke. After a few conversations, I could tell that he not only had common sense, but also a peace about him that I envied. (He also had a healthy sense of humor, which is why I got away with calling him "Father Flapjack.") We got to be friends but then he was transferred and I lost track of him. One day, out of the blue, he walked into a soup kitchen where I was working in Berkeley, California. The moment I saw him, I knew. Knew that I'd been on the path to the religious life all along.

When I turned around again, I was Father Bonaventure, a Franciscan priest. My namesake was the successor of St. Francis of Assisi, whose name is said to have originated from the exclamation of St. Francis— *"O buona ventura!"* (Oh, what good fortune!)—upon seeing Bonaventure when he was brought as an infant to be cured of a life-threatening illness. This account has never been proven but I liked the name even before I liked the person.

The Franciscan Order has ever regarded Bonaventure as one of the greatest doctors of the Church, but I was impressed with his singular humility, the way he steadfastly refused honors, appointments and nominations. He was held in great esteem and respected by his peers because of his pure character and of the miracles attributed to him. Respected as he was, his secretary believed that he was poisoned to death in 1274. In 1434, when Bonaventure's remains were sent to the new church erected in Lyons in honor of St. Francis, his head was found in a perfect state of preservation, his tongue being as red as in life. A great philosopher and theologian, Bonaventure's writings are numerous, and what shines forth in all of his works was his tender piety and profound learning. And so it was in the spirit of this man, that I took my vows.

I have been a Franciscan priest for eight years now and whether I'm serving a small rural church in Ohio or a huge suburban parish in New York, my method of ministry madness has been the same: feed and pray. Over the years, friends have suggested that I write down some of my recipes. I tell them, first of all, they are not *my* recipes but family recipes that have been handed down from generations of Italian mothers. But who would want recipes from a cooking priest? Someone suggested a praying cookbook (a cookbook that prays? I asked). Someone else suggested a cooking prayer book (a prayer book that cooks?). We finally came up with this little Food and Prayer Book.

My tenure as a priest has been most rewarding. Over the years, my friend and mentor Father Luke has encouraged me to keep cooking, to keep feeding people, to keep feeding the faith. And that is exactly what I have been doing in this wonderful parish to which I have been assigned. I would like to share with you the fruits of this feeding and praying ministry. In this little book, you will find nurturing recipes, simple prayers, relevant Bible verses, and pithy quotations.

One hundred percent of the proceeds from the sale of this book will go directly to the St. Anthony Fund, a trust set up to benefit the needs of our parish, St. Anthony of Padua Church in New Bremen, Ohio. You see, like so many other small parishes in the country, we are struggling. Some say we are a dying parish, but hopefully, this little book will help save us. Every penny will be spent on the parish. (Franciscan priests take a vow of poverty in addition to chastity, so I have no bank account.)

So do a little cooking and do a lot of praying and if you can, do them simultaneously. Pray and Eat! *Pax et Boum!* (Peace and all good.)

Yours in Christ, Father Bonaventure

It's All About Food

Food should be treated with respect, since Our Lord left Himself to us in the guise of food. —Dorothy Day

Business underlies everything in our national life, including our spiritual life. Witness the fact that in the Lord's Prayer the first petition is for daily bread. No one can worship God or love his neighbor on an empty stomach. —Woodrow Wilson

If man can be sensible and one fine morning, while he is lying in bed, count at the tips of his fingers how many things in this life truly will give him enjoyment, invariably, he will find food is the first one. —Lin Yutang

If your enemy be hungry, give him food to eat, if he be thirsty, give him to drink. —Proverbs 25:21

HAVEN'T WE ALL at some time in our lives asked the question "What's it all about?" My parishioners ask me this question often. Some Catholics think priests have all the answers, but let me tell you this: I not only do not have all the answers, I don't even have all the questions. For example, a young parishioner asked me the other day—he must be five or six—how heaven smells. I have never even thought to ask the question!

Annie Dillard said this: "You were made and set here for this, to give voice to your own astonishment." Isn't that a wonderful reason to be here? We are the audience of the greatest show on earth—God's creation. (Have you applauded lately?) And it is astonishing—astonishingly beautiful, astonishingly ugly, astonishingly joyous, and astonishingly sad. Life is drama, comedy and tragedy. We are here for the show anyway, we might as well get a soda, some popcorn and a box of chocolate-covered raisins, and find someone to share them with.

The answer to the "what's-it-all-about" question has come to me over the years in small epiphanies. Little revelations that come as great AH-HAs! I believe the big picture is this: God made us spiritual beings, created in His image and likeness, and then deemed it important, no essential, for us, as spiritual beings, to experience *physical* life. We are not, even though we often live like it here on earth, physical beings attempting to live a spiritual life.

What's it all about? Why are we here? Jesus said: "I have come that you may have life, and have it more abundantly."

So we are called to live life abundantly, but how does one live life in the full? By passionately embracing the blessings that are constantly and abundantly bestowed upon us. Live with a passionate, grateful heart. Savor everything: nature, people, food, music, art, dance, literature, athletics, science, prayer, good health, the sacraments. Be aware of every second of your life. Love with every cell of your body. Taste with all of your senses. Speak with a strong voice. See with twenty-twenty vision. Read in between the lines. Hear what is not said in words. And do all of this in spite of the pain and sorrow and suffering and boredom that is a part of your everyday life, just as it is a part of all of our lives.

Mme. de Maintenon said it this way: "The true way to soften one's troubles is to solace those of others." Do we not often comfort our friends with food?

Over the years, I have met a good number of people who have had near death experiences. Their stories are fascinating in both content and similarity. They see the tunnel and the bright lights, and they are embraced by a peace, a peace that goes beyond all understanding. One man I know had been in a hunting accident and was undergoing surgery to remove a bullet from his chest. He coded on the table and he saw the tunnel and the bright lights and felt the peace embrace him. But he heard a voice say that it was not his time to die, to go back to the living. Even though the man had a young wife and three small children, he wanted to continue on his journey—the light and the peace were so fulfilling, so comforting. But the messenger said: "Life is about giving and receiving love; your job is not yet finished."

So it's all about giving and receiving love, is it? YES! But what does that mean? Our society has diluted the word "love" so that its meaning has been rendered ambiguous. We use the same word to express our fondness for God, humankind, animals, plants and things. "I love God, I love my kids and I love my big screen TV."

Here's my humble epiphany: I think it's really all about food. Yes, food. And contrary to what the nutritionists say, there are only two kinds of food groups: physical food and spiritual food. And we humans are unique among the animal world in that we need both.

So how can it all be about food? Food is our most basic bodily need. I believe the best way we can love each other—figuratively and literally—is to take turns feeding each other. Sometimes we are the servers in the restaurant of life and sometimes we are the patrons enjoying the meal. Michel Bourdin said: "Cooking is a way of giving." Loving each other means tending to each other's daily needs. This is how we feed the faith: through actions of love, the operative word here, being *actions*.

Food is to be celebrated both in its simplicity and its splendor. So that every time you peel an orange, take a moment to enjoy its vibrant color, its citrus fragrance and its sweet-tart taste. And every time you sit down to a holiday table, resplendent in special festive dishes, savor each taste and thank God for His bounty!

Reflect on the beauty of food: the colors, shapes, smells, textures, flavors. Imagine if God had been only half as generous when creating food for the earth. What if He'd skimped on color, making all produce the color green? What if He were in a hurry and made all fruits and vegetables spherical in shape? Or what if we still had color and shape variety, but every fruit and every vegetable had the texture of musk melon? Or what if we had variety in color, shape, and texture, but everything tasted like bananas?

How can we not be in awe of a God that loves us so much He gives us food that is not only nourishing to our bodies, but is pleasing to all of our senses. Just the other day I was snacking on a perfect banana. And as I peeled back the gorgeous yellow skin, I wondered: what if the meat of this banana were purple instead of ivory? Would it taste different? I think it would. And this reminded me of a question a first-grader at our school asked me the other day. He said, "Father B., how did God know that a banana should be yellow?" What could I say? I said, "He just did." And he does.

I sincerely believe that part of the way that we satisfy our spiritual hunger and thirst for God's holiness and righteousness is through partaking of His physical food. I pray that you will find beauty in the cultivation of, in the preparation of, and most importantly, in the sharing of beautiful food.

I once read that a person spends about nine years of his or her life simply eating. Let's make that time count, for even in eating, a base bodily function, and cooking, a daily chore, we can praise God.

A man hath no better thing under the sun, than to eat, to drink, and to be merry... —Ecclesiastes 8:15

First Thing in the Morning...............

Preparation Prayers:
- Gentle God, all food comes from You and has something of the miraculous in it. By Your gracious providence I am blessed with the ingredients I need to prepare this morning meal. May my work become my prayer.

- "That it may please Thee to give and preserve to our use the kindly. fruits of the earth, so as in due time we may enjoy them." —The Litany

- Loving Father, You bless us in every way. You give to us all good things. Our hearts sing out in gratitude. Bless those of us who provide and prepare as we bring Your bounty to the table.

- Lord, bless these cooking hands, that they may create savory meals that satisfy eyes, nose, mouth, and stomach.

Partaking Prayers:
- Gentle God, bless us this morning as we break our fast and renew our strength with this blessed food.

- Thus I will bless You while I love; lifting up my hands, I will call upon Your name. As with the riches of a banquet shall my soul be satisfied, and with exultant lips my mouth shall praise You. — Psalm 63:5-6

- What should we be without our meals? They come to us in our joys and sorrows and are the most blessed break that dullness can ever know. —Anonymous

- Loving Creator, You bring blessings to our table. You have filled the hungry with good things. Bless us who eat and bless those who live in want.

Sfingi—Fried Pastry Puffs

Our version of "coffee and doughnuts" after Mass at Our Lady of Pompei in Chicago's Little Italy was "coffee and *Sfingi.*" My mother and the other ladies of the parish would whip up these fried pastry puffs in the church kitchen for just pennies. They'd mix the batter before Mass and then sneak out before the recessional song to prepare them.

2 2/3 cups all-purpose flour, sifted
2 tsp vanilla extract
1 ¼ cups milk
olive oil
4 large eggs
1 cup confectioner's sugar
6 TBSP granulated sugar
ground cinnamon
3 TBSP baking powder

Whisk milk, eggs, sugar, and vanilla in a medium bowl. Add flour and baking powder and blend until smooth like cake batter. Cover bowl with a clean dishtowel and set away from drafts for half hour to hour, or until batter has risen at least fifty percent. Pour olive oil three inches deep into a medium pot. Heat oil to 350°. To test the oil, drop in a bit of batter; if it instantly floats to the top, the oil is ready. Drop 1 TBSP of batter at a time into hot oil. Don't crowd the pot. Cook about 1 minute on each side or until puffs are golden brown. Remove puffs with slotted spoon. Drain on a paper-towel lined plate for a few seconds. Transfer hot puffs to a plate. Using a sieve, sprinkle generously with confectioner's sugar and cinnamon. Serve hot.

Sfingi di San Giuseppe (St. Joseph's Day Doughnuts)

Pastry: 1 cup flour
        1 cup water
        ¼ tsp salt
        1 tsp vanilla
        1 quart oil for frying
        1 TBSP butter
        4 eggs

Filling: 1 lb. fresh *ricotta* cheese
       ½ cup powdered sugar
       1 tsp vanilla
       ¼ tsp cinnamon
       2 TBSP chopped semi-sweet chocolate
       powdered sugar for dusting doughnuts

For Filling: Beat *ricotta* cheese in medium bowl until smooth and creamy. Mix in the remaining filling ingredients and chill until needed.

For Pastry: Heat water, butter and salt in a saucepan until butter melts. Remove from flame. Stir in flour all at once and return to heat. Stir and cook until mixture leaves the sides of pan. Add eggs, one at a time, beating after each addition. Stir in vanilla.

To Fry: Heat oil in frying pan to 350°. Drop batter by tablespoonful and fry until golden brown—about 3 to 4 minutes. Remove with slotted spoon and place on paper towels.

To Fill: Make a slit in the center of the pastry and fill with *ricotta* mixture. Dust with powdered sugar and serve.

Sara Salina's Quick Company Coffee Cake

In my neighborhood, kids were always outside and doors were always open to neighbors. This is a simple and quick coffee cake my mother seemed always to have on hand.

> 2 cups flour
> 1 cup sugar
> 1 cup vegetable oil
> 1 tsp vanilla
> 4 eggs
> 2 tsp baking powder
> ¼ tsp salt
> sugar and cinnamon to sprinkle
> 1 can of fruit pie filling (cherry, apple or peach)

Preheat oven to 350°. Beat well sugar, oil, eggs and vanilla. In separate bowl, mix flour, baking powder and salt. Pour dry ingredients into egg mixture. Blend until all ingredients are incorporated. Pour half of mixture into greased and floured 9 x 13 cake pan. Sprinkle with cinnamon and sugar. Spoon 1 can of pie filling over crust layer. Cover with remaining mixture. Sprinkle top with cinnamon and sugar. Bake at 350° for 40 minutes.

Nana Lilli's Quick Peach Cobbler
A treat my grandmother would make me anytime I asked.

> 1 slice of Italian bread
> ½ cup milk
> 1 egg
> 6 canned peach slices
> ½ tsp cinnamon
> 1 tsp sugar
> 1 tsp margarine or butter

Place bread in a greased, one-serving, oven-safe bowl. Arrange peach slices on bread. Beat egg and milk and pour over bread and peaches. Sprinkle with sugar and cinnamon. Add tsp of butter. Bake at 350° for 20 minutes.

Pancetta and Ricotta Strata
Great for breakfast, brunch—even lunch or dinner.

> 12 slices of Italian bread
> 1 lb. *ricotta* cheese
> 4 cups milk
> 8 eggs, beaten
> 1 small onion, minced
> salt and pepper to taste
> 1 cup *Romano* or *Asiago* cheese, grated
> 3 TBSP butter
> 2 cups of cooked *pancetta*, chopped

Line a greased 9 x 13 pan with bread slices. Spread *ricotta* cheese. Layer with *pancetta*. Sprinkle with grated cheese. Beat egg, milk, salt and pepper. Add onions. Pour over bread and cheese. Dot with butter. Bake one hour at 350°. Let set for 10 minutes. Cut into squares.

Sausage and Red Pepper Strata
Men seem to love this version.

12 slices of Italian bread
½ cup chopped red pepper
4 cups milk
8 eggs, beaten
1 small onion, chopped
3 TBSP butter
salt and pepper to taste
1 cup *Parmesan* cheese, grated
1 lb. Italian sausage, removed from casing, cooked
     and crumbled
1 cup shredded *Mozzarella*

Line a greased 9 x 13 pan with bread slices. Sprinkle with the two cheeses. Layer with crumbled sausage, onion and red pepper. In separate bowl beat egg, milk, salt and pepper. Pour over bread and cheese. Dot with butter. Bake one hour at 350°. Let stand for 10 minutes to set before cutting into squares.

Potato and Red Pepper *Frittata*

Another great anytime dish.

4 large eggs
1 clove garlic
4 medium potatoes
Salt and pepper to taste
2 red peppers
1 TBSP water
1 large onion
¼ cup extra virgin olive oil for pan

Wash and peel potatoes. Slice 1/4 inch thick. Cut peppers into 1-inch pieces. Slice onion and chop garlic. In a 10-inch skillet, sauté onion and garlic in olive oil till golden. Add potatoes and peppers. Cover and fry on low heat until tender. Beat eggs with water and pour over potatoes and peppers. Cover and cook until partially set. Loosen frittata by sliding a pancake turner under and around it. To turn, place a plate over the skillet, and with one hand on top of the plate and the other holding the skillet, turn upside down. Slip frittata back into skillet to brown other side. To remove frittata, turn onto a plate again. Cut in wedges like a pie. Serves 4.

Italian Scrambled Eggs
What makes 'em Italian? Cheese and garlic, of course!

    8 fresh eggs
    2 TBSP water
    ½ cup Romano cheese, cubed
    salt and pepper to taste
    pinch of garlic powder

Beat eggs with water. Add cheese cubes, garlic powder, salt and pepper.
Cook in skillet.

Asparagus *Frittata*
A favorite Italian classic.

    ¼ cup olive oil
    1 lb. fresh asparagus, cut up
    5 fresh eggs
    Salt and pepper to taste
    ½ lb. *ricotta* cheese
    1 TBSP water

Cut washed asparagus spears into 1-inch pieces. Cook in salted water until
tender.   Strain and set aside.   Beat eggs, *ricotta*, salt and pepper until
blended. Add cooked asparagus to egg and cheese mixture. Heat oil on
high in skillet, then reduce heat to medium. Pour blended mixture into pan.
Cover and cook until partially set. Loosen frittata by sliding a pancake
turner under and around it. To turn, place a plate over the skillet, and with
one hand on top of the plate and the other holding the skillet, turn upside
down. Slip frittata back into skillet to brown the other side for a few
minutes. To remove frittata, turn onto a plate again. Cut in wedges like a
pie. Serves 4.

Mozzarella in *Carroza*
The best "French Toast" you'll ever have!

    8 slices of rustic Italian bread
    5 beaten eggs, plus 1 TBSP milk
    8 thick slices of *Mozzarella* cheese
    pinch of salt

In a bowl, beat eggs with milk and salt. Dip bread slices into egg mixture and cook in greased skillet till golden brown. Place cheese slice between two cooked bread slices. Serve with butter and syrup.

Frittata with Cabbage and Garden Mint
Honestly, this dish is more delicious than it sounds! Try it and you'll see.

    4 large eggs
    3 TBSP grated *Parmesan* cheese
    1 TBSP water
    half medium onion, chopped
    salt and pepper to taste
    1 tsp dried garden mint
    ¼ head of boiled cabbage—squeezed of liquid

Heat oil on high in skillet. Reduce heat to medium. Sauté onions till tender. Add cooked cabbage to pan, spreading evenly. In a bowl, beat eggs with salt, pepper and cheese. Pour egg mixture over cabbage and onions. Cover and cook until partially set. Loosen frittata by sliding a pancake turner under and around it. To turn, place a plate over the skillet, and with one hand on top of the plate and the other holding the skillet, turn upside down. Slip frittata back into skillet to brown the other side for a few minutes. To remove frittata, turn onto a plate again. Cut in wedges like a pie. Serves 4.

THE SPICE OF LIFE

We cannot imagine eating one single flavor all the time, the reason being that we have been created with taste buds, a delicate sense of smell, and a sensitive appreciation of and response to texture and colour.
—Edith Schaeffer

The earth was made so various, that the mind of desultory man, studious of change, and pleased with novelty, might be indulged.
—William Cowper

Countless the various species of mankind; countless the shades that separate mind from mind; no general object of desire is known; each has his will, and each pursues his own. —Gifford

Here hills and vales, the woodland and the plain,
Here earth and water seem to strive again,
Not Chaos-like together crush'd and bruis'd,
But as the world, harmoniously confus'd:
Where order in variety we see,
And where though all things differ, all agree.
—Alexander Pope

VAREITY REALLY IS the spice of life. We have this little dog here at the rectory—he came with the place. He's a mixed breed, but I detect a lot of collie in him. His name is Abraham. He's a good-natured old boy and I appreciate his pleasant company. He came with a bag of dried dog food and a doggie dish. "Ack," I said out loud the first time I opened the bag of food. "This stuff isn't fit for a dog." And so I inquired around the parish and found out what kind of chow my dog-loving parishioners recommended. We came up with a canned food—a gourmet equivalent in dog food. The good news is it comes in five different flavors.

Think about it. Most animals don't enjoy the unlimited varieties of food we humans do. Carnivores eat meat—maybe a few different kinds. Herbivores eat plants—a few varieties. But look what God has provided for the human palate! He has set his table for a feast—an endless variety of food!

God is so generous! We, his children, would have surely been content with one kind of apple. But there are countless varieties of apples cultivated and exported around the world. The authors of *The Gourmet Atlas, The History, Origin, and Migration of Foods of the World*—Susan

331

Ward, Claire Clifton and Jenny Stacey—tell us that over ten thousand varieties of apples have been identified internationally. Imagine, ten thousand different kinds of apples! Of those ten thousand, only two- to three-thousand are suitable for commercial exploitation, and only fifty to sixty named varieties are actually marketed. There's the Red Delicious, Golden Delicious, Granny Smith, McIntosh, Jonathan, Redstar, Elstar, Starkimson, Ida Red, Cortland—just to name a few.

What about lettuce? If you only eat iceberg lettuce, you don't know what you are missing. Lettuces are classified into three main groups: crisphead, romaine, and butterhead. There's the Chicory family, which includes the slightly bitter or peppery tasting radicchio, French frisee and escarole. There's sorrel, corn salad, spinach (actually a member of the beet family), watercress, endive, arugula, bib, red leaf, green leaf. The list goes on.

Look at what we can put on our pasta: tomato sauce, oil and garlic sauce, marinara sauce, Pesto, clam sauce, plain butter, *ricotta*, white sauce, Alfredo sauce. Or on our bread: butter, margarine, jam, cream cheese, olive oil, peanut butter.

Endless variety…to keep life interesting!

Make no mistake about this, my dear brothers. Every worthwhile gift, every genuine benefit comes from above, descending from the Father of the heavenly luminaries, who cannot change and who is never shadowed over. He wills us to birth with a word spoken in truth so that we may be a kind of first fruits of His creation.
—James 1:16-18

Just Before the Meal.....................

Preparation Prayers:

- Everything God created is good; nothing is to be rejected when it is received with thanksgiving, for it is made holy by God's word and by prayer. —1Timothy 4:4,5

- Father in heaven, we give thanks for variety. For color and shape, for texture and taste. For Your abundant love and grace.

- Whether therefore ye eat, or drink, or whatsoever ye do, do all to the glory of God. —1 Corinthians 10:31

- Lord, help me to enjoy the preparation of this meal as much as I will enjoy the meal itself.

Partaking Prayers:

- The earth is replete with the fruit of your works. You raise grass for cattle, and vegetation for men's use, producing bread from the earth, and wine to gladden men's hearts. So that their faces gleam with oil, and bread fortifies the hearts of men. –Psalm 104:13-15

- Bless this table, Lord, and all who gather round it
  May they be nourished by food and fellowship
  By kind and comforting words; by great love.

- Creator of all things that taste good
  Let me be forever mindful that my kitchen table is an altar
  All that I set upon it is a gift
  Passed from You to me,
  and from me to my family and friends.

- Father of us all, this meal is a sign of Your love for us.
  Bless us and bless this food
  And help us to give You glory each day.

Olive *Crustini*
A wonderful hors d'oeuvres

    ½ loaf of French bread, cut into 1/4 inch thick slices
    1 can pitted black olives
    1 small bottle green olives with pimentos
    ½ cup grated *Parmesan* or *Asiago* cheese
    1 clove garlic
    salt and pepper to taste
    ½ cup olive oil

Process black and green olives with garlic clove in food processor. Add cheese, salt and pepper. Blend. Add olive oil. Spread mixture on bread slices. Broil until lightly browned in broiler, checking after two minutes. Serve hot or at room temperature.

Sausage and Cheese Stuffed Mushrooms
Delicious!

    1 lb. large mushrooms
    1 cup *Gorgonzola*, crumbled
    ½ lb. Italian sausage, removed from casing

Wash mushrooms. Remove stems. (Save to use in another dish.) In a bowl, mix sausage meat with *Gorgonzola* cheese, using your hands to blend well. Stuff each mushroom cap with meat/cheese mixture. Cook under broiler until sausage is cooked (from pink to brown) and mushrooms are juicy. Serve hot with cocktail picks.

Pancetta-Mascarpone New Potatoes

These mini twice-baked potatoes make a nice addition to an antipasti platter.

12 small unpeeled new potatoes
2 TBSP olive oil
¼ cup minced green onion
1 clove garlic, minced
3 oz. of *Mascarpone* (Italian cream cheese)
salt and pepper to taste
8 oz. of *pancetta*, cooked and finely chopped
1 cup shredded cheddar cheese
¼ cup grated *Parmesan* or *Asiago* cheese
½ cup milk
2 TBSP dried parsley

Heat oven to 400°. Rub potatoes with olive oil and place on an ungreased cookie sheet. Bake potatoes for one hour or until tender. Cut each in half. With teaspoon or melon baller, scoop out small amount of potato pulp. Combine pulp and all ingredients except the *pancetta*. Blend with mixer then stir in *pancetta*. Spoon mixture into each potato half. Place back on cookie sheet. Bake 5 to 7 minutes, until browned. Serve warm.

Garlic Anchovy Dip

    1 cup extra virgin olive oil
    salt and pepper to taste
    1 stick (1/2 cup) butter
    8 canned anchovies, chopped
    2 garlic cloves, finely chopped

In a skillet, heat ingredients and simmer for 5 minutes. Serve with bread, breadsticks or vegetables such as carrots, celery, green onions, and red, yellow and green pepper strips.

Sicilian Olive Salad

    2 ½ lb. Sicilian green olives
    1 medium red onion, sliced fine
    2 stalks celery, cut ½ thick
    1 large red pepper, cut into strips
    4 cloves garlic, cut into small dice
    1/3 cup white wine vinegar
    1 tsp balsamic vinegar
    ½ cup extra virgin olive oil
    1 tsp dried oregano, crushed
    salt and pepper to taste

Crack olives slightly with a wooden meat tenderizer. Combine all ingredients in a large bowl. Cover and refrigerate for at least 1 day. Serve at room temperature.

Spinach Artichoke Dip

    2 boxes of frozen creamed spinach
    1 can artichoke hearts, drained, and chopped
    1 cup grated *Asiago* cheese
    ¼ cup *Parmesan* cheese
    ¼ cup milk
    salt and pepper to taste
    1 tsp crushed red pepper

Thaw spinach and squeeze out excess liquid. Mix all ingredients in a bowl. Transfer to a greased casserole. Bake covered at 350° for 40 minutes. Remove cover to brown for 5 to 10 more minutes.

Caponatina (Eggplant Relish)

Delicious on crackers or crusty bread.

4 medium eggplants
6 medium tomatoes
12 black Italian olives, pitted and chopped
6 tsp sugar
1 cup virgin olive oil
salt and pepper to taste
1 ½ cups red wine vinegar
½ tsp salt
½ tsp pepper
2 cups celery, coarsely chopped
½ cup drained capers
1 TBSP pine nuts
4 onions, sliced thin
2 cloves garlic, minced

Peel and dice eggplants, then soak in salted cold water for 1 hour to draw out the bitter juices. Rinse under cold water, drain and dry on paper towels. In skillet brown eggplant cubes in ½ cup olive oil. Remove; place on paper towels. Pat dry. Place in medium bowl. Add ½ cup of olive oil to skillet and sauté onions. Blanch tomatoes for 1 minute, peel, core and cut up. (Or you can puree in a food processor or blender for 2 minutes.) Add tomatoes to onions in skillet, along with celery. Simmer for 15 minutes, or until tender. Add capers, olives, garlic, eggplant, sugar, vinegar and pine nuts. Season lightly with salt and pepper. Simmer for 10 minutes, stirring frequently. Cool before serving. Serve with grilled or toasted Italian bread. Can be refrigerated.

BE CREATIVE!

The discovery of a new dish does more for the happiness of mankind than the discovery of a star. —Brillat-Savarin

Imagination is more important than knowledge. —Albert Einstein

To love what you do and feel that it matters—how can anything be more fun? —Katharine Graham

Curiosity is the key to creativity. —Akio Morita

ONE OF THE most awesome gifts that God has shared with His people is our ability to create. We are all co-creators; partners with God, if you will. How can we not be overcome with thankfulness when we reflect on this? That a man and a woman can come together in love and that their love can create a human life is no small miracle. God has given us creative powers so that we can uniquely contribute to the world, whether we create children, art, music, gardens, laughter, machines, medicines, harmony, literature, love, prayer or simply delicious food.

What's your talent? How do you create? Do you paint? Garden? Write? Cook? Teach? Act? Decorate? Can you build things, fix things, wire things, compute things? Do you have a knack for listening? For numbers? Are you musical? Athletic? Comical? Use your creative talents to bring your own special beauty to the world. Ask the Holy Spirit to guide your creative efforts. And He will.

Don't you admire creative cooks? Those who can whip up incredibly good dishes without following a recipe and with whatever ingredients are on hand? These are the real gourmets. But anyone can be a creative cook. Yes, even you!

It's not just about following a recipe, but if that's your style, that's fine. But don't forget to experiment and substitute along the way—that's what personalizes your cooking.

Cooking is a creative act that fulfills a yearning— not just to eat, but to savor, to surrender to the pleasure of food.
—Christopher Wormell

Doing Lunch.............................

Preparation Prayers:

- How beautiful are all His works! The universe lives and abides forever; to meet each need, each creature is preserved. All of them differ, one from the other, yet none of them has He made in vain. For each in turn, as it comes, is good. —Sirach 42:23-25

- Lord, we give thanks for all our benefits. Thank you for gardens and grocery stores. Thank you for farmers and factories. Thank you for butchers and breweries.

- Sing to the Lord with thanksgiving; sing praise with the harp to our God, who covers the heavens with clouds, who provides rain for the earth; who makes grass sprout on the mountains and herbs for the service of men. Who gives food to the cattle, and to the young ravens when they cry to him. —Psalm 147:7-9

- How blessed we are that in this fruitful land we can pull from the earth and pluck from the trees so many wonderful things!

Partaking Prayers:

- Loving Father, we praise You for all the gifts You give us. For life and health, for faith and love, and for this meal we will share together.

- Save Thy people, and bless Thine inheritance: feed them also, and lift them up forever. —Psalm 28:9

- Lord, we give thanks for those who cooked this meal. In doing so they have provided nourishment, satisfaction and contentment to both body and soul.

- Our hearts are filled with gratitude for good company and food imaginatively and lovingly prepared. Thank you for these blessings.

Classic Chicken Soup with Arborio Rice

8 to 10 cups water
1 large cooking chicken, cleaned
1 large onion, chopped
2 carrots, chopped
2 celery ribs, chopped
3 plum tomatoes, chopped
salt and pepper to taste
2 cups cooked *Arborio* rice

Fill a large soup pot with water. Add chicken and chopped vegetables. Salt and pepper to taste. Simmer for one hour. When chicken is done, remove and transfer to plate. Cut into bite-sized pieces and add back to the broth. Add the rice before serving. Sprinkle with *Asiago, Romano,* or *Parmesan* cheese.

Hidden Vegetable Chicken Soup

My mother made this soup for my sister Becky who turned her nose at carrots and onions and such. By pureeing the vegetables and then adding them back to the broth, Mama got the required nutrients into my sister, and Becky was none the wiser.

8 to 10 cups water
1 large cooking chicken, cleaned
1 large whole onion
2 whole carrots, peeled
2 whole celery ribs
3 whole plum tomatoes
salt and pepper to taste
½ lb. *stelline* or other small pasta

Fill a large soup pot with water. Add chicken and vegetables. Salt and pepper to taste. Cook chicken until it pulls from the bone and vegetables until done. Remove chicken, transfer to plate and cut into pieces to be served with the soup. Remove vegetables with slotted spoon. Puree vegetables in food processor or blender and add back to the broth. Stir. Cook pasta and add to finished soup before serving. Sprinkle with *Asiago, Romano,* or *Parmesan* cheese.

Meatball and Cabbage Soup
People rave about this soup!

8 to 10 cups homemade or good canned chicken stock
½ head of cabbage, chopped into 1-inch pieces
1 large onion, chopped
2 carrots, chopped
2 ribs celery, diced
¼ lb. *tubetti, ditali,* or other small pasta

Meatballs:
1 lb. ground round or ground chuck
1 cup Italian style breadcrumbs
1 egg
1 TBSP McCormick's SeasonAll
1/2 tsp garlic powder
1 tsp minced onion
salt and pepper to taste
2 TBSP of dried garden mint leaves
1/2 cup grated *Parmesan* cheese

Heat chicken stock in large soup pot. Add chopped cabbage, onion, carrots and celery. To prepare meatballs, combine all ingredients in a bowl and mix well with hands. Form into 1-inch balls and drop into boiling stock. Simmer for at least one hour. Taste test for doneness. Cook pasta in a separate pot (*al dente)* and add to stock before serving. Yields six servings.

Tortellini Sausage Soup

> 8 to 10 cups homemade or good canned chicken stock
> 1 lb. Italian rope sausage, grilled or fried and cut into 1/8-
>   inch thick slices
> 1 large onion, chopped
> 2 carrots, chopped
> 2 celery ribs, diced
> 1 lb. small cheese *tortellini*
> salt and pepper to taste

Heat chicken stock in a large soup pot. Add cooked sausage, onion, celery, and carrots. Simmer for one hour. Cook *tortellini* separately then add to the finished soup. Sprinkle with *Asiago, Romano*, or *Parmesan* cheese.

White Bean *Pancetta* Soup

> 8 to 10 cups homemade or low-salt canned chicken stock
> 2 - 16 o z. cans of Great Northern Beans with liquid
> 2 - 14.5 oz. cans of whole tomatoes with liquid
> 1 TBSP olive oil
> 1/2 lb. *pancetta*, cut small
> 2 cloves garlic, pressed
> 6 cups fresh chopped Swiss chard
> salt and pepper to taste
> 1 package frozen cheese *tortellini*
> 1 medium onion

Sauté *Pancetta* and garlic in olive oil in Dutch oven. Remove *Pancetta* and garlic from the pan and cook the Swiss chard in the pan dripping for 2 minutes. Stir in stock, beans, tomatoes, onions and bring to boil. Reduce heat. Simmer for 1 hour. Stir in cooked *tortellini*. Serve with fresh grated cheese of your choice.

Briolotta—Sausage Bread

1/2 cup warm water
1 1/2 tsp salt
4 cups flour
1 1/2 lb. Italian sausage, casing removed
1 1/2 pkg dry yeast
2 cups *Parmesan* cheese, grated
4 TBSP sesame seeds

In large skillet, fry sausage, drain, and set aside. Dissolve yeast in warm water. Combine flour, salt and yeast mixture. Knead for 15 minutes. Place dough in bowl. Brush top with olive oil, cover with a clean, floured dishtowel, and set in a warm place to rise for two hours, until dough doubles in size. Divide dough into 4 equal portions. Roll each piece out on floured surface until thin. Spread sausage evenly on dough. Sprinkle with salt and pepper. Add ½ cup cheese, spreading evenly. Roll up like a jelly roll. Seal the edges. Brush tops of loaves with a beaten egg, then sprinkle with sesame seeds. Place loaves on a baking stone sprinkled with cornmeal. Bake at 350° until golden brown—about 30 minutes.

Summer Tomato Salad

4 large fresh garden tomatoes
2 cloves of garlic
10 fresh garden mint leaves
salt and pepper to taste
2 TBSP extra-virgin olive oil
6 TBSP red wine vinegar

Cut tomatoes into bite-size slices and place in a bowl. Salt the tomatoes liberally and set aside for at least two hours. (The salt will bring out the juices of the tomatoes.) Crush the garlic cloves and mint leaves in a mortar and pestle, then add to the tomatoes. Drizzle with the oil and vinegar. Add pepper and stir, coating the tomatoes thoroughly in the juices. Serve at room temperature with fresh crusty bread.

Pressed Italian Sandwich

1 loaf fresh Italian or Vienna bread
8 slices of *Provolone* cheese
2 to 3 large Romaine lettuce leaves
20 *Kalamata* olives, pitted and halved
8 slices *prosciutto*
8 slices Genoa *salami*
Extra virgin olive oil—to drizzle
Balsamic vinegar—to drizzle

Cut loaf in half, lengthwise. With your fingers, pinch out some of the center of the bread. Drizzle bottom loaf half with vinegar and oil. Layer *prosciutto, salami, Provolone*, olive halves, and lettuce leaves. Drizzle top loaf half with vinegar and oil and put in place. Wrap the loaf in wax paper and then in aluminum foil. Set in the refrigerator with something heavy on top of it—2 gallons of milk work nicely—for 24 hours. Slice and serve. Vary the meat, cheese and olives for other wonderful versions of this sandwich.

Panzanella—Italian Bread Salad

This is a wonderful use of day-old bread. (Do not use store-bought tomatoes.)

> 1 loaf Italian bread, 3-4 days old, cut into 1-in. thick slices
> 1 seedless cucumber, peeled, cut into ½-inch cubes
> 5 or 6 ripe garden tomatoes (about 2 lbs.) seeded and cut
>   into ½-inch cubes
> ½ cup cold water
> 2 cloves garlic, minced
> salt and pepper to taste
> ½ cup red-wine vinegar
> ¼ cup plus 1 TBSP extra-virgin olive oil
> 1 medium onion, diced
> ½ cup loosely packed fresh torn basil leaves

Sprinkle the bread slices with water and let stand for five minutes. Squeeze the water from the bread gently as you tear the slices into 1-inch pieces. Lay the pieces out on a paper towel to dry slightly. In a large bowl, whisk together the vinegar, oil, and garlic. Salt and pepper to taste. Add the tomatoes, cucumbers, onions, basil and the bread pieces. Toss and then let stand about fifteen minutes so that the bread can absorb some of the dressing. Some delicious additions to this basic recipe: tuna, capers, celery, anchovies, hard-cooked eggs.

Summer *Siciliano Sugo* (No cook sauce)

> ¼ cup extra virgin olive oil
> ¼ cup pine nuts
> ¼ cup freshly grated *Parmesan* or *Asiago* cheese
> 2 cloves garlic, minced
> 2 cups loosely packed fresh basil leaves, chopped
> 1 ½ lbs. ripe tomatoes, peeled, seeded, and chopped
> salt and pepper to taste

Rinse and drain basil. Combine garlic and oil in a food processor and process until garlic is finely chopped. Add basil and nuts and process until smooth. Add remaining ingredients—except the tomatoes—and process until blended. Mix processed ingredients into tomato chunks. Serve over penne or *mostaccioli.*

Zucchini Stew

Here's a great recipe for that summertime surplus of zucchini.

> 4 small zucchini or 2 large zucchini, cubed
> 4 plum tomatoes, chopped
> 1 medium onion, chopped
> salt and pepper to taste
> pinch of garlic powder
> 1 can of peas or ½ bag of frozen peas
> shredded *Asiago* cheese
> (optional—1/2 pound ground beef, browned)

Spray 2 quart pot with olive oil. Add zucchini, tomatoes and onions. Season. Cover and cook until tender. Vegetables will make a nice juice. Add peas. Cook ten minutes more. Serve topped with shredded cheese. (Sometimes my mother would add ground beef to make it a heartier stew.)

Karla Clark

THE FAMILY DINNER

*There is a communion of more than our bodies when bread is broken and
wine is drunk. And that is my answer, when people ask me: Why do you
write about hunger, and not wars and love.*
—*M. F. K. Fisher*

*Heavenly Father, bless us, and keep us all alive,
There's ten of us to dinner, and not enough for five. —Anonymous*

*As a child, my family's menu consisted of two choices:
take it or leave it. —Buddy Hacket*

*At table people enjoy one another; above all when one has managed to
enchant them. —Fernand Point*

IT FILLS ME with sadness to think that nowadays few families sit down to
meals together. But Father, they tell me, this one has soccer practice and
that one has Girl Scouts and I say, yeah, yeah. But my parishioners will tell
you that on this subject I am unyielding. I ask our students at our all-school
Masses on Friday mornings, "What did you have for dinner last night?"
Their answers provide a sad commentary on our society. Many can't
remember what they had because it wasn't a memorable meal. Some say
they didn't eat dinner, others say they grabbed a sandwich on the run or a
bowl of cold cereal before bed.

Bear with me because this is a topic that raises my blood pressure.
If there was such a thing as the Last Supper for Jesus then there must have
been a lot of other suppers. Jesus knew that sharing a meal with people you
love creates a special bond. Breaking bread together. He deemed this so
important that He bid us to "do this in memory of me." And so we do, every
time we celebrate Mass and partake in the Holy Eucharist. It's *that*
important. So why don't we think it's important to break bread together at
home with the people we love the most? I know Susie has basketball
practice and Jimmy has Chess Club but what about the other six days of the
week?

These are busy times in which we live. But I ask the families in my
parish to do this: make it a priority to sit down to a meal together at least
three nights a week and on Sundays. That's four days out of seven. Maybe
Monday, Wednesday, Friday and Sunday. That leaves three days for fast
food and carryout. And that doesn't necessarily mean Mom has to do all the
cooking. Some families assign nights and this is a great thing. The kids

learn not only how to cook, but how much is involved, and they are more appreciative when they sit down to a meal someone else has prepared for them.

I urge you. Eat together. Break bread together. And if you're so inclined, cook together. My grandma, Nana Lilli, used to say that there's something about eating that loosens up your lips. When I was small, I thought she meant that literally, but later, after I was a bit seasoned, I realized that what she meant was this: eating and talking go together. Watching television and talking do not. Playing video games and talking do not. When you're eating, your lips are flapping anyway, so keep them flapping, and ask your kid how his day was or tell the cook how good the meal is.

Okay, I'm done lecturing. Let me conclude by saying that I practice what I preach. I sit at the rectory dining room table three nights a week with our pastor, Monsignor Bill. On Sundays Monsignor and I are guests for dinner at various parishioners' homes—something we look forward to with great anticipation. It is the only day that we indulge in desserts—Monsignor due to mild diabetes and me due to a mildly generous waistline.

A final note on this eating together issue. I teach a religion class at our high school: Christian Marriage and Family. I tell my students that I can't offer a lot of advice about dating—I dated only two girls in my life—but I can say that the best date is a restaurant date. You can't carry on a conversation at a movie, a play, a sports event, a concert, or a dance, but you can talk over food, and you can learn a lot about a person just by eating together. Try it! And heed this good advice from Leigh Hunt: "If you are ever at a loss to support a flagging conversation, introduce the subject of eating."

Delicious Entrees..........................

Preparation Prayers:

- Lord, sometimes cooking is the only part of our day that puts us in touch with nature. Let me think about the fruitful earth, so kind to man, that we but plant a seed and eat forever.

- Great God, how selfless are the cooks! Those who wash and chop and knead and stir. Those of us who eat must never forget the cooks.

- Father, bless these raw ingredients as I attempt to transform them into a delicious meal for my family.

- Great Giver, I thank Thee for the conveniences that I have come to take for granted in the kitchen. Just think of those around the world who can't just open up a cupboard or a refrigerator. There are those who still hunt and gather, those who still must rub sticks together to make fire, those who still eat food in its simplest form. How easy it is to eat for most of us in this country. Help me not to forget.

Partaking Prayers:

- Blessed are you, O Lord God, King of the Universe, for You give us food to sustain our lives and make our hearts glad.

- Lord, bless this beautiful food to our bodies and our bodies to Your service.

- Be present at our table, Lord! Be here among those who have gathered in Your name and break bread together in Your memory.

- For good food and those who prepare it, for good friends with whom to share it.

Pasta with Basil and Pine Nut Pesto

2 cups lightly packed basil leaves
2 cloves garlic
½ cup of extra virgin olive oil
1/3 cup pine nuts
¼ tsp each salt and pepper
½ cup freshly grated *Parmesan* cheese

Rinse and drain basil. Combine garlic and oil in a food processor and process until garlic is finely chopped. Add basil and nuts and process until smooth. Add remaining ingredients and process until blended. Toss into fresh hot pasta, such as *linguini*, angel hair, or *fettuccini.*

Pasta and Seafood

1 medium onion, chopped
3 TBSP olive oil
2 large cans (29 oz) tomatoes, drained and chopped
6 fresh basil leaves
1 cup heavy cream
1 TBSP sugar
salt and pepper to taste
1 lb. fresh scallops
1 lb. fresh shrimp, peeled and deveined
6 cups cooked pasta
1 cup frozen peas
½ cup freshly grated *Parmesan* cheese
½ cup crumbled *Gorgonzola* cheese

In a large saucepan, cook onion in oil until golden, stirring often. Add tomatoes and basil. Cook ten minutes. Add cream, salt, pepper and sugar. Simmer ten minutes and add next four ingredients. Toss and heat. Serve garnished with cheeses.

Garlic-Lemon Chicken with Rosemary

> 3 lb. fryer, cut into eight pieces
> 4 large cloves garlic, minced
> 4 TBSP olive oil
> 1 TBSP dry rosemary or two fresh sprigs
> ½ cup fresh squeezed lemon juice
> salt and pepper to taste
> ¼ cup water

Clean and cut fryer and place in greased baking dish. Mix together garlic, olive oil and lemon juice. Brush chicken with garlic-lemon-oil mixture and broil under broiler until golden. Turn, brush and broil other side. When chicken is browned lightly, transfer to baking dish. Pour remaining mixture and water over pieces. Sprinkle with rosemary leaves. Salt and pepper to taste. Cover and bake in 325° oven for one hour.

Pork Chops with Roasted Potatoes & Peas

> 4 to 6 lean pork chops
> salt and pepper to taste
> McCormick's SeasonAll
> 4 medium potatoes, quartered
> garlic powder
> 1 can peas or one pkg of frozen peas
> 2 medium onions, quartered
> olive oil
> ½ cup water or white wine

Sprinkle chops and potatoes with salt, pepper and SeasonAll. Heat olive oil in a large skillet and brown chops on both sides. Transfer to greased baking dish. Add potatoes, onions, water. Bake at 350° for 45 minutes. Add peas. Cook 15 more minutes.

Sfinciuni—Sicilian Stuffed Pizza

Sfinciuni is a closed pizza stuffed with a variety of wonderful things. Choose a filling or come up with one of your own.

Dough recipe:
>   2 cups flour (semolina works best)
>   1 TBSP salt
>   1 TBSP olive oil
>   1 TBSP dry active yeast
>   ½ tsp sugar
>   1 cup hot water

Preheat oven to 450°. Mix yeast and sugar together in small glass bowl. Add a bit of hot water and stir. Let sit until yeast is foamy, approximately 10 minutes. Mix flour and salt in large bowl. Mix in olive oil, yeast mixture and rest of water. Mix until ball is formed. (Add more flour if dough is too sticky and more water if dough is too stiff.) Knead dough for 10 minutes. Place dough in floured bowl; cover with a clean cotton dish cloth that has been dusted with flour, and set in a warm place for two or three hours, or until the dough has doubled in size. Divide the risen dough in half and roll the two pieces into circles, one slightly bigger than the other. Place the larger circle (about a foot in diameter) on a semolina-dusted baking stone. Spread with filling. Cover with top circle of dough and roll edges of both circles together to form a tight seal. Brush the top of the crust with a beaten egg and bake for 20 to 25 minutes. Let stand for a few minutes before serving.

Filling Recipe Number One:

>   6 slices of *prosciutto*
>   1 ½ lbs. *ricotta*
>   2 TBSP extra virgin olive oil
>   2 TBSP breadcrumbs
>   salt and pepper to taste
>   ½ tsp garlic powder
>   ¼ cup grated *Asiago* cheese
>   6 to 8 spinach leaves (washed, dried, stems removed)

Spread 1 TBSP olive oil on circle of dough. Sprinkle with half of breadcrumbs. Spread *ricotta*, layer *prosciutto* and spinach leaves. Drizzle TBSP of olive oil. Sprinkle with *Asiago* cheese and remaining breadcrumbs. Cover with second circle of dough.

Filling Recipe Number Two:

>½ lb. Italian sausage, removed from casing, browned, drained
>2 cups shredded *Mozzarella*
>1 cup sautéed mushrooms
>½ medium onion, chopped and sautéed
>½ cup chopped black olives
>1 TBSP olive oil
>salt and pepper to taste
>½ cup grated *Romano* cheese
>1 cup homemade *sugo*

Spread 1 TBSP olive oil on circle of dough. Next layer sausage, mushrooms, olives, and cheeses. Salt and pepper to taste. Drizzle with the *sugo*. Cover with second circle of dough.

Breaded Pork Chops

     1 to 1 ½ lbs. lean pork chops
     1/3 cup Italian-seasoned breadcrumbs
     1/3 cup grated *Parmesan* cheese
     salt and pepper to taste
     ¼ cup milk
     ½ tsp garlic powder
     ¼ tsp onion powder
     1 TBSP dried garden mint leaves
     olive oil for frying

In a small bowl, beat egg and milk. Mix cheese, breadcrumbs, salt, pepper, garlic powder and mint in another small bowl. Dip pork chops in egg/milk mixture, then in cheese and breadcrumbs. In a skillet, brown on both sides in hot olive oil. Transfer chops to a covered baking dish and complete cooking in a 350° oven for one hour.

Eggplant *Parmigiana*

3 eggplants (approximately 1 lb. each)
salt and pepper to taste
olive oil for frying
5 to 6 cups of fresh *sugo*
1 cup freshly grated *Asiago* cheese
2 cups shredded *Mozzarella*
1 lb. ground round or chuck, sautéed, rinsed, drained

Peel eggplants and slice lengthwise, about 1/2 inch thick. Salt liberally and stack slices on plate. Place another plate on top of the slices and weigh it down with something heavy, such as canned goods. This salt-press process removes the acidic liquid from the eggplant that causes it to taste bitter. Press for approximately 2 hours. (Please do not skip this process as the pressing also helps keep the eggplant slices from absorbing too much fat when frying.) Rinse eggplant slices and pat dry with a paper towel. Dust each slice with flour and fry to a golden brown in half inch of olive oil. (You will need to add a little more oil to the pan at times.) Place cooked slices on paper towels. In a greased baking dish, layer in this order: *sugo*, eggplant, ground beef, *Asiago* cheese. Repeat as many times as dish will accommodate, ending with a layer of sugo. Bake at 375° for 1 hour. Sprinkle *Mozzarella* cheese on top 10 minutes before removing from oven.

THE MIRACLE OF BREAD

What hymns are sung, what praises said, for the homemade miracles of bread. —Louis Untermeyer

Cast thy bread upon the waters: for thou shalt find it after many days. —Ecclesiastes 11:1

Man doth not live by bread only, but by every word that proceedeth out of the mouth of the Lord doth man live.
—Deuteronomy 8:3

He was known of them in breaking of bread. —Luke 24:35

WHEN I WAS a child I used to watch people baking bread. It was like watching magicians at work. Think about it. They took some flour, salt, water, and yeast and they created this whole new thing—this thing we call bread. While watching I was so caught up in the fun of it that I never really thought much about the chemistry going on inside a ball of dough. Later I learned about the synergy involved in the seemingly simple but surprisingly complex process of making bread. Back then, I just wanted to mix and knead and braid and slash. Most of all, I wanted to try my hand with the twelve foot baker's peel, that wooden shovel that bakers use to remove the loaves from the oven. I knew at an early age that there was something magical about bread.

Later, in culinary school, when I finally got to the second part of the program—Baking and Pastry Arts—I knew where my heart was…in dough.

God sent a great opportunity my way after I was out of school and working at a high-end restaurant in Chicago: the chance to help a young Italian-American man start up a bakery cafe. I jumped at the chance, even though it meant cutting my income by a third. The cafe was a casual little place, offering breads and simple sandwiches, until my employer decided he wanted to go into desserts—authentic Italian and mostly rustic Sicilian desserts. He told me to pack a bag and he sent me on the most extraordinary trip in my life—a culinary journey through Italy, Sicily and the Aeolian Islands.

I came back from my trip a different person. I'd changed as a cook, as a baker, as a human. The beauty, elegance and simplicity of the Italian people touched my heart right through to the ventricles. I developed an increased reverence for bread. Did you know that the word Bethlehem or *Beth Lechem* means "house of bread?"

I have meditated for long periods of time simply on the subject of bread. How beautiful is the loaf of bread! In Italy, the highest compliment one can pay to a man is to liken him to bread. And so a down-to-earth man is described as "*buono come il pane*"—good, like bread. And a man with a heart of gold is "*unu cantu de pane*"—a piece of bread. And an informal, friendly man is "*pane e salami*"—bread and salami.

To an Italian, life could not exist without bread, and it is served at all three meals of the day. Other foods are viewed almost as an accompaniment to bread. Italians have an all-purpose term to describe what one eats with bread—*companatico*. And so if you ask, "What's for dinner?" The answer would be: "*Pane e companatico*"—bread and something that goes with it.

When I visited Italy and Sicily, one of the very first things I discovered on the streets and in the kitchens was the fact that bread is synonymous with well-being. Bread makes the world go round. Bread is so respected it is treated with a sense of reverence. And it was my trip to Italy that helped me to understand some of the superstitions my own grandmother had about bread. Nana never wasted a crumb of bread. Stale bread could be grated into breadcrumbs, used in *Panzanella* (Italian bread salad), scattered for the birds, but never, ever thrown away. Nana thought a loaf of bread placed upside down on the table would bring bad luck. And the worst thing one could ever do to a loaf of bread was to jam a knife into the crust and leave it there. "*Pane* is the body of *Jesu*!" she would tell me. And Nana would never, ever bake bread when the moon was full, but she never knew why not, it was simply something her mother had forbidden.

Bread is beautiful to behold, delicious to eat, and satisfying like no other food is. It is now a scientific fact that bread (and other carbohydrates) can actually elevate our mood. But my Nana knew this all along. She used to say when I was distressed: "Don't worry; eat bread."

It's no wonder that Jesus chose to continue his presence in the world in the form of bread, his pledge of eternal life.

Pane—Bread..............................

Nana Lilli's Bread

2 cakes dry yeast
½ cup lukewarm water
1 cup milk
1/3 cup sugar
1 TBSP salt
1/3 cup butter or margarine
8 cups flour
1 ¼ cups cold water
1 egg yolk
sesame seeds

Bring milk, sugar (reserve 1 tsp), salt, margarine almost to boil. Remove from heat and add water. Cool down to room temperature. Mix together 1 tsp sugar, yeast cakes, and lukewarm water. Add yeast mixture to cooled milk mixture. Mix with flour. Knead into a soft dough. Let sit for twenty minutes. Knead again. Place in greased bowl and cover with clean dishcloth. Let rise for one hour. Punch down. Let rise another hour if desired. Divide dough and place in pans. Let rise another hour in pans. Brush with beaten egg and sprinkle with sesame seeds. Bake at 375 for 40 to 45 minutes. Remove from pans immediately.

Nana's Cloverleaf Rolls

1 cake compressed or 1 pkg dry yeast
½ cup lukewarm water
½ cup scalded milk
2 TBSP salt
¼ cup butter or margarine
3 cups flour
1 egg, beaten

Soften yeast in lukewarm water. (Use warm water for dry yeast.) Pour scalded milk over sugar, salt, and butter. Stir occasionally, until butter melts; cool to lukewarm. Stir in 1 cup flour. Add softened yeast and egg; beat until blended. Stir in more flour – enough to make a soft dough. Turn out on lightly floured board. Knead for about 10 minutes. Round dough into ball; place in greased bowl. Cover and let rise in warm place until double in size, about 1 hour. Punch down. Cover and let rest 10 minutes. Pinch off pieces of dough and form into balls about 1 inch in diameter. Place three balls in each greased cup of muffin pan. Cover and let rise in warm place until nearly double in size, about 1 hour. Bake in preheated 400 oven, fifteen to twenty minutes. Remove from pan immediately.

All sorrows are less with bread.
–Miguel de Cervantes, Don Quixote

THESE PEOPLE
ACTUALLY LIKE EACH OTHER

Strange to see how a good dinner and feasting reconciles everyone.
—Samuel Pepys

Better is a dinner of herbs where love is than a fatted ox and hatred with it.
—Proverbs 15:17

The cold truth is that family dinners are more often than not an ordeal of nervous indigestion, preceded by hidden resentment and ennui and accompanied by psychosomatic jitters.—M. F. K. Fisher

After a good dinner, one can forgive anybody,
even one's own relations. —Oscar Wide

MY PARISHIONERS HAVE been so good to me. I have been adopted by so many families since coming to St. Anthony's.

I'll never forget my very first dinner here. The invitation came from our organist, Valerie Greness, a woman whom upon my first impression seemed a little stiff and reserved. I was nervous, being the new priest and all. I clutched the hostess gift—a bottle of wine of which I wasn't even sure Valerie would approve—and rang the doorbell. I was greeted by a slew of kids and then by the real Valerie... the wife and a mother of six. She was warm and welcoming. The evening was wonderful and when I left I couldn't help but think about how well this family all got along. I chalked it up to the probability that all the children were instructed to be on their best behavior in front of the new priest. But over the years, I have come to know the Greness family as a unit of people who actually like one another.

A family in which the members actually like each other is a true gift. Think about it. If a stranger walked into your kitchen tonight for supper, what would he find? Squabbling and indigestion? Or conversation and satiation. When families like each other, it really shows. What a valuable gift from God!Sometimes parents get so bogged down they forget about injecting fun into their family life. But kids need fun. And parents that provide some fun are the parents whose kids come round years later for the holidays. Have some fun with your kids!

Sunday Dinners.........................

Preparation Prayers:

- You have visited the land and watered it; greatly have You enriched it. God's watercourses are filled; You have prepared the grain. — Psalm 65:10

- Lord, help me to find time in my day to cook. It's hard sometimes with our busy lives. Help me to shop smarter, plan better, and serve healthier meals.

- Dear Lord, company is coming. Calm my nerves and help me to enjoy the preparation time as much as the time shared with friends.

- They all look to You to give them food in due time. When You give it to them, they gather it; when You open Your hand, they are filled with good things. —Psalm 104:27-28

Partaking Prayers:

- Thus I will bless You while I live; lifting up my hands, I will call upon Your name. As with the riches of a banquet shall my soul be satisfied and with exultant lips my mouth shall praise You. —Psalm 63:5,6

- Lord, God, Creator of the first and last supper, help me to make time in my life to gather my family to the table. May our meals and conversation nurture our bodies and buoy up our souls. And may we know that each morsel we bring to our lips is imbued with Your perfect love.

- Whoever observes the day, observes it for the Lord. Whoever eats, eats for the Lord, since he gives thanks to God. Whoever abstains, abstains for the Lord and gives thanks to God. —Romans 14:6

- Bless this table, Lord, and those who gather round it.
  May they be nourished by food and fellowship.
  May I always keep it clean and inviting,
  May harsh words never pass from chair to chair.

Nana's *Sugo*

My Nana's Tomato Sauce, or *Sugo* as we called it, is a very simple sauce. It's less spicy than many, and my grandmother never, ever used oregano. Every Sunday, the aroma of this sauce filled her house.

>   3 TBSP extra virgin olive oil
>   2 large (29 oz) cans of tomato puree
>   2 large (29 oz) cans of crushed tomatoes
>   2 small (6 oz) cans of tomato paste
>   3 cloves of garlic, chopped
>   1 small onion
>   3/4 cup freshly grated *Parmesan* cheese or *Asiago* cheese
>   1/2 cup of red wine
>   1 wooden spoonful of sugar
>   10 fresh basil leaves, chopped
>   1 tsp. McCormick's SeasonAll seasoned salt
>   salt and pepper to taste
>   water

Heat oil in large sauce pot. Sauté onion and garlic. Add canned items. Add 1/2 can (use empty 29 oz can) of water. Add cheese, wine, sugar, and basil. Sprinkle SeasonAll. Salt and pepper to taste. Bring to boil. Reduce heat to low. Add cooked meatballs, pork, beef or sausage. Simmer on low for at least two hours. (For thinner sauce, add more water.)

Nana's Meatballs

2 lbs. ground sirloin
2 eggs
1 cup freshly grated *Parmesan* cheese
2 cups Italian seasoned breadcrumbs
3 TBSP of dried garden mint
½ tsp garlic powder
½ tsp minced onion
1 tsp McCormick SeasonAll seasoned salt
salt and pepper to taste

Mix all ingredients well. Roll into 2 inch balls. Brown in skillet sprayed with olive oil. Add to sauce pot.

Rollini Di Carne (Bruscioluni)
Sirloin Steak Roll

1 (2 lb) slice of sirloin steak or round steak,
½ inch thick, cut into 2 equal halves
4 cloves garlic, minced
salt and pepper to taste
1 TBSP dried garden mint
½ cup seasoned breadcrumbs
½ cup grated *Asiago* cheese
4 slices *salami*
salt and pepper to taste
4 slices *prosciutto*
4 slices *Provolone*
½ cup shredded carrot
½ cup minced celery
½ cup minced onion
6 TBSP olive oil for frying
4 hard cooked eggs, peeled (optional)
clean white string for tying

Pound the steak to make it slightly thinner. Heat 3 TBSP of olive oil and sauté onion, carrots, and celery until tender. Add garlic and sauté. To this, add the breadcrumbs, *Asiago* cheese, salt, pepper and mint. Add 1 TBSP of olive oil to breadcrumb mixture. Spread the mixture on the two steaks. Layer *Salami, Prosciutto* and *Provolone*. (Optional step: Place two whole (peeled!) hard cooked eggs at one end of steak. Roll meat around egg carefully to keep ingredients from falling out. If omitting eggs, simply roll meat up.) Hold together while you tie up with string, going around several times to seal well. Knot securely. Brown in 2 TBSP olive oil on all sides. Add to your pot of sugo and cook for 2 to 3 hours. To serve, remove string with an electric knife, and cut into round slices. Serve with a little sugo drizzled on top.

Meat Stuffed Pasta Shells

1 pot of *sugo*
1 box of large pasta shells
2 lbs. of ground round or chuck
1 large onion, chopped
6 slices of bread (fresh or stale)
1 cup milk
1 cup of freshly grated *Parmesan* cheese
3 cups shredded *Mozzarella* cheese
3 eggs
1 cup of Italian seasoned breadcrumbs
½ tsp garlic powder
1 tsp. McCormick's SeasonAll seasoned salt
salt and pepper to taste

Brown ground beef and chopped onions in skillet. Drain and cool. Soak bread in the milk, then break up with hands. Add remaining ingredients to meat and onion and mix well. Cook pasta shells *al dente*. Drain and rinse under cold water. Stuff each shell with ground beef dressing. Cover the bottom of a greased glass 9 x 13 baking dish with a layer of sugo. Place stuffed shells (open side up) in pan. Cover with sugo. Bake at 350° for 45 minutes. Sprinkle with *Mozzarella* cheese. Bake for 15 more minutes.

Cheese Stuffed Shells

1 box large pasta shells
2 lbs. fresh *ricotta* cheese
3 eggs
1 cup freshly grated *Parmesan* cheese
2 TBSP dried parsley

Combine all ingredients in mixing bowl. Cook pasta shells *al dente*. Drain and rinse under cold water. Stuff each shell with cheese mixture. Cover the bottom of a greased glass 9 x 13 baking dish with layer of sugo. Place stuffed shells (open side down) in pan. Cover with sugo. Bake at 350° for 45 minutes. Top with *Mozzarella* cheese and bake for 15 more minutes.

Roast Capon with Ground Beef Dressing

A capon is a neutered male chicken that is wonderfully tender and tasty. My family preferred capon to turkey and so it was this bird that generally graced our holiday tables. Capons are typically larger and plumper than other chickens, usually weighing between eight and ten pounds. My Nana roasted four birds on holidays.

Dressing:

> 1 lb. ground round or ground chuck
> 4 celery ribs, sliced thinly
> 1 large onion, halved and then sliced
> 1 tsp. McCormick's SeasonAll
> 1 cooking apple, cut into 1/8 inch cubes
> salt and pepper to taste
> 4 slices of bread, soaked in milk and squeezed
> 1 cup Italian style breadcrumbs
> 1 egg, beaten
> 1 cup milk
> 1 TBSP olive oil
> 1 cup dry white wine
> ½ cup butter, melted
> ½ cup *Parmesan* cheese

Season ground beef with SeasonAll, salt and pepper. Brown in skillet. Drain grease and set aside. Sauté onions and celery in olive oil until transparent. In mixing bowl, combine meat, onions, cheese, celery, apple, bread and breadcrumbs. Add egg and milk and mix with your hands until ingredients are well-incorporated.

After cleaning, sprinkle cavities of capon with 1 tsp of salt. Stuff with dressing and truss. Bake any extra dressing in a covered baking dish during the last 45 minutes of baking time. Spray roasting pan with non-stick spray. Roast at 400° for 20 minutes to brown. Reduce heat to 325°. Add the wine and brush with melted butter. Baste occasionally. Allow approximately 20 minutes cooking time per pound. Use thermometer. Capon is done if legs loosen at the joints when pulled. Make gravy from drippings.

Karla Clark

PRAY ALWAYS

This is what I think, in essence, prayer is. It is the breaking of silence. It is the need to be known and the need to know. Prayer is the sound made by our deepest aloneness
—Frederick Buechner

Heaven is full of answers to prayers
which no one has bothered to pray. —Billy Graham

Let your prayer be very simple. For the tax collector and the prodigal son, just one word was enough to reconcile them to God.
—St. John Climacus

When I was young, I thought that prayer could be—should be—only in thankfulness and adoration. A prayer of supplication seemed to be something unworthy. Afterwards, I changed my opinion completely. Today, I ask very much. —Pope John Paul II

I LOVE TO preach about prayer. It's my favorite subject—yes, even before food. All people have a built-in desire for intimacy with God. And certainly God speaks to us through Scripture, through the sacraments, through the people that love us, and through His creations that surround us. But God also speaks to us through prayer. Prayer is a dialogue, a two-way conversation. You talk to God and God talks back. But some people forget to wait for God's response. If you were seeking advice from a friend, would you walk away before he responded? If you wrote a letter to a friend and then received one in return, would you stick it in a drawer and not open it? When you talk on the telephone, do you only speak into the mouthpiece? Of course the answer to all of these questions is no, but that, in effect, is what we do when we pray to God and do not listen for His answer. We cut Him off; we negate our prayer!

Whenever I cook, I pray. To me, they go hand in hand. Mostly I cook alone, which may not be the case with many of you, dear readers. Often there may be little hands helping you. Then I say pray together! Something as simple as, "Thank you for this gorgeous tomato, Lord," is a really big prayer.

Show-Stealing Side Dishes..............

Preparation Prayers:

- O God, You are my God whom I seek. For You my flesh pines and my soul thirsts like the earth, parched and lifeless and without water. —Psalm 63:2

- Lord, I reflect on how these ingredients got to my kitchen. There were countless people involved, each playing an important part. For the farmer, the trucker, the grocer, I thank you.

- Bless my hands, bless my heart. What to cook? Where to start? Help me feed my hungry bunch breakfast, dinner, snacks and lunch.

- The Lord provides. No matter what our family situation, there is always good food on the table. No matter what is going on in our lives, our family can gather together, share warm food, and talk of the day.

Partaking Prayers:

- Happy are you who fear the Lord, who walk in His ways! For you shall eat the fruit of your handiwork, happy shall you be, and favored. —Psalm 128:1,2

- You have crowned the year with Your bounty, and Your paths overflow with a rich harvest; the untilled meadows overflow with it, and rejoicing clothes the hills. The fields are garmented with flocks and the valleys blanketed with grain. —Psalm 65:12-14

- Ask, and you shall receive. Seek, and you will find. Knock, and it will be opened to you. For the one who asks, receives. The one who seeks, finds. The one who knocks, enters. —Matthew 7:7,8

- When our souls are happy, we seek food. Celebrations would not be celebrations without feasts. How much pleasure man derives from food!

Sicilian-Style Stuffed Artichokes

When making this dish, choose artichokes with closed leaves. Open leaves mean the artichoke has begun to go to seed and will be tough.

> 4 fresh artichokes
> 1 cup Italian-seasoned breadcrumbs
> 4 cloves of garlic, diced
> 3 TBSP extra virgin olive oil
> salt and pepper to taste
> 4 TBSP *Parmesan* cheese, grated
> 4 ounces of *Asiago* cheese, chopped into 1/8 inch cubes

Using a serrated knife and a cutting board, cut 1 inch off the tops of each artichoke. Cut off stems and a little of the bottoms (so the artichokes will sit upright). Snap off any bottom leaves that have pulled away and trim the points of the remaining leaves with kitchen shears. Using both hands, gently spread back the leaves of the artichokes. (Many recipes call for removing the inner purple spiny leaves and the choke with a spoon. You can leave it intact and remove it when eating the artichoke.) Rinse artichokes and drain upside-down while preparing cheese and garlic. Moving from the outer leaves to the center (but not the choke) stuff each leaf with a piece of garlic and a cube of cheese. Spoon each artichoke with ¼ cup of breadcrumbs, shaking artichokes slightly so that the breadcrumbs will fall down between the leaves. Sprinkle each with 1 TBSP *Parmesan* cheese. Salt and pepper each, then drizzle with a little of the olive oil. It's important to use a pot in which the artichokes fit snugly, upright. Fill the pot with an inch of water and drizzle in rest of olive oil. Position the artichokes, cover and cook on low heat for one hour. Check the water level from time to time as some of the water will evaporate. (My mother used to add the stems and sometimes potato wedges to the pot to fix artichokes in place—these can also be eaten.) Serve hot. To eat, remove the leaves one by one and scrape the delicious pulp from the leaf against your teeth. Once you get to the center leaves and the choke, take a spoon and remove the entire choke section, leaving the tender and delectable artichoke bottom. If you loved the leaves, you'll love the concentrated flavor of the bottom. I had a cousin who would pay his siblings anywhere from fifty cents to a dollar for their artichoke bottoms.

The Best Ever Tossed Salad

1 head each red and green leaf lettuce
½ head iceberg lettuce
1 cucumber
1 small bottle pimento, drained
½ medium red onion
1 can artichoke hearts (reserve liquid)
4 plum tomatoes
homemade croutons
½ can black olives
homemade vinaigrette dressing

Wash and shred lettuces. Peel and slice cucumber and tomato. Chop red onion. Cut artichoke hearts into bite-sizes. Drain pimento. Break olives into two pieces with your fingers. Combine in large bowl. Toss with dressing. Serve with croutons.

Italian Vinaigrette Salad Dressing

½ cup extra-virgin olive oil
¼ cup apple-cider vinegar
1 TBSP balsamic vinegar
1 tsp garlic powder
salt and pepper to taste
½ of liquid from canned artichokes
2 TBSP water
½ cup coarsely grated *Asiago* cheese

Whisk together all ingredients and pour over salad. Toss and serve.

Homemade Croutons

½ loaf Italian bread
½ cup extra virgin olive oil
1 TBSP Dijon mustard
¼ cup grated *Parmesan* cheese
juice of one fresh lemon
1 garlic clove, crushed
salt and pepper to taste

Cut bread into 2-inch square pieces. Spread out on cookie sheet. Whisk together all other ingredients. With pastry brush, brush all four sides of each crouton. Brown in broiler, turning every few minutes, so that all sides get toasted. Cool and serve.

Sicilian Green Bean Potato Salad

2 lb. fresh string beans
3 lbs. new potatoes
2 cloves garlic, chopped finely
salt and pepper to taste
¼ cup extra virgin olive oil
½ cup red wine vinegar
1 small red onion, sliced

In a large pot, boil the beans in salted water till *al dente.* Drain and rinse immediately under cold water. Boil the new potatoes in salted water until overcooked—where the skins crack and the potato falls apart easily. Drain and rinse potatoes in cold water. Sauté garlic and onions in a skillet sprayed with olive oil. Mix all cooked ingredients in a large bowl. Salt and pepper to taste. Drizzle with vinegar and oil. Toss. Keep refrigerated until serving. Sometimes my Nana added hard-cooked eggs to the salad. Crumbled *pancetta* also gives it a nice taste.

Sicilian Green Beans

1 lb. fresh string beans
3 TBSP olive oil
1 medium white onion, sliced
¼ cup of grated *Parmesan* cheese
½ cup of Italian seasoned breadcrumbs
¼ tsp garlic powder
salt and pepper to taste
2 slices of fried *Pancetta*, crumbled

Boil beans in salted water and cook *al dente.* Drain and set aside. Heat oil in skillet and sauté onion until brown. Add green beans and cook until done. Add cheese and breadcrumbs, salt, pepper and garlic powder. Stir. As the cheese melts, the breadcrumbs, cheese and oil will coat the beans. Cook until coating becomes golden. Sprinkle with *pancetta* crumbles and serve hot.

Karla Clark

KISS THE COOK

I declare that a meal prepared by a person who loves you will do more good than any average cooking. —Luther Burbank

There is one thing more exasperating than a wife who can cook and won't and that's a wife who can't cook and will.
—Robert Frost

There is no sight on earth more appealing than the sight of a woman making dinner for someone she loves. —Thomas Wolf

No mean woman can cook well, for it calls for a light head, a generous spirit, and a large heart. —Paul Gauguin

WHO HANDLES THE cooking in most homes? The woman, of course. It goes without saying, right? It also goes without thanks sometimes, too. My own grandfather—a man of few words—never found the right ones to praise my grandmother's wonderful cooking. A grunt here, a sigh there. That's all he thought was necessary to show his pleasure. Once, after years of cooking for my grandfather without a single word of praise or thanks, my grandmother stood up from the table, threw down her napkin and asked: "Why don't you ever say anything about my cooking?" My grandfather simply looked up and said, "I eat it, don't I?"

FOR SHE WHO COOKS
Lest they forget to thank you as they eat your tender meat
sitting at your table with full bellies and warm feet.
Know this: God loves a cook.
When no one claims the meal delicious as they lap it up,
putting their forks down only to swallow, burp, or hiccup.
Don't forget: God blesses a cook.
When it's time to clear the table and you can't find a picker-upper
don't don your rubber gloves and proclaim this the last supper!
Just remember: God rewards a cook.

Best For Last.............................

Preparation Prayers:
- I will bless the Lord at all times. Praise shall be always in my mouth. My soul will glory in the Lord that the poor may hear and be glad. Magnify the Lord with me; Let us exalt His name together. —Psalm 34:2-4

- Whatever we hear, but also whatever we see, taste, touch, or smell, vibrates deep down with God's song. —David Steindl-Rast

- Do not labor with food that perishes, but for the food which endures to eternal life, which the Son of Man will give to you; for on Him has God the Father set His seal. —John 6:27

- You cannot love God's sweetness if you have never tasted it. Rather, embrace the food of life with the palate of the heart so that, having made trial of God's sweetness, you may be empowered to love. —St. Gregory the Great

Partaking Prayers:
- God our heavenly Father, You send rain and sun to descend upon the earth, that it may bring forth fruit for our use. We give You humble thanks, for You send us just what we need, just when we need it.

- That it may please Thee to give and preserve to our use the kindly fruits of the earth, so as in due time we may enjoy them. —*The Litany*

- Remember always to welcome strangers, for by doing this, some people have entertained angels without knowing it. —Hebrews 13:2

- Lord, I taste Your love in this delicious food. I savor every flavor! Your bounty is as endless as my appetite.

Italian Sesame Cookies

(I only have the recipe my mother used to make giant quantities for weddings and Christmas.)

    3 lb. flour
    3 TBSP baking powder
    1 ½ lb. sugar
    2 TBSP vanilla extract
    1 dozen eggs
    1 tsp orange extract
    1 ¼ lb. butter or margarine
    1 lb. sesame seeds

In medium bowl, blend flour and baking powder. Cut butter or margarine into sugar and then into the flour/baking powder with pastry blender. In another bowl, beat eggs; add orange and vanilla extracts. Add to flour mixture. Shape dough into balls. Elongate the balls into size of a man's thumb. Dip in milk, roll in sesame seeds. Place on greased cookie sheet and bake in preheated 400° oven for 10 minutes or until golden brown.

Arborio Rice Pudding

    1 cup *Arborio* rice
    2 quarts plus 1 cup milk
    4 fresh egg yolks
    1 cup sugar
    4 TBSP cornstarch
    1 tsp vanilla
    ground cinnamon to taste
    raisins (optional)

Pre-heat oven to 350°. Cook rice until almost done in lightly salted boiling water. Keep covered and set aside. In a mixing bowl, whisk cornstarch into milk until it is lump free, then set aside. In separate bowl, beat sugar and egg yolks until well blended. Whisk in cornstarch mixture and vanilla. Stir in rice and raisins. Pour into greased baking dish and bake at 350° for 1 hour.

Bread Pudding

    1 loaf of 2-day old Italian or Vienna bread
    4 cups milk
    4 eggs, beaten
    2 cups sugar
    3 TBSP butter or margarine
    2 TBSP vanilla
    1 cup raisins (optional)
    pinch of salt
    1 tsp ground cinnamon (optional)

Preheat oven to 350°. Tear bread into shreds. In large bowl, soak shredded bread in milk. Set aside. In a separate bowl, beat eggs with sugar, butter, vanilla, salt, and if desired, raisins and/or cinnamon. With hands, crush and mix bread into the milk until clumpy. Add soaked bread to the egg mixture. Mix until well blended. Transfer to greased baking dish. Bake at 350° for 1 hour or until knife inserted to center comes out clean. Serve with one of the following sauces:

Whiskey Sauce for Bread Pudding

    ¼ cup butter or margarine
    2 TBSP whiskey
    ½ cup sugar
    2 TBSP water
    1 tsp vanilla

Melt butter in small saucepan. Stir in sugar and water. Cook, stirring constantly over medium-low heat until sugar dissolves and mixtures boils. (About 5 minutes.) Remove from heat; stir in whiskey and vanilla extract. Drizzle over pudding.

Brandy Sauce for Bread Pudding

    1 stick butter or margarine
    1 cup sugar
    3 TBSP brandy

Melt butter and sugar in saucepan. Stir in brandy. Serve warm.

Italian Wild Cherry Sauce for Bread Pudding

8 oz. Amarene Fabbri cherries (found at good Italian market), finely diced, juices saved
½ cup of Italian sweet dessert wine—Marsala,
1 TBSP cornstarch

Drain cherry juice into a small bowl and whisk in cornstarch. Heat diced cherries in a small saucepan on low, then add wine and cornstarch mixture. Heat until slightly thickened. Serve warm.

Italian Pasta Pudding

Pasta pudding? Okay, okay, no laughing. You like bread pudding, right? You like rice pudding, right? Pasta is just another starch. Try this. You'll love it.

½ lb. *fettuccini* or *linguini* noodles
3 eggs, beaten
¼ cup butter or margarine, melted
½ cup sugar
½ tsp cinnamon
½ tsp vanilla
1 ½ cups warmed milk
8 oz. *Mascarpone*
salt to taste
1 cup raisins

Preheat oven to 350°. Cook pasta until *al dente* in lightly salted water. Drain. Blend *Mascarpone* with milk until creamy. Mix with pasta. In separate bowl, blend eggs, sugar, cinnamon, and salt. Pour over pasta mixture. Add melted butter, raisins and vanilla. Blend. Pour into greased baking dish. Sprinkle with cinnamon and sugar and dot with butter. Bake for 50 minutes. Serve with dollop of *Mascarpone*.

Chocolate Crazy Cake

My mother loved to whip up this cake. It's so easy—you just throw everything into one bowl.

3 cups flour
2 cups sugar
½ cup cocoa
1 tsp salt
2 tsp baking soda
2 tsp vinegar
2 tsp vanilla
2/3 cup oil
2 cups cold water

Preheat oven to 350°. In a large mixing bowl, mix all ingredients with blender until smooth. Bake at 350° for 30 to 35 minutes.

Mascarpone-filled Chocolate Cupcakes
A grown-up version of the cupcake, but kids will love them, too!

For cupcake batter:

> 2 cups cake flour, sifted
> 1 tsp baking powder
> 2 cups sugar
> ½ cup cocoa
> 1 cup buttermilk or plain yogurt
> ½ cup butter
> 2 eggs
> 1 tsp baking soda
> 1 tsp vanilla

In a mixing bowl, combine flour, cocoa, salt, baking soda and baking powder. In a separate bowl, cream sugar and butter. Beat in eggs and gradually add the buttermilk or yogurt. Add the flour mixture gradually and beat just until smooth.

For filling:

> 1 lb. *Mascarpone*
> 1/3 cup sugar
> 1 egg
> 1/8 tsp salt
> 1 - 6 oz pkg of chocolate chips
> 1 TBSP sugar for top

Beat egg and sugar until creamy. Add *Mascarpone* and salt. Beat well. Stir in chocolate chips.

Fill 24 cupcake liners half full with batter. Drop 1 TBSP of cheese mixture on top of the batter. Sprinkle with sugar and bake at 350° for 30 to 35 minutes.

Taylor Street Mothers' Brownies
Okay, so brownies aren't Italian, but this recipe went through my neighborhood when I was a kid, and everyone, including my mother, wanted to claim it as her own. These are the best brownies I have ever tasted. One bite and I'm back in the old neighborhood...

For batter:

1 cup sugar
4 eggs
1 stick butter
1 cup flour
pinch salt
1 can Hershey syrup
12 pecan halves for jumbo brownies or
24 pecan halves for regular size brownies

Preheat oven to 350°. In a mixing bowl, cream butter and sugar. Add eggs one at a time, blending with each addition. Add the flour and salt. Blend. Pour in the can of syrup. Blend. Pour into a greased and floured 9 x 13 pan and bake at 350° for 20 to 23 minutes—until toothpick comes out clean. Do not overcook.

For icing:
1 ½ cups sugar
1/3 cup 2% milk
1 stick butter
1 cup chocolate chips

Combine sugar, butter and milk in saucepan. Boil for 2 minutes. Add chocolate chips and stir until melted. When brownies are cool and icing is almost cool, ice brownies. Top with 12 pecan halves. Makes 12 jumbo brownies or 24 regular size brownies.

22

Firing up the Ovens

By the time I close the book it's four a.m. No problem I tell myself, I'll just head to bed and sleep the whole day tomorrow. What better day than New Year's Day to sleep in?

Before I climb into bed, I unplug the phone on my nightstand. I burrow down deep under the covers. I can't figure out how I feel about this whole Vito thing. I guess I feel a lot of different things. First of all, I'm disappointed: I thought Vito's book would provide some answers to my questions. But since the small amount of personal information Vito shared didn't include his childhood, or me, or the accident, there were no answers. Then there's the part of me that's ticked-off royally about Vito stealing many of my mother's recipes. There goes my cookbook idea. I entertain the thought of suing him but I read somewhere that you can't copyright recipes.

The priest thing I can see; I can live with. It would have been much more difficult to find out that he'd married and had children. From his book, it seems as if his life suits him. And although I wish I could say that this news makes me happy—the fact that he has recovered from his illness and has been able to move on—I just can't. How can he be so happy, so joyful? Was he able to just sweep the past under the rug? Forget about me so easily? He had the power to release me, with a simple phone call, a brief letter, a quick visit. I hung on to those three words—"I love you"— for so long. But he never released me. He's had such power over me all these years.

The thing is, Vito completely wiped us off the face of the earth when he didn't mention my family or me in his book. I know this will hurt Mama and Papa. He said the food he ate up and down Taylor Street was what made him change his mind about becoming a priest. Ha! It was *me* that made him change his mind. Or, maybe it was my father and my father's bread.

Now I'm almost certain that it was Vito Nino saw looking in our window Christmas Eve night. I know that this idea is irrational, but somehow the thought comforts me, feeds into my thinking that maybe over the years he has tried to make contact, but for whatever reason—fear, embarrassment, shame, guilt—was not ever able to bring himself to go through with it.

I close my eyes and prepare for hibernation.

Nobody bothers me—I sleep for twelve hours with only one bathroom break. When I get up, it's dinnertime and dark again. I'm glad. I'll eat a little something and then I'll do some laundry and maybe take down the tree for Mama. I can get through the rest of the day. I just won't answer the door or the phone.

There's a note waiting for me on the kitchen table. It's Papa's writing: *"We're at Uncle Silvio and Aunt Anna's for dinner. Your mother's been playing secretary all day."* I wonder what the heck that means, but then I turn over the note and see that I've had eleven phone calls throughout the day. Three from Ted, two from Virgie, and one each from Rosa, Marina, Colina, Angie, Jimmy, and Nino. The phone rings now and makes me jump. I let the machine pick it up and hold my breath. It's Nino. "Aunt B, I'm missing one LEGO piece that I really need. It's black and it looks like an 'L' with two bumps on each side. Do you remember seeing it? I really need it. Call me as soon as you can. It really stinks when you can't find a piece you need."

The bowl of bran flakes hits the spot and when I pour a little more cereal in the bowl to even out the milk, I can't help but think of what Virgie said about Pauly and then I can't help but wonder if living alone (without a partner) has caused me to have some idiosyncrasies of my own. The phone rings again and once more I let the machine pick it up. "Bina, it's Jimmy. I'm giving a speech tomorrow in my Communications class and I want to see what you think. It's supposed to be a persuasive speech and so mine's about breaking all the wine rules, you know, about only drinking red with beef and white with chicken and holding the glass by the stem and using a three ounce glass for white and a four ounce glass for red and all that garbage. My goal is to persuade people to drink whatever friggin' kind of wine they want, whenever and however. Call me."

I lift the cereal bowl to my lips—something Mama never allowed us to do—and slurp up the last bit of milk. It's mean not to call them all back, I know, but I'm tired of being needed. The phone rings again but I'm in the bathroom with the shower running before I hear who it is. Can't people tell when someone is hiding? Geez, it should be obvious.

After my shower, I slip into a clean flannel nightgown, put fresh sheets on my bed, climb in, and set a new record for the Guinness World Book: I sleep another twelve hours, waking up just in time to get dressed and get downstairs and back to work. I know what you're thinking: some restaurant manager she'll make, but I assure you the present circumstances are extenuating.

It doesn't take me to long to realize I should have tried for another twelve-hour stretch—anyone who is anyone is angry with me. Mama is quiet and pretends to be hyper-interested in Aunt Lina's weekend report (her youngest son, his wife, and their two kids stayed with her for the last three days). Jimmy's mad that I didn't call him back and won't let me read his speech now. Says it's too late, he got someone else to listen to it. And Papa, well, he's looking at me like I'm some sort of pessimistic disappointment. I just carry on: brewing five different flavors of coffee and then pouring them into the pump-style thermoses at the coffee bar.

Every time I enter the hot yeasty kitchen Aunt Lina has another rotten story to share with Mama about her daughter-in-law Ruth. "I tell you, Luna, she can't even make a *salami* sandwich right. My son does all the cooking. The kids make their own lunches. She can't even bring herself to pour dog food into the dog dish. She says, 'food is food,' and she just eats to survive, and that's it."

"No!" Mama says. She's incredulous when people don't share our family's reverence for food.

"You could put a cold TV dinner in front of her or *Chateaubriand* and you'd get the same reaction."

I stay only long enough to get today's specials—*Polenta* Pizza and Stuffed Yellow Peppers with Roasted Red Pepper Sauce. I leave the kitchen just as Aunt Lina tells Mama how Ruth poured water over her son's breakfast cereal this morning because Aunt Lina had run out of milk.

I unlock and open the front door and Mr. Barbiere greets me with a chipper "Good morning!" which means he must be mad at me, too. But everyone else seems happy to see me. Our regulars hate when we shut the place down for the holiday, so as they straggle in they hug me and slap Jimmy on the back. Some wander back to the kitchen to talk to Mama and Papa and Aunt Lina. I find myself perking up a bit. There is comfort in routine. I'm living proof that one can come to terms with boredom. Maybe I am happiest here in the store. Maybe this is my destiny—where I'm meant to be—dishing out comfort and comfort food.

Charlie Gradezzi shows up smiling, still running on the high of having all his family gathered together for the holidays. He asks me how Colina is doing and says that his son is the best damn lawyer in town. I feel bad because I didn't even remember that today was the day Colina was meeting with Charlie's son, Frank, about the divorce arrangements. Poor Colina.

I'm pouring coffee and listening to Mr. Roan tell about his New Year's Eve mugging. "I chased the kid three blocks, but then I thought I was having a heart attack so I had to stop. The bastard."

Mrs. Zinsia, who has just arrived with her granddaughters, tells Mr. Roan to watch his language. Makes me wonder what's going to happen when the two little girls are finally in school and nobody has to watch his language anymore. It also makes me wonder why it is that Mrs. Zinsia has a hard time hearing everything except bad language.

My perk-up has peaked. And now I'm back to where I have to force a smile. All of a sudden, everybody and everything is bugging me. Even the music. Perry Como singing "*I'll be Home For Christmas,*" usually one of my favorite songs, is grating on my nerves. Papa insists on playing Christmas music for the full twelve days of Christmas, something that will change when I take over. I could go for some blues right about now.

The Randanza brothers are telling me about their New Year's Eve dates. I'd like to ask these two exactly which planet they visit to find these women, but I'm nothing if not tactful. These guys are just too sweet. Tony and Nick own a truck and auto repair shop down the street. Honest to a fault, they turn away business each and every day. "Just use better gas and that knock'll go away," Tony will say. Or, "Why fix the air conditioner if you're gonna trade this car in?"

Soon the time for chit-chat and catching-up is over—the lunch throng is upon us. We are busier than ever and I feel the rush of adrenaline. I speed up my engine. Thankfully the tables are turning over quickly. Half of Little Italy has decided to eat lunch at Mela's today. Even Penny,

Mama's friend from the bakery across the street, is here munching on Polenta Pizza. I recognize many of the lunch guests and it occurs to me that they are now becoming regulars themselves.

A visit to the kitchen tells me that we've run out of Polenta Pizza, or at least out of polenta. Papa has to run out to get more cornmeal. Somehow Aunt Lina has talked Mr. Maggio into staying on to help with the rush. I'm almost out the kitchen door when Aunt Lina shouts to me, "Is he gone yet?"

"Who?" I ask.

"Joey the Baldy."

"Yeah, he left about an hour ago."

"Thank God," she says. She turns to Mama and grabs her by both arms with her polenta-dusted hands. "I did something stupid, Luna."

"What? What did you do that was stupid?"

"I told Joey the Baldy I'd go out with him tonight."

"What?!" Mama screams.

"What?!" I scream.

Aunt Lina covers her face with her hands, now dusting *it* with polenta. "I know, I know. But he bought tickets to Andrea Bocelli and I just adore him! More than Pavorotti, more than Julio! Luna, what should I do? I don't want to go. Did you see him this morning, smiling like the cat that got the mouse. He just caught me at a weak moment."

"I don't know how you can get out of it," Mama says.

"You love opera," Aunt Lina says to Mama, "why don't you go?

"Don't be ridiculous," Mama says.

"How about Sunny? They're supposed to be such good friends. Maybe Sunny will go." I've never seen Aunt Lina desperate before. "Or, hey, Maggio, do you like opera?"

Mr. Maggio won't even dignify the question with an answer. He snorts and then he gives Aunt Lina what could be something like a smile, but I can't be sure.

"Lina," Mama says while she sprinkles cheese on a pizza, "you accepted, now you have to go. Go and enjoy yourself. He's not that bad."

"He's worse. I don't know what I was thinking. It's just that I haven't had a date since before Christmas," she says, like it's some kind of deep, dark confession. I guess I am a little surprised.

Mama pats her on the back to comfort her but then she says, "You have to go. Remember what Sunny said about your dating—that it better not jeopardize customer relationships. He'll kill you! Or at least fire you, and I need you."

"Well, if I play my cards right, cancel legitimate-like, then nobody will kill me. I'm going to tell him I'm sick. I am feeling rather nauseated."

"Lina!"

"And feverish, too."

I would love to stay and hear more of this juicy stuff, but I know I'd better get back out front. When I return to the counter, Ted and Clay are just approaching. My heart decides to do somersaults. Who needs this at forty? I thank Jimmy for covering for me and he saunters off to clean a table. Ted smiles at me, but it's Clay who seems excited to see me. He says, "Hey, it's you!"

"It's me?" I say, stupidly pointing to myself.

"Yes, I knew I knew you. Remember? The let's-cook-naked book?"

I feign confusion. Ted looks shocked. I'm certain that I am *visibly* perspiring.

"At the bookstore, the other night," Clay says. "Remember?"

Ted is staring at me, waiting to be enlightened. "Oh, yes, sure. Silly me. How did your wife like the book?"

"*We* loved the book," he says with a naughty laugh. "Better than a second honeymoon." He turns to Ted. "Remind me to show you this new cookbook I picked up for Sharon." He turns back to me. "So, what do you recommend today?"

"Oh, definitely, my mother's Stuffed Yellow Peppers," I say with the Chicago Magazine restaurant review in mind. "They're huge, stuffed with ground round, cheese and bread crumbs, and they're served with *Arborio* rice and covered with a roasted red pepper couli." I say *couli* rather than *sauce* just because I know who they are. Ted gives me a look but I don't care because Clay and I now have a past, and quite possibly more of a future than Ted and I.

They both order the peppers and Clay pays. He thinks he's so smug using a credit card with one of his aliases: Jonathan Jordan. What would he think if he knew that I knew that Jonathan and Jordan are the names of his two sons? Or that I know the significance of all his pseudonyms? Thor Addison: his two cats. Harvey Augustana: his (Harvard) and his wife's (Augustana) alma maters. Perry Josseloux: his father's first name and his mother's maiden name (I think). I give Clay-Jonathan-Thor-Harvey-Perry back his credit card and his receipt. I flash both men a big smile and say, "The soft drinks are in the refrigerator in the corner. Help yourself and enjoy your lunch."

I take two more orders then hightail it to the kitchen and announce as calmly as I can to Mama, Aunt Lina, and Mr. Maggio (Papa's not back yet from the polenta run) that there are food writers in the house. They all look at me like I'm crazy. "Restaurant reviewers!" I almost shout. "Don't ask me how I know. Don't ask me any questions. Just get me the two most beautiful peppers you have, be generous with the couli, I mean sauce, and for Pete's sake garnish the plates!" Aunt Lina gives me a look that says who died and made you executive chef, but I ignore it. "And whatever you do, do not come out of this kitchen. And do not tell Papa that we've got foodies in the house—he'll just lose it!" Oh, yes, the adrenaline is surging. I feel like a tri-athlete.

Mama, who knows I don't go ballistic unless there's good reason, springs into action and when I come back a few minutes later after serving other customers, two perfect pepper dishes await me. I serve them at just the right time. I even come back to clear away the plates—something we don't typically do at Mela's. Ted explained to me how dining critics visit a restaurant at least three times before reviewing it, and I want three to be the charm. For Papa's sake.

On my way back to the kitchen, Clay stops me. "You know what? Oh, I'm sorry, I never did get your name."

"Sabina."

"Sabina. That's pretty. Well, Sabina, we've decided we actually have room for dessert today. What do you suggest?"

I rattle off a couple of our more unique desserts all the while wondering if I'll get points deducted for not introducing myself, but I'm sorry, I do not do the "Hello, I'm Sabina, and I'll be your server today" thing. I just don't.

Clay chooses the Cappuccino Hazelnut Cheesecake. Ted can't seem to decide. He sits there drumming his fingers on his lips until finally he orders the Raspberry Cream Cheesecake. He follows me to the counter to pay for the desserts and to grab mugs for coffee. He hands me one of his bogus credit cards and I almost smile while he signs his alias to the receipt. I wonder if he ever forgets and signs his real name. You have to wonder if food critics ever suffer from identity crises later on in life. He takes the mugs and I tell him I'll bring the desserts out in a minute. He nods but doesn't say anything, not even thank you.

Just as I am about to open the kitchen door, a loud crash reverberates from the kitchen and every eye in the place gapes at the door with curiosity. I go in. Mr. Maggio is on the floor along with several broken lunch plates. "He slipped on some pizza sauce," Aunt Lina says, squatting near him, helping him to sit up.

"Are you hurt, Mr. Maggio?" Mama asks, holding his hand.

"Should I call 911?" Papa, who has just returned with the cornmeal, asks.

"No, no," Mr. Maggio says, shaking his head. I see him hold his left wrist. He says something to Mama in Italian that I can't make out.

"He hurt his wrist," Mama says, "trying to save the fall."

Aunt Lina's wiping up the floor. "It's my fault, Maggio. I dribbled *sugo* all over the floor over here. I'm sorry."

"Well, we better get you to the Emergency Room," Papa says, helping Mr. Maggio to his feet. "Get it looked at."

Mama gets a bag of ice and lays it on Mr. Maggio's wrist.

"I'll drive him," says Aunt Lina, wiping her hands on a towel, "it's the least I can do."

Mama and I look at her suspiciously. You don't have to tell us how many teaspoons are in a tablespoon. We both know exactly what's going on here: Aunt Lina is somehow going to use poor Mr. Maggio's accident as a way out of her hot date with you-know-who. Just wait and see. If I were a betting woman, I'd bet a lot of money on this one. Papa isn't privy to the hot date information, so he thinks it's a great idea. "Thanks Lina, I'll help finish up lunch. You know where to go?"

"Yes, yes, we had to bring my grandson there the other day when he cut his finger. I told that boy not to cut the pepperoni, that I'd cut the pepperoni, but he had to cut the pepperoni."

They go out the back door and only then do I remember Ted and Clay's desserts, which I was just about to dish out when we heard the crash. I hurry out to the front, grab the cheesecakes from the refrigerated display case and direct my eyes to their table as I cut a generous slice of each. They are both looking around. They've waited, what, five minutes, ten tops? I know now that I have blown the review to pieces—first by not introducing myself and now with poor service.

I set the two plates down in front of them, almost giving each the other's dessert, but catching myself just in time.

"Everything all right in the kitchen?" Clay inquires.

"Let's just say it's all right now," I say and leave it at that. Oh, Geez, I think as I walk away, I can just see the review now: "Mom and Pop joint has superb authentic Sicilian food but suspicious crashing noises come from the kitchen and the service is inconsistent." Or something like that. Imagine Papa's face when he reads about the sporadic service after grilling us daily all these years about proper table service. Yikes!

I tell Jimmy to take the counter and I go to the kitchen to get the next order. I go in and out a few times and finally Ted and Clay, or should I say George and Jonathan, are gone.

Later, when I lock the front door, we all sigh in relief. We haven't had a day like today in a long time. Even so, Jimmy asks Papa if he can leave a little early to study for a test. Papa says, "Go ahead," without a smidgen of sarcasm in his voice, so Jimmy heads out, without so much as a "good-bye" to me. Mama, Papa, and I start cleaning up. Everything seems so quiet without Jimmy and Aunt Lina around.

Sometimes I can't help wondering how many times I have washed this same pot or pan. Or how many times I have swept this floor or run this dishwasher. Well, I've been working in the store since I was ten—thirty years—so the number must run in the high thousands. If I were my nephew Nino I would calculate the exact number. But why? It's not the number that's important, it's the fact that I'm not sure I want to wash this same pot for another thirty years. I never wanted to run this place by myself—that was never the plan. The whole idea was to be like Mama and Papa: a team.

When everything is in order Mama suggests to Papa that they drop by Mr. Maggio's to bring him some food and check on his wrist. Papa says, "Good idea. And we can stop by the bank and save Bina the trip."

"Hey thanks," I say. I don't usually mind taking over the deposit but last I heard it was three below zero so I am in no hurry to go outside. "I think I'm just going to take a bath, read, and go to bed early," I say. They both give me a look, but say nothing. Their faces say everything; their faces say: "I wonder if Bina is having some kind of breakdown."

They gather the "care package" as Mama calls it and head out the back door. I am headed upstairs for bath and bed when there is a knock on the front door. I know I flipped the sign around to closed. I pull back the shade ever so gently knowing damn well it's Ted. But it's not, it's Mama. I open the door for her, thinking she knocked differently. That wasn't her usual, gentle one, two, three.

"I forgot the bread. Can you imagine not bringing the breadmaker bread?" I follow her to the kitchen. "Hey, I forgot to ask you, what ever happened with those food writers? What was that commotion all about?"

"Can't tell you and don't mention it to Papa," I say bluntly, like I mean it.

"I won't. But I already know that Rosa must be behind it. Papa's birthday is coming up in a few weeks and I'm sure she's probably hired someone…wait a minute, it's Jimmy, isn't it? He showed me that review he wrote about *Volare* the other day and it was pretty good."

I give her a purposely-misleading smile. I hug her and ask her to tell Mr. Maggio I hope he feels better. After she leaves I lock the door and turn to head upstairs. But there's another knock on the door. I just know that this time it's Ted. But it's not; it's Mama again. She says, "Just thought I'd let you know that Ted's walking up the street as we speak. And that after the bank and Mr. Maggio's, Papa and I have some shopping to do—Christmas returns—and we're stopping by Colina's after that, and so don't expect us until, oh, around eight." She gives me a thumbs-up and gets into the car. I'm tempted to peep my head out to see if she's telling the truth or not, but I know Mama wouldn't lie about something like that. I close the door just to bide for time, that and because it's damn cold outside.

I open the door before Ted even has the chance to knock. His eyebrows arch up. "Mama saw you coming," I say.

"Oh," he says.

"Come on in."

"Thanks."

Next I say, "So what's going on?" but the edge in my voice makes it sound more like "What are *you* doing here?"

"Well, I'd like to talk, but first, could I get an antacid?"

"Ha!" I say. "An antacid? You come back to the source of your indigestion for an antacid? Don't you think that's a little rude?"

"Sabina, it wasn't your mother's food that gave me indigestion. Clay and I had lunch at two other places after we left here. Two more lunches and two more desserts and neither of them nearly as good as what we had here. Clay thought so, too."

"Oh, sorry. Yeah, come on upstairs and I'll get you something."

We climb the back stairs, Ted two steps behind me. My hands are shaking. I'm so nervous. My legs feel so rubbery that I have to think about putting my foot firmly down on each stair. I'm not sure I'm ready to deal with this—whatever it is that's going to happen. For certainly it will be emotional. Why does everything have to be so complicated? I'm almost to the top of the stairs, when, just like he did on Christmas Eve, Ted suddenly grabs my arm and pulls me to him.

"Bina," is all he says as he holds me. And really, it's all he has to say.

***

After the Alka-Seltzer, Ted builds a nice fire in the fireplace and now we're sitting on the couch. He didn't want anything to drink, but I poured myself a glass of ginger ale. We avoid the painful stuff that we really need to talk about and go right for the small talk. He tells me all about his trip and I fill him in on my New Year's Eve date with Virgie and about bumping into Clay at the bookstore.

"Clay likes you," he says.

"Clay knows about me?"

"No, today at lunch he just said, 'There's something about that girl I like.'"

"Geez, just the fact that he called me a *girl* is wonderful."

"So anyway, don't worry about Clay."

"I'm not worried about Clay."

"When are your parents getting home anyway?"

"Don't get any ideas."

"I always get ideas."

"We have a lot to talk about before you get any ideas."

"Why do girls like to talk so much?" he whines.

"Because we're more verbally adept. We speak and read sooner and faster than boys. And because we use dual-hemisphere language processing while men use only their left-hemisphere for language processing."

Ted looks at me funny.

I smile and say, "I just read an article on the differences between male and female brains. I guess I retained more of it than I thought."

"*Dual-hemisphere*," he says in pretend mockery.

"That's what it said."

"Well, did they say anything about why talking is so painful for men?"

"Something to do with your neuron activity not being as greatly distributed throughout the brain as ours. That and the fact that the male brain shrinks faster than the female brain."

"Written by a female, I'm sure."

"Written by a male M.D."

"Ha!"

"Ha!"

He grabs my glass of ginger ale and takes a sip. "It was Lizette's chief complaint about me, that I was closed up, that I couldn't share my feelings. But I'm just not put together that way. *Men* aren't put together that way. Hell, back then we didn't have all this scientific data proving that men and women's brains are different. Lizette just decided that I was abnormal, sub-human, because I had, *have*, a hard time putting my feelings into words. It doesn't mean I'm not feeling."

"I know that."

"Listen, Sabina, I actually practiced on the plane what to say to you. I was ready to talk but then *someone* wouldn't return my phone calls."

"I know. I'm sorry. Sometimes I sleep off the stress. It's like a defense mechanism thing with me."

"Anyway, I'm ready to talk and so please listen because it's not easy for me. Okay, here it is. It was a shock at first, when you told me about *him*. And see, it was kind of like this double blow, because I'd already started disliking the guy after you told me what he did to you. So when you told me who he was—as it relates to me—all the hate and anger came back. All those things that I have pushed down just came shooting back up. And it's not just about you and who you are or who he is—part of all of this emotional stuff is just from moving back here. Memories just saturating everything. I even drove through the very intersection where it happened the other day. I've been avoiding that route since I've been back, but then the other day I'm driving over to a cafe to eat with Clay and all of a sudden it's *deja vu* and I'm back there. I started hyperventilating. And the acid jumped up into my throat. And so when you told me about him, I just didn't know if I could be with you, which was totally unfair to you since you had nothing at all to do with it."

I start to interrupt him. I want to tell him that I was the one who made Vito get behind the wheel that night when he didn't want to, but he raises his hand in the air to stop me.

"I was relieved that I had to go away with Clay. I was glad for the excuse to run away. I guess that's what I have always done. But then on the plane and at the hotel I had to listen to Clay talk about his wife and his two sons. He called home several times. He's like this really devoted husband and father—started beating himself up when he realized that he'd forgotten to buy Sharon a gift. And all of a sudden it hits me: I want what Clay has. I want someone to call when I'm away from home, someone to buy presents for."

I smile. "That's a nice way to put it." He kisses me and a tingle shoots up my back. This is a wonderful man.

"Sabina, I want to be with you, in every way I can be with you. And I think I can get past *him*, but I have to ask you again, can you get past him?"

I already told him I was past him but obviously he needs to hear it again. Fortunately I have something better than my words to convince him—I have Vito's words. "Hold on a minute," I say. I go grab the book from my night stand.

I come back and hand the book to Ted and sit down next to him. He flips through it, confused, and says, "You want me to pray about this? Believe me, I've prayed long and hard."

"Look at the picture of the author on the back," I tell him.

"Father Bonaventure...so?"

"It's Vito."

"No shit!"

"It's him. My friend Virgie found the book when we were at the bookstore New Year's Eve. Right after Clay took that naked cooking book from me."

"He's a fucking priest!"

"Fine choice of words to use, Ted. I would hope it's an oxymoron."

"I'm sorry, it's just that this guy is full of surprises. A priest—and the St. Francis kind no less. Brown robe, sandals and all that. Wow!"

"My reaction exactly: wow."

"How do you feel about this? Finding out about him like this, all these years later?"

"I don't know. I feel a lot of things: anger, sadness, resentment, curiosity, even relief. But I definitely do not feel love, I can honestly tell you that. But I feel stuff—hurt and regret, I guess. And I don't feel stuff—like closure. I still don't feel the closure."

"Closure's a biggy, I know."

"Ted, I want to go see him. I have to go see him, just once. And then I think I can finally get beyond it. I just need to talk to him. To get all my questions answered. He's had this hold on me."

He shakes his head. "You know what, he's had a hold on me, too. Where is he anyway?"

"Ohio. New Bremem, Ohio. Wherever that is."

"I'd like to go with you. I could use a little closure myself."

We sit on the couch and look through the book. I can't help it, I get mad all over again. Vito should have mentioned my family somewhere in this book. What kind of priest is he, if he can't even be honest about where he's come from?

"Hey," I say, "I'm hungry. Are you?"

Ted shrugs. "I am, but I'm afraid to eat."

"How about some chicken soup? That's not spicy."

He says fine, so I leave him to read the book while I head to the kitchen to warm up some soup.

When I come back with two bowls of soup on a tray, Ted slaps the book closed, sets it on the table and shrugs. "It's a nice little book, isn't it? Some great recipes."

"Of course they are, he stole them from my mother."

"What?"

"Well, not really, I guess. My mother and Vito's mother were best friends. They had the same recipes handed down to them and they always cooked the same dishes."

We eat our soup and think our own thoughts. I'm thinking how terribly strange it will be to see Vito again, how even more strange to see Vito again with *Ted*. But I know it's what I need to do. I load our dirty dishes onto the tray and tell Ted to relax while I throw them into the dishwasher. I rinse the bowls under hot water and reflect on the fact that more has happened to me in these last couple of months than has happened to me in the last eighteen years.

Ted and I lie on the couch and watch the fire, the hot flames jumping as if they were alive, their casted shadows keeping us company in the quiet room. My eyelids are getting heavy and I almost drift off when

Ted asks, "What time did you say your parents are getting home?" He kisses my hair, my neck.

"Ted, I told you, I'm an old-fashioned girl. I have to be ready. I'm not ready—not emotionally anyway."

"I know, I know. You're just driving me crazy, that's all."

"Well, I don't mean to."

"I know you don't mean to. It's just your nature. Just tell me something."

"Hmmm?'

"Just what kinds of things will an old-fashioned girl allow a modern man to do?"

I whisper in his ear.

"Oh," he says laughing, "I wished you would have said something sooner."

We both doze off on the couch and never even hear Mama come in. "Whoops!" she says when she discovers us. "I'm sorry, I didn't know you two were here."

It's not fair that some people blush and some don't because I can feel my face being colorized. I sit up quickly and pull down my sweater, which had hiked up. Ted sits up, too, rubs his eyes, and says sheepishly, "Hi, Luna, how are you?"

"I'm fine, how are you?"

Ted laughs, not at all embarrassed. I am embarrassed, but I laugh, too.

"I guess you're both fine," she says.

"Where's Papa?" I ask, looking at my watch. It's almost nine.

"Downstairs getting some things ready for baking."

"And how's Mr. Maggio?"

"Oh, Sabina," she says. "You're not going to believe this!" She comes around and sits in Papa's recliner. "Well, first, Ted, did you hear what happened to our breadmaker today?"

"No, what happened?"

I tell him, "Remember that crash in the kitchen today? Well, Mr. Maggio slipped and fell and—what did he do Mama, break his wrist?"

"Yes. They casted it at the emergency room."

"So what won't I believe?" I ask her.

"Your Aunt Lina."

"Lucy?" Ted says with a smile.

"He calls her Lucy, Ma. What did she do now?"

"Well, when Papa and I stopped by Mr. Maggio's to bring him dinner guess whose car was there?"

"Lucy's," I say.

"Right. So I said to Papa, well, after all, she did have to drive him home. And Papa said yes, but that would have been hours ago. So we rang the bell and Mr. Maggio came to the door and invited us in. And Bina, there were candles on the dining room table and the remains of a nice roasted chicken. And there was a wine bottle and glasses on the coffee table. There's Lina lounging on the sofa, with her nyloned feet tucked up nice and cozy, and when we all go to sit down, Mr. Maggio sits next to Lina, real close. And I look at my sister and I notice that her face is red, not blushing red, mind you, but irritated, you know, and then I look at her closer and I see that her hair is mussed up and her clothes look a little wrinkled, and she looks kind of like..." (I'm waiting for Mama to say something like "kind of like you look right now" and I run my fingers through my own mussed up hair.) "I don't know, younger or something. And then it hits me like a brick—they've been *necking*!"

"No!" I scream and cover my mouth with my hand.

"No!" Ted screams and imitates me doing the hand thing.

"Yes, and your father is beside himself. He's not as surprised at Lina as he is at Mr. Maggio."

"Mama, Mr. Maggio is a man, after all," I say.

"Yes," Ted adds, "and no offense Luna, but your sister doesn't strike me as an old-fashioned girl. At least not like the old-fashioned girls that I know."

I take the opportunity to smack him on the shoulder.

"You should have seen the smug look on her face when we left. I think she just may spend the night!" Mama says.

"No!" Ted says. I smack him again.

"Listen," says Mama, "I'm not a prude, and what people do is their own business, and I know that Mr. Maggio has been alone for years, well, almost forever, but can you imagine what will happen when we all are back together in that kitchen! Then what? What happens after Lina moves on to the next one? What's going to happen to Mr. Maggio?"

"Mama, listen, don't get all worked up about this. Mr. Maggio is going to retire soon anyway, right? Papa told me that I'm going to have to hire a new breadman. Maybe he'll just retire now. We'll work it out."

"Bina," she says, "you're forgetting about Mr. Barbiere!"

"Oh, geez, Mr. Barbiere! Aunt Lina was supposed to go to the opera with him tonight," I tell Ted. "I hope she at least had the decency to call him."

"I don't know what she did—there wasn't a chance to ask her."

"Can I have the day off tomorrow?" I ask, half-kidding.

"No, I want the day off tomorrow," Mama says. "I told Papa on the way home, let's get this place transferred over to Sabina as soon as possible."

"Is it getting too much for you, Luna?" Ted asks.

"I can still handle the work, Ted, I just can't handle the politics." Mama shakes her head and then yawns.

"Go to bed Mama," I tell her. "I'll go help Papa."

"Goodnight you two." She starts off down the hall but then turns back to say, "There's food in the refrigerator if you're hungry." Ted waits until we hear the bathroom door close before he rubs his stomach and groans. Then he sneaks in some more kisses.

"Hey, listen, I have to go help my father."

"Yeah, you'd better get going," he says, not releasing me.

"I have to. It's going to be a long night. I saw the book—he's got a couple of big orders for tomorrow."

"Okay, I'll walk you down and say hello."

I take the stairs, fast, enjoying both the sound and the sensation of the click of my shoes on the steel strips that hold down the linoleum. Ted follows behind. Halfway down, he burps loudly.

"Sorry," he says when I look back surprised. "I think maybe I need to see a gastroenterologist. Something is going on with my stomach. It's been perennial heartburn for the last three or four months."

"Maybe you have that reflux thing or lactose intolerance. My brother-in-law Ross has reflux. He had to give up coffee and spicy foods."

"Oh, great. A food critic that can't eat spicy foods. That would be about as bad as a chef who's lost his sense of smell. Or like this one guy at cooking school who was colorblind and couldn't tell when the meat was cooked. I'm not kidding, he couldn't distinguish the gray from red or pink. He ended up dropping out."

I tell him he needs to get checked out and that I'd call Ross to get the name of a good specialist for him.

In the kitchen Papa is tending to the fire in the oven. Getting and keeping the dragon at just the right temperature is a tricky matter. Papa burns a variety of woods in his oven, but favors eucalyptus. He fusses with the oven constantly—moving the large logs around to prevent hot spots, damping the flames with an old pan, throwing in handfuls of hazelnut shells for fuel and flavor—as if there is some part of him that needs to feel the merciless heat that it radiates. The heat is all-encompassing. It hits you when you walk in the door and then it holds you like a squeezing hand. The fire in my father's oven could hypnotize a person. I developed respect for the oven early on. As a child, I thought it looked like a hungry monster, a bread monster, waiting open-mouthed for its next feeding of shaped and proofed loaves.

Papa turns when he sees us, his face red with heat, moist with perspiration. You can tell by his face that he's surprised to see us, and he produces a half-smile. I kiss his cheek, which feels sunburned hot. When people ask him how he weathers the heat of his dragon oven (the ambient temperature can reach over a thousand degrees Fahrenheit) he just laughs. "Ha! This is nothing. My Sicilian sun was much hotter than this." He reaches out to shake hands with Ted, squeezing Ted's shoulder with his other hand. This is something I love about Italians, the fact that a handshake isn't enough touch for them, they have to touch you somewhere else as well. "Ted, good to see you," he says, mustering up some cheerfulness, and then giving him the ol' slap on the back.

Papa would never discuss the dysfunctions (we never had any until Aunt Lina came from New York) of our family with an outsider, so no mention is made of "Aunt-pain-in-the-ass" in front of Ted. Papa turns his attention back to the fire. Armed with a spray-bottle, he spritzes the oven— something bakers do to provide the steam breads need as they bake, but something probably only my father does when there isn't even bread in the oven. I've wondered if it's a quirk, or a way of symbolically telling the oven who is in charge. Now he checks his thermometer to see if the temperature has reached six hundred degrees Fahrenheit. He shakes his head, grabs his wheelbarrow and heads out the backdoor to the alley to fill it again with the split logs that are delivered weekly.

Ted says, "Should I go?"

"No, stay a bit longer. Please?"

He smiles. I grab a clean apron from the hook near the kitchen door and I tie it around me. Ted leans against the door and pats his chest absentmindedly. Heartburn.

Papa comes back with the wheelbarrow piled with wood and starts jamming huge hunks into the oven. "Broken wrist," he says and then laughs this off-balance kind of laugh. "Ever break a wrist, Ted?"

Ted sort of springs from his position of holding up the wall and says, "No, not a wrist. Broke my foot once, and a couple of fingers playing basketball, and I got my nose broken by a...well, by this guy that didn't like what I'd written about him. But no, never a wrist."

"My breadmaker broke his wrist today," Papa says and then laughs that weird little laugh again.

"Yes, Luna told me about it."

"Oh," he says and pushes in the last hunk of wood. He pulls a white hanky from his back pocket and wipes his brow. "You know, I don't know what it is, but I just don't feel like baking tonight."

"What?!" I say, incredulous. Papa, not want to bake? That's like Papa not wanting to breathe. "Are you sick?" I want to feel his forehead but that would be silly because of course it would feel feverish.

"No, no."

"Tired? You're probably exhausted. The holidays have taken a toll on all of us. Listen, I can handle the baking—maybe we'll be a little short tomorrow but we'll make it work."

"Have you seen the book? I got orders." He glances at the oven, at the mixers, and at the bags of flour stacked one on top of the other by the back door. They all await his hands. "I don't know, I guess I am tired or something."

My father, tired! My father, who has lived happily all these years among flour, water, salt, and fire. Never tiring of it. He has lived his life in awe of bread. "Maybe you caught the bug Mama had," I say.

"My arms feel like lead. Feet, too."

"All right, that's it," I say. "You go on up to bed. Come down later if you feel better. I can handle it. Listen I have to learn how to run this place on my own, don't I? Some day when my breadman gets sick, I'll have to do the baking myself, won't I? Now go." I don't often talk to Papa this way, but he looks so fatigued.

"You can't do it on your own, *bedda*. This is no job for one per—"

"I can help. I'll be glad to help her, Sunny," Ted says, before Papa can finish his sentence. He pulls another apron from the hook and ties it around him.

Papa and I both look at him.

"I know how to bake. Just tell me what to do."

Papa looks back at me. I know what he's thinking—that bread is alive, and bread needs to be massaged and caressed, and bread needs soft music, and bread needs happy thoughts. And most importantly, not just anyone can make Mela's Market bread. But Papa unties his apron, throws it on the counter and says, "The oven is ready. Have it at." He gives me a hug and heads upstairs.

"I can't believe it!" I say to Ted.

Ted just shrugs. "He's burned out, Sabina. He's tired."

"But this has been his whole life!"

"Art was Michelangelo's whole life and he got tired."

"Michelangelo was still going until he died at seventy-nine, so he couldn't have been all that tired. Papa's only sixty-three."

"Actually, Michelangelo died at *eighty*-nine and he *was* tired. I read that at age seventy-five, after he finished painting two frescoes for Pope Paul, he said that he painted at the cost of great fatigue. You of all people know how this business can age a person."

"Oh thanks, are you saying I look older than I am?"

"No, I'm just saying that you have firsthand knowledge. Your father is tired, that's all."

"And old. I better face the fact. But I don't want to."

"Tell me about it. Yesterday Deidra was doing the limbo with Howard at my cousin's wedding and today she sits perfectly still in a nursing home. It stinks."

"Are you really going to help me?" I ask as I wash my hands.

He rolls up his sleeves and washes his hands, too. "Yes, I am."

"What about sleep?"

"It's overrated."

"No, really."

"I've done without sleep before."

"What about work?"

"I don't have anything until noon. I can sleep in a little. Besides I'm a pyromaniac at heart."

"Well just don't burn yourself," I say as he heads over to check out the fire.

We load the twenty sesame-sprinkled braided loaves that Papa has shaped and proofed into the oven, then start on mixing the next batch of dough for the *Asiago* Pepper Bread. After that, we'll mix some wheat dough for our Cinnamon Raisin Walnut Bread. Then we'll make the Cappuccino-Cheese Bread and finish up with the assorted breakfast muffins.

Our work is ahead of us. I tell Ted that if he would like a little music to pop a cassette into the tape player. He does and now Dean Martin is serenading us with *Memories Are Made of This*. I tell Ted that he's chosen my parent's theme song, the song that used to bring them dancing out of the kitchen and into the store. I tell him how they would dance and twirl around the store and how everyone but my sisters and I would cheer them on and applaud. We would hide behind the refrigerator we were so embarrassed. I tell him how I made them stop doing it when Aunt Lina came.

Ted surprises me by saying, "Why? That is so cool. It's stuff like that that makes a place like Mela's so unique. Man, I wished I'd known about that for the review. Better yet, I wish they would have danced while Clay and I were here."

Suddenly, I am ashamed of myself. I feel as if I just had my hand slapped. Maybe I had no right to break such a tradition. Who the heck was I to break such a tradition?

Soon we are in the groove of baking and whenever Ted passes me he gives me a peck on the lips. We're both sweaty and dusted with flour. It's funny though, with Ted, I don't get overly concerned with how I look.

He acts as if I look good, period. I should be wiped out, but we've got this rhythm going and I am wide-awake. Not one bit tired. In fact, my body feels about thirty right now. Thirty-one tops.

Ted has stripped down to his tee shirt. His arms are strong and still tan from all those years of exposure to California sunshine. We don't say much: he accepts my simple instructions, asks a few pertinent questions.

He was right when he said he wasn't fast. Vito was much, much faster, but there's a calmness about Ted that you find only in true bakers, like Papa and Mr. Maggio, that just wasn't there with Vito. Ted's deft hands are now removing the golden brown loaves from the oven. Sliding the peel under as many loaves as he can, he pulls them out, and then slips them onto the wire cooling rack. He looks like he's been doing this for years. He said he lacked the passion, but right now, as he's taking on Papa's oven, there's an intensity or fervor in his eyes. Maybe passion. For a moment I fantasize that maybe the object of his passion is not the bread. Quite possibly *I* could be the object of his passion. I'm deep in this thought when he shouts, "Bina, what about these?" He's balancing several loaves on the peel, unable to fit them on the rack, which is full. I grab another rack and wheel it over. He unloads the last of the loaves and they crackle and pop as they state their intent.

Ted smiles, like a proud little boy, but then he must see something in my face or my eyes, because he smiles and says, "What?"

"Nothing," I say.

He pulls me to his sweaty self and kisses me with what I would have to call passion. Down right passion. We are interrupted by my father's multiple-setting digital cooking timer (it allows you to time three items at once), which I set for the proofing of the next batch of dough. We break apart and I say, fanning myself, "Is it hot in here or is it just me?"

I punch down some dough and then run upstairs to get myself a tee shirt. I tell Ted to put on some more music, that I'll be right back. While upstairs, I peek in on my parents. They're both sound asleep, snoring in unison: Papa louder on the intake and Mama louder when she exhales. They've got their own rhythm going, I think, as I head back downstairs.

When I push through the kitchen door, I find Ted shirtless and rummaging through the basket of cassette tapes. I like how he's a little on the meaty side. He holds up a tape and smiles. "Engelbert Humperdink?"

"It's Aunt Lina's. Honest. Please say you believe me."

"Tom Jones?"

"Hers."

"Barry Manilow?"

"Barry Manilow?" I echo. I don't remember hearing any Barry Manilow in this kitchen.

He holds up a Paul Simon tape. "Just kidding."

"That one I'll claim," I say. He pops it in and we shape loaves to Paul's *Kodachrome* and *Fifty Ways to Leave Your Lover.* I pat the last loaf and then catch Ted yawning. I don't dare look at the clock because then my body will know that it should be tired. Right now I have it fooled. I bribe Ted awake with an offer of cold caffeine and so we head out to the front of the store to rev up, cool down, and wait for bread to rise.

I grab two bottles of pop from the refrigerator and climb up onto a stool next to him.

"Damn!" he shouts, after swigging.

"What's wrong?"

"Nothing's wrong. This is great. What we're doing."

"What are we doing?"

"Baking! I mean, I've always preferred baking to cooking, but I don't know, I just never enjoyed it so much. Your father's kitchen is special. And that oven is unbelievable! You know this experience gives me a behind-the-scenes perspective that could really add to the review of Mela's. Too bad I can't use it."

"Why can't you?"

"How would I explain it to Clay that once upon a time I baked bread all night at Mela's Market?"

"Oh, right," I say. Clay is starting to sound like a dirty word to me.

"Still, this has been an awesome experience. I just hope the bread turns out okay."

"Me too." I've been thinking about that all night, especially after we put on the Paul Simon tape—not that anyone would consider Paul Simon music hard rock, but I think all would agree that it's a bit jumpier than Perry Como. I just hope the bread isn't jumpy, or nervous, or thinking bad thoughts. I can just hear Papa tomorrow after he tastes the bread: "But Sabina, Paul Simon's not good bread music. Franky makes good bread. Dean makes good bread. Perry, excellent bread, except for the hot-diggity-dumb-diggety song—forget-about-that song."

We drink down our pops and resume our work, for now we realize we are racing against the clock and we still have much to do. We barely look at each other as we mix, knead, divide, shape, proof, bake, and cool. All of a sudden, I feel forty again. My bones and muscles say: you're old, you're old, you're old as mold. Then a flash of panic slashes through my body: I can't do this! How did I think I could do this? How am I going to work a whole day tomorrow? What was I thinking? I haven't pulled an all-nighter since college!

We pull the last of the Cherry Almond Muffins from the conventional oven. The fire in Pap's oven is finally dying out and Ted and I are dead on our feet. It's almost three in the morning. A new day is on its way, but after brushing ourselves down and washing our hands and arms, we can barely make it out of the kitchen. I don't think my feet can carry me up the stairs to my bed, for what might be, with a little luck, a whole two or three hours of sleep.

When we walk out of the heat of the kitchen and into the coolness of the store, the temperature change and the fatigue make me feel like I might faint. I stop to catch my breath. I lean up against the wall for a second while Ted gives me a funny look. And I don't plan to do it, but with my back still against the wall, I find myself sliding slowly down until I'm sitting on the cool wood floor. Ted watches me, then practically falls down beside me. And to tell you the truth what happens next is just as much of a surprise to me as it will be to you. Suffice it to say, that for the second time in my life, behind the counter in my father's store, I have found love on hardwood flooring.

23

Elbows off The Table

I wake up on top of the packing table in front of the oven. My back hurts and muscles I didn't even know I had are aching. It seems like only minutes ago that Ted left. I lacked the energy to climb the stairs so I pushed a few items off the table and was asleep before I pulled my left leg up and over. I hold my watch close to my face to check the time, but it's no use, I can't focus. Then I hear someone. I spring to a sitting position and find Papa sweeping out the oven.

Instead of good morning he says, "You did good, you and Ted. Everything looks good." I'm thankful that he doesn't lay into me about being on the table. Papa never allowed us to climb on, sit on, much less fall asleep on, any table in the store. If only the health inspector could see me now. I head to the closet for some sanitizer.

As I spritz away my germs, I decide it will be better to be straight forward about the music. "Pa, we played a little Paul Simon music."

"Awwwww," he waves his hand, "Paul Simon's not so bad."

What is happening to Papa? He's always been so protective of his bread. Maybe he is trying to let go.

"Let's have a taste," he says and grabs a perfectly brown loaf of *Asiago* Pepper Bread. He pulls off a hunk and hands it to me, then twists off a piece for himself. *"Delizioso!"* he proclaims. And he's right, it's good. Tastes almost just like it's supposed to taste—like Papa's.

"It doesn't taste quite as good as yours though, Papa."

He smiles. "How late did he stay?"

"Until we finished," I say, purposely vague. I'm afraid of making eye contact, afraid that he'll see my latent but all the same raging hormones. "Ted's a natural, Papa. Not fast, really, but a very skilled baker."

"He has good hands for bread, *bedda.* After all, he's a CIA graduate. Ask him if he'd like a night job."

"Yeah, right. Do I have time for a quick shower?"

"Hell no!" he says and then smiles. "Of course, it's only twenty to six."

Climbing the back stairs feels like tackling Mount Everest. After I shower and dress I feel a little better. When I find my way back down the stairs, I am ready for a new day. My body may be tired but the rest of me is invigorated. Last night was the best night of my life, so far. It was how I always thought it would be for Vito and me—running the store together, baking the bread together, living out our married life together, and making babies together. Great plan; wrong man.

I pray on my way down the stairs that the events of the day will not be too hard for my parents to swallow. I wonder if Aunt Lina knows that she has brought stormy weather with her from Long Island. I have to laugh a little. Hell, of course she knows. It's her life intention to shake things up.

"You're here early," I say to Jimmy when I come around the corner. I can tell by his face that he's still pouting about the speech I didn't listen to.

"I told Uncle Sunny I'd come in early since he let me leave early yesterday to study for that test," he says flatly.

"How'd you do?"

"Fine," he says, pretending to concentrate on his mopping.

"Hey, Jimmy, come on. Don't be mad. You have no idea what's been going on with me."

"What?"

I want to tell him that I'd rather not get into it right now but that would only make things worse, so I give him the short version of the last few days: about who Ted is, about my New Year's Eve outing with Virgie and her discovery of Vito's book, and about Ted and I being reunited.

"Wow, heavy stuff. I didn't mean to bug you."

"You weren't bugging me."

"Sabina!" Mama calls from the kitchen.

"Coming Mama," I call. "Hey Jimmy, remind me to fill you in on what's going on in the kitchen."

"Oh, thanks," he says. "Keep me in suspenders, why don't you."

I find Mama cracking eggs in a big stainless-steel bowl. Papa is tending to his oven, which he has started up again for the day's baking. I look around: no sign of Mr. Maggio or Aunt Lina. Not that I actually expected Mr. Maggio to show up. If he had, God forbid, he would have walked in on Ted and me on the floor. But Aunt Lina has no excuse to be a half-hour late.

"Should I call her?" Mama asks as she cracks the eggs against the side of the bowl with a little more force than necessary.

I want to say, yeah, call her and fire her, but I'm nothing if not too happy with my own life right now. "Did she say 'See you in the morning' when you left her yesterday?"

"No, but she didn't say she wouldn't be here either."

"Well, she's often late, at least two out of five days."

"That's true, but if she's not here in a half-an-hour, I'm going to call Rosa to see if she can come in and help. Just in case, I've changed today's specials. Keep it simple. A soup and a pasta dish. If I have to do it by myself, I can do it."

In walks Aunt Lina. "Do what by yourself?"

"The specials. Who knew if you'd show up," Mama says and slams another egg against the edge of the bowl.

"Why wouldn't I show up?" Aunt Lina asks as she scrubs her hands at the sink. "I still have a job, don't I? Or have you already transferred the store over to Sabina?"

The room gets quiet. Papa stops throwing wood in the oven and turns to look at us. I never told Aunt Lina, I tell him with my eyes. I honestly assumed Mama would tell her.

"Sammy told me all about it," Aunt Lina announces. "Imagine how I felt being the last to know." If I didn't know her better, I'd say Aunt Lina's eyes were moist. I want to ask who the hell Sammy is but I have a strong suspicion that Sammy is Mr. Maggio.

Mama sets down the egg in her hand, wipes her hands on a towel, and walks over to her sister. "Now Lina, listen, we don't have an official date yet, and Sunny and I just thought it would be best not to say anything until we got a little closer. I wasn't aware that Sunny had discussed it with Mr. Maggio."

Papa comes over to defend himself. "It just happened to come up in conversation the other day, that's all. He was talking about retiring and I asked him to stick around for a few more months to help train a new breadman for Sabina."

"So what does that mean, Sabina, that you're replacing everyone?" Aunt Lina asks. "You don't want me working for you?"

"Now Aunt Lina, no one has said that. You're welcome to work here for as long as you like. I just didn't think you'd want to without Mama." I muster up some bull: "You two make such a great team."

"Well you know I'm only working here for the fun," Aunt Lina says. "I certainly don't need the meager pay."

"We know that," Mama says. "But Lina, you know we've been talking about turning the place over to Sabina."

"Yes, of course, but I thought it was still years away."

Mama shrugs and says, "We're tired, Lina. That's the long and short of it. I'm getting to the age where I would like someone to cook for me for a change."

Aunt Lina's eyes lighten up. "Good for you, Luna!"

"And we want to do a little traveling," Papa adds.

"Now you're talking. You've both been chained to this place forever. There's a whole world out there. I'll show you around New York, we can go visit our cousins in Sicily, and I'll take you two on a cruise. Talk about letting someone else cook for you!" She claps her hands together. "Oh," she says, "I feel so much better! Here I'm thinking you don't want me around anymore and now you want to vacation with me!"

Papa rolls his eyes and sings this as he walks back to his oven:

> *"This is my sweet wife's big sister,*
> *We've got to find her a mister,*
> *If someone don't come quick and kiss her*
> *I'll have no choice but to dismiss her."*

"Hey, you!" Aunt Lina shouts to Papa's back. "You don't have to worry about me. I found my own mister. And you don't have to worry about dismissing me either because I QUIT!"

"What?" Mama says. "You aren't serious."

"Ha! Just watch me," Aunt Lina says to Mama but she's looking at Papa for some kind of reaction. He gives none. Just calmly spritzes his oven with water.

"You wouldn't do this to me, would you, Lina?" Mama says almost crying. "Just walk out and leave me without help?"

Aunt Lina stands there breathing heavily. "I don't want to. Oh, of course not. But honestly, Luna, are you and Sunny going to be able to handle Sammy and me?"

"What about Sammy and you?" Mama says, pretending she doesn't know what she knows.

"That Sammy and me are together?"

"Together? One broken wrist, one drive to the hospital, one dinner, and you're together?"

"Luna, these things happen, nobody plans them. I've been working in the same kitchen with this man for months now and not once did I give him a second look. Then I take him to the emergency room and, well, I don't know, it was like he needed me, and then the nurse took off his shirt and all of a sudden I saw this other person, this other person that wasn't Maggio, the old baker in the kitchen. It was Sammy, this attractive man with this unbelievable seventy-year-old physique!"

I wait for Mama to blurt out something like, "It's always about sex with you Lina," but she doesn't. Instead, she walks around the counter and wraps her arms around Aunt Lina and says, "Lina, it's wonderful!" I look at Aunt Lina. She's actually glowing. I look at Papa. He's glowing, too—not from a touch of romance, but from heat and what looks like elevated blood pressure. I shoot him a look that says don't wreck the moment.

Almost in a daze I walk out front. Before the door closes behind me I hear Aunt Lina start to tell Mama all about it in this high-pitched school-girl voice that I've never heard before. Jimmy throws me the keys and a "think fast." I catch the key ring on the end of my pinkie. "Nicccceeee," he says.

I unlock the door and actually hold my breath. If he's there—Mr. Barbiere—it means Aunt Lina called him and gave him some lame excuse. If he's not there, she either didn't call him or she told him the truth about Mr. Maggio. Jimmy's counting down the seconds to open—annoying and sophomoric, yet vintage Jimmy. "Six. Five. Four. Three. Two..." Sometimes, just to be mean, I'll open on two and really tick him off, but I'd better not press my luck today. "One!"

The door is open. No Mr. Barbiere. "Awww, geez!" I cry out. "This is not good," I say to Jimmy who doesn't know what the heck I'm talking about. "My brain cells are sleep-deprived. I cannot handle this today."

"What do you mean?" Jimmy asks. "You slept the entire New Year's Day."

"Turn the page Jimmy," I snap at him, sounding suddenly like the redhead in the kitchen. "That was two days ago!"

I leave Jimmy to greet the regulars as I make my way back to the kitchen. "Just so everybody knows," I shout, "he's not here."

"Give him a few minutes, he'll be here," Aunt Lina says, knowing exactly who I'm talking about. She doesn't even bother to look up from her chopping.

"How can you be so sure?" I ask.

"Don't worry about Joey the Baldy."

"Please stop calling him that!" Papa calls from the mixer.

"Everything is A-OK with JOEY THE BALDY," she says even louder, for Papa's benefit. "Go Sabina, don't worry about a thing." She continues telling Mama everything. "And Sunny must pay him well, Luna, because the man's got money. Loads of it, socked away! Who'd have thought, huh? So what I'd like to know is how come my pay is so low."

I wait at the door to hear if Mama will say something like, "It's always about money with you," but she doesn't. I push through the door and bump into Jimmy. He makes his eyes go big as saucers and then jerks his head in the direction of the counter. I look over that way. Praise the Lord! Mr. Barbiere is here, sitting on his stool, chattering cheerfully to an attractive silver-haired woman on the stool next to him. I've never seen her before. I saunter over in their direction with the coffee pot. "Sabina!" Mr. Barbiere says when he sees me. "Good-a morning. I'd like-a you to meet-a Marion. Marion Frederick," he says.

"Hello, Marion. Nice to meet you," I say.

"Nice to meet you. Giuseppe has told me so much about you."

"He has?"

"Yes. And about your parents as well. I'm looking forward to meeting them. I already met your Aunt. She's a doll."

"Aunt Lina?"

"Oh, yes. We met in the ER yesterday."

"Marion is a nurse-a!" Mr. Barbiere exclaims proudly.

"Oh, I see," I say, but I don't.

Mr. Barbiere, or whoever this masked man is, must intuit my confusion so he explains. "Yesterday, your Aunt-a was-a supposed to accompany me-a to the opera. Well-a, I get a call-a at-a the shop. She's at-a the hospital-a with-a Mr. Maggio who broke-a his wrist-a and she-a has to drive-a him home, and she doesn't tink-a she should leave-a him alone-a. Well-a, I say-a to your aunt, I say, be straight-a with-a me, don't take-a Giuseppe Barbiere for a fool. So she tells-a me that-a out of the blue-a, she has-a feelings for the baker. I say-a okay, I-a understand. But really, I'm-a mad, mad-a as hell-a. And I have-a these-a tickets. Expensive tickets. Then-a she tells me that there's-a this nurse-a at-a the ER room-a that loves-a Andreo Bocceli and that she-a would love-a to accompany me to see-a him. I ask-a Lina, what the hell-a does she look-a like? And Lina says-a, she looks-a good. So I drove-a over to-a the hospital and we-a had a cup-a coffee, Marion and me-a, and we went-a for dinner. Had a nice-a time. Then we went-a to the show, and guess-a what? She still looks-a good this-a morning!"

"Well," I say, cocking my ear, listening for that haunting Twilight Zone music—do-do-Do-do, do-do-Do-do, do-do-Do-do—but I don't hear anything. "That's a great story," I say and mean it. "I'll get your toast for you, Mr. Barbiere. And what would you like, Marion?"

"No, no toast-a this-a morning, Sabina. Please-a ask-a your dear Mama to make-a us two of-a her *delizioso* frittatas, if-a you please-a. Oh, and would-a you also be-a so kind-a as to ask-a your father to step-a out-a so that-a I may introduce him-a to Marion?"

Over at the end stool, Charlie Gradezzi is cracking up. He just can't hold it in. Mr. Barbiere leans over and says, "Charlie, I'd like-a you to meet-a Marion. And what's-a so funny, anyway?"

Charlie pulls himself together. "Nothing Joey, nothing at all. Nice to meet you Marion," he says, coming over to shake her hand.

Marion smiles and says, "Giuseppe, you were right, everyone is so nice."

"I'll go get Papa," I say.

In the kitchen, Mama and Aunt Lina are fussing over the frittatas and French Toast. "He's here," I announce. Papa looks at me for clues. "He's happy and he has a new friend with him."

Aunt Lina says, "Told you. It's Marion, right?"

"Yes," I say, "It's Marion. I'm not sure if it's really Mr. Barbiere, but it's Marion."

Papa hands me the peel. "Pull them out in three minutes," he says and heads out front to greet his oldest customer. Quite possibly he's thinking what I'm thinking, that all of a sudden his friends are all getting women. Is there something in the air? The water? The bread?

I stand near the oven and the heat instantly starts to melt my makeup. The timer goes off and I begin to pull out the loaves and transfer them to the cooling rack. I'm not dressed for this—I put on tee-shirt and a crew-neck sweater this morning—and now the sweat is running down my forehead and into my eyes, blurring my vision, but not enough to where I can't see Mr. Maggio walk in through the alley door. He removes his coat, hangs it on the hook, and then pulls an apron over his head, leaving it untied. He extends his good hand to me indicating that he wants the peel. I hand it over to him. He actually thanks me, says, "*Grazie.*"

All I can think of is that some city employee slipped a "nice" pill into the water supply. If this keeps up, before we know it, Aunt Lina will be running around performing random acts of kindness and then where we will be? Maybe this will all wear off by morning. Remnants of Christmas.

Aunt Lina catches a glimpse of Mr. Maggio and runs over to him. "You're here. How's your wrist?" she asks, and then switches to Italian. She talks so fast I can't follow.

I seek out Mama's eyes as I leave the kitchen, but she is all smiles. The phone rings and Mama, who is at the stove, asks me to grab it. It's Virgie, all breathless and apologetic for bothering me at work, but she had to tell someone: "I told him, Bina. I told Pauly that I want a divorce."

"What did he do, what did he say?"

"He cried!"

"He cried?! You said it wouldn't faze him. You said he wouldn't care."

"I know, I know. He's never cried before. Ever. We talked and we're going to get some help. He's going to deal with the obsessive-compulsive stuff and we're going to see a marriage counselor. I told him about your offer Bina and I still want to come and cook for you, if the offer is still open." All I can think of is how glad I am that I didn't bash him. Mama is so right about not bashing boyfriends and husbands.

"Of course, of course," I say, thinking that I'd better tell Aunt Lina about Virgie right away, before she gets the news second-hand again. "I'm glad, Virgie. It's best if people can work it out. I hope you guys can. I bet you can."

"I don't know, but we have to try. Anyway, I just wanted to tell you. I know you got to get back to work. Call me tonight."

"Virgie?"

"Yeah?"

"Everything's all right with Ted, too."

"Oh, good Sabina, I've been praying for you. I can't wait to meet him." I hang up. It must be the moon, because it's affecting the whole town, maybe the whole country, the world for all I know.

Out front, Jimmy is frantic, trying to pour coffee, take orders, and keep everyone happy. Papa is talking leisurely with Mr. Barbiere and Marion. What Marion sees in Mr. Barbiere I'll never know, but as I look at him sitting on the stool, I notice that his hair looks fuller, his posture is straighter, and the lines on his face aren't nearly so deep. I ask myself this question: can one single female human being be responsible for such visible changes in a man? This is a rhetorical question but I answer it anyway inside my own head with a resounding "I guess so!"

Mr. Barbiere is laughing out loud. "And Sunny, you won't-a believe-a this: Marion also has a son-a who is-a gay!"

This statement rises up, amplifies, and then settles on the room like a nuclear bomb. What we can't believe—and I think I can speak for all of us who are here day in and day out, year in and year out—is that Mr.

Barbiere has finally admitted to the world what we have known about Joey Jr. for years and what Mr. Barbiere has denied for decades. I just about have to manually return my lower jaw to a normal position. This I have to tell Mama. I know it's not fair to Jimmy, but I leave him once again to handle things out front. Even I can't explain the powerful force that keeps shooting me through this kitchen door this morning.

I'm about to tell Mama about Mr. Barbiere's revelation when I smell something so delicious it makes me forget what I was going to say. Breakfast pasta! Every so often, when Mama and Aunt Lina are getting along in the kitchen exceptionally well (about a dozen times in all) they'll call me into the kitchen mid-morning and inform me of an additional special. Aunt Lina likes to call it the "Brunch Special." Today she tells me to add breakfast pasta to the chalkboard out front. "A Nice Breakfast Pasta" she tells me to call it. It's really just plain old Pasta Carbonana, but I'm not about to tell her that.

Aunt Lina simply cooks up some diced *pancetta* (don't even *try* using American or Canadian bacon), maybe one forth of a pound or so. She pours off the remaining fat and then sweats a half cup of minced onions until transparent. Two eggs are beaten with six tablespoons of grated Asiago cheese, some chopped Italian parsley, and coarse black pepper. Aunt Lina takes cooked pasta—*rigatoni* works well with this dish—drains it and then adds the pasta and the egg mixture to the cooked onions in the saucepan. She stirs it over low heat for about a minute until the eggs and cheese form a coating around the pasta and *voila!*—you have bacon and eggs with your pasta.

Before heading out to the chalkboard, I check out the two men of the kitchen. Mr. Maggio is wielding a razor, scoring the tops of some molded dough, the perfect task for a one-handed baker. Papa is loading *Pane Mela*—two pound round loaves of his signature bread—into a huge wicker basket to bring out front. To the untrained eye, he looks fine, happy in his work. But I'm nothing if not a detective and I discover two missing personality tags: the smile and the whistle. I think I know how Papa's mind works and right about now I suspect he's brooding about his new vacation pal. That or else he's considering what it would be like to be Mr. Maggio's brother-in-law.

No sooner do I write the pasta special on the chalkboard do I get four orders. When I return from the kitchen, I notice that Mr. Barbiere and Marion have gone. "So they left?" I ask Charlie.

"Just now," he says. "Joey the Barber said he had 'many, many heads of hair' to attend to."

"*Heads-a hair-a,*" Mr. Roan corrects.

Charlie and Mr. Roan would rather die than admit to jealousy, so instead they are making fun. "Just wait until she goes to run her fingers through his hair and finds out that it's just one strand that's about twenty-two feet long," says Charlie, laughing.

"I give her two days to see his true malevolent colors," says Mr. Roan.

Charlie nods and adds, "When she sees that the man has the first dollar bill he ever earned framed and hanging in his barber shop, she'll realize that Joey the Baldy is the Merriam-Webster definition of C-H-E-A-P."

"Cheat? Who's cheating?" asks Mrs. Zinsia.

Charlie looks at me and shakes his head. He speaks loudly into Mrs. Zinsia's right ear, which is the better of the two. "No, Camalla, not *cheat—cheap.*"

"Oh," she says, "Cheep, cheep, like a chicken?"

"No! Cheap, cheap, like a Barbiere," he says, laughing.

"Now, Charles," she says, "be nice."

Charlie breathes heavily and rolls his eyes. He turns away from Mrs. Zinsia and toward me. "Why do I bother?"

I look over at Mrs. Zinsia, who might have been an attractive older woman had she stayed away from sun and cigarettes. As it is, her face is the hue and texture of tree bark. But then again, Marion sees something in Mr. Barbiere and Aunt Lina sees something in Mr. Maggio. So who's to say? I lean over the counter and whisper to Charlie, "Why don't you invite her to the opera? If it worked for Mr. Barbiere, it might work for you."

He smiles and raises his eyebrows up and down a few times. But then he frowns. "Here's what's stopping me, Sabina. If I ask her in here, I'll have to scream in order for her to hear me. Everyone in the place will hear my question and her answer. I couldn't take that kind of public humiliation."

"Well then call her at home. Tonight. Honest, Charlie, there's something in the air or in the moon or in the coffee. I'm serious. Now is your chance!"

"I don't have her phone number. It's unlisted," he grouses.

"Well, I do. It's in the kitchen. I'll get it for you."

"Thanks, Sabina. Hey, Sabina. Tell me something. Is it true about Sam Maggio and your aunt?"

"It's true all right."

"Well I'll be damned," Charlie says.

"Charles, watch your language!" Mrs. Zinsia says.

How come she can hear the swear words just fine, I wonder again as I go to fetch her phone number for Charlie, my all-time favorite customer whom I used to have a crush on.

***

At six o'clock Ted picks me up for dinner and I nearly choke on my breath mint when I open the door and see him. He's wearing an impeccably-tailored suit, with this funky fluorescent green tie, John Lennon-esque eye-glasses, a diamond stud in one ear, and his hair is slicked back with gel.

"And whom are we tonight, John Travolta?"

He ignores me and tells me that I look great. Now I feel bad for laughing at him. "Well, you said get dressed up," I say, fidgeting with the lapel on my black suit with the animal print collar and cuffs. All of a sudden, I feel like the cat lady.

"I did and you look wonderful," he says and kisses me.

"Well you didn't say anything about funky—spiked and studded. Do you want me to run back upstairs and apply a temporary tattoo? Insert a nose-ring?"

"All right now. Hey, this is nothing. You should see some of my other disguises."

"This is a disguise?" I say, pointing to his slick hair and pulling on his pierced earlobe.

"Not a disguise as much as a distraction of sorts. See, you'd like to be invisible, but you can't, so you just try to blend in with the rest of your dinner party."

"The rest of our dining party is going to look like you?"

He laughs and says, "Sort of. Kind of. Actually no, I just felt like wearing this I guess."

"Well, you look very GQ."

"Well, you look great. I wish it was just going to be the two of us tonight, but to pull off a review at Arun's, you have to have at least three or four other people with you. I'll take you there some time, just the two of us."

We walk out into a mild January night filled with stars. Ted squeezes my hand. "Been thinking about you all day. How you holding up? Tired?" he asks as he opens the car door for me.

"Yes and no. You?"

He waits to answer until he goes around and gets in the driver's side. Then he says, "Woman, I've been bouncing off the walls. Couldn't sit still at a meeting this morning. Couldn't concentrate. Shelia, one of the other critics, brought in cherry nut muffins, and well, everything reminded me of last night."

As we drive to the restaurant, I tell Ted about my day and about the new romances that have blossomed in the front and the back of the house. He tells me about the people who will be joining us for dinner. "Josh and Lisa Lindsey are old friends from college. Josh loves to cook and has experimented quite a bit with Asian food. The other couple, Mick and Norrie Stevens, used to run a small diner down in Carbondale. So we're just a bunch of foodies out for a delicious meal to celebrate the twentieth wedding anniversary of our good friends, Mick and Norrie. Okay? Got it?"

"Got it. Wait, is it really their anniversary?"

"No! That's just an excuse to eat at someplace as special as Arun's. Actually, Arun's is really more of a business casual place, but sometimes something as simple as attire can really throw them off. Often I'll overdress for a casual place and under dress for a more formal place. You have to distract the staff—fool them into thinking you are just a typical diner."

"It's just kind of funny," I tell him. "I feel like I'm doing something on the sly. I don't know, like spying."

"Well, *you* don't have to spy. You just enjoy yourself. I'll do the spying. But you're right. Clay says this job is one part espionage, one part drama, and two parts entertainment."

"Clay," I say and scrunch up my nose.

"I know, I know."

I have only eaten in a couple of storefront Thai restaurants in Chicago so when we walk into Arun's, I am surprised. It gives one the feel of an art museum. The maitre d' seats us in a cozy, small paneled nook, where the others are waiting. Ted asked Mick to make the reservations and arranged for his friends to arrive ahead of us—so that Mick would appear to be the host of the evening. "Sorry we're late guys," Ted says, as he shakes the two men's hands and kisses the two ladies' cheeks. "I took I-94 North and then got fumbled up at the East and West entrance signs. Hope you haven't been waiting long."

I know this comment is for the benefit of the restaurant staff, but I can't help but take note of what a smooth liar Ted is. We actually took Lake Shore Drive, North—no problems. Ted smiles at me as he pulls out my chair. He makes a round of introductions and presents me simply as "Sabina Giovanotti."

They're all very nice, very welcoming, but all of a sudden I am jittery. After all, this is more than just a dinner with Ted's friends—which is cause enough for a bit of anxiety—this is also espionage, drama, and entertainment. My biggest worry is that somehow I will end up being part of the entertainment.

Lisa is all smiles, but her eyes are all over me, sizing me up. She's a study in urbanity, city chic in an all-black velour ensemble—straight black dress, tights, boots, hat. The other woman, Norrie, looks a little more casual, a little less put-together, but then I realize that that is precisely the look she is going for. She smiles at me, too, but then opts for a more direct approach, saying, "We want to know all about you, Sabina. Everything—from your current age and weight to your true hair color."

Lisa laughs. I do, too, but more due to nerves than humor.

"Lay off," Ted says. "They always think they have to screen my dates for me," he says to me.

"What dates?" says Lisa. "There haven't been any dates in years. That's why we're so glad to meet you, Sabina."

"Oh, great, I was trying for a man-about-town image, but you've gone and blown my cover," Ted says.

"Seriously, Sabina," Norrie says, "We're just glad to meet you. And glad that you could join us tonight to share in our celebration of twenty years of marital bliss." She clicks her wine glass with her husband's and gives me a wink.

"It's nice to finally meet all of you, too," I say. I look over at Ted and find that he is mumbling into his tie. I catch something about the Thai artwork that decorates the walls.

He looks up and smiles and then leans in close to whisper this: "I forgot to tell you about the microphone in my tie." I raise my eyebrows. I think I'm in for an interesting evening.

Lisa and Norrie tell me about their jobs and children. Lisa and Josh have three girls and Norrie and Mick have four boys and a girl. Lisa tells me that she is a set director for a local photographer, which brings my envy cells to surface. Norrie does bookkeeping for her and Mick's business, an office furniture store, which they took over from her parents. I tell them that I will be doing the same thing soon, taking over my parent's place. They are curious about Mela's—where it is, what we serve—and say that they will stop in some time for lunch. In the course of the conversation, we realize that all three of us are UIC alumni. We reminisce about our college days and discover that my sister Marina dated Lisa's roommate's brother for a short time junior year. We laugh and say what a small world it is after all.

Then we eat. Huge platters of food start arriving to our table. This food is a thing of beauty. Mick (upon Ted's prior instructions) has ordered the *degustation* menu for all of us—the chef's own creation, which Mick says includes something like thirteen or fourteen tasting courses. At this moment, I'm wishing I hadn't worn a skirt that's so constricting in the waist.

First our server comes with these gorgeous little edible baskets filled with chicken, shrimp, and corn. Norrie pronounces the tiny masterpieces too beautiful to eat, but her husband insists. What is hard to believe is that they taste even better than they look! A nice combination of flavors and textures. Ted mumbles something about plating artistry into his tie.

I decide to forget about the microphone and enjoy the food—rice dumplings filled with ground crabmeat and shrimp with jicama. There are shrimp rolls, and something like a spring roll, steamed noodle rolls filled with honey-roasted barbecued pork, prawns, minced pork and rice, chicken curry with coconut milk, a whole red snapper in pepper sauce and veal medallions with rice. I ask myself why I haven't been eating more Thai food.

Since I know that Chicago Magazine is underwriting dinner, I lean over and ask Ted just exactly how much the chef's *degustation* dinner is. "Seventy-five each," he whispers, then raises and lowers his eyebrows a few times. "Wine not included." I realize that I'm sharing in a six- or seven-hundred dollar meal. I could eat dinner here for the rest of my life.

"The chef is a genius," Lisa says to one of our servers.

"Self-trained," the young man says, smiling, hands behind his back, rocking on his heels.

It's obvious to me that Mick has played the role of host for Ted before. He talks about each dish with the servers but makes it appear that he is simply a die-hard gourmand, interested only in the food and the experience. It makes me feel a little guilty. Ted must sense my discomfort. "Don't worry about it, Sabina, this place is always top-notch—they'll get a wonderful review," he whispers.

I breathe a little easier, knowing now that this evening will have a good ending. Ted has told me about what happens sometimes when the review is not good, that a bad review by an important dining critic can literally make or break a place. On the ride over, I had teased Ted about writing a review tonight that wouldn't result in a punch in the nose. I was thinking about Ted's review that closed down that small Italian restaurant in San Francisco. I told Ted (I probably sounded like Papa) that I found it hard to believe that an Italian could serve awful food. Ted said he had never tasted worse. The cook was using inferior ingredients—spoiled produce and questionable meats. I found it even harder to believe that someone actually stalked Ted and then broke his nose. Ted told me it was nice to know that someone was worried about his nose, but not to worry, that now it was his policy not to review small restaurants at all, because a bad review is just too devastating. Small places will either succeed or fail on their own, he explained. I told him I couldn't imagine having that kind of power. He said, "It can be frightening."

"So, what about Mela's?" I asked him as we pulled up to Arun's. "We're a small place."

"Well, there are exceptions. Don't you worry about Mela's," he said, smiling.

Before I know it, it's time for dessert. I find myself anticipating something both unique and delicious. At first, I'm a little disappointed when our server sets the plate in front of me: slices of mango served with a clump of what he calls "sweet sticky rice." But then he tells us to eat the two together for the full effect and I am surprised and pleased with the synergy.

I put down my spoon ceremonially. "I cannot eat another thing," I announce. But then the server arrives with a tray of demitasse—"fruit soup" he calls it—and I am so intrigued I sample it. Tiny bits of fresh mango, blueberries, raspberries, and blackberries float in a light green lemon-grass broth. The taste is so delicious it makes me close my eyes, and for a second I am brought to a wonderfully warm and tropical place.

Ted has been keeping himself busy with eating and microphoning. I can certainly appreciate the challenge of balancing the work part and the social part of a critiquing dinner. It can't be easy—to be analyzing everything: the color, taste, temperature, texture, and quality of the food, the pace and skill of the service, the lighting, ambiance, seating arrangements, music, and noise level of the physical environment, the wine lists, the parking, the prices, the accommodations of special diets, not to mention interacting with your dining companions. I always thought that the life of a dining critic would be wonderfully glamorous—wielding power, eating for free. But from what Ted has told me and from what I have just witnessed, I can see it for what it is: damn hard work. And this is at a great restaurant. What about repeating this same evening at a mediocre or crappy restaurant? Not to mention the dangerous element. He's not only suffered a punch in the nose, but hate mail and harassing phone calls as well. One crazy chef even hired a private detective to track Ted down once and photograph him. The chef's intention was to have the photographs published by the local newspaper so as to sabotage Ted's anonymity. It never happened.

One more cup of decaf and Ted and Mick pretend to fight over the bill. Ted wins and hands the server one of his many credit cards. We say our good-byes and nice-to-meet-yous and I wish Mick and Norrie a happy anniversary. In the parking lot, Ted promises to take us all back to Arun's next year, for Mick and Norrie's *real* twentieth anniversary. Before we leave we get an invitation to Josh and Lisa's in two weeks for dinner. On the way home, I fall asleep in the car. I feel full all over, and it's not just from the food.

24

Beware of Flying Plates

So here's the current update. Aunt Lina hasn't slept at home in over three weeks. And she doesn't even bother hiding it or at least being discreet about it. The other day my Aunt Connie came in for lunch, and when she left she told Aunt Lina she'd call her to confirm something or other. Aunt Lina called out to her, so that everyone in the whole place could hear, "You know where to find me: either here or at Sammy's."

As wonderful as it has been for Mama—she's been enjoying working alongside of a cheerful, happy human being for a change—that's how miserable it's been for Papa. All of a sudden the optimist is worried about how Aunt Lina and Mr. Maggio's relationship will affect life at Mela's, and more importantly, how it will affect his bread.

Things *have* changed. Like this morning. I walked into the kitchen and was encouraged by what I thought was the sound of Papa whistling. As it turns out, Papa was wearing a silent scowl as he kneaded bread and it was

Mr. Maggio who was whistling the happy tune. So later, after Mr. Maggio went home—for he can't do much with one hand—I asked Papa what he is so worried about. He rattled off a list that would have convinced you the man had lived his life as a pessimist. "Here's what stinks, Bina: sooner or later she's going to drop him like a hot potato," he said. "You know her track record, a new man every week."

"Oh, Papa," I said, for I have also been appreciative of this new and improved version of my aunt, "it's not like she sleeps around or anything."

"No, but she eats around. And that's almost worse. Look at all the men—my customers—that have wined and dined her, spent a lot of money on her, only to find themselves snubbed when she gets bored with them after a few days or a week."

Eating around! I'm still laughing about that. Only my father would think that eating around was worse than sleeping around. I thought I'd be the last to say it, but I think it's great about Aunt Lina and Mr. Maggio. This morning I told her as much. I told her that maybe a man of few words is just what she needed. She replied that "Sammy" is more talkative if you speak Italian. "Plus, he doesn't like to talk while he is working, you know, out of respect for the bread."

Last I heard, Aunt Lina was trying to set up some kind of double date with Mama and Papa for dinner and a movie. Papa's resisting. I guess he doesn't want to eat with someone who's been eating around.

I should talk about eating around. I've been joining Ted for dinner—almost five nights out of seven—for the last three weeks. It's been a hectic schedule, not to mention that I've gained five pounds. But it's been fun, too. We had our dinner at Josh and Lisa's and we met up with Mick and Norrie for another dinner together so I feel like I'm getting to know Ted's friends. One night he invited Virgie and Pauly (who actually acted like a human being in spite of not being able stop himself from eating clockwise around his plate). Mama wants to know why we eat out so much, but of course I can't tell her until the review is out.

Tonight Ted's dining out with Clay and some other people from work and so I get the night off. I would like to just go to bed early since I've been burning the candle at both ends, working all day, going out with Ted at night, and then getting up at four to help Papa with the baking, but I promised Nino, Carl, and Marc that I would take them out to eat and then to the latest Star Trek movie. I'm not a "Treky" but I pretend to be for their benefit. They take Star Trek very seriously.

I take the three boys to California Pizza Kitchen even though I detest the place and feel that it should have stayed in LA. It's busy—overrun with teenagers with rings in their eyebrows, noses, you name it—but my nephews love it. They think they've died and gone to heaven.

The Star Trek movie isn't half bad. Even so, I am asleep before Captain Picard can say, "Make it so, Number One." Now the movie is over and someone is tugging at my arm. "Aunt B, wake up. Wake up!" I open my eyes to see Nino's angry ones. "You missed the whole thing, didn't you?"

"No, no," I say, sitting up straighter.

"Well, what happened then?" Carl says.

"Yeah, what happened then?" Nino echoes.

"Well, those weird looking people were trying to take over the planet but through quick-thinking, state-of-the-art weapons, and fantastic heroics, Captain Jean-Luc Picard and team saved the planet—but not without some pretty close calls."

They look at each other and shrug. I know I lucked out. I also know that I just described the plot of every Star Trek movie ever created. Marc, the oldest, is on to me. "Major mistake to 'dis' Star Trek, Aunt B. Major mistake."

I take the boys home, spend about ten minutes with Marina, who is hooked up to her heating pad. "The worst cramps I've ever had. Four hundred milligrams of ibuprofen hasn't even come close to touching the pain." I tell Marina that I'm beat, which is the truth, and make a quick escape. I head for home, but all of a sudden I turn off in the direction of Ted's apartment—a totally spontaneous move. Then I think that maybe I had better phone first before I go twenty minutes out of my way, so I fish my cell phone out of my purse and punch in his number.

He answers on the first ring.

"You are home!" I say.

"Just walked in the door."

"Up for a little company?"

"It'll be the best part of a bad old day."

"What's wrong?"

"I'll tell you when you get here."

I decide I'd better let my parents know my plans, so I call home and talk to Mama. "I might just stay," I tell her honestly.

"Sabina, you are an adult. You certainly don't need my permission."

"I know that. This is simply a courtesy call. You and Papa would do the same for me. Tell Papa I'll be there at four."

"You need to start getting more sleep. And you and Papa better start thinking about advertising for a breadman. You're both going to wear yourselves out."

"I'll be okay, Mama, I'm young. Ha. Ha."

I get to Ted's apartment around ten o'clock and he buzzes me in. I take the elevator up and when I get off I can see him standing at his door, holding it open for me. The first thing I think is that he's sick. His face is flushed and he's perspiring, even though he's wearing gym shorts and a tee shirt that says, "I am not a human billboard."

"Hi," he says, and, "come on in." Then he walks over to the sofa and plops down on it. He sprawls out and sighs a terrific sigh, a weight-of-the-world kind of sigh. I kick off my boots and follow him over to the sofa. I sit on the edge, coat still on. The room is dark and quiet.

"What's wrong? What's going on?"

"It's complicated."

"What?" Maybe he got fired. My brother-in-law Ross's face looked exactly like this once when he got fired.

"I hate to tell you because I don't want to scare you."

"Well, you are scaring me."

He sits up. Always a gentleman, even in times of distress, he helps me remove my coat. "Remember I told you about that guy in San Francisco that broke my nose?"

"The one you wrote the bad review about?"

"Yes, him. He's here, in Chicago."

"What? How do you know?"

"I saw him. I think he's been following me, Sabina."

"Oh my God!" I say. "What does he want?"

"Revenge!"

"How do you know?"

"Well, tonight we had dinner at Bistro 110—Clay and Sharon, Shelia and Trenton Wiston, Mark and Janey Sandburg, and Vanessa and me."

I feel my eyebrow arch up at "Vanessa and me." I know she's just the secretary in his office, but I can't help it. Ted catches this and says, "Don't even go there Sabina; it's just work."

"I didn't say a thing," I respond, though it's a fact that my facial expressions never lie.

"Anyway, we're eating dinner—and by the way, we're pushing Bistro 110 up a notch because everything was quality—and all of a sudden this guy is walking toward our table and I realize it's him. I'd know that face anywhere: dark eyes, curly hair, full, dark beard. He sees me and screams, 'Kallista!' and then he attacks me."

"Ted!"

"He didn't hurt me, Sabina. He just kind of fell on top of me. Well, it turned into a huge scene. The police came and the night was ruined. Clay is so pissed-off because then someone recognized Sheila, and Clay is scared to death that the papers will expose us all, so-to-speak. Who could blame them? I mean it makes for good copy."

"This is terrible! Did they arrest the guy?"

"Yes, this time I pressed charges. The first time, in California, I didn't because I felt bad for his cousin who co-owned the restaurant. His cousin paid the doctor bills and I let it go at that."

"And all because of one negative review?"

"He claims it closed the place down, ruined his life, but like I said, the place was on its way out. It had been reviewed negatively before. My review was just the nail in the coffin. The guy is wacko."

"Do you know what he's doing in Chicago?"

"Stalking me. It's weird, but for some time now I've had this strange feeling that someone was following me. And I even saw him once before but didn't realize it was him until I saw him tonight. It was on Christmas Eve, on my way to your party. That guy peeping in the windows that scared the hell out of Nino."

"Oh my God, Ted!"

"I know, I know. He must have seen me drop you off there. I feel terrible about getting you involved in this. Not to mention poor Nino."

"Well, it's not your fault. But it is scary. He didn't have a gun or anything, did he?"

He looks at me with those blue-green eyes. "No, but he had a camera. He's been threatening to take my picture and get it printed in the paper and ruin my career just as I ruined his."

"Would that really ruin you?"

"It depends. It's happened before. There have been a couple instances where some magazine or newspaper prints a photograph of a critic. Maybe it doesn't ruin the person's career but it makes the anonymity part more difficult."

"How do you think he found you?"

"Sabina, it's easier to track someone down than you think. You can do it on the Internet, even. To be honest, that's why I was surprised that you never tried to track down Vito. You could have you know, even with his priest name."

"Well, now that you brought the subject up, I have to tell you, I got to thinking that maybe the guy peeping in our window Christmas Eve was Vito."

"Thinking or hoping?"

"Thinking. I just thought maybe God was throwing a bit of irony into my life. He does that every now and then. You know, just when I'm head over heels with someone else…"

"Head over heels?"

"Mmmm. Hmmm."

Ted hugs me to him and kisses me. We're quiet for a while. I'm thinking about how scary this all is. He reads my thoughts. "He doesn't want me dead, Sabina, he just wants to hurt me a little, scare me a little, get my picture printed somewhere."

"Did he get a picture of you?"

"No, he tried though." He laughs a little. "I had him pinned on the ground until the police came. He's just a little guy."

"Geez, I was pouting all night about not being there and now I'm glad I wasn't there. I would have had a heart attack."

"Don't pout about not being there," he says, rubbing my arm up and down. "Just a few more weeks and then everyone gets to meet you. For now, you're my secret and in light of what happened tonight I think that it's a good thing. Anyway, I don't mean to dump on you. It will work itself out. I'll know tomorrow how bad things are when I open up the Tribune." He pecks me on the lips. "Do you want some wine or something?"

"No, I'm fine. It'll make me too sleepy."

"That's the idea," he says, smiling, and then disappears into the kitchen. "Hot tea?" he shouts.

"Sure, that sounds good, but I can make it," I say, getting up.

"Stay put," he says, and because I'm so tired, I plop back down. I don't dare close my eyes, because I'm on the verge of sleep. Sleep is knocking on my door. I am visited by a tinge of guilt when I think about how I faked sleeping on this very sofa Christmas night. But my eyes are so heavy…

For the second time this evening, someone is pulling on my sleeve. "Sabina, wake up. Sabina. It's eleven, honey. Don't you need to get home?"

"Hmmm? What? Oh, sorry. How rude of me."

"Hey, it's all right. I know how wiped out you must be. Listen, why don't I follow you home?"

"Don't be silly."

"I'm not being silly. I'm looking out for your safety."

"That's sweet, but you know, I think I need to sleep a little more. I don't have to be at the store until four."

"Are you saying you want to sleep over?"

"Yes, I am. Think you could set your alarm for three?"

"Three it is," he says taking my hand and pretending he has to heave me up.

It's a funny thing, but afterward, I'm not tired at all. I must take after my sister Rosa in this way. She always says that afterward, she has to get up and do something: clean a closet or a drawer or run a load of laundry.

I'm not looking for any activities, but I am wide-awake. Next to me, Ted is breathing in a comfortable rhythm, but I can't sleep. He told me he loved me. I told him back. He said he's never been happier. I told him me too. And that's the truth.

I snuggle up closer to him. He stirs and sighs and then resumes a nice, even breathing. I love to watch a person sleep. When you look at Ted with his eyes closed, you would guess that his eyes were brown by the overall coloring of his face. That's what makes him so striking—those eyes surprise you. I am filled with love for this man. I never thought I could love like this again. And just maybe I never loved like this ever. Anyone else would be happy, but all of a sudden, I am visited by worries. How will Ted and I be able to blend our two lives together. How am I going to manage taking over the store, working all day, and then joining Ted for dinner almost every night of the week? It will not be possible. I've seen she-works-all-day-he-works-all-night unions and they just don't work. And Ted doesn't just work all night, he works all the time.

And there's still this Vito—Father Bonaventure—thing. I just won't be able to feel peace about my life until I see him and talk to him. I admit to myself that I am a little disappointed that the guy that scared Nino was the crazy chef from California and not Vito.

I must sleep for a while because I wake up when Ted gets up to go to the bathroom. He comes back and says, "Oh, I woke you up, sorry." He slides in, warming his cold feet on my legs.

"No, I haven't really been sleeping. Too much on my mind."

"You'll never guess what I dreamed." He scoots closer and now we're face to face.

"That some nutcase attacked you in a restaurant? Sorry to tell you, it wasn't a dream."

"No, I'm through losing sleep over that idiot. I didn't sleep for a week the first time. I almost quit the business, too—that's how much it got to me. But no, I dreamed that you and I were on a plane to Ohio. We meet him, Father Adventure—"

"Bonaventure," I correct.

"Yeah, whatever. Anyway, we meet him and we talk to him and I let him take you out to dinner, but then I follow you to the restaurant to spy on you and then I walk up to your table and punch him in the face."

"Oh Ted!" I cover my mouth with my hand, because I don't want to smile.

"And then I grab you and take you back to the rectory, where we were invited to stay, and we make loud, sloppy love, banging against the wall and breaking the bed and ooohing and aaaahing and laughing all along."

Now I can't help but laugh. "Wow. Quite a dream."

"I'll say—kind of a super-sized combo of all my fears and desires."

"What does it mean?"

"It means that I know you want to see him, and I still want to go with you, but I'm scared about, I don't know, how it will affect you."

"I know, and I'm scared, too. It will be so weird. But I know it's something I have to do."

"I've been thinking about it a lot. It's something I have to do, too. I mean he wrote that letter asking us to forgive him and we just couldn't. All these years I've been blaming him and it really wasn't his fault. I see that now."

"It will mean so much to him, Ted. I know it will."

"Let's just do it then. Let's go this weekend. If we wait, we won't do it."

"I can't just up and go. What with Mr. Maggio and everything. I can't leave Papa in a lurch."

"Sabina, your sisters will help you. You said Rosa helps out often."

"I know, but she can't go in at four in the morning—she's got five kids, remember?"

He strokes my hair, my cheek, tickles my earlobes. "I'd like to get this step over with so we can get on to the next step."

"What's the next step?"

"Dinner with Deidra."

"Who's Deidra?" I tease.

***

Papa is so far along with the baking when I show up at four-fifteen that I think he must have been down here since two. He nods and I can't tell if he's mad at me for being fifteen minutes late or still mad at Mr. Maggio and Aunt Lina. Geez, I feel like a teenager out past curfew.

Gradually, his mood lightens up a little. We've been enjoying this time together the last few weeks. While we work, Papa and I talk business. I told him earlier about my offer to Virgie and he thinks it's a great idea.

We decide we need to run an ad for a baker immediately since neither Papa nor I can tolerate this schedule much longer. While the loaves are proofing, I draft an ad for the Sunday Tribune. Papa reads it over and makes a couple of small changes and then tells me to run it ASAP. "It will be odd having someone other than Mr. Maggio in here, won't it?" he asks, squeezing my shoulder. "It makes me a little nervous. You'll have to hire someone trustworthy. He'll have a key to the place, after all."

As we work Papa tells me that in the spring—in a couple of months—he's going to have a new furnace put in. "A new roof, too," he says. "I don't want you to inherit any of my procrastinations."

I sigh. I didn't even know we needed a new roof. Or a new furnace. Papa looks at me. He walks over and pats my cheek. I'm expecting his usual hard pat, but tonight, Papa's touch is light. "You're going to do great," he assures me.

"The pressure is on," I say, honestly.

"Yeah, but I can feel it sliding off of me, minute by minute, and it feels good."

"I'm glad, Papa."

I step back a moment. Have you ever stopped to look at your father or your mother and all of a sudden, out of the blue, with no warning whatsoever, he or she looks old? That has happened to me, right now, this minute. I look at Papa's face as he pulls some loaves out of the oven. There are lines and creases where there didn't used to be. His voice sounds weak and tinny. Geez, I love him. When the last loaf is set to cool on the rack, I broach the subject of my impending travel plans.

"Papa, I'm thinking about going to see Vito in Ohio."

"I think you should. You want Mama and me to go, too?"

"Actually, Pa, Ted's going to go with me. We feel like this could be healing for both of us."

"Yes, I can see how it would be, *bedda*. Still can't believe that he never came back. I would like to say a few things to that boy myself."

"Papa, he's not a boy anymore. He's as old as me."

"Yeah, yeah, but in my mind's eye, you know. When do you want to go?"

"This weekend? Get a late flight out Friday night." I'm nervous, twirling my apron strings. "See him on Saturday and fly back Sunday."

"Go," he says, pushing the air with his hand. "I can handle Sunday morning. Don't worry about it."

"You cannot. Not by yourself. I thought I'd ask Rosa to help."

"I'm not sure, but I think your mother said something about Ed taking Rosa away for the weekend for their anniversary."

"Oh, yeah. You're right. Hey! What about Virgie? I think she only works every other Sunday at the bookstore. It would be a great way for her to get acquainted with the kitchen."

"That would work. You set it up, *bedda,* and let me know. That's one redhead I won't mind having in this kitchen."

***

427

Ted calls me at the store the next morning—before I even have a chance to get a look at the newspaper to see if he and his Chicago Magazine cohorts have been exposed. "Good news!" he almost screams in my ear. "Well, good new for us. Not good news for Aurelio Campanella."

"That's his name? The guy who attacked you?

"Yes, such a beautiful name for such a scummy guy. But anyway, they checked this guy out and he's in hot water. Problems with his Visa. They're trying to deport him on the grounds of marriage fraud and failure to register and falsification of documents and firearms violation."

"Geez, I thought you said he didn't have a gun on him!"

"He didn't; it was in his glove compartment. I am so relieved. They'll deport him and we'll be done with this affair. And there was nothing in the paper about it, so we lucked out there, too. Vanessa—you know, from work—well her brother's wife's brother, or maybe it was her sister's husband's sister, works at the paper and helped to put the kibosh on the story. So all is well in the world."

"I'm so glad Ted. I haven't been able to think about anything else. Listen, I better go. Jimmy is trying to talk Italian to some little old guy and I think he just told him that today's breakfast special is *French feet.*"

After lunch when there is a lull, I call Virgie to ask her about helping Papa out this weekend. She tells me she is off this Sunday and agrees to come in Saturday night and Sunday. She is so excited, says she needs a change. When I ask her how things are going with Pauly and with counseling, she just says, "So-so." That could mean anything I guess.

After we close I call my cousin Ambra, who is a travel agent, and have her set up the trip to Ohio for Ted and me this Friday. After that, the only thing left to do is to decide whether Ted and I should be announced guests or unexpected surprises.

***

"*Bedda matre*, Sabina, you have to tell him you're coming. Do you want to give the poor boy a heart attack?"

We're in my room, Mama and me, and I'm packing a suitcase. Mama is following me as I move from closet to bed, dresser to bed, packing sloppily. She refolds and tucks and even removes a couple of items she deems too shabby to take. "Mama, he's not a boy—everyone still thinks he's a boy. He's a man, a forty-year-old man. You saw his picture, he has gray hair and crow's feet."

"All the more reason *not* to surprise him. Besides, what if he's not even there? You're not bringing that old robe are you? Where's that pretty one Rosa bought you?" She digs around in my closet until she comes up with it, this loud, purple satin thing that is not me. "What if he's away for the weekend or something?"

"I had Rosa call the church secretary for me. She said that Father Bonaventure would be available all weekend, other than from one to three on Saturday for a wedding, and from three-thirty to four-thirty for confessions."

"I still say a simple phone call would be the right thing to do," she says, examining my slippers. "These aren't even fit for a dog to play with." She flings them one by one to the wastebasket near the door, making both shots.

"I'm too scared to call. I'm afraid if I hear his voice I might chicken out. This way I have to go. I'll just go."

"It's not fair, Sabina!" Mama says.

"Fair?! Fair?! As if leaving me without a word was fair? As if years of waiting and wondering and never hearing from him was fair? Geez, Mama, remember who we're talking about here."

She's quiet. She knows I have her on that one. She purses her lips and plops down on my bed, deep in thought. Meanwhile I keep packing. "All right," Mama says, putting her hands together. "What do you think of this idea? After you leave, I call Vito—Father Bonaventure—and tell him that you are on your way to surprise him, but that I just had to call and warn him, no not warn, but inform him, of your visit."

"Mama!" I say, looking at her out of the corner of my eye. "You've been hanging around with Aunt Lina too long!" We both laugh, but then I'm quiet for a minute, giving her idea consideration. I sit down next to her on the bed and sling my arm around her soft neck. "You know what Mama? This time I'm going to do this *my* way. He's going to get the surprise of his life."

"Sabina!"

"Well! Now listen, Ma, it would be one thing if I was going to bring him pain, but I'm going to bring him what he always wanted—Ted and forgiveness." I grab Vito's book from the nightstand and pack it in my suitcase. I close the suitcase and zip it up.

"Wish I was going with you," Mama says. "I would love to see him."

"I know."

***

It's Friday morning and the day looms ahead. Ted and I have to leave for O'Hare by three o'clock. He's picking me up here at the store. I keep wondering if there's any way I can back out. I have to keep steering my mind back to what I'm doing: serving coffee and breakfast.

This morning, Mama and Aunt Lina have whipped up something special for breakfast—a Sicilian-style brioche, which is flatter than the French version, sliced almost in half and filled with a scoop of Papa's homemade coffee ice cream. Oh, if everyone could start the day like this, with a little bit of ambrosia, the world would be a better place. But it's February, you say. And I say, exactly. I don't know how something so cold can warm you up, but it does.

Even Mr. Barbiere will break tradition and skip his almost-burnt toast on a morning when brioche is offered. Now he and his girlfriend—for it's been over a month now that they've been together—are sharing one. Marion is moaning and groaning with each bite. "Oh my God! Oh my God!"

"Tastes-a good, doesn't it?" Mr. Barbiere says.

"Yesterday I had cornflakes and milk, today a slice of heaven," Marion proclaims. "Oh my God!"

I look around the room. At the counter and at the tables, our customers are smiling and sighing, wanting to take their time eating their brioche, but afraid the ice cream will melt. It makes me think Mama did this on purpose—made this particular breakfast so we'd have a cheerful morning, and I wouldn't feel bad about leaving a whole hour before we close.

Mama, Papa, and Aunt Lina come out front carrying small plates of brioche and ice-cream, followed by Mr. Maggio. Mr. Maggio stands back in a corner to eat his bioche, but it's something that he's even come out front. It's almost festive in here.

I look around at everyone—these people are really like family to me: Charlie, Mr. Roan, the Radanza brothers, Mrs. Zinsia. Even Mr. Barbiere and Mr. Maggio feel like family today. They all know where I'm going this afternoon. Not all of them knew Vito, but all of them know *about* Vito. It's like they want closure, too. I don't know why I'm getting so melancholy all of a sudden, but there is change in the air. Things are happening around here. I can feel it.

Suddenly, Aunt Lina sets her plate on the counter and grabs my arm. "Sabina, I need you to help me with something. Come here," she pulls me along by the arm. Mama gives me a look. All I can do is arch my eyebrows. Aunt Lina tells Jimmy to cover for me and she ushers me off to her office—the ladies' room. Here we go again.

She closes the door forcefully and locks it up. She flushes the toilet and turns the cold water faucet on full stream. Then she starts talking in a low voice.

"I wanted to speak with you before you left."

"Why are you talking so quietly?" I ask, because Aunt Lina never speaks quietly.

"Just listen to me, will you? This is important. I don't want you getting on that plane without knowing everything you need to know."

"What are you talking about?"

"All right now, listen. You know that Sammy and I have become very, very close. But before Sammy, there were others."

"You don't have to brag, Aunt Lina."

"*Marona*! I'm not bragging. I certainly could, but I'm not. Just listen to me. A few months back I allowed Charlie Gradezzi to take me to see that interactive dinner thing everybody was talking about, that *Joey and Rita's Wedding Show.*"

"Tony and Tina's Wedding."

"Joey and Rita, Tony and Tina. Everyone said it was hysterical, you got to see it. Pssshhhh—there was more theatrics at my son Luke's wedding, but that's not what I want to talk to you about."

"What then?" I'm growing impatient. I want out of here.

"Anyway Charlie and I had a very, very nice time that night. Now don't think bad of me, Sabina, but afterward, I invited him up. And then *afterward-afterward* we got to talking."

"Soooooooo."

"We got to talking about you."

Maybe it has something to do with receiving this news here in the bathroom—that Charlie and Aunt Lina were in bed together and talking about me—but suddenly I become a bit queasy. "Talking about me? Oh, geez, Aunt Lina, why?"

"I can't even remember how your name came up. The point is Charlie Gradezzi thinks the world of you and he's always felt bad that he couldn't tell you what he knew about Vito."

Now she has my attention. The nausea subsides. "What? He knew all these years that Vito was a priest?"

"No, not that. He just learned about that from you."

"What then?"

"Well, I guess before he was a priest, Vito was out in California, living with this woman and their little girl."

"Vito has a baby?"

"That's what Charlie said. Said that Vito contacted his son, the one that's a lawyer."

"Frank," I say.

"Yes, Frank. Something about the woman getting mixed up with drugs and Vito wanting to try to get custody of the child."

431

"Oh my God," I say and sit down on the toilet seat lid, which I thought was down, but in fact is up. The seat is up as well and I fall in. Yes, I am in the toilet. I scream and Aunt Lina covers her mouth with her hands and starts to laugh uncontrollably. I want to cry, but her laughter is contagious, and so now I'm laughing, too. And the more I laugh the harder it is to keep my rear end above sea level.

"That a girl," Aunt Lina says. "Laugh about it."

"Wow," I say again, finally pulling myself up from the toilet. I'm dripping and queasy all over again. Still laughing, Aunt Lina hands me some paper towels. "You've got to go upstairs and get me some different pants," I tell her. I'm wearing black wool slacks. My other black dress slacks are packed so I tell her to get the black jeans from my second dresser drawer.

Aunt Lina looks at me funny. "You don't hang your jeans in your closet? I hang all my jeans."

"Aunt Lina!"

"Okay, okay. Black jeans, second drawer."

"And hurry. Oh, and my underwear are in the top right-hand drawer of my dresser. Hurry!" She's just about to close the door behind her when I say, "Aunt Lina, wait!" She peeks her head around the door. "Why didn't Charlie tell me? I don't understand—all these years. It might have saved me some precious time."

With her Roman nose in the air, she says, "Sabina, there is a thing called attorney-client confidentiality."

"Well then how come he told you?" I ask. It's a simple question.

She smiles, shrugs. "Maybe I just got him at a weak moment."

I want to say, "Yeah, flat on his back," but I also want dry clothes so I keep my mouth shut. I close the door and quickly lock it. Now I'm standing here wondering what kind of microorganisms are crawling around on the skin of my butt. I shudder. Eeeeee-uuuuu! I stand perfectly still and think about Vito living with a woman. About Vito with a baby? About Vito mixed up with someone on drugs and with custody battles and God knows what else.

There's a knock and then, "Open up, it's me." But when I open the door, it's Mama, not Aunt Lina.

"Mama!"

She squeezes her way through the door. "Bina, what's going on? Where's Lina? We're getting busy."

I lock the door again and then turn around and show her my wet butt. "I fell in the toilet. Aunt Lina ran upstairs to get me some clean clothes."

"What! How?"

"I thought the lid and seat were down, but they were up."

Mama asks me why her sister has trapped me in here this time. But before I can tell her, there's another knock at the door. This time it is Aunt Lina. I unlock the door and let her in and now there are three of us in a dinky bathroom that's even small for one. I'm getting a little claustrophobic.

"Hi, Luna," Aunt Lina says to Mama as if the three of us gathered in this place regularly. She shoves underwear and a pair of tan jeans at me. "I couldn't find any black jeans," she says.

"You packed your black jeans," Mama says to me. To Aunt Lina she says, "So what did you tell my daughter that made her fall in the toilet?"

Aunt Lina starts laughing again. "You should have seen her!" She starts to jump up and down like a five year old. "You should have seen her face!" I smile so Mama knows it's okay to laugh.

Aunt Lina reenacts the scene for Mama, but never answers the question so I tell Mama, "She told me that Mr. Gradezzi has had information about Vito for years. Before he was a priest he lived in California with some woman. And that he has a child, Mama, a daughter!"

"*Bedda matre!*" my mother says. "How did Charlie know?"

Aunt Lina tells what she knows. "But all of this is confidential. Neither one of you can tell Charlie that you heard it from me. I swore on my dead husbands' souls."

My mother gives her sister the dirtiest look. Unlike me, Mama knows when to stop asking Aunt Lina questions, thereby saving herself from—take your pick—shock, shame, embarrassment. She shakes her head slowly, knowing exactly how Aunt Lina came by this information.

"I just wanted Sabina properly equipped before she leaves for who-in-the-hell-ever-heard-of-it Ohio. That's all."

I slip out of my slacks and quickly change into the fresh clothes while Mama politely overts her eyes. Not Aunt Lina, she politely asks me if I would like to borrow some miracle cellulite cream she has recently discovered.

Well, I'll tell you. It makes me cringe to think of myself as the topic of conversation over the years. But it makes me cringe even more to think about Vito, recovered enough to be with some woman, to have a baby, to go on with his life. Now I don't even want to go to Ohio. I don't think I care to even see his face. I have spent the last eighteen years giving him the benefit of the doubt—that he wasn't well, that he was punishing himself. But this information changes everything. The worst part of all is that I really have only myself to blame. No one was forcing me to wait. I wash my hands and then push my way around Aunt Lina. "Let me out of here," I say. "I can't breathe."

Jimmy practically knocks me down as I turn the corner. "*Minguine!*" he says, "I was just coming to get you. I thought maybe you'd fallen in or something."

"Fallen in the toilet? Give me a break, will you, Jimmy?"

25

Tastes Like Airplane Food

I brace myself for take-off, which for me is the worst part of flying. Landing is a cinch, but I lose my stomach on take-off. I'll confess, I don't really understand how a big hunk of metal like this can sail through the air and then, even more astonishing, safely touch ground again. If Vito occupied the seat next to me instead of Ted, he would gently elucidate upon the idea of air travel, starting out with a very technical explanation: "See Bina, an aircraft is driven by either a screw propeller or by a jet engine and it is supported by the dynamic reaction of the air against its wings." Then he would scan my face for comprehension. Satisfied that he found none, he would say, "Let me explain in layman's terms," which was a nice way of saying, "Let me bring this down to a fifth grade reading level." And then he would patronize me, using hand motions and saying, "The air goes over the wings and at a certain speed, it causes the craft to lift up off the ground. Flight is a function of speed. Go below a certain speed and down you go."

I lean over and ask Ted, "Do you get this whole flying thing?"

He arches an eyebrow. "Are you asking me if I understand the concept of air flight?"

"Yes, I am."

"No, I don't," he says, just like that, not even embarrassed that he doesn't. He closes his eyes, leans his head back against the headrest, then opens them. "But I do know why jets leave those long cloudlike trails in the sky when they fly at high altitudes. You know what I'm talking about?"

"That long trail? I thought it was smoke."

"I always did, too. It's not smoke, it's called a *contrail*. It's formed from condensed water vapor. Anyway, why are you asking? You're not afraid to fly, are you?"

"No, not really. Well, sort of. I'm just amazed by the very idea of it."

A voice says please prepare for take-off, so I sit stiffly in my seat, sandwiched between Ted in the aisle seat and a walking bottle of aftershave in the window seat. I am not kidding; this guy next to me must have doused his entire body with aftershave. The fragrance (more like odor) is a blend of cinnamon, apples, campfire, and musk. I might gag if I'm not careful. I close my eyes. Ted reaches for my hand. I try to take short, shallow breaths, so as not to breathe in the air surrounding my stinky seatmate, but I almost start to hyperventilate, so I lean way over by Ted and inhale some of his air instead.

"You okay?" he asks.

"I'm fine," I lie. "You?"

"I'm feeling guilty about being so evasive to Clay about this trip."

"What did you tell him?"

"Just that I had some personal business—of a rather delicate nature—to attend to, and that it couldn't wait."

"That about sums it up."

"Clay's a good friend, Sabina. Once you get to know him, you'll really like him."

"I'm sure I will. Just so he doesn't try to get us to cook naked with him and his wife."

Ted laughs and squeezes my hand. "It's going to be a late night. Once we land in Dayton, we'll still have an hour's drive to the Holiday Inn in Sidney. I can't believe New Bremen doesn't even have a hotel. We should both try to get some sleep."

He doesn't have to twist my arm. Right now I'd rather close my eyes than talk. I'm in no hurry to discuss with Ted the bomb that Aunt Lina dropped on me in the bathroom this morning. I guess he'll find out soon enough. I'm feeling unsure of this whole thing, thinking that maybe I should have come alone. Poor Ted. I mean really, he's sitting on a plane with his girlfriend, flying to the tiny town of New Bremen, Ohio, population three thousand, to meet with her ex-fiancé, a Franciscan priest, the very man who was instrumental in his baby daughter's death. To make matters worse, he insisted on paying for my ticket.

***

In the morning the sun shines down on us as we make our way to New Bremen in a rented silvery blue sedan. It's one of those deceivingly cold sunshiny February days. When we arrive in town about ten o'clock Saturday morning, I am struck by how quiet it is, and how clean. I try to take it all in as it whizzes by me. I want to see what kind of place this is where Vito lives and serves. It's a pretty little town. Cliché adjectives come to mind such as *wholesome* and *quaint.* You'd bet money these people hold block parties and picnics and talk about family values and community pride. Ted drives a little slower, as if out of respect. He looks this way and that at the tidy houses, the immaculate storefronts, the old restored buildings, then looks at me and says, "Sabina, we're not in Kansas anymore."

"I think we're in Mayberry R.F.D.," I say, and when I say it, I am not making fun of this sweet little town. I've never been so drawn to a place before. I bet they all know each other's names. I bet they don't even have to lock their doors at night. I bet there's not one homeless person. I bet they don't even know what crack is or road rage. And I bet there aren't many traffic fatalities either. On the other hand, I'd bet money there's not a decent Thai or Indian or Greek restaurant in town, and I'd also bet you couldn't get a good *cappuccino* if your life depended on it.

Ted keeps calling me "Ang"—what Barney Fife used to call Andy Taylor—so I'm calling him "Barn." All this talk about Mayberry makes Ted finally remember what the *R.F.D.* in *Mayberry R.F.D.* stood for: *Rural Free Delivery.* But our attempt at a little light humor does nothing to cut the nervous tension that permeates the air.

"What street is the church on?" Ted asks.

I fish out a sheet of paper from my purse. "Eastmore Drive," I say. "Go two more blocks, then turn left."

When we pull up in front of St. Anthony Church, my stomach jumps up to my throat and I have to open the car door and spit up some of my oatmeal breakfast. Ted hands me a tissue to wipe my mouth and says, "We don't have to do this, you know. We could turn around right now. We could take a quick tour of the Bicycle Museum of America and then head back to Dayton. It's your call."

"Let's just go," I say, but I don't move from the seat. Now I'm thinking that maybe Mama was right, maybe we should have called first. I'm nothing if not a second-guesser, always questioning even my best-laid plans. All of a sudden I am bombarded with conflicting thoughts. *Go in one at a time. Send Ted in first. No, I should go first. Don't tell him about Ted and me right away. Tell him about Ted and me right away. Leave and go to the Bicycle Museum of America. Leave and go straight home. Or, just go.*

I make the sign of the cross and say a prayer. Ted waits patiently. Another sign of the cross and I open the car door. I wait for Ted to come around from the driver's side and then we start walking up to the rectory. Ted hands me half of a stick of spearmint gum. As we approach, I see the mini-blind in the front window of the rectory flutter. My chest feels like it's housing a Ping-Pong table. I pat it and take a deep breath. Eighteen years has been a lifetime.

The rectory door opens before we can knock or ring or even swallow, and it's him, it's Vito, or Father Bonaventure, who opens it. He looks the same! Behind his glasses I can tell that his eyes are bright and sparkly. His cheeks still look like a Nana just pinched them. He's meaty, robust. The only thing different is his salt and pepper hair, which to me looks like someone just sprinkled a little talcum powder in it. He looks good. I expected him to be in a friar's robe and sandals, but he is simply dressed in a black long-sleeved shirt, black slacks, and black Nike's.

He looks at me, eyes wide, mouth hanging open in surprise, but then his eyes lock onto Ted and they don't move from him. He's trying to put this all together, I'm sure. Suddenly, the brain cells in his memory bank must kick in, because his face registers recognition and he says tentatively, "Mr. Kallistophulos?" as he comes around from behind the dark wooden door.

Ted stops in his tracks, his face goes white, but he nods, looks as if he's going to extend his hand for a shake, but then doesn't, lets it hang limply at his side.

And then, perhaps because I'm feeling suddenly out of the loop (I am after all the person who connects all the dots in this little scenario) or perhaps because I can actually *feel* the nerve endings in my fingers and toes, or possibly because I know that the only way I can survive this meeting is if I am in control, I say, as if I am savior and private detective all rolled into one: "Look, Vito, I found Ted for you!" Poor Ted hasn't moved from the third step. He's gripping the iron railing with his right hand, looking bewildered. It was a stupid thing to say, I know it the moment I say it. Makes it look like I've been searching for Theodore Kallistaphulos for eighteen years and I finally delivered him to Vito so that he could grant the forgiveness Vito has so desperately needed. Makes it look like I'm here to please Vito.

I look at Vito, but his eyes remain on Ted, greedily holding him in his sight, and it's then I know that Vito wants and needs Ted's forgiveness more than he wants or needs mine. Finally he turns to me and says, "Sabina! Man, I cannot believe this!" Before I can say anything, he has me in a bear hug. I've waited so long to be back in these arms, never dreaming it would be like this, feel like this. It feels so strange and yet so familiar. He pats me on the back a few times and then releases me, saying, "Looks like you found me, too, huh?"

"I found your book. Well, actually, Virgie found your book."

"Virginia Rossini?"

"Yes."

"Man! How is she doing?"

"She's doing fine, just fine."

"And Pauly?"

"He's fine, too," I say. Of course this is not true, but I haven't traveled all this way to discuss Virgie's marital problems.

There's a moment of awkward silence, a pregnant pause, where none of us knows what to say. Our eyes cast downward, we all study the concrete slab upon which we stand. Finally, Vito thrusts out his hand to Ted and says, "Vito Salina." Then he laughs and says, "But of course you already know that. I'm also known as Father Bonaventure, or, as the kids around here call me, Father Bike."

"Bike?" Ted says, as he shakes Vito's hand firmly. His single word comes out in a puff of steamy breath.

"Because I always use a bicycle to get around."

"Oh," Ted says. "Well I'm also known as Ted Kallista."

"Kallista?" Vito repeats.

"Because I'm a writer. Needed a shorter byline."

Vito looks from Ted to me. Looks me up and down, taking in the whole of me. It's unnerving. I tell him, "Well, I'm still Sabina Giovanotti."

"Well of course you are!" he states, a little too emphatically. Being coatless and gloveless, he's probably freezing. But he doesn't say anything, just rubs his hands together, rocking on the heels of his feet.

"Would it be all right if we came in?" Ted asks.

"Oh! Oh! I'm sorry. Of course. It's colder than I thought out here. That sun is deceiving." He opens the door then steps back to hold it open for Ted and me. "Pardon me, please, I'm just so shocked. I still can't believe it's really you, Sabina. Man, it's been a long time."

"Eighteen years," I say as I pass him.

He nods and holds the door for Ted. He strains his neck to look out at the car we drove in. "Anyone else with you? Waiting in the car?" he asks.

"No," Ted says and I am left wondering who else he could be expecting—maybe Mama or Papa, or one of my sisters.

"It's just the two of us," I say.

He nods and closes the door. The air inside the old rectory is dusty, warm and strangulating. I pull at my scarf to loosen it. Vito says, "Head down the hall there," and points the way. "My office is the second door on the right. Have a seat. I'm just going to make some coffee. I'll be right with you."

When we walk into Vito's office, a drab room with shabby furniture, we walk back into the cold. I notice the window is open a crack. I don't want to give up my coat, but I know it would be rude to sit here with it on, so I hand it over to Ted who hangs it on the coat tree next to his. We take a seat on the love seat that faces Vito's desk. The springs are shot and so we sink toward the middle, toward each other. In order not to look like teenagers glued to each other at the waist, I have to lean outward a bit, away from Ted, which causes a tightness to develop in my right side. "Geez," I whisper, "It's cold in here."

He moves in closer and rubs my hands. "This is really weird, Sabina."

"I know. I'm sorry."

This office could belong to anybody—it lacks any personality at all. Beige walls, yellowed window shades, worn brown carpet, threadbare upholstery. A watercolor of the facade of the church hangs on one wall, a religious calendar on another. Even his desk tells nothing about Vito—no photographs, or plants, or plaques, none of the usual desk-type paraphernalia one would expect to find. There's just a clutter of papers and pens. I hear a little jingle, and then a large dog, a Collie perhaps, peeps his head in at us.

"Here Abraham," Ted calls, holding out an open palm. The dog trots over to Ted and gives his hand a sniff.

"Hey, how'd you know his name?" I ask, surprised.

"Don't you remember? This guy made a cameo appearance in the book."

The book, I'm thinking, the book. Oh, Vito's book. I think my brain cells are frostbitten. "Oh, yeah," I say.

The dog likes the look and smell of Ted. He puts on the stance and demeanor that dogs assume when they want someone to pet them. "You're a good boy. Yes. Yes," Ted says, stroking the dog's head and back. "Look at you. You eat well, don't you? *Gourmet* doggy food." The way Ted says the word "gourmet," the way the word kind of bends in sarcasm, reveals his feelings.

"Ted," I say softly. He doesn't look up from the dog, in fact, he starts to stroke him even harder, scratching him between the eyes. The dog is in dog heaven.

"Ted," I try again. "It didn't come out right, out there. What I said. I hope you didn't feel like—"

"Like Abraham? Like a lost dog you found for Vito?" He looks at me now, straight at me.

I hide my face in my hands. "That's how it sounded, didn't it? That's not what I planned on saying. Not at all. But then I didn't plan on him recognizing you right off the bat like that. That really threw me for a loop." Ted shrugs and continues to pet the dog. This leads me off on a tangent, reflecting upon how odd it is that humans often treat canines better than they treat each other. I mean here we are, Ted and I, with frayed nerves, dry mouths, and palpitating hearts, both in need of each other's touch for comfort and moral support, and it's the dirty old dog that gets the love massage. How stupid is it to be jealous of a dog?

I'm just about to whisper to Ted what I had planned to say to Vito when Abraham springs up to greet his master, who is standing in the doorway holding a silver tray with silver coffee service. "All right now, Abe, settle yourself down," Vito says to the dog as he sets the tray on the desk. I can't help but smile when I notice the basket of muffins on the tray—lined with a checkered napkin. Of course he would have to feed us.

Abraham looks at Ted, his new friend, then looks at Vito again. He doesn't move. "Go on now, go. Go see what Father Bill's doing. Go on. Atta boy." Abraham leaves, and as Vito presses the door shut, I realize that I am now trapped in this cold room with the only two men in this world of billions whom I have ever loved and known in the biblical way. The cold has left me and now I'm clammy.

Ted says, "Nice dog," as Vito pours coffee.

"He's a great dog, but I really can't take any credit for him—he came with the place so-to-speak."

"I know," Ted says, "from your book."

Vito sits up straighter and carefully hands me a cup of coffee, having added the cream without even needing to ask. "Oh yes, the book. Cream or sugar, Ted?"

"Just black, thanks." Vito's hand shakes a bit as he passes the cup to Ted. He's nervous. We're all nervous.

"The book. Yes. It's astonishing what a little book can do. That little thing has really taken off. Can you believe someone from *The Today Show* called? Wanted me on the show. Wanted me to cook. Said they thought their viewing audience would find a cooking priest very entertaining."

"Are you going to do it?" I ask.

"No way! I may be many things but I've never been very entertaining." He laughs and pours a cup of coffee for himself. "Who would have thought the book would do so well? The whole thing started as a lark. At a monthly pastoral council meeting, our rector went over the financial report. Bad news. We were in the red every month but December when parishioners dig a little deeper. We let go some staff. Cut a couple of positions down to part-time. We even considered closing the school. Everyone was throwing out ideas on how to raise some money to keep our doors open and someone said what about a cookbook. That's how the whole thing started. So all the proceeds from the book go to our church and school." He shakes his head. "God has blessed us so abundantly." He says this and I try to see him as the priest that he is, as Father Bonaventure. I try…but he's still Vito. "How about a cranberry walnut muffin?" he asks, holding out the basket. "I made them myself."

Ted declines the offer but I know how Vito feels when people refuse his food so I accept the muffin on the plate he offers. I'm sorry I do though once I try to eat and talk at the same time. I feel very self-conscious.

"Well, listen," Vito says, clapping his hands together with a nice solid *swack.* "I know you didn't come all the way from Chicago to listen to me talk about my humble little cookbook slash prayer book. So what brings you here?"

He asks this question just as I am swallowing a bite of his cranberry walnut muffin. My whole body can't fathom where he gets the nerve to even ask such a question, as if he doesn't know the answer. A piece of muffin gets stuck in the back of my throat. I start choking and Ted has to bang me on the back to dislodge the glomp of muffin. "Are you all right?" Ted asks.

"I'll get you some water," Vito says and disappears down the hall.

Just as I am composing myself the phone rings—and rings—and then the machine on the desk picks it up. "Hey-ya, Father Bike! It's Donny. I'm serving today at the wedding at one-o'clock? And I don't have a ride? My Mom can drive me if I come a little early, like at noon? Is that okay? And as long as I'm there, can you make me lunch?"

Father Bike comes back in with a glass of water for me. As I drink, Ted plays secretary: "Donny called and he can serve your wedding Mass, but in order to get a ride over he has to come at noon. Oh yeah, and he wants lunch."

"Oh, he does, does he?" Vito says, smiling. "I never should have started cooking for these kids. I've gotten my share of mothers angry with me. The kids go home and suggest cooking lessons. Well, you can imagine how that goes over. Donny's mother doesn't know how to cook. Can you imagine? Anyway, I was sort of hoping you two would stay for lunch, an early lunch in light of the one o'clock wedding."

Ted and I exchange glances and I say, "Oh, no, I'm sorry, we won't be able to stay for lunch. Really, this was just a friendly visit. We were just in the area and thought we would..."

"Sabina!" Ted says in a way that makes me feel five years old. He sets his coffee cup on the desk and says, "Look, we might as well stop this pretending. We all know why we're here. And it's not easy for any of us." He stands up and says, "You two need to talk and so I'm going to head over to that bicycle museum and check it out because I understand that you can't come to New Bremen, Ohio, without visiting the Bicycle Museum of America." I start to protest. I want Ted here with me, but he's already got his coat in his hand. Vito gets up and puts a hand on the doorknob and then a hand on Ted's arm. "Ted, please stay." Tables turned, I think Vito would have let me go so that he could talk to Ted alone.

I nod to Ted and he hangs his coat back up and walks slowly back to the couch. He sits, sinking low, the couch eating him. Vito drags his chair out from behind the desk and moves it nearer to us. I take a deep breath. I fiddle with my fingernails. Where do we start? Who will be brave enough to start?

Ted breathes in and out, looks at Vito. He says, "Eighteen years ago, you wrote a letter to my wife and me. You asked for forgiveness and we never answered your letter. It was wrong of us not to. Truth is, we blamed you just as much as we blamed Bob Pendall. But it wasn't your fault. I'll be honest though, if it wasn't for Sabina, I'd still be blaming you today." He grabs my hand and gives it a little squeeze, which causes Vito's eyebrows to elevate. Something about his surprise makes me feel good. "And so that's why I'm here—well, one of the reasons—to tell you that I forgive you, even though you really don't need to be forgiven."

Vito's eyes are moist. He leans forward, rests his elbows on his thighs. "We all need forgiveness, Ted, and I can't tell you what your words mean to me. I never in my life expected to hear them, not after all these years." He wipes his eyes with the back of his hand. "I have prayed every night for you, and your wife and little—"

"Grace. It's okay. You can say it," Ted says gently.

"Grace. It's a terrible thing to live with, this kind of guilt. I wasn't well for years."

"I'm sorry for that. I could only see things from my side. It must have been living hell for you," Ted says in a low voice.

Vito nods in answer. He closes his eyes and sits silently. I don't know what to do. I want to get up and hug him, but suddenly my legs lack the strength. Ted's legs still work. He gets up and walks over to Vito. He places his hand on Vito's shoulder and just lets it sit there while Vito bobs up and down in noiseless sobs. It's too sad to watch so I squeeze my eyes shut and cover them with my hand. I peek out every few seconds to see what's going on.

After a while, Vito gathers his composure. Ted lets his hand drop to his side. He walks back to me, leans down and says softly, "I'm going to go look at some bicycles. Be back in an hour." He kisses me lightly on the forehead and walks out the door.

Minutes upon minutes upon minutes go by. The coffee gets cold; the muffins, hard. Vito still sits. Eyes closed. Head down. To fill the time, I start thinking about revenge. I tell myself that's not why I came here, but isn't it? Isn't it, really? Ted was merciful. How much mercy can a person expect in one day? There can be no denying it. I saw that hint of surprise in Vito's eyes when Ted squeezed my hand. Maybe he was expecting Lizette to be with us, maybe that's who he thought might be waiting in the car. Surprised by a little squeeze of the hand. What about my surprise? That he has a child? How could they let him be a priest, a man who fathered a child out of wedlock? Well, maybe he's in for a few surprises of his own today.

Then, his voice breaks through the cold air. "Sabina," he says, "Let me show you my church."

He leads me down a hall and through the sacristy. It is so quiet I am afraid he can hear my thoughts. My first view of the church is from the altar, from the priest's vantage point. I imagine it filled with people singing and praying and listening to Vito preach.

The church is small, much smaller than Our Lady of Pompei, but it is warm and quaint and it smells like Our Lady of Pompei—a blend of old wood, candles, hymnals, and dust. Vito gives me the grand tour, pointing things out with the tenderness of a first-time homebuyer. Finally, he slips into a pew and gestures for me to sit beside him. I do, but not too close.

He looks at me and sighs. It's a long time before he speaks. Maybe he's praying. I am. I am praying for strength to keep my composure. I'm vacillating between an urge to cry shamelessly and a strong desire to slap Vito's face—something I'm sure would be blasphemous or sacrilegious, whichever applies.

I pretend to be interested in a hymnal, fanning the pages back and forth. "Sabina," he says. I look at him and he removes his glasses, just like he used to all those years ago. "Lord knows I'm glad you're here. It's a shock, yes, but I'm glad you're finally here. I looked out my window and saw you walking up the path, and I thought I was seeing things. My first thought was how brave you are." I shrug. He smiles. "Well you are. How can you even look at me? Sabina, please look at me."

I do, but I can't maintain eye contact for more than a second. I pick at the clear polish on my nails. My nails actually look pretty good for this time of year. They usually crack and peel in the winter but I found this new strengthening polish and it's really helped. Okay, I'm stalling. "It has nothing to do with courage, Vito. Once Virgie discovered your book, I knew I had to see you."

"I know you won't believe me, but back in my office, in the right-hand drawer of my desk, there's a package addressed to you. It's a copy of the book. I didn't want you to have to find out about me the way you did. But the book's been sitting in my drawer for weeks now. I couldn't even bring myself to walk two blocks over to the post office to get it weighed and stamped."

"Well, geez, it was a shock. I open up this book and there's your face. After all those years, there's your face."

"Could you believe I was a priest?"

"Actually, that wasn't so shocking. What I couldn't believe is how happy you looked. That's what ticked me off, that you could actually be happy. Are you?"

"If you consider happiness to be an attitude rather than a state of being, then, yes, I am happy. I savor each day. I celebrate each day. I try to serve God each day. Do I have regrets? Yes, I do. Are there skeletons in my closet? A few. Am I completely at peace? No, I'm not. Have you been unhappy, Bina?"

Inside I'm boiling. I feel as if someone put me on a high burner and then forgot to remove me from the heat. I chew on my thumbnail for a moment. This is not what I wanted—for me to get ruffled while he stays calm and cool. I exhale and try to speak but the words won't come out. I want to tell him that the more accurate question would be: when *have* I been happy? But I don't want to talk about me right now so I quickly shift the focus back to him. I pull a "Colina" and put on my professional voice. "Listen, Vito, or Father—"

"It's all right, Bina, you can call me Vito."

"Well, you asked why I came. I guess I've come to get some answers to some questions, that's all.

"I was sick, Bina."

"I know that, but that's the answer to the "why did you go?" question. I'm looking for the answer to the "why didn't you ever come back?" question. So, why didn't you ever come back? Or at least contact me to end it? I wasted so much time waiting. Years of my life."

"Please don't tell me that. No. My sisters told me you were dating. Years ago Becky told me you were serious with someone."

"Becky told you that?"

"Yes."

"Well, she lied."

"Why would she lie?"

"You know very well that Becky had it out for me ever since your father's funeral."

"But Jenny said so as well. And she had no reason to lie. Jenny always loved you."

"Maybe she just thought it would be easier for you to get on with your life if you stopped worrying about me. I don't know. I dated a little, but nothing serious, at least not until Ted."

"Ted? You and Ted?"

"Yes, Vito, me and Ted."

"Oh," he says, nodding his head and doing this funny twisty thing with his lip. "What happened to his wife? Please don't tell me that she died, too."

"No, she's alive, but they divorced years ago."

"Because of the accident?"

"It happens to a lot of couples who lose a child."

"I know, I know, but I prayed it wouldn't happen to them. I still feel so responsible," he says and pounds a fist on his thigh.

I grab his clenched fist, unravel his fingers and say, "Vito, everyone has forgiven you. Now you have to forgive yourself."

"I'm afraid that's easier said than done."

Still holding his hand, I ask him again, "Tell me why you never came back. Please, tell me."

He sighs, shakes his head, and pulls his hand back. "How can I explain it? I don't know if I can. See, at first I was just out-of-it, Bina. For a long time I couldn't feel anything, didn't care about anything. Just numb to the world. You can't feel joy or pain. It's like you're just in neutral. Then, Becky found me a good therapist. I started to make progress, which was encouraging. Then I really wanted to get better. And then every thought, all my energy was focused on getting better. I wanted to get better for you but then I'd have these setbacks. Then they started fooling around with my medications, trying this new one in combination with that one, upping dosages, lowering dosages, and I got worse again. I was anxious all the time. I couldn't work, was living off my sister and brother-in-law and the money my Nana had left me. Finally, Becky told me that Jerome said I go or he goes. So I had to go. So I said to myself: It's time to go home. By this time I'd been gone, I'd don't know, almost two years. I actually flew to

Chicago, which was a huge accomplishment in itself. Two or three panic attacks later, we landed. I got my luggage and walked outside to catch a bus to Mela's. It's the truth, I was just going to show up at your door. But then, man, I walked outside into this fantastic windstorm. It was *so* windy. And that wind just whipped the last bit of courage I had right out of me. I walked back inside and bought a ticket to San Francisco. And I remember this like it was yesterday: it was over the Rocky Mountains that I'd realized what I'd become—an anxious, depressed, sleep-deprived coward. And I was so ashamed. So ashamed. I knew I could never face you after what I'd done to you. Never."

I squeeze my eyes tight. I am composed. I am in control. I will not cry. He seems to be waiting for me to say something, so I say, "Go on, keep talking." I'm waiting for him to tell me about the woman and their baby.

"I tried a couple of cooking jobs, but my hands were always shaking and I couldn't keep up with the pace. I'd lost the edge. Since I couldn't work, what else was there to do, but go back to school? So Berkeley accepted me and I became one of those professional students. Took Philosophy as my major, which was a huge mistake because it was just one more thing that served to confuse my brain, my emotions, and how I dealt with the world. I was sort of a hippy. Then I met Julianna."

Here it comes, I think. He's going to tell me about the woman and the baby.

"Julianna was a med student. A brilliant girl, she was studying to be a psychiatrist. She didn't so much fall in love with me as she did with my mental illness. She was fascinated with me. I guess I was her first case study. And I guess it would be fair to say that I didn't really fall in love with her either, but I fell head over heels in love with her eight-month-old daughter, Caroline."

"*Her* daughter?" I ask.

"Yeah. The father was never in the picture. Julianna had fallen bad for one of her professors. I guess he fell for her, too, but he had a wife and kids. I cared about Julianna, but it was Caroline who tore out my heart. I mean here it was—my opportunity for reparation! This little girl needed a father. But Julianna wouldn't marry me—she knew I didn't love her. But we did move in together and I helped her get through med school. Not with money—Julianna was a rich girl from L.A. I helped her with the baby. I took care of Caroline during the day, took classes at night and ran a soup kitchen on the weekends. It was a good time in my life. I really thought I was better. I was on a new combination of drugs that seemed to be working well with fewer side effects. I was sleeping better. I'd gained some weight back. I felt almost normal again. You sure you want to hear all this?"

"That's why I'm here."

"When Caroline was almost three, Julianna found someone who really did love her, a first year resident. I told her I'd move out but she asked me to stay. Caroline loved me and Julianna was in residency, too, by then, working crazy hours. She said she'd pay me to keep watching Caroline. I really loved Caroline and I really needed the money, so I did it. But then this terrible thing happened with Julianna—she started doing drugs. She and her boyfriend were stealing psych drugs from the hospital where they both worked. I guess they were both having a hard time coping with the hours and the caseload and lack of sleep. Anyway, they got caught. The hospital kept it hush, didn't press charges, but they kicked them out of the program. He and Julianna were going to take the baby and move to Portland. I was worried about Caroline. When I confronted Julianna about her drug problem, she denied it. I told her she needed to get some help. She said she didn't need help and to mind my own business. I knew it was crazy but I threatened to try to get custody of Caroline if she didn't get help. She just laughed at me. But I was serious. I called Frank Gradezzi because I figured he knew my background, he'd give it to me straight. He told me I didn't have a chance in hell. So they left with Caroline and I went downhill again. I started having what they call "intrusions," started reliving the accident all over again."

"I'm sorry," I say. "You've suffered a lot."

"I spent another few years in bad shape—everything out of wack again—just skimming by, working on my degree. Two things finally saved me: the FDA approved a new drug for persistent anxiety and a Franciscan priest came to help me one day at the soup kitchen. This priest finally helped me turn my life around. I hadn't thought about the priesthood since eighth grade. But a year and a half after Julianna left, I entered the seminary and embarked on months and months of study and reflection and meditation and contemplation. That's when I started thinking about you again, in the seminary. I attended the Franciscan seminary in Chicago. It was weird being back in the city. I would fantasize about just arriving at your door one day. Out of the blue. But I was a first-class coward! I know that now. I was in this self-preservation mode, which is this all-consuming, all-encompassing self-centered state of being. Finally, I got to the stage in my life where I could put the past behind me. I had to do it. It's the only way I have survived. I stopped asking people about you—my sisters, Frank Gradezzi. I convinced myself that you'd put the past behind you as well. I knew you were working at the store and I was glad because that had always been your dream. I just knew in my heart that you'd moved on, that you would marry and have children."

I shake my head. "I waited. I waited all the way up until I met Ted, a few months ago."

"I'm so sorry, Bina. It was just too painful. The accident, you canceling the wedding—"

"Vito, I did not *cancel* the wedding, I *postponed* the wedding. You couldn't even get out of bed. You wouldn't even talk to me. What else could I do?"

"I'm not blaming you."

"It sure sounds like it."

"Well, I didn't think you'd really do it."

"Do what?"

"Cancel the wedding. And then when you did, I panicked. I called Mikey. I didn't know what to do. So I just ran, like I did when I was a kid."

I stand up, forgetting about the hymnal in my lap. It drops to the floor with a loud *smack*. Vito bends over to pick it up as I step out into the aisle. Suddenly I have an urge to pace. "I just can't believe how we both messed up, how we hurt each other so badly. I always felt that I could have nursed you back to health. But you never gave me the chance."

"It's not like that, Bina. It's a solitary journey."

"But I wanted you!" I say, a bit too loudly. And my voice seems to expand, reaching to every corner of the church, to the ears of every statue. I look him right in the eye, and in a lower voice, I say: "Now, I just want closure."

"And I want your forgiveness," he says, walking over to me and taking my hand in his. "I need—I guess I have always needed—your forgiveness."

"All you had to do was ask," I say and I move toward him and hug him. Finally, I let the tears fall—all over Vito's shirt. When I come up for air, Vito pulls out a handkerchief from his pocket and hands it to me. While I'm blotting my face he suddenly takes me by the chin, holds my head up a little, and then pushes back my hair. I know what he's looking for—the scar he put on my forehead with the baseball bat over twenty-five years ago. I don't want him to dwell on scars, so I say, "You know, I need your forgiveness, too."

"You? Whatever for?"

"I've always felt guilty about losing it that night and *making* you drive over to the tuxedo shop. I should have driven you myself."

"Not one bit of it was your fault, Bina, not one bit. I take all the blame."

"Who the hell are *you*?" I ask, then remember where I am and say, "Oh, sorry."

"Excuse me?"

"Who do you think you are?"

"What are you talking about?"

449

"Well, you must be pretty important if you have so much power over the world, if you were responsible for everything that happened. You were responsible for Ben Pendall's rotten life and for his heroin addiction, and you were responsible for his car crashing into yours and throwing yours into Ted's, and you were to blame for Ted and Lizette's divorce. Well, just who do you think you are?"

He's standing there, staring at me, with his mouth hanging open. Then he laughs a little. "Man, Bina, you've changed."

I laugh, too, the anger leaving me now like water swirling down a drain. "I guess I have. I'm a lot older now, you know."

"But you don't look it. You look exactly the same."

"I wasn't fishing for a compliment," I say.

"I know that. But it's true. You still look…what did Brad Burns call you that time in high school…luminous?"

I smile. That word sounds like a million dollars to these forty-year-old ears.

"Or was it luminescent?" I tease.

"I'm pretty sure it was luminous. You love him don't you?"

"Brad Burns? Not my type."

"You know who I'm talking about."

"Yes, I do, very much. He's a good man."

"Do Sunny and Luna like him?"

"They really do."

"Then he's a breadman, huh?"

"Yes, I think so."

"How in heaven's name did you two meet?"

"Total coincidence," I say, laughing a little, picturing in my mind the image of Ted in his swimming trunks, "shame-shaming" me with his fingers.

"You know what, Bina, I have come to believe that there are no coincidences."

"You know what, Father Bonaventure, so have I."

We walk to the back of the church and we each light a candle for Grace Kallistaphulous. "Lord," Father Bonaventure prays, "please designate this day as one of forgiveness and mercy. We have so much for which we need to be forgiven. Show mercy on me, your humble servant, for my sins of the past, my sins of the present, for my sins of the future. Forgive me my part in the accident that took the life of little Grace Kallistaphulous. Forgive me my cowardice, for never facing Sabina. Forgive Sabina, for waiting too long, for wasting the precious gift of time, time that can never be retrieved. Lord, you have brought Ted and Sabina together, two hurting people. Only your love can turn two hurts into a healing. In your name, we pray. Amen."

"Amen," I whisper and I then I let the tears flow again. Cleansing and comforting tears. We stand in the vestibule and I fill in Father Bonaventure on Mama and Papa, my sisters and their husbands, and all my nieces and nephews. He tells me about the two families in his parish that have adopted him. He tells me that Becky and Jerome usually visit at Christmastime and that they made the trip once last summer.

"I miss Chicago," he tells me. "My dreams are always set in Chicago. There's no place like it, really. Remember that Carl Sandburg poem? How did he describe Chicago? I think it was 'coarse and strong and cunning.' I miss the life I had there. With you. Do you ever talk to Carl DiMontaggio?"

I shake my head. I don't want to tell him how *C. V. Sweets* failed without him and how shortly after that Carl closed down *The Bread and Salami* and moved to Madison, Wisconsin. Just more to feel guilty about.

But I do find the nerve to ask him the question that has been driving me crazy all these years. "Vito," I say (I have to revert back to calling him *Vito* because I can't call him *Father* when I ask him this question), "I have to ask you. I always wondered about where you were taking me on our honeymoon?"

"Door County," he says sheepishly.

"*Door County!*" I say, surprised. Door County, a thumb-shaped peninsula on Lake Michigan and Green Bay, in Wisconsin, while a gorgeous vacation spot, is as un-Italian as a smorgasbord. A honeymoon in Door County would have been wonderful—just different from what I'd imagined.

"I had it all planned, Bina. Mikey Pinotta's folks had a little cottage up there in Fish Creek. Mikey's brother, Tom, you remember Tom, don't you, the pilot? He was going to fly us there so we wouldn't have to drive. And then we could have rented mo-peds and bikes. It was going to be great."

I'm starting to visualize Vito and me in Door County: sailing on Lake Michigan, hiking in Peninsula State Park, riding the go-carts, sunning at White Fish Dunes State Park, eating at the fish boils, retiring at night in a cozy little cottage. I shake the pictures out of my head. "We better see if Ted is back," I say.

Father Bonaventure leads the way to the front door of the church. Before he opens the door, I pull at his sleeve. I didn't plan on asking him this, it just kind of slips out: "Vito, you did love me, didn't you?"

He closes his eyes for a couple of seconds and sighs. He opens his eyes and touches my cheek with the back of his hand. "Very, very much."

I brace myself for take-off. This time, it's easier. The plane is not completely full and since no one claimed the window seat, Ted and I have both scooted over one, me to the window seat and he to the middle seat. For a micro-minute I wish he would have stayed in the aisle seat. I need some space. I have needed space since yesterday, since our visit with Father Bonaventure—and I say *Father* specifically, once and for all, because he will never be Vito to me again.

Ted and Father had the opportunity to talk while I waited in the car, listening to a CD of Van Morrison's greatest hits. It had warmed up by then and so they sat on the rectory steps, the two of them, in the just-before-spring sunshine and talked for maybe fifteen or twenty minutes. At times, they laughed. There was a moment I thought they would hug, but they didn't. They might have talked longer but a car pulled up and a boy of about eleven or twelve walked up the sidewalk and I assumed it was Donny the altar boy. Father looked at his watch and then greeted Donny by messing up his hair. Ted and Father shook hands and then Father looked over at me and waved. I was glad that he didn't come to the car to say good-bye. We'd said our good-byes. By the time Ted had gotten back, I was talked out and cried out. I didn't want to make a big tearful good-bye scene in front of Ted, so I gave Father a casual hug—the kind of hug you give someone when you know you'll be seeing him or her again soon. I hugged him this way even though I knew damn well that I would probably never see him again after today. I walked out the door, thinking that Ted was behind me, but when I got to the car, I realized that he wasn't. When I'd turned to look, there they were talking on the steps. I was glad they had the chance to talk in private.

When Ted walked over to the car, I could see that his eyes were moist and so I hopped out and asked if he minded if I drove. He said of course not. We pulled away just as Father and Donny were heading inside for lunch. We drove in silence for a while. I asked Ted what they had talked about. He told me that they mostly talked about the Bicycle Museum of America. "He loves that place. He loves bicycles. I guess they have one of the world's largest collections. I didn't get to see it though; it was closed. He doesn't drive, Bina. He hasn't driven in eighteen years—ever since the accident. He's been biking it everywhere. Or he walks. And sometimes his parishioners chauffeur him around."

"Are you okay? Are you glad you came?" I asked him.

"I am, I really am. He's a good guy. For the first time in so long, I think maybe I can deal with this healthily. There's just one thing."

"What?"

"I wished I would have brought Lizette."

"Lizette?!" I said, not even trying to hide my surprise.

"She should have been here. Talking with him would have helped her, too."

"Of course," I told him. But all of a sudden, Lizette—who until then had seemed to be so out of the picture all the way out in L.A.—became threatening to me. The old "what ifs" kicked in. What if Lizette talks to Father and she feels a healing, too, and what if this somehow leads her back to Ted? And what if, deep down that's what Ted wants? In about three seconds, I had them reunited and married with children.

I drove, keeping my eyes on the road. Ted sighed heavily a couple of times. And thinking about it now, it is really uncanny how this man who has known me for such a short time could already read—or at least anticipate—my thoughts.

He said to the windshield: "I don't want her back, Sabina, but I do want her to feel like I feel. And I can't even explain how I feel. Free or something. New, even. She's been engaged for five years to some judge. But she can't bring herself to go through with the wedding. She's still frozen. She calls me every year on Grace's birthday and we have this cry-athon thing. It's not good for either of us, but every year she calls."

"The poor thing," I said, genuinely feeling sorry for her, this woman who had her little girl ripped away from her. "Oh, Ted, you're right, of course. She should talk to Father," I said. All the way to the hotel I had to bite my lips to keep from asking him if he was already planning another trip to Ohio.

We could have had a romantic weekend. We could have splashed in the hotel pool, dined in the fancy dining room, enjoyed the firm king-sized bed. We could have talked, listened, and planned. Instead we were both edgy and pensive. I just really wanted to be alone to sift through everything that had happened. I tried not to think about Lizette, but the image of this blond (I don't even remember if she is a blonde), tall, skinny woman kept butting into my thoughts. I didn't want to think about her. I wanted instead to think positively—about the door that had been closed and the other that seemed to be opening.

We ordered room service and watched a mediocre movie, me in bed and Ted in a chair. Later, we made love but we were both just going through the motions. We fell asleep on opposite sides of the bed. Then we slept, not even touching.

This morning, we arrived at the airport two hours before our flight, just so we would have other people to look at besides each other. Now I look up and see the perky face of the flight attendant, who has just awakened me from a sound sleep to ask if I would care for a beverage. "No, thank you," I say.

I watch Ted sip his can of Coke and think about yesterday. I thought closure would be different. I imagined it to be satisfying, like the ending to a good novel. But now closure just seems like a mandate to stop getting even with the past. And getting even with the past has been the centerpiece of my life thus far.

"Almost home," Ted says and pats my hand.

"Good," I say.

"This is going to be a killer week," he informs me. "Clay has packed four lunches and four dinners into one week. Also, I have that doctor's appointment tomorrow to see what's going on with my stomach and this heartburn. I've got to do something quick or else I might be out of a job. Out of a career."

"I'm sure they have medications that can help," I say. "I'm going to be busy, too. We're going to start interviewing this week for a new bread man. And Virgie is going to start coming in one day a week to cook with Mama and Aunt Lina. Geez," I say, rubbing my eyes, "everything is changing so fast!"

We land, endure the chipper "bye-byes" of the flight attendants, and since we both just have carry-on, we by-pass baggage claim and head for Ted's car. It seems like we've been away for a week instead of just two and a half days.

I look at my watch as we pull up to the store. Nine-fifteen p.m. Rosa's car is in the parking lot. Marina's and Colina's are there, too. They're waiting to hear all about the weekend, all about Father Bonaventure. Mostly, they want to make sure that I haven't blown things with Ted.

Ted kills the engine and asks if I want help with my bag. He's really only asking to be nice. I've managed it just fine on my own the entire trip; I'm certainly capable of carrying it up a flight of stairs.

"Listen," I say, "I don't know how to thank you for coming with me."

"It wasn't just for you."

"I know that, but I know it wasn't easy either."

"I think we both need some time to process it all."

"I think you're right."

We kiss, but it's kind of a sad interaction. It feels like kissing at a funeral or something. He pulls away. "Sabina, I want to be straight with you. I'm going to call Lizette and tell her about Vito. See if she wants to see him. I talked to Vito—Father—about her coming."

"Would you go with her?" I want to know.

"Maybe. I don't know if she'd go by herself. But she needs to go. Maybe the judge will take her. We'll see. But it would be healing for her, I know it would. The good thing is that then we'll have come full circle with this, with Grace's accident. We'll at least have had something good come of it. Nothing more than just some decent people forgiving each other, which I guess is nothing more than a miracle when you think about it." And then Ted surprises me by just breaking down. His face is pensive one minute, then contorted with pain the next. Tears start to slide down his cheeks. I hold him, pat him on the back and think, how did I ever come to deserve this wonderful man?

"It's okay," I say. "You take Lizette, okay? Don't worry about me. I'll try to act like an adult, I promise."

"It's not that, Sabina. It's just... Grace would have turned twenty yesterday."

"Yesterday was her birthday?"

He nods. "We had the same birthday."

"Oh my gosh! Ted!"

"And I'm feeling guilty because Lizette calls me every year on Grace's birthday and we have this cry-athon, and of course I wasn't home yesterday for her call."

"Ted, I feel so bad. I can't imagine how it must feel."

"The weird thing—and I've heard other people say it—is how it hits you when you least expect it. The pain comes from out of nowhere and throws you into a funk. I don't know."

I hug him again. Hard. "What can I do? How can I help?"

"Just being with you helps," he says.

"Well, I feel awful about your birthday. I'm going to make it up to you."

"Hey, I got my wish. Remember? I wanted a slumber party on my birthday and I got one."

"Ted, last night was awful. I know I was distant. Well, you pick a night and I'll take you out to a great restaurant. Oh, wait, you go to great restaurants all the time. That would be like taking a mailman out for a nice walk on his birthday. Well, you name it. Anything you want to do. We'll celebrate. A movie. A show. Opera. Jazz bar. Symphony. A nice, home cooked meal. A big, loud party with my family. Laser tag. Sledding with my nieces. A night on the town. Breakfast in bed. A massage. Come on, what would make it a perfect birthday?"

He smiles, closes one eye and drums two fingers on his lips, pretending to be in deep thought. Then he holds up one finger and says, "I know exactly what I'd like to do." I watch as a mischievous smile overtakes his face. "I'd like to bake bread with you again."

I look at him. And I know I'm blushing.

When he opens the trunk to get my suitcase, he says, "Do you know what other important date you're forgetting about?"

"Oh, geez, what else have I forgotten? Tell me."

"Tomorrow, Miss Giovanotti, is the day the March issue of Chicago magazine hits the stands. Tomorrow is when Clay and the rest of the world can know about us," he says and then slams the trunk door shut.

"I think that's the best news I've had all day." I kiss him. I tell him that I love him. I walk to the front door, unlock it and wave as he drives away. I'm about to go upstairs to my mother and my sisters, but something makes me leave my bag at the door and walk back out onto the sidewalk. It's the moonlight. I stand here for a while, staring at the full moon—this huge white beautiful ball of light suspended in the sky—and it makes me wonder what it would look like through Ted's telescope. And I wonder if Father Bonaventure has as good a view of it in Ohio as I do from here. I can just hear him describing it to me back when we were young…"The moon, Bina, is the planet earth's only known natural satellite. It shines by the sun's reflected light. It revolves around the earth from west to east in about twenty-nine-and-a-half days…"

I laugh out loud. Maybe Vito spent too much of his life trying to figure everything out. Sometimes there aren't any answers. Sometimes there are only the questions. And if you're lucky, some surprises. Look at that moon! *"Che bella luna!"* I say out loud. I don't need to know the science of the moon to appreciate its beauty. To me, the moon is simply that thing which gives balance and light to the night. I turn back to my front door. I run up the stairs, eager for Mama and my sisters to hug me while I tell them all about how Father Bonaventure cooks for his altar servers, how the kids call him Father Bike, how he serves coffee on a silver tray, and how once, he loved me.

26

Everybody Loves a Cook

Monday morning brings evidence of last night's full moon. First, Jimmy comes in with a pierced earlobe. A small diamond stud adorns his slightly pink and puffed lobe. I tug on it gently and he winces. "And what is the meaning of this?" I ask.

"Hands off, cuz, it's a fresh wound. Marcella likes a guy with an earring. It's a real diamond." Marcella is the current "babier babe" of night-school-dom.

Then, Mr. Barbiere saunters in wearing a wig. A wig! Not a tasteful, discreet toupee, mind you, but a not-kidding-nobody dark brown, wiry wig. I about faint. He smiles big, showing his yellow teeth and then gives me an uncharacteristic wink. I don't know why, but I wink back.

A little while later, Charlie shows up with Mrs. Zinsia on his arm. And her granddaughters are nowhere to be seen. "Where are the girls?" I ask after they welcome me back from my trip.

"I told my daughter it was time for daycare," Mrs. Zinsia informs me. "I have a life, too, you know." She says this like I'm the one who needs convincing.

"Well of course you do," I say, but I realize that a part of me will miss Rachel and Elizabeth. Things *are* changing.

I pour coffee for Charlie and Mrs. Zinsia, look up as the bell rings on the front door, and blink a couple of times to test my vision. Yes, it's Joey Jr. with Marion. Behind her is another man, a man I have never seen before. "Joey," I call out. "How nice to see you. To what do we owe this honor?"

"Hey Sabina! No honor, just that my old man said enough with the toast. If I want to start out my day visiting with him, I have to come here for toast."

"That's-a right!" sings Mr. Barbiere, "I'm-a through with-a the deliveries."

"Besides," Joey says and winks (is there something, a new type of pollen in the air that is causing everyone to wink?), "Pop and Marion introduced me to Jerry here." He points to the man that came in behind Marion. "Marion's son."

I nod and smile. You don't have to tell me how many pints are in a quart.

I take orders noting that Joey Jr. has moved up the menu from toast to *French Toast.* Don't let anyone tell you people can't change. People can change right before your eyes. You go away for five minutes and look what happens.

The next thing I know, Dean Martin's vintage voice is coming over the speakers singing Mama and Papa's favorite song, *Memories Are Made of This.* Suddenly, the kitchen door flings open and Mama and Papa emerge dancing cheek-to-cheek, just like they used to. They weave in and out of the tables while Dean croons. When the song ends the applause is loud and generous. Papa bows and Mama curtsies. I smile. Ted was right. I never should have stopped their dancing.

Charlie clinks his coffee mug against Mrs. Zinsia's and shouts, "Tradition!" Then he looks directly at me and winks.

At eleven-thirty Aunt Lina comes out from the kitchen to inform me that April thirtieth will be her last day. "Sammy has given your father the same date. I love you *bedda* but you don't need me anymore. You found a man without my help, you can certainly run this place without me. Sammy and I are going to travel. I'm trying to convince your mother and father to join us on a cruise the first week of May. Don't you think that would be good for them?"

Yes, I do, I tell her. Then I hug her and tell her that the place just won't be the same without her, which is the truth. Every place needs a character and Aunt Lina has played that role flawlessly. And there's no denying that the woman *can* cook. When she pulls back from my hug, I see tears. She wipes them away quickly, saying, "I was just dicing onions," and heads back to the kitchen.

I lean against the counter and think about the timing. The store will be transferred to me on March thirtieth. I'll have Mama and Papa, Aunt Lina, and Mr. Maggio for a month after that. Then I go solo. This is really getting scary. What if I can't pull this off?

The sight of Ted and Clay walking through the front door interrupts my daydreaming. "Sarina!" Clay says with a big smile. "Nice to see you again."

I don't bother correcting him. "Nice to see you, too," I say. Inside I'm screaming: *Why do they keep coming in here?* People in here know Ted now and someone is going to say something, I just know it. I look to Ted for cues, wondering if the March issue is out yet and if Clay knows about us. His eyes say nothing, but he looks nervous.

"I was thinking about you the other day," Clay says. I look at Ted for help but he just shrugs.

"You were thinking about me?" I say, placing my hand on my chest.

"Yes, my wife and I were in Borders and we came across another interesting book. This one is called: *InterCourses: An Aphrodiasiac Cookbook.* It's by Martha Hopkins and Randall Locbridge." He winks and says, "Very interesting" with a German accent and I can't help but think that the man is flirting with me. I am by no means an expert in the art of flirtation, but damn it, I'm pretty sure that Clay is hitting on me!

"Clay, let's eat. I'm starved," Ted says, pointing to the chalkboard featuring today's specials: Green Bean-Artichoke-*Froscia* (a frittata of sorts but made with more vegetables than eggs), and Meatball Lasagna (layers of lasagna noodles, *ricotta*, Asiago cheese, and tiny meatballs instead of sausage).

"Okay, okay," Clay laughs, "I didn't mean to make you blush, Sarina."

"Her name is Sa*bina*," Ted says, "not Sa*rina.*"

"Oh," Clay says, looking a little confused. "Sorry." They both order Mama's *Froscia* and sit down at a table near the kitchen.

The suspense is killing me. I find Jimmy and tell him to run down the street to the drugstore and get a copy of the March issue of Chicago Magazine. "If all they have is the February issue, don't bother," I say to a pair of eyes that are squinting suspiciously at me. "Just do it for me, please—I'll explain later."

He holds out his hand and I open the register, grab a ten, and slap it into his palm. "Hey, Ted's here," he informs me, just noticing him now.

"Yes, but don't talk to him, okay, he's with his boss."

Jimmy shakes his head but obeys. As he passes Ted I see him nod slightly. Jimmy's a good boy. While he's gone I take orders and serve five more tables. I don't realize how nervous I am until a customer tells me I have given her the wrong change—five dollars too much. I am nervous!

Jimmy comes back empty-handed. "All they had was February," he says, handing me back the ten dollar bill. I thank him and ask him to mop up a spill near the dessert case. "And please don't dance with the mop in front of customers," I tease. Then I grab him by the shoulder and say, "Wait! Jimmy, soon this place will be mine. I am so glad you are staying. I couldn't do it without you, you know. You are so important to me. You know that don't you?"

He says, "Awwww," and goes to get the mop.

Ted and Clay both order dessert and so I serve them generous scoops of bread pudding dripping with whiskey sauce. I hope they eat fast and get out of here before someone—Mama, Papa, Aunt Lina—comes out of the kitchen and talks to Ted. But then it happens, just when it looks like they're about to get up to leave, that damn Dean Martin song comes on again, the kitchen door opens, and Mama and Papa come waltzing out. Well, our lunch crowd has never seen the likes of this before and at first people are looking around with questioning eyes. Then they start clapping. Then Mama sees Ted and she directs Papa over his way, leaves Papa's hold for one second, leans down and plants a big one on Ted's cheek. "Dance with Sabina, Ted!" she calls out over the music.

All the blood circulating through my body rushes to my face. Clay looks at Ted, Ted looks at Clay, and then Clay looks over at me. Then he starts laughing. I quickly make my getaway to the kitchen. I decide the walk-in refrigerator would make a good place to hide but when I open the door I find Aunt Lina and Mr. Maggio inside necking. And I could be wrong about this part, but I believe her skirt is hiked up. They don't even notice me, so I just slam the door shut and exit the back door to the alley.

The cold air slaps me in the face. I stay outside until my breathing returns to normal. Two shocks in a matter of minutes is a lot for this old heart to take. I estimate that maybe six or seven minutes have gone by so I decide to head back in. But stupid me forgot to unlock the door before I exited and now I am locked out. I knock. Hard. But I know Aunt Lina and Mr. Maggio certainly won't be able to hear me, so I walk around to the front of the store just in time to see Ted and Clay walking down the street.

"Thank God," I say out loud. Then I head inside to do damage control.

Jimmy gives me a play-by-play—all in headlines. *"Dance Number Ends. Mom and Pop Retreat to Kitchen. Busboy Slyly Eavesdrops. Boss Says, "You Know Her, Don't You?" Ted Confesses. Boss Laughs. Ted and Boss Leave Cafe.* That's it, that's all I know. What's the big secret? Shouldn't Ted know you?" Jimmy, who usually lets me mind my own business, is full of questions, but what with the dance number and my game of hide and seek, we are running behind. There are four customers who have not been served so we have to put first things first. I promise Jimmy I'll fill him in later. It will be a happy day when the March issue of Chicago Magazine is in my hand, that's all I have to say.

After the lunch rush, Papa comes out from the kitchen to ask me why Ted was acting so funny. "Everything okay with you two?"

"Yes, Papa, don't worry. He was just with his boss, that's all." I change the subject quickly. "So, I'm glad things went well with Virgie."

"Virgie was great, *bedda.* I told her that I think she's taking the wrong position though—she's a natural at baking. But she told me she couldn't take the hours." He shakes his head. Hiring a new breadman is not going to be easy for him. He tells me that he has five interviews set up for Wednesday after we close. "Wow!" I say. "That was fast. I'll type up a job description tonight. You just have to let me know about the salary."

"I know, I know." Papa is having a hard time coming up with a figure for the salary. Mr. Maggio has been here so long that he's probably one of the highest paid bakers in town—or at least in a small place like ours. Papa wants someone young but someone with a little experience. He wants someone who has "an honest face and good hands for bread." He wants someone who loves and respects bread the way he does. I may be wrong but the baker Papa wants may not even exist.

I enter the interview times into my day planner, the one Ted gave me for Christmas, which I now bring downstairs with me each morning. Papa tells me to also enter four o'clock, March thirtieth. "That's when we transfer everything over. I hired Joey Barbiere's nephew to help us. He'll meet us at the title company. Billy Angelo is his name. I wanted Frank Gradezzi, but now I guess he just specializes in divorces. He's helping Colina with the divorce, you know." And just as Papa says Colina, there she is walking through the door with her three little girls.

"Speak of an angel!" Papa says, taking her into his arms.

I take Chelsea from her and bend down to kiss Morgy and Nicole. I can tell Colina's been crying. "I'll get Aunt Lina to get the girls some ice cream," I say.

Aunt Lina's in the kitchen applying lipstick while Mr. Maggio watches in awe. I announce that Colina is here and ask Aunt Lina if she'll watch the girls out front for a few minutes. She says, "Sure." No questions asked, no complaints voiced. She takes Chelsea from me and Mr. Maggio follows her out. Mama and I exchange looks of surprise.

When Colina comes in with Papa, she gushes this out: "John got demoted at work. Demoted! Someone caught Monica and him *doing it* in someone's office. Can you believe it? How stupid can he be?" I decide my mouth will stay in the closed position for the benefit of everyone in the room. "They demoted him and reduced his salary and so now Frank Gradezzi tells me that I'll be getting *less* child support. Good Lord, I think I'm going to have to get a job!"

"We'll help you *bedda*," Mama says, holding her hand. "Don't you worry now. We'll help you find a job and we'll help you with the kids. Whatever you need. Don't cry, *bedda*."

"But what can I do? All I ever did was social work and I just couldn't go back to that. I can't even help myself right now, how could I help other people? And I have no other skills. I'm a pokey typist, I can't run a computer, I'm not good with money, and everyone knows I can't cook."

When she says that, that last thing about not being able to cook, I remember what Virgie said about an assistant—she wanted someone who knew her way around a kitchen, but really didn't know how to cook that well. Colina fit the bill. But of course I would have to let Virgie decide. I announce my idea but it only makes Colina cry even harder.

"What? You don't want to cook?"

"No, just the opposite. I came here with the intention of asking you for a job, but I was thinking of something like what Jimmy does. I even asked Angie already if she'd watch the girls for me. And I've talked to Rosa and she's volunteered to be my backup when the girls get sick. But I can't believe you'd actually want me to cook! Are you sure? Have you eaten over lately?"

I smile at her. I tell her how she fits Virgie's description of the perfect assistant. "But are you sure you want to come back here? You never enjoyed working here that much as a kid."

"I know, but the older I get the more I appreciate this place. Oh, Bina, do you really think it could work?" she asks. I look at her: an almost anorexic, soon to be divorced, mother of three who doesn't like to eat, much less cook. I look at Mama and Papa, who taught us above everything else to be loyal to one another. I'm nothing if not a loyalist, so I tell her sure, why not?" But I know that hiring Colina is the wrong thing to do for a million different reasons, but especially because the wrongness of it will ultimately come out in the food.

So, what's a sister to do? Papa always said to try to do the right thing over the best thing. I try to have faith that if I do the right thing, everything else will work out for the best. I hug Colina tightly. Papa winks at me. "Just let me run it by Virgie. I promised her the final word in choosing an assistant."

"Of course," Colina says. "And tell her that she'd be the boss. I'd do whatever she says. I wouldn't be like Aunt Lina, trying to compete with her or anything. You tell her, okay?"

"Okay," I say.

Then Nicole peeks her head into the kitchen and screams, "Mr. Man is here! Mr. Man is here!"

Ted enters with a sheepish grin, holding the Chicago Magazine, front cover out, to his chest. "Finally!" I say, walking toward him. I go to grab it but he pulls it up and out of my reach

"This copy is for Sunny and Luna," he says, and hands it to Papa. "Open it up to page eighty, Sunny."

Aunt Lina, Mr. Maggio, Jimmy, and my nieces join us in the kitchen as Papa flips through the pages. "What's this all about?" Papa asks. Ted just smiles. We crowd around him until he finds the page. He reads out loud: *"Joints That Put the* Pop *in Mom 'N' Pop."* He still doesn't get it, even after reading the sub-head and a couple of paragraphs, so Ted points to the heading on the next page—*Mela's Market.*

"What? You gotta be kidding me!" Papa starts to get choked up. "You mean they actually reviewed us?" Papa looks as if he might faint so I drag over a stool. He sits down and says, "I can't believe this! Look Luna and Lina, look what they say about your soup and your *Brusiluni* and your cheesecake and...*Jesu mio*, my bread!"

I hug Ted. He doesn't know the gift he has given me. "Can I tell them?" I whisper. He nods. "Papa, Mama, Ted wrote this. I told you that he's a writer but actually he's a food writer for Chicago Magazine. He's a restaurant reviewer. And his boss couldn't know about us until today, that's why we were so secretive."

"But he found out about Sabina today when we were here for lunch," Ted adds, shaking his head. He explains to Papa how dining critics usually try not to fraternize with the staff of the restaurants they are reviewing. "But Clay was fine about it; said I should have told him months ago."

There's cheering and pats on the back, and then Papa runs out to the front of the house to get a bottle of Italian sparkling wine. I grab my camera.

"It's not chilled, but who the hell cares?" he says, popping the cork. "Luna, get some glasses, I feel a toast coming on."

For a person who hates surprises, I have to admit, this one I like. I look at my mother and my father, sipping their wine and hugging, with everyone huddling around them trying to get a look at the article. Ted says he has more copies in his car and Jimmy volunteers to run out to get them.

Now Ted is holding Chelsea and it is truly a sight to behold. She, like her sisters, is enamored with him. He bounces her a little in his arms and then kisses her hair, while Papa asks him all about the life of a dining critic. Jimmy comes back and passes out the other copies, and now that he knows the truth about Ted's occupation, he is enamored with Ted as well.

Morgy and Nicole are pulling at Mr. Man's shirtsleeve. They want some of his attention, too. I watch all of this and smile, thinking, Mama may be the moon, Papa may be the sun, but today Ted Kallista is the star.

After everybody goes home, and just Mama, Papa, Ted, and I are left in the store, Ted invites the three of us over to his place for a celebratory dinner.

Mama says she'd accept the invitation only if he promised not to fuss.

"I was thinking pizzas from *Volare*," he says.

"Perfect!" Mama says.

Papa slaps Ted one of his hard ones on the back. "This," he says, still holding onto the magazine (he hasn't set it down once) "this really pleases me. This is like my Academy Award. I'm going to frame this thing and hang it right there," he says, pointing to the thick beam positioned directly across from the front door, "so that it's the first thing you see when you walk in."

Ted gently warns Papa about what can happen after a positive review. "I just want you to be prepared, Sunny. Sometimes a small restaurant can be inundated with new people. Every once in a while, a positive review can actually hurt a place. I do remember this one instance in San Francisco. We gave this little Mexican place a great review and then the next day they served lunch to fifty people instead of their usual twenty to thirty. It was a madhouse and of course under the circumstances the food and the service were not up to par. This went on for a couple of weeks. Well, the family that owned the place, husband and wife and two daughters, couldn't keep up. They ended up closing their doors. Said the review wrecked their lives, and I hate to admit it, but it really did."

"I'll call Rosa to come help out," Mama says. "And maybe a couple of my sisters, too."

"That's a good idea," Ted tells her. Then he turns to Papa and says, "And Sunny, I'd like to help out, too. Let me bake with Sabina tonight so you can get a good night's rest to prepare for your big day tomorrow." He gives me a little wink.

Papa protests. "That's not necessary. I can handle it."

"I know that. I just really feel like baking bread tonight. You'd be doing me a favor," Ted says, staring straight at me. I have to look away quickly or I know my face will turn crimson.

Papa says, "Well, since you put it that way…"

***

Mama and Papa and I arrive at Ted's at little before seven. Papa is so excited, Mama has to tell him three times that he's speeding. He's been hyped up all afternoon. After Ted left to go back to the office, Papa took his copy of the magazine over next door to show Mr. Barbiere, and then he made Mama drive him around the neighborhood so that he could make quick stops at Charlie Gradezzi's, Mr. Roan's, Nick and Tony's garage, Our Lady of Pompei, and Uncle Silvio and Aunt Anna's.

Now, sitting on Ted's sofa eating *Volare* anchovy and mushroom pizza and watching Wheel of Fortune, Papa finally settles down a little. He looks worn out, kind of like a little kid who has had too much birthday. He drinks a little too much wine and ends up falling asleep.

Mama doesn't look tired at all. She probably is exhausted, but she just doesn't look it. Earlier today, after Ted left the store, I told Mama about how I forgot his birthday. She actually slapped me on the cheek. "How could you, Bina? You better treat him like a king. He's good as bread." Then she went upstairs and "threw together" a *Cassatta* for Ted. When I came out of the bathroom after my bath and found her in the kitchen, I asked her what she was doing, why she wasn't resting with Papa. "The man's got to have a birthday cake, doesn't he?" she said, not even looking up. "I hope you at least bought him a present."

"Of course I did," I tell her. I'd bought a present for him even before we went to Ohio, but then just completely forgot about it. I brought the gift with me tonight. Papa carried it in and hid it in a closet while Mama and I distracted Ted. I'll surprise him after dessert.

After dessert, Mama does get tired. She can't stop yawing. She pulls Papa up from the sofa by the hand. "Come on you, or you'll never get up to make bread."

"I don't have to tonight, remember," Papa tells her, "Ted's going to help Sabina."

"And I promise, Sunny," Ted says, "no more Paul Simon."

Papa laughs. "No, go ahead, go ahead. You know that bread had a little jump to it. It was good bread."

465

They leave about nine-thirty and Ted and I prepare for a rigorous night of baking by cuddling up on his leather sofa and falling asleep. I wake up first, rub my eyes and look at the clock. Eleven-thirty. I can't believe we slept for two hours. I get up to get his gift from the closet. I bring it back and set it on the coffee table. Then I start tickling Ted awake.

He loves my present. Okay, I splurged a little. I found a great Expresso/Cappuccino Maker like the one we have at the store in a chef's catalog. I point out all the features of the Baby Gaggia—the commercial grade pump, electronic push button operation, and the turbo frother jet stream.

"Just what we need for our night of baking!" Ted says. "A turbo blast of caffeine. Let's try it out!" We do and it works great. "Thanks for the little party," he says as we sit on the sofa with our mugs.

"You're welcome. Thanks for making Papa the happiest man on earth. My mother says I better treat you like a king."

"Your mother is a very wise woman."

"What a day this has been!" I say, rewinding the day's events in my brain. "Oh, I almost forgot about your doctor's appointment. What did he say?"

"He gave me a prescription and set up some tests next week. He said it sounds like that reflux thing you were talking about," he says. "But see," he says, rubbing his chest, "even with the medicine, I'm still burning up after that pizza."

"I hate to say it, but you might have to give up pizza."

"I don't want to talk about it," he says, pulling me to him. "But I do want to talk to you about Lizette. I'd like to call her now and get this out of the way."

"Now?" I look at my watch. "Isn't it too late?"

He shakes his head. "It's two hours earlier in L.A. I tried her a couple of times this morning, but she was in court. I feel like this is the last step I need to take before I can move on."

I sit down next to him on the sofa and make him take his medicine first. He punches in the number and I watch him as he listens to the ringing. He fidgets a little. He's nervous. "Hi," he says into the phone. "Larry? Yeah, this is Ted. Is Lizette available? Thanks."

"Are you sure you don't want me to go in the other room while you talk to her?" I whisper. He shakes his head and grabs my hand. It's a while before she comes to the phone.

Of course I hear only Ted's end of the conversation but it's easy to fill in the blanks. "Liz. Yeah, how you doing? No, I wasn't screening my calls. The machine was on because I wasn't home. I was out of town. Ohio. Listen, it's a long story. But it has a good ending...for all of us." He squeezes my hand. With the tables turned, I guess I know now how Ted felt sitting in Vito's office. It's unnerving.

"First of all, I met someone…"

***

He told her I was amazing. Told her I owned this great little cafe and bakery. The "owned" part is a little premature but I'm glad he said it. We're almost done with the bread. It's been an incredible night. Again we worked so well together. There's this synergy when we bake bread. It's funny, we started out the night with Paul Simon, and now we're finishing up with Clapton. Our bread should be quite interesting.

Papa's fancy timer goes off and now Ted's about to pull the last of tonight's loaves out of the oven. Just as he sticks the peel in, that song comes on, Tears in Heaven, and he freezes. "Do you want me to fast forward it?" I ask, now knowing the reason the song is so painful to listen to.

"No, leave it on," he says. "Maybe it's good for me to hear it sometimes. To face it." He removes the bread to what I think is one of the saddest songs ever written. I finish wiping down all the work areas. I know I can never imagine what it feels like to lose a child, but I can't understand why Lizette refused to go talk to Vito. She told Ted she wasn't interested. Ted pleaded with her, but she wouldn't give in. Upon Ted's insistence, she did take Father Bonaventure's phone number.

Our work is completed. All is well in the kitchen of Mela's Market. Ted comes over and hugs me. I stay in his arms, loving the sweaty feel of him. We begin to sway a little and I wonder if Mama and Papa ever had romantic interludes in this kitchen. I'd bet money. And I also wonder about my Nano Melarosso. Could he also have danced around the kitchen with my Nana? The thought comes to me again that this place was meant to be run by two people who love each other. Suddenly we are dancing, Ted and I, slowly, to no audible music. But I'm quite sure he's dancing to the same song that I am: Tears in Heaven. And I'm quite positive when he starts to softly hum the very song that has been haunting him. Free is a wonderful way to feel.

27

A Place Where You Can Eat Well

I'm standing at the top of the back stairs that lead from our apartment down to my store. I'm not stalling so much as just catching my breath. It just occurred to me that I have spent a good portion of my life climbing up and down these back stairs: something like thirty-nine years and seven months if you subtract the first year of my life. If I were Nino, I would pause and take a few seconds to figure out how many steps I have actually taken on this staircase in my lifetime: thirty-nine years (forget the seven months—I'm not as exact as Nino) times three hundred and sixty-five days in a year times fourteen stairs times four trips a day brings the figure somewhere in the neighborhood of just under eight hundred thousand steps. Steps that I always thought would lead me to a life with Vito. Instead they have led me to forgiveness and of course to Ted.

Let me update you. A lot has happened in a few short months. Some things you know about. Some things you don't.

All hell broke loose once the March issue of Chicago Magazine came out. Thank goodness Ted prepared us and thank goodness the review came out before the store was transferred to me because I would not have been able to handle it. As it was, we needed help. Ted came in and helped bake. Virgie left the bookstore a week early to help out. Rosa and Colina helped. Even my Aunt Connie pitched in. It was crazy, but wonderful, too. Mama and Papa were in their glory. Papa said: "What a way to go out!"

Things settled down after a couple of weeks, but by then it was apparent that Colina was not working out in the kitchen. I knew it. Virgie knew it. Even Colina knew it. The solution was simple—Colina and I simply traded places: I started cooking with Virgie and I gave Colina my old job out front. She's much better at it than I ever was with her natural gift of gab.

March thirtieth loomed before me and still Papa and I had not been able to come up with a replacement for Mr. Maggio. We interviewed twelve applicants and each one of them fell short in one way or another. I thought we had one, a young kid, just graduated from the College of DuPage with a two-year AAS degree in Food Service Administration & Culinary Arts. He was so nervous, the poor kid. With trembling hands he offered his resume to me—a one page, neatly typed report of his two years of schooling and zero experience. Glen Ellison was his name and he looked younger than Jimmy, even though he was twenty-three. I was thinking how the zero experience did not weigh in his favor when he started to bite his nails and this alone completely eliminated him from the running. You absolutely cannot have a nail-biting breadman!

But here's the good part, no, the great part: Ted started coming in to help bake and somehow he never left. You see, the diagnostic tests that he underwent showed that he did indeed have a fairly severe case of gastroesophagal reflux disease and two ulcers. He's on medication now and that has helped, but there was no getting around an immediate and lifelong change in his diet. "What's a hired stomach without a stomach?" he'd asked Clay. He did both jobs—breadmaker and food critic—for about three months and then quit the magazine all together. His decision was also influenced by the fact that the guy who was stalking him was not deported after all.

Clay was devastated by Ted's leaving. "Sure, drag me to this cold and windy city and then leave me." But of course he understands, and he and Ted get together once a week or so for lunch or racquetball.

My cousin Jimmy thought he actually had a shot at getting Ted's job at Chicago Magazine (was all set to type up a resume and dig up his restaurant review of *Volare)* but Ted gently explained that the best thing to do was to stay in school and learn as much as he could about food and the food industry if he really wanted to be a food writer.

I don't know if he's just trying to make me feel better about it, but Ted says he doesn't miss his old job. "The stress is finally off," he says. And reducing the amount of stress in his life has reduced the severity of the reflux. "At times it was overwhelming," he explained to me the night he asked me for a job. "A few written words could change someone's life forever. I never did handle that part of the job very well. Maybe I never really had the stomach for it."

So now it's Ted, Virgie, and me in the kitchen until we hire an assistant baker to help out Ted—someone who will eventually come in at three in the morning so Ted can come in at six, like Papa always did. We've got three more interviews tomorrow so I'm keeping my fingers crossed.

Mama, Papa, Aunt Lina, and Mr. Maggio are on that vacation that Aunt Lina was pushing for—only they didn't go on a cruise, they went to Sicily. They've been gone for two whole weeks now! They're supposed to be home around noon today. Rosa is picking them up and driving them here. I've missed them so much. But I have enjoyed having the place to myself—well, I should say Ted and I have enjoyed having the place to ourselves.

I finally got to meet Ted's mother. We brought her dinner from her favorite Greek restaurant, the *Parthenon.* We ate *dolmades* (rice stuffed grape leaves) and broiled sea bass brushed with olive oil, lemon, and oregano, in the nursing home cafeteria. The moment I met her I could see why my Aunt Lina reminded Ted of his mother. Like my aunt, Deidre is a tell-it-like-it-is woman, verbalizing every little thought—good or bad—that pops into her head. She was pleasant enough to me, though, and afterward I told Ted that she wasn't half as bad as he'd made her out to be. This is what he said: "Deidra is like balsamic vinegar—delicious in small drizzles."

I continue my way down the steps, clicking my heels on the metal strips. The thought comes to me that someday I should replace this flooring. I'm looking at things differently now that they're mine. Soon the apartment will be mine, too. Mama and Papa are looking at condos.

When I reach the bottom of the stairs, I hear laughter coming from the kitchen. Virgie's already here and she and Ted are laughing it up. They go at each other all day long—just like Papa and Aunt Lina, only they really are just teasing. Ted calls Virgie "Big Red" and she calls him "Teddy." She's the only person to get away with it besides his mother. He doesn't even let *me* call him Teddy! He's taken over Papa's tradition of singing in the kitchen. Yesterday his serenade went something like:

This is the new chef Big Red-a

she likes to cook things that are dead-a
Don't stick your fingers into her bread-a
She'll slap you across-a your head-a.

Or something like that.

I pause at the kitchen door to listen to more of their laughter. It sounds so good. Not so long ago, the tension in this kitchen was so thick you could slice it. Now this kitchen is a happy place again. I say a silent prayer of thanks. I can't explain how proud it makes me to be a part of this place. There were times in my life when I questioned my dream—was it really my dream to run this place or was it Vito's dream all along? Now I know the answer.

No, it's not the same place it was; it could never be. But Mela's has been evolving for years—reinventing itself as necessary. We're still folksy, just maybe a little more chic. And we're still catering to the Italian food craze that's been taking over Chicago. But first and foremost, Mela's is still what Papa calls *un posto dove si mangia bene*—a place where you can eat well.

We *have* made some changes. Papa kept his promise and had the building re-roofed and also replaced the ancient furnace. He had the entire kitchen painted with a special type of insecticide paint that helps to prevent infestation. We had our tabletops covered with thick plates of glass, which allows for easier clean-up and less wear-and-tear on our tablecloths. And Papa surprised me by having new light fixtures installed in the dining area. I know I said I hate surprises, but sometimes surprises can be nice. As a matter of fact I have a surprise for Papa. He will discover it when he returns home from his trip this afternoon. This is sure to be the surprise of his life! I have my camera loaded and ready.

So the place looks great and I am thankful for the improvements because, as luck would have it, the city inspector came about a week after I took over. While my heart missed beats, he went through the place with a fine-toothed comb. When he finally handed me the *Food Service Establishment Inspection Report*, it took me a couple of seconds before I could open my eyes and read it. Not one violation! Which really shouldn't have surprised me—Papa has always kept this place squeaky-clean.

All in all, I think we've maintained what was essential about Mela's Market—the great food, the sublime bread, and the family-like atmosphere. Our morning regulars still show up religiously, so if that's any indication, I think we're doing okay. I should also tell you that our customers really like Ted and they adore Colina who sees not only to their hunger but to their socio-psychological needs as well.

I push through the door. *"Buon giorno!"* says Ted, who has been learning Italian by listening to cassette tapes while he bakes. He holds his doughy hands up, like a surgeon, and pecks me on the cheek. Virgie smiles at me, her big hair tucked inside a White Sox cap. I get a kiss on the cheek from her, too.

"You've made me a happy person," she tells me. I am thoroughly enjoying cooking with her, too. Mama and Aunt Lina taught her to recreate our customers' favorite dishes, plus she has added some things of her own. In the kitchen, she's the chef—plans the specials, orders the food, get things going—and I am happy to be her assistant. She's fast, too. And this leaves me time to be up front for parts of the day because unfortunately, Colina isn't so fast. Mainly because she talks too much. But everyone loves her. And they heed her advice. Yesterday I heard her ask Tony Radanza if he did the decent thing and broke up with Dawn, seeing that he had been dating Judy for over a month. I also heard him tell her, yes, he did.

My pal Mr. Gradezzi has transferred the crush he's had on me all these years over to Colina. But that doesn't only have to do with her gift of gab, winning smile, and charming personality. He has his eyes on Colina for his future daughter-in-law. His son, Frank, the attorney, has been coming in for lunch quite frequently lately. He's got it bad for Colina, who told him—I think these were her exact words—"You're driving way too fast for conditions, mister." Frank's slowed it down. Now he only comes in a couple of times a week. But I can tell, Colina likes him.

I hear the bell ring on the front door and I peek out. Colina and Jimmy enter together. I wait for their respective greetings as they push through the door.

"Damn, something smells good!" Jimmy says, inhaling deeply, tasting the air.

"Bina," says my sister, "that lock keeps sticking. Everyday I have trouble with it."

Some things don't change. The music hasn't changed. I tried to change it—put on some Beatles and some Billy Joel, but I got complaints. And it wasn't just from the morning crowd. I expected *them* to complain. It was our young lunch crowd that wanted Dean and Frank and Perry and Tony. So I guess I'll be listening to these guys until I die.

Jimmy puts the music on and he and Colina start their day with sweeping and mopping and a game of ABC Whatever. I'm not sure how long this will last though. Jimmy told me that even after detailed instructions, Colina just doesn't really get the game. "I say okay, today let's play ABC Green Vegetables and I start out with artichoke and asparagus and she says bamboo shoots, black beans, broad beans. And I say, *green* vegetables and continue with brussel sprouts, cabbage and cardoon, hoping

472

she'll catch on. But she just says, 'Oh, I forgot butter beans.' I say butter beans aren't green and she says, 'celery, chives, and cucumber.' And I say cucumber isn't really considered a green vegetable even though it has a green skin. And then we get into an argument about that and she says, 'Whatever' just like a valley girl. And I say what kind of answer is that? And she says, 'I thought the name of the game was ABC Whatever.' So this is what I'm dealing with, Bina. It's just not the same."

I slapped his cheek and said, "Endive, escarole, leeks, okra, peas, peppers, raddicchio, spinach, swiss chard, watercress and zucchini."

"Not bad," he said. "Although I think the same would hold true for the zucchini as for the cucumber."

"Whatever," I said, imitating Colina.

I grab a bottle of cleaner and spray down the glass tabletops. Colina could do this—usually does this—but I find myself gravitating out here into the dining area every morning at this time. I like to watch Jimmy's silhouette as he sweeps the front stoop and sidewalk, just like Papa always did. He's sweeping now, with his Frank Sinatra swagger. A mop or a broom—it's all the same to him.

The suns filters in around the window shades and when I pull them up—SNAP!—the whole room is filled with spring sunshine. A few weeks ago, on May first, Colina brought in paper May baskets filled with dandelions that Morgy and Nicole made for me. The flowers (dandelions are *not* weeds in children's eyes) are long gone, but the baskets I have kept and Colina brings in a few springs from her garden and fills them each morning and they sit next to the cash register and remind me of spring and children and second chances. I straighten the place up, pushing in some chairs, picking up some leaves the fig tree has dropped, and adjusting a frame or two on the wall. I finally have my wall of black and white photographs of customers eating at Mela's. Ted had a good idea for the other big wall too—we covered it with the menus we have both collected over the years.

On the wide beam across from the front door, strategically placed so you can't miss it, hangs a framed copy of the review of Mela's. I adjust the frame, proudly.

It's still my job to write the day's specials on the chalkboard. Even left-handed, my penmanship is better than Colina's. And Jimmy's—forget about it. I print neatly: Pan-Fried Marinated Swordfish (made with white wine, garlic, olive oil, breadcrumbs, and capers) and Pasta Norma (a Sicilian pasta dish made with penne pasta, fresh plum tomatoes, onion, garlic, eggplant, and basil). I wipe my chalk-dusted fingers on my apron and head back to the kitchen where Virgie and I work on *Pancetta and Ricotta Cheese Stratas* for breakfast and Ted makes beautiful brown brioches.

I didn't hear the bell on the front door ring, but it must be seven o'clock because I hear Mr. Barbiere's gruff voice calling out to us. I shout over to Ted, who has just pulled the last of the brioches out of the oven, "He's heeeeeeere." We both wipe our hands on our aprons and head out front. Virgie smiles and shakes her head, glad to be able to stay put.

"Sunny! Luna! *Dove sono tu?*" Mr. Barbiere calls out loudly. "Sunny! Luna!" he calls again, even though Ted and I are standing directly in front of him.

"Oh, it's you," Ted says. "I thought maybe we had a real customer."

"I want-a to talk-a to Sunny," he says. "The sign-a out-a front-a says *Sunny and Luna's.*"

"Now you know as well as I do, Mr. Barbiere, they won't be back until noon today," I say.

He winks at me. "I like-a your new sign-a. It looks-a real nice-a. Your Papa, well, he's-a gonna flip-a when-a he sees it. I canceled all-a my appointments today between-a twelve o'clock-a and one-o'clock-a just-a so I could-a see his-a face."

Our other customers make their way in and also give us positive feedback on the new sign. So now you know—I took advantage of Mama and Papa's absence and had a new sign installed out front. A big, lighted, expensive new sign that says *Sunny and Luna's.* I actually ordered it over a month ago. Other stuff as well, such as paper bags, bakery boxes, stickers, napkins, receipts, purchase orders, and even aprons.

Ted tried to talk me out of changing the store name. "It's unheard of to change the name of an eating establishment after you've just received rave reviews from Chicago Magazine. It's madness, Sabina. You'll confuse your customers. You'll confound your vendors. The phone will ring off the hook with questions. You'll be tampering with forty years of tradition. Doesn't that translate into like eighty years of bad luck?"

I used Papa's own words to explain to Ted why in spite of all that I had to change the store name from Mela's Market to Sunny and Luna's: "*Uno parola,* Ted, *onore!*" It was worth a little confusion, a few questions, even breaking tradition, to honor my father, who has looked at that sign every day for forty years and wished he saw his own name on it. Papa deserves a nice surprise.

Mr. Barbiere knows about honor but he pretends that he doesn't. "What-a I don't-a understand though, is why-a the sign-a out-a front-a never has-a the right-a names of-a the owners. The sign-a says *Mela's Market* when it-a belongs to-a Sunny Giovanotti. Now-a the sign-a says *Sunny and Luna's* when it-a belongs to you-a! What? You two-a will probably have-a to wait-a until you have-a kids-a of your own-a and then they will name-a the store *Ted and Sabina's.*"

I laugh and say, "Don't you mean *Sabina and Ted's?*"

"Atta girl," Charlie says as he climbs onto his stool.

Ted smiles as we retreat to the kitchen. When we're out of sight, he says, "*Ted and Sabina's* sounds better, you know."

"It does not. *Sabina and Ted's* sounds way better, doesn't it Virgie."

Virgie, who is removing a huge pan of *strata* from one of the ovens, scrunches up her face, and says, "Neither one sounds right. It's not balanced. You see, you got three syllables in Sabina and only one in Ted. You need balance. But the solution is easy—just call it *Teddy and Bina's.*"

"Yeah! I'd even let you have top billing if you'd use *Teddy,*" I say.

"Actually," Ted says, "*Sabina and Ted's* does sound better."

At about eleven-thirty, Rosa calls from her cell phone pretending that she's calling her dentist to confirm an appointment. "Think you'll be here at noon?" I ask.

"Yes, thank you very much," she says. See you then."

I'm working on the *Pasta Norma.* My camera is loaded and sitting on the counter within easy reach. Jimmy is out front standing lookout. My plan is to sit outside on Mr. Barbiere's bench at ten to twelve with my camera and catch them pulling up. But I really get into the *Past Norma.* I'm not liking the way the eggplant is cooking up so I shuck it and start over with a new one. Jimmy must have gotten distracted himself because next thing I know Papa is pushing through the kitchen door, saying, "Where is she? Where's my girl?"

"Oh, Papa, I'm over here." I start crying even before I see his tears. I hug him—a tanner, meatier Papa. "You like it? Only the best for my father." Mama enters and I add quickly, "And mother."

"*Bedda!* It's wonderful!" Papa says.

"I can't believe it," says Mama. "I thought we took a wrong turn!" They give me what our family calls a *double*—Mama gives me ten or twelve kisses on one cheek while Papa does the same on the other. It tickles!

Aunt Lina barrels her way through the door with Mr. Maggio behind her. "I like the sign and all the new changes, Sabina, but tell me, did you fix the damn lock on the front door?"

Ted and Virgie come over to hug Mama and Papa and we're all talking at once. Lunch may be a held up a few minutes today because now Jimmy's holding open the kitchen door and waving us out. "They're playing your song!" he yells.

What else can we do? We—Mama and Papa, Aunt Lina and Mr. Maggio, and Ted and me—all go out front and dance to Dean's *Memories Are Made of This.* Before the song ends, Jimmy and Rosa join us. And then Colina and Mr. Gradezzi. Seeing them makes me wish that Marina and Angie were here, too. The song ends and we all hold hands and bow to the applause that doesn't seem to let up. Just then Aunt Lina notices the ring on my finger. "I see you're finally wearing the ring I gave you," she says, bringing my hand closer to her.

Aunt Lina grabs me and whispers, "Egads, Sabina, it's bigger than the one Joey number three gave me!" She looks at Ted with her head cocked to one side. She always liked him; I suspect that now she respects him as well.

Papa kisses me, hugs Ted, and then runs over to his wine shelves for another bottle of Asti. "Luna," he shouts, "get some glasses, I feel another toast coming on!" While Mama passes out paper cups and Papa pours a sip for everyone, the front door opens and in runs Nino ("Mom says I have a sore throat so she kept me home from school") with Marina and Angie following. Marina has little Victor in her arms and Angie's carrying Alexandria. I smile and bend down to give Nino a kiss, but just as my lips get within an inch of his cheek, he shrieks, "No lipstick allowed!" and shields his face with his hands. Everyone laughs. I muss up his hair instead, then grab Victor with one arm and Alexandria with the other. I alternate giving them kisses and then hug Angie and Marina. Now all of my sisters are here. And I know that they really came to see Mama and Papa, but it feels like they are all here for me. Just for me. Marina tugs at my left hand to get a peek at the ring. She gives an approving wink, then whispers, "We just got to get you some nails, girl."

I walk over to Ted with a kid on each hip, and right away Victor stretches out his arms. They all love Mr. Man. Ted gives me a little peck on the forehead and the tears just keep rolling down my cheeks. I keep wiping my eyes, but I can't stop. It hasn't totally sunk in yet: I got my breadman. Maybe twenty years later than the average girl, but I got him. I guess I know deep down in my heart that moments such as this—so infused with happiness—are few and far between. Maybe Virgie was right all along—that I was just between courses. I'm savoring this. I kiss the top of Alexandria's head. She smells like baby shampoo and I am visited by the thought that I am nothing if not insatiable: I still want a baby more than anything else in the whole wide world.

Ted and I have talked about children, and I understand his honesty when he says he's not sure he could emotionally handle a child, especially a girl. I'm nothing if not understanding, but that doesn't mean I can't work on him a little. Maybe he's just not ready. I can wait until he's ready. I can't wait too long because I'm over forty and a half now. But I can wait. I'm good at waiting. Matter of fact, I'm an expert.

About The Author

Karla Manarchy Clark grew up in Rockford, Illinois, where her relatives owned grocery stores, Italian restaurants, and bakeries. She holds a Journalism degree and has worked as a freelance writer. *Between Courses* is her first novel. She recently completed a collection of short stories called *Knotted Pearls*. Karla lives in Rockford with her husband and her two sons.

Printed in the United States
16002LVS00002B/31-222